Lecture Notes in Computer Science   10327

Commenced Publication in 1973
Founding and Former Series Editors:
Gerhard Goos, Juris Hartmanis, and Jan van Leeuwen

More information about this series at http://www.springer.com/series/7410

Michalis Polychronakis · Michael Meier (Eds.)

Detection of Intrusions and Malware, and Vulnerability Assessment

14th International Conference, DIMVA 2017
Bonn, Germany, July 6–7, 2017
Proceedings

 Springer

Editors
Michalis Polychronakis
Stony Brook University
Stony Brook, NY
USA

Michael Meier
University of Bonn and Fraunhofer FKIE
Bonn
Germany

ISSN 0302-9743   ISSN 1611-3349 (electronic)
Lecture Notes in Computer Science
ISBN 978-3-319-60875-4   ISBN 978-3-319-60876-1 (eBook)
DOI 10.1007/978-3-319-60876-1

Library of Congress Control Number: 2017943061

LNCS Sublibrary: SL4 – Security and Cryptology

Printed on acid-free paper

This Springer imprint is published by Springer Nature
The registered company is Springer International Publishing AG
The registered company address is: Gewerbestrasse 11, 6330 Cham, Switzerland

Preface

On behalf of the Program Committee, it is our pleasure to present the proceedings of the 14th International Conference on Detection of Intrusions and Malware and Vulnerability Assessment (DIMVA), which took place in Bonn, Germany, during July 6–7, 2017. Since 2004, DIMVA has been bringing together leading researchers and practitioners from academia, industry, and government to present and discuss novel security research in the broader areas of intrusion detection, malware analysis, and vulnerability assessment. DIMVA is organized by the Special Interest Group – Security, Intrusion Detection, and Response (SIDAR) – of the German Informatics Society (GI).

This year, DIMVA received 67 valid submissions from academic and industrial organizations from 25 different countries. Each submission was carefully reviewed by at least three Program Committee members or external experts. The submissions were evaluated on the basis of scientific novelty, importance to the field, and technical quality. The final selection of papers was decided during a day-long Program Committee meeting that took place at Stony Brook University, USA, on April 7, 2017. In all, 18 full papers were selected for presentation at the conference and publication in the proceedings, resulting in an acceptance rate of 26.9%. The accepted papers present novel ideas, techniques, and applications in important areas of computer security, including enclaves and isolation, malware analysis, cyber-physical systems, detection and protection, code analysis, and Web security. Beyond the research papers, the conference program also included two insightful keynote talks by Thomas Dullien (Google) and Prof. Christopher Kruegel (University of California at Santa Barbara).

A successful conference is the result of the joint effort of many people. We would like to express our appreciation to the Program Committee members and external reviewers for the time spent reviewing papers, participating in the online discussion, attending the Program Committee meeting in Stony Brook, and shepherding some of the papers to ensure the highest quality possible. We also deeply thank the members of the Organizing Committee for their hard work in making DIMVA 2017 such a successful event, and our invited speakers for their willingness to participate in the conference. We are wholeheartedly thankful to our sponsors ERNW, genua, Google, Huawei, Rohde & Schwarz Cybersecurity, Springer, and VMRay for generously supporting DIMVA 2017. We also thank Springer for publishing these proceedings as part of their LNCS series, and the DIMVA Steering Committee for their continuous support and assistance.

Finally, DIMVA 2017 would not have been possible without the authors who submitted their work and presented their contributions as well as the attendees who came to the conference. We would like to thank them all, and we look forward to their future contributions to DIMVA.

July 2017

Michalis Polychronakis
Michael Meier

Organization

DIMVA was organized by the special interest group Security – Intrusion Detection and Response (SIDAR) of the German Informatics Society (GI).

Organizing Committee

General Chair

Michael Meier   University of Bonn and Fraunhofer FKIE, Germany

Program Chair

Michalis Polychronakis   Stony Brook University, USA

Steering Committee (Chairs)

Ulrich Flegel	Infineon Technologies, Germany
Michael Meier	University of Bonn and Fraunhofer FKIE, Germany

Steering Committee (Members)

Magnus Almgren	Chalmers University of Technology, Sweden
Herbert Bos	Vrije Universiteit Amsterdam, The Netherlands
Danilo M. Bruschi	Università degli Studi di Milano, Italy
Roland Bueschkes	RWE AG, Germany
Juan Caballero	IMDEA Software Institute, Spain
Lorenzo Cavallaro	Royal Holloway, University of London, UK
Herve Debar	Telecom SudParis, France
Sven Dietrich	City University of New York, USA
Bernhard Haemmerli	Acris GmbH and HSLU Lucerne, Switzerland
Thorsten Holz	Ruhr University Bochum, Germany
Marko Jahnke	CSIRT, German Federal Authority, Germany
Klaus Julisch	Deloitte, Switzerland
Christian Kreibich	ICSI, USA
Christopher Kruegel	University of California, Santa Barbara, USA
Pavel Laskov	Huawei European Research Center, Germany
Federico Maggi	Trend Micro, Italy
Konrad Rieck	TU Braunschweig, Germany
Robin Sommer	ICSI/LBNL, USA
Urko Zurutuza	Mondragon University, Spain

Program Committee

Magnus Almgren	Chalmers University of Technology, Sweden
Leyla Bilge	Symantec Research Labs, France

Herbert Bos	Vrije Universiteit Amsterdam, The Netherlands
Lorenzo Cavallaro	Royal Holloway, University of London, UK
Mauro Conti	University of Padua, Italy
Baris Coskun	Amazon, USA
Lucas Davi	University of Duisburg-Essen, Germany
Herve Debar	Telecom SudParis, France
Sven Dietrich	City University of New York, USA
Brendan Dolan-Gavitt	NYU, USA
Adam Doupé	Arizona State University, USA
Zakir Durumeric	University of Michigan, USA
Manuel Egele	Boston University, USA
Ulrich Flegel	Infineon Technologies AG, Germany
Cristiano Giuffrida	Vrije Universiteit Amsterdam, The Netherlands
Martin Johns	SAP Research, Germany
Alexandros Kapravelos	North Carolina State University, USA
Vasileios Kemerlis	Brown University, USA
Christian Kreibich	ICSI, USA
Christopher Kruegel	University of California, Santa Barbara, USA
Andrea Lanzi	University of Milan, Italy
Pavel Laskov	Huawei European Research Center, Germany
Corrado Leita	Lastline, UK
Zhiqiang Lin	University of Texas at Dallas, USA
Martina Lindorfer	University of California, Santa Barbara, USA
Federico Maggi	Trend Micro, Italy
Stefan Mangard	Graz University of Technology, Austria
Michael Meier	University of Bonn and Fraunhofer FKIE, Germany
Collin Mulliner	Square, USA
Nick Nikiforakis	Stony Brook University, USA
Roberto Perdisci	University of Georgia, USA
Jason Polakis	University of Illinois at Chicago, USA
Konrad Rieck	TU Braunschweig, Germany
Christian Rossow	Saarland University, Germany
Gianluca Stringhini	University College London, UK
Urko Zurutuza	Mondragon University, Spain

Additional Reviewers

Tooska Dargahi	Panagiotis Ilia	Srdan Moraca
Michalis Diamantaris	Mikel Iturbe	Raphael Otto
Patrick Duessel	Daniele Lain	Pablo Picazo-Sanchez
Hossein Fereidooni	Clémentine Maurice	Tobias Wahl
Daniel Gruss	Veelasha Moonsamy	

Contents

Enclaves and Isolation

Malware Guard Extension: Using SGX to Conceal Cache Attacks 3
    Michael Schwarz, Samuel Weiser, Daniel Gruss,
    Clémentine Maurice, and Stefan Mangard

On the Trade-Offs in Oblivious Execution Techniques 25
    Shruti Tople and Prateek Saxena

MemPatrol: Reliable Sideline Integrity Monitoring
for High-Performance Systems 48
    Myoung Jin Nam, Wonhong Nam, Jin-Young Choi,
    and Periklis Akritidis

Malware Analysis

Measuring and Defeating Anti-Instrumentation-Equipped Malware 73
    Mario Polino, Andrea Continella, Sebastiano Mariani,
    Stefano D'Alessio, Lorenzo Fontana, Fabio Gritti,
    and Stefano Zanero

DynODet: Detecting Dynamic Obfuscation in Malware 97
    Danny Kim, Amir Majlesi-Kupaei, Julien Roy, Kapil Anand,
    Khaled ElWazeer, Daniel Buettner, and Rajeev Barua

Finding the Needle: A Study of the *PE32* Rich Header
and Respective Malware Triage 119
    George D. Webster, Bojan Kolosnjaji, Christian von Pentz,
    Julian Kirsch, Zachary D. Hanif, Apostolis Zarras,
    and Claudia Eckert

Cyber-physical Systems

Last Line of Defense: A Novel IDS Approach Against Advanced Threats
in Industrial Control Systems 141
    Mark Luchs and Christian Doerr

LED-it-GO: Leaking (A Lot of) Data from Air-Gapped Computers
via the (Small) Hard Drive LED 161
    Mordechai Guri, Boris Zadov, and Yuval Elovici

A Stealth, Selective, Link-Layer Denial-of-Service Attack Against
Automotive Networks   185
   Andrea Palanca, Eric Evenchick, Federico Maggi, and Stefano Zanero

Detection and Protection

Quincy: Detecting Host-Based Code Injection Attacks in Memory Dumps . . .   209
   Thomas Barabosch, Niklas Bergmann, Adrian Dombeck,
   and Elmar Padilla

SPEAKER: Split-Phase Execution of Application Containers   230
   Lingguang Lei, Jianhua Sun, Kun Sun, Chris Shenefiel, Rui Ma,
   Yuewu Wang, and Qi Li

Deep Ground Truth Analysis of Current Android Malware.   252
   Fengguo Wei, Yuping Li, Sankardas Roy, Xinming Ou,
   and Wu Zhou

Code Analysis

HumIDIFy: A Tool for Hidden Functionality Detection in Firmware   279
   Sam L. Thomas, Flavio D. Garcia, and Tom Chothia

BinShape: Scalable and Robust Binary Library Function Identification
Using Function Shape   301
   Paria Shirani, Lingyu Wang, and Mourad Debbabi

SCVD: A New Semantics-Based Approach for Cloned Vulnerable
Code Detection.   325
   Deqing Zou, Hanchao Qi, Zhen Li, Song Wu, Hai Jin, Guozhong Sun,
   Sujuan Wang, and Yuyi Zhong

Web Security

On the Privacy Impacts of Publicly Leaked Password Databases   347
   Olivier Heen and Christoph Neumann

Unsupervised Detection of APT C&C Channels
using Web Request Graphs   366
   Pavlos Lamprakis, Ruggiero Dargenio, David Gugelmann,
   Vincent Lenders, Markus Happe, and Laurent Vanbever

Measuring Network Reputation in the Ad-Bidding Process.   388
   Yizheng Chen, Yacin Nadji, Rosa Romero-Gómez,
   Manos Antonakakis, and David Dagon

Author Index   411

Enclaves and Isolation

Malware Guard Extension:
Using SGX to Conceal Cache Attacks

Michael Schwarz(✉), Samuel Weiser, Daniel Gruss, Clémentine Maurice,
and Stefan Mangard

Graz University of Technology, Graz, Austria
michael.schwarz@iaik.tugraz.at

Abstract. In modern computer systems, user processes are isolated
from each other by the operating system and the hardware. Additionally,
in a cloud scenario it is crucial that the hypervisor isolates tenants from
other tenants that are co-located on the same physical machine. However,
the hypervisor does not protect tenants against the cloud provider and
thus the supplied operating system and hardware. Intel SGX provides a
mechanism that addresses this scenario. It aims at protecting user-level
software from attacks from other processes, the operating system, and
even physical attackers.

In this paper, we demonstrate fine-grained software-based side-
channel attacks from a malicious SGX enclave targeting co-located
enclaves. Our attack is the first malware running on real SGX hardware, abusing SGX protection features to conceal itself. Furthermore, we
demonstrate our attack both in a native environment and across multiple Docker containers. We perform a *Prime+Probe* cache side-channel
attack on a co-located SGX enclave running an up-to-date RSA implementation that uses a constant-time multiplication primitive. The attack
works although in SGX enclaves there are no timers, no large pages, no
physical addresses, and no shared memory. In a semi-synchronous attack,
we extract 96% of an RSA private key from a single trace. We extract
the full RSA private key in an automated attack from 11 traces.

1 Introduction

Modern operating systems isolate user processes from each other to protect
secrets in different processes. Such secrets include passwords stored in password managers or private keys to access company networks. Leakage of these
secrets can compromise both private and corporate systems. Similar problems
arise in the cloud. Therefore, cloud providers use virtualization as an additional
protection using a hypervisor. The hypervisor isolates different tenants that are
co-located on the same physical machine. However, the hypervisor does not protect tenants against a possibly malicious cloud provider.

Although hypervisors provide functional isolation, side-channel attacks are
often not considered. Consequently, researchers have demonstrated various side-
channel attacks, especially those exploiting the cache [15]. Cache side-channel

© Springer International Publishing AG 2017
M. Polychronakis and M. Meier (Eds.): DIMVA 2017, LNCS 10327, pp. 3–24, 2017.
DOI: 10.1007/978-3-319-60876-1_1

attacks can recover cryptographic secrets, such as AES [29] and RSA [33] keys, across virtual machine boundaries.

Intel introduced a new hardware extension SGX (Software Guard Extensions) [27] in their CPUs, starting with the Skylake microarchitecture. SGX is an isolation mechanism, aiming at protecting code and data from modification or disclosure even if all privileged software is malicious [10]. This protection uses special execution environments, so-called enclaves, which work on memory areas that are isolated from the operating system by the hardware. The memory area used by the enclaves is encrypted to protect application secrets from hardware attackers. Typical use cases include password input, password managers, and cryptographic operations. Intel recommends storing cryptographic keys inside enclaves and claims that side-channel attacks "are thwarted since the memory is protected by hardware encryption" [25].

Hardware-supported isolation also led to fear of super malware inside enclaves. Rutkowska [44] outlined a scenario where an enclave fetches encrypted malware from an external server and executes it within the enlave. In this scenario, it is impossible to debug, reverse engineer, or analyze the executed malware in any way. Costan et al. [10] eliminated this fear by arguing that enclaves always run with user space privileges and can neither issue syscalls nor perform any I/O operations. Moreover, SGX is a highly restrictive environment for implementing cache side-channel attacks. Both state-of-the-art malware and side-channel attacks rely on several primitives that are not available in SGX enclaves.

In this paper, we show that it is very well possible for enclave malware to attack its hosting system. We demonstrate a cross-enclave cache attack from within a malicious enclave that is extracting secret keys from co-located enclaves. Our proof-of-concept malware is able to recover RSA keys by monitoring cache access patterns of an RSA signature process in a semi-synchronous attack. The malware code is completely invisible to the operating system and cannot be analyzed due to the isolation provided by SGX. We present novel approaches to recover physical address bits, as well as to recover high-resolution timing in absence of the timestamp counter, which has an even higher resolution than the native one. In an even stronger attack scenario, we show that an additional isolation using Docker containers does not protect against this kind of attack.

We make the following contributions:

1. We demonstrate that, despite the restrictions of SGX, cache attacks can be performed from within an enclave to attack a co-located enclave.
2. By combining DRAM and cache side channels, we present a novel approach to recover physical address bits even if 2 MB pages are unavailable.
3. We obtain high-resolution timestamps in enclaves without access to the native timestamp counter, with an even higher resolution than the native one.
4. In an automated end-to-end attack on the wide-spread *mbedTLS* RSA implementation, we extract 96% of an RSA private key from a single trace.

Section 2 presents the required background. Section 3 outlines the threat model and attack scenario. Section 4 describes the measurement methods and the online phase of the malware. Section 5 explains the offline-phase key recovery. Section 6 evaluates the attack against an up-to-date RSA implementation. Section 7 discusses several countermeasures. Section 8 concludes our work.

2   Background

2.1   Intel SGX in Native and Virtualized Environments

Intel Software Guard Extensions (SGX) are a new set of x86 instructions introduced with the Skylake microarchitecture. SGX allows protecting the execution of user programs in so-called enclaves. Only the enclave can access its own memory region, any other access to it is blocked by the CPU. As SGX enforces this policy in hardware, enclaves do not need to rely on the security of the operating system. In fact, with SGX the operating system is generally not trusted. By doing sensitive computation inside an enclave, one can effectively protect against traditional malware, even if such malware has obtained kernel privileges. Furthermore, it allows running secret code in a cloud environment without trusting hardware and operating system of the cloud provider.

An enclave resides in the virtual memory area of an ordinary application process. This virtual memory region of the enclave can only be backed by physically protected pages from the so-called Enclave Page Cache (EPC). The EPC itself is a contiguous physical block of memory in DRAM that is encrypted transparently to protect against hardware attacks.

Loading of enclaves is done by the operating system. To protect the integrity of enclave code, the loading procedure is measured by the CPU. If the resulting measurement does not match the value specified by the enclave developer, the CPU will refuse to run the enclave.

Since enclave code is known to the (untrusted) operating system, it cannot carry hard-coded secrets. Before giving secrets to an enclave, a provisioning party has to ensure that the enclave has not been tampered with. SGX therefore provides remote attestation, which proves correct enclave loading via the aforementioned enclave measurement.

At the time of writing, no hypervisor with SGX support was available. However, Arnautov et al. [4] proposed to combine Docker containers with SGX to create secure containers. Docker is an operating-system-level virtualization software that allows applications to run in separate containers. It is a standard runtime for containers on Linux which is supported by multiple public cloud providers. Unlike virtual machines, Docker containers share the kernel and other resources with the host system, requiring fewer resources than a virtual machine.

2.2   Microarchitectural Attacks

Microarchitectural attacks exploit hardware properties that allow inferring information on other processes running on the same system. In particular, cache attacks exploit the timing difference between the CPU cache and the main memory. They have been the most studied microarchitectural attacks for the past 20 years, and were found to be powerful to derive cryptographic secrets [15]. Modern attacks target the last-level cache, which is shared among all CPU cores. Last-level caches (LLC) are usually built as n-way set-associative caches. They consist of S cache sets and each cache set consists of n cache ways with a size of 64 B. The lowest 6 physical address bits determine the byte offset within a cache way, the following $\log_2 S$ bits starting with bit 6 determine the cache set.

Prime+Probe is a cache attack technique that has first been used by Osvik et al. [39]. In a *Prime+Probe* attack, the attacker constantly primes (*i.e.*, evicts) a cache set and measures how long this step took. The runtime of the prime step is correlated to the number of cache ways that have been replaced by other programs. This allows deriving whether or not a victim application performed a specific secret-dependent memory access. Recent work has shown that this technique can even be used across virtual machine boundaries [33, 35].

To prime (*i.e.*, evict) a cache set, the attacker uses n addresses in same cache set (*i.e.*, an *eviction set*), where n depends on the cache replacement policy and the number of ways. To minimize the amount of time the prime step takes, it is necessary to find a minimal n combined with a fast access pattern (*i.e.*, an *eviction strategy*). Gruss et al. [18] experimentally found efficient eviction strategies with high eviction rates and a small number of addresses. We use their eviction strategy on our Skylake test machine throughout the paper.

Pessl et al. [42] found a similar attack through DRAM modules. Each DRAM module has a row buffer that holds the most recently accessed DRAM row. While accesses to this buffer are fast, accesses to other memory locations in DRAM are much slower. This timing difference can be exploited to obtain fine-grained information across virtual machine boundaries.

2.3   Side-Channel Attacks on SGX

Intel claims that SGX features impair side-channel attacks and recommends using SGX enclaves to protect password managers and cryptographic keys against side channels [25]. However, there have been speculations that SGX could be vulnerable to side-channel attacks [10]. Xu et al. [50] showed that SGX is vulnerable to page fault side-channel attacks from a malicious operating system [1].

SGX enclaves generally do not share memory with other enclaves, the operating system or other processes. Thus, any attack requiring shared memory is not possible, e.g., *Flush+Reload* [51]. Also, DRAM-based attacks cannot be performed from a malicious operating system, as the hardware prevents any operating system accesses to DRAM rows in the EPC. However, enclaves can mount DRAM-based attacks on other enclaves because all enclaves are located in the same physical EPC.

In concurrent work, Brasser et al. [8], Moghimi et al. [37] and Götzfried et al. [17] demonstrated cache attacks on SGX relying on a malicious operating system.

2.4   Side-Channel Attacks on RSA

RSA is widely used to create asymmetric signatures, and is implemented by virtually every TLS library, such as OpenSSL or *mbedTLS*, which is used for instance in cURL and OpenVPN. RSA essentially involves modular exponentiation with a private key, typically using a square-and-multiply algorithm. An unprotected implementation of square-and-multiply is vulnerable to a variety of side-channel attacks, in which an attacker learns the exponent by distinguishing the square step from the multiplication step [15,51]. *mbedTLS* uses a windowed square-and-multiply routine for the exponentiation. Liu et al. [33] showed that if an attack on a window size of 1 is possible, the attack can be extended to arbitrary window sizes.

Earlier versions of *mbedTLS* were vulnerable to a timing side-channel attack on RSA-CRT [3]. Due to this attack, current versions of *mbedTLS* implement a constant-time Montgomery multiplication for RSA. Additionally, instead of using a dedicated square routine, the square operation is carried out using the multiplication routine. Thus, there is no leakage from a different square and multiplication routine as exploited in previous attacks on square-and-multiply algorithms [33,51]. However, Liu et al. [33] showed that the secret-dependent accesses to the buffer b still leak the exponent. Boneh et al. [7] and Blömer et al. [6] recovered the full RSA private key if only parts of the key bits are known.

3   Threat Model and Attack Setup

In this section, we present our threat model. We demonstrate a malware that circumvents SGX and Docker isolation guarantees. We successfully mount a *Prime+Probe* attack on an RSA signature computation running inside a different enclave, on the outside world, and across container boundaries.

3.1   High-Level View of the Attack

In our threat model, both the attacker and the victim are running on the same physical machine. The machine can either be a user's local computer or a host in the cloud. In the cloud scenario, the victim has its enclave running in a Docker container to provide services to other applications running on the host. Docker containers are well supported on many cloud providers, e.g., Amazon [13] or Microsoft Azure [36]. As these containers are more lightweight than virtual machines, a host can run up to several hundred containers simultaneously. Thus, the attacker has good chances to get a co-located container on a cloud provider.

Figure 1 gives an overview of our native setup. The victim runs a cryptographic computation inside the enclave to protect it against any attacks. The attacker tries to stealthily extract secrets from this victim enclave. Both the attacker and the victim use Intel SGX features and thus are subdivided into two parts, the enclave and loader, *i.e.*, the main program instantiating the enclave.

The attack is a multi-step process that can be divided into an online and an offline phase. Section 4 describes the online phase, in which the attacker first

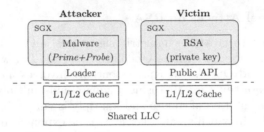

Fig. 1. The threat model: both attacker and victim run on the same physical machine in different SGX enclaves.

locates the victim's cache sets that contain the secret-dependent data of the RSA private key. The attacker then monitors the identified cache sets while triggering a signature computation. Section 5 gives a detailed explanation of the offline phase in which the attacker recovers a private key from collected traces.

3.2   Victim

The victim is an unprivileged program that uses SGX to protect an RSA signing application from both software and hardware attackers. Both the RSA implementation and the private key reside inside the enclave, as suggested by Intel [25]. Thus, they can never be accessed by system software or malware on the same host. Moreover, memory encryption prevents physical information leakage in DRAM. The victim uses the RSA implementation of the widely deployed *mbedTLS* library. The *mbedTLS* library implements a windowed square-and-multiply algorithm, that relies on constant-time Montgomery multiplications. The window size is fixed to 1, as suggested by the official knowledge base [2]. The victim application provides an API to compute a signature for provided data.

3.3   Attacker

The attacker runs an unprivileged program on the same host machine as the victim. The goal of the attacker is to stealthily extract the private key from the victim enclave. Therefore, the attacker uses the API provided by the victim to trigger signature computations.

The attacker targets the exponentiation step of the RSA implementation. The attack works on arbitrary window sizes [33], including window size 1. To prevent information leakage from function calls, *mbedTLS* uses the same function (`mpi_montmul`) for both the square and the multiply operation. The `mpi_montmul` takes two parameters that are multiplied together. For the square operation, the function is called with the current buffer as both arguments. For the multiply operation, the current buffer is multiplied with a buffer holding the multiplier. This buffer is allocated in the calling function `mbedtls_mpi_exp_mod` using `calloc`. Due to the deterministic behavior of the tlibc `calloc` implementation, the used buffers always have the same virtual and physical addresses and thus the same cache sets. The attacker can therefore mount a *Prime+Probe* attack on the cache sets containing the buffer.

In order to remain stealthy, all parts of the malware that contain attack code reside inside an SGX enclave. The enclave can protect the encrypted real attack code by only decrypting it after a successful remote attestation after which the enclave receives the decryption key. As pages in SGX can be mapped as writable and executable, self-modifying code is possible and therefore code can be encrypted. Consequently, the attack is completely stealthy and invisible from anti-virus software and even from monitoring software running in ring 0. Note that our proof-of-concept implementation does not encrypt the attack code as this has no impact on the attack.

The loader does not contain any suspicious code or data, it is only required to start the enclave and send the exfiltrated data to the attacker.

3.4 Operating System and Hardware

Previous work was mostly focused on attacks on enclaves from untrusted cloud operating systems [10, 46]. However, in our attack we do not make any assumptions on the underlying operating system, *i.e.*, we do not rely on a malicious operating system. Both the attacker and the victim are unprivileged user space applications. Our attack works on a fully-patched recent operating system with no known software vulnerabilities, *i.e.*, the attacker cannot elevate privileges.

We expect the cloud provider to run state-of-the-art malware detection software. We assume that the malware detection software is able to monitor the behavior of containers and inspect the content of containers. Moreover, the user can run anti-virus software and monitor programs inside the container. We assume that the protection mechanisms are either signature-based, behavioral-based, heuristics-based or use performance counters [12, 21].

Our only assumption on the hardware is that attacker and victim run on the same host system. This is the case on both personal computers and on co-located Docker instances in the cloud. As SGX is currently only available on Intel Skylake CPUs, it is valid to assume that the host is a Skylake system. Consequently, we know that the last-level cache is shared between all CPU cores.

4 Extracting Private Key Information

In this section, we describe the online phase of our attack. We first build primitives necessary to mount this attack. Then we show in two steps how to locate and monitor cache sets to extract private key information.

4.1 Attack Primitives in SGX

Successful *Prime+Probe* attacks require two primitives: a high-resolution timer to distinguish cache hits and misses and a method to generate an eviction set for arbitrary cache sets. Due to the restrictions of SGX enclaves, implementing *Prime+Probe* in enclaves is not straight-forward. Therefore, we require new techniques to build a malware from within an enclave.

High-Resolution Timer. The unprivileged `rdtsc` and `rdtscp` instructions, which read the timestamp counter, are usually used for fine-grained timing outside enclaves. In SGX, these instructions are not permitted inside an enclave, as they might cause a VM exit [24]. Thus, we have to rely on a different timing source with a resolution in the order of 10 cycles to reliably distinguish cache hits from misses as well as DRAM row hits from row conflicts.

To achieve the highest number of increments, we handcraft a counter thread [31, 49] in inline assembly. The counter variable has to be accessible across threads, thus it is necessary to store the counter variable in memory. Memory addresses as operands incur an additional cost of approximately 4 cycles due to L1 cache access times [23]. On our test machine, a simple counting thread executing 1: `incl (%rcx)`; `jmp 1b` achieves one increment every 4.7 cycles, which is an improvement of approximately 2% over the best code generated by gcc.

We can improve the performance—and thus the resolution—further, by exploiting the fact that only the counting thread modifies the counter variable. We can omit reading the counter variable from memory. Therefore, we introduce a "shadow counter variable" which is always held in a CPU register. The arithmetic operation (either `add` or `inc`) is performed on this register, unleashing the low latency and throughput of these instructions. As registers cannot be shared across threads, the shadow counter has to be moved to memory using the `mov` instruction after each increment. Similar to the `inc` and `add` instruction, the `mov` instruction has a latency of 1 cycle and a throughput of 0.5 cycles/instruction when copying a register to memory. The improved counting thread, 1: `inc %rax; mov %rax, (%rcx)`, `jmp 1b`, is significantly faster and increments the variable by one every 0.87 cycles, which is an improvement of 440% over the simple counting thread. In fact, this version is even 15% faster than the native timestamp counter, thus giving us a reliable timing source with even higher resolution. This new method might open new possibilities of side-channel attacks that leak information through timing on a sub-`rdtsc` level.

Eviction Set Generation. *Prime+Probe* relies on eviction sets, *i.e.*, we need to find virtual addresses that map to the same physical cache set. An unprivileged process cannot translate virtual to physical addresses and therefore cannot simply search for virtual addresses that fall into the same cache set. Liu et al. [33] and Maurice et al. [35] demonstrated algorithms to build eviction sets using large pages by exploiting the fact that the virtual address and the physical address have the same lowest 21 bits. As SGX does not support large pages, this approach is inapplicable. Oren et al. [38] and Gruss et al. [18] demonstrated automated methods to generate eviction sets for a given virtual address. Due to microarchitectural changes their approaches are either not applicable at all to the Skylake architecture or consume several hours on average before even starting the actual *Prime+Probe* attack.

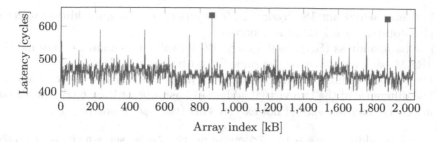

Fig. 2. Access times when alternately accessing two addresses which are 64 B apart. The (marked) high access times indicate row conflicts.

We propose a new method to recover the cache set from a virtual address without relying on large pages. The idea is to exploit contiguous page alloca- tion [28] and DRAM timing differences to recover DRAM row boundaries. The DRAM mapping functions [42] allow to recover physical address bits.

The DRAM organization into banks and rows causes timing differences. Alternately accessing pairs of two virtual addresses that map to the same DRAM bank but a different row is significantly slower than any other combination of virtual addresses. Figure 2 shows the average access time for address pairs when iterating over a 2 MB array. The highest two peaks show row conflicts, *i.e.*, the row index changes while the bank, rank, and channel stay the same.

Table 1. Reverse-engineered DRAM mapping functions from Pessl et al. [42].

		Address Bit															
		22	21	20	19	18	17	16	15	14	13	12	11	10	09	08	07	06
2 DIMMs	Channel				⊕	⊕					⊕	⊕	⊕	⊕	⊕	⊕		⊕
	BG0								⊕							⊕	
	BG1	⊕				⊕											
	BA0				⊕			⊕									
	BA1		⊕			⊕											
	Rank			⊕			⊕										

To recover physical address bits we use the reverse-engineered DRAM map- ping function as shown in Table 1. Our test machine is an Intel Core i5-6200U with 12 GB main memory. The row index is determined by physical address bits 18 and upwards. Hence, the first address of a DRAM row has the least-significant 18 bits of the physical address set to '0'. To detect row borders, we scan memory sequentially for an address pair in physical proximity that causes a *row conflict*. As SGX enclave memory is allocated contiguously we can perform this scan on virtual addresses.

A virtual address pair that causes row conflicts at the beginning of a row satisfies the following constraints:

1. The least-significant 18 physical address bits of one virtual address are zero. This constitutes a DRAM row border.
2. The bank address (BA), bank group (BG), rank, and channel determine the DRAM bank and must be the same for both virtual addresses.
3. The row index must be different for both addresses to cause a row conflict.
4. The difference of the two virtual addresses has to be at least 64 B (the size of one cache line) but should not exceed 4 kB (the size of one page).

Physical address bits 6 to 17 determine the cache set which we want to recover. Hence, we search for address pairs where physical address bits 6 to 17 have the same known but arbitrary value.

To find address pairs fulfilling the aforementioned constraints, we modeled the mapping function and the constraints as an SMT problem and used the Z3 theorem prover [11] to provide models satisfying the constraints. The model we found yields pairs of physical addresses where the upper address is 64 B apart from the lower one. There are four such address pairs within every 4 MB block of physical memory such that each pair maps to the same bank but a different row. The least-significant bits of the physical address pairs are either (0x3fffc0, 0x400000), (0x7fffc0, 0x800000), (0xbfffc0, 0xc00000) or (0xffffc0, 0x1000000) for the lower and higher address respectively. Thus, at least 22 bits of the higher addresses least-significant bits are 0. As the cache set is determined by the bits 6 to 17, the higher address has the cache set index 0. We observe that satisfying address pairs are always 256 KB apart. Since we have contiguous memory [28], we can generate addresses mapping to the same cache set by adding multiples of 256 KB to the higher address.

In modern CPUs, the last-level cache is split into cache slices. Addresses with the same cache set index map to different cache slices based on the remaining address bits. To generate an eviction set, it is necessary to only use addresses that map to the same cache set in the same cache slice. However, to calculate the cache slice, all bits of the physical address are required [34].

As we are not able to directly calculate the cache slice, we use another approach. We add our calculated addresses from the correct cache set to our eviction set until the eviction rate is sufficiently high. Then, we try to remove single addresses from the eviction set as long as the eviction rate does not drop. Thus, we remove all addresses that do not contribute to the eviction, and the result is a minimal eviction set. Our approach takes on average 2 s per cache set, as we already know that our addresses map to the correct cache set. This is nearly three orders of magnitude faster than the approach of Gruss et al. [18]. Older techniques that have been comparably fast do not work on current hardware anymore due to microarchitectural changes [33, 38].

4.2 Identifying and Monitoring Vulnerable Sets

With the reliable high-resolution timer and a method to generate eviction sets, we can mount the first stage of the attack and identify the vulnerable cache sets. As we do not have any information about the physical addresses of the victim, we have to scan the last-level cache for characteristic patterns corresponding to the signature process. We consecutively mount a *Prime+Probe* attack on every cache set while the victim is executing the exponentiation step.

We can then identify multiple cache sets showing the distinctive pattern of the signature operation. The number of cache sets depends on the RSA key size. Cache sets at the buffer boundaries might be used by neighboring buffers and are more likely to be prefetched [20,51] and thus, prone to measurement errors. Consequently, we use cache sets neither at the start nor the end of the buffer.

The measurement method is the same as for detecting the vulnerable cache sets, *i.e.*, we again use *Prime+Probe*. Due to the deterministic behavior of the heap allocation, the address of the attacked buffer does not change on consecutive exponentiations. Thus, we can collect multiple traces of the signature process.

To maintain a high sampling rate, we keep the post-processing during the measurements to a minimum. Moreover, it is important to keep the memory activity at a minimum to not introduce additional noise on the cache. Thus, we only save the timestamps of the cache misses for further post-processing. As a cache miss takes longer than a cache hit, the effective sampling rate varies depending on the number of cache misses. We have to consider this effect in the post-processing as it induces a non-constant sampling interval.

5   Recovering the Private Key

In this section, we describe the offline phase of our attack: recovering the private key from the recorded traces of the victim enclave. This can either be done inside the malware enclave or on the attacker's server.

Ideally, an attacker would combine multiple traces by aligning them and averaging out noise. From the averaged trace, the private key can be extracted more easily. However, most noise sources, such as context switches, system activity and varying CPU clock, alter the timing, thus making trace alignment difficult. We pre-process all traces individually and extract a partial key out of each trace. These partial keys likely suffer from random insertion and deletion errors as well as from bit flips. To eliminate the errors, we combine multiple partial keys in the key recovery phase. This approach has much lower computational overhead than trace alignment since key recovery is performed on partial 4096-bit keys instead of full traces containing several thousand measurements.

Key recovery comes in three steps. First, traces are pre-processed. Second, a partial key is extracted from each trace. Third, the partial keys are merged to recover the private key. In the pre-processing step we filter and resample raw measurement data. Figure 3 shows a trace segment before (top) and after pre-processing (bottom). The pre-processed trace shows high peaks at locations of cache misses, indicating a '1' in the RSA exponent.

To automatically extract a partial key from a pre-processed trace, we first run a peak detection algorithm. We delete duplicate peaks, e.g., peaks where the corresponding RSA multiplications would overlap in time. We also delete peaks that are below a certain adaptive threshold, as they do not correspond to actual

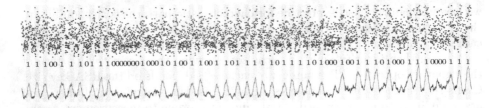

Fig. 3. A raw measurement trace over 4000000 cycles. The peaks in the pre-processed trace on the bottom clearly indicate '1's.

multiplications. Using an adaptive threshold is necessary since neither the CPU frequency nor our timing source (the counting thread) is perfectly stable. The varying peak height is shown in the right third of Fig. 3. The adaptive threshold is the median over the 10 previously detected peaks. If a peak drops below 90% of this threshold, it is discarded. The remaining peaks correspond to the '1's in the RSA exponent and are highlighted in Fig. 3. '0's can only be observed indirectly in our trace as square operations do not trigger cache activity on the monitored sets. '0's appear as time gaps in the sequence of '1' peaks, thus revealing all partial key bits. Note that since '0's correspond to just one multiplication, they are roughly twice as fast as '1's.

When a correct peak is falsely discarded, the corresponding '1' is interpreted as two '0's. Likewise, if noise is falsely interpreted as a '1', this cancels out two '0's. If either the attacker or the victim is not scheduled, we have a gap in the collected trace. However, if both the attacker and the victim are descheduled, this gap does not show up prominently in the trace since the counting thread is also suspended by the interrupt. This is an advantage of a counting thread over the use of the native timestamp counter.

In the final key recovery, we merge multiple partial keys to obtain the full key. We quantify partial key errors using the edit distance. The edit distance between a partial key and the correct key gives the number of bit insertions, deletions and flips necessary to transform the partial key into the correct key.

The full key is recovered bitwise, starting from the most-significant bit. The correct key bit is the result of the majority vote over the corresponding bit in all partial keys. To correct the current bit of a wrong partial key, we compute the edit distance to all partial keys that won the majority vote. To reduce the performance overhead, we do not calculate the edit distance over the whole partial keys but only over a lookahead window of a few bits. The output of the edit distance algorithm is a list of actions necessary to transform one key into the other. We apply these actions via majority vote until the key bit of the wrong partial key matches the recovered key bit again.

6   Evaluation

In this section, we evaluate the presented methods by building a malware enclave attacking a co-located enclave that acts as the victim. As discussed in Sect. 3.2, we use *mbedTLS*, in version 2.3.0.

For the evaluation, we attack a 4096-bit RSA key. The runtime of the multiplication function increases exponentially with the size of the key. Hence, larger keys improve the measurement resolution of the attacker. In terms of cache side-channel attacks, large RSA keys do not provide higher security but degrade side-channel resistance [41,48,51].

6.1   Native Environment

We use a Lenovo ThinkPad T460s with an Intel Core i5-6200U (2 cores, 12 cache ways) running Ubuntu 16.10 and the Intel SGX driver. Both the attacker enclave and the victim enclave are running on the same machine. We trigger the signature process using the public API of the victim.

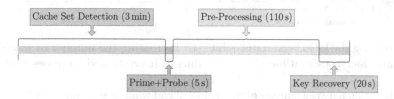

Fig. 4. A high-level overview of the average times for each step of the attack.

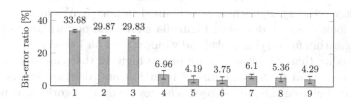

Fig. 5. The 9 cache sets that are used by a 4096-bit key and their error ratio when recovering the key from a single trace.

Figure 4 gives an overview of how long the individual steps of an average attack take. The runtime of automatic cache set detection varies depending on which cache sets are used by the victim. The attacked buffer spans 9 cache sets, out of which 6 show a low bit-error ratio, as shown in Fig. 5. For the attack we select one of the 6 sets, as the other 3 suffer from too much noise. The noise is mainly due to the buffer not being aligned to the cache set. Furthermore, as already known from previous attacks, the hardware prefetcher can induce a significant amount of noise [20,51].

Detecting one vulnerable cache set within all 2048 cache sets requires about 340 trials on average. With a monitoring time of 0.21 s per cache set, we require a maximum of 72 s to eventually capture a trace from a vulnerable cache set. Thus, based on our experiments, we estimate that cache set detection—if successful—always takes less than 3 min.

One trace spans 220.47 million CPU cycles on average. Typically, '0' and '1' bits are uniformly distributed in the key. The estimated number of multiplications is therefore half the bit size of the key. Thus, the average multiplication takes 107662 cycles. As the *Prime+Probe* measurement takes on average 734 cycles, we do not have to slow down the victim additionally.

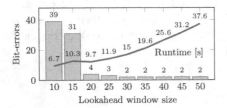
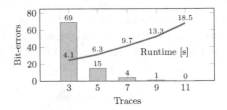

(a) Increasing the lookahead reduces bit errors and increases runtime.

(b) Increasing the number of traces reduces bit errors and increases runtime.

Fig. 6. Relation between number of traces, lookahead window size, number of bit errors, and runtime.

When looking at a single trace, we can already recover about 96% of the RSA private key, as shown in Fig. 5. For a full key recovery we combine multiple traces using our key recovery algorithm, as explained in Sect. 5. We first determine a reasonable lookahead window size. Figure 6a shows the performance of our key recovery algorithm for varying lookahead window sizes on 7 traces. For lookahead windows smaller than 20, bit errors are pretty high. In that case, the lookahead window is too small to account for all insertion and deletion errors, causing relative shifts between the partial keys. The key recovery algorithm is unable to align partial keys correctly and incurs many wrong "correction" steps, increasing the overall runtime as compared to a window size of 20. While a lookahead window size of 20 already shows a good performance, a window size of 30 or more does not significantly reduce the bit errors. Therefore, we fixed the lookahead window size to 20.

To remove the remaining bit errors and get full key recovery, we have to combine more traces. Figure 6b shows how the number of traces affects the key recovery performance. We can recover the full RSA private key without any bit errors by combining only 11 traces within just 18.5 s. This results in a total runtime of less than 130 s for the offline key recovery process.

Generalization. Based on our experiments we deduced that attacks are also possible in a weaker scenario, where only the attacker is inside the enclave. On most computers, applications handling cryptographic keys are not protected by SGX enclaves. From the attacker's perspective, attacking such an unprotected application does not differ from attacking an enclave. We only rely on the last-level cache, which is shared among all applications, whether they run inside an enclave or not. We empirically verified that such attacks on the outside world are possible and were again able to recover RSA private keys.

Table 2 summarizes our results. In contrast to concurrent work on cache attacks on SGX [8,17,37], our attack is the only one that can be mounted from unprivileged user space, and cannot be detected as it runs within an enclave.

Table 2. Our results show that cache attacks can be mounted successfully in the shown scenarios.

Attack from	Attack on		
	Benign userspace	Benign kernel	Benign SGX enclave
Malicious userspace	✓ [33,39]	✓ [22]	✓ **new**
Malicious kernel	—	—	✓ **new** [8,17,37]
Malicious SGX enclave	✓ **new**	✓ **new**	✓ **new**

6.2 Virtualized Environment

We now show that the attack also works in a virtualized environment. As described in Sect. 2.1, no hypervisor with SGX support was available at the time of our experiments. Instead of full virtualization using a virtual machine, we used lightweight Docker containers, as used by large cloud providers, e.g., Amazon [13] or Microsoft Azure [36]. To enable SGX within a container, the host operating system has to provide SGX support. The SGX driver is then simply shared among all containers. Figure 7 shows our setup where the SGX enclaves communicate directly with the SGX driver of the host operating system. Applications running inside the container do not experience any difference to running on a native system.

Considering the performance within Docker, only I/O operations and network access have a measurable overhead [14]. Operations that only depend on memory and CPU do not see any performance penalty, as these operations are not virtualized. Thus, caches are also not affected by the container.

We were successfully able to attack a victim from within a Docker container without any changes in the malware. We can even perform a cross-container attack, *i.e.*, both the malware and the victim are running inside different containers, without any changes. As expected, we require the same number of traces for a full key recovery. Hence, containers do not provide additional protection against our malware at all.

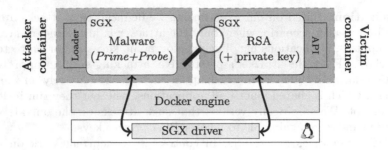

Fig. 7. Running the SGX enclaves inside Docker containers to provide further isolation. The host provides both containers access to the same SGX driver.

7   Countermeasures

Most existing countermeasures cannot be applied to a scenario where a malicious enclave performs a cache attack and no assumptions about the operating system are made. In this section, we discuss 3 categories of countermeasures, based on where they ought to be implemented.

7.1   Source Level

A generic side-channel protection for cryptographic operations (e.g., RSA) is exponent blinding [30]. It will prevent the proposed attack, but other parts of the signature process might still be vulnerable to an attack [45]. More generally bit slicing can be applied to a wider range of algorithms to protect against timing side channels [5,47]

7.2   Operating System Level

Implementing countermeasures against malicious enclave attacks on the operating system level requires trusting the operating system. This would weaken the trust model of SGX enclaves significantly, but in some threat models this can be a viable solution. However, we want to discuss the different possibilities, in order to provide valuable information for the design process of future enclave systems.

Detecting Malware. One of the core ideas of SGX is to remove the cloud provider from the root of trust. If the enclave is encrypted and only decrypted after successful remote attestation, the cloud provider has no way to access the secret code inside the enclave. Also, heuristic methods, such as behavior-based detection, are not applicable, as the malicious enclave does not rely on malicious API calls or user interaction which could be monitored. However, eliminating this core feature of SGX could mitigate malicious enclaves in practice, as the enclave binary or source code could be read by the cloud provider and scanned for malicious activities.

Herath and Fogh [21] proposed to use hardware performance counters to detect cache attacks. Subsequently, several other approaches instrumenting performance counters to detect cache attacks have been proposed [9,19,40]. However, according to Intel, SGX enclave activity is not visible in the thread-specific performance counters [26]. We verified that even performance counters for last-level cache accesses are disabled for enclaves. The performance counter values are three orders of magnitude below the values as compared to native code. There are no cache hits and misses visible to the operating system or any application (including the host application). This makes it impossible for current anti-virus software and other detection mechanisms to detect malware inside the enclave.

Enclave Coloring. We propose enclave coloring as an effective countermeasure against cross-enclave attacks. Enclave coloring is a software approach to partition the cache into multiple smaller domains. Each domain spans over multiple cache sets, and no cache set is included in more than one domain. An enclave gets one or more cache domains assigned exclusively. The assignment of domains is either done by the hardware or by the operating system. Trusting the operating system contradicts one of the core ideas of SGX [10]. However, if the operating system is trusted, this is an effective countermeasure against cross-enclave cache attacks.

If implemented in software, the operating system can split the last-level cache through memory allocation. The cache set index is determined by physical address bits below bit 12 (the page offset) and bits >12 which are not visible to the enclave application and can thus be controlled by the operating system. We call these upper bits a color. Whenever an enclave requests pages from the operating system (we consider the SGX driver as part of the operating system), it will only get pages with a color that is not present in any other enclave. This coloring ensures that two enclaves cannot have data in the same cache set, and therefore a *Prime+Probe* attack is not possible across enclaves. However, attacks on the operating system or other processes on the same host would still be possible.

To prevent attacks on the operating system or other processes, it would be necessary to partition the rest of the memory as well, *i.e.*, system-wide cache coloring [43]. Godfrey et al. [16] evaluated a coloring method for hypervisors by assigning every virtual machine a partition of the cache. They concluded that this method is only feasible for a small number of partitions. As the number of simultaneous enclaves is relatively limited by the available amount of SGX memory, enclave coloring can be applied to prevent cross-enclave attacks. Protecting enclaves from malicious applications or preventing malware inside enclaves is however not feasible using this method.

Heap Randomization. Our attack relies on the fact, that the used buffers for the multiplication are always at the same memory location. This is the case, as the used memory allocator (dlmalloc) has a deterministic best-fit strategy for moderate buffer sizes as used in RSA. Freeing a buffer and allocating it again will result in the same memory location for the re-allocated buffer.

We suggest randomizing the heap allocations for security relevant data such as the used buffers. A randomization of the addresses and thus cache sets bears two advantages. First, automatic cache set detection is not possible anymore, as the identified set will change for every run of the algorithm. Second, if more than one trace is required to reconstruct the key, heap randomization increases the number of required traces by multiple orders of magnitude, as the probability to measure the correct cache set by chance decreases.

Although not obvious at first glance, this method requires a certain amount of trust in the operating system. A malicious operating system could assign only pages mapping to certain cache sets to the enclave, similar to enclave coloring. Thus, the randomization is limited to only a subset of cache sets, increasing the probability for an attacker to measure the correct cache set.

Intel CAT. Recently, Intel introduced an instruction set extension called CAT (cache allocation technology) [24]. With Intel CAT it is possible to restrict CPU cores to one of the slices of the last-level cache and even to pin cache lines. Liu et al. [32] proposed a system that uses CAT to protect general purpose software and cryptographic algorithms. Their approach can be directly applied to protect against a malicious enclave. However, this approach does not allow to protect enclaves from an outside attacker.

7.3   Hardware Level

Combining Intel CAT with SGX. Instead of using Intel CAT on the operating system level it could also be used to protect enclaves on the hardware level. By changing the `eenter` instruction in a way that it implicitly activates CAT for this core, any cache sharing between SGX enclaves and the outside as well as co-located enclaves could be eliminated. Thus, SGX enclaves would be protected from outside attackers. Furthermore, it would protect co-located enclaves as well as the operating system and user programs against malicious enclaves.

Secure RAM. To fully mitigate cache- or DRAM-based side-channel attacks memory must not be shared among processes. We propose an additional fast, non-cachable secure memory element that resides inside the CPU.

The SGX driver can then provide an API to acquire the element for temporarily storing sensitive data. A cryptographic library could use this memory to execute code which depends on secret keys such as the square-and-multiply algorithm. Providing such a secure memory element per CPU core would even allow parallel execution of multiple enclaves.

Data from this element is only accessible by one program, thus cache attacks and DRAM-based attacks are not possible anymore. Moreover, if this secure memory is inside the CPU, it is infeasible for an attacker to mount physical attacks. It is unclear whether the Intel eDRAM implementation can already be instrumented as a secure memory to protect applications against cache attacks.

8 Conclusion

Intel claimed that SGX features impair side-channel attacks and recommends using SGX enclaves to protect cryptographic computations. Intel also claimed that enclaves cannot perform harmful operations.

In this paper, we demonstrated the first malware running in real SGX hardware enclaves. We demonstrated cross-enclave private key theft in an automated semi-synchronous end-to-end attack, despite all restrictions of SGX, e.g., no timers, no large pages, no physical addresses, and no shared memory. We developed a timing measurement technique with the highest resolution currently known for Intel CPUs, perfectly tailored to the hardware. We combined DRAM and cache side channels, to build a novel approach that recovers physical address bits without assumptions on the page size. We attack the RSA implementation of *mbedTLS*, which uses constant-time multiplication primitives. We extract 96% of a 4096-bit RSA key from a single *Prime+Probe* trace and achieve full key recovery from only 11 traces.

Besides not fully preventing malicious enclaves, SGX provides protection features to conceal attack code. Even the most advanced detection mechanisms using performance counters cannot detect our malware. This unavoidably provides attackers with the ability to hide attacks as it eliminates the only known technique to detect cache side-channel attacks. We discussed multiple design issues in SGX and proposed countermeasures for future SGX versions.

Acknowledgments. This project has received funding from the European Research Council (ERC) under the European Unions Horizon 2020 research and innovation programme (grant agreement No 681402).   This work was partially supported by the TU Graz LEAD project "Dependable Internet of Things in Adverse Environments".

References

1. Anati, I., McKeen, F., Gueron, S., Huang, H., Johnson, S., Leslie-Hurd, R., Patil, H., Rozas, C.V., Shafi, H.: Intel Software Guard Extensions (Intel SGX) (2015). Tutorial Slides presented at ICSA 2015
2. ARMmbed: Reduce mbed TLS memory and storage footprint, February 2016. https://tls.mbed.org/kb/how-to/reduce-mbedtls-memory-and-storage-footprint. Accessed 24 Oct 2016
3. Arnaud, C., Fouque, P.-A.: Timing attack against protected RSA-CRT implementation used in PolarSSL. In: Dawson, E. (ed.) CT-RSA 2013. LNCS, vol. 7779, pp. 18–33. Springer, Heidelberg (2013). doi:10.1007/978-3-642-36095-4_2
4. Arnautov, S., Trach, B., Gregor, F., Knauth, T., Martin, A., Priebe, C., Lind, J., Muthukumaran, D., O'Keeffe, D., Stillwell, M.L., et al.: SCONE: secure Linux containers with Intel SGX. In: 12th USENIX Symposium on Operating Systems Design and Implementation (OSDI 2016) (2016)

5. Biham, E.: A fast new DES implementation in software. In: International Workshop on Fast Software Encryption, pp. 260–272 (1997)
6. Blömer, J., May, A.: New partial key exposure attacks on RSA. In: Boneh, D. (ed.) CRYPTO 2003. LNCS, vol. 2729, pp. 27–43. Springer, Heidelberg (2003). doi:10. 1007/978-3-540-45146-4_2
7. Boneh, D., Durfee, G., Frankel, Y.: An attack on RSA given a small fraction of the private key bits. In: Ohta, K., Pei, D. (eds.) ASIACRYPT 1998. LNCS, vol. 1514, pp. 25–34. Springer, Heidelberg (1998). doi:10.1007/3-540-49649-1_3
8. Brasser, F., Müller, U., Dmitrienko, A., Kostiainen, K., Capkun, S., Sadeghi, A.: Software grand exposure: SGX cache attacks are practical (2017). http://arxiv. org/abs/1702.07521
9. Chiappetta, M., Savas, E., Yilmaz, C.: Real time detection of cache-based side-channel attacks using hardware performance counters. Cryptology ePrint Archive, Report 2015/1034 (2015)
10. Costan, V., Devadas, S.: Intel SGX explained. Technical report, Cryptology ePrint Archive, Report 2016/086 (2016)
11. Moura, L., Bjørner, N.: Z3: an efficient SMT solver. In: Ramakrishnan, C.R., Rehof, J. (eds.) TACAS 2008. LNCS, vol. 4963, pp. 337–340. Springer, Heidelberg (2008). doi:10.1007/978-3-540-78800-3_24
12. Demme, J., Maycock, M., Schmitz, J., Tang, A., Waksman, A., Sethumadhavan, S., Stolfo, S.: On the feasibility of online malware detection with performance counters. ACM SIGARCH Comput. Archit. News 41(3), 559–570 (2013)
13. Docker: Amazon web services - docker (2016). https://docs.docker.com/machine/ drivers/aws/
14. Felter, W., Ferreira, A., Rajamony, R., Rubio, J.: An updated performance comparison of virtual machines and linux containers. In: 2015 IEEE International Symposium On Performance Analysis of Systems and Software (ISPASS) (2015)
15. Ge, Q., Yarom, Y., Cock, D., Heiser, G.: A survey of microarchitectural timing attacks and countermeasures on contemporary hardware. Technical report, Cryptology ePrint Archive, Report 2016/613 (2016)
16. Godfrey, M.M., Zulkernine, M.: Preventing cache-based side-channel attacks in a cloud environment. IEEE Trans. Cloud Comput. 2(4), 395–408 (2014)
17. Götzfried, J., Eckert, M., Schinzel, S., Müller, T.: Cache attacks on Intel SGX. In: Proceedings of the 10th European Workshop on Systems Security (EuroSec 2017) (2017)
18. Gruss, D., Maurice, C., Mangard, S.: Rowhammer.js: a remote software-induced fault attack in JavaScript. In: Caballero, J., Zurutuza, U., Rodríguez, R.J. (eds.) DIMVA 2016. LNCS, vol. 9721, pp. 300–321. Springer, Cham (2016). doi:10.1007/ 978-3-319-40667-1_15
19. Gruss, D., Maurice, C., Wagner, K., Mangard, S.: Flush+Flush: a fast and stealthy cache attack. In: Caballero, J., Zurutuza, U., Rodríguez, R.J. (eds.) DIMVA 2016. LNCS, vol. 9721, pp. 279–299. Springer, Cham (2016). doi:10.1007/ 978-3-319-40667-1_14
20. Gruss, D., Spreitzer, R., Mangard, S.: Cache template attacks: automating attacks on inclusive last-level caches. In: USENIX Security Symposium (2015)
21. Herath, N., Fogh, A.: These are not your grand Daddys CPU performance counters - CPU hardware performance counters for security. In: Black Hat USA (2015)
22. Hund, R., Willems, C., Holz, T.: Practical timing side channel attacks against kernel space ASLR. In: S&P 2013 (2013)
23. Intel: Intel® 64 and IA-32 Architectures Optimization Reference Manual (2014)

24. Intel: Intel® 64 and IA-32 Architectures Software Developer's Manual, Volume 3 (3A, 3B & 3C): System Programming Guide 253665 (2014)
25. Intel Corporation: Hardening Password Managers with Intel Software Guard Extensions: White Paper (2016)
26. Intel Corporation: Intel SGX: Debug, Production, Pre-release what's the difference? https://software.intel.com/en-us/blogs/2016/01/07/intel-sgx-debug-production-prelease-whats-the-difference. Accessed 24 Oct 2016
27. Intel Corporation: Intel Software Guard Extensions (Intel SGX) (2016). https://software.intel.com/en-us/sgx. Accessed 7 Nov 2016
28. Intel Corporation: Intel(R) Software Guard Extensions for Linux* OS (2016). https://github.com/01org/linux-sgx-driver. Accessed 11 Nov 2016
29. Irazoqui, G., Inci, M.S., Eisenbarth, T., Sunar, B.: Wait a minute! a fast, cross-VM attack on AES. In: Stavrou, A., Bos, H., Portokalidis, G. (eds.) RAID 2014. LNCS, vol. 8688, pp. 299–319. Springer, Cham (2014). doi:10.1007/978-3-319-11379-1_15
30. Kocher, P.C.: Timing attacks on implementations of Diffie-Hellman, RSA, DSS, and other systems. In: Koblitz, N. (ed.) CRYPTO 1996. LNCS, vol. 1109, pp. 104–113. Springer, Heidelberg (1996). doi:10.1007/3-540-68697-5_9
31. Lipp, M., Gruss, D., Spreitzer, R., Maurice, C., Mangard, S.: ARMageddon: cache attacks on mobile devices. In: USENIX Security Symposium (2016)
32. Liu, F., Ge, Q., Yarom, Y., Mckeen, F., Rozas, C., Heiser, G., Lee, R.B.: Catalyst: defeating last-level cache side channel attacks in cloud computing. In: IEEE International Symposium on High Performance Computer Architecture (HPCA 2016) (2016)
33. Liu, F., Yarom, Y., Ge, Q., Heiser, G., Lee, R.B.: Last-level cache side-channel attacks are practical. In: S&P 2015 (2015)
34. Maurice, C., Scouarnec, N., Neumann, C., Heen, O., Francillon, A.: Reverse engineering intel last-level cache complex addressing using performance counters. In: Bos, H., Monrose, F., Blanc, G. (eds.) RAID 2015. LNCS, vol. 9404, pp. 48–65. Springer, Cham (2015). doi:10.1007/978-3-319-26362-5_3
35. Maurice, C., Weber, M., Schwarz, M., Giner, L., Gruss, D., Boano, C.A., Mangard, S., Römer, K.: Hello from the other side: SSH over robust cache covert channels in the cloud. In: NDSS 2017 (2017)
36. Microsoft: Create a Docker environment in azure using the docker VM extension, October 2016. https://azure.microsoft.com/en-us/documentation/articles/virtual-machines-linux-dockerextension/
37. Moghimi, A., Irazoqui, G., Eisenbarth, T.: CacheZoom: how SGX amplifies the power of cache attacks. arXiv preprint arXiv:1703.06986 (2017)
38. Oren, Y., Kemerlis, V.P., Sethumadhavan, S., Keromytis, A.D.: The spy in the sandbox: practical cache attacks in JavaScript and their implications. In: CCS 2015 (2015)
39. Osvik, D.A., Shamir, A., Tromer, E.: Cache attacks and countermeasures: the case of AES. In: CT-RSA 2006 (2006)
40. Payer, M.: HexPADS: a platform to detect "stealth" attacks. In: ESSoS 2016 (2016)
41. Pereida García, C., Brumley, B.B., Yarom, Y.: Make sure DSA signing exponentiations really are constant-time. In: Proceedings of the 2016 ACM SIGSAC Conference on Computer and Communications Security (2016)
42. Pessl, P., Gruss, D., Maurice, C., Schwarz, M., Mangard, S.: DRAMA: exploiting DRAM addressing for Cross-CPU attacks. In: USENIX Security Symposium (2016)
43. Raj, H., Nathuji, R., Singh, A., England, P.: Resource management for isolation enhanced cloud services. In: Proceedings of the 1st ACM Cloud Computing Security Workshop (CCSW 2009), pp. 77–84 (2009)

44. Rutkowska, J.: Thoughts on Intel's upcoming Software Guard Extensions (Part 2) (2013). http://theinvisiblethings.blogspot.co.at/2013/09/thoughts-on-intels-upcoming-software.html. Accessed 20 Oct 2016
45. Schindler, W.: Exclusive exponent blinding may not suffice to prevent timing attacks on RSA. In: Güneysu, T., Handschuh, H. (eds.) CHES 2015. LNCS, vol. 9293, pp. 229–247. Springer, Heidelberg (2015). doi:10.1007/978-3-662-48324-4_12
46. Schuster, F., Costa, M., Fournet, C., Gkantsidis, C., Peinado, M., Mainar-Ruiz, G., Russinovich, M.: VC3: trustworthy data analytics in the cloud using SGX (2015)
47. Sudhakar, M., Kamala, R.V., Srinivas, M.: A bit-sliced, scalable and unified montgomery multiplier architecture for RSA and ECC. In: 2007 IFIP International Conference on Very Large Scale Integration, pp. 252–257 (2007)
48. Matsui, M., Zuccherato, R.J. (eds.): SAC 2003. LNCS, vol. 3006. Springer, Heidelberg (2004)
49. Wray, J.C.: An analysis of covert timing channels. J. Comput. Secur. 1(3–4), 219–232 (1992)
50. Xu, Y., Cui, W., Peinado, M.: Controlled-channel attacks: deterministic side channels for untrusted operating systems. In: S&P 2015, May 2015
51. Yarom, Y., Falkner, K.: Flush+Reload: a high resolution, low noise, L3 cache side-channel attack. In: USENIX Security Symposium (2014)

On the Trade-Offs in Oblivious Execution Techniques

Shruti Tople$^{(\boxtimes)}$ and Prateek Saxena

National University of Singapore, Singapore, Singapore
{shruti90,prateeks}@comp.nus.edu.sg

Abstract. To enable privacy-preserving computation on encrypted data, a class of techniques for input-oblivious execution have surfaced. The property of input-oblivious execution guarantees that an adversary observing the interaction of a program with the underlying system learns nothing about the sensitive input. To highlight the importance of oblivious execution, we demonstrate a concrete practical attack—called a logic-reuse attack—that leaks every byte of encrypted input if oblivious techniques are not used. Next, we study the efficacy of oblivious execution techniques and understand their limitations from a practical perspective. We manually transform 30 common Linux utilities by applying known oblivious execution techniques. As a positive result, we show that 6 utilities perform input-oblivious execution without modification, 11 utilities can be transformed with $O(1)$ performance overhead and 11 other show $O(N)$ overhead. As a negative result, we show that theoretical limitations of oblivious execution techniques do manifest in 2 real applications in our case studies incurring a performance cost of $O(2^N)$ over non-oblivious execution.

1 Introduction

Many emerging techniques provide privacy preserving computation on encrypted data. These techniques can be categorized into two lines of work—secure computation and enclaved execution. Secure computation techniques enable operations on encrypted data without decrypting them. Examples of such techniques include fully homomorphic encryption [24–26], partially homomorphic encryption [20,31,50,52,61], garbled circuits [34,36,68] and so on. A second line of research uses hardware-isolation mechanisms provided by Intel SGX [48], TPM [5], Intel TXT [4], ARM Trustzones [7,44]. Systems such as Haven [10], XOM [60], Flicker [47] use these mechanisms to provide *enclaved execution*. In enclaved execution the application runs in a hardware-isolated environment in the presence of an untrusted operating system. The sensitive data is decrypted only in the hardware-isolated environment and the computation result is encrypted before it exits the enclaved execution. Enclaved execution can be achieved via hypervisor-based mechanisms as well (cf. OverShadow [14], Inktag [32]).

One fundamental challenge in privacy preserving computation is to make the program execution *input-oblivious*. Input-oblivious execution guarantees that the

© Springer International Publishing AG 2017
M. Polychronakis and M. Meier (Eds.): DIMVA 2017, LNCS 10327, pp. 25–47, 2017.
DOI: 10.1007/978-3-319-60876-1_2

execution profile of a program observed by an adversary reveals nothing about the sensitive input. This challenge goes beyond the mechanism of enabling individual operations on encrypted inputs, whether done in enclaved execution environments or via cryptographic techniques for secure computation. In concept, it is easy to show that making all programs oblivious may be undecidable; such a result is neither surprising nor particularly interesting to practice. We study this problem from a practical perspective—whether it is feasible to make existing commodity applications execute obliviously without unreasonable loss in performance. If so, to what extent is this feasible and whether any theoretical limitations manifest themselves in relevant applications.

We explain the problem conceptually, considering various channels of leakage in the scenario of enclaved execution. To highlight the importance of oblivious execution, we show that enclaved execution is highly vulnerable to leakage of sensitive data via a concrete attack—called a logic-reuse attack. Specifically, we show that chaining execution of commonly used utilities can leak every byte of an encrypted input to the enclaved application.

Next, we study how existing oblivious execution techniques such as padding of dummy instructions [46], hiding message length [19] or hiding address accesses using Oblivious RAM [28] proposed in different contexts can be used to block the leakage in enclaved execution. Our work explains the symmetry among these lines of research, systematizing their capabilities and explaining the limits of these techniques in practical applications. Specifically, we manually transform 30 applications from the standard CoreUtils package available on Linux operating system. As a positive result, we show that 6 utilities perform input-oblivious execution without modification, 11 utilities can be transformed with $O(1)$ performance overhead and 11 other show linear performance overhead of $O(N)$.

As a negative result, we show that theoretical limitations of oblivious execution techniques do manifest in 2 utilities which incur an exponential performance overhead of $O(2^N)$. Of course, they can be made oblivious conceptually, since everything on a digital computer is finite—in practice, this is hard to do without prohibitive loss in performance.

Contribution. We summarize our contributions as follows:

- 1. *Logic-reuse attack:* We demonstrate a concrete attack in the enclaved execution setting that leaks every byte of encrypted input by chaining execution of common applications.
- 2. *Systematization of oblivious execution techniques:* We systematize existing defenses for oblivious execution and show new limitations for enclaved execution of practical applications.
- 3. *Study of practical applications:* To study an empirical datapoint, we manually transform 30 applications from CoreUtils package to make them input-oblivious using existing defenses and find that 28 applications can be transformed with acceptable overhead. The limitations of oblivious execution techniques manifest in 2 applications which cannot be transformed without prohibitive loss in performance.

2   The Problem

Baseline Setting. Various existing solutions such as OverShadow [14], SecureMe [15], Inktag [32], SGX [48], Haven [10] and Panoply [57] support enclaved execution of applications. Here, the OS is untrusted whereas the underlying processor is trusted and secure. The file system is encrypted under a secret key K to protect the data on the untrusted storage. The trusted application executes in an enclaved memory which is inaccessible to the untrusted OS. The secret key K is available to the enclaved memory for decrypting the sensitive data. This system guarantees confidentiality and integrity of sensitive content using authenticated encryption. However, the application still relies on the OS to interact with the untrusted storage using *read-write channels* such as file system calls, memory page management and others.

Our baseline setting (shown in Fig. 1) is a system (such as Panoply [57]) where the read-write channels correspond to the read and write system calls. Although our discussion here is for the system call interface, our attack and defenses are applicable to other read-write operations that expose information at the granularity of blocks or memory pages, when caching or swapping out pages (for eg. in Haven [10], OverShadow [14]).

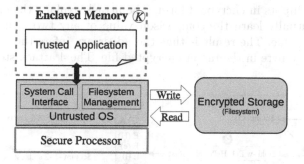

Fig. 1. Baseline setting for enclaved execution with untrusted read-write channels

Attack Model. In our model, the untrusted (or compromised) OS acts as a "honest-but-curious" adversary that honestly interacts with the application and the underlying encrypted storage. It passively observes the *input/output (I/O) profile* of the execution, but hopes to infer sensitive encrypted data. The I/O profile of an application is the "trace" of read-write file system calls made during the execution. The execution of an application A with sensitive input I and output O generates an I/O profile $P = (P_1, P_2, ...P_n)$. Each P_i is a read/write operation of the form $[type, size, address, time]$ requested by the application A. Each P_i consists of four parameters:

- (**C1**) type of operation (read or write)
- (**C2**) size of bytes read or written
- (**C3**) address (e.g. file name/descriptor) to read or write the content
- (**C4**) time interval between current and previous operation.

We assume the application A is publicly available and known to the adversary. Thus, the attacker's knowledge set consists of $\psi = \{A, |I|, |O|, P\}$ where $|I|$ and $|O|$ are the total input and output size, and A is the application logic. We assume the OS is capable of initiating the execution of any pre-installed application on encrypted inputs, in any order.

Goal. The goal is to make a benign enclaved application input-oblivious. An application that exhibits I/O profile P which is independent of the sensitive inputs exhibits the above security property. This security property guarantees that an adversary cannot distinguish between any two encrypted inputs of the same size when executed with the same application, leaking nothing beyond what is implied by knowledge of ψ.

2.1 Logic-Reuse Attack

To emphasize the importance of input-oblivious execution in the enclaved execution scenario, we demonstrate a concrete attack called the *logic-reuse attack*. In this attack, the adversary chains the execution of permitted applications to do its bidding (as shown in Fig. 2). Specifically, we show the use of four applications: `nl`, `fold`, `split` and `comm` from the CoreUtils package commonly available in commodity Linux systems [3]. These applications accept sensitive user arguments and file inputs in encrypted form. The attack exploits the execution I/O profile to eventually learn the comparison value of any two characters in the input encrypted file. The result is that the adversary infers the frequency and position of every byte in the target encrypted file. The 4 attack steps are:

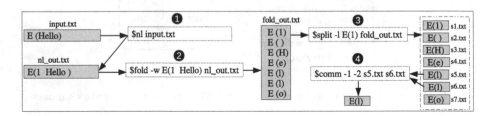

Fig. 2. Attack example that leaks the frequency and position of characters in an encrypted file

Step 1 - Get a known ciphertext value: The `nl` command in CoreUtils adds a line number to each line in the input and writes the modified line to the output. The attacker executes this `nl` program with the target encrypted file (`input.txt` in Fig. 2) as its input. Every ciphertext is of 16 bytes given the use of AES encryption. Thus, the adversary learns that the first ciphertext of each write call contains the encryption of a number along with other characters (see `nl_out.txt` in Fig. 2).

Step 2 - Generate the ciphertext for individual characters: This step uses the `fold` program that folds input lines according to the given width size. The adversary runs this command on the output of the previous step. The ciphertext for encryption of number "1" (along with other characters) learned in Step 1 is used as encrypted input argument to the width size. This step folds the input file such that every line contains the ciphertext of a single character and makes a separate call to write it. After this step, the ciphertext for every individual character in the file is available to the adversary (as shown in `fold_out.txt` in Fig. 2).

Step 3 - Save each ciphertext in a separate file: In this step, the adversary uses the `split` program that splits an input file either line-wise or byte-wise and writes the output to different files. The command is run on the output of Step 2. The ciphertext of the character "1" learned in Step 2 is passed as an option to it. It generates separate files as output each having encryption of a single character (`s1.txt` - `s6.txt` in Fig. 2). Thus, the adversary learns the total number of characters and their positions in the input file.

Step 4 - Compare the characters in each file: Finally, the adversary executes the `comm` program that takes two files as input and writes the lines present in both the files as output. Any two files generated as output in the previous step can be provided as input to this command. The program does not perform a write call if there are no common lines in the input files. Thus, the I/O profile leaks whether two lines (or characters) in the input files are the same.

Result: In the end, this allows the attacker to infer a histogram of encrypted bytes. Once the histogram is recovered, it can be compared to standard frequency distribution of (say) English characters [1]. Using the values in the histogram and the positions learned in Step 3, the adversary learns the value of every byte in the encrypted file!

Remarks. Note that, the adversary neither tampers the integrity of the sensitive input nor disrupts the execution process in any manner throughout the attack. It simply invokes the applications on controlled arguments and honestly executes the read-write operations from the application without tampering any results. The adversary only passively observes the input-dependent I/O profile of the execution. Thus, we establish that it is practical to completely leak every byte in an encrypted file system in the absence of input-oblivious execution, when program logic running in enclave is sufficiently expressive.

3   Analysis of Information Leakage Channels

Recall that in our model, parameters in I/O profile P form the four channels **C1** to **C4** discussed in Sect. 2. The *type* parameter is either R (read) or W (write) call, *size* is the bytes read or written to the untrusted storage, and the *address* signifies the file descriptor (fd) in use. Let *time* be the difference in the time-stamp[1] for the occurrence of present and previous call. This section analyses the channels **C1** to **C4** in P for information leakage and their role in expanding attackers knowledge set ψ.

```
1    rsize = read(infile, inbuffer, 1, infilesize);
2    line1 = getline(inbuffer);
3    while ((line2 = getline(inbuffer)) != NULL)
4      if ((linecompare(line1, line2)) == true)
5        match = true;
6      else
7        if (match == true)
8          wsize = write(repeat_out, line1, 1, strlen(line1));
9          match = false;
10       else
11         wsize = write(uniq_out, line1, 1, strlen(line1));
12     line1 = line2;
```

Fig. 3. Sample program which writes repeated lines in the input to repeat_out file and the non-repeated lines to uniq_out file.

Throughout the rest of the paper, we consider a running example similar to the **uniq** Unix utility (refer to Fig. 3) that has 4 information leakage channels. The example reads the data from an input file (line 1) and writes out consecutive repeated lines to **repeat_out** file (line 8) and non-repeated lines to **uniq_out** file (line 11). The code performs a character-by-character comparison (line 4) to check whether two lines are equal. Figure 4 shows the I/O profile that this program generates for two different inputs of the same size and the overall information learned about each input file. The I/O profile leaks the total number of input lines, output lines, repeated and non-repeated lines in the encrypted file.

Sequence of Calls (C1). The sequence of calls is an *input-dependent* parameter that depends on the **if** and loop terminating conditions in the application. In particular, the sequence of calls in the example are control-dependent on the bits from the sensitive input used in branch conditions.

Example. The program in Fig. 3 uses a separate write call (highlighted) to output a new line[2]. Every time the adversary observes a **write** call in the I/O profile, it learns that a newline is written to the output file. This is beyond the allowed set ψ because it leaks the total number of lines in the output. From the I/O profiles in Fig. 4, the adversary learns that input 1 and 2 yield total of 3 and 4 lines as output respectively.

---

[1] The granularity of the clock is units of measurement as small as what the attacker can measure (e.g., ms, ns or even finer).

[2] This is a common programming practice observed in legacy applications such as CoreUtils as shown later in Sect. 6.

Difference in Size of Bytes (C2). The return values of the read and write system calls act as the *size* channel for information leakage. As the *size* parameter in the I/O profile P shows a direct data dependency on the input values, any difference in the value of this parameter leaks information about the encrypted inputs.

Example. In Fig. 4, the adversary observes that the difference in the size of total read and write bytes for input 1 is 130 bytes, inferring that 1 line is repeated. For input 2 the difference is 185 (90 + 95) bytes. Observing the size values in the profile for input 2, the adversary can infer that it has 2 lines repeated since no other combination of sizes result in a difference of 185 bytes.

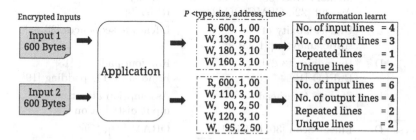

Fig. 4. I/O profiles generated for two different inputs Input1 and Input2 of size 600 bytes. The numbers 1, 2 and 3 in the I/O profile are the file descriptors for infile, repeat_out and uniq_out respectively. The last part shows the information learned by observing the I/O profile.

Address Access Patterns (C3). We consider the file descriptor (fd) to the read and write system call as the *address* parameter in the I/O profile P. This is assuming the OS organizes its underlying storage in files. The untrusted OS infers the input dependent accesses patterns to different files from this parameter, as shown in the example below.

Example. In Fig. 4, the *address* parameter in P leaks that input 1 reads the repeat_out file (fd = 2) once and input 2 reads it twice leaking that they contain 1 and 2 repeated lines respectively. Similar observation for uniq_out file (fd = 3) leaks that input 1 and input 2 both have 2 unique lines.

Side Channels - Time (C4). There are several well-known side channels such as power consumption [41], cache latency [51], time [11,42] that could leak information about sensitive inputs. We focus on the computation time difference between any two calls as a representative channel of information leakage. Our discussion applies more broadly to other observed channels too.

Example. In Fig. 4, readers can see that the computation time before a call that writes to repeat_out file is 50 units and uniq_out file is 10 units. A careful analysis of the time difference between all consecutive calls reveals that input 1 and 2 have 1 and 2 repeated lines respectively. This is because for repeated lines the character-by-character comparison (line 4 in Fig. 3) proceeds till the end of the line, thus taking more time. However, the comparison fails immediately if the lines are not the same, reducing the time difference.

The above explanation with our running example establishes that every parameter in the I/O profile acts as an independent channel of information leakage. Each channel contributes towards increasing the ψ of an adversary.

Table 1. Systematization of existing defenses to hide leakage through I/O profile and their known limitations. 'D' and 'L' denote defenses and limitations.

Channel	D/L	Determinising I/O Profile	Randomizing I/O Profile
Type	D	Memory trace obliviousness [46] Ascend [22], CBMC-GC [34]	RandSys [38] RISE [9]
	L	Undecidability of static analysis [21,43]	Infeasible sequences [33,64]
Size	D	Rounding [13,67], BuFLO [19]	Random padding [13], Random MTU padding [19]
	L	Storage Overhead	Assumption about input distribution
Address	D	Linear Scan [30,40,63,71]	ORAM [28], [59]
	L	Access Overhead [30,63]	*polylog N* overhead [56]
Time	D	Normalized timing [11,37] Language-based Approach [6,17,49,70]	Fuzzy Time [35]
	L	Worst Case Execution Time [65]	Insufficient Entropy [27]

4 Defense: Approaches and Limitations

To block the above information channels (**C1** to **C4**), the execution of an application should be input-oblivious i.e., the adversary cannot distinguish between two inputs by observing the I/O profile. We formally define the security property of "input-oblivious execution" as:

Definition 1 (Input-Oblivious Execution). *The execution of an application A is input-oblivious if, for any adversary $\mathcal{A}$ given encrypted inputs $E(i), E(j)$ and a query profile P, the following property holds:*

$$Adv\mathcal{A} := |Pr[\mathcal{P} = \mathcal{P}[E(i)]] - Pr[\mathcal{P} = \mathcal{P}[E(j)]]| \leq \epsilon \qquad (1)$$

where ϵ is negligible.

There are two common approaches to achieve input-oblivious execution: (a) determinising the I/O profile and (b) randomizing the I/O profile. We study these existing defenses and show whether their limitations manifest in practical applications. Table 1 systematizes existing defenses and their limitations.

4.1   Approach 1: Determinising the Profile

The idea is to make the execution of an application input-oblivious by determinising the parameters in the I/O profile. This forces a program operating on different inputs of the same size to generate equivalent I/O profiles. Figure 5 shows the modified code for our example (in Fig. 3) and its determinised I/O profile.

Channel C1 - Type. To determinise the *type* parameter in P, a program should have the same sequence of calls for different inputs irrespective of the path it executes. This requires making the execution of read/write calls independent of the sensitive data used in the branches or loops of a program. One way to achieve this is to move the read/write calls outside the conditional branches or the loop statements. This removes their dependence on any sensitive data that decides the execution path. The other method is to apply the idea of adding dummy instructions to both the branches of an `if` condition, as proposed in works on oblivious memory trace execution [22, 46]. This makes the I/O profile input-oblivious with respect to the `if` statements in the program. Loops can be determinised by fixing a upper bound on the number of iterations. Previous work on privacy preserving techniques use this method to remove the input-dependence in loops [34, 46].

Example: We show how to apply this idea to our running example. In Fig. 5, we determinise the sequence of calls by moving the write call outside the loop making them data-indpendent. All the lines are combined into a single buffer and are written outside the loop. This makes the profile P deterministic with respect to the *type* parameter while retaining the performance.

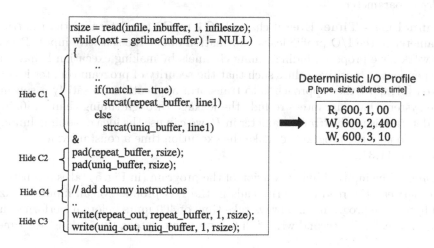

Fig. 5. Modified code with the defense to hide the channels of information leakage in I/O profile and a deterministic I/O profile for input of size 600 bytes.

Channel C2 - Size. To hide the leakage through *size* parameter, a straight-forward method is to pad the data with dummy bytes up to a certain maximum value. Padding technique is used in several other contexts to hide leakage through message length. Chen et al. and Wright et al. use the idea of rounding messages to fixed length to prevent information leakage in web applications and encrypted VoIP conversations [13,67]. Dyer et al. proposed the idea of BuFLO (Buffered Fixed Length Obfuscator) as a countermeasure against traffic analysis [19]. Similarly, in program execution, padding can be used to determinise channel **C2** by forcing the same value of *size* parameter in profile *P*.

Example: In Fig. 5, we pad the arguments to the write calls upto the size of total read bytes. This is because in our running example, the maximum output size equals the total input size when none of the input lines are repeated.

Channel C3 - Address. The pattern of *address* (file descriptor) parameter in profile *P* acts as a channel of information leakage. This is analogous to the memory access patterns observed in RAM memory. A memory address in the RAM model corresponds to a file descriptor in our setting. The simple approach to hide the address access patterns is to replace each access with a linear scan of all addresses [40]. In the context of secure two-party computations, Wang et al. and Gorden et al. show that linear scan approach is efficient for small number of addresses [30,63]. Privacy preserving compilers such as PICCO use the linear scan approach to access encrypted indexes [71]. Linear scanning approach can be used to determinise the I/O profile with respect to the *address* parameter.

Example: In Fig. 5, we modify the program to access both the `repeat_out` and `uniq_out` file for every execution no matter whether the input file contains any repeated or unique lines. This makes the execution oblivious with respect to the *address* parameter.

Channel C4 - Time. Even if channels **C1** to **C3** are deterministic, the *time* parameter in the I/O profile leaks information about the sensitive input. Previous work have proposed hiding timing channels by making execution behaviour independent of sensitive values such that the security of program counter is preserved [17,49]. Other approach is to transform applications to satisfy a specific type system that guarantees to hide the leakage through timing channel [6,70]. For determinising the *time* parameter in *P*, we can use the idea of adding dummy instructions in the program to make the execution time a constant value as suggested in [11,37].

Example: The input-oblivious version of the program (in Fig. 5) takes a constant time between the read and write calls in the I/O profile. For all inputs of size 600 bytes, the program will always take time of 400 units before it performs the first write call. The second write call follows immediately, thus taking less time.

4.2   Limitations of Determinising I/O Profile

Readers will notice that all the defenses to determinise the channels **C1** to **C4** exhibit one common characteristic. Each of the solution modifies their corresponding parameters in the I/O profile to the worst-case execution time. This introduces a performance trade off in most of the applications. Deterministic approach requires statically deciding the upper bound for the worst-case values of all the profile parameters. This is not always possible due to the theoretical limitations of static analysis [21]. Statically identifying the upper bounds for loops is itself an undecidable problem and notoriously difficult in practice too [43,54]. To explain the limitations, we use the split utility from CoreUtils package (shown in Fig. 6) which reads from an input file (line 1), splits a given input file line-wise (line 3) and writes the maximum B bytes as output to N different files (line 8).

```
1   n_read = safe_read (STDIN_FILENO, buf, bufsize);
2   while (true)
3       bp = memchr (bp, '\n', eob - bp + 1);
4       if (bp == eob)
5           break;
6       ++bp;
7       if (++n >= n_lines)
8           cwrite (new_file_flag, bp_out, bp - bp_out);
9       bp_out = bp;
10      new_file_flag = true;
11      n = 0;
```

Fig. 6. split program code that splits the lines in input file and writes to different output files

Type. In Fig. 6, it is difficult to statically decide a "feasible" upper bound on the number of loop iterations. In the worst case, a file can have a single character on each line in the input file. To explicitly decide an upper bound for a file of size around 1 GB, a determinised profile will execute the loop for $N = 2^{30}$ times (assuming one byte on each line) which is not a reasonable solution.

Address. The simple strategy of linearly accessing all addresses suffers from an overhead proportional to the maximum addresses an application uses during the execution [63]. In split program performing linear access incurs a total overhead of N^2 i.e., accessing N files for each of the N loop iterations (where $N = 2^{30}$ in worst case). This is impractical for real usage, unless N is small.

Size. Padding data with dummy bytes up to a maximum output size incurs huge storage overhead as shown in previous work [13,19]. In our split example, for a 1 GB input file, the maximum possible bytes in a line is $B = 1$ GB, when no newline characters are present in the file. Thus, determinising the split program results in total storage overhead of N GB. It becomes N^2 GB when the I/O profile is determinised with respect to *address* channel.

Time. Determinising the *time* channel results in worst case execution time for the application for different inputs of the same size [11,65]. For a file of 1 GB, `split` program will take equal time for input file having single character on every line or the whole file having just a single line.

4.3   Approach 2: Randomizing the I/O Profile

The second approach to making application execution input-oblivious is transforming the original I/O profile to a randomized profile. Randomizing the I/O profile involves addition of sufficient noise to every parameter in P. One advantage of randomization over determinising the profile is that it scales better in terms of performance for most of the applications. We explain this paradigm of randomization techniques using the `split` example in Fig. 6.

Oblivious RAM. A strategy for randomizing the address access patterns which is the focus of many current research works is to use Oblivious RAM (ORAM) [28,56,58,59,62]. ORAM technique replaces each read/write operation in the program with many operations and shuffles the mapping of content in the memory to hide the original access patterns [28]. With the best ORAM techniques, the application only needs to perform *poly log N* operations to hide the access pattern where N is the total address space [56,58]. This is strictly better as compared to linear overhead of N operations in the trivial approach. Use of ORAM has been proposed in various areas such as cloud storage [29], file system [66] and so on. Similarly, we can apply ORAM to randomize the file descriptor parameter in the I/O profile during program execution.

Example: In Fig. 6, `split` program splits the input file and writes the output to N files, we can make the I/O profile oblivious by making the program write only to *poly log N* files using ORAM. Thus, the overhead reduces to $N.polylog\ N$ and is strictly better than N^2 in the case of determinising the profile.

Addition of Noise. Randomization involves addition of random noise to the parameters in profile P such that the I/O profiles for two different inputs are indistinguishable. For this to work, we assume the enclaved application has access to a secure source of randomness. We can employ the techniques similar to those used in determinising the profile such as insertion of calls, padding of bytes and addition of dummy instructions to randomize the I/O profile as well. Randomization as a defense is popularly used in Instruction Set Randomization (ISR) and Address Space Layout Randomization (ASLR) techniques to prevent attacks on execution of benign applications [9,39,55]. RandSys combines these two techniques and proposes randomization at the system call interface layer [38]. This approach can be used to randomize the sequence of calls in the I/O profile of applications. Hiding of message length using random padding is explored in depth in previous work in the context of web applications [13,19]. Effects of using same random number for all messages versus different random number for each message was shown in [19]. Recent work has focussed on use of differential privacy techniques [18], to randomly pad the traffic in web application [8]. We can apply similar techniques to randomize the bytes in the I/O profile of an application. Finally, to randomize the *time* channel, we can use existing ideas that makes all the clocks available to the adversary noisy for reducing the leakage through timing channels [35].

Example: For a file size of 1 GB, an efficient random padding technique for split program in Fig. 6 writes bytes less than the maximum value for most of the write calls. This requires storage less than the worst case scenario.

4.4 Limitations of Randomizing I/O Profile

Although randomizing I/O profile provides better performance in most applications, it does not imply ease of deployment in real applications.

Infeasible Sequence. Randomizing the *type* parameter in the I/O profiles may introduce sequence of system calls which are not possible for a given application. An adversary detecting such infeasible sequences learns about the additional (fake) system calls inserted to make the profile input-oblivious. This is a valid threat as adversary has access to the application logic and hence can notice any irregular sequences. We call this as the "infeasible profile detection" attack. To avoid this, an application needs to guarantee that a randomized sequence is always a subset of feasible sequences. This requires generating a complete set of feasible sequence of calls for a given application which is a theoretical and practical limitation using path-feasibility analyses (eg. symbolic execution) [43].

Example: A simple example is the split program in Fig. 6 which compulsorily performs a read operation followed by a series of writes to different files. A randomized sequence of calls such as read, write, write, read, write alarms the adversary that the second read call is a fake. This immediately leaks that at most 2 lines are written out by the program before the occurrence of the fake call i.e., the value of variable n (at line 7 in Fig. 6) is at most 2. The adversary can iterate the execution sufficient number of times and collect different samples of I/O profile for the same input. With the knowledge of infeasible sequences and identifying the fake calls in each profile, the adversary can recover the original sequences in finite time and learn the actual number of lines in the encrypted input file.

Assumption About Input Distribution. The randomization approach often performs better than determinising the profile as it does not always effect the worst case behaviour. However, to reap the performance benefits of randomization, it is necessary to know the input distribution [13].

Example: To efficiently pad the *size* channel in the split program, the distribution of output bytes (B) for an input file with English sentences can be known using possible sentence lengths in English [53]. But the distribution is different for a file that contains numerical recording of weather or genome sequence information. When we compile the application, we may not know this distribution. However, a significant challenge is to know beforehand the appropriate distribution of all possible inputs to an application. It is practically infeasible for common applications such as found it CoreUtils which take variety of input.

Insufficient Entropy. With insufficient entropy, the adversary can perform repeated sampling to remove the randomization effect and recover the original profile. Gianvecchio et al. show how entropy can be used to accurately detect covert timing channel [27]. Cock et al. perform empirical analysis to show that although storage channels are possible to eliminate, timing channels are a last mile while thwarting leakage through side channels [16]. Similarly, other channels can be recovered if the source of randomness does not provide sufficient entropy— well-known from other randomization defenses [55]. It is necessary to ensure that the source of random number which the application uses is secure and the amount of entropy is large enough.

5   Insufficiency of Hiding Selective Channels

Defenses for both determinising and randomizing the profile have limitations that affect their use in practical applications. One might hope to selectively hide one or more leakage channels so that the transformed applications are still practical to use. This hypothesis assumes that blocking one channel as well hides the leakage through other channels. This section attempts to answer the question: Is it sufficient to hide partial channels to get input-oblivious execution? Or, does hiding one channel affect the amount of leakage through another channel?

Hiding Only the Address Channel. In the logic-reuse attack (Sect. 2.1), recall that the split application writes the ciphertext of each character in the input to a separate output file (refer Fig. 2). Using ORAM in the split program hides the exact file to which the ciphertext is written. It replaces every write call with *poly log N* calls where N is the total number of characters in the input file. But this is not sufficient to mitigate the attack. The adversary can get the ciphertext for number "1" by brute forcing all the ciphertexts written by the first *poly log N* calls. ORAM just makes it harder for the adversary to get exactly the required ciphertext. With ORAM, the adversary has to try the Step 2 of attack with poly-log input ciphertext. This is expected as ORAM only blocks the leakage through *address* parameter but does not hide the sequence of calls. Recall that the leakage through other parameters like *type*, *size* and *time* are sufficient for the attack to succeed. The adversary can observe the partially oblivious I/O profile and still infer every byte in the encrypted file. Our logic-reuse attacks even works in the presence of ORAM defense for hiding address access patterns.

Hiding Only the Type Channel. Let us assume that the *size* parameter for write calls in our running example in Fig. 3 always has the same value. This is possible when all the lines in an input file have the same length. Such an I/O profile is deterministic with respect to the size channel. To hide the leakage through *type* channel, let us move the write calls outside the loop (as shown in Fig. 5). In this case, the *type* channel is determinised but the leakage is not actually blocked. The leakage is shifted to the *size* channel which now has different values depending on the number of repeated lines and unique line. This shows that in determinising the *type* channel the leakage simply gets "morphed" to the

```
1  while  (( bytes_read = fread (buf, 1, BUFLEN, fp)) > 0)
2    unsigned char *cp = buf;
3    length += bytes_read;
4    while (bytes_read--)
5      crc = (crc << 8) ^ crctab[(( crc >> 24) ^ *cp++) & 0xFF];
6    if (feof (fp))
7      break;
8  printf ("%u %s", (unsigned int) crc, hp);
```

Fig. 7. cksum code with no channel of information leakage

```
1  for (int i = 0; i < n_lines; i++)
2    char *const *p = line + permutation[i];
3    size_t len = p[1] - p[0];
4    if ( fwrite (p[0], sizeof *p[0], len, stdout) != len )
5      return -1;
```

Fig. 8. shuf utility code that leaks the number of lines in input file

size channel, not really eliminated. This shows that its often misleading to selectively hide some subset of information channels due to this channel morphism problem.

In summary, transforming an application to input-oblivious execution involves two important steps: (a) correctly identifying all the channels of information leakage in profile P and (b) applying either deterministic or randomization approach to hide all the channel simultaneously.

6   Case Studies

Selection of Benchmarks. We select CoreUtils and BusyBox that are commonly available on Unix system as our benchmarks [2,3]. We choose all the 28 text utilities[3] from GNU CoreUtils package, 1 utility (grep) from BusyBox and the file utility as our case studies. All of them perform text manipulation on input files. With this benchmark, our goal is to answer the following questions.

(a) Does information leak through I/O profile in practical applications?
(b) Is it possible to convert practical applications to input-oblivious execution?

6.1   Analysis Results

We analyze these 30 applications for read/write channels and manually transform them to perform input-oblivious execution. We use the strace utility available

---
[3] The class of utilities that operate on the text of the input files. Other classes in coreutils include file utilities that operate on file metadata and shell utilities.

```
1   if ((m = file_is_tar(ms, ubuf, nb)) != 0)  /*Tar check*/
2     file_printf(ms, "%s", code_mime);
3
4   if ((m = file_trycdf(ms, fd, ubuf, nb)) != 0)/*CDF check*
5     file_printf(ms,"%s", code_mime);
6   /*text check*/
7   if ((m = file_ascmagic(ms, ubuf, nb, looks_text)) != 0)
8     file_printf(ms, "%s", code_mime);
```

Fig. 9. `file` utility code that leaks the file type through the *time* channel

in Linux system to log all the interactions of the application with the untrusted OS. The "-tt" option of strace gives the time-stamp for every system call made by the application. We categorize each application into one or more channels (discussed in Sect. 3) which need to be blocked for providing input-oblivious execution. The *type*, *size*, *address* and *time* channel leak information in 22, 11, 2, 24 applications respectively. Table 2 summarizes our analysis results.

No Channels. Out of the 30 case studies, 6 applications perform nearly input-oblivious execution without modification. These programs include sum, cksum, cat, base64, od and md5sum. Figure 7 shows the code for cksum program as a representative to describe the behaviour in these applications. The while loop at line 1 uses the input size for termination which is a part of adversary's knowledge set ψ. Therefore the program generates the same sequence of calls for different inputs of the same size. As the same computation is performed on every character (line 5), the time interval between the calls is the same for different inputs. Thus, the I/O profile of the program execution does not depend on sensitive input. These 6 applications generate deterministic profiles by default and thereby exhibit the property of input-oblivious execution.

Type. Of the remaining 24, 22 generate sensitive input-dependent sequence of calls. We observe that 8 of the 22 applications specifically leak the number of newline characters present in the input file. Figure 8 shows the code for shuf utility that shuffles the arrangement of lines in the input file and outputs every line with a separate write call (line 4). These 8 applications include ptx, shuf, sort, expand, unexpand, tac, nl and paste. Other applications such as cut, fold, fmt, tr, split and so on leak additional information about the sensitive input depending on the options provided to these applications. Recall that in our logic-reuse attack, the command "fold -w E(1 Hello)" leaks the ciphertext for individual characters in the input file.

Size. In our case studies, applications that writes as output either partial or complete data from the input file are categorized as leaking channel through *size* parameter. 11 of our 30 case studies fall under this channel namely tr, comm, join, uniq, grep, cut, head, tail, split, csplit and tsort. All these applications as well leak information through the *type* parameter. This means that none of the 11 utilities leak information exclusively through *size* parameters.

Such a behaviour indicates that even if one of the channels is blocked, information is still leaked and shifted over to another channel (refer Sect. 5).

Address. Most of the applications in our case studies read and write to a single file with the exception of two utilities. The `split` and `csplit` programs access different output files during the execution process. Thus, these two application leak information via the address access pattern. From Table 2, readers can see that these are the only two applications that leak information through all the four channels in the I/O profile.

Time. All the 24 applications that do not fall in the no channel category leak information through the *time* parameter in the I/O profile. Readers can observe from Table 2 that only two programs i.e., `wc` and `file` leak information explicitly through timing channel. The code snippet of `file` utility in Fig. 9 explains this behaviour. The `file` reads the input and checks it for each file type (line 1, 4 and 7). The I/O profile contains only one read and write call but the time difference between the them leaks information about the input file type.

Table 2. Categorization of CoreUtils applications into different leakage channels. ✓ denotes that the channel should be blocked to make the application input-oblivious

	paste	sort	shuf	ptx	expand	unexpand	tac	grep	cut	join	uniq	comm
Type	✓	✓	✓	✓	✓	✓	✓	✓	✓	✓	✓	✓
Size								✓	✓	✓	✓	✓
Address												
Time	✓	✓	✓	✓	✓	✓	✓	✓	✓	✓	✓	✓
	fold	fmt	nl	pr	split	csplit	tr	head	tail	tsort	file	wc
Type	✓	✓	✓	✓	✓	✓	✓	✓	✓	✓		
Size					✓	✓						
Address					✓	✓						
Time	✓	✓	✓	✓	✓	✓	✓	✓	✓	✓	✓	✓
No Channel	-		cat , cksum , sum , base64 , md5sum , od									

6.2   Can Be Transformed to Input-Oblivious Execution?

To answer our second evaluation goal, we manually transform the applications using the defenses discussed in Sect. 4. Since all the applications leak information through timing channel for a fine grained measurement by adversary, we ignore the timing channel in our manual transformation. We find some positive results where the existing defenses can be directly applied to make commonly used applications input-oblivious. Surprisingly, our findings yield negative results as well. We show that the limitations of oblivious execution techniques do manifest in 2 real applications.

Transformed with $O(1)$ Overhead. We find that 11 applications can execute obliviously by the determinising the profile with respect to the *type* parameter.

These are the applications in Table 2 which fall only under *type* and *time* channels and no others. In all these applications the sequence of call can be made independent of the loops that use sensitive data for termination. The code for shuf in Fig. 8 is an example of such an application. Thus, there is no performance overhead due to determinising the *type* channel. We consider this to be a positive result as the applications can be transformed with $O(1)$ overhead.

Transformed with $O(N)$ Overhead. We find that 11 applications that leak information through both the *type* and *size* channel can be converted to input-oblivious execution by making the sequence of calls loop independent as well as padding the output bytes to the total input size. These transformed applications incur a performance penalty of $O(N)$ i.e., linear to the size of input file.

Transformed with Exponential Performance Penalty. We find that 2 applications namely split and csplit show the limitation of statically deciding a feasible upper bound for loops. In these programs, the number of loop iteration depends on the number of newline characters present in the input file (line 3 in Fig. 6) which is not known at the compile time. Hence, transforming these applications to input-oblivious execution is not possible without exponential performance overhead of $O(2^N)$. We explain this behaviour for split program earlier in Sect. 4. The csplit application is similar to split with additional options to it and therefore exhibits same limitations. This confirms that limitations of existing oblivious execution techniques do manifest in practical applications.

7   Related Work

Attacks on Enclaved Systems. On a similar setting as this paper, Xu et al. demonstrate controlled-channel attack using page faults that can extract complete text documents in presence of an untrusted OS [69]. This confirms that enclaved execution techniques are vulnerable to information leakage through different channels. Our work specifically focuses on file system calls as the read-write channels in these systems. Iago attacks [12] demonstrate that untrusted OS can corrupt application behaviour and exploit to gain knowledge about sensitive inputs. This attack however assumes the OS is malicious and can tamper the parameter of return values in memory management system calls like mmap. In this paper, we have shown that information leakage is possible even with a weaker i.e., semi-honest adversarial model.

Oblivious Execution Techniques. A discussion of closely related oblivious execution techniques is summarized in Sect. 4 (see Table 1). Here we discuss a representative set of recent work on these defenses. Liu et al. [46] propose a type system for memory-trace oblivious (MTO) execution in the RAM model. In their solution, they add padding instructions to 'if' and 'else' branches to achieve memory trace obliviousness. We use this technique to hide the system call sequences in I/O profile. Along with this, they use the ORAM technique to hide address access patterns. GhostRider [45] provides a hardware/software platform for privacy preserving computation in cloud with the guarantees of memory-trace oblivious execution. Along with hiding address access pattern Ghostrider determinises the time channel by making the application take worst case execution time. Ascend [22] is a secure processor that uses randomizes access pattern using ORAM and determinises the time channel by allowing access to memory at fixed intervals. The fixed interval is a parameter chosen at compile time. It uses the idea of inserting dummy memory access to hide the timing channel. Fletcher et al. have proposed a solution that provides better performance while still hiding the timing channel [23]. However, their solutions leaks a constant amount of information, thus introducing a tradeoff between efficiency and privacy.

8 Conclusion

In this paper we demonstrate a concrete attack called—a logic-reuse attack—to highlight the importance of oblivious execution. We systematize the capabilities and limits of existing oblivious execution techniques in the context of enclaved execution. Finally, our study on 30 applications demonstrate that most of the practical applications can be converted to oblivious execution with acceptable performance. However, theoretical limitations of oblivious execution do manifest in practical applications.

Acknowledgements. We thank the anonymous reviewers of this paper for their helpful feedback. We also thank Shweta Shinde, Zheng Leong Chua and Loi Luu for useful feedback on an early version of the paper. This work is supported by the Ministry of Education, Singapore under Grant No. R-252-000-560-112 and a university research grant from Intel. All opinions expressed in this work are solely those of the authors.

References

1. http://letterfrequency.org
2. BusyBox. http://www.gnu.org/software/coreutils/
3. GNU CoreUtils. http://www.busybox.net/
4. Intel Trusted Execution Technology: Software Development Guide. www.intel.com/content/dam/www/public/us/en/documents/guides/intel-txt-software-development-guide.pdf
5. Trusted Computing Group. Trusted platform module, July 2007
6. Agat, J.: Transforming out timing leaks. In: Proceedings of the 27th ACM SIGPLAN-SIGACT Symposium on Principles of Programming Languages, POPL 2000 (2000)
7. ARM: ARM Security Technology – Building a Secure System using TrustZone Technology. ARM Technical White Paper (2013)
8. Azab, T.: Differentially private traffic padding for web applications. Ph.D. thesis, Concordia University Montreal, Quebec (2014)
9. Barrantes, E.G., Ackley, D.H., Palmer, T.S., Stefanovic, D., Zovi, D.D.: Randomized instruction set emulation to disrupt binary code injection attacks. In: Proceedings of the 10th ACM conference on Computer and communications security (2003)
10. Baumann, A., Peinado, M., Hunt, G.: Shielding applications from an untrusted cloud with haven. In: OSDI (2014)

11. Brumley, D., Boneh, D.: Remote timing attacks are practical. Comput. Networks **48**(5), 701–716 (2005)
12. Checkoway, S., Shacham, H.: Iago attacks: why the system call API is a bad untrusted RPC interface. In: ASPLOS (2013)
13. Chen, S., Wang, R., Wang, X., Zhang, K.: Side-channel leaks in web applications: a reality today, a challenge tomorrow. In: IEEE Symposium on Security and Privacy (SP), pp. 191–206. IEEE (2010)
14. Chen, X., Garfinkel, T., Lewis, E.C., Subrahmanyam, P., Waldspurger, C.A., Boneh, D., Dwoskin, J., Ports, D.R.: Overshadow: a virtualization-based approach to retrofitting protection in commodity operating systems (2008)
15. Chhabra, S., Rogers, B., Solihin, Y., Prvulovic, M.: SecureME: a hardware-software approach to full system security. In: ICS (2011)
16. Cock, D., Ge, Q., Murray, T., Heiser, G.: The last mile: an empirical study of timing channels on sel4. In: Proceedings of the 2014 ACM SIGSAC Conference on Computer and Communications Security, CCS 2014 (2014)
17. Coppens, B., Verbauwhede, I., De Bosschere, K., De Sutter, B.: Practical mitigations for timing-based side-channel attacks on modern x86 processors. In: 30th IEEE Symposium on Security and Privacy, pp. 45–60. IEEE (2009)
18. Dwork, C., van Tilborg, H.C.A., Jajodia, S.: Differential privacy. Encyclopedia of Cryptography and Security, pp. 338–340. Springer, New York (2011)
19. Dyer, K.P., Coull, S.E., Ristenpart, T., Shrimpton, T.: Peek-a-boo, i still see you: why efficient traffic analysis countermeasures fail. In: IEEE Symposium on Security and Privacy (SP), pp. 332–346. IEEE (2012)
20. ElGamal, T.: A public key cryptosystem and a signature scheme based on discrete logarithms. In: Blakley, G.R., Chaum, D. (eds.) CRYPTO 1984. LNCS, vol. 196, pp. 10–18. Springer, Heidelberg (1985). doi:10.1007/3-540-39568-7_2
21. Fairley, R.E.: Tutorial: static analysis and dynamic testing of computer software. Computer (1978)
22. Fletcher, C.W., Dijk, M.V., Devadas, S.: A secure processor architecture for encrypted computation on untrusted programs. In: Proceedings of the seventh ACM workshop on Scalable trusted computing, pp. 3–8. ACM (2012)
23. Fletchery, C.W., Ren, L., Yu, X., Van Dijk, M., Khan, O., Devadas, S.: Suppressing the oblivious ram timing channel while making information leakage and program efficiency trade-offs. In: 2014 IEEE 20th International Symposium on High Performance Computer Architecture (HPCA), pp. 213–224. IEEE (2014)
24. Gentry, C., Halevi, S.: Implementing gentry's fully-homomorphic encryption scheme. In: Paterson, K.G. (ed.) EUROCRYPT 2011. LNCS, vol. 6632, pp. 129–148. Springer, Heidelberg (2011). doi:10.1007/978-3-642-20465-4_9
25. Gentry, C.: Fully homomorphic encryption using ideal lattices. In: 41st Annual ACM Symposium on Theory of Computing (2009)
26. Gentry, C., Halevi., S.: A working implementation of fully homomorphic encryption. In: EUROCRYPT (2010)
27. Gianvecchio, S., Wang, H.: Detecting covert timing channels: an entropy-based approach. In: Proceedings of the 14th ACM conference on Computer and communications security. ACM (2007)
28. Goldreich, O., Ostrovsky, R.: Software protection and simulation on oblivious RAMs. J. ACM **43**(3), 431–473 (1996)
29. Goodrich, M.T., Mitzenmacher, M., Ohrimenko, O., Tamassia, R.: Practical oblivious storage. In: Proceedings of the second ACM conference on Data and Application Security and Privacy (2012)

30. Gordon, S.D., Katz, J., Kolesnikov, V., Krell, F., Malkin, T., Raykova, M., Vahlis, Y.: Secure two-party computation in sublinear (amortized) time. In: Proceedings of the 2012 ACM Conference on Computer and Communications Security, CCS 2012 (2012)

31. Henecka, W., Kogl, S., Sadeghi, A.R., Schneider, T., Wehrenberg, I.: TASTY: tool for automating secure two-party computations. In: ACM CCS (2010)

32. Hofmann, O.S., Kim, S., Dunn, A.M., Lee, M.Z., Witchel, E.: InkTag: secure applications on an untrusted operating system. In: ASPLOS (2013)

33. Hofmeyr, S.A., Forrest, S., Somayaji, A.: Intrusion detection using sequences of system calls. J. Comput. Secur. **6**(3), 151–180 (1998)

34. Holzer, A., Franz, M., Katzenbeisser, S., Veith, H.: Secure two-party computations in ANSI C. In: Proceedings of the 2012 ACM Conference on Computer and Communications Security, CCS 2012 (2012)

35. Hu, W.M.: Reducing timing channels with fuzzy time. In: IEEE Computer Society Symposium on Research in Security and Privacy, Proceedings, pp. 8–20, May 1991

36. Huang, Y., Evans, D., Katz, J., Malka, L.: Faster secure two-party computation using garbled circuits. In: USENIX Security Symposium (2011)

37. Hund, R., Willems, C., Holz, T.: Practical timing side channel attacks against kernel space ASLR. In: IEEE Symposium on Security and Privacy (SP) (2013)

38. Jiang, X., Wang, H.J., Xu, D., Wang, Y.M.: RandSys: thwarting code injection attacks with system service interface randomization. In: 26th IEEE International Symposium on Reliable Distributed Systems, SRDS 2007, pp. 209–218. IEEE (2007)

39. Kc, G.S., Keromytis, A.D., Prevelakis, V.: Countering code-injection attacks with instruction-set randomization. In: Proceedings of the 10th ACM Conference on Computer and Communications Security, pp. 272–280. ACM (2003)

40. Keller, M., Scholl, P.: Efficient, oblivious data structures for MPC. In: Sarkar, P., Iwata, T. (eds.) ASIACRYPT 2014. LNCS, vol. 8874, pp. 506–525. Springer, Heidelberg (2014). doi:10.1007/978-3-662-45608-8_27

41. Kocher, P., Jaffe, J., Jun, B.: Differential power analysis. In: Wiener, M. (ed.) CRYPTO 1999. LNCS, vol. 1666, pp. 388–397. Springer, Heidelberg (1999). doi:10.1007/3-540-48405-1_25

42. Kocher, P.C.: Timing attacks on implementations of Diffie-Hellman, RSA, DSS, and other systems. In: Koblitz, N. (ed.) CRYPTO 1996. LNCS, vol. 1109, pp. 104–113. Springer, Heidelberg (1996). doi:10.1007/3-540-68697-5_9

43. Landi, W.: Undecidability of static analysis. ACM Lett. Program. Lang. Syst. **1**(4), 323–337 (1992)

44. Li, X., Hu, H., Bai, G., Jia, Y., Liang, Z., Saxena, P.: DroidVault: a trusted data vault for android devices. In: 19th International Conference on Engineering of Complex Computer Systems (ICECCS), pp. 29–38. IEEE (2014)

45. Liu, C., Harris, A., Maas, M., Hicks, M., Tiwari, M., Shi, E.: GhostRider: A hardware-software system for memory trace oblivious computation. In: Proceedings of the Twentieth International Conference on Architectural Support for Programming Languages and Operating Systems, pp. 87–101. ACM (2015)

46. Liu, C., Hicks, M., Shi, E.: Memory trace oblivious program execution. In: CSF 2013, pp. 51–65 (2013)

47. McCune, J.M., Parnoy, B., Perrig, A., Reiter, M.K., Isozaki, H.: Flicker: an execution infrastructure for TCB minimization. In: EuroSys (2008)

48. McKeen, F., Alexandrovich, I., Berenzon, A., Rozas, C.V., Shafi, H., Shanbhogue, V., Savagaonkar, U.R.: Innovative instructions and software model for isolated execution. In: Proceedings of the 2nd International Workshop on Hardware and Architectural Support for Security and Privacy, HASP (2013)

49. Molnar, D., Piotrowski, M., Schultz, D., Wagner, D.: The program counter security model: automatic detection and removal of control-flow side channel attacks. In: Won, D.H., Kim, S. (eds.) ICISC 2005. LNCS, vol. 3935, pp. 156–168. Springer, Heidelberg (2006). doi:10.1007/11734727_14

50. Osadchy, M., Pinkas, B., Jarrous, A., Moskovich, B.: SCiFI - a system for secure face identification. In: Security and Privacy (2010)

51. Osvik, D.A., Shamir, A., Tromer, E.: Cache attacks and countermeasures: the case of AES. In: Pointcheval, D. (ed.) CT-RSA 2006. LNCS, vol. 3860, pp. 1–20. Springer, Heidelberg (2006). doi:10.1007/11605805_1

52. Paillier, P.: Public-key cryptosystems based on composite degree residuosity classes. In: Stern, J. (ed.) EUROCRYPT 1999. LNCS, vol. 1592, pp. 223–238. Springer, Heidelberg (1999). doi:10.1007/3-540-48910-X_16

53. Quirk, R., Crystal, D., Education, P.: A Comprehensive Grammar of the English Language, vol. 397. Cambridge University Press, Cambridge (1985)

54. Saxena, P., Poosankam, P., McCamant, S., Song, D.: Loop-extended symbolic execution on binary programs. In: Proceedings of the Eighteenth International Symposium on Software Testing and Analysis, pp. 225–236. ACM (2009)

55. Shacham, H., Page, M., Pfaff, B., Goh, E.J., Modadugu, N., Boneh, D.: On the effectiveness of address-space randomization. In: Proceedings of the 11th ACM Conference on Computer and Communications Security, pp. 298–307. ACM (2004)

56. Shi, E., Chan, T.-H.H., Stefanov, E., Li, M.: Oblivious RAM with $O((\log N)^3)$ worst-case cost. In: Lee, D.H., Wang, X. (eds.) ASIACRYPT 2011. LNCS, vol. 7073, pp. 197–214. Springer, Heidelberg (2011). doi:10.1007/978-3-642-25385-0_11

57. Shinde, S., Le Tien, D., Tople, S., Saxena, P.: Panoply: Low-TCB linux applications with SGX enclaves. In: NDSS (2017)

58. Stefanov, E., van Dijk, M., Shi, E., Fletcher, C., Ren, L., Yu, X., Devadas, S.: Path oram: an extremely simple oblivious ram protocol. In: Proceedings of the 2013 ACM SIGSAC Conference on Computer and Communications Security, CCS 2013 (2013)

59. Stefanov, E., Shi, E., Song, D.: Towards Practical Oblivious RAM. CoRR (2011)

60. Thekkath, D.L.C., Mitchell, M., Lincoln, P., Boneh, D., Mitchell, J., Horowitz, M.: Architectural support for copy and tamper resistant software. In: Proceedings of the Ninth International Conference on Architectural Support for Programming Languages and Operating Systems, ASPLOS IX (2000)

61. Tople, S., Shinde, S., Chen, Z., Saxena, P.: AUTOCRYPT: enabling homomorphic computation on servers to protect sensitive web content. In: Proceedings of the 2013 ACM SIGSAC Conference on Computer and Communications Security, CCS 2013 (2013)

62. Wang, X.S., Chan, T.H., Shi, E.: Circuit ORAM: on tightness of the Goldreich-Ostrovsky lower bound (2014)

63. Wang, X.S., Huang, Y., Chan, T., Shelat, A., Shi, E.: SCORAM: Oblivious RAM for secure computation. In: Proceedings of the 2014 ACM SIGSAC Conference on Computer and Communications Security, pp. 191–202. ACM (2014)

64. Warrender, C., Forrest, S., Pearlmutter, B.: Detecting intrusions using system calls: alternative data models. In: Proceedings of the 1999 IEEE Symposium on Security and Privacy, pp. 133–145. IEEE (1999)

65. Wilhelm, R., Engblom, J., Ermedahl, A., Holsti, N., Thesing, S., Whalley, D., Bernat, G., Ferdinand, C., Heckmann, R., Mitra, T., et al.: The worst-case execution-time problem–overview of methods and survey of tools. ACM Trans. Embed. Comput. Syst. (TECS) **7**(3), 36 (2008)
66. Williams, P., Sion, R., Tomescu, A.: PrivateFS: a parallel oblivious file system. In: Proceedings of the 2012 ACM Conference on Computer and Communications Security, CCS 2012
67. Wright, C.V., Ballard, L., Coull, S.E., Monrose, F., Masson, G.M.: Spot me if you can: uncovering spoken phrases in encrypted VoIP conversations. In: Proceedings of the 2008 IEEE Symposium on Security and Privacy, SP 2008 (2008)
68. Yao, A.C.: Protocols for secure computations. In: 23rd Annual IEEE Symposium on Foundations of Computer Science (1982)
69. Xu, Y., Cui, W., Peinado, M.: GhostRider: Controlled-channel attacks: deterministic side channels for untrusted operating systems. In: IEEE Security and Privacy 2015 (2015)
70. Zhang, D., Askarov, A., Myers, A.C.: Language-based control and mitigation of timing channels. In: Proceedings of the 33rd ACM SIGPLAN Conference on Programming Language Design and Implementation, PLDI 2012 (2012)
71. Zhang, Y., Steele, A., Blanton, M.: PICCO: a general-purpose compiler for private distributed computation. In: Proceedings of the 2013 ACM SIGSAC Conference on Computer and Communications Security, CCS 2013 (2013)

MemPatrol: Reliable Sideline Integrity Monitoring for High-Performance Systems

Myoung Jin Nam[1]([✉]), Wonhong Nam[2], Jin-Young Choi[1],
and Periklis Akritidis[3]

[1] Korea University, Seoul, South Korea
{mjnam,choi}@formal.korea.ac.kr
[2] KonKuk University, Seoul, South Korea
wnam@konkuk.ac.kr
[3] Niometrics, Singapore, Singapore
akritid@niometrics.com

Abstract. Integrity checking using inline reference monitors to check individual memory accesses in C/C++ programs remains prohibitively expensive for the most performance-critical applications. To address this, we developed *MemPatrol*, a "sideline" integrity monitor that allows us to minimize the amount of performance degradation at the expense of increased detection delay. Inspired by existing proposals, *MemPatrol* uses a dedicated monitor thread running in parallel with the other threads of the protected application. Previous proposals, however, either rely on costly isolation mechanisms, or introduce a vulnerability window between the attack and its detection. During this vulnerability window, malicious code can cover up memory corruption, breaking the security guarantee of "eventual detection" that comes with strong isolation. Our key contributions are (i) a novel userspace-based isolation mechanism to address the vulnerability window, and (ii) to successfully reduce the overhead incurred by the application's threads to a level acceptable for a performance-critical application. We evaluate *MemPatrol* on a high-performance passive network monitoring system, demonstrating its low overheads, as well as the operator's control of the trade-off between performance degradation and detection delay.

Keywords: Integrity monitoring · Isolation · Buffer overflow attacks · Concurrency · Cryptography

1 Introduction

The inlined reference monitor approach [7] has become indispensable for finding memory errors in C/C++ programs during development and testing. By embedding checks into the binary code during compilation or via binary rewriting, inline reference monitors can enforce integrity guarantees for the program's memory accesses or control-flow. Violations are detected promptly, with the instruction at fault identified, which greatly facilitates debugging.

© Springer International Publishing AG 2017
M. Polychronakis and M. Meier (Eds.): DIMVA 2017, LNCS 10327, pp. 48–69, 2017.
DOI: 10.1007/978-3-319-60876-1_3

However, the performance overhead of inline monitoring applied at so fine a granularity makes it unattractive for production deployment in performance-critical applications, such as passive network monitoring systems. Widely used debugging solutions such as Google's AddressSanitizer [31] typically slow down applications to roughly 2× of the original run-time. Other performance-optimized solutions for inline monitoring also incur high and unpredictable overheads [11].

The unpredictability of the performance overhead incurred from inline reference monitoring is a problem by itself. Its runtime overhead is highly dependent on the code being instrumented. A few instructions inserted in a tight loop can translate to a large number of dynamic instructions during runtime, causing a significant performance impact. Moreover, additional memory accesses for security checks may increase memory bandwidth and cache misses. Inlined checks cannot abstain from using the cache hierarchy without slowing down the application.

To avoid the costs of inlined reference monitors, researchers proposed replacing inline security enforcement with concurrent monitors [33,37]. In principle, such approaches can minimize the performance overhead on the protected application by offloading checks to the concurrent monitor. Detection, however, now happens asynchronously, introducing a detection delay. This weaker security guarantee is nevertheless still useful. For example, in the case of passive network monitoring systems, it helps validate the integrity of the system's past reports.

Existing proposals, however, face significant challenges. For some, the delay introduced before the detection of memory safety violations opens up a vulnerability window during which the attackers have control of the program's execution and may attempt to disable the detection system. This undermines the guarantee of eventual detection. For others, attempts to isolate the monitor during the vulnerability window degrade performance. Finally, these solutions have been designed for general purpose systems, and their communication and synchronization overheads between the monitor and the application threads can be prohibitive for high-performance applications.

In this paper, we present *MemPatrol*, a sideline memory integrity monitoring system that detects a class of memory corruption attacks with very low performance overhead, using available Linux kernel primitives and Intel CPU encryption facilities. *MemPatrol* aims (i) to guarantee the eventual detection of integrity violations regardless of the detection delay, by reliably protecting itself against a compromised application during the time window between the occurrence of the attack and its eventual detection, and (ii) to give engineers the flexibility of tuning the cost of integrity monitoring in a reliable and predictable way by configuring the desired amount of computational resources allocated to it.

MemPatrol implements a userspace-based isolation mechanism by using CPU registers as the integrity monitor's private memory, allowing the monitor to safely run as a thread inside the address space of the protected application. The CPU registers cannot, obviously, hold all the information required to run an integrity monitoring system, such as the addresses and expected values of memory locations. However, they are sufficient to store cryptographic material and run a register-only message authentication code (MAC) algorithm to reliably access the rest of the data required for the monitor's operation.

Attackers in control of a compromised application thread cannot tamper with the monitor thread's information that is offloaded to memory without detection, because they lack access to the key used to authenticate it. The authentication key is only available to the integrity monitor, and threads cannot address each other's registers. The key and intermediate states of the MAC algorithm stay only in registers, never being flushed into userspace memory. The monitor's code never spills registers and does not use primitives such as `setjmp/longjmp`. The registers may only be flushed to kernel-space memory during a context switch, where they remain unreachable to a potentially compromised userspace application. Besides this main idea, we discuss how we prevent replay attacks, and the mechanisms based on SELinux and the `clone` Linux system call which are required to protect the monitor thread from forced termination by its parent process using `kill` or modification of its code memory to alter its execution.

We study a concrete special case of sideline integrity monitoring for detecting heap buffer overflows in a commercial high-performance passive network monitoring system [23] where existing memory safety techniques are too expensive to apply. We believe, however, that periodic integrity checking of memory locations in a program's memory can have additional applications. For example, it could be used to detect malicious hooks installed by modifying persistent function pointers.

Of course, even a concurrent monitoring system incurs performance overheads that may affect application threads, for example, memory bandwidth overheads from increased reads, cache coherency overheads, and other cross-CPU communication in NUMA systems. The low overhead imposed by our isolation mechanism, however, enables engineers to minimize monitoring overheads arbitrarily by throttling integrity monitoring without compromising eventual detection.

In summary, we make the following contributions:

1. An effective, userspace-based isolation mechanism for the monitor thread that does not require new Linux kernel modifications
2. Demonstration of tunable and predictable allocation of resources to security monitoring, in particular memory bandwidth
3. Avoidance of synchronization overheads for heap monitoring by taking advantage of the memory allocation mechanisms used in performance-critical systems

The remainder of the paper is organized as follows. Section 2 describes our threat model. Section 3 presents our monitor thread isolation mechanism. Section 4 applies our mechanism to monitoring of heap integrity, and Sect. 5 evaluates its performance. Section 6 reviews related work, and Sect. 7 concludes with final remarks on the current limitations and future directions of this work.

2 Threat Model

In this section we discuss *MemPatrol*'s threat model. Firstly, we discuss the threat model for integrity monitoring using a concurrent thread in general. Secondly, we discuss the threat model for heap memory corruption attacks that we use as a concrete case study of integrity monitoring.

2.1 Sideline Integrity Monitoring

Our threat model for integrity monitoring in general considers attacks as malicious modification of memory contents, whether on the stack, heap, or static variables. It divides the life cycle of a protected application into two phases: the *trusted* and the *untrusted phase*. We assume the program starts in the trusted phase, during which the application is responsible for registering all memory locations to be monitored and then launching the monitor. The program, then, enters its untrusted phase before the application receives any inputs from potentially malicious third parties that could compromise it.

We assume that at some point after entering the untrusted phase of its lifetime, the application becomes vulnerable, for example, by starting to process external input. After this point, it is no longer trusted by the monitor that was launched before the process became vulnerable. In particular, we assume that a compromised process may access any memory location that lies in its address space, and may attempt to restore any data corrupted during the attack leading to the compromise, in order to avoid detection. A compromised process may also invoke any system calls, such as `kill` to terminate other processes or threads, subject to OS controls. Attacks against the OS kernel, however, are outside the scope of this paper.

Finally, while the application is under the control of the attacker, we assume the attacker may perform replay attacks, meaning that older contents of the memory can be saved and reused to overwrite later contents.

2.2 Heap Integrity

We built a concrete case study of *MemPatrol* by applying it to heap buffer overflow detection based on detecting canary data modifications, and evaluated it with a high-performance passive network monitoring system [23]. Other threats such as stack-based buffer overflows are handled by existing defences, such as GCC's stack protector (`-fstack-protector` set of options), or fall outside the scope of this case study.

The program is assumed to be compromised through heap buffer overflows employing only contiguous overwrites. Buffer overflows often belong to this category, and we do not consider other memory safety violations, such as those enabling corruption of arbitrary memory locations.

The attacker may corrupt any kind of data in heap objects by overruns across adjacent memory chunks. For instance, attackers can overwrite a function pointer, virtual function table pointer or inlined metadata of a free-list-based memory allocator by overflows. We assume that attackers may overwrite contents across multiple buffers in both directions, i.e. underflows and overflows.

Finally, we assume that the canary value cannot be learned through memory disclosure attacks. However, note that the standard form of memory disclosure attack is impractical with passive network monitoring systems, such as [23], because there is no request-response interaction with an attacker to exfiltrate the data. An "indirect" elaboration of the attack is conceivable, that deposits the contents of the canary to another buffer inside the process, used later to restore the canary. For this to work, the copy must not corrupt another canary, so it must be achieved using random access, which the current solution does not cover. These attacks are outside the scope of this case study.

In summary, we assume the attacker can gain control of the execution of the application through heap buffer overflows, but we cannot defend against overflows that stride over heap canaries without overwriting them, other kinds of memory safety violations, or against information leakage through memory disclosure attacks.

3   Monitor Thread Isolation

Sideline integrity monitoring systems offer asynchronous detection with a delay. Crucially, if this detection latency can be exploited to disable the monitor, no deterministic security guarantees can be made. To avoid this, we need to anticipate all possible scenarios under which a compromised application can disrupt the monitor thread, and thwart them. We have identified the following ways that an attacker with full control of the application can disrupt a monitor thread running in the same address space:

1. Tampering with the monitor's data structures on heap or its stack
2. Hijacking the control flow of the monitor by manipulating the monitor thread's stack
3. Hijacking the control flow of the monitor by altering the monitor thread's executable code in memory
4. Terminating the monitor thread via the `kill` system call
5. Faking application termination

In the following sections, we discuss how to block these attacks.

3.1   Protection of Data Structures in Memory

Attackers may attempt to subvert the monitor thread by corrupting data in the program's memory used by the monitor, such as the list of memory locations to monitor. This would effectively disable monitoring. Besides these data structures that are stored on the heap, an attacker could alter local variables or spilled registers on the stack of the monitor thread.

Our solution is for the monitor thread to only trust data in its registers. Of course not all data can be saved in the register file due to the limited space of

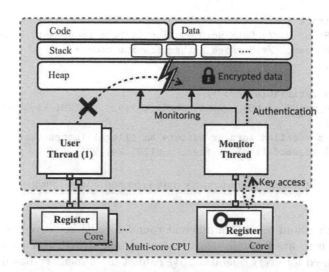

Fig. 1. The cryptographic key is only accessible to the monitor thread by storing it in a register, and additional information stored in memory is authenticated cryptographically.

registers. Instead, any data stored outside of registers must be authenticated to prevent tampering. We achieve this using cryptographic techniques. The cryptographic key used for authentication is stored only in a register as shown in Fig. 1. Compromised application threads cannot succeed in corrupting data without detection, because they do not have access to the cryptographic key required for counterfeiting the stored information. Of course, it is not sufficient to merely protect the key in a register. It is also required that the entire authentication mechanism is implemented using only registers, and that the main loop of the monitor thread also only trusts registers and authenticates any memory used. Next, we describe the memory authentication primitives and the methodology followed to implement the monitor code using only registers for its trusted data instead of memory.

Authenticated Memory Accesses. To secure data stored in untrusted memory from being counterfeited, we use AES-based Message Authentication Codes (MAC) to sign the value and its location. We chose AES because we can utilize the AES-NI [8] instruction set of Intel processors which provides a hardware implementation of AES using the `aesenc` and `aesenclast` instructions for the encryption operation. Each of them performs an entire AES round without any access to RAM. We use the compiler's intrinsics to access these instructions. Note however that these hardware extensions are used in this work for convenience and performance. In principle, our solution does not depend on the availability of dedicated cryptographic instructions, as CPU-only implementations of AES on processors without AES-NI exist [32].

```
typedef struct {
    __m128i m;      /* Data word and its (albeit redundant) address */
    __m128i mac;    /* Message authentication code */
} sec64_t;

/* Store a verifiable word */
void store_sec64(uint64_t word, sec64_t *sec, __m128i key);

/* Return a verified word or execute an illegal instruction */
uint64_t load_sec64(sec64_t *sec, __m128i key);
```

Fig. 2. Untrusted-memory data type and access routines

Every AES round requires a different round-specific key expanded from the initial key. These are typically expanded once and stored in a memory-based array and reused for every operation. We cannot use a memory-based table and we also avoid using 10 registers, one for each round's key, by interleaving the key expansion with the encryption rounds. This technique cannot be used with decryption, because decryption requires the expanded key in reverse order, so all the stages would have to be kept in registers. Fortunately, the decryption operation is not required for implementing message authentication codes.

Figure 2 illustrates the authenticated memory access routines used by the monitor thread. The routines can store and load data in units of 64-bits expanded into 256 bits of memory, namely the sec64_t type that includes the value and its signature. Specifically, we pack the 64-bit address of the sec64_t object and the 64-bit value into 128 bits of data, and produce an additional 128 bits of MAC by encrypting the concatenation of the address and value using the key with the help of the store_sec64 routine.

To retrieve the value, the load_sec64 routine regenerates the signature using the address of the sec64_t passed to it, the value from the sec64_t, and the key passed to it in a register. If the signature does not match, it raises a trap, otherwise it returns the value.

Replay Attacks. To block attackers from maliciously overwriting an entry with a signed datum from a different memory location, we include the memory address in the authenticated data. To block attackers from reusing signed data representing previous values of the same memory location, we avoid storing new data to the same address. Note, however, that we can enable a limited form of secure updates by using append-only tables and keeping the table size in a register.

Writing Register-Only Code. While it is entirely possible to implement the monitor thread in assembler by hand, we found that this was not necessary. Here we describe the methodology used to achieve the same result and to verify its correctness.

First, we isolated the code that must avoid using unauthenticated memory into its own source file, compiled with a controlled set of GCC options, and manually inspected the generated assembly. Initially we attempted to instruct GCC to use specific registers by using asm annotations on variable definitions. This achieved control of the registers used, but unfortunately it generated memory accesses for superfluous temporaries. Instead, we had to rely on GCC eliminating register usage through optimization, by compiling the code with -O3 (and also -msse4 -maes for SSE2 and AES-NI). Using stock AES-NI routine implementations for the MAC routines produced code with register spilling. Obviously these routines must not use any memory, as they are the ones that we rely on for authenticating memory use elsewhere. We solved this by modifying the stock encryption routines to interleave the round-key generation with the encryption rounds. This was sufficient for implementing a MAC algorithm and the memory access routines.

Next, we worked in a similar way on the register-only implementation of the main loop of the monitor thread. We could not use functions calls, because they would use the stack to save their return address and temporary variables from registers, so we placed the previously crafted store_sec64 and load_sec64 routines in a header file and annotated them with the always_inline GCC attribute. After some experimentation, we achieved the desired code. Of course, the solution does not rely on these techniques, as we could always write the core routines of the system directly in assembler.

Finally, besides manual verification of the generated assembly code, we zero out the rsp register at the start of the integrity checking loop using inline assembly, forcing any stack frame access to cause a crash. This ensures we do not accidentally introduce memory accesses due to spilled local or temporary variables as the code evolves, or in subsequent recompilations.

3.2 Protection of Code

Another way the application's threads can subvert the monitor thread is by modifying its executable code in memory while it runs. On x86 there is no need to flush instruction caches for program memory modifications like this to take effect. Code segments are write-protected by default, but attackers in control of the process could easily call mprotect on a vanilla Linux kernel to gain write access to the code section of the monitor thread. They could then neutralize the monitor thread without causing it to exit by replacing its code with a version that does not perform integrity checks.

With a vanilla Linux kernel, this attack is entirely possible. However, solutions to prevent the modification of program code are already included in most Linux distributions. For example, the PaX project introduced MPROTECT [25], a kernel patch designed to prevent the introduction of new executable code into the task's address space by restricting the mmap and mprotect interfaces. Security-Enhanced Linux (SELinux) [30] also contains the execmem access control, to prevent processes from creating memory regions that are writable and executable. One of these common solutions needs to be used to prevent this attack. We use Red Hat Enterprise Linux which provides SELinux.

3.3 Terminating or Tracing the Monitor Thread

A trivial attack scenario that must be tackled is termination of the monitor thread by the compromised process using the `kill` system call, or subverting it using `ptrace`. We address this scenario by using the Linux `clone` system call which allows fine grained control over sharing parts of the execution context. We start the application as a privileged user and, instead of the regular POSIX thread interfaces, we use `clone` with the `CLONE_VM` flag to create the monitor thread. After the monitor thread is launched, the main application drops its privileges by executing `setuid` and `setgid`. This results in two threads/processes (the distinction between thread and process is not so clear when using `clone`) running in the same address space without sharing user credentials. The monitor thread retains the privileged user credentials, while the rest of the application is running with reduced privileges, and thus cannot use the `kill` system call to signal the privileged thread, nor `ptrace` to debug it.

3.4 Faking Application Termination

Under this scenario the attacker may call `exit` in order to terminate the process before the monitor thread had a chance to detect the attack. Uninitiated termination of the application process could be considered sufficient grounds for raising an alarm, but we also address this scenario by ensuring that a final integrity scan is performed on exit.

3.5 Detection of Normal and Abnormal Termination

The monitoring system needs to detect normal application termination, in order to also terminate, as well as abnormal termination triggered by a MAC failure in order to raise an alarm.

Unfortunately, it is impossible to receive notification of the termination of the process by a signal through the `prctl` mechanism with the `PR_SET_PDEATHSIG` option, because of the different user credentials used for isolation with the explicit purpose of disallowing signals. Instead, the monitor needs to detect the termination of its application by polling its parent PID using `kill` with a signal number of 0.

As we have discussed, the execution of the monitor thread is severely constrained, to the extent that calling the libc wrapper for `kill` can compromise it by dereferencing the return address saved on the stack. It is technically possible to send a signal to another process in a safe manner on x86 Linux by running the `syscall` machine instruction directly. It accepts its input parameters in registers and stores the return address in a register. However, it is more convenient to use a more flexible scheme described next.

To detect termination, we use an additional monitor *process*, spawned as a child of the monitor thread using the normal `fork` mechanism. Unlike the monitor thread, this process does not share its address space with the monitored application. Therefore it is free of the draconian execution constraints imposed on the monitor thread. This process can poll the main application using `kill` in a loop to detect its termination and signal the monitor thread, which is possible, as they are running under the same UID. The monitor thread must perform a final integrity check of the application before exiting, to handle the possibility of a process termination initiated by the attacker, as discussed earlier.

As for abnormal termination, once the monitor thread detects an integrity violation, it has limited options due to its constraints. We call the `__builtin_trap` intrinsic instruction which on x86 Linux compiles to an illegal instruction and generates a `SIGILL` signal, terminating the monitor thread. The termination is detected by the monitor *process*, which has the flexibility required to alert operators.

3.6   Minimizing Performance Impact

The execution of a concurrent monitor thread, unlike inline reference monitors, does not increase the dynamic instruction count of the monitored program's threads. However, its presence may still incur other kinds of overheads affecting them including cache pollution, memory bandwidth increases, and cross-CPU communication.

To minimize last-level cache pollution, we ensure that the monitor thread is using non-temporal memory accesses, which are available to C code by using the `__builtin_prefetch` intrinsic. Unlike inline monitoring, refraining from cache use only affects the performance of the monitor thread itself, which translates to detection delays, rather than slow down of application threads.

Moreover, network monitoring systems go to great lengths to avoid paging overheads because the jitter introduced to execution time by having to walk the page tables on a miss may lead to packet loss. For example, they utilize so-called huge pages introduced in modern processors, typically sized at 2 MiB or 1 GiB instead of the default page size of 4 KiB on x86. We additionally avoid any such overheads by sharing the entire address space, page tables included, with the monitored threads.

To avoid hogging memory bandwidth and minimize cross-CPU communications, the monitor thread should pace its memory accesses. In fact, we allow the rate of memory accesses to be configurable as a means to allow the user to select the desired level of overhead, at the expense of detection delay. This allows the user to tune for minimal impact on the application threads.

In summary, we explore a set of design trade-offs to avoid overheads to the application threads at the cost of the monitor thread's speed. This highlights the importance of protecting the monitor thread itself so that this trade-off does not result in invalidating the approach.

4   Case Study: Heap Integrity

Heap canaries can be used for detecting heap buffer overflows. They are fashioned after stack-based canaries and work in a similar way. Typically the canaries are checked on deallocation, which for our use case would lead to frequent checking and overhead to the main application threads for short-lived objects, or excessive detection delays for long-lived ones.

As a case study of integrity monitoring, we apply *MemPatrol* to canary-based heap integrity checking. We use the monitor thread to patrol heap buffers, and detect illegal memory overwrites across boundaries between heap objects by checking corruption of canary values placed strategically between heap-allocated objects. In this section we describe our implementation of sideline integrity checking for heap canaries.

4.1   Memory Pools

To check heap canaries, the monitor needs to keep track of heap allocations. Existing sideline heap buffer overflow detection systems achieve this by intercepting heap allocation functions to collect the addresses and sizes of live heap buffers. This can be a significant source of overhead, slowing down the main application threads.

High-performance applications typically use fixed-size memory pools for performance, such as the memory pool library for network monitoring systems provided by the DPDK [10] toolkit. We designed our monitoring system to take full advantage of such memory pools. Instead of tracking individual object allocations, we track information at the granularity of memory pools: the base address of each pool, the number of blocks, and the size of a block in the pool are included in an entry and added to the append-only table used by the monitor thread. This enables the bulk setup of heap canaries before their use in the fast path of the program. Memory pools also enable reusing canaries between allocation lifetimes (since typically the object size is fixed per memory pool). Such *canary recycling* eliminates synchronization overheads suffered by existing solutions designed around a `malloc`-style arbitrary object size interface.

4.2   Integration with the Monitored Application

MemPatrol is implemented in the form of a library offering an API for integration with applications. To use *MemPatrol* the application needs to augment its memory pool implementation with canary objects. These are defined in the *MemPatrol* library by the `canary_t` type. The monitored application is responsible for registering all its canaries using the `patrol_register` function provided by our library. This integration effort is similar to what is required for using debugging solutions such as Google's AddressSanitizer [31] with custom memory allocation schemes.

In the current implementation, all canaries must be registered before the application enters its untrusted execution phase, signified by starting the monitor

```
typedef int8_t canary_t[16]; // Data type for canaries

void patrol_init(void); // Called at system startup

// Used for registering canary locations
void patrol_register(void *base, size_t stride, size_t count);

void patrol_start(int cpu); // Start monitoring
```

Fig. 3. Canary-monitoring integration API

thread with the `patrol_start` function and dropping its privileges. Figure 3 illustrates the API used by the application to integrate with *MemPatrol*.

Upon calling the `patrol_register` function, the value of the base address as a 64-bit integer and the values of the pool's object size and object count, as 32-bit integers concatenated into a 64-bit integer, are stored in a table using two `sec64_t` entries generated using the `store_sec64` function. The monitor thread has not been started yet, so the key, generated by the `patrol_init` function on program startup, is temporarily stored in memory inside the *MemPatrol* library.

Once the `patrol_start` function is called, it loads the key into a register, zeroes out the copy in memory, and launches the monitor thread. The number of table entries is also kept in a register to prevent it from being tampered to trick the monitor into ignoring table entries.

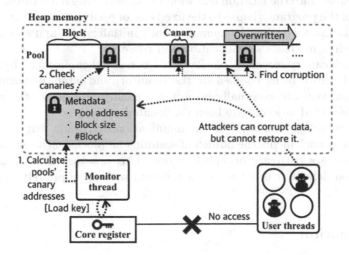

Fig. 4. Secure canary checking

4.3 Cryptographically Generated Canary Values

Some existing approaches [22] using random valued canaries safely store the original copies in the kernel or a hypervisor. In our technique, we generate canaries using cryptographic techniques to prevent attackers from inferring the original canary values and recovering them to prevent detection after a compromise. We use 128 bits for a canary, storing a MAC of the address of the canary. Unlike using random canary values, this does not require storing copies of canary values for comparison.

Since possibly compromised threads of the application do not have access to the key, even if attackers succeed in exploitation through heap buffer overflows, they cannot recover the overwritten canary's expected value. The overall checking procedure is illustrated in Fig. 4.

We place one canary at the end of each block. Memory blocks are typically padded to match a requested alignment. This has to be done after the addition of the canary size to the allocation size. There is a choice on whether to place the canary back-to-back with the actual object, or to align the canary in memory. We chose to pack canaries tightly, to detect even small, accidental heap buffer overflows and to save memory, at the cost of unaligned memory accesses from the monitor thread.

4.4 Canary Recycling

The integrity monitor does not have to track the life cycle of each heap buffer. This is possible since the location and values of canaries are fixed throughout the execution of the program, thanks to the fixed size of pool elements. This allows us to setup all canaries during the memory pool's initialization, and avoid updates on every individual block's deallocation and reuse.

With such canary recycling, blocks with a corrupted canary may be returned to the pool before being checked by the monitor, and later re-allocated. The monitor, however, will eventually inspect the canary and detect the violation, even if the affected objects have been deallocated.

Canary recycling eliminates the communication overheads, but on the other hand, this approach incurs the burden of scanning all blocks of the memory pool, whether they are currently occupied or not. This has the effect of increasing the detection delay but is not a serious problem with appropriately provisioned memory pools.

5 Evaluation

We evaluated *MemPatrol*'s performance by integrating it with NCORE [23], a proprietary Deep Packet Inspection (DPI) system, and running experiments using high bandwidth network traffic.

5.1   Integration with NCORE

We modified NCORE's memory pool library to reserve 16 bytes for one canary at the end of each block, and to call `patrol_register` when the memory pool is created to register all its canaries. Each canary also helps protect against buffer underflows in the next block. NCORE does not store allocator metadata between blocks, but stores free-list pointers at the start of free blocks. These are protected since canaries are active even when their block is free. Finally, we added a call to the *MemPatrol* initialization routine (`patrol_init`) at the beginning of NCORE's startup, and a call to *MemPatrol*'s monitor thread launching routine (`patrol_start`) after the NCORE has initialized but before it drops privileges. The system's memory pools are initialized between these two calls.

5.2   Experimental Results

We ran NCORE on an iXsystems Mercury server with 2 Intel(R) Xeon(R) E5-2690 v4 CPUs, nominally clocked at 2.60 GHz (but running at 3.20 GHz thanks to Turbo Boost) with HyperThreads enabled and 256 GiB of RAM at 2133 MHz distributed over all four memory channels of the two CPUs. This system has 56 logical cores, out of which NCORE was configured to use 41 logical cores for pattern matching, and 5 logical cores for packet capture and internal load balancing, with their sibling logical cores left idle to avoid interference. One logical core on the first CPU was assigned to the *MemPatrol* monitor thread, and one physical core per CPU (4 logical cores in total) was left for general purpose use, such as user shells and OS services. We configured NCORE for a pattern matching workload inspecting all network traffic against a list of 5 million random substring patterns with an average pattern length of 100 bytes.

Space Overhead. After launch, NCORE had registered 203 million heap canaries in 120 contiguous ranges. Thanks to memory pools, the overhead of metadata kept for each contiguous range of canaries is low. Also, the system used 129 GB of heap memory for objects and their canaries. Thus the average object size without canaries is 619 bytes, and the 16 bytes used for each canary amount to a memory overhead of 3.25 GB or 2.58%.

CPU Overhead. We used another iXsystems server as a traffic generator replaying an 650 MB real traffic trace with a tool that rewrites the IP addresses on the fly to simulate an unlimited supply of flows. To evaluate the performance overhead, we generated traffic at the rate of 50 Gb/s at 9.3 M packets/s and 170 K bidirectional flows/s. Under this load, the baseline NCORE without *MemPatrol* had 77% CPU utilization on the pattern matching cores. The traffic capture cores are constantly polling a network interface so are always at 100% utilization irrespective of actual load. There was no packet loss observed in this baseline setup. We repeated the experiment with the monitor thread running, and observed no increase in CPU utilization, with packet loss also remaining zero. By running on a separate core and performing non-temporal memory accesses, *MemPatrol* did not interfere with the instruction count of the application's processing threads.

Cache Overhead. We used the Intel Performance Counter Monitor (PCM) tool [35] to measure the cache hit rates on each logical core. The results are shown in Table 1. We show separate results for the traffic capture threads (RX), the pattern matching threads (Workers) and the monitor thread (Patrol). The first row is the baseline without the monitor thread. The second row shows the results with the monitor thread running and using non-temporal memory accesses. We observe that there is a small decrease of the L3 cache hit rate. If we disable the non-temporal memory access hinting, or instead we specify a high degree of temporal locality using the value 3 to the third argument of the GCC prefetch intrinsic, we measure a slightly higher degradation. We further justify adding the hints for non-temporal memory access to the monitor thread by observing that its cache hit rate is zero.

Table 1. Cache hit rates for different types of application threads and different temporal locality hints used by the monitor thread.

	RX		Workers		Patrol	
	L3 Hit	L2 Hit	L3 Hit	L2 Hit	L3 Hit	L2 Hit
No patrol	0.31	0.10	0.64	0.66		
Prefetch 0	0.31	0.10	0.62	0.66	0.00	0.00
No prefetch	0.30	0.10	0.59	0.66	0.00	0.00
Prefetch 3	0.30	0.10	0.60	0.66	0.00	0.00

Memory Bandwidth Overhead. Subsequently, we used the PCM tool to measure the system memory throughput. The measurement was done over a 60 s interval to smooth out variations. As expected, there was no impact on the memory write throughput, but we could observe the effects of the patrol thread on the system's memory read throughput: An 18.1% increase over the baseline read throughput of 15.5 GB/s.

Detection Delay. Running at full speed, *MemPatrol* required 5 s to scan all 203 million canaries. This corresponds to the worst-case detection delay after the corruption of a canary. We confirmed the detection capability end-to-end by introducing an artificial buffer overflow.

Overhead Control. Next, we ran experiments to demonstrate control of the overhead by trading-off detection latency. We slowed down the monitor thread by a configurable amount by adding `pause` hardware instructions (via the `_mm_pause` compiler intrinsic). Figure 5 illustrates the effect of different delays determined by the number of additional `pause` instructions executed in each iteration of *MemPatrol*'s monitoring loop that is checking one canary. Insertion of a single delay instruction results in a sharp drop of the read throughput overhead from 18.1% to 5.2% and a roughly proportional increase in detection latency from 5 to 17.7 s. By further tweaking the number of `pause` instructions we can bring down

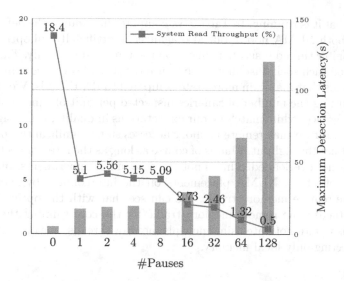

Fig. 5. Relation between System Read Throughput and Maximum Detection Latency (time to scan all canaries). The user can select the trade-off by controlling the number of pause instructions inserted to throttle the monitor thread.

the memory throughput overhead to 0.65% for an increased detection delay of 120 s. This experiment confirms that the user can decide the amount of overhead that is acceptable for the application, at the cost of detection delay. At the same time, the design of the system does not allow an attacker to disable detection by exploit the detection delay introduced for performance reasons.

NUMA Effects. Modern multi-processor systems employ non-uniform memory access (NUMA). We investigated the performance effects of the CPU socket placement of the monitor thread. In the baseline setup we use a single monitor thread running on socket 0 to monitor memory on both NUMA sockets. We wish to evaluate the performance of a monitor thread only inspecting local memory on

Table 2. Effects of the NUMA placement of the monitor thread on the detection latency and local/remote memory bandwidth of the monitor thread's core.

	Monitored sockets		
	Both	Local	Remote
#Canaries	203, 159, 920	76, 184, 970	126, 974, 950
Scan Duration (μs)	5, 151, 152	1, 865, 777	3, 553, 998
#Canaries/μs	39.4	40.8	35.7
Remote memory bandwidth	1, 576	0	3, 339
Local memory bandwidth	915	3, 399	0.1

the socket that it is running. In Table 2 we compare this against the default setup inspecting both NUMA nodes, but also against an artificially suboptimal setup where a monitor thread inspects memory on the remote socket only. The number of canaries on each socket is different, because the second socket is running more worker threads that maintain more state compared to RX threads. We normalize this by reporting the number of canaries inspected per unit of time, and observe that the difference, while matching our expectations in quality, is not significant. The reason must be that remote memory accesses suffer significantly in terms of latency, but not throughput. That is of course as long as the interconnect between the CPUs is not overloaded. This is not the case in our experiments, but we can observe the effects of NUMA placements on the interconnect by showing the local vs. the remote memory traffic. We can see that with the optimal NUMA placement there is no remote memory traffic for the core running the monitor thread. This would motivate using multiple monitor threads, one on each NUMA node, inspecting only local memory.

6   Related Work

Concurrent Monitoring. With the advent of multicore machines, utilizing spare CPU cores for security became an attractive approach. Multi-Variant Execution Environments (MVEE) [28,29] use spare cores to run several slightly different versions of the same program in lockstep, monitoring them for discrepancies. This approach, however, is impractical for high-performance multicore programs utilizing the majority of the CPU's cores.

Cruiser [37] is one of the original system to decouple security checks from program execution, running them instead in a thread inside the address space of the monitored process. Unlike *MemPatrol*, Cruiser's guarantees are probabilistic. Its low detection latency, for the programs it was evaluated on, helps defend against tampering with its data structures, but is not a reliable solution on its own. Moreover, for performance critical applications using large amounts of heap memory, like NCORE, the detection latency would increase significantly due to the sheer number of canaries, and should not be relied upon for security. Cruiser also employs pseudo-isolation using ASLR and surrounding its data structures with inaccessible guard pages, in the hope that blind access will trigger segmentation faults. Recent techniques [24], however, demonstrate that faith in ASLR-based information hiding is misplaced. Therefore, these systems do not offer a strong guarantee against tampering with the monitor's execution before a compromise is detected. Without reliable isolation, the risk of exploitation remains as long as there is detection delay.

Other software-based techniques utilizing spare CPU cores include ShadowReplica [12] and TaintPipe [17], which aim to improve the performance of dynamic information flow tracking (DIFT) for security. DIFT is a comprehensive protection mechanism, and these solutions demonstrated significant performance improvements over inline DIFT, but the remaining overhead due to the presence of inline stub code remains significant ($> 2\times$ slowdown over native execution).

Monitor Isolation. The problem of the isolation of monitoring systems has been addressed by using OS kernel or VM hypervisor mechanisms [5,22,33]. These are comparatively safer, but come with additional overheads and engineering costs. Instead, we present a userspace solution sharing the address space of the main application. Our solution minimizes the overhead to the execution of the main application threads while at the same time it allows monitoring the entire memory of the application if so required. Finally, it avoids any engineering costs for the maintenance of custom kernel modifications.

Other software-based isolation mechanisms using Software Fault Isolation (SFI) (e.g. NativeClient [36]) suffer from overheads because they inline checks to the code that needs to be contained (in our case the application's code). Native-Client has an average overhead of 5% for CPU-bound benchmarks. *MemPatrol's* overheads on the other hand are taxing mostly the monitor thread, which we can afford.

Kernel Integrity Monitors. Kernel integrity monitors (KIMs) periodically inspect critical kernel memory regions, such as syscall tables and persistent function pointers, isolating themselves from the kernel by residing in hypervisors [9] or hardware such as PCI cards [26]. Some KIMs tackle transient attacks by snooping the bus traffic using PCI cards [18] or even commodity GPGPUs [14]. *MemPatrol* is quite similar to KIMs using periodic memory inspection, but monitors applications, so does not require a hypervisor or dedicated hardware.

Cryptographic Key Protection. *MemPatrol* takes advantage of the AES instruction set of Intel processors [8] to implement CPU-only cryptographic message authentication codes (MACs), and stores critical information in regular registers of user-mode programs. TRESOR [19], a disk encryption system that defends against main memory attacks, uses a similar CPU-only cryptographic mechanism based on AES-NI, but stores its secret key in special CPU debug registers in each core and is kernel-based.

Note that the availability of the AES-NI instruction set is not a hard requirement, but rather an optimization and implementation convenience. For example, Loop-Amnesia [32], a disk encryption system similar to TRESOR, does not rely on AES-NI. We could avoid the dependency on the special AES instruction set by using their CPU-only implementation of AES.

MACs have been previously used in Cryptographic Control Flow Integrity (CCFI) [16] to protect control flow elements such as return addresses, function pointers, and vtable pointers. CCFI also takes advantage of the AES-NI instruction set. Compared to *MemPatrol*, CCFI offers comprehensive protection against control flow violations but does not protect against some non-control-flow data corruptions that *MemPatrol* can detect. Moreover, CCFI is an inline solution, hence it directly affects the performance of the application threads (3–18% decrease in server request rate).

Memory Safety. Much research has been done on enforcing *spatial* [4,13,20] and *temporal* [2,21] memory safety in C/C++ programs. Some of these solutions offer extensive memory safety, but they slow down applications significantly. For example, SoftBound [20], a solution for comprehensive spatial memory safety, incurs an average execution time overhead of 79% for CPU-bound benchmarks. Our target, however, is to protect applications where almost any execution overhead must be avoided.

A number of approaches aim for a favourable security-to-overhead ratio rather than complete memory safety. For example, some focus on preventing illegal control flow, e.g. [1,15,16], and can block the majority of attacks, but still incur inline overheads (21% on average for CPU-bound benchmarks for [1] and 8.4% for [15]). Other solutions focus on preventing buffer overflows that overwrite adjacent memory locations. StackGuard [6] detected exploitations of stack-based buffer overflows by placing a *canary* word before the return address, and checking it when the stack frame is deactivated. Similar solutions are currently widely deployed due to their effectiveness and simplicity, and the idea has been extended to heap buffer overflow detection [22,27] with canary checks triggered by memory management routines, library routines, or system calls.

Our case-study for heap memory integrity is based on heap-canary countermeasures, and specifically those that use a monitor running in parallel with the protected application [33,37]. Note, however, that NCORE also uses stack-based overflow protections on top of *MemPatrol*, and the mere use of memory pools also offers some level of protection against temporal-safety violations through the reuse of memory only for objects with identical layout, which can prevent most abuses of function pointer fields [2].

Finally, it is worth comparing *MemPatrol* with inline solutions offering similar security guarantees. For example, inline heap canary checking [27] can be very efficient, but suffer from unbounded detection delay, as detection relies on checks triggered by events such as deallocations. In the case of NCORE, heap allocations for certain objects such as host state may linger for several days. *MemPatrol*, on the other hand, puts a bound on the detection delay. Other inline solutions detect buffer overflows immediately by instrumenting every memory write to check whether it overwrites a canary. WIT [3], for example, uses this approach, which contributes the bulk of its runtime overhead of 4–25% for CPU bound benchmarks, which is prohibitive for some performance-critical applications.

Tunable Overhead. *MemPatrol* offers developers and operators control over its runtime overhead. A similar idea was pursued by ASAP [34], which automatically instruments the program to maximize its security while staying within a specified overhead budget. Unlike *MemPatrol*, ASAP controls the overhead by decreasing coverage, while *MemPatrol* achieves this by increasing detection delay without compromising eventual detection. Cruiser [37] also discussed a possible approach to increase its efficiency using back-off strategies to pace the monitor thread with `nop` instructions or `sleep` calls. However, without proper isolation of the monitor thread, this approach undermines Cruiser's security guarantees.

7 Conclusion

In summary, we applied our integrity monitoring solution, *MemPatrol*, to a high-performance network monitoring system, demonstrating 0% CPU-time overhead for the application's threads. The hidden memory bandwidth overheads also concerned us, but we demonstrated how to minimize them to under 1%. We conclude with some remarks on current limitations and future directions.

Importantly, our case study's memory safety guarantees are limited to heap buffer overflow detection, and can be thwarted by memory disclosure attacks. Future work is required to identify additional memory integrity applications.

Moreover, the current *MemPatrol* prototype cannot register additional memory locations to monitor after initialization, but this limitation is not fundamental. We could intermix monitoring with processing of registration requests received through a message queue. As long as bookkeeping data structures are append-only, the threat of replay attacks is averted. A general solution for supporting arbitrary updates, however, is an interesting future direction.

Creating the binary code for a system like *MemPatrol* is currently a tedious, manual process. As pointed out in Loop-Amnesia [32], some level of compiler support, e.g. to control register spilling, would help.

Finally, the full security of AES may be overkill given the bound on detection latency, and lowering the number of AES rounds used could be considered as a way to increase the monitor thread's performance.

Acknowledgment. The authors would like to thank our shepherd, Vasileios Kemerlis, and the anonymous reviewers for their valuable feedback.

References

1. Abadi, M., Budiu, M., Erlingsson, U., Ligatti, J.: Control-flow Integrity. In: ACM CCS 2005, Alexandria, VA, USA (2005)
2. Akritidis, P.: Cling: a memory allocator to mitigate dangling pointers. In: USENIX Security 2010, Washington, DC, USA (2010)
3. Akritidis, P., Cadar, C., Raiciu, C., Costa, M., Castro, M.: Preventing memory error exploits with WIT. In: IEEE S&P 2008, Oakland, CA, USA (2008)
4. Austin, T.M., Breach, S.E., Sohi, G.S.: Efficient detection of all pointer and array access errors. In: ACM PLDI 1994, Orlando, FL, USA (1994)
5. Bauman, E., Ayoade, G., Lin, Z.: A survey on hypervisor-based monitoring: approaches, applications, and evolutions. ACM Comput. Surv. **48**(1), 10 (2015)
6. Cowan, C., Pu, C., Maier, D., Hintony, H., Walpole, J., Bakke, P., Beattie, S., Grier, A., Wagle, P., Zhang, Q.: StackGuard: automatic adaptive detection and prevention of buffer-overflow attacks. In: USENIX Security 1998, San Antonio, TX, USA (1998)
7. Erlingsson, U.: The inlined reference monitor approach to security policy enforcement. Ph.D. thesis, Cornell University (2004)
8. Gueron, S.: Intel Advanced Encryption Standard (AES) Instruction Set White Paper, Rev. 3.0 edn. (2010)

 9. Hofmann, O.S., Dunn, A.M., Kim, S., Roy, I., Witchel, E.: Ensuring operating system kernel integrity with OSck. In: ACM ASPLOS XVI, Newport Beach, CA, USA (2011)
10. Intel: Data Plane Development Kit (DPDK). http://DPDK.org
11. Intel: MPX Performance Evaluation. https://intel-mpx.github.io/performance
12. Jee, K., Kemerlis, V.P., Keromytis, A.D., Portokalidis, G.: ShadowReplica: efficient parallelization of dynamic data flow tracking. In: ACM CCS 2013, Berlin, Germany (2013)
13. Jones, R.W.M., Kelly, P.H.J.: Backwards-compatible bounds checking for arrays and pointers in C programs. In: ACM AADEBUG 1997, Linköping, Sweden (1997)
14. Koromilas, L., Vasiliadis, G., Athanasopoulos, E., Ioannidis, S.: GRIM: leveraging GPUs for kernel integrity monitoring. In: Monrose, F., Dacier, M., Blanc, G., Garcia-Alfaro, J. (eds.) RAID 2016. LNCS, vol. 9854, pp. 3–23. Springer, Cham (2016). doi:10.1007/978-3-319-45719-2_1
15. Kuznetsov, V., Szekeres, L., Payer, M., Candea, G., Sekar, R., Song, D.: Code-pointer integrity. In: USENIX OSDI 2014, Broomfield, CO, USA (2014)
16. Mashtizadeh, A.J., Bittau, A., Boneh, D., Mazières, D.: CCFI: cryptographically enforced control flow integrity. In: ACM CCS 2015, Denver, CO, USA (2015)
17. Ming, J., Wu, D., Xiao, G., Wang, J., Liu, P.: TaintPipe: pipelined symbolic taint analysis. In: USENIX Security 2015, Washington, DC, USA (2015)
18. Moon, H., Lee, H., Lee, J., Kim, K., Paek, Y., Kang, B.B.: Vigilare: toward snoop-based kernel integrity monitor. In: ACM CCS 2012, Raleigh, NC, USA (2012)
19. Müller, T., Freiling, F.C., Dewald, A.: TRESOR runs encryption securely outside RAM. In: USENIX Security 2011, San Francisco, CA, USA (2011)
20. Nagarakatte, S., Zhao, J., Martin, M.M., Zdancewic, S.: SoftBound: highly compatible and complete spatial memory safety for C. In: ACM PLDI 2009, Dublin, Ireland (2009)
21. Nagarakatte, S., Zhao, J., Martin, M.M., Zdancewic, S.: CETS: compiler enforced temporal safety for C. In: ACM ISMM 2010, Toronto, ON, Canada (2010)
22. Nikiforakis, N., Piessens, F., Joosen, W.: HeapSentry: kernel-assisted protection against heap overflows. In: Rieck, K., Stewin, P., Seifert, J.-P. (eds.) DIMVA 2013. LNCS, vol. 7967, pp. 177–196. Springer, Heidelberg (2013). doi:10.1007/978-3-642-39235-1_11
23. Niometrics: NCORE DPI System. http://www.niometrics.com
24. Oikonomopoulos, A., Athanasopoulos, E., Bos, H., Giuffrida, C.: Poking holes in information hiding. In: USENIX Security 2016, Austin, TX, USA (2016)
25. PaX: MPROTECT (2003). https://pax.grsecurity.net/docs/mprotect.txt
26. Petroni, Jr., N.L., Fraser, T., Molina, J., Arbaugh, W.A.: Copilot - a coprocessor-based kernel runtime integrity monitor. In: USENIX Security 2004, San Diego, CA, USA (2004)
27. Robertson, W., Kruegel, C., Mutz, D., Valeur, F.: Run-time detection of heap-based overflows. In: USENIX LISA 2003, San Diego, CA, USA (2003)
28. Salamat, B., Gal, A., Jackson, T., Wagner, G., Manivannan, K., Franz, M.: Multi-variant program execution: using multi-core systems to defuse buffer-overflow vulnerabilities. In: IEEE CISIS 2008, Barcelona, Spain (2008)
29. Salamat, B., Jackson, T., Gal, A., Franz, M.: Orchestra: intrusion detection using parallel execution and monitoring of program variants in user-space. In: ACM EuroSys 2009, Nuremberg, Germany (2009)
30. SELinux Wiki: Main Page – SELinux Wiki (2013). http://selinuxproject.org
31. Serebryany, K., Bruening, D., Potapenko, A., Vyukov, D.: AddressSanitizer: a fast address sanity checker. In: USENIX ATC 2012, Boston, MA, USA (2012)

32. Simmons, P.: Security through amnesia: a software-based solution to the cold boot attack on disk encryption. In: ACM ACSAC 2011, Orlando, FL, USA (2011)
33. Tian, D., Zeng, Q., Wu, D., Liu, P., Hu, C.: Kruiser: semi-synchronized non-blocking concurrent kernel heap buffer overflow monitoring. In: ISOC NDSS 2012, San Diego, CA, USA (2012)
34. Wagner, J., Kuznetsov, V., Candea, G., Kinder, J.: High system-code security with low overhead. In: IEEE S&P 2015, Oakland, CA, USA (2015)
35. Willhalm, T., Dementiev, R., Fay, P.: Intel Performance Counter Monitor - A better way to measure CPU utilization (2012). http://www.intel.com/software/pcm
36. Yee, B., Sehr, D., Dardyk, G., Chen, J.B., Muth, R., Orm, T., Okasaka, S., Narula, N., Fullagar, N., Inc, G.: Native client: a sandbox for portable, untrusted x86 native Code. In: IEEE S&P 2009, Oakland, CA, USA (2009)
37. Zeng, Q., Wu, D., Liu, P.: Cruiser: concurrent heap buffer overflow monitoring using lock-free data structures. In: ACM PLDI 2011, San Jose, CA, USA (2011)

Malware Analysis

Measuring and Defeating
Anti-Instrumentation-Equipped Malware

Mario Polino$^{(\boxtimes)}$, Andrea Continella$^{(\boxtimes)}$, Sebastiano Mariani, Stefano D'Alessio,
Lorenzo Fontana, Fabio Gritti, and Stefano Zanero$^{(\boxtimes)}$

DEIB, Politecnico di Milano, Milano, Italy
{mario.polino,andrea.continella,stefano.zanero}@polimi.it,
{sebastiano.mariani,stefano.dalessio,
lorenzo2.fontana,fabio1.gritti}@mail.polimi.it

Abstract. Malware authors constantly develop new techniques in order
to evade analysis systems. Previous works addressed attempts to evade
analysis by means of anti-sandboxing and anti-virtualization techniques,
for example proposing to run samples on bare-metal. However, state-of-
the-art bare-metal tools fail to provide richness and completeness in the
results of the analysis. In this context, Dynamic Binary Instrumentation
(DBI) tools have become popular in the analysis of new malware samples
because of the deep control they guarantee over the instrumented binary.
As a consequence, malware authors developed new techniques, called
anti-instrumentation, aimed at detecting if a sample is being instrumented. We propose a practical approach to make DBI frameworks more
stealthy and resilient against anti-instrumentation attacks. We studied
the common techniques used by malware to detect the presence of a
DBI tool, and we proposed a set of countermeasures to address them.
We implemented our approach in ARANCINO, on top of the Intel Pin
framework. Armed with it, we perform the first large-scale measurement
of the anti-instrumentation techniques employed by modern malware.
Finally, we leveraged our tool to implement a generic unpacker, showing
some case studies of the anti-instrumentation techniques used by known
packers.

1   Introduction

Malware is still one of the Internet's major security threat and dynamic analysis
systems are an essential component to a defend from it. By running malicious
samples in a controlled environment, security analysts can observe their behavior [30], unpack obfuscated code [25], identify command and control (C&C)
servers, generate behavioral signatures, as well as remediation procedures for
infections [12]. However, modern malware samples present many techniques,
called *anti-debugging* and *anti-sandboxing*, to hide their behavior when they
detect that they are running in a controlled environment. Generally, such malware is known as "evasive".

Previous research proposed different mechanisms to defeat evasive malware, mainly based on two approaches. A first approach draws upon techniques

M. Polychronakis and M. Meier (Eds.): DIMVA 2017, LNCS 10327, pp. 73–96, 2017.
DOI: 10.1007/978-3-319-60876-1_4

(commonly known as "multi-path execution") used to increase the coverage of dynamic analysis tools [10,28,42]. Binaries are executed multiple times, either providing different inputs that invert the outcomes of conditional branches (i.e., trying to disarm detection triggers) [10,28], or simply forcing the execution along a different path [42]. The second approach tries to analyze malware samples in environments that minimize the artifacts that can be exploited to detect the analysis system, for instance running samples on bare-metal [20], or porting the instrumenting framework in hardware [37]. While the former approach is more generic, it is often unfeasible since it leads to an explosion in the need of computational resources. Instead, the latter is more practical and, in fact, it has been recently adopted by security researchers [20,21,37].

To evaluate a malware analysis system, one should consider three factors: quality, efficiency, and stealthiness [20]. Quality refers to the richness and completeness of the analysis results. Efficiency measures the number of samples that can be analyzed per unit time. Stealthiness refers to the undetectability of the presence of the analysis environment. Intuitively, there is a constant trade-off between these factors. Despite the effort of the research community in developing approaches and tools to enforce the stealthiness of malware analysis systems, state-of-the-art tools provide either stealthiness or quality. For instance, Kirat et al. [20] proposed a framework for performing analyses on bare-metal. However, such systems cannot guarantee a good quality, i.e., they do not provide the analysts a good level of details in the inspection of the malware behavior. Instead, in some specific scenarios (e.g., manual and automated reverse engineering) we need deeper control of the running binary. In fact, the use of Dynamic Binary Instrumentation (DBI) frameworks has become a valid alternative for analyzing malware samples [4,16,26,27]. By injecting instrumentation code inside the binary under analysis, DBI tools give a deep control over the analyzed program, providing both a low-level (i.e., instruction) and a high-level (i.e., system call) view. Given that, in order to keep on hindering the reverse engineering of their code, malware authors developed a new series of techniques, called *anti-instrumentation*, aimed at detecting the presence of a DBI tool at runtime.

We propose a dynamic protection framework to defend a generic DBI Tool against anti-instrumentation attacks. First, we classified state-of-the-art techniques in four categories (code cache artifacts, environment artifacts, just in time compiler detection, and overhead detection); then, we designed a set of generic countermeasures to defeat every identified class. In order to achieve this, we leverage the power of DBI tools to fully control the execution flow of the instrumented process. This allow us to detect and dismantle possible evasion attempts. We implemented our approach in ARANCINO, on top of the Intel Pin framework [23].

We tested our system against eXait [15], a tool containing a set of plugins that aim at detecting when a program is instrumented by Intel Pin, showing that ARANCINO is able to hide Intel Pin, allowing the analysis of evasive binaries. Then, we used our tool to perform a large-scale study of the anti-instrumentation techniques used by malware: we collected and analyzed 7,006 malware samples, monitoring the evasive behaviors that triggered our system. Finally, to show a useful application scenario of our system, we leveraged ARANCINO to implement a generic, dynamic, unpacker that can handle anti-instrumentation-equipped packers. Moreover, we show case studies of known packers that employ anti-instrumentation techniques in the unpacking process.

In summary, we make the following contributions:

- We proposed an approach to practically defeat the techniques that malware employs to detect instrumentation systems (i.e., DBI tools).
- We performed a study of the common techniques adopted by modern malware authors to perform evasion of instrumentation systems. We measured how malware detects DBI tools on a dataset of 7,006 samples.
- We leveraged our anti-evasion approach to implement a generic, dynamic, evasion-resilient unpacker, showing some case studies of the evasion techniques used by know packers.

In the spirit of open science, we make our datasets and the code developed for ARANCINO publicly available[1].

2   Background and Motivation

Dynamic Binary Instrumentation (DBI) is a method to analyze the behavior of a binary application at run-time by injecting instrumentation code, which executes transparently as part of the normal instruction stream after being injected. Commonly, DBI tools exploit a Just In Time (JIT) compiler to instrument the analyzed binary at run-time, translating originally x86 code into an intermediated representation. Translation units used by different frameworks differ in size. For instance, Valgrind [29] uses standard basic blocks as traces, caches the translation, and jumps inside the corresponding cache each time a basic block is hit. DynamoRIO [9], instead, uses an extended definition of basic block as trace, including all instructions until a conditional jump. This includes also code inside function calls or after an unconditional jump. Intel Pin, uses traces defined as all the code between the previous trace and the next unconditional jump.

DBI tools turned out to be particularly useful in malware analysis, for instance to detect malicious software [4], identify cryptographic primitives [16], or to efficiently perform taint analysis [26]. However, DBI tools are not completely transparent to the analyzed malware, and, in fact, anti-instrumentation techniques have been developed to detect the instrumentation process. We classified such anti-instrumentation techniques in four categories.

Code Cache Artifacts. These techniques aim at detecting artifacts that are inherent of a DBI cache. For example, the Extended Instruction Pointer (EIP) is different if a binary is instrumented. In fact, in a DBI Tool the code is executed from a different memory region, called *code cache*, rather than from the main module of the binary.

---

[1] https://github.com/necst/arancino.

Environment Artifacts. The memory layout of an instrumented binary is deeply different respect to the one of a not instrumented one. Searching for DBI artifacts such as strings or particular code patterns in memory can eventually reveal the presence of a DBI tool inside the target process memory. Also, the parent process of an instrumented binary is often the DBI tool itself.

JIT Compiler Detection. JIT compilers make a lot of noise inside the process in terms of Windows API calls and pages allocation. These artifacts can be leveraged by the instrumented program to detect the presence of a DBI tool.

Overhead Detection. Instrumentation adds an observable overhead in the execution of a target program. This overhead can be noticed by malware by estimating the execution time of a particular set of instructions.

3   ARANCINO: Approach

A DBI tool can work at three granularities: (1) Instruction, a single instruction inside a collected trace; (2) Basic block, a sequence of instructions terminated by a conditional jump; (3) Trace, a sequence of basic blocks terminated by an unconditional jump. Our approach leverages the complete control that a DBI tool has on the instrumented binary to hide the artifacts that the DBI tool itself introduces during the instrumentation process. In fact, by instrumenting a binary, we can identify when it tries to leverage such artifacts to evade the analysis. In practice, we designed a set of countermeasures for the anti-instrumentation techniques we mentioned in Sect. 2. We implemented our approach in ARANCINO using Intel Pin. While we developed our countermeasures specifically targeting Intel Pin, the approach on which such countermeasures are based is generic and can be adapted to any DBI tool.

3.1   Code Cache Artifacts

DBI tools do not execute the original code of a program. Instead, they execute a particular memory region called code cache in which they copied an instrumented version of the original code.

EIP Detection. A malware sample can detect if the Instruction Pointer (EIP) is different from the expected one. This technique exploits particular instructions that save the execution context, including the current value of the EIP register. Once obtained the effective value inside EIP register, this value is compared with the base address in which the program expects the Instruction Pointer to be (main module of the program). If these two values are different, the program under analysis become aware that it has been instrumented. Here we report the currently working methods we identified to retrieve EIP. Examples of such instructions are `int 2e`, `fsave`, and `fxsave`. An easier technique to retrieve the EIP is monitoring the stack after a `call` instruction. However, this scenario is already inherently handled by Intel Pin, which does not alter the original EIP value on the stack. In order to defeat this technique, since there are a set of instructions that expose the presence of the DBI by leaking the effective EIP, we track these instructions in the collected trace and block the information leakage. Specifically, when we detect such instructions we execute a user defined function that patches the value inside registers or memory with the expected one, so that the analyzed program can be fooled.

int 2e is the legacy instruction used in Windows in order to perform a system call (now replaced by sysenter). The interrupt handler called as consequence of the int 2e saves the current state information parameters, such as the EIP and the EFLAGS, in order to eventually return correctly from kernel-mode to user-mode after the execution of the syscall. Practically, this behavior has the side effect to store the EIP in the EDX register. When we detect the presence of int 2e, we insert a call to a function right after its execution that patches the value stored in EDX with the real EIP of the current instruction inside the main module.

fsave/fxsave/fstenv instructions save the floating-point context, including the effective EIP, at the moment of the execution of the last floating-point operation. When we detect one of these instructions in a trace, we insert a call to a function that manipulates the floating-point context by modifying the value of EIP with the correct address inside the main module of the program.

Self-modifying Code. Another way to detect the presence of a code cache is using self-modifying code, i.e., code that changes the instructions at run-time by overwriting itself. Because a DBI tool executes the cache where the code is not modified, it will execute a wrong trace breaking the semantic of the program. This violates the property of semantic equivalence between the original program and the instrumented one. To handle this technique, we force the DBI tool to build a new trace with the correctly patched code and abort the execution of the wrong one. When a new trace is collected, we first retrieve its boundaries, then for each write instruction we check if the written address is inside the boundaries of the current trace. If this happens, the address is marked as *written*. At the same time, for each instruction we check if the EIP that has to be executed is marked as *written* and, if so, we force the DBI tool to discard the trace and build a new one.

3.2 Environment Artifacts

DBI tools introduce further environment artifacts during instrumentation.

Parent Detection. Since the instrumented program is launched by the DBI tool as its child, it can obtain its parent process and check if it is not the expected one. In order to hide the parent process name, we took into account the possibility to get the parent process not only by using the standard Windows APIs, but also using more advanced methods. Analyzing the various techniques aimed to retrieve the process list we have identified two countermeasures that can correctly defeat this type of attacks. The first one consists in hooking the `NtQuerySystemInformation` and faking the returned `SYSTEM PROCESS INFO` structure by replacing every process named `pin.exe` with `cmd.exe`. Second, we deny the instrumented program to open the process `CSRSS.exe`. In fact, this process is responsible to maintain its own process list in user-space. To do so, we create a list of PID of processes that we want to hide from the target program, then we hook the `NtOpenProcess` to check if the target PID is included in the list. If so, we trigger an `NTSTATUS_ACCESS_DENIED`.

Memory Fingerprinting. Malware can identify the presence of several artifacts that a DBI tool unavoidably leaves in memory. The most straightforward technique is to scan the entire memory of the process looking for allocated pages and searching inside these pages for a set of DBI-related artifacts (like strings and code patterns). This kind of attack is thwarted by hiding all the memory regions where the DBI-related code and data reside. This is done by intercepting and controlling the results of the functions (`VirtualQuery`, `NtQueryVirtualMemory`) used to determine the state of a particular memory page. We check if the queried memory is inside a whitelist of addresses that the instrumented process is authorized to access. In the case the address is in the whitelist, we return the correct value, otherwise we return a `MEM_FREE` value. In other words, the memory space inside the whitelist is the only part that the analyzed program can see as allocated.

The whitelist is created at the beginning of the instrumentation process and updated at run-time when we detect a new dynamic memory allocation made by the analyzed program. Initially, the whitelist contains the main module of the executable. Then, when we detect that a new library is being loaded, we update the whitelist including such memory region. The heap and stack memory space is also whitelisted. We use `getProcessHeaps` at start-up in order to add to the whitelist the heap memory addresses created during the initialization process. We hook heap allocation functions to keep track of the dynamically allocated contents. By hooking the `NtAllocateVirtualMemory`, `RtlAllocateHeap`, and `RtlReAllocateHeap` functions we can actually cover all allocation functions since all the higher level APIs end up using one of them. Instead, to identify the stack we recover the address from `ESP` register and, using the default stack size (1048576 bytes), we whitelist its memory address space. Moreover, we need to add to our whitelist the PEB and TEB data structures, which contain information about the current process and threads. While analyzing these structures we also whitelist different memory regions pointed by fields in these structures. Last, we whitelist mapped files. Mapped files are particular memory structures in which the content of a file is associated with a portion of the process memory space. Some memory mapped files are created during the loading process of the executable, e.g., `locale.nls`, while others are created at run-time using the `MapViewOfFile` function, which at a lower level invokes the `NtMapViewOfSection` system call. Therefore, we scan the memory of the process as soon as it is loaded whitelisting all the memory regions marked as `MEM_MAPPED`. This allows us to consider the memory mapped files which are created before we get actual control of the execution. Moreover, we hook the `NtMapViewOfSection` system call to track the mapped files which are created by the application itself at run-time.

Note that a sample could detect our system by trying to allocate memory that is already allocated but hidden by our system. To this end, malware should allocate and deallocate through the entire address space to identify such memory regions. However, this is inefficient for the malware, and ARANCINO could easily detect such weird behavior.

3.3 JIT Compiler Detection

As briefly explained in Sect. 2, DBI tools use JIT compilers to instrument a binary. Malware can leverage JIT artifacts to spot the presence of a DBI tool.

DLL Hook. DBI tools need to hook functions in order to intercept the execution at the end of a not instrumented trace. Specifically, they insert jumps (Hooks) at the beginning of some functions. Consequently, an instrumented program can check if the initial instructions of common functions have been modified. In order to hide these differences, at the beginning of the instrumentation we retrieve the addresses in memory of the hooked functions (for example using the Windows API `GetModuleHandle`). Using this method, we can correctly retrieve addresses even if Address Space Layout Randomization (ASLR) is active on the machine. Once we know these addresses, we label them as *protected*, and we store the original values in a different memory region. When the binary wants to read a protected memory region, we simply redirect the read to our fake pages. In this way, the instrumented binary obtains the original value.

Memory Page Permissions. A JIT compiler needs to write and then execute a significant amount of code, hence the number of pages marked as RWX inside the address space is substantially larger respect to the not-instrumented execution of the program. A binary can scan the entire process address space counting the number of page encountered with RWX permissions. If this number is considerably high, it can spot the presence of the DBI. To address this technique, we leverage a whitelist of memory pages as we described in Sect. 3.2. When the instrumented binary performs a query of a memory region, we check if the address of such region is included in the whitelist of authorized addresses. If not, we return a `MEM_FREE` value, hiding the pages used by the JIT compiler.

Memory Allocations. As we mention before, the JIT compiler intensely uses RWX memory pages to instrument and cache instrumented traces. To this end, the DBI tool allocate the memory to fulfill the need. All these allocations are executed going through the low-level Windows API `ZwAllocateVirtualMemory`. A detection mechanism is to count the number of invocations of the `ZwAllocateVirtualMemory` and compare it with the number of invocations performed during a non-instrumented execution; if the difference is considerably high, the program can spot the presence of the JIT compiler. Usually, a program that wants to implement this anti-instrumentation technique inserts a simple assembly routine at the beginning of the `ZwAllocateVirtualMemory` which increments a counter every time the function is invoked; if the counter exceeds a predefined threshold then the JIT compiler is detected. The approach we used to defeat this technique aims at (1) redirecting every write attempt of the process inside the `.text` segment of libraries, and (2) faking the results of suspicious read instructions that have their target addresses inside the `.text` segment of libraries. This (1) prevents the insertion of hooks (e.g., in `ZwAllocateVirtualMemory`), and (2) denies the possibility to check if an hook is in place or not. Note that this approach is generic and can defeat every attempt to overwrite the original code of functions and to insert hooks inside protected memory regions.

3.4 Overhead Detection

Despite DBI tools' effort to reach good instrumentation performance, they introduce an observable overhead, which can be detected by performing small benchmarks tests. To do so, malware leverages Windows APIs such as `NtQueryPerformanceCounter`, `GetTickCount`, `timeGetTime` to obtain execution times and reveal the presence of instrumentation tools. Our countermeasure tries to fool the process to think that the elapsed time is less despite the introduced overhead. We can achieve this by lowering the results returned from the previously described functions.

Windows Time. Windows APIs, such as `GetTickCount` and `timeGetTime`, retrieve the time information by accessing different fields in a shared user page mapped at the end of the process memory space. In this memory area, we can find the structure `KUSER_SHARED_DATA`. Our approach is to implement a "Fake-Memory" in the locations that these functions access, lying about its content to cause the functions to return controlled time values. Hooking the API is not enough, because it is possible to read such data structure directly from the memory without calling any API. The strategy adopted in order to return fake values varies for the `GetTickCount` and the `timeGetTime`, because in order to calculate the elapsed time they employ two different methods.

   `GetTickCount` accesses the fields `TickCountMultiplier` and `TickCountQuad` and performs a computation that returns the number of milliseconds elapsed since the start of the system. Our approach is to intercept the read of the `TickCountMultiplier`, retrieve the real value, divide it by a user defined `TICK DIVISOR` and finally return this value to the read instruction. This approach relies on a user defined divisor that must be tuned in order to successfully defeat this technique. `timeGetTime` accesses the field `interrupt_time` that is represented by a struct called `_KSYSTEM_TIME`. The time is retrieved by concatenating two fields of this struct: the `High1Time` and the `LowPart` as `High1Time:LowPart`. We reassemble the value, divide it by the user defined divisor, split it again in high and low part, and finally return to the read instruction the part that it was reading.

The second way that can be followed in order to retrieve the time elapsed is to employ the `QueryPerformanceCounter`. Since it is only a wrapper of `NtQueryPerformanceCounter`, we hooked directly the system call. Following this strategy after the execution we divide the value of the field `QuadPart` (a signed 64-bit integer) inside the `LARGE_INTEGER` struct returned by the syscall, with a user defined constant.

CPU Time. The last technique that we consider in order to defeat the time attack is the use of the assembly instruction `rdtsc`. This assembly instruction returns the processor timestamp defined as the number of clock cycles elapsed since the last reset. Since this is a 64-bit integer it returns, in a i386 architecture, the high part and the low part respectively in `EDX` and `EAX` registers. In order to fake the value returned from this instruction we recognize the `rdtsc` in a trace, then after its execution, we insert a call to a function that compose the 64-bit integer as specified (`EDX:EAX`), divide it by a user defined constant, and patch the value of the two registers according to their new value.

4 Large-Scale Anti-Instrumentation Measurement

We performed a study to measure which anti-instrumentation techniques are used by recent, malware samples found in the wild. To do this, we refer to the techniques that we described in the previous sections.

Environment Setup. We prepared a set of identical VirtualBox virtual machines running Windows 7 (64-bit), in which we installed common utilities such as Adobe Reader, alternative Web browsers, and media players. We also included typical user data such as saved credentials and browser history and, at runtime, our analysis system emulates basic user activity (e.g., moving the mouse, launching applications). This is useful to create a legitimate-looking environment. As suggested by Rossow et al. [32], we followed the best practices for malware experiments. We let the malware samples run for 5 min allowing samples to communicate with their control servers, and denying any potentially harmful traffic (e.g., spam). We automated our analysis environment to manage and control such VMs. For each analysis, our agent inside the VM receives the sample to be analyzed and executes it, instrumenting it with ARANCINO. After each execution, we save the logs produced by ARANCINO and roll back each virtual machine to a clean snapshot.

Dataset. Between October 2016 and February 2017, we used the VirusTotal Intelligence API to obtain the most recent Windows executables labeled as malicious by at least 3 AVs. We obtained a dataset of 7,006 samples. We then leveraged AVClass [34] to cluster AV labels and identify each sample's family. Table 1 shows the top 20 malware families in our dataset.

Table 1. Top 20 malware families in our dataset.

Family	No. Samples	No. Evasive	No. Techniques
virlock	619 (8.8%)	600 (96.9%)	2
confidence	505 (7.2%)	68 (13.5%)	4
virut	242 (3.5%)	13 (5.4%)	2
mira	230 (3.3%)	9 (3.9%)	1
upatre	187 (2.7%)	2 (1.1%)	1
lamer	171 (2.4%)	0 (0.0%)	0
sivis	168 (2.4%)	0 (0.0%)	0
installcore	164 (2.3%)	0 (0.0%)	0
ipamor	164 (2.3%)	0 (0.0%)	0
vtflooder	152 (2.2%)	2 (1.3%)	1
downloadguide	135 (1.9%)	1 (0.7%)	1
bladabindi	103 (1.5%)	22 (21.4%)	2
dealply	98 (1.4%)	1 (1.0%)	1
mydoom	88 (1.3%)	0 (0.0%)	0
parite	86 (1.2%)	18 (20.9%)	1
zusy	84 (1.2%)	10 (11.9%)	3
installmonster	79 (1.1%)	2 (2.5%)	1
allaple	68 (1.0%)	0 (0.0%)	0
razy	66 (0.9%)	10 (15.2%)	3
neshta	62 (0.9%)	0 (0.0%)	0
Others	3,535	335	4
Total	7,006	1,093 (15.6%)	5

Table 2. Top 10 most evasive malware families in our dataset. We considered only the families with at least 10 samples.

Family	No. Samples	No. Evasive	No. Techniques
sfone	19	19 (100.0%)	1
unruy	11	11 (100.0%)	1
virlock	619	600 (96.9%)	2
vilsel	13	8 (61.5%)	2
urelas	19	9 (47.4%)	2
confuser	18	8 (44.4%)	1
vobfus	52	19 (36.5%)	1
swisyn	29	10 (34.5%)	1
softcnapp	17	5 (29.4%)	1
downloadsponsor	24	7 (29.2%)	1

Table 3. Anti-instrumentation techniques used by malware in our dataset.

Category	Technique	No. Samples
Code Cache Artifacts	Self-modifying code	897
Environment Artifacts	Parent detection	259
JIT Compiler Detection	Write on protected memory region	40
Environment Artifacts	Leak DEBUG flag	5
Environment Artifacts	Memory fingerprinting	3

Results. We found out that 1,093 (15.6%) samples presented at least one anti-instrumentation technique. In particular, as shown in Table 3, we identified malware employing 5 different techniques, with the majority of the samples exposing self-modifying code capabilities. Table 2 shows the 10 most evasive malware families in our dataset. We leveraged AVClass [34] to determine the most likely family of each sample, and then we ranked families with more than 10 samples by the percentage of samples showing at least one anti-instrumentation technique. Interestingly, from Tables 1 and 3 we can see that, in some cases, not all the samples of a given family presented anti-instrumentation capabilities. This might mean that, at a certain point, malware authors decided to update their samples providing them with such features.

As further discussed in Sect. 7, we cannot assure that some of the detected anti-instrumentation techniques were added for the precise purpose of DBI evasion (instead of generic evasion techniques). Intuitively, this is dependent from the specific technique. For instance, while the detection of parent process could be performed by malware for different reasons (e.g., detecting a debugger or a specific agent inside a known sandbox) other than spotting the presence of Intel Pin, detecting writes and reads on protected memory regions is more specific to DBI-evasion.

From our study, we conclude that ant-instrumentation techniques, are employed by a significant amount of malware samples, motivating the effort in enforcing DBI tools and showing that systems such as ARANCINO can be useful in defeating these evasion techniques.

5   Application Scenario: Unpacker

On top of ARANCINO, we implemented a generic, anti-instrumentation-resilient unpacker. Our tool leverages the functionality provided by Intel Pin to track, with an instruction level granularity, the memory addresses that are written and then executed. As explained in Sect. 5.1, first of all, we identify a subset of instructions that are relevant for our analysis. Then, we keep track of each written memory region in order to create a list of contiguous written memory ranges, defined as *write intervals*. At the same time, we check if each executed instruction belongs to a write interval—this is the typical behavior of a packed binary that is executing the unpacked layer. If so, we trigger a further stage that consists of: (1) Dumping the main image of the PE and a memory range of the heap; (2) Reconstructing the Import Address Table (IAT) and generating the correct Import Directory; (3) Applying a set of heuristics (entropy, long jump, jump outer section, pushad popad, init function calls) to evaluate if the current instruction is the Original Entry Point (OEP). The result of our tool is a set of memory dumps or reconstructed PEs (depending on the success of the IAT fixing phase), and a report which includes the values of each heuristic for every dump. Based on those heuristics we can choose the best dump.

5.1   Unpacking Phases

In this section, we describe more in detail our unpacking approach.

Instructions Filtering. Since our tool works with an instruction level granularity, limiting our analysis to the relevant instructions of the program is critical. For this reason, we have introduced some filters, based on the common behaviors showed by packers. Specifically, we do not track two kinds of instructions: (1) write instruction on the Thread Environment Block (TEB) and on the stack, and (2) instruction executed by known Windows libraries.

The write instructions on the stack are ignored because unpacking code on the stack is not common. The same consideration can be applied to the instructions that write on the TEB, since most of these writes are related to the creation of exception handlers. The instructions executed by known Windows libraries are never considered when checking if the current instruction address is contained inside a write interval because this would mean that the packer writes the malicious payload in the address space of a known Windows library. This behavior has never been identified in the analyzed packers; moreover, this approach would break the application if it explicitly uses one of the functions which have been overwritten.

Written Addresses Tracing. In order to correctly operate, most packers need to write the original program in memory and then execute it. We can detect this behavior by tracing each write operation performed by the instrumented program and annotating a set of memory ranges that identify contiguously written memory addresses.

WxorX Addresses Notifier. As expressed before, packers need to both write and execute a specific memory region. Indeed, this behavior is distant from how common benign programs act during execution. Although some benign programs may present such behavior, e.g., JIT compiler, virtual machine, programming languages interpreters, we can exploit such behavior as an evidence of something that was unpacked. Therefore, the first time we detect that the instruction pointer is inside one of the traced memory ranges, we trigger the analysis and dumping routines, and mark the memory range as *unpacked*. We call the property of having a memory region that is either written or executed *WxorX rule*.

Dumping Process. While many memory dumping tools only look at the *main module* of the target program, which includes sections containing code, data, and the resources used by the binary, in order to handle more unpackers, we need to collect also code that has been unpacked on dynamic memory regions such as the heap. If the packer's stub unpacks new code on the heap and then redirects the execution there, a naive dump strategy that only looks at the sections of the PE would miss the unpacked code. We correctly catch this behavior by using the *WxorX address notifier*, and including in the dump all the memory regions that contain the unpacked code.

IAT Fixing and Import Directory Reconstruction. We focus our attention on three different techniques. The first technique we have to deal with is called *IAT redirection*: instead of having the addresses of the APIs directly in the IAT, entries contain addresses that point to jump instructions to the real API functions. The second technique is known as *stolen API*: it copies N instructions of the API function code at the address pointed by the IAT entry and then inserts an unconditional absolute jump to the N+1 instruction to the real API function code. The last one is a generalization of the stolen API technique. It differs from stolen API function because multiple parts of the original API functions are copied and they are connected together by absolute jumps until the last one reaches the original API code (Fig. 1).

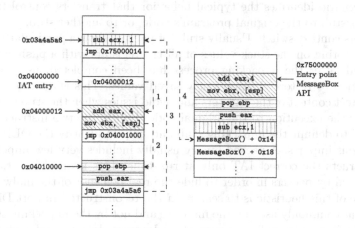

Fig. 1. (1) The execution is redirected to the address inside the IAT entry. (2) The first two instructions of the original API are executed followed by a jump to the next chunk of instructions. (3) The chunk is executed together with another jump instruction. (4) The last instruction is executed and finally a jump goes inside the original memory space of the API. (Color figure online)

Thanks to Intel Pin, our system can deal with all these techniques using static analysis. Indeed, for each IAT entry we statically follow the control flow counting the number of instructions different from jumps, those are instructions belonging to the real API function (green, yellow and orange instruction in Fig. 1). We follow the control flow until the target of a jump is inside a memory region occupied by the DLL. When the target address and the instructions count are retrieved, the value of the current analyzed IAT entry is replaced with the difference between the target address and the instructions count.

Heuristics Description. We used a set of heuristics during the unpacking process to understand when the program reaches the Original Entry Point (OEP) and can be considered fully unpacked. Howewer, as demonstrated in [33], understanding if the unpacking process is finished is not a decidable problem. The heuristics we have collected come from different works and books [24,36], and we use them to tag a taken dump. These tags are useful at the end of the work of our tool in order to understand if a taken dump and the associated reconstructed PE represent the original program or not (since often the number of taken dumps is more than one). Here we describe the heuristics that we used:

- Entropy. We trace the entropy evolution of the main module of the target program and trigger a flag when the difference of the current entropy compared with the original one is greater than a threshold, as shown by Arora et al. [6].
- Jump outer section. A *long jump* is defined as a jump in which the offset between the target address and the previous EIP is larger than a threshold. This scenario identifies the typical behavior that transfers control from the packer's stub to the original program's code, or to another stub.
- Registers context switch. Usually stubs of packers show a particular behavior that is storing on the stack values of all the registers with a **pushad** instruction and, after the unpacking process has been completed, using a **popad** instruction to restore the previously saved values. This is done to maintain the correct context of the registers and avoid issues when the stub of a packer resumes the execution to the original code. Hence, the two instructions can be used to delimit the unpacking stub and help to identify the OEP.
- Suspicious imports. A packed binary usually includes very few imports, and reconstructs the correct IAT only at run-time. This is an obfuscation technique used by packers in order to hide the real behavior of the malware. The purpose of this heuristic is to search, in the reconstructed Import Directory, functions commonly used by the malware and not by the unpacking stub. For example, if a malware has to contact an Internet domain to download some malicious code, it has to have in its imports some Internet communication APIs, such as **connect** and **send**. Since the unpacking stub generally does not need them to perform its job, when the binary is packed, it does not have these API functions in its Import Directory initially. In some cases, the packed binary has as imports only the **GetProcAddress** and **LoadLibrary** functions, because these two are then used to dynamically load further functions.

6 Testing and Validation

6.1 Defeating Anti-instrumentation Techniques

We tested ARANCINO to evaluate its capabilities in defeating anti-instrumentation techniques. To do so, we leveraged eXait [15], a benchmark tool specifically designed to highlight different techniques aimed at spotting the presence of Intel Pin instrumentation. First, we instrumented and executed eXait with Intel Pin, then we did the same using ARANCINO. In both cases, we looked at the output of eXait to check if any of the techniques detected the instrumentation framework. Specifically, eXait implemented the following detection techniques: detecting common JIT API calls, detecting code and string artifacts, leaking the effective EIP, detecting by page permission, detecting ntdll hooks, detecting parent process, measuring overhead. While instrumented with Intel Pin, eXait flagged all of these techniques, spotting the presence of the DBI. Instead, when we instrumented it using ARANCINO, eXait did not produce any positive results, showing that our system successfully hid the presence of Intel Pin.

6.2 Unpacking Capabilities

Testing Known Packers. We tested our unpacker against 14 known packers, used to pack two binaries: a simple Message-Box (100 KB) and WinRAR (2 MB). We used different programs with different sizes because the behavior of a packer can be influenced by the size of the target program. Table 4 shows the effectiveness of our generic unpacking algorithm and PE reconstruction system against the different packers. For some packers, such as ASProtect, eXpressor and Obsidium we managed to take a dump at the correct OEP but, due to the presence of IAT obfuscation techniques, we were not able to reconstruct a working PE.

Unpacking Malware Samples Found in the Wild. We downloaded random samples from VirusTotal and we classified them with Exeinfo PE [1], a packer detection tool, in order to discard not packed samples. Eventually, we obtained a dataset of 1,066 packed samples, protected by known or custom packers, the latter tagged by Exeinfo PE as "unknown." Then, we tested the effectiveness of our unpacker against malicious samples spotted in the wild protected with both known and unknown packers. We automated the analysis of such samples using a VirtualBox VM and letting each sample, instrumented with our unpacker, run for 5 min. After the analysis performed by our tool, all the results were manually validated. Our unpacker managed to successfully unpack 808 (75.8%) samples, producing a working executable in 669 cases, while it failed to unpack the remaining 258 ones. The reasons of the failures can be different: evading the virtual environment, messing with the environment in a way that our script cannot manage to collect results, employing IAT obfuscation techniques, or exploiting packing techniques with a level of complexity out of our scope.

88   M. Polino et al.

Table 4. Results of our tests against known packers. For each packer, here we show the packed program, if the original code of the binary has been successfully unpacked (U), if the reconstructed PE is a working executable (EX), the number of imports observed in the packed program, and the number of imports observed in the reconstructed PE.

Packer	Binary	U	EX	Packed Imports	Recon/Tot Imports
Upx	MessageBox	✓	✓	8	55/55
FSG	MessageBox	✓	✓	2	55/55
Mew	MessageBox	✓	✓	2	55/55
Mpresss	MessageBox	✓	✓	2	55/55
Obsidium	MessageBox	✓	✗	4	4/55
PECompact	MessageBox	✓	✓	4	55/55
EXEpacker	MessageBox	✓	✓	8	55/55
WinUpack	MessageBox	✓	✓	2	55/55
ezip	MessageBox	✓	✓	4	55/55
Xcomp	MessageBox	✓	✓	5	55/55
PElock	MessageBox	✓	✗	2	3/55
Asprotect	MessageBox	✓	✗	7	46/55
Aspack	MessageBox	✓	✓	3	55/55
Hyperion	MessageBox	✓	✓	2	55/55
Upx	WinRAR	✓	✓	16	433/433
FSG	WinRAR	✓	✓	2	433/433
Mew	WinRAR	✓	✓	2	433/433
Mpress	WinRAR	✓	✓	12	433/433
Obsidium	WinRAR	✓	✗	2	0/433
PEcompact	WinRAR	✓	✓	14	433/433
EXEpacker	WinRAR	✓	✓	16	433/433
WinUpack	WinRAR	✓	✓	2	433/433
ezip	WinRAR	✓	✓	12	433/433
Xcomp	WinRAR	✓	✓	5	433/433
PElock	WinRAR	✓	✗	2	71/433
Asprotect	WinRAR	✓	✓	16	433/433
Aspack	WinRAR	✓	✓	13	433/433
Hyperion	WinRAR	✓	✓	2	433/433

6.3   Case Studies

In this Section, we present two case studies that show how known packers employ anti-instrumentation capabilities, and how ARANCINO successfully managed to overcome these techniques and instrument the binaries.

Obsidium. We found that Obsidium [2] performs a call to the function `QueryInformationProcess` using as `ProcessInformationClass` argument an undocumented class called `ProcessDebugFlags`. When `QueryInformation-Process` is called with this parameter, it returns the inverse of the field `EPROCESS.NoDebugInherit`, i.e., `TRUE` if the process is debugged, `FALSE` otherwise. Since this flag is set when a program is instrumented with Intel Pin, this attack can successfully reveal the presence of the DBI in memory. Instead, using ARANCINO, we managed to defeat this anti-instrumentation technique. In fact, by hooking the `NtQueryInformationProcess` system call and patching the `ProcessInformation` struct, as described in Sect. 3, ARANCINO correctly managed to instrument and execute a test binary. As result, our dynamic unpacker successfully unpacked samples packed with Obsidium.

PEspin. We found that PEspin [3] makes use of self-modifying code. In fact, when we instrumented a test binary packed with PEspin without ARANCINO, the program crashed. Instead, when using our tool, the execution reached its normal end flawlessly. To understand precisely the reason of the crash, we manually analyzed the packed binary. We ran it in a debugger and we identified two instructions, `IN` and `OUT` that provide a direct access to I/O devices and require to be executed in protected mode. As a consequence, a program running in user space, which is not allowed to do it, crashes. During normal executions, these instructions are overwritten before `EIP` reaches them, so they are never executed and they never cause the crash of the program. However, when the binary is instrumented, Intel Pin places a trace composed by the two instructions in the code cache, eventually running them. Instead, as explained in Sect. 3.1, ARANCINO is able to detect if instructions are modified, and discard the current trace forcing Intel Pin to collect a new one. This avoids the crash of the program.

6.4 Performance

The efforts made to improve the transparency of Intel Pin come with a performance cost. We measured three different times. First, the execution time of the program when not instrumented, used as reference to estimate the final overhead. Second, execution time of the instrumented executable without ARANCINO, used to evaluate the overhead introduced by Intel Pin alone. Finally, the execution time of the executable instrumented with ARANCINO, used to evaluate the overhead introduced by our tool. As shown in Table 5 the overhead introduced by our countermeasures is strictly dependent from the specific technique. For instance, while handling `int2e`, `fsave`, `fxsave`, `fstenv` instructions, ARANCINO introduces a low overhead. On the other hand, when we defeat detection of DLL hooks or memory fingerprinting, the overhead introduced by ARANCINO is high, because ARANCINO has to analyze each read instruction to find its destination address and check if it belongs to the whitelist.

7   Discussion of Limitations

Our work presents some limitation that we describe in the following paragraphs.

Table 5. Overhead introduced by ARANCINO to defeat each technique.

Technique	Execution time [s]	Instrumentation time [s]	ARANCINO time [s]	ARANCINO overhead [%]
EIP Detection - int2e	0.01	0.71	1.15	61%
EIP Detection - fsave	0.01	0.90	1.20	33%
EIP Detection - fxsave	0.01	0.90	1.15	27%
EIP Detection - fstenv	0.01	0.82	1.05	28%
Memory Page Permissions	0.01	0.82	0.90	9%
DLL Hook	0.01	0.81	2.00	145%
Memory Allocations	0.01	2.00	2.90	45%
Windows Time	0.01	2.93	5.51	88%
Parent Detection	0.02	0.85	0.87	2%
Memory Fingerprinting	0.04	2.00	7.09	254.5%

ARANCINO's Artifacts. Even if ARANCINO correctly hides a vast number of DBI artifacts, we cannot guarantee that it is completely immune to detection attempts. In fact, some of the anti-evasion techniques that we proposed might be leveraged as detection criteria. For instance, malware could exploit that fact that ARANCINO hides all the protected memory pages. Specifically, a malicious sample could try to allocate memory through the entire address space failing to access memory regions that are already allocated for those hidden pages. This does not tell the analyzed sample which libraries are loaded or the reason the OS is denying memory allocation, but it is a particular behavior that could be fingerprinted. Another example is the denied access to CSRSS.exe. On one side this prevents to know the list of running processes, on the other side this could be detected by a malware sample. However, although these limitations are present in the current implementation of ARANCINO, it is possible to implement more sophisticated mechanisms to hide such artifacts (e.g., allowing access to CSRSS.exe and altering its internal data structures) and partially overcome these limitations. In summary, we believe that ARANCINO definitely raises the bar for the attacker, making DBI evasion much harder.

Anti-Instrumentation vs. General Artifacts. The techniques we observed to identify DBI-evasion attempts are indicators of potential anti-instrumentation attacks, but they do not capture the intention of the malware authors. For instance, a self-modifying behavior, even if it breaks the use of code cache, may be used as an obfuscation technique as well as an anti-instrumentation feature. Similarly, the detection of parent process could be performed for different reasons (e.g., detecting agents of a known sandbox) other than spotting the presence of a DBI tool. We can only speculate why malware authors are adopting the techniques that we identified in our study. Independently from the intention of malware authors, our experiments showed that ARANCINO is able to hide many artifacts that malware uses to evade analysis systems.

Measurements. We based our approach and our study on the known techniques employed to detect instrumented environment. While we cannot assure that the current version of ARANCINO covers all the possible techniques used to detect the presence of a DBI tool, our approach and our tool can be easily extended in order to add support for new ones.

Environment Setup. We performed our study running malware on a virtualized environment (i.e., VirtualBox). While we setup our VMs to minimize the presence of VirtualBox artifacts, sophisticated malware samples can detect they are running in a virtualized environment and hide their malicious behavior. However, this is not a fundamental limitation of our approach, in fact, ARANCINO can perfectly work on top of bare-metal system such as [20,21,37] improving the quality of such systems without affecting the stealthiness.

Implementation. ARANCINO currently supports only 32-bit binaries. Extending ARANCINO to 64-bit binaries can introduce a new attack vector that exploits the Windows 64-bit backward compatibility with 32-bit applications to spot the presence of a DBI, making it crash. In fact, in order to implement the backward compatibility Windows runs each application using two different code segments, one for the execution in 32-bit compatibility mode and one for the 64-bit mode. Each segment has a flag indicating in which mode its instructions have to be interpreted. Particular instructions, such as far `jmp` or far `ret`, can be used to jump from one segment to the other. This behavior can cause the program to switch between the 32- and the 64-bit segments. Unfortunately, DBI tools cannot correctly handle this behavior and, consequently, they may disassemble and instructions wrongly or, in the worst case, they may be unable to disassemble them at all. While we leave the implementation of 64-bit support for future work, the majority of malware samples nowadays are 32-bit binaries.

Performance. As shown in Sect. 6.4, ARANCINO inevitably introduces an overhead on the execution of the instrumented binary. While this overhead is often acceptable, it is quite high when ARANCINO handles some particular techniques.

Unpacker. First, our unpacker does not handle the process hollowing techniques, so runtime unpacking that injects the payload inside new processes and/or make use of DLL injection techniques are not considered by our tool. Second, if a packer implements a custom IAT obfuscation technique, we cannot reconstruct a runnable PE. Third, it does not track unpacking on the stack, so if the original code of the program is written on the stack our tool cannot dump the correct memory region and consequently it cannot reconstruct a working PE. However, this technique is not commonly employed by known packers. Finally, referring to the packer taxonomy presented in [38], our unpacker can handle packers with a maximum level of complexity of 4. To handle more sophisticated packer, our approach could be combined with approaches such as [39], which is less generic and targets specifically complex packers.

8 Related Work

DBI-Evasive Malware. Despite the fact that it is theoretically impossible to build a completely transparent analysis tool, different works have been done regarding the development of stealthy instrumentation systems.

SPiKE [41] adopts an approach completely different from other DBI tools, such as Intel Pin or DynamoRIO, because it does not use a JIT compiler in order to instrument traces. Instead, it places a series of breakpoints in memory, called *drifters*, that, when are hit, trigger appropriate hooks, called *instruments*. The drifters are implemented following the technique explained in VAMPiRE [40], which guarantees a certain level of transparency and the impossibility of removal by the malware—they are placed in not accessible memory regions. While this work is stealthier than other DBI tools, it is also much less powerful than the aforementioned ones, because it offers very few APIs. Another work that relies on setting stealthy breakpoint is

SPIDER [14]. It duplicates the program in two different views: the code view, and the data view. The former can be modified by the instrumentation framework with the insertion of breakpoint and it is where the instructions are fetched, while the latter is where all the write and read operations made by the program are redirected and it can be modified only by the program itself, ensuring transparency of the framework. If the instruction fetched and executed from the code view hits a breakpoint, then a user-defined hook is invoked. As the work described before, SPIDER is less powerful than other DBI tools, as it only works at function-level.

Malware Unpacking. Ugarte-Pedrero et al. [38] recently proposed a taxonomy to classify packers by their complexity. Generally, we can classify unpackers in three categories: static [13], dynamic and hybrid unpackers. Most of the recent proposed works are dynamic unpackers [7,8,17,18,31,43,44]. These approaches leverage the fact that packers need of unpack the code in memory at runtime to obtain the unpacked code.

Omniunpack [25], monitors memory page writes, exploiting a memory protection mechanism provided by the operating system, to access unpacked code pages and notify external tools when such pages are ready to be analyzed. Another attempt of exploiting operating system capabilities was made in Eureka [35]. This tool uses a kernel driver to trace system calls and identify the time when the analyzed sample is unpacked in memory. Similarly to our tool, Renovo [19] instruments a packed binary to trace writes in memory and execute until the instruction pointer fall inside written regions. Unfortunately, Renovo is easily detectable by anti-instrumentation techniques. Moreover, its output is a not working PE because it is does not try to recover the IAT table. Rambo [39] exploits a multi-path execution technique to trigger the unpacking of code regions. This is useful to defeat those packers who check the environment to understand if they are under analysis. Complementary to our approach, Rambo tries to solve this problem by forcing the execution of not executed code, while our unpacker exploits ARANCINO to hide artifacts.

Hybrid unpacking mixes some static analysis techniques with dynamics ones. The strategy for hybrid unpacking can generally follow two approaches. First, static analysis followed by dynamic analysis: An initial static analysis phase is performed in order to extract a model of how the execution will look like and, after that the program is executed, the static model built before is checked against the dynamically executed instructions [33]. Second, dynamic analysis followed by static analysis: This scheme relies on collecting traces of the execution of the packed program, and eventually extracting, by static analysis, the interface and the body of the unpacking function [11].

Our dynamic unpacker provides, respect to the existing solutions, a richer synergy of heuristics aimed to automatically detect a possible OEP. Following the taxonomy proposed in [38], our unpacker is able to handle packers up to type 4. These packers are multi-layer, cyclic and interleaved. This means that they use different layers with both forward and backward transitions. Moreover, our unpacking algorithm is more generic respect to solution such as [22] since we remove the assumption about the last written at page: We do not assume that the last written and executed page is the one that contains the OEP; in fact, as demonstrated in [5], this is not always necessarily true. Finally, while previous approaches aim only at unpacking obfuscated code, our tool is able, in most of the cases, to produce a working (i.e., runnable) executable.

9   Conclusions

Dynamic Binary Instrumentation (DBI) frameworks provide useful features in the analysis of malware samples. However, modern malware samples implement anti-instrumentation techniques to detect if they are being instrumented. We proposed a practical approach to enforce DBI frameworks and make them stealthier against anti-instrumentation attacks by studying the common techniques used by malware to detect their presence, and proposing a set of countermeasures to address such techniques. We implemented our approach in ARANCINO on top of Intel Pin. Then, we used ARANCINO to perform a measurement of the anti-instrumentation techniques employed by malware. We analyzed 7,006 recent malware samples showing that 15.6% of them employ at least one anti-instrumentation technique. Moreover, we leveraged our evasion-resilient approach to implement a generic unpacker showing interesting case studies of the anti-instrumentation techniques used by known packers. Combining ARANCINO with our unpacker we provided a tool that can successfully analyze malware that employs both anti-static-analysis and anti-instrumentation techniques.

Acknowledgements. We would like to thank our reviewers and our shepherd Alexandros Kapravelos for their valuable comments and input to improve our paper. We would also like to thank Alessandro Frossi for his insightful feedback and VirusTotal for providing us access to malware samples. This work was supported in part by the MIUR FACE Project No. RBFR13AJFT. This project has also received funding from the European Union's Horizon 2020 research and innovation programme under grant agreement No 700326.

References

1. Exeinfo PE. http://exeinfo.atwebpages.com/
2. Obsidium. https://www.obsidium.de/show/download/en
3. PESpin. http://www.pespin.com/
4. Aaraj, N., Raghunathan, A., Jha, N.K.: Dynamic binary instrumentation-based framework for malware defense. In: Proceeding of the International Conference on Detection of Intrusions and Malware, and Vulnerability Assessment (DIMVA) (2008)
5. Arne, S., Alaeddine, M.: One packer to rule them all: Empirical identification, comparison and circumvention of current Antivirus detection techniques. https://www.blackhat.com/docs/us-14/materials/us-14-Mesbahi-One-Packer-To-Rule-Them-All-WP.pdf
6. Arora, R., Singh, A., Pareek, H., Edara, U.R.: A heuristics-based static analysis approach for detecting packed PE binaries. Int. J. Secur. Appl. **7**(5), 257–268 (2013)
7. Bania, P.: Generic unpacking of self-modifying, aggressive, packed binary programs. arXiv preprint arXiv:0905.4581 (2009)
8. BromiumLabs. The Packer Attacker is a generic hidden code extractor for Windows malware. https://github.com/BromiumLabs/PackerAttacker
9. Bruening, D., Duesterwald, E., Amarasinghe, S.: Design and implementation of a dynamic optimization framework for windows. In: ACM Workshop on Feedback-Directed and Dynamic Optimization (FDDO-4) (2001)
10. Brumley, D., Hartwig, C., Liang, Z., Newsome, J., Poosankam, P., Song, D., Yin, H.: Automatically identifying trigger-based behavior in malware. In: Botnet Detection (2008)
11. Caballero, J., Johnson, N.M., McCamant, S., Song, D.: Binary code extraction and interface identification for security applications. Technical report, DTIC Document (2009)
12. Continella, A., Guagnelli, A., Zingaro, G., De Pasquale, G., Barenghi, A., Zanero, S., Maggi, F.: Shieldfs: a self-healing, ransomware-aware filesystem. In: Proceeding of the Annual Conference on Computer Security Applications (ACSAC) (2016)
13. Coogan, K., Debray, S., Kaochar, T., Townsend, G.: Automatic static unpacking of malware binaries. In: Proceeding of Working Conference on Reverse Engineering (WCRE). IEEE (2009)
14. Deng, Z., Zhang, X., Spider, D.: Stealthy binary program instrumentation and debugging via hardware virtualization. In: Proceeding of the Annual Computer Security Applications Conference (ACSAC) (2013)
15. Falcon, F., Riva, N.: Dynamic binary instrumentation frameworks: i know you're there spying on me. In: Proceeding of Reverse Engineering Conference (2012)

16. Gröbert, F., Willems, C., Holz, T.: Automated identification of cryptographic primitives in binary programs. In: Sommer, R., Balzarotti, D., Maier, G. (eds.) RAID 2011. LNCS, vol. 6961, pp. 41–60. Springer, Heidelberg (2011). doi:10.1007/978-3-642-23644-0_3

17. Guo, F., Ferrie, P., Chiueh, T.-C.: A study of the packer problem and its solutions. In: Proceeding of International Workshop on Recent Advances in Intrusion Detection (RAID) (2008)

18. Hex-Rays. IDA Universal Unpacker. https://www.hex-rays.com/products/ida/support/tutorials/unpack_pe/index.shtml

19. Kang, M.G., Poosankam, P., Yin, H.: Renovo: a hidden code extractor for packed executables (2007)

20. Kirat, D., Vigna, G., Kruegel, C.: Barebox: efficient malware analysis on bare-metal. In: Proceeding of the Annual Computer Security Applications Conference (ACSAC). ACM (2011)

21. Kirat, D., Vigna, G., Kruegel, C.: BareCloud: bare-metal analysis-based evasive malware detection. In: Proceeding of USENIX Security (2014)

22. Lenoir, J.: Implementing Your Own Generic Unpacker (2015)

23. Luk, C.-K., Cohn, R., Muth, R., Patil, H., Klauser, A., Lowney, G., Wallace, S., Reddi, V.J., Hazelwood, K.: Pin: building customized program analysis tools with dynamic instrumentation. In: ACM Sigplan Notices. ACM (2005)

24. Lyda, R., Hamrock, J.: Using entropy analysis to find encrypted and packed malware. In: Proceeding of IEEE symposium on Security and Privacy (SP). IEEE (2007)

25. Martignoni, L., Christodorescu, M., Jha, S.: OmniUnpack: fast, generic, and safe unpacking of malware. In: Proceeding of the Annual Computer Security Applications Conference (ACSAC). IEEE (2007)

26. Ming, J., Wu, D., Xiao, G., Wang, J., Liu, P.: TaintPipe: pipelined symbolic taint analysis. In: Proceeding of USENIX Security (2015)

27. Ming, J., Xu, D., Wang, L., Wu, D.: Loop: logic-oriented opaque predicate detection in obfuscated binary code. In: Proceeding of the ACM SIGSAC Conference on Computer and Communications Security (CCS). ACM (2015)

28. Moser, A., Kruegel, C., Kirda, E.: Exploring multiple execution paths for malware analysis. In: Proceeding of IEEE symposium on Security and Privacy (SP) (2007)

29. Nethercote, N., Seward, J.: Valgrind: a program supervision framework. Electron. Notes Theor. Comput. Sci. **89**(2), 44–66 (2003)

30. Polino, M., Scorti, A., Maggi, F., Zanero, S.: Jackdaw: towards automatic reverse engineering of large datasets of binaries. In: Proceeding of the International Conference on Detection of Intrusions and Malware, and Vulnerability Assessment (DIMVA) (2015)

31. Quist, D.: Circumventing software armoring techniques. https://www.blackhat.com/presentations/bh-usa-07/Quist_and_Valsmith/Presentation/bh-usa-07-quist_and_valsmith.pdf

32. Rossow, C., Dietrich, C.J., Grier, C., Kreibich, C., Paxson, V., Pohlmann, N., Bos, H., Van Steen, M.: Prudent practices for designing malware experiments: status quo and outlook. In: Proceeding of IEEE symposium on Security and Privacy (SP) (2012)

33. Royal, P., Halpin, M., Dagon, D., Edmonds, R., Lee, W.: PolyUnpack: automating the hidden-code extraction of unpack-executing malware (2006)

34. Sebastián, M., Rivera, R., Kotzias, P., Caballero, J.: AVCLASS: a tool for massive malware labeling. In: Monrose, F., Dacier, M., Blanc, G., Garcia-Alfaro, J. (eds.) RAID 2016. LNCS, vol. 9854, pp. 230–253. Springer, Cham (2016). doi:10.1007/978-3-319-45719-2_11

35. Sharif, M., Yegneswaran, V., Saidi, H., Porras, P., Lee, W.: Eureka: a framework for enabling static malware analysis. In: Jajodia, S., Lopez, J. (eds.) ESORICS 2008. LNCS, vol. 5283, pp. 481–500. Springer, Heidelberg (2008). doi:10.1007/978-3-540-88313-5_31

36. Sikorski, M., Honig, A.: Practical Malware Analysis. No Starch Press, San Francisco (2012)

37. Spensky, C., Hu, H., Leach, K.: LO-PHI: low observable physical host instrumentation. In: Proceeding of the Network and Distributed System Security Symposium (NDSS) (2016)

38. Ugarte-Pedrero, X., Balzarotti, D., Santos, I., Bringas, P.G. SoK: deep packer inspection: a longitudinal study of the complexity of run-time packers. In: Proceeding of IEEE symposium on Security and Privacy (SP). IEEE (2015)

39. Ugarte-Pedrero, X., Balzarotti, D., Santos, I., Bringas, P.G.: RAMBO: run-time packer analysis with multiple branch observation. In: Caballero, J., Zurutuza, U., Rodríguez, R.J. (eds.) DIMVA 2016. LNCS, vol. 9721, pp. 186–206. Springer, Cham (2016). doi:10.1007/978-3-319-40667-1_10

40. Vasudevan, A., Yerraballi, R.: Stealth breakpoints. In: Proceeding of the Annual Computer Security Applications Conference (ACSAC). IEEE (2005)

41. Vasudevan, A., Yerraballi, R.: Spike: engineering malware analysis tools using unobtrusive binary-instrumentation. In: Proceeding of the 29th Australasian Computer Science Conference, vol. 48. Australian Computer Society Inc. (2006)

42. Wilhelm, J., Chiueh, T.: A forced sampled execution approach to kernel rootkit identification. In: Kruegel, C., Lippmann, R., Clark, A. (eds.) RAID 2007. LNCS, vol. 4637, pp. 219–235. Springer, Heidelberg (2007). doi:10.1007/978-3-540-74320-0_12

43. Yadegari, B., Johannesmeyer, B., Whitely, B., Debray, S.: A generic approach to automatic deobfuscation of executable code. In: Proceeding of IEEE symposium on Security and Privacy (SP). IEEE (2015)

44. Yu, S.-C., Li, Y.-C.: A unpacking and reconstruction system-agunpacker. In: Proceeding of International Symposium on Computer Network and Multimedia Technology, (CNMT). IEEE (2009)

DynODet: Detecting Dynamic Obfuscation in Malware

Danny Kim[1]($^{(\boxtimes)}$), Amir Majlesi-Kupaei[1]($^{(\boxtimes)}$), Julien Roy[2]($^{(\boxtimes)}$), Kapil Anand[2]($^{(\boxtimes)}$), Khaled ElWazeer[2]($^{(\boxtimes)}$), Daniel Buettner[3]($^{(\boxtimes)}$), and Rajeev Barua[1]($^{(\boxtimes)}$)

[1] University of Maryland, College Park, USA
dannykim@terpmail.umd.edu
[2] SecondWrite LLC, College Park, USA
[3] Laboratory of Telecommunications Sciences, College Park, USA

Abstract. Malicious software, better known as malware, is a major threat to society. Malware today typically employ a technique called obfuscation. Obfuscation detection in malware is a well-documented problem and has been analyzed using dynamic analysis. However, many tools that detect obfuscation in malware make no attempts to use the presence of obfuscation as a method of detecting malware because their schemes would also detect benign applications. We present three main contributions. First, we conduct a unique study into the prevalence of obfuscation in benign applications. Second, we create discriminating features that can distinguish obfuscation in benign applications versus malware. Third, we prove that using the presence of obfuscation can detect previously hard-to-detect malware. Our results show that for our set of programs, we are able to reduce the number of malware missed by five market-leading AV tools by 25% while only falsely detecting 2.45% of tested benign applications.

Keywords: Malware detection · Dynamic analysis · Binary instrumentation

1 Introduction

Malicious software, better known as malware, is a problem in today's growing cyber community. Malware has continued to grow at an increasingly rapid rate, which brings the need for advanced and innovative defenses to an all-time high. Symantec reported discovering more than 430 million unique pieces of malware in 2015 alone [7]. The sheer number of malware with their growing complexities make detecting them a difficult task. Malware has been a cornerstone for cyberthieves and attackers to steal money, compromise information and undermine the security of all people. In order to combat advanced malware today, security companies use a combination of static and dynamic techniques for extracting unique indicators of maliciousness (IOM) from malware. Static techniques refer to analyzing a program without execution whereas dynamic techniques involve

© Springer International Publishing AG 2017
M. Polychronakis and M. Meier (Eds.): DIMVA 2017, LNCS 10327, pp. 97–118, 2017.
DOI: 10.1007/978-3-319-60876-1_5

executing the program. These techniques are used to extract malicious indicators that can be employed to differentiate malware from benign programs.

Malware writers have used a technique called obfuscation [22] to thwart extraction of such IOM from malware and evade static detection [21]. Examples of obfuscation techniques are self-modifying code, and dynamic code generation. Although dynamic analysis tools have detected most types of obfuscation, obfuscation successfully thwarts static techniques such as [37] when analyzing malware. Obfuscated malware is a heavily studied subset within the field of malware [30]. The tools mentioned here [3,9,18,26–28,33,34,36] are capable of detecting and, in some cases, reversing obfuscation in malware. However, such tools are largely forensic tools and cannot be used for automatically distinguishing malware from benign programs because their schemes would detect obfuscation in both.

In this paper, we study obfuscations present in programs with a goal of automatically distinguishing malware and benign programs. First, we present our study of the presence of six different obfuscation types in 6,192 benign applications. This study is the first that looks at which obfuscations (or code patterns that appear indistinguishable from obfuscation) are present in benign programs. Next, obfuscation is classified in two ways – allowed obfuscations (present in benign applications) vs. disallowed obfuscations (usually only in malware). Through the study, we find that three of the six obfuscations we analyze are regularly present in benign applications. For these three, we create a set of *discriminating features* that reduce false positives. The remaining three obfuscation types are found to be largely restricted to malware. With our set of six obfuscations with discriminating features, we produce a malware detection technique, which is able to detect malware with high confidence. This includes the ability to detect previously missed malware using the presence of disallowed obfuscations as an IOM.

We present DynODet, a dynamic obfuscation detection tool built as an Intel Pin DLL [17] that detects binary-level obfuscations, and uses discriminating features to filter out benign application behaviors. When configured with discriminators, DynODet is not a general obfuscation detection tool and is not meant to generically detect obfuscation in all programs. Rather, DynODet is the first tool of its kind that can detect advanced malware, and hence is meant to be used in addition to existing detection tools. DynODet is meant for use in a sandbox [39], such as those in widely used sandbox based malware detectors. Enhancing the sandbox with DynODet increases malware detection without significantly increasing false positives. We present the following contributions:

- A unique study into the prevalence of obfuscations in benign applications
- Methods, implemented in our tool DynODet, to classify obfuscation types into two types - allowed obfuscations that are prevalent in benign programs and disallowed obfuscations that are present in malware
- Results showing that 33% of malware in a set of 100,208 have at least one of the six disallowed obfuscations DynODet detects

- Results showing a false positive rate of below 2.5% in a test of 6,192 real world benign applications
- Results showing a decrease of 24.5% in malware missed by five market-leading AV tools by using DynODet's disallowed obfuscations

The paper is structured as follows: Sect. 2 discusses the theoretical idea behind detecting obfuscation in malware. Sections 3 through Sect. 8 give an in-depth explanation of each of the six obfuscation types, including related work. Section 9 discusses DynODet's capabilities. Section 10 discusses current findings. Section 11 looks ahead at future work.

2   Detecting Dynamic Obfuscation

Obfuscation is defined as the deliberate attempt of programs to mislead a static analysis tool. Obfuscation works by thwarting or misleading static disassembly that is used in static analysis tools to understand the instruction-level structure of the program. Obfuscation has become a widespread tool in malware given its ability to defeat static analysis [21]. DynODet leverages the strength of dynamic analysis in order to improve static analysis efforts against obfuscated programs.

Although static analysis has been shown to be ineffective against obfucsation, it is still useful in determining a program's expected path. Using *just-in-time recurisive-traversal disassembly* is advantageous because it allows DynODet to produce a limited expected path of the program prior to its execution. Then during execution, for some of the obfuscations, *DynODet can compare the expected path to the actual path to detect if any obfuscation is present.* DynODet implements just-in-time disassembly at run-time, which is the process of performing disassembly recursively during execution. It uses this in order to disassemble portions of the program just before they are executed in groups of code called *frontiers.* A frontier is the set of instructions reachable from the current instruction using direct control-transfer instructions (CTIs) only[1]. Hence frontiers terminate at a set of indirect CTIs. Frontiers are disassembled when execution reaches the current instruction at its beginning. Because indirect branch targets cannot be always determined until just before the instruction executes, just-in-time disassembly stops at all indirect branches. When an indirect branch target at the end of a frontier becomes known because the execution reaches that point, DynODet then restarts recursive traversal disassembly at its target.

DynODet chose to detect the following six obfuscations because these were among the obfuscations studied in academic papers, as shown through the related work sections below, and were discovered through our program-analysis of malware. The six chosen obfuscations are not an exhaustive list, but do show the potential of using the presence of obfuscations as IOMs. Also, by detecting these obfuscations, DynODet limits the ability of malware to escape static analysis.

---

[1] A CTI is called direct where the CTI's target is a constant; otherwise it is called indirect.

3   Self-modification

Definition. Self-modifying code is when a program overwrites existing instructions with new instructions at run time. Self-modification defeats static analysis by producing instructions at run time that were not present during static analysis.

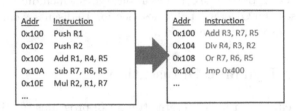

Fig. 1. Example of Self-modification

Malware can implement this behavior by first changing the write permission on a region of existing code. Then the malware can overwrite the existing instructions with new instructions as seen in the example in Fig. 1. The malware can then re-execute the same region with the new instructions in place.

Presence in Benign Applications. When detecting self-modification by comparing an initial snapshot of a program with a current one after some execution time, we found that self-modification occurs in benign applications, in part because of dynamic address relocation. Dynamic address relocation is the process of updating a program with the runtime addresses for functions that exist in other DLLs or binary images. Static linking does not cause self-modification. In order to perform this relocation, the operating system loader overwrites instruction operands that are dependent on the addresses of other DLL functions because the addresses is unknown statically. By naively implementing self-modification detection, this dynamic address relocation behavior would be flagged. DynODet uses the comparison of two snapshots of the program's code from different points of execution as its overall detection scheme, but also incorporates two discriminating features to distinguish malware from benign programs.

Detection Scheme. First, DynODet detects self-modification by comparing only the opcodes of instructions rather than the instructions along with their operands. We found that the dynamic linking process described above only modifies operands, whereas malware may modify both the operands and opcodes. Detecting only opcode modification reduces the detection of self-modification in benign programs while still detecting it in malware. By not being able to change the opcodes, malware is limited in its ability to perform malicious actions.

Second, DynODet does not flag a dynamic optimization found in a small percentage of benign programs as malicious. The dynamic optimization allows programs to overwrite the first instruction of a function with a JMP instruction. At run-time, a program may decide that it can reduce the runtime of the program by simply jumping to some other location every time this particular function is called [23]. A program can also overwrite a JMP instruction in order to enable a function to execute based on a runtime decision. Thus, DynODet allows a single instruction per frontier of code to be replaced by a JMP instruction or have a JMP instruction replaced without it being considered malicious. DynODet's goal is not to generally detect self-modification, but to only distinguish self-modification in malware vs. benign applications.

DynODet does not detect self-modification in any dynamically allocated memory outside of the program's main image because it found this behavior in both benign applications and malware without a clear discriminating feature. During the course of execution, a program in Windows can allocate memory with read/write/execute permissions, which allows a program to use the region as a code cache where it can write code, execute it, and repeat. Benign interpreter programs will do this as confirmed in Sect. 10.2.

At first, it may seem like malware can simply mimic benign programs in order to evade detection. However, it has been shown in studies such as [32] that static analysis of opcode sequences can be used to detect malware. Thus, malware can either only modify its instructions' operands and be detected by their opcode sequences, or it can overwrite its instructions and be caught by DynODet.

Related Work. Previous work, as explained below, detecting self-modification has largely focused on detecting it in a forensic setting, rather than using it as an IOM. Previous schemes would not be a viable detection tool because their methods of detecting self-modification would also detect it in benign applications.

PolyUnpack [31] detects self-modification by performing static analysis on a program, then comparing the dynamically executed instructions to those in the static disassembly. If they do not match, then PolyUnpack outputs the code. MmmBop [2] is a dynamic binary instrumentation scheme that uses a code cache to help unpack a program and determine the original entry point. It detects self-modification by checking the write target of every write instruction to determine if the program wrote to a code cached instruction. However, both of these tools do not use the detection of self-modification as a method of catching malware, since their goals were malware understanding, not malware detection.

The following works [1,8,19] also detect self-modifying code, but do not propose their techniques as a method of detecting malware. [1,19] in particular did not build their tools with the intention to use it on malware. [8] is a forensic tool and not meant for live detection. Work from the University of Virginia [10] provides a way, such as using a dynamically generated check-sum, to protect binaries against self-modification to preserve software integrity, but do not use the presence of self-modification as an IOM.

4   Section Mislabel Obfuscation

Definition. Section mislabel obfuscation is the process of dynamically changing the permissions of a section within the binary to execute a non-code region. By marking some sections of its binary as a non-code section, a static analyzer may not analyze it for instructions, thus missing potentially malicious code.

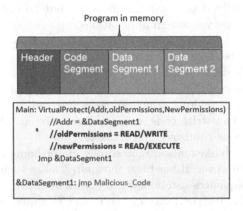

Fig. 2. Example of permission change

As an example of section mislabel obfuscation, Fig. 2 shows a malware that first changes the permissions on a data section to executable, then it executes from the data region. This type of obfuscation allows malware to avoid statically marking sections of code in their binary, which can help evade static detection. It also allows the malware to possibly make changes to the non-code regions prior to changing the permissions on the section to further its obfuscation.

Self-modification, explained in Sect. 3, can include the changing of permissions on a memory region. However, section mislabel obfuscation is distinct because it tracks when a malware intentionally mislabels a section or sections of a binary as a non-code region, only to later modify the permissions to execute the section. Self-modification, per our definition, only occurs in code sections.

Presence in Benign Applications. From our study of benign applications, section mislabel obfuscation does not occur in most benign programs. This is most likely due to the use of standard compilers when compiling benign applications. Thus, DynODet does not employ a discriminating feature for this obfuscation.

Detection scheme. DynODet detects section mislabel obfuscation by using Pin's API to determine a program's sections when first loaded into memory. Each binary has several sections such as code, and data. DynODet stores which address ranges are marked as code regions and which are not. It then monitors the execution of the program and if the PC lies within a non-code region then section mislabel obfuscation has occurred. DynODet does not detect the actual request of the program to change the permissions on its section, but is still able to determine if such an event did occur by watching the execution of the program.

Because DynODet does not employ a specific discriminating feature in order to detect this obfuscation, there is no way for malware to hide this obfuscation.

Related Work. We are not aware of any tool that explicitly detects section mislabel obfuscation in the manner that DynODet does, but there are existing schemes that try to prevent the execution of non-code sections.

Windows and other OSs have implemented a protection called data execution prevention (DEP) [6]. DEP prevents programs from executing code from non-executable memory regions such as data sections. Although it seems DEP employs a similar goal to our method, the goals are not identical – DEP is primarily meant to prevent hijacking of control of critical Windows system files using data execution, for example in a stack smashing attack. DynODet aims to detect malware payload files. Consequent to its goals, most DEP implementations do not prevent adding execute permissions to segments. DynODet will detect such permission changes. Another drawback of DEP with regard to Dyn-ODet's goals is that with DEP, if a piece of malware on an end point performs some malicious actions prior to attempting to execute data, then those prior will be allowed. In contrast, DynODet is meant to be an integral part of a sandbox mechanism, which means detection of section mislabeling will imply that the malware will be prevented from reaching the end point in its entirety.

5   Dynamically Generated Code

Definition. Dynamically generated code is the process of creating code in a dynamically allocated memory region. Malware dynamically generates code because it wants to hides its malicious instructions from static analysis. As in Fig. 3, malware can first allocate a new region of memory with read/write/execute permissions. It can then copy over instructions to the new memory region and then execute it. To add a level of obfuscation, malware could also decrypt a data section that holds malicious instructions prior to copying over the instructions. Static analysis is defeated here because it cannot reliably decrypt the data section to reveal the instructions in addition to its inability to know with high confidence that the data section is encrypted.

Dynamically generated code differs from self-modification because dynamically generated code is the action of allocating new memory, copying code to it, then executing that region. Self-modification refers to overwriting existing instructions (*i.e.* instructions that have already executed) with new instructions and then executing the new instructions.

Presence in Benign Applications. In our experiments, we found that benign applications also dynamically generate code for a variety of reasons. For example, we found that some benign programs generate jump tables that can only be built after the linking of other DLLs at runtime because the addresses of DLL functions

```
Main: addr = VirtualAlloc(size,permissions)
         //size = 0x100
         //permissions = READWRITE_EXECUTE
         //addr = 0x800
      Copy(destAddr,srcAddr,size)
         //srcAddr = &DataSegment
         //destAddr = addr
         //size = 0x100
      Call 0x800

0x800: //Code copied from data segment of the program
```

Fig. 3. Example of dynamically generated code

are not known statically. Benign applications may also copy a function to a new region of memory to create a wrapper function. In the cases where a benign program dynamically generates code, we found that the code that is copied to new memory is in an existing code section of the binary image loaded at run time. This is because the dynamically generated code that is copied to new memory is often generated by a compiler, which naturally places code in a code section. Understanding that dynamically generated code occurs in benign applications, discriminating features are needed in order to eliminate false positives.

Detection Scheme. DynODet detects dynamically generated code in a three-step manner. First it hooks into Windows systems calls that are related to the allocation and changing of permissions of memory. DynODet begins to track any region that is marked as executable and is not a part of any loaded binary image. Second, it instruments any write instructions to tracked memory regions from the program so that right before it executes, DynODet can determine if such a memory region is written to. If such a write occurs, DynODet checks to see if the source address of the write instruction is from one of the program's non-code regions. If so, DynODet watches for the newly copied code to execute at which point DynODet detects dynamically generated code.

With DynODet's unique method of detecting dynamically generated code, malware cannot simply try to mimic the behavior of benign applications in order to evade detection. If the malware tried to specifically evade DynODet's detection, it would only be allowed to copy code into the newly allocated region of memory from statically-declared code sections. If the code is copied from a code section, then the code is discoverable statically and thus defeats the purpose of dynamic code generation. In regards to self-modification in external memory regions, if the code that is replacing existing code is from a data section inside of the main image of the binary, then DynODet will detect it. If the code is from a code section, then static analysis can discover it.

Just-in-time (JIT) compilation and interpretation of code are two types of programs that are closely tied to dynamically generated code. JIT compilation and interpretation of code are present in platforms that take an input of data or bytecode and translate it into machine code. Unfortunately, interpretation of code is a powerful tool that malware can misuse. For example, malware can use tools such as Themida and VMProtect to obfuscate attacks [33]. Further research is needed to mitigate this risk. The current implementation of our detection scheme for dynamically generated code with discriminating features does not flag interpretation or JIT compilation as malicious. However, one potential solution to this problem is to whitelist benign interpreter and JIT-platform programs, which is feasible given their small number and well-known nature- this has the added benefit of preventing the malicious use of interpreters unknown to the user.

Related Work. As noted above, detecting and tracking dynamically generated code is a solved problem. However, none of the following tools are able to use their detection of dynamically generated code to catch malware.

OllyBonE [36], a plug-in to OllyDbg [41] is a kernel driver which reports when pages are written to then executed. However, OllyBonE was only tested on common packer code and not on benign applications. OmniUnpack [20] is a similar tool that tracks memory page writes and then analyzes the contents when a dangerous system call is made. When such a call is made another malware analysis tool is invoked to analyze the written pages. ReconBin [40] also analyzes dynamically generated code. Renovo [13] attempts to extract hidden code from packed executables by watching all memory writes, and determining if any instructions executed are generated. It does not check the source of the writes and was not tested on benign applications. None of these tools use the presence of dynamically generated code as an IOM, since, lacking our discriminant, they would have found such code in several benign applications as well. These tools are also limited in their malware analysis only to dynamically generated code.

6   Unconditional to Conditional Branch Obfuscation

Definition. Unconditional to conditional branch obfuscation is the process of converting an unconditional branch to a conditional branch by the use of an opaque predicate [5]. An opaque predicate is an expression that always evaluates to true or false and thus can be used in a conditional branch to always transfer control one way. This obfuscation can be used to thwart static analysis by adding more control-paths that static analysis has to analyze.

For example, in Fig. 4, malware can take an unconditional branch and convert into a conditional branch. The malware can set the R1 and R2 registers such

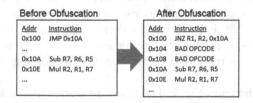

Fig. 4. Example of Unconditional to Conditional Obfuscation

that they are never equal thus always jumping to the target address of 0x10A. Now the malware can insert junk code or invalid opcodes at the always not-taken direction of the conditional branch in order to confuse the static disassembler.

This type of obfuscation is generally defeated by any dynamic analysis tool by watching the actual execution of the program, and seeing which paths were taken and never taken. *However, merely having one outcome of a conditional branch never execute is not indicative of the presence of this obfuscation, since benign program may have branches outcomes which never happen (for example error checks that never trigger in a particular run).* In order to detect this obfuscation specifically, some additional analysis has to be done.

Presence in Benign Applications. Although benign programs rarely use this obfuscation, having one side of a branch in a benign program never execute is common. Thus, we need a discriminating feature to distinguish this behavior in malware vs. benign applications.

Detection Scheme. To distinguish malware from benign applications, DynODet uses the observation that if malware uses this obfuscation, then the untaken path is likely not code, and can be detected as such by just-in-time disassembly. DynODet disassembles both the target and fall through address of each conditional branch until an indirect branch is reached. If either control flow path contains an invalid instruction prior to reaching an indirect branch, this obfuscation is detected. DynODet stops inspecting the control flow paths at indirect branches because the targets of indirect branches are unknown statically.

This is as far as DynODet is able to detect unconditional to conditional branch obfuscation because it is hard to determine whether code is doing useful work or not. However, it does eliminate the malware's ability to place junk code at either the target or fallthrough address of a conditional branch, which can thwart some static disassemblers.

Related Work. DynODet is not aware of any work that explicitly detects this obfuscation. In most dynamic analysis tools, this obfuscation is partially detected as a by-product, but is not documented as being used to distinguish malware from benign programs.

7   Exception-Based Obfuscation

Definition. Exception-based obfuscation is the process of registering an exception handler with the OS then causing an exception intentionally. Static analyzers fail to see this because exceptions can occur in programs in ways that are not statically deducible. For example, a divide instruction, which usually take registers as operands, can have the divisor equal to zero. It is very difficult for static analysis tools to reliably confirm that the divisor register will be set to zero.

An example is shown in Fig. 5. The malware first registers an exception handler that jumps to harmful code. Then, the malware causes an intentional exception such as division by zero. In Fig. 5, R6 would be equal to zero. The registered

```
Main: //register Div_trap_handler function as exception handler
      call Foo

Foo:  Add  R1, R2, R3
      Div  R4, R5, R6    /* R4 = R5 ÷ R6 */
      Xor  R7, R8, R9
      ...

Div_trap_handler: Jmp Harmful_function
```

Fig. 5. Example of exception-based obfuscation

exception handler will then execute and the program will jump to the harmful code. This instruction execution sequence would not have been predicted or analyzed by static analyzers due to the dynamic nature of exceptions.

Presence in Benign Applications. Exception-based obfuscation has been studied in the past as the related work section below shows, but we are not aware of any work that uses this as an IOM for malware. Unsurprisingly, handled exceptions do occur inside of benign applications. Legitimate exception handlers may execute because of an invalid input from the user or bad input from a file. Because of this, simply classifying any exception handler execution as exception-based obfuscation is not a viable detection technique.

Detection Scheme. Benign applications do not intentionally cause exceptions, such as divide by zero, in their programs because these would cause a system error. Malware, however, to ensure that its malicious exception handler executes, will cause an intentional exception. Using this, DynODet incorporates the following discriminating features to catch exception-based obfuscation in malware.

DynODet detects exception-based obfuscation by monitoring exception handler registration followed by an exception occurring. During execution, DynODet monitors two methods of registering an exception handler. One is the standard Windows API *SetUnhandledExceptionFilter*. The other method is directly writing to the thread information block (TIB). In order to detect this method, DynODet watches all writes to the TIB and detects any changes to the current exception handler. Once an exception handler is registered, DynODet instruments the beginning of it and is notified when it runs. Next, DynODet strengthens the probability of detecting a malicious exception by catching an *unexpected control flow exception*. DynODet defines an unexpected control flow exception as when the control-flow of the program does not follow the expected path. In order to detect an unexpected control flow exception, DynODet instruments every Pin basic block and keeps track of the first and last instruction addresses. Prior to the dynamic execution of each basic block, DynODet checks if the entire prior basic block executed. A basic block is a sequence of instructions that should execute from top to the bottom, unless an exception occurred. If DynODet determines that a previous basic block did not execute in its entirety, it turns an internal flag on. If the next basic block executed is in a registered exception handler and the internal flag is on, exception-based obfuscation has occurred. The internal flag is used because DynODet is only concerned with exceptions that occur within the application because malware, when employing this obfuscation, triggers the exception in its code to ensure that the exception will occur.

This type of obfuscation is rare, as will be seen in the results below. The point of this obfuscation is to hide a malware's true path of execution from a static analysis tool. If malware chose to implement exception-based obfuscation in a manner that deliberately evades DynODet's detection scheme, such as by using an explicit interrupt instruction, the interrupt could be discovered through static analysis, thus making the obfuscation less useful. DynODet's detection scheme allows it to broadly detect most exception-based obfuscation scenarios such as divide by zero or writes to address zero.

Related Work. There have been a few works that looked at how exception-based obfuscation may be present in malware, but none have created a general solution and used it as an IOM. Prakash [25] introduced an x86 emulator that attempts to detect exception-based obfuscation in attempts to generically unpack malware. The emulator only detects common exception-based obfuscations, such as using the x86 interrupt instruction or a divide by zero, to ensure that the emulator continues running. It does not use exception-based obfuscation as a detection mechanism and did not study it in benign programs. Work from the University of Arizona [24] proposes using exception handlers as a method of obfuscation, but does not propose or deliver a mechanism of detecting it.

8 Overlapping Code Sequences

Definition. Overlapping code sequences occur when jumping into the middle of an existing instruction. This method allows malware to hide instructions within other instructions, which can trick static disassemblers. In the complex instruction set computing (CISC) x86 architecture, instructions have variable length so the same range of addresses can have several different instruction sequences.

As shown in Fig. 6, to implement this behavior, a malware can use an instruction with an immediate value that is an encoding of an instruction. A static disassembler will not be able to see the hidden instruction because it is not located at a natural instruction address and could miss malicious behavior.

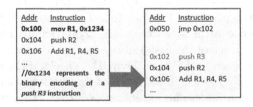

Fig. 6. Example of Overlapping Code Sequences

A push instruction is represented in the immediate value of a MOV instruction as a proof-of-concept in Fig. 6.

Presence in Benign Applications. During benign testing, DynODet found a very small number of benign programs with this behavior. To the best of our knowledge, there are no high-level construct that would produce this behavior when compiled by a standard compiler. Thus, no discriminating feature is needed to use this as an IOM.

Detection Scheme. During disassembly, DynODet checks if the current PC is in the middle of an existing instruction in the disassembly map produced by recursive traversal. If it is, DynODet checks if all bytes of the current instruction match the original code. If they do not match, self-modification has occurred. If they do, overlapping code sequences are present.

Related Work. Work at the University of Louisiana at Lafayette [14] implements segmentation to produce a collection of potentially overlapping segments, where each segment defines a unique sequence of instructions. Their tool attempts to uncover all potential sequences of instructions. Their tool does not provide much insight into which sequence of instructions actually ran, and provides superfluous instructions that may never be executed dynamically. Their scheme also does not try to detect overlapping code sequences as an IOM.

9 DynODet Capabilities and Limitations

9.1 Capabilities

Multithreaded Applications: DynODet can handle multithreaded applications so long as the underlying dynamic binary instrumentation (DBI) tool it uses (such as Pin) handles multi-threading. Pin assigns each created thread a thread ID that is used to distinguish which thread is executing and being instrumented. DynODet analyzes each thread's dynamic execution separately, and combines all detections found in all threads.

Spawned Child Processes: DynODet is able to handle programs that spawn other processes. This is a common behavior for many programs so DynODet is injected by Pin into each child process and each process gets its own unique analysis, but ultimately gets grouped into the parent process's analysis.

9.2 Limitations and Assumptions

Malware detection is a constant arms race between the malware writers and cybersecurity companies. As with any new scheme, malware can specifically target to defeat our scheme and bypass our detections. However, our detection schemes do make it considerably more difficult for malware to bypass both conventional static detection and our tool's detections.

10   Results

10.1   Test Set up

Our tool is currently built as an Intel Pin [17] dynamically linked library (DLL). Pin is a DBI tool that provides all of the necessary capabilities described above. Although the current implementation of DynODet is tied to Pin, our detection mechanisms are universal and can be implemented using other dynamic binary rewriters. As a Pin DLL, DynODet gets injected into the program being monitored in a sandbox environment. After the program is finished running or killed by our timeout, the results are collected and sent back to the host computer.

The Cuckoo Sandbox [11] is a popular malware analysis environment that provides an infrastructure for dynamic malware testing. We perform all of our malware testing in duplicated Cuckoo sandboxes, one sandbox per malware, which are reverted to a clean environment prior to each execution. We give our Cuckoo Sandbox process 32 KVM [15] instances, which are running Windows 7 with 1 GB of RAM each. We also set up INetSim [12] in order to give the KVM machines a fake Internet connection to trick malware into thinking it has access to Internet. INetSim is used here to get better code coverage in malware. DynODet has an internal timeout of one minute per malware.

10.2   Benign Applications

We performed benign application testing for 6,192 Windows programs. In order to ensure that our testing was comprehensive, we tested two sets of benign programs. First were 119 programs that had to be installed prior to executing (referred to as the installed benign set). Second was a set of 6,073 benign programs from a list produced by the National Institute of Standards and Technology (NIST) [35].

For the installed benign set, some of the installed programs tested were Adobe Acrobat, Mozilla Firefox, QuickTime Player, Notepad++, Google Chrome, WinScp, Open Office, 7zip, and Java Virtual Machine (JVM). The other installed programs were a mix of media players, music players, text editors, IDEs, mail clients, digital recorders, and standard system tools. When testing these installed benign applications, there was no easy method of interaction automation because these programs require a complex level of input. A generic interaction script cannot be created to robustly test all of the benign applications. In our best attempt, we modified human.py, Cuckoo's python script that is responsible for simulating human interaction, to click in a grid pattern, left to right, top to bottom, in fixed intervals across the window of the benign application in order to click as many buttons as possible. Human.py also input random text in order to give input into text fields of applications. Although this was a simple method of interaction, the purpose of this was to increase code coverage in each application.

For the second part of our dataset, we obtained a list of Windows executables from the National Software Reference Library (NSRL) produced by NIST. The NSRL set contains millions of hashes of benign software. From the initial list, we extracted the unique hashes of Windows 7 compatible executables and queried Virus Total in order to download the binaries. This resulted in 6,073 benign applications that we were able to test. The NSRL Set is largely considered to be a set of known benign software as noted in [16,38]. However, there is a small subset of known hacker tools and other unknown software that are considered to be malicious [29]. For testing purposes, we removed these programs to ensure that our benign dataset was truly benign in order to evaluate our tool properly. Ground truth is important, thus we felt that the preceding precautions were justified. Additionally, due to the sheer number of samples, it was not feasible to test and install each by hand. The ability to thoroughly test benign applications that arrive as standalone executables is outside of the scope of DynODet.

NSRL Set. The results for the 6,073 programs from the NSRL set are listed below in Table 1. In Table 1, the second column shows the obfuscation types that were detected in benign applications when no discriminating features were implemented. Without discriminating features, 8.35% of benign programs tested contain at least one type of obfuscation. The third column shows the obfuscations present with discriminating features. With discriminating features, the false positive rate is reduced by nearly 70% for programs with one or more obfuscations to 2.45% and 75% for programs with two or more obfuscations to .13%. As with any detection tool, the false positive rate is important and using these obfuscation types without discriminating features as IOM of malware is not viable.

The 149 programs falsely flagged, from manual inspection, seem to have no single attribute that explain their false detection. Using PeID, a popular packer identifier, we were able to determine that 58 of the 149 programs were packed with a variety of packers and compressors. Our conjecture is that these falsely flagged programs are very uncommon and do not follow standard compilation tools as supported by our testing results. These programs, rather than intentionally implementing unallowed obfuscations, are most likely flagged due to some extreme corner cases that our current implementation does not allow. A possible solution to this problem is addressed in Sect. 11.

The subset of programs tested from the NSRL set were obtained from Virus Total. This leads us to believe that the programs tested in this dataset are more representative of the types of executables that would be tested in an intrusion detection system. Thus, the results here show the versatility of DynODet in that it can work for both large, installed programs as well as standalone executables such as those arriving at a network's firewall.

Standard Installed Applications. The results for 117 out of the 119 applications are also listed in Table 1. Only 117 were tested here because two of the programs, JVM and Python interpreter, cannot be run without input. These are tested and explained in the next sub-section. Out of the 117 benign applications tested, only one program had a false positive in any of our obfuscation detectors, namely a section mislabel obfuscation. The program with the false positive was a graphical viewer called *i_view.exe*. This false positive is caused by Pin's inability to detect a code region along with the program's possible use of a non-standard

Table 1. Benign application results

Detection	W/O discriminating features		W/ discriminating features	
	NSRL	Installed	NSRL	Installed
Self-modification	135	5	2	0
Section Mislabel	51	1	51	1
Dynamically Generated Code	296	29	86	0
Unconditional to Conditional	12	0	12	0
Exception-based	27	1	5	0
Overlapping Code Sequences	5	0	5	0
Had 1 or more obfuscations	507/6,073 (8.35%)	34/117 (29.05%)	149/6,073 (2.45%)	1/117 (.85%)
Had 2 or more obfuscations	33/6,073 (.54%)	2/117 (1.71%)	8/6,073 (.13%)	0/117 (0%)

compiler that may have produced an irregular header. As shown in Table 1, none of the indicators outside of the one explained above, were detected in 117 benign applications. This shows that the modifications that were made in DynODet reduce false positives for three of the indicators to nearly 0%.

Interpreters and JIT-platform Programs. We also studied interpreter programs, which are programs take in data containing executable code. For example, Adobe Acrobat Reader (AR) takes in a PDF as input, which can contain executable code. *DynODet's goal is not to detect malicious PDFs*. Rather, we aimed to find out whether DynODet detects behaviors such as dynamically generated code in the interpreter program.

Each interpreter program was tested with a small set of inputs. AR was tested with 12 PDFs that included scripts, such as a template form. The Python interpreter (PyInt) was tested with a set of nine python scripts that performed small tasks such as analyzing a directory for mp3s or printing the date and time. Firefox was tested with eight websites running javascript such as www.cnn.com, www.youtube.com, and www.amazon.com. JVM was tested with 11 benchmarks out of Decapo Benchmarks, a Java open-source benchmark suite [4].

As Table 2 shows, when our tool did not use discriminating features, it detected dynamically generated code in AR, Firefox and JVM. With our discriminating features incorporated, there were no detections. This proves that our discriminating features are valuable in not detecting obfuscation in benign applications.

As noted in Sect. 3, we did not test for self-modification in dynamically allocated memory. We found that Firefox and JVM allocate memory outside of their main images to use as a code cache when executing chunks of interpreted code. As mentioned in Sect. 5, there are other methods of detecting malicious interpreter and JIT-platform programs.

Table 2. Benign interpreter results

Detection	W/O discriminating features				W/ discriminating features			
	AR	PyInt	Firefox	JVM	AR	PyInt	Firefox	JVM
Self-modification	0/12	0/9	0/8	0/11	0/12	0/9	0/8	0/11
Section Mislabel	0/12	0/9	0/8	0/11	0/12	0/9	0/8	0/11
Dynamically Generated Code	12/12	0/9	8/8	11/11	0/12	0/9	0/8	0/11
Unconditional to Conditional	0/12	0/9	0/8	0/11	0/12	0/9	0/8	0/11
Exception-based	0/12	0/9	0/8	0/11	0/12	0/9	0/8	0/11
Overlapping Code Sequences	0/12	0/9	0/8	0/11	0/12	0/9	0/8	0/11
Had 1 or more obfuscations	**12/12 (100%)**	**0/9 (0%)**	**8/8 (100%)**	**11/11 (100%)**	**0/12 (0%)**	**0/9 (0%)**	**0/8 (0%)**	**0/11 (0%)**

10.3 Malware

The malware samples were collected by our group from Virus Total, a database of malware maintained by Google. We tested in total of 100,208 malware selected randomly from 2011 to 2016. The malware test set used is a comprehensive set including viruses, backdoors, trojans, adware, infostealers, ransomware, spyware, downloaders, and bots. It is worth noting that Virus Total does contain some benign applications as well; hence we only tested samples that had at least three detections in their corresponding Virus Total report to filter out false positives.

As seen in Table 3, DynODet found examples of each obfuscation in malware. The table shows the number of detections in the 100,208 malware tested when discriminating features are used. With discriminating features enabled, 32.7% of malware are detected. *DynODet here is not claiming that the results below show the true number of malware that have these characteristics.* Rather, DynODet is showing the number of malware that can be detected despite having made modifications to some of the dynamic obfuscation detection schemes.

Although some of the detections such as overlapping code sequences and exception-based obfuscation were not that common in malware, it is still useful to include them as malware detectors for two reasons. The first is that these are rarely found in benign programs so adding to the list of distinguishable characteristics between malware and benign applications will always be useful. Second, an advantage of DynODet is that it uses all of these detections in combination in order to catch malware. Thus, although the detections of individual obfuscations may be small, when combined, they can be substantial.

As seen in Table 3, DynODet found that 32.74% of malware tested had at least one disallowed obfuscation. When compared to benign programs, in which less than 2.5% had at least one indicator, there is a clear distinction between malware and benign programs. This allows DynODet to be employed as a detection tool, rather than just an analysis tool. If a use case of DynODet could not tolerate any false positives, then it can be altered to only classify programs with 2 obfuscations as malware, which still results in a 5.74% detection rate.

Table 3. Obfuscation in malware results

Detection for 100,208 Malware		
Detection	W/ discriminating features	
Self-modification	10,264	10.24%
Section Mislabel	19,051	19.01%
Dynamically Generated Code	7,106	7.09%
Unconditional to Conditional	7,889	7.87%
Exception-based	334	0.33%
Overlapping Code Sequences	1,710	1.71%
Had 1 or more obfuscations	**32,811**	**32.74%**
Had 2 or more obfuscations	**5,750**	**5.74%**

Table 4. Malware detection improvement

Detection of 12,833 missed malware			
W/O discriminating features		W/ discriminating features	
4,445	**34.64%**	**3,141**	**24.48%**

Another indication of the capability and novelty of DynODet is shown in Table 4. We analyzed the detections of the following five market-leading AV tools: Kaspersky, ClamAV, McAfee, Symantec, and Microsoft Security Essentials and gathered the subset of malware that were not detected by any of the tools. The set resulted in 12,833 malware. We are able to show that DynODet is able to detect 4,445 (34.63%) without discriminating features and 3,141 (24.48%) with discriminating features out of the previously missed malware. This also shows the efficacy in using obfuscation detection in order to detect malware that was previously hard to catch. The detection rate of each tool listed below was obtained through Virus Total's reports for each malware.

10.4 Limitations with Evasion

As with any detection scheme, there are ways for malware to evade our tool specifically. We have listed below possible evasion techniques for three of the obfuscations detected in DynODet.

– Section mislabel obfuscation: In order to evade section mislabel detection, malware can mark all sections in their program executable so that regardless of which section it executes from, it will not be caught by our detection. However, this becomes problematic for the malware for two reasons. First, from our analysis of benign programs, we found that almost no program had all executable sections. If malware, in order to evade our detection scheme, started to mark all sections executable, this would be an easy sign for analysis tools to pick up on. Second, if malware marks all sections as code, every analysis tool will analyze all of its sections expecting code. This leads to two scenarios. Either the malware's malicious code will be revealed, or in attempts to hide its code, the malware's code sections will have high entropy due to encryption or no valid code at all, which is suspicious and will also be caught by detection schemes.

– Exception-based obfuscation: Our tool currently detects all hardware exceptions that lead to the execution of a registered exception handler as a potentially malicious indicator. Although hardware exceptions can occur in benign programs, through our study, we found that the frequency of occurances in benign programs differ from those in malware. As supported by our data, this occurs about three times more often in malware than in benign applications. Although this is not a great indicator, we conjecture that it might be useful in a machine-learning framework as one feature among many used to weigh the likelihood of a program being malicious.

– Unconditional to conditional obfuscation: Malware can evade this detection by putting legitimate code at every conditional branch in the program. As mentioned in Sect. 6, DynODet is unable to prevent this evasion. However, it does constrain the malware writer's flexibility in placing data in the code section, since not all data values also represent valid instructions. Moreover, it increases the work of the malware writer.

11 Future Work

Although our current scheme above has shown promise in being able to detect malware solely based on the presence of these features, this is not how real-world malware detection tools operate. They use a combination of features in order to classify a program as malicious or benign. Using this, we propose to first expand our list of obfuscations to other program-level features in order to detect more malware. Second, we will incorporate other static and dynamic features that have already been discovered to enhance our tool. We plan to feed these features into a machine learning algorithm to help distinguish the difference in the presence of these features in malware versus benign. The machine learning algorithm, based on statistical data, will choose which combinations of obfuscations are indicators of maliciousness, eliminating the need to manually inspect what allowed versus disallowed obfuscations look like. Our work thus far shows there is a viable avenue for using program-level obfuscations to detect advanced malware.

12 Conclusion

DynODet, a dynamic obfuscation detection tool, is able to detect that 33% of malware contain at least one disallowed obfuscation while less than 2.5% of benign applications contain any. Without our unique discriminating features, at least one of the six obfuscations we measure are found in over 29% of installed benign applications. This has prevented the use of obfuscation as an IOM for malware. By categorizing obfuscations into allowed and disallowed obfuscations, DynODet is able to accurately detect versions of self-modification, section mislabel obfuscation, dynamically generated code, overlapping code sequences, exception-based obfuscation, and unconditional to conditional obfuscation that are specific to malware. Additionally, DynODet makes it more difficult for malware to use these obfuscations to hide from static analysis. Previous work did not make any attempts to distinguish obfuscations that can occur in both benign applications and malware. DynODet was also able to decrease the number of malware missed by five market-leading AV tools by nearly 25%. DynODet is a deployable detection tool that contains the technology to strengthen today's defenses against malware.

Acknowledgments. The research was sponsored in part by contracts H9823013D00560016 and H9823013D00560037 from the US Department of Defense via the Maryland Procurement Office. The ARCS Foundation has also played a role in funding the research.

References

1. Anckaert, B., Madou, M., Bosschere, K.: A model for self-modifying code. In: Camenisch, J.L., Collberg, C.S., Johnson, N.F., Sallee, P. (eds.) IH 2006. LNCS, vol. 4437, pp. 232–248. Springer, Heidelberg (2007). doi:10.1007/978-3-540-74124-4_16
2. Bania, P.: Generic unpacking of self-modifying, aggressive, packed binary programs. arXiv preprint (2009). arXiv:0905.4581
3. Bayer, U., Moser, A., Kruegel, C., Kirda, E.: Dynamic analysis of malicious code. J. Comput. Virol. **2**(1), 67–77 (2006)
4. Blackburn, S.M., Garner, R., Hoffmann, C., Khang, A.M., McKinley, K.S., Bentzur, R., Diwan, A., Feinberg, D., Frampton, D., Guyer, S.Z., et al.: The dacapo benchmarks: java benchmarking development and analysis. In: ACM Sigplan Notices, vol. 41, pp. 169–190. ACM (2006)
5. Collberg, C., Thomborson, C., Low, D.: A taxonomy of obfuscating transformations. Department of Computer Science, The University of Auckland, New Zealand, Technical report (1997)
6. Microsoft Corporation: What is data execution prevention? May 2016
7. Microsoft Corporation: Internet security threat report 21, 5, April 2016
8. Debray, S., Patel, J.: Reverse engineering self-modifying code: unpacker extraction. In: 2010 17th Working Conference on Reverse Engineering (WCRE), pp. 131–140. IEEE (2010)
9. Dinaburg, A., Royal, P., Sharif, M., Lee, W.: Ether: malware analysis via hardware virtualization extensions. In: Proceedings of the 15th ACM Conference on Computer and Communications Security, pp. 51–62. ACM (2008)
10. Ghosh, S., Hiser, J., Davidson, J.W.: Software protection for dynamically-generated code. In: Proceedings of the 2nd ACM SIGPLAN Program Protection and Reverse Engineering Workshop, p. 1. ACM (2013)
11. Guarnieri, C., Tanasi, A., Bremer, J., Schloesser, M.: The cuckoo sandbox (2012)
12. Hungenberg, T., Eckert, M.: Inetsim: internet services simulation suite (2013)
13. Kang, M.G., Poosankam, P., Yin, H.: Renovo: a hidden code extractor for packed executables. In: Proceedings of the 2007 ACM Workshop on Recurring Malcode, pp. 46–53. ACM (2007)

14. Kapoor, A.: An approach towards disassembly of malicious binary executables. Ph.D. thesis, University of Louisiana at Lafayette (2004)
15. Kivity, A., Kamay, Y., Laor, D., Lublin, U., Liguori, A.: KVM: the Linux virtual machine monitor. In: Proceedings of the Linux Symposium, vol. 1, pp. 225–230 (2007)
16. Kwon, B.J., Mondal, J., Jang, J., Bilge, L., Dumitras, T.: The dropper effect: insights into malware distribution with downloader graph analytics. In: Proceedings of the 22nd ACM SIGSAC Conference on Computer and Communications Security, pp. 1118–1129. ACM (2015)
17. Luk, C.K., Cohn, R., Muth, R., Patil, H., Klauser, A., Lowney, G., Wallace, S., Reddi, V.J., Hazelwood, K.: Pin: building customized program analysis tools with dynamic instrumentation. In: ACM Sigplan Notices, vol. 40, pp. 190–200. ACM (2005)
18. Madou, M., Van Put, L., De Bosschere, K.: Understanding obfuscated code. In: 14th IEEE International Conference on Program Comprehension (ICPC 2006), pp. 268–274. IEEE (2006)
19. Maebe, J., De Bosschere, K.: Instrumenting self-modifying code. arXiv preprint cs/0309029 (2003)
20. Martignoni, L., Christodorescu, M., Jha, S.: OmniUnpack: fast, generic, and safe unpacking of malware. In: Twenty-Third Annual Computer Security Applications Conference (ACSAC 2007), pp. 431–441. IEEE (2007)
21. Moser, A., Kruegel, C., Kirda, E.: Limits of static analysis for malware detection. In: Twenty-third Annual Computer Security Applications Conference (ACSAC 2007), pp. 421–430. IEEE (2007)
22. O'Kane, P., Sezer, S., McLaughlin, K.: Obfuscation: the hidden malware. IEEE Secur. Priv. 9(5), 41–47 (2011)
23. Pike, R., Locanthi, B., Reiser, J.: Hardware/software trade-offs for bitmap graphics on the blit. Softw. Pract. Exper. 15(2), 131–151 (1985)
24. Popov, I.V., Debray, S.K., Andrews, G.R.: Binary obfuscation using signals. In: Usenix Security (2007)
25. Prakash, C.: Design of x86 emulator for generic unpacking. In: Assocation of Anti-Virus Asia Researchers International Conference, Seoul, South Korea (2007)
26. Quist, D.A., Liebrock, L.M.: Visualizing compiled executables for malware analysis. In: 6th International Workshop on Visualization for Cyber Security (VizSec 2009), pp. 27–32. IEEE (2009)
27. Quist, D., Smith, V.: Covert debugging circumventing software armoring techniques. Black hat briefings USA (2007)
28. Rabek, J.C., Khazan, R.I., Lewandowski, S.M., Cunningham, R.K.: Detection of injected, dynamically generated, and obfuscated malicious code. In: Proceedings of the 2003 ACM Workshop on Rapid Malcode, pp. 76–82. ACM (2003)
29. Rodrigues, T.: Extracting known bad hash set from nsrl. https://digital-forensics.sans.org/blog/2010/02/22/extracting-known-bad-hashset-from-nsrl/
30. Roundy, K.A., Miller, B.P.: Binary-code obfuscations in prevalent packer tools. ACM J. Name 1, 21 (2012)
31. Royal, P., Halpin, M., Dagon, D., Edmonds, R., Lee, W.: PolyUnpack: automating the hidden-code extraction of unpack-executing malware. In: Null, pp. 289–300. IEEE (2006)

32. Santos, I., Devesa, J., Brezo, F., Nieves, J., Bringas, P.G.: Opem: a static-dynamic approach for machine-learning-based malware detection. In: Herrero, A., et al. (eds.) International Joint Conference CISIS '12-ICEUTE '12-SOCO '12 Special Sessions. AISC, vol. 189, pp. 271–280. Springer, Heidelberg (2013). doi:10.1007/978-3-642-33018-6

33. Sharif, M., Lanzi, A., Giffin, J., Lee, W.: Automatic reverse engineering of malware emulators. In: 2009 30th IEEE Symposium on Security and Privacy, pp. 94–109. IEEE (2009)

34. Song, D., et al.: BitBlaze: a new approach to computer security via binary analysis. In: Sekar, R., Pujari, A.K. (eds.) ICISS 2008. LNCS, vol. 5352, pp. 1–25. Springer, Heidelberg (2008). doi:10.1007/978-3-540-89862-7_1

35. National Institute of Standards and Technology: National software reference library. Online

36. Stewart, J.: Ollybone: semi-automatic unpacking on IA-32. In: Proceedings of the 14th DEF CON Hacking Conference (2006)

37. Wang, X., Jhi, Y.C., Zhu, S., Liu, P.: Still: exploit code detection via static taint and initialization analyses. In: Annual Computer Security Applications Conference (ACSAC 2008), pp. 289–298. IEEE (2008)

38. Wang, Y.M., Vo, B., Roussev, R., Verbowski, C., Johnson, A.: Strider ghostbuster: why it's a bad idea for stealth software to hide files. Technical report, Technical Report MSR-TR-2004-71, Microsoft Research (2004)

39. Willems, C., Holz, T., Freiling, F.: Toward automated dynamic malware analysis using CWSandbox. IEEE Secur. Priv. **2**, 32–39 (2007)

40. Ying, L., Su, P., Feng, D., Wang, X., Yang, Y., Liu, Y.: Reconbin: reconstructing binary file from execution for software analysis. In: Third IEEE International Conference on Secure Software Integration and Reliability Improvement (SSIRI 2009), pp. 222–229. IEEE (2009)

41. Yuschuk, O.: Ollydbg (2007)

Finding the Needle: A Study of the *PE32* Rich Header and Respective Malware Triage

George D. Webster[✉], Bojan Kolosnjaji, Christian von Pentz, Julian Kirsch, Zachary D. Hanif, Apostolis Zarras, and Claudia Eckert

Technical University of Munich, Munich, Germany
webstergd@sec.in.tum.de

Abstract. Performing triage of malicious samples is a critical step in security analysis and mitigation development. Unfortunately, the obfuscation and outright removal of information contained in samples makes this a monumentally challenging task. However, the widely used Portable Executable file format (*PE32*), a data structure used by the Windows OS to handle executable code, contains hidden information that can provide a security analyst with an upper hand. In this paper, we perform the first accurate assessment of the hidden *PE32* field known as the Rich Header and describe how to extract the data that it clandestinely contains. We study 964,816 malware samples and demonstrate how the information contained in the Rich Header can be leveraged to perform rapid triage across millions of samples, including packed and obfuscated binaries. We first show how to quickly identify post-modified and obfuscated binaries through anomalies in the header. Next, we exhibit the Rich Header's utility in triage by presenting a proof of concept similarity matching algorithm which is solely based on the contents of the Rich Header. With our algorithm we demonstrate how the contents of the Rich Header can be used to identify similar malware, different versions of malware, and when malware has been built under different build environment; revealing potentially distinct actors. Furthermore, we are able to perform these operations in near real-time, less than 6.73 ms on commodity hardware across our studied samples. In conclusion, we establish that this little-studied header in the *PE32* format is a valuable asset for security analysts and has a breadth of future potential.

1 Introduction

The shear volume of malware samples that analysts have to contend with makes thorough analysis and understanding of every sample impractical. As a result, effective and timely triaging techniques are vital for analysts to make sense of the collective information and focus their limited time on agglomerated tasks through uncovering commonalities and similar variants of malicious software. This in turn, allows analysis to better hone in their effort and avoid wasting costly cycles on previously analyzed or unrelated samples. Unfortunately, it is common practice for malware authors to design malware that hinders automated analysis

© Springer International Publishing AG 2017
M. Polychronakis and M. Meier (Eds.): DIMVA 2017, LNCS 10327, pp. 119–138, 2017.
DOI: 10.1007/978-3-319-60876-1_6

and otherwise thwart triaging efforts; thereby allowing malware to operate under the radar for a longer period of time.

One of the common practices used in triaging samples is to leverage header information from the Portable Executable file format (*PE32*) [3,6,7]. This is primarily done as the derived information can: (*i*) reveal how the executable was built and who built it, (*ii*) provide an understanding of what the executable does, and (*iii*) identify entry points for disclosing packed and obfuscated code. For example, when investigating the *Rustock* Rootkit, the *PE32* Headers identified the location of the first deobfuscation routine [3]. Additionally, numerous clustering and similarity matching algorithms are often exclusively based on the data derived from the *PE32* file format [5,11,24,26].

Unfortunately, malware authors are well aware of the valuable data contained in the *PE32* file format. As a result, they routinely take steps to strip or otherwise distort any useful information from the *PE32* format through packing binaries, adjusting compiler flags, and manually removing data in the header [1,10]. While unpacking malware and performing manual reverse engineering can recover this useful information, the process is extremely costly. As stated by Yan et al. [27], "Who has the time to reverse all the bytecodes given that security researchers are already preoccupied with a large backlog of malware?" Needless to say, stripping the headers leaves little useful information available for triage.

Fortunately for security analysis, the *PE32* Header contains information that is often poorly understood or simply hidden. In this work, we perform an in-depth study of one of these hidden attributes commonly known as the Rich Header. While rich in information, this header is also common in malware, present in 71% in our random sample set, and is found in any *PE32* file assembled by the Microsoft Linker. Through the knowledge we derive from our in-depth study, we show how to properly dissect the information and explain what the resulting data means. We then study the extracted headers from malicious samples, which we gather from four distinct datasets. Leveraging this information, we present proof of concept methods to demonstrate the significant value the Rich Header can provide for triage.

Overall, in this paper, we show that the Rich Header field is valuable in triage and can be a catalyst for past and future work. As such, we provide the first accurate assessment of the Rich Header and detail how to extract its clandestine data. We then present a series of statistical studies and describe two proof of concept methods in which the Rich Header can be used in triage. The first method allows for the rapid detection of post-modified and packed binaries through the identification of anomalies. The next method leverages *machine learning* to perform rapid and effective triage based solely on the values in the Rich Header's *@comp.id* field; specifically the 516 unique *ProdID*, 29,460 distinct *ProdID* and *mCV* pairs, and their *Count* values we have identified across 964,816 malicious samples. This method can identify *similar malware variants* and *build environments* in 6.73 ms across 964,816 malware samples using only a consumer grade laptop. In summary, we prove that leveraging the data contained in this often forgotten and overlooked aspect of the *PE32* file format, called the Rich

Header, establishes a major boon for performing analytic triage operations and opens the door for a plethora of future work.

In summary, we make the following main contributions:

- We present the first accurate and in-depth study of the Rich Header field and describe how to extract its data.
- We demonstrate how anomalies in the Rich Header can identify 84% of the known packed malware samples.
- We present a proof of concept approach that utilizes machine learning techniques to identify similar malware variants and build environments in near real-time, 6.73 ms, by only leveraging the Rich Header.

2   Background

In this section, we provide a background on the Portable Executable file format, commonly known as *PE32*.[1] We then present an overview of the compiler linking and describe how it creates the sections contained in the header.

2.1   Portable Executable File Format Headers

The Portable Executable file format was introduced by Microsoft to provide a common format for executable files across the Windows Operating System family [17]. As such, the format is the primary standard used for shared libraries, binaries, among other types of executable code or images in Windows. The Portable Executable file format is also often called the Common Object File Format (*COFF*), *PE/COFF*, and *PE32*.

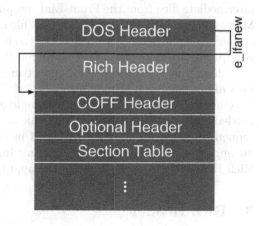

Fig. 1. High level view of the *PE32* format

The *PE32* format includes an MS-DOS stub for backwards compatibility, with the e_lfanew field pointing to the beginning of the COFF Header, as Fig. 1 illustrates. The COFF Header, in turn, is followed by optional headers that control (among others) imports, exports, relocations, and segments [14]. Together, these headers contain valuable information for program execution, identification, and debugging. Including the base address of the image in virtual memory, the execution entry point, imported

---

[1] For simplicity, we will use the 32 bit version of the Portable Executable file format. The 64 bit version behaves similarly.

and exported symbols, and information on the code and data sections that form the program itself.

The *PE32* Header is openly documented by Microsoft and as such its internal mechanics are well understood by the development community [13]. However, as we will discuss in this work, the *PE32* format does contain undocumented sections that have eluded understanding.

2.2 Compiler Linking

The typical process of building an executable image is subdivided into two parts: the compilation phase in which the compiler translates code written in a high-level language into machine code and the linking phase where the linker combines all produced object files into one executable image. These are both compartmentalized processes introducing a one-to-one relation between compile units (usually files containing source code) and the resulting object files.

The Microsoft Visual C++ (MSVC) Compiler Toolchain is a commonly used solution for building executable images from source code written in a variate of programming languages. During the compilation phase `cl.exe` provides the interface to the Front-End compilers (`c1.dll` and `c1xx.dd`) as well as the Back-End compiler `c2.dll`. Then, `c2.dll` will create object files (`.obj`) from intermediate files from the Front-End compilers. While creating the objects, the Microsoft Compiler assigns each object file an ID, which in this work referred to as the *@comp.id*, and stores the ID in the header of the respective object file. It is important to note that also the Microsoft assembler as well as the part of the tool chain that is responsible for converting resource files into a format suitable for linking generated *@comp.id*s.

Once the compilation phase is complete, `link.exe` will collect the objects needed and begin to stitch the *PE32* file or static library (`.lib`) together. Consequently, static libraries consisting of more than one object contain multiple *@comp.id*s. For executables and dynamic link libraries, `link.exe` builds up the Rich Header during generation of the appropriate *PE32* headers.

3 Rich Header

The Rich Header name originates from the fact that one of the elements in the header contains the ASCII values for *"Rich."* The header is an undocumented field in the *PE32* file format that exists between the MS-DOS and the COFF Headers. While rumors of its existence and speculation on its purpose have existed across multiple communities for a long time, it was not until July of 2004 that an article by *Lifewire* started to unveil information about the Rich Header [8]. Unfortunately, this article provided limited technically correct information and the drawn conclusions—especially regarding the purpose of the *@comp.id* field—were incorrect. Four years later, on January 2008, Trendy Stephen furthered the understanding of Rich Header by discovering some of the meaning behind the *@comp.id* field and a relatively correct assessment of how the checksum is generated [22]. Few months later, Daniel Pistelli released an article that provided a guide for extracting the Rich Header and portions of the *@comp.id* field [18]. Then, two years later, in November 2010, Daniel Pistelli updated his article with information describing how the high value bits in *@comp.id* correspond to a "Product Identifier" (referred to in this paper as *ProdID*) [18].

While the work of these pioneers provided crucial details on how to reverse engineer the Rich Header, aspects of the header are still poorly understood. Specifically, the full structure of the *@comp.id* has not yet been identified, information about how to map the *ProdID* is unknown, and mistakes were made regarding how to extract the fields. In this section we perform a technical deep dive of the Rich Header, which has not previously been completely and accurately described in any single source. We then explain how the header is added to *PE32* files, reveal the meaning behind the *ProdID*s, and present our algorithm for generating the hashes used to obfuscate the header.

3.1 Core Structure

During building, the Microsoft Linker (`link.exe`), via calling the function *CbBuildProdidBlock* [18], adds the Rich Header to the resulting binary. Although this action is performed during the building of the COFF Header, it is undocumented in the Microsoft specification [13] and begins before the official start of the COFF Header, as designated by the symbol e_lfanew in the MS-DOS stub. Additionally, this field is ubiquitous and cannot be disabled by compilation flags or by selecting

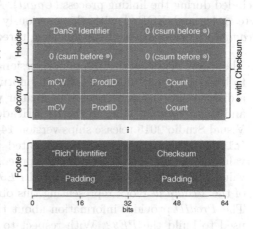

Fig. 2. Structure of the Rich Header

different binary formats. The only notable exception is when the linker is not leveraged. For example, *.NET* executable files do not use the MSVC linker and these executables do not contain a detectable Rich Header.

The Rich Header has been added as far back as 1998 with the release of Microsoft VC++ 6. Since then, each iteration of the Microsoft Toolchain adjusts how the header is generated and updates the *ProdID* mapping that the MSVC can generate. However, we suspect that this header has been included prior to VC++ 6. This is because we can have seen evidence of a potential Rich Header like field in samples that were generated before the release of VC++ 6. Unfortunately, it was not possible to confirm this belief because we were unable to obtain an older version of the Microsoft Linker and received only a smattering of samples generated before 1998.

Diving deeper, the generated structure of the Rich Header is composed of three distinct sections: the header, an array of *@comp.id* blocks, and the footer, as Fig. 2 depicts. Together, these provide four core pieces of information: (*i*) a checksum composed from a subset of the *PE32* MS-DOS header and the *@comp.id*s, (*ii*) the *ProdID* used when building the binary, (*iii*) the minor version information for the compiler used when building the product, and (*iv*) the number of times the linker leveraged the product during building.

The header of the Rich Header is composed of four blocks where each is 0x04 bytes in length. The first block contains the ASCII representation of *"DanS"*— it is speculated that *"DanS"* probably refers to *Daniel Spalding* who ran the linker team in 1998 [2]—while the next three blocks contain null padding. During linking, this section is XORed with a generated checksum value that is contained in the footer of the Rich Header.

The next section of the Rich Header is represented by an array of *@comp.id* blocks. Each block is 0x08 bytes in length and contains information related to the Product Identifier (*ProdID*), the minor version information for the compiler used to create the product (*mCV*), and the number of times the product was included during the linking process (*Count*). All fields are stored in little endian byte order and XORed with the previously mentioned checksum value. The *@comp.id* block consists of the following three values:

1. The *mCV* field contains the minor version information for the compiler used to build the *PE32* file. This version information allows the establishment of a direct relationship between a particular version of the Microsoft Toolchain and this *@comp.id* block in the Rich Header. For example, Microsoft's latest Visual Studio 2015 release ships version 14.00.23918 of the MSVC compiler (cl.exe). Therefore, object files created by this compiler will contain the value of 0x5d6e. During the linking process for the building of a *PE32*, the value will be added into the produced *PE32*'s Rich Header in the *mCV* field of the *@comp.id* block representing this object.
2. The *ProdID* provides information about the identity or type of the objects used to build the *PE32*. With respect to type, each Visual Studio Version produces a distinct range of values for this field. These values indicate whether the referenced object was a C/C++ file, an assembly blob, or a resource file before compilation as well as a subset of the compilation flags. For example, a C file compiled with Visual Studio 2015 will result in the value 0x104 being copied into the Rich Header as *ProdID* in all *PE32* files that include the respective object file.
3. The *Count* field indicates how often the object identified by the former two fields is referenced by this *PE32* file. Using a simple C program as an example, this fields will hold the value 0x1 zero-extended to span 32 bits, indicating that the object file is used once by the *PE32*.

The final section of the Rich Header, the footer, is composed of three blocks of information. The first block is 0x04 bytes in length and represents the ASCII equivalent of *"Rich"*. The next 0x04 bytes are the checksum value that are used as the XOR key for enciphering the Rich Header. The final block section is used as padding, typically null, and ensures that the total length of the Rich Header is a multiple of 8. Unlike the previous two sections, the footer is not XORed with the checksum value.

3.2   Hashes Contained Within the Rich Header

In the Rich Header, the checksum value appears at four distinct places, as shown in Fig. 2. The first three occurrences are located immediately after the ASCII equivalent of "DanS". As the linker initially places null values in this location, they only appear after the header is XORed with the checksum value. The final checksum is located in the footer and immediately after the ASCII equivalent of "Rich".

While checksum values are traditionally straight forward to generate, the Rich Header's checksum has interesting properties. Specifically, only 37 of each *@comp.id*'s 64 bits are calculated. As such, we present the following algorithm[2], based on our reverse engineering work, which produces a valid Rich Header checksum.

The Rich Header checksum is composed of two distinct values c_d and c_r that are summed together. To calculate c_r, we define the rol operator, which zero extends its first argument to 32 bits and then performs a rotate left operation equal to the second arguments value of the first argument's bits. We define rol as:

$$\mathrm{rol}(val, num) := ((val \ \texttt{<<} \ num) \ \texttt{\&} \ \texttt{0xffffffff}) \ | $$
$$| \ (val \ \texttt{>>} \ (32 - num))$$

where << and >> denote logical left and right shift, and | and & are the binary OR/AND operators. Then, the distinct parts of the checksum *csum* are calculated in the following way:

1. For c_d, all bytes contained in the MS-DOS header with the "*e_lfanew*" field (offset 0x3c) set to 0 are rotated to the left by their position relative to the beginning of the MS-DOS header and summed together. Zeroing the "*e_lfanew*" field is required as the linker can not fill in this value because it does not know the final size of the Rich Header. Therefore is unable to calculate the offset to the next header. Let n denote the length of the MS-DOS header in bytes (most commonly 0x80) and let DOS$_i$ be the i-th byte of the (modified) MS-DOS header:

$$c_d = \sum_{i=0}^{n} \mathrm{rol}(\mathrm{DOS}_i, i)$$

---

[2] For a copy of the checksum algorithm, please see Sect. 8.

2. To calculate c_r, the algorithm first retrieves the list of m @comp.id blocks. Then the algorithm combines the corresponding mCV and ProdID parts into one 32 bit value. Finally, this value is rotated to the left by its respective Count value:

$$c_r = \sum_{j=0}^{m} \text{rol}(ProdID_j \text{ << } 16 \mid mCV_j, Count_j \text{ \& } \texttt{0x1f})$$

It is noteworthy that despite the fact that Count beings as a 32 bit field, the checksum algorithm only considers the least significant byte value (& 0xff). Combined with the fact that $m \equiv n \mod 32 \implies \text{rol}(v, n) = \text{rol}(v, m)$, it is sufficient to perform the calculation as indicated above.

The two values c_d and c_r, and the size of the MS-DOS header (0x80) are then added together to form the final checksum value:

$$\text{csum} = \texttt{0x80} + c_d + c_r$$

3.3 Generation of @comp.id and ProdID

The @comp.id is generated for each object file before linking. The type of the object being created is determined during the creation of the object file. With this information, the respective generator (see Table 1) will then assign a ProdID and mCV that map to object type and the Visual Studio release version in

Table 1. Subset of ProdIDs generated by Visual Studio 2015

ProdID	VS Release	Object Type	Generator
0x105	2015	C++	c2.dll via cl.exe
0x104	2015	C	c2.dll via cl.exe
0x103	2015	Assembly	c2.dll via ml.exe
0x102	2015	Linker	link.exe
0x101	2015	Imported sym	c2.dll via cl.exe
0x100	2015	Exported sym	c2.dll via cl.exe
0xff	2015	Resource file	cvtres.exe

which the object was compiled.[3] For instance, a ProdID value of 255 to 261 corresponds to a Visual Studio 2015 Resource, Export, Import, Linker, Assembler, C, and a C++ file respectively. The same range of values can be shifted to base values 0xab, 0xcf, and 0xe1 which correspond to Visual Studio 2010, 2012, and 2013. Additionally, the ProdID is adjusted based on the compilation flags used to create the object. To date we have identified that the MSVC Toolchain is capable of assigning 265 ProdID. During our research we found that the generated ProdIDs cannot be manually changed without patching the compiler backend.

In cases where a ProdID is already present, such as a third party static library (.lib) containing multiple object files, the linker uses the preexisting ProdIDs and mCVs. Inside of the library, the data is represented as a linked list. Interestingly enough, in our research we have found that these ProdIDs do not

---

[3] For a mapping of ProdIDs that the MSVC Toolchain can generate, see Sect. 8.

necessarily correlate to what the MSVC Toolchain can generate. Specifically, we have identified 251 *ProdID*s that cannot be generated by MSVC and appear to map to either a bundled library or the libraries supplied by major corporations.

3.4 Adding the Rich Header to the *PE32* File Format

During the build process, the section that generates the data contained in the Rich Header is located in the Microsoft Compiler backend (c2.dll). The Microsoft Linker (link.exe) then collects the data required to build the Rich Header and places it in the generated *PE32* file.

4 Statistical Analysis

To study the effectiveness of using the Rich Header for triage operations, we developed a custom extractor and studied the values extracted across approximately one million malware samples.

4.1 Data Sources

We leveraged four sets of *PE32* samples during our evaluation. The first set is composed of 964,816 randomly selected malicious *PE32* samples from 2015 and is supplied by VirusShare [19]. The second set contains 1875 samples from the Mediyes dropper [28]. The third set contains 2031 samples related to the Zeus derivative Citadel [21]. The final set is composed of 293 samples associated to the APT1 espionage group [4].

In total, these binaries represent a diverse set of malware types that range from traditional criminal malware, highly advanced state-sponsored malware, and programs which have not been confirmed to be malicious but are highly suspicious. It is worth to mention that in order to study the effectiveness of the Rich Header during triage, we made no efforts towards unpacking or deobfuscating these samples.

4.2 Extracting the Rich Header

While the Rich Header has been identified for a number of years, to our knowledge, no articles have completely and accurately explained the header's structure. As a result, we found that most common triage engines and libraries that parse the *PE32* Headers either ignore, do not fully process, or perform incorrect parsing of the Rich Header. For example, two of the most common and openly available malware triage systems, Viper and MITRE's CRITs, do not properly extract this field. In the case of Viper, the supplied *PE32* Header extractor ignores the Rich Header field entirely, whereas CRITs will attempt to process the Rich Header but performs an incomplete extraction. Specifically, CRITs will only process the first 0x80 bytes of the Rich Header and does not extract the fields contained in the @comp.id data structure. Unfortunately, this is not unique to triage systems. When looking at major *PE32* parsing libraries, we found that the very popular PEFile has a similar issue to CRITs in that it also only parses the first 0x80 bytes of the Rich Header and also does not extract the values contained in the *@comp.id*. Furthermore, the *PE32* extraction script, `pescanner.py`, from the Malware Analyst's Cookbook [9] ignored the Rich Header field entirely. Last, when the Rich Header is attempted to be parsed, we have found it to be common to only attempt to identify the Rich Header at location 0x80. As a result, we developed a custom service to accurately extract the Rich Header information.

4.3   Information Gathering

To generate our information we used an automated infrastructure based on SKALD that executed five services across our datasets [25]. These services (*i*) extracted the Rich Header using our custom tool, (*ii*) performed Yara signature matching with 12,693 signatures provided by YaraExchange [15], (*iii*) retrieved malicious scan results from VirusTotal, (*iv*) performed identification on the compiler and any potential packer used to create the sample, and (*v*) generated pseudocode via IDA Pro.

4.4   Statistical Results

With our gathered information we performed a series of statistical studies. This was done to better understand the Rich Header's prevalence in malicious samples and identify which packers or compilers omit the Rich Header. Additionally, we developed a statistical check that is capable of rapidly identifying packed and post-modified *PE32* files, leveraging data only contained within the Rich Header.

Samples with a Rich Header. We identified that a surprisingly high percentage of samples contain the Rich Header, as shown in Table 2. For instance 71% of the random sample set and 98% of APT1 sample set contained parseable versions of the Rich Header.

Table 2. Samples containing a Rich Header with total percentages rounded

Family	Total	Rich Header	Percent
Random Set	964,816	683,238	71%
APT1	292	286	98%
Zeus-Citadel	1928	717	37%
Mediyes	1873	30	2%

This is surprising as our initial assumption was that malware authors would use a variety of compilers when creating samples and potentially attempt to strip the Rich Header. However, the results show that the majority of malware authors are in fact leveraging the Microsoft Linker and pay no mind to the Rich Header.

Based on the above information, we conclude that the Rich Header is commonly found in malware and that malware authors do not deliberately strip the Rich Header. Furthermore, we can conclude that compilation of malicious binaries are most often done using compilers that leverage the Microsoft Linker.

Compilers and Packers without a Rich Header. While the high rate for malware containing a Rich Header is positive for triage, this was not a uniform result. Specifically, some malware variants reported a low match for samples containing the Rich Header, such as Mediyes reporting 2%. In Sect. 2.2 we discussed that the Rich Header is generated by the Microsoft Linker. This implies that compilation tools not using the official Microsoft Linker should not generate the Rich Header. While this can explain why some samples do not include the Rich Header, in this section we further explore other reasons behind the absence of the field. Specifically, we identify common tools and packers used by malware to either strip or corrupt the Rich Header.

To do this we used our service that performs compiler and packer identification to scan all samples without a Rich Header. This was done to identify if there are any commonalities with these sample. As Table 3 shows, the percentage of samples built by either Borland C++ Builder or MinGW, which is based on GCC, is relatively high and accounts for approximately a third of all samples that do not contain a Rich Header in the random and Zeus-Citadel datasets. However, this was not the case in the APT1 and Mediyes dataset. Upon further analysis, we identified that most packers, while sometimes introducing anomalies, did not often strip the Rich Header from samples. With respect to the Mediyes set, we had a high rate of matches for the Themida Packer [23]. As we discuss further in Sect. 4.4, Themida is one of the packers that rewrites the entire *PE32* file and does not include the Rich Header. Instead, we identified that the absence of a Rich Header was a result of corruption caused during the packing of the sample.

Table 3. Samples not containing a Rich Header

Family	Total	Rich Header	Percent
Random Set	964,816	683,238	71%
APT1	292	286	98%
Zeus-Citadel	1928	717	37%
Mediyes	1873	30	2%

To identify if other packers caused similar corruption, we leveraged our identification service again to detect the most common packers used by our malware datasets. Our results showed that UPX, ASPacker, mingw, dUP, and the Nullsoft Scriptable Install System were the top five most commonly used packers. As we already understood that samples created with mingw and dUP will remove or otherwise corrupt the Rich Header, we manually created test samples with variants of UPX (v1, v2, and v3.91), ASPacker, and Nullsoft. In every manual test case, we were unable to cause a corruption or exclusion of the Rich Header field.

Identifying Modified Binaries Based on Rich Header Corruption. In our previous results, we found that it was uncommon for malware authors to deliberately strip the Rich Header. As such, we re-evaluated our samples to search for cases where the Rich Header was inadvertently corrupted.

The first approach we took was to identify cases where the Rich Header contained duplicate *@comp.id* blocks. We took this approach because under normal operation, the Microsoft Linker should never produce duplicate entries. This is because during the linking process, the Microsoft Linker will search for existing instances of the *ProdID* and *mCV* and if identified, will increment the number of times it was used, *Count*, to the existing entry.

The second approach we took was to re-calculate the Rich Header checksum and compare it to the sample's reported Rich Header checksum. This was done as an unsuccessful check would indicate that either the MS-DOS Header or the Rich Header was modified after the linking process; potentially revealing Trojanized or post modified binaries.

As Table 4 shows, the amount of malicious samples containing a corrupted Rich Header varies and can rise upwards to 50% based on the malware family. Additionally, across the random one million dataset, this corruption occurred approximately 31% of the time. Knowing this and the fact that no official Microsoft Linker should produce these forms of corruption, identifying corruption of the Rich Header can be a fast and efficient triage step to use for screening samples for potential maliciousness.

@comp.id and mCV Values Present in Malware. To develop an understanding of how we can potentially leverage the Rich Header for more advanced triage operations, we studied the *@comp.id* values in our malware datasets. By doing so, we identified 516 unique *ProdID*s. This was surprising as all versions of the MSVC Toolchain, dating back to VS++ 6, are only capable of generating 265 *ProdID*s. While researching the 251 unknown *ProdID*s, we identified that these appear to more than likely correlate to bundled libraries and major corporations. However, while in practice this assumption appears to be accurate, we cannot conclusively confirm this.

Digging in deeper, we discussed in Sect. 3 that the *ProdID* is paired with the *mCV*. Thus, potentially providing more fine grained information for identifying specific objects. To confirm this we created tuples of all the *ProdID* and *mCV* pairings. We then single out

Table 4. Samples containing a Rich Header that have duplicate entries and invalid checksums

Family	Total	Dup. ID	csum Err
Random Set	683,238	15,006	137,965
APT1	286	0	34
Zeus-Citadel	717	17	357
Mediyes	30	0	0

29,460 distinct *ProdID* and *mCV* pairs across our approximately one million malware samples. These numbers show relatively substantial variability in the *@comp.id*s found in malware and malware authors build environments.

5   Case Study

The data obtained in Sect. 4 showed promise in using the Rich Header for more complex triage operations. This is especially true considering the vast majority of our datasets are from the same date range and the fact that the Rich Headers of malicious samples contain numerous *@comp.id*s along with the number of times the object was used during linking.

In order to demonstrate the potential of leveraging the Rich Header in future work, we created a basic proof of concept machine learning algorithm. The algorithm was designed to only process the *@comp.id* values contained in the Rich Header. Specifically, the values for *ProdID, Count*, and *mCV*. As the Rich Header identifies linked object and version information of the build environment, our algorithm is specifically focused on identifying similar samples, based on linked objects, and also samples using a similar build environment. In crafting the algorithm, we used a feature hashing strategy which transformed the features into a *50-dimensional* vector. We then leveraged a *Stacked Autoencoder* to turn our data into a denser, lower-dimensional space. Finally, in order to improve performance and allow us to scale to support datasets containing millions of malware samples, we utilized a *Ball Tree* for fast storage and retrieval of the vectors.

In the following case studies, we demonstrate the ability of solely using the Rich Header to perform similarity matching leveraging our proof of concept machine learning algorithm. In the case studies, we compare the exemplar samples, selected at random, with the collected vector similarities from the *Ball Tree* populated by the random one million, APT1, and Zeus-Citadel datasets, and analyze their closest matches. For our ground truth in the case studies, we compare the results of our algorithm to the results returned by Kaspersky and Symantec Antivirus, as implemented by VirusTotal, and perform manual reverse engineering. We selected this ground truth method primarily due to the limited matches across Yara and the high percentage of no detection or generic signatures across the other popular AV vendors.

5.1   Similarity Matching with the APT1 Dataset

We selected three exemplar samples from the APT1 dataset for our first case study. APT1 was selected as the actor is a relatively skilled APT and 98% of the samples in the APT1 dataset contain a Rich Header.

We randomly selected our first exemplar sample, E1. Kaspersky classifies this sample as *HEUR:Trojan.Win32.Generic* which means that through heuristic analysis, Kaspersky believes that this is a Trojan but has not classified the sample further. When querying our algorithm, we identified that it had an identical Rich Header feature vector with another APT1 sampled, which we will refer to as E1-R1. Inspecting E1-R1, Kaspersky classified the sample also as *HEUR:Trojan.Win32.Generic*. While a generic classification does not tell us much, manual analysis of the generated source code, produced by IDA Pro, confirmed that these two samples were in fact identical.

Going a step further, we then queried the nearest neighbor to E1. This returned three samples: E1-N-R1, E1-N-R2, and E1-N-R3. All three matches were also contained in the APT1 dataset and shared the *HEUR:Trojan.Win32.Generic* Kaspersky classification. Our algorithm reported that the distance between these vectors was 1; the smallest possible difference without the vectors being identical.

We then performed manual analysis and identified that the generated source code produced by IDA Pro for E1-N-R1 was identical to our exemplar. However, as the vectors were slightly off, we further analyzed the cause for this and concluded that the variance was caused by slightly different build environments when compiling the binaries.

The other two nearest neighbor matches, E1-N-R2 and E1-N-R3, produced even more interesting results. In both cases, the generated source code produced by IDA Pro had slight differences. In the case of E1-N-R3, E1-N-R3 adds a call to function $FlushFileBuffers$ right after it writes the buffer to a file. Furthermore, E1-N-R2 seemed to build upon the changes made to E1-N-R3. Specifically, E1-N-R2 includes an additional change in that E1-N-R2 adjusted how it wrote the buffer to files. In our exemplar sample, E1 first writes the buffer to the file and then performs a second write that adds \r\n to the file. In the case of E1-N-R2, the sample does not write \r\n to the file and instead calls strcat on the buffer in order to add \n to the buffer before it writes the buffer to the file.

Our second exemplar, E2, was selected from the APT1 dataset because its signature was different than E1 and it shares its feature vector with no other samples. After running our algorithm, we identified E2-N-R1 as the nearest neighbor to E2 at a distance of 1.732. While it is reasonable to argue that the distance is very near, it is indicative of a clear similarity between the samples.

When analyzing the results, both E2 and E2-N-R1 are classified by Kaspersky as "Agents". However, the generated source code produced by IDA Pro for both samples is quite different and the programs have different functionality. To understand why our algorithm identified this as a match, we performed additional research on the binaries and found that both E2 and E2-N-R1 are very small, had a nearly identical import table with only one variation, and were packed with Armadillo v1.71. Looking at the Rich Header vectors we found that the vast majority of the objects imported all had identical version information; which led us to conclude that the samples were more than likely built on the same machine or the machines at least had an identical build environment. Open-source research further validated this opinion as both samples were used by APT1 in cyber operations [20]. While not a direct match in terms of functionality, this example demonstrates the power in using the Rich Header to identify not only similarly behaving malware but also malware that is related because the malware is presumably built on the same machine.

Our final exemplar, E3, was selected as it had five samples that shared the same Rich Header feature vector: E3-R1, E3-R2, E3-R3, E3-R4, and E3-R5. In all cases, these samples ended up being members of the APT1 dataset and shared the $HEUR:Trojan.Win32.Generic$ Kaspersky classification. Manual reverse engineering also showed that the samples shared a nearly identical code base and performed the same functionality.

We then queried our algorithm for the nearest neighbors to E3 that were not in the APT1 sample set. The query returned six samples at a distance of 2.236: E3-N-R1, E3-N-R2, E3-N-R3, E3-N-R4, E3-N-R5, and E3-N-R6. Kaspersky classified E3-N-R2, E3-N-R4, E3-N-R5, and E3-N-R6 as

HEUR:Trojan.Win32.Generic. E3-N-R1 and E3-N-R3 were classified by Kaspersky at *Net-Worm.Win32.Cynic.in* and *Net-Worm.Win32.Cynic.am*, respectively. However, although the Kaspersky classifications were different, manual analysis revealed that all E3-N-R* samples were nearly identical to themselves. The only differences between the samples in this cluster were caused by artifacts left by the obfuscation engines and by the language settings on the build environment. Furthermore, the two clusters for the same vector, E3 and E3-R*, and nearest neighbors, E3-N-R*, were remarkably similar in functionality.

During the evaluation we identified that the similarity matching algorithm produced very strong results for the exemplar samples E1 and E3. However, with E2 and E3, the algorithm further identified samples of similar nature and with a similar build environment.

5.2   Similarity Matching with the Zeus-Citadel Dataset

In this case study we opted to explore the results of two exemplar samples from the Zeus-Citadel botnet. We selected this dataset because the Zeus-Citadel actors are typical of basic cyber criminals and as such have a different target and mission than the actors behind the first test case.

Kaspersky classified our first exemplar, E4, as a generic Trojan. Our algorithm though was able to identify 23 similar samples, E4-R*, that shared the feature vector of E4. Kaspersky classified them as either *HEUR:Trojan.Win32.Generic* or *not-a-virus:AdWare.Win32.FakeDownloader.ac* whereas Symantec identifies all the E4-R* samples as *Trojan.Gen* or *Trojan.Zbot*. When comparing the IDA Pro generated source code, we confirmed that the E4 and E4-R* samples were nearly identical; the differences in E4 and E4-R1 are that sections of the code has moved under different functions and that E4 uses a "for loop" while R4-R1 uses a "do while" for their XOR algorithm. Thus, the difference in E4 and E4-R* appear to be related to slightly different version, compiler optimization, or artifacts left by the obfuscation engines.

When looking at the nearest neighbor cluster for E4 we identified four additional samples: E4-N-R1, E4-N-R2, E4-N-R3, E4-N-R4. While Kaspersky classified the sample as *HEUR:Trojan.Win32.Generic*, Symantec identified E4-N-R1 and E4-N-R3 as clean. However, when looking at the samples, we observed only a slight variation in that E4-N-R* ran the XOR loop 220,712 times where E4 and E4-R* ran the XOR loop 51,700 times. As with E4-R*, E4-N-R* also moved code segments into different functions. When verifying the Rich Header we observed that the reason for being classified as a nearest neighbor was because of variations in the number of times one product was included. This is a clear example where using Rich Header values as a triage system could prove useful for an investigative team by identify similar malware samples from potentially different version.

The next exemplar, E5, shares its vector hash with 36,606 samples. This is notably high, no less so due to the fact that Kaspersky fails to identify 16,123 of those samples with a classification of any kind, not even the most generic of names. However, when comparing the IDA Pro generated source code, we observed only small variations; specifically the value for a constant was changed.

The nearest neighbor grouping for, E5, has a distance of 2 and contained a total of 1,567 samples, where 511 samples have no Kaspersky listing. In fact, the majority of samples in both groups are listed as generic Trojans, *HEUR:Trojan.Win32.Generic*. While the inclusion of a known Zeus-Citadel sample is not enough to convict these samples as Zeus-Citadel members, it provides an interesting jumping off point for analysis.

5.3   Similarity Matching with the Mediyes Dataset

In our final case study, we selected a random Mediyes sample, E6, to use as our exemplar. We chose this sample because it would allow us to perform an out-of-set comparisons as the Mediyes dataset was not originally vectorized and included in the *Ball Tree*.

Querying our algorithm for identical Rich Header feature vectors, we received a list of 266 other samples: E6-R*. When querying for the nearest neighbors we receive 86 additional samples, E6-N-R*, with a distance of 1. Analysis of the IDA Pro generated source code showed a strong correlation between the samples. Furthermore, the vast majority of both E6-N-R* and E6-R* were classified by Kaspersy as Zango samples; an instance of adware frequently associated with Mediyes.

6   Future Work and Limitations

In this paper we present an important yet little-studied header of *PE32*, the Rich Header. We show that the Rich Header has been largely ignored by malware authors and is not removed by most packers and obfuscation engines. In fact, 71% of the 964,816 samples in our random dataset include the Rich Header. Our experiments revealed that the Rich Header contains useful information that can be leveraged by defenders; analysis of the data contained within the header allows for the rapid triage of samples using a cost effective approach. This is true even for samples that are stripped and contain little to no *PE32* Header information.

We strongly believe that by leveraging the Rich Header, current and future triage algorithms will perform a more accurate and cost effective triage functionality. In future work, we will explore how to combine the Rich Header features with other aspects of the *PE32* file format to generate robust similarly matching and clustering algorithms. As the Rich Header artifacts helps to identify similar malware as well as characterizing the build environment in which the malware was built, this presents new opportunities for attribution and tool-chain identification.

Furthermore, as knowledge of the Rich Header grows, it is understandable that malware authors will attempt to obfuscate this field. This is an expected outcome but also presents interesting future work potentials when the Rich Header is combined with additional features. This is because leveraging compiler finger-printing and additional *PE32* header information can be used to determine if the Rich Header should be included and approximate the expectant values of this field. As such, future algorithms can identify anomalies in the Rich Header field. This increases the complexity required when performing obfuscation and adds resiliency.

7   Related Work

Leveraging the data derived from the *PE32* file format has been widely explored for triage purposes. One common technique, as shown by Mandiant's Imphash, is to generate a hash of the values located in the *PE32* Import Address Table (IAT) [11]. These hashes are then used in analytic queries and by machine learn-ing algorithms to identify similar strains and families of malware. In this vein, JPCERT recently released Impfuzzy to improve upon this technique through incorporation of a fuzzy hash [24]. However, these algorithms require accurate IAT and their accuracy is greatly reduced if the malware strips or otherwise provides a misleading IAT.

In light of this issue, more advanced techniques use additional meta data that can be derived from the *PE32* file format. For example, PEHash uses the structural characteristics of the *PE32* file format to generate hashes that are then used in clustering operations [26]. Unfortunately, the above methods only work well when the data is available and not being misconstrued.

Identifying the weaknesses in this approaches, specifically PEHash's lack of robustness, Jacob et al. [5] expand upon these method by focusing their efforts on the *PE32*'s code section. While this approach is more tamper resistant, it is still not immune. On the other side of the spectrum, Perdisci et al. [16] focused their efforts on using patter recognition to identify packed samples and then send those samples to universal unpacking algorithms before matching occurs. However, while this process does reduce the cost and improve the accuracy in clustering and similarity matching, unpackers are known to be unreliable and exceedingly expensive [12, 16].

In a change of pace, our work illustrates a hidden aspect of the *PE32* file format, the Rich Header, that has been largely ignored by malware authors. Using this section of the *PE32* file formation, we show how to cheaply identify packed malware, perform similarity matching solely using this field, and identify malware that was created using similar build environments. Our work does not aim to directly compete with the existing research. Instead the knowledge gained from our novel approach aims to be a catalyst for triage when combined with these, and other, triage techniques. In turn, this work enables existing and future algorithms to provide better results, be more resistant to tampering due to the wider scope, and improve returned information by allowing matching based not just on the samples characteristics but also the characteristics of the build environment used to create the samples.

8   Conclusion

In this paper we performed an in-depth study of the Rich Header and showed its significant potential in being leveraged for triaging malicious samples. To the best of our knowledge, this assessment of the Rich Header is the most complete and accurate report for this hidden and undisclosed section of the *PE32* header so far. With this knowledge, we created a custom Rich Header parser and extracted the headers' contents in over 964,816 malicious samples. We demonstrated the Rich Header's potential in enabling the rapid triage of malicious samples. By doing so, we showed how to leverage the Rich Header to identify post-modified and packed *PE32* files, detecting 84% of the known packed malware samples. We also demonstrate the value in leveraging the Rich Header by developing a proof of concept machine learning algorithm and performing three case studies. In these studies we are capable of rapidly returning results in 6.73 ms using a single CPU core, identifying similar malware variants, and highlight malware developed under the same build environments.

Availability

The feature extraction methods and additional reference material have been open-sourced under the Apache2 license. They can be freely downloaded at the following location:
    https://holmesprocessing.github.io

Acknowledgments. We thank our shepherd Pavel Laskov and the reviewers for their valuable feedback. We are thankful to the Technical University of Munich for providing ample infrastructure to support our development efforts. Additionally, we thank the the German Federal Ministry of Education and Research under grant 16KIS0327 (IUNO) and the Bavarian State Ministry of Education, Science and the Arts as part of the FORSEC research association for providing funding for our infrastructure. We would also like to thank the United States Air Force for sponsoring George Webster in his academic pursuit. Lastly, we would like to thank Microsoft Digital Crimes Unit, VirusTotal, and Yara Exchange for their support and valuable discussions.

References

1. Binsalleeh, H., Ormerod, T., Boukhtouta, A., Sinha, P., Youssef, A., Debbabi, M., Wang, L.: On the analysis of the zeus botnet crimeware toolkit. In: Annual International Conference on Privacy Security and Trust (PST) (2010)
2. RCE Cafe. Microsoft's Rich Signature (Undocumented) - Comments, February 2008. http://rcecafe.net/?p=27
3. Chiang, K., Lloyd, L.: A case study of the rustock rootkit and spam bot. In: The First Workshop in Understanding Botnets (2007)
4. Mandiant Intelligence. APT1: Exposing One of China's Cyber Espionage Units. 2013. Mandian.com

5. Jacob, G., Comparetti, P.M., Neugschwandtner, M., Kruegel, C., Vigna, G.: A static, packer-agnostic filter to detect similar malware samples. In: Flegel, U., Markatos, E., Robertson, W. (eds.) DIMVA 2012. LNCS, vol. 7591, pp. 102–122. Springer, Heidelberg (2013). doi:10.1007/978-3-642-37300-8_6

6. Kendall, K., McMillan, C.: Practical malware analysis. In: Black Hat Conference, USA (2007)

7. Kolosnjaji, B., Zarras, A., Lengyel, T., Webster, G., Eckert, C.: Adaptive semantics-aware malware classification. In: Caballero, J., Zurutuza, U., Rodríguez, R.J. (eds.) DIMVA 2016. LNCS, vol. 9721, pp. 419–439. Springer, Cham (2016). doi:10.1007/978-3-319-40667-1_21

8. Lifewire. Things They Didn't Tell You About MS Link and the PE Header (29A) (2004)

9. Ligh, M., Adair, S., Hartstein, B., Richard, M.: Malware Analyst's Cookbook and DVD: Tools and Techniques for Fighting Malicious Code. Wiley Publishing, Indianapolis (2010)

10. Lyda, R., Hamrock, J.: Using entropy analysis to find encrypted and packed malware. IEEE Secur. Priv. **2**, 40–45 (2007)

11. Mandiant. Tracking Malware With Import Hashing, January 2014. https://www.fireeye.com/blog/threat-research/2014/01/tracking-malware-import-hashing.html

12. Martignoni, L., Christodorescu, M., Jha, S.: OmniUnpack: fast, generic, and safe unpacking of malware. In: Annual Computer Security Applications Conference (ACSAC) (2007)

13. Microsoft. Microsoft Portable Executable and Common Object File Format Specification, Rev. 8.3 (2013)

14. Microsoft. Common Object File Format - KB121460 (2016). https://support.microsoft.com/en-us/kb/121460

15. Parkour, M., DiMino, A.: Deepend research, May 2015. http://www.deependresearch.org/2012/08/yara-signature-exchange-google-group.htm

16. Perdisci, R., Lanzi, A., Lee, W.: Classification of packed executables for accurate computer virus detection. Pattern Recognit. Lett. **29**(14), 1941–1946 (2008)

17. Pietrek, M.: An in-depth look into the win32 portable executable file format. MSDN Mag. **17**(2), 80–90 (2002)

18. Pistelli, D.: Microsoft's Rich Signature (Undocumented) (2012)

19. Roberts, J.-M.: Virus share, April 2016. https://virusshare.com/

20. Sarméjeanne, S.: The HTran tool used to hack into french companies, August 2011. https://www.lexsi.com/securityhub/the-htran-tool-used-to-hack-into-french-companies/?lang=en

21. Sherstobitoff, R.: Inside the world of the citadel trojan. Emergence **9** (2012)

22. Stephen, T.: Rich Header, January 2008. http://trendystephen.blogspot.de/2008/01/rich-header.html

23. Oreans Technologies. Themida - Advanced Windows Software Protection System, January 2016. http://www.oreans.com/themida.php

24. Tomonaga, S.: Classifying malware using import API and fuzzy hashing -impfuzzy-, May 2016. http://blog.jpcert.or.jp/2016/05/classifying-mal-a988.html

25. Webster, G.D., Hanif, Z.D., Ludwig, A.L.P., Lengyel, T.K., Zarras, A., Eckert, C.: SKALD: a scalable architecture for feature extraction, multi-user analysis, and real-time information sharing. In: Bishop, M., Nascimento, A.C.A. (eds.) ISC 2016. LNCS, vol. 9866, pp. 231–249. Springer, Cham (2016). doi:10.1007/978-3-319-45871-7_15

26. Wicherski, G.: peHash: a novel approach to fast malware clustering. In: USENIX Workshop on Large-Scale Exploits and Emergent Threats (LEET) (2009)

27. Yan, W., Zhang, Z., Ansari, N.: Revealing packed malware. IEEE Secur. Priv. **6**(5), 65–69 (2008)
28. Zakorzhevsky, V.: Mediyes - the dropper with a valid signature, March 2012. https://securelist.com/blog/research/32397/mediyes-the-dropper-with-a-valid-signature-8/

Cyber-physical Systems

Last Line of Defense: A Novel IDS Approach Against Advanced Threats in Industrial Control Systems

Mark Luchs[1]($\boxtimes$) and Christian Doerr[2]($\boxtimes$)

[1] Department of Offshore and Dredging Engineering, Delft University of Technology,
Mekelweg 4, 2628 CD Delft, The Netherlands
m.luchs@tudelft.nl
[2] Cybersecurity Group, Delft University of Technology,
Mekelweg 4, 2628 CD Delft, The Netherlands
c.doerr@tudelft.nl

Abstract. Industrial control systems are becoming increasingly inter-connected, and with it their vulnerability to malicious actors. While intrusion detection systems are suited to detect network-based attacks, they remain unable to detect more sophisticated attacks against control systems, for example a compromise of the PLCs. This paper makes the case that the evolving landscape of threats such as the Stuxnet malware requires an alternative approach to intrusion detection in industrial control systems. We argue that effective control of such advanced threats needs to happen in the last link of the control network, hence building a last line of defense. A proof of concept of this new paradigm was implemented for the control system of a dredging vessel, and we describe main lessons learned and pose open research questions we find based on these experiences for ICS intrusion detection.

Keywords: Cyber physical security · Intrusion detection · Industrial control systems

1 Introduction

Industrial control systems (ICS) monitor and control physical systems, forming a cooperative bond between the digital and the physical world. They are to be found, amongst others, in critical infrastructures, building monitoring or production systems [1]. In recent years these systems are becoming increasingly connected to IP-based networks or even the Internet, either indirect through corporate networks or by direct connection. As such these systems are exposed to much of the same weaknesses as traditional IT systems. The effects of their failure, though, are potentially much more severe. Causing irreparable harm to the physical system being controlled, its environment, and to the people who depend on said system [2].

M. Polychronakis and M. Meier (Eds.): DIMVA 2017, LNCS 10327, pp. 141–160, 2017.
DOI: 10.1007/978-3-319-60876-1_7

Unfortunately this potential for abuse is no longer just speculation. There exists numerous incidents resulting in significant damage, ranging from the flooding of a water treatment facility in Maroochy Australia caused by a disgruntled ex-employee with knowledge of the system and old access credentials [3], the often referenced attack on the Natanz nuclear facility in Iran by the Stuxnet malware [4–6], to the massive damage to a blast furnace in a steel mill in Germany after an attacker gained access to the control systems [7,8].

Industrial control systems security is still in its infancy [9]. Although the topic is now attracting significant attention and there are many technical solutions to protect IT environments, controls such as intrusion detection systems or firewalls are not easily bridged to ICS systems. As we argue in this paper, many of the classic IT controls are not directly applicable to ICS or would actually not provide effective mitigation against the kind of real-world attacks listed above. While firewalls, intrusion detection systems and packet inspection tools are capable of filtering out unusual traffic in regular IT systems in terms of origin, access destinations and content, this defense is less applicable for ICS systems as packets will only flow between the programmable logic controllers (PLCs) and the ICS control node. As past attacks have compromised the control node and used this host to inject malicious commands or upload malicious binaries to the field devices, these types of attacks would not stand out from a network-packet analysis: packets are still flowing between the authorized control host and the ICS devices, and also in terms of packet sizes or from a protocol-interaction standpoint no anomalies would stand out.

Given these new types of threats and potential attack vectors, we argue that a new type of intrusion detection system is needed. As intrusion detection cannot successfully detect and mitigate such advanced vectors on the process network by looking at traffic between the controller and the PLCs, ICS defense needs to move closer towards the field devices that have actually been compromised in past incidents. It is necessary to (also) apply detection and mitigation on the last link of the field network, hence drawing a last line of defense that is difficult to subvert.

This paper contains three main contributions: first, we propose the idea of rethinking IDS approaches to meet advanced threats in industrial control systems, and argue that advanced vectors can only effectively be met deep inside the control network. Together with placing an IDS deeper into the ICS, it is also necessary to extend the current approach of anomaly detection in terms of packets and network flows, by interpreting the content and context of the packets and adding knowledge about the actual ICS process into the anomaly detection. Second, we have implemented this new paradigm for the control system of a dredging vessel and evaluated in extensive simulations the utility of this new IDS paradigm. Since detection rates are highly system- and model-specific and difficult to abstract, we do not go into the performance results in this paper, but rather present a number of observations and lessons learned about building intrusion detection for industrial control systems and discuss in our view open research challenges to solve. This is our third contribution.

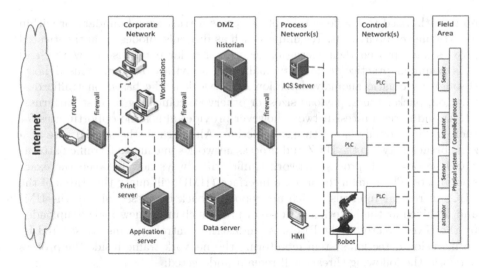

Fig. 1. Security zones and components of an industrial control system and corporate network.

The remainder of this paper is structured as follows: Sect. 2 describes the new threat model industrial control systems face, and reviews current approaches to ICS intrusion detection. Section 3 discusses related work. Section 4 presents an alternative approach to IDS design for ICS. Section 5 briefly introduces the evaluation of a prototype built to test the new design, while Sect. 6 discusses the major lessons learned. Section 7 concludes and summarizes our work.

2   Threat Model

Although industrial control systems have always posed high value targets, three major developments over the last decade have greatly increased the attack surface and risk of these systems: First, previously entirely separated systems are now routinely furnished with remote access possibilities, allowing the continuous retrieval of measurements and statistics from the industrial processes inside the business operations. Second, increased value opportunities from cyber crime have resulted in a steadily increasing influx of actors, as well as a continuously growing specialization and sophistication of these actors [10]. Third, originally state-sponsored activities such as the Stuxnet incursion have demonstrated to a wider audience the general vulnerability of these systems. We have already seen in the recent past that the ideas and source code developed by nation-state actors have proliferated towards cyber criminals, and interactions of cyber criminals [11] with ICS – accidental or intentional – such as [8] thus need to be considered in the risk analysis of such systems.

Figure 1 shows the typical system architecture of an organization operating an industrial control network inside its perimeter. The different security zones are typically enforced by firewalls or network diodes, and meant to ensure that no unauthorized traffic flows take place across a trust zone boundary or within a particular compartment. Techniques such as firewalls, diodes, or authenticated proxies have proven their merit for securing regular enterprise networks, and it is common practice to identify malicious activities or compromised hosts through automatic anomaly detection of network traffic based on traffic destination, packet types, payload sizes, or otherwise coinciding request patterns.

An industrial process network however provides almost no opportunities for such traffic anomaly-based threat detection. Although in the special case of a zone breach between the DMZ and process network some unusual traffic patterns could be observed, process network traffic will always flow between the exact same hosts. The human-to-machine-interface (HMI) will query the status of the PLCs in regular intervals, which are reported back by these units to the HMI and archived at the historian. In case of process changes, new logic is uploaded by the HMI directly to the PLCs. As industrial control systems are secured by an intrusion detection system monitoring the network traffic inside the process network, the following threats will remain undetected:

- **Incorrect operational process instructions.** Intentionally malicious or a benign operational mistake, the person controlling the system from the HMI could send incorrect commands to the devices in the field area, triggering a situation with severe consequences. From the perspective of the network there would be no anomalous flows, as commands – although unsafe ones – would be issued from the operator's station and sent to the field devices as usual. A problem could however be detected if the IDS would go beyond network-flow analysis, and parse and interpret the content of the network packets. While the packets are compliant to the protocol and also unlikely to be matched by a signature database of known threats (as commonly used by IDS), an IDS *with* knowledge about the physical process model as proposed in this paper would be able to spot a deviation from the expected state.
- **Malicious control software on PLCs.** In the example of the Natanz facility, the Stuxnet malware uploaded modified program code to the PLCs which executed malicious process logic in addition to the normal program [6]. When the devices were queried by the control host, the PLCs reported back incorrect values and did not reveal the presence of the malicious additions to the control program. Viewed from a network perspective, none of these activities would typically be flagged as abnormal: the control system would routinely upload new program code to the PLCs, query the devices and receive packets back. Even for a protocol-aware IDS, any of the packets are valid, and completely compliant with the access policy of such control network.

The sober conclusion, especially from the latter example, is that against advanced threats with the ability to modify the behavior of the PLCs itself, a mitigation approach centered around the process network is unlikely to provide merit, unless the scope of detection is greatly extended to include in-depth verification of control logic before application, as well as stringent access control and supply chain security of the field devices. Given the changing threat profile and documented instances of such incidents, we believe it is necessary to extend the risk analysis and mitigation plans for industrial control systems towards these potential threats, and given the difficulty in achieving threat localization in the process network build up an additional layer of defenses one layer deeper inside the field network. Although an advanced adversary might in theory launch an attack in which all process control variables and sensor values would remain identical to the benign scenario, a pervasive tracking of the system at the process level will reduce the degree of freedom drastically, thereby eliminating most adversaries and slowing attack progressing down significantly. The proposed IDS should only be one of many techniques in a portfolio of controls. It may however augment and complement existing controls and address other operational questions, for example the detection of wear and tear, with the additional use cases and added benefit making an adoption more likely. The following section will describe current practices in industrial control system security, Sect. 4 describes our alternative proposal for introducing security in the last link of the ICS network.

3   Related Work

Two areas of existing work are relevant for the design proposed in this paper, (a) security challenges for control systems, and (b) intrusion detection systems.

3.1   Challenges Faced by ICS

Despite the similarities between control and IT systems, such as basic components used, the challenges they face in securing them are very different. As are their responses to security breaches [2,12–14]. Three challenges which must be faced to strengthen control networks are identified; improving access controls, security inside the network, and the security management of control networks. Despite the similarities between control and IT systems, the challenges they face in securing them are quite different. Cheminod [14] additionally raises the challenge that while most ICS security studies focus on prevention and/or detection, there is relatively little research available into the response to threats. Historically these threats originate from the inside, these days this is shifting to the majority of security threats emanating from the outside.

3.2   Intrusion Detection Systems

Historically, the origin of intrusion detection systems evolved out of a set of tools mostly intended to help administrators review audit trails such as user access logs. In 1987 Denning published a paper titled "An intrusion-detection model"[15], describing what to this day remains the basis for many monitoring systems. Today, there is a large body of IDS related research available. Almost all of these focus exclusively on IT-based environments, where the offered solutions are not directly suitable for ICS environments. This applies even when underlying protocols and infrastructure used are the same [2, 12–14, 16].

Research investigating monitoring solutions for ICS environments are not completely absent, however almost all of these make use of IT based approaches such as network traffic analysis and packet inspection [17–20]. These proposed solutions are thus focussing on the protocols utilized and ignore the physical domain entirely. As such a large and presumable the most important resource is missed. Researchers have however suggested to utilize this resource and incorporate knowledge of the physical system into the workings of the IDS itself [19, 20]. By understanding the network traffic it is possible to simulate the physical, the result of which can then be used to take the physical state into account [21]. Research investigating a direct tap into the physical state by going directly to the field devices (sensors and actuators) seems to be missing however. [19] presents a taxonomy of ICS security related work. Besides presenting a new validation metric, they look into the advantages and disadvantages of different evaluation setups. Simulations here have the benefit that they are easily adaptable, and possibly provide the best method for initial proof-of-concept work. This is also reflected by the majority of the taxonomy, which rely on simulation for their validation step. Especially noteworthy is the conclusion by Urbina et al. [19] about the untreated risk if an attacker can falsify readings from the field devices itself, an issue that is mitigated by the work in this paper.

Change Detection. As part of a series of studies into the security of ICS systems, Cardenas concluded that only limited research into ICS security is available and that what is published are generally tweaks of solutions aimed at an IT environment [2, 13, 22]. As such, incorporating knowledge of the physical system might very well trigger a paradigm shift in the sector. This realization leads to the proposal of a linear mathematical model which is used to analyse the actual system and determine if an attack is ongoing. Their main aim being to *"protect the operational goals from a malicious party attacking our cyber infrastructure"*, which they separate into a two stage process: first, the detection of attacks on cyber-physical infrastructures, and second their survival [16, 23].

For the detection problem Cardenas suggest that when having knowledge on how the output sequences should react to the control input sequence it is probably possible to detect an attack by comparing this expected output with the actual received output signal. The effectiveness of this idea will depend on the quality of the estimated output signal. Further investigating this idea they created a model of a physical system and formulated an anomaly detection algorithm based on change detection. Change detection works under the assumption that a set of measurements starts out under the normal hypothesis, H_0. The thought is that this hypothesis will then be rejected in favor of the attack hypothesis H_1 at a certain measurement. To avoid making any assumptions on the probability of an actual attacker their work does not assume a parametric distribution but only puts mild constraints on the measured sequence.

Virtual Image. Having researched the effects that malware has on industrial control systems, both for the case of IT malware as samples specifically targeting ICS, [21] suggests to leverage available knowledge on the physical system to enhance its protection. Following this suggestion [24,25] does exactly that by creating an new intrusion detection system which maintains an internal representations of the physical state of the controlled systems in a virtual image. To define and build this virtual image a new formalized language has been specifically defined, which has been named Industrial State Modeling Language (ISML) [24]. The virtual image is meant to operate parallel to the monitored system, providing real time insights and analysis. At start-up the IDS will load the systems model from an XML file which comes with predefined settings and values. During operation, the IDS received a copy of the network traffic which it scans for ICS protocols. The ICS packets are then processed and the commands they contain send on towards the virtual image where they are used to update the internal representation of the control system. Each update also triggers a monitoring module that compares the (virtual) system state to a list of predefined critical states. If a match is found the IDS will raise an alarm. Implementation of a prototype and conducting of experiments have demonstrated that the proposed solution is successful, proving the approach has merit.

By adding a multidimensional metric that provides a parametric measure of the distance between a given state and the set of critical states further extends the IDS, giving it the ability to estimate future instability in the system [26]. Conducting experiments using a prototype implementation of the extended IDS demonstrated the improved functionality and that the approach indeed has merit.

Network Based. The solutions given by the research above operate on the control network, which also applies to the research discussed by [19]. These solutions obtain their information on which their system works from the network traffic between controllers and the larger ICS systems. This means that their effectiveness directly builds on the security and trust placed upon the controllers within the system. If an malicious entity is able to compromise such devices the previous solutions can be evaded.

4   A Cyber-Physical IDS Architecture

In this section we present an alternative approach for intrusion detection in control systems. Previous work such as [19,20,24,25] is centered around an anomaly detection based on information flows over the network connecting PLCs and the larger control network, which we have seen in the discussion of the threat model would not detect malicious or accidental instructions sent to the field devices or an upload of malicious control programs to the PLC. By moving intrusion detection one level deeper into the industrial control network, the field network, intrusion detection can also exploit the physical state of equipment - such as temperature and pressure readings -, as opposed to looking at network traffic

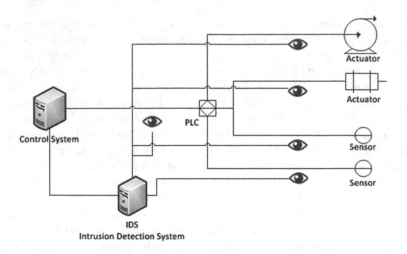

Fig. 2. The concept architecture

solely. As "communication" with the field network is analog only, a sensor would map temperature into a voltage and an actuator would switch depending on the voltage level applied to the control wire, the absence of more sophisticated data exchange provides a number of advantages for defense: first, as there is no digital communication link this makes it much harder for malware to compromise the system. Second, by monitoring these lines it is possible to obtain the raw values measured in the field area, and in combination with an analysis of packets on the control network thereby also find faulty or maliciously acting PLCs.

Figure 2 shows a conceptual view of the shift to the last link. In addition to passively observing the communication between the control system and the PLC, values are taken from all or the most important sensor and actuator connections on the other side of the PLC. This design approach provides a number of distinct advantages:

1. **Extensibility and Multi-vector Detection.** The system may be extended to include more sensors to accommodate evolving attacks and new vectors, including sensors not connected to the ICS system such as a microphone listing to the acoustics of machinery, sensors reading power usage and output of equipment, or even radio frequencies readings. One of Stuxnet's attack vectors for example cause damages by changing the spinning speed of centrifuges, causing mechanical damage. While a microphone could have easily recognized such changes, it is exemplary for additional types of sensors that are (normally) not providing input to an ICS system, but would help within the context of our IDS to detect abnormal events, making it significantly harder to launch attacks that would go unnoticed by other off-the-ICS sensors.
2. **Unmodified signal path.** Existing network-based IDS are located in between devices (here the controller and the PLCs) to scan and block malicious traffic. As scans however change the latency of communication messages,

may in some cases change packet order and the blocking of select packets within a larger control packet train may cause significant side effects, control engineers in our pre-study voiced concerns about placing such devices inside a production environment. As the proposed system does not interfere with IDS communication and control messages are interpreted off the bus, timings, packet order and the integrity of packet trains remain unmodified.

3. **Ability to detect compromised ICS infrastructure.** As the Stuxnet malware compromised both the control system as well as the PLCs reading and responding to sensor values, it was able to send back falsified sensor readings and remain unnoticed while bringing the ICS outside of the safe operating context. An IDS system reading both the state of actuators and sensor readings at the last line (which are assumed to be analog voltages) and comparing them with the readings reported by the regular control infrastructure has the ability to detect malfunctioning or purposely compromised equipment. While this would seem like a duplication of the control infrastructure, the additional expenditures for such an approach are actually minimal: they simply require a single microcontroller per group of sensors and actuators digitizing analog voltages and reporting them cryptographically-signed via Ethernet to the IDS.

4. **Upgrade without compliancy issues.** As no changes to the existing ICS infrastructure are necessary, the approach would allow for an effective upgradability of existing legacy systems. Note that since nothing is placed into the signal path that may intercept or alter its behavior, no compliancy issues or the necessity of re-certify the system would arise which would make a roll-out within certain critical infrastructures very expensive or time consuming.

From Network Anomalies to Physical Process Knowledge

The other main modification that is necessary to accommodate today's threat landscape is to move away from a detection solely based on network anomalies and include information about the physical processes and their behavior into an IDS. As discussed during Sect. 2, several relevant threats in IDS would not deviate in terms of communication endpoints or packet sizes from normal traffic, nor trigger any exception in terms of protocol or access policy compliance. While this complicates the design of IDS, and means that instead of short training of off-the-shelf an extensive customization period of the IDS to the system at hand is necessary, an IDS with information about the physical processes can evaluate how a command sent from the control system to the PLCs would play out and thus be able to stop these threats previously uncovered.

In our work we implemented the physical model behind a general trailing suction hopper dredger design, which will be briefly introduced in Sect. 5. Ultimately though, the last line of defense approach can be adapted to any kind of ICS given some knowledge of the underlying system. In the following we will briefly discuss four detection strategies we apply in our prototype system. These strategies are basic and generic and cover different information sources available in system operation, as well as the design, engineering and control process.

When the physical system is designed, we know from the engineering documentation the boundary conditions under which the system is designed to operate. A monitoring system can directly apply these values to maintain process safety and security, as deviations from the normal are cause for concern. In the next step, it is meaningful to compare the consistency between the action and values of the devices in the field area, and those being reported on the control network and inside the control system. This uncovers faulty devices, as well as those operating with malicious hard- and software. Finally, in case of a physical process (e.g., a chemical reaction), detailed knowledge of how the process will behave based on changes in input. Based on this information, an internal representation of the ICS can be kept by the IDS. This allows commands be evaluated for their potential effect and an evaluation whether the obtained sensor values would be feasible and expected from the current state of the system. Incoming sensor values and events, either input from a monitoring point such as an I/O measurement or communication and control messages, are subjected to four analysis methods in the proposed architecture: consistency comparison, value and signature analysis and envelope escalation. Each method is explained in further detail below:

Consistency Comparison. In a first step, the value emitted by an instrument is compared to the value in the control system, as assuming the PLC and/or control system is not tampered with these values should match up. Any deviations are thus a basis for alarm and further investigation, indicating a malfunction or deliberate action.

Value Analysis. In addition to a basic consistency check, instrument readings are compared against the device, component and system level specifications, describing the minimum/maximum operating context for specific components or the rating alarm and trip setting (RATS) list for the entire design. Think for example of the flow rate in a pipeline, which the control system only monitors for a lower bound value - no flow for example. There is also an physical upper limit though, which could be the maximum capacity the pumps can sustain. Any deviations from this are flagged for immediate investigation, especially if not reported as such by the main ICS control system.

Signature Analysis. Industrial control systems run very structured processes, onto which a form of signature analysis is applied. The value under consideration and the context in which it appeared is matched against a list of logic rules and reference traces, raising an alarm when deviations are encountered. These rules can take any form, as long as they can be specified in a machine-readable and -interpretable format. Within this initial proof-of-concept we are considering (a) timing analysis of ICS control packets (since PLCs will show a different answer time and deviations from their otherwise exact response patterns in case they are executing different software branches than usual), (b) request-responsive-sequence analysis of packets (PLCs communicate in set intervals status messages to which other devices hen react), and (c) power-trace analysis of PLCs (as PLCs

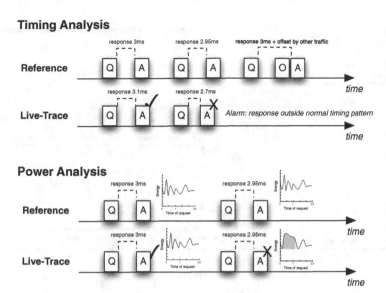

Fig. 3. Signature detection for timing analysis of request-response packets, as well as power consumption during the servicing of requests

execute other code branches than usual their relative power consumption over time will change). Figure 3 shows a schematic representation of this method.

Envelope Escalation. As in control engineering the various states of the system, the failure domains and safe operating conditions are well defined, we can utilise knowledge of the system's secure and insecure states to follow the actions and reactions in a multi-level multi-dimensional model, thereby creating a safe-state envelope. Envelopes have been used for dependability engineering of communication networks to provide hard performance guarantees during challenge events [27,28], however the method may directly be applied to control engineering as well. Each independent subcomponent of an ICS is described by one or more envelopes, which are defined by a set of metrics assessing a particular component from various angles. Each envelope hence captures an N-dimensional state space, which is annotated based on the system specifications indicating which operating context is safe or not.

Figure 4 shows this concept in a two-dimension plot for 2 independent metrics, with green indicating a safe operating context, red an unsafe system condition and yellow an operation outside norm values which may be temporarily acceptable or after a legitimate operator override. As can be seen in the figure, the IDS system monitors the development of the system's status based on the envelope specification and tracks whether it can still be considered safe. As commands are issued and controls are actuated that would take it into an unsafe condition, an alarm is generated. This tracking and detection can be done in two ways: First, many control processes are well defined, i.e., it is possible to

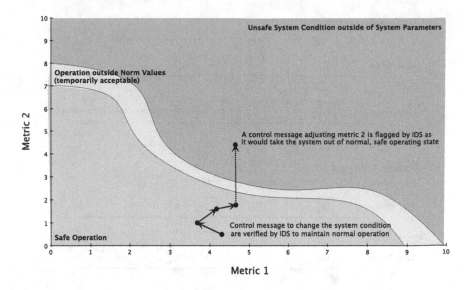

Fig. 4. Envelope escalation (Color figure online)

determine before-hand how say a chemical process will change given a particular change in input variables. Second, in case such information is not directly modelable, it is usually generated and available after the testing period during a system's commissioning, during which normal and various boundary cases of a system are being tested.

Both cases will let the IDS directly flag a command as abnormal to the operator, and in case an actor conducts a previously unknown attack a comparison with historical commands and system responses will help the system maintainer to at least identify, where and how things went out of the ordinary with concrete pointers on how to roll back.

5   Experiments

To verify that our proposed new IDS approach has validity and can detect malicious tampering within an ICS, we implemented and evaluated a proof-of-concept prototype. This prototype is based on a generic trailing suction hopper dredger design. As the prototype is subjected to intentional tampering of the control systems, it is for security reasons not running on any production systems, but in an simulated environment. This has the additional advantage of enabling us to control system state and repeat scenarios under identical circumstances, and evaluate the performance of different detection strategies.

The remainder of this section will further elaborate on the source model, followed by a discussion of the experiments and the obtained results.

Source Model

The source model can be created using three approaches: (1) first principles[1], (2) empirical input and output obtained from the field, and (3) a combination of both. This quickly narrows down to first principles as obtaining such empirical data is infeasible within this works scope. The approach used is to start out with the most simplistic first principles model with the option to increase complexity after initial evaluation. Reasoning for this is that the goal is to evaluate the IDS system and not to create the most complex and realistic TSHD model.

A TSHD has either a fixed or dynamic overflow system. Within the generic design use is made of a dynamic overflow system, which will also be used in the model as this offers a possible vector for malicious behaviour. The main risk within the loading cycle is that this overflow does not work as intended. This has the potential to cause the system to overload and sink the vessel. There are other parts that could malfunction, such as a suction pump not turning off. In those cases however lowering the overflow would win time and safety by simply ensuring excess cargo is discharged overboard.

The source model is built in such a way that there is a physical model representing the TSHD, and a separate controller that influences the state of the modeled THSD. This mimics the functionality of a real controller, which also operates on a process. The physical model includes the following main components: the hopper, the dynamic overflow and the inflow pipeline. In reality there would be many other parts involved but for the purposes of the evaluation these are not required and will be presented abstractly within the model.

The control network receives the sensor information from the physical model and processes this. After processing the controller computes the required change and sends a control message that influences the state of the source system. This has been represented with Fig. 5, displaying the field devices in play and their connection to the controller.

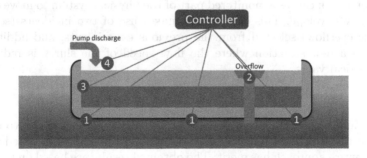

Fig. 5. The THSD modeled network.

---

[1] In physics the first principles approach relates to something which is based directly on established science.

Experiments

There is a total of three experiments which aim to evaluate the prototype and the proposed detection strategies. Each is based on vulnerabilities identified by the threat model and inherent weaknesses in the source model. These experiments are cyber incident, manipulation attack and envelope escalation, each targeting a specific detection strategy.

Cyber Incident. A cyber incident occurs when a unwanted situation occurs but there is no malicious intent trying to cause the situation. An example is the overflowing of a tank because a control engineer has entered the wrong maximum volume for said tank. While these events might resemble a cyber attack, the differentiator is intent. The evaluation is accomplished by introducing two incidents that each target a different part of the system. During each iteration one of these is randomly selected. The two incidents used are then: The first case mimics the changing of a system set-point. The second case alters process logic used within the controller. Both of these incidents mimic an operator, engineering or operational error which can cause the physical process to move outside of its (safe) operating specification.

Manipulation Attack. An manipulation attack is said to have occurred when a malicious entity manipulates a controller to act in a malicious way. For example by ignoring specific sensor reading and always reporting all is safe. This experiments implements three attacks: the first is a controller that thinks the cargo is not changing, the second is where the controller will effectively keep the overflow static and the final where the controller has access to a misleading draught. This produces three possible incidents, one of which is chosen at random during each iteration.

Envelope Escalation. An envelope incident has occurred when either a cyber incident or attack causes a monitored part of the physical system to move outside of the safety envelope. This experiment makes use of two incidents (set-point and static overflow) selected from the previous experiments, and additionally implements a new situation where the flow speed of the slurry is reduced to below a critical value.

Results

The main aim behind the proof-of-concept and the experiments was to demonstrate that the idea to reframe intrusion detection from a network-based view to a process-aware approach has merit. The obtained results are based on the initial experiments, without improvements, and simply marking a sample as malicious when somewhere in the model an unwanted situation was occurring. For each proposed analysis method, the results are as follows:

It is important to note here that the signature method, as mentioned earlier, is not included in the experiments. The reason for this is the implementation of a model instead of making use of an actual control system and hardware.

Method	True positive rate	False alarm rate
Value analysis	88.7%	1.31%
Consistency analysis	100%	$6.3 \cdot 10^{-6}\%$
Envelope analysis	92.3%	10.7%

As this approach does not directly allow for signature detection, it was decided to keep it for future work.

It is evident that a system protected by the last-line-of-defense approach will be somewhat more complex than a design where a single IDS module monitors the flow of packets on the system's network, after all additional wires are needed from sensors and actuators to devices that cryptographically sign and report sample values to the main IDS component. This requirement in deployment complexity needs however be weighted against the added operational complexity when intrusion detection were to be deployed right into the system's signal path, potentially necessitating re-certification and measures to deal with dropped and modified control messages as discussed in Sect. 4. Whether such an approach should be pervasively deployed or only a few sensors covered on the last line of defense is subject to a risk and cost-benefit analysis, a solution could be to cover the most essential sensors and parts of the process whose deviation would result in the highest impact, or instead redefine the measurement strategy by measuring multiple properties through orthogonal sensors not otherwise included in the control system. This point will be further elaborated in the lessons learned in the next section.

Regardless of the placement and coverage, the resulting defense in depth will increase the resilience of the system. In case where no formal description of an underlying process is available, a detection of process deviation can to some extent be accomplished by empirical learning of sensor values at the expense of loosing the predictive power of the IDS.

6   Lessons Learned and Open Research Questions

Based on the experiences building the proof of concept for the dredging hopper and the evaluation of the prototype with practitioners, we did find the alternative approach to have merit, but also raise a number of interesting aspects that have not found consideration in the academic literature. In the following we discuss five of the most important lessons learned and open research questions we identified.

Measuring ICS Intrusion Detection Success

Coming from a traditional network-security background, measuring the performance of an intrusion detection system is straight forward. Given a number of packets, some of which are tagged as malicious, success is easily quantified by means of the true/false positive and true/false negative ratios. While we

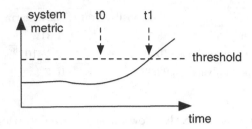

Fig. 6. In many contexts, ICS intrusion detection can be more efficiently measured by time-to-detect, instead of benchmarks such as TPR or FPR.

may attach benign and malicious labels to packets on the control network, this packet-driven view on IDS success is however less expressive when viewed from the operational side of industrial control system owner.

To demonstrate this issue imagine some metric measuring one particular aspect of an industrial process which is monitored over time as shown in Fig. 6. At some point in time t0, a command is sent from the HMI to the PLCs that will guide the system to an undesired operating condition. At the scale of most industrial processes, the effects are however not immediately visible but will only manifest in time, for example a closed value will lead to a build up in pressure that will ultimately raise an alarm once a predefined threshold is exceeded. We see from this example that a packetized view to measure the success of intrusion detection may be rethought in case of ICS. While a single packet may be the root cause for an developing issue, categorizing packets as malicious and non-malicious is not straight forward. Although the system state could be defined as "infected" at any point after t0, the problem would only be detected as soon as the metric exceeds the tolerance and detection threshold at t1. By definition samples between t0 and t1 could thus be seen as false negatives as the IDS was unsuccessful in detecting the compromised system state. Even when counting packets, changing the sampling and reporting rates of the field units will change the TPR and FPR of the system without changing the IDS performance in itself. We believe that a better approach for ICS IDS evaluation would be operational characteristics such as the time to detect an issue, or the time between false positives as suggested by [19].

Rethinking Detection with Orthogonal Sensor Inputs

A recurring principle in IT security is the principle of "defense in depth", in which multiple layers of control require an adversary to circumvent multiple defenses thus slowing down the attack progression and increasing the likelihood of detection. The ideal defense in depth scenario would contain a set of complementary detection and defense mechanisms, so that any attempt to bypass one layer would be detected by another.

Industrial control system intrusion detection could embrace this principle of orthogonal detection at comparatively low complexity and overhead. While the sensors connected to a PLC and control network are all directly process related, there exist a plethora of other industrial sensor types that can be leveraged for asserting the process' stability. With sensors measuring the ship engine's rotations per minute and fuel consumption, an attacker could still change the parameters of the fuel injection process and increase the wear and tear. Although invisible in the existing measurements, an additional microphone and a fingerprint of the engine's sound would add an additional dimension to the attack, drastically increasing the complexity to successfully complete the compromise without being detected and remain invisible to the adversary as these additional sensors are not connected to the regular process network and thus do not show up in the HMI.

While not directly stopping attack progression, such additional sensory values significantly reduce the available attack surface, a malicious actor would need to account for the monitoring of multiple process variables while pursuing the attack. This will address unintentional misconfiguration incidents, eliminate most adversaries, and slow down the attack progression of advanced ones. As augmenting today's systems with additional sensory capabilities will increase both cost and complexity of such deployments, deployment of these sensors then depends on a risk evaluation of a control system and limited to the most critical failure points or processes with the highest impact upon failure.

Slow Response Time Reduces Urgency of Comprehensive Detection
When a command is executed to change the state of a physical system this change does not happen instantly, some amount of time will transition between the initial state and the resting state. This passing of time means that in the event of a malicious command the system will not instantly transition into an unwanted state. This "extra" time reduces the urgency for instant, and extremely, accurate detection as multiple samples can be taken and even combined for analysis, prior the system actually transitioning into the unwanted state.

Digital Sensor Security
While the bulk of sensors and actuators we found in practice were analog, newer types of sensors are increasingly making the transition to a digital integrated system. Basic building blocks such as pressure gauges that used to translate the measured quantity into an output voltage, now frequently include a network interface to stream out data independently, as well as extensive embedded software stacks such as a web server to control and configure the device. This additional software does not only introduce new features, but likely also new vulnerabilities and the possibility for an attacker to compromise the sensor itself. Attacks can thus be embedded even one layer deeper into an industrial control system, if a compromise of the firmware of digital sensors and actuators cannot be effectively mitigated by an IDS operating anywhere in the field network.

Additional Value Provided by ICS IDS
A significant portion of the use cases sought after by current IDSes is also accomplished by safety systems in industrial control systems. Based on the values provided by the PLC, redundant backups monitor the correct behavior of the

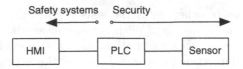

Fig. 7. Current safety systems do not extend beyond the control network into the field network.

primary control and raise an alert if the behavior of the primary deviates from the actions considered appropriate by the safety system.

Current safety systems however do not extend beyond the control network into the field network, and typically do not establish the correct functioning of the field devices and their embedded software as shown in Fig. 7. Such deviations of sensor values from the actual process state may be the result of two causes, either a malicious attack or the result of malfunctioning devices and instrumentation.

As it can be expected that in most operating contexts, the likelihood of sensor and actuator failure will significantly outweigh the likelihood of a device failure caused by an intentional attack, an intrusion detection system that includes the last line of defense has the potential to extend the scope of safety systems and augment them, for example by detecting a malfunctioning sensor device or a component damaged by wear and tear, ultimately leading to a merging of safety and security in ICS. The fusion of these two domains will both cut costs and result in more comprehensive coverage of the system, and the simultaneous view of the network on both sides of the PLCs also enables new functionality, such as the detection of faulty sensors or the measurement of wear and tear. These aspects might create a sufficiently attracting selling proposition as it can lower the operational costs, allow for better maintenance scheduling, and entice the development of new detectors and controls in ICS, and ultimately be less expensive even when considering the additional costs for extra instrumentation.

Still, in situations with malicious intent, the components in the process network will be the first ones to be targeted, and research results and practical experiences – such as the steel mill incident – highlight that existing controls are unsuited to stop advanced adversaries, requiring in addition to orthogonal detection extra rings of security beyond the current ones implemented by network-based IDS and safety systems.

7   Conclusion

This paper presents a novel intrusion detection system for industrial control systems which exploits their well defined nature and physicality. Our approach differentiates from related research in that it also exploits the physical state of the system, as opposed to the network traffic between PLC and control system. This state information is then analyzed by three detection strategies: (a) value comparison that compares actual instrument values to what the control system reports, deviation of which could indicate a faulty or compromised controller; (b) signature analysis which checks the instrument value(s) to pre-set and state independent rules; (c) an envelope escalation strategy where a multi-level multi-dimensional envelope is created depending on the actual system state, checking if each sensor reading is still within this envelope from a system operation context. We built a working prototype of our IDS, for which initial validation experiments demonstrated the general feasibility of this approach. Although this research is a work in progress the initial results are promising and indicate that approaching intrusion detection from the physical instead of the networking side is indeed feasible and provides additional detection capabilities not existing in current solutions. As with all security research it will not provide a catch-all solution, but used along side other strategies offers a firm last line of defense.

References

1. Hadziosmanovic, D.: The process matters: cyber security in industrial control systems. Ph.D. thesis, Universiteit Twente (2014)
2. Cárdenas, A.A., Amin, S., Sastry, S.: Research challenges for the security of control systems. In: Conference on Hot Topics in Security (2008)
3. Abrams, M., Weiss, J.: Malicious control system cyber security attack case study-maroochy water services, Australia, July 2008
4. Falliere, N., Murchu, L.O., Chien, E.: W32.stuxnet dossier. Technical report, Symantec, February 2011
5. McDonald, G., Murchu, L.O., Doherty, S., Chien, E.: Stuxnet 0.5: the missing link. Technical report, Symantec (2013)
6. Langner, R.: The Langner Group. Technical report, November 2013
7. Lee, R.M., Assante, M.J., Conway, T.: Technical report, SANS ICS (2014)
8. BSI. Die Lage der IT-Sicherheit in Deutschland 2014 (2014)
9. Radvanovsky, R., Brodsky, J.: Handbook of SCADA/Control Systems Security. CRC Press, Boca Raton (2013)
10. Anderson, R.J.: Security Engineering. Wiley, Indianapolis (2008)
11. Goodin, D.: Stepson of stuxnet stalked kaspersky for months, tapped iran nuke talks. Februari 2017. arstechnica.com
12. Igure, V.M., Laughter, S.A., Williams, R.D.: Security issues in SCADA networks. Comput. Secur. **25**(7), 498–506 (2006)
13. Cardenas, A., Amin, S., Sinopoli, B., Giani, A., Perrig, A., Sastry, S.: Challenges for securing cyber physical systems. In: Workshop on Future Directions in Cyber-physical Systems Security, DHS, July 2009
14. Cheminod, M., Durante, L., Valenzano, A.: Review of security issues in industrial networks. IEEE Trans. Ind. Inf. **9**(1), 277–293 (2013)
15. Denning, D.: An intrusion-detection model. IEEE Trans. Softw. Eng. **SE–13**(2), 222–232 (1987)
16. Cárdenas, A.A., Amin, S., Lin, Z.-S., Huang, Y.-L., Huang, C.-Y., Sastry, S.: Attacks against process control systems: risk assessment, detection, and response. In: Symposium on Information, Computer and Communications Security (2011)
17. Etalle, S., Gregory, C., Bolzoni, D., Zambon, E., Trivellato, D.: Monitoring industrial control systems to improve operations and security. Technical report, Security Matters (2013)

18. Etalle, S., Gregory, C., Bolzoni, D., Zambon, E.: Self configuring deep protocol network whitelisting. Technical report, Security Matters (2013)
19. Urbina, D.I., Giraldo, J.A., Cardenas, A.A., Tippenhauer, N.O., Valente, J., Faisal, M., Ruths, J., Candell, R., Sandberg, H.: Limiting the impact of stealthy attacks on industrial control systems. In: SIGSAC Conference on Computer and Communications Security (2016)
20. Hadžiosmanović, D., Sommer, R., Zambon, E., Hartel, P.H.: Through the eye of the PLC: semantic security monitoring for industrial processes. In: Annual Computer Security Applications Conference (2014)
21. Fovino, I.N., Carcano, A., Masera, M., Trombetta, A.: An experimental investigation of malware attacks on scada systems. Crit. Infrastruct. Protection **2**(4), 139–145 (2009)
22. Cardenas, A., Baras, J., Seamon, K.: A framework for the evaluation of intrusion detection systems. In: 2006 IEEE Symposium on Security and Privacy, pp. 15–77, May 2006
23. Cardenas, A., Amin, S., Sastry, S.: Secure control: towards survivable cyber-physical systems. In: Distributed Computing Systems Workshops, pp. 495–500, June 2008
24. Fovino, I.N., Carcano, A., Murel, T.D.L., Trombetta, A., Masera, M.: Modbus/dnp. 3 state-based intrusion detection system. In: International Conference on Advanced Information Networking and Applications (2010)
25. Carcano, A., Fovino, I.N., Masera, M., Trombetta, A.: State-based network intrusion detection systems for SCADA protocols: a proof of concept. In: Rome, E., Bloomfield, R. (eds.) CRITIS 2009. LNCS, vol. 6027, pp. 138–150. Springer, Heidelberg (2010). doi:10.1007/978-3-642-14379-3_12
26. Carcano, A., Coletta, A., Guglielmi, M., Masera, M., Fovino, I.N., Trombetta, A.: A multidimensional critical state analysis for detecting intrusions in scada systems. Trans. Ind. Inf. **7**, 179–186 (2011)
27. Doerr, C., Hernandez, J.M.: A computational approach to multi-level analysis of network resilience. In: Third International Conference on Dependability, DEPEND (2010)
28. Doerr, C.: Challenge tracing and mitigation under partial information and uncertainty. In: Communications and Network Security (CNS) (2013)

LED-it-GO: Leaking (A Lot of) Data from Air-Gapped Computers via the (Small) Hard Drive LED

Mordechai Guri[✉], Boris Zadov[✉], and Yuval Elovici[✉]

Cyber Security Research Center,
Ben-Gurion University of the Negev, Beer-Sheva, Israel
{gurim, elovici}@post.bgu.ac.il, borisza@gmail.com

Abstract. In this paper we present a method that allows attackers to covertly leak data from isolated, air-gapped computers. Our method utilizes the hard disk drive (HDD) activity LED which exists in most of today's desktop PCs, laptops, and servers. We show that a malware can indirectly control the HDD LED, turning it on and off rapidly (up to 5800 blinks per second) – a rate that exceeds the visual perception capabilities of humans. Sensitive information can be encoded and leaked over the LED signals, which can then be received remotely by different kinds of cameras and light sensors (Demonstration video: https://www.youtube.com/watch?v=4vIu8ld68fc). Compared to other LED methods, our method is unique, because it is also *covert;* the HDD activity LED routinely flickers frequently, and therefore the user may not be suspicious of changes in its activity. We discuss attack scenarios and present the necessary technical background regarding the HDD LED and its hardware control. We also present various data modulation methods and describe the implementation of a user-level malware that doesn't require a kernel component. During the evaluation, we examined the physical characteristics of different colored HDD LEDs (red, blue, and white) and tested different types of receivers: remote cameras, 'extreme' cameras, security cameras, smartphone cameras, drone cameras, and optical sensors. Finally, we discuss hardware and software countermeasures for such a threat. Our experiment shows that sensitive data can successfully be leaked from air-gapped computers via the HDD LED at a maximum bit rate of 120 bit/s (bits per second) when a video camera is used as a receiver, and 4000 bit/s when a light sensor is used for the reception. Notably, the maximal speed is 10 times faster than the existing optical covert channels for air-gapped computers. These rates allow rapid exfiltration of encryption keys, keystroke logging, and text and binary files.

Keywords: Covert channel · Air-gap · Exfiltration · Optical · LED · Hard drive · Network security

1 Introduction

In the modern cyber era, attackers have proven that they can breach many organizations thought to be secured. They employ sophisticated social engineering methods and exploit zero-day vulnerabilities in order to infiltrate the target network, while bypassing

© Springer International Publishing AG 2017
M. Polychronakis and M. Meier (Eds.): DIMVA 2017, LNCS 10327, pp. 161–184, 2017.
DOI: 10.1007/978-3-319-60876-1_8

defense measures such as intrusion detection and prevention systems (IDS/IPS), firewalls, antivirus programs, and the like. For that reason, when highly sensitive information is involved, so-called air-gap isolation is used. In air-gap isolation, a network is kept separate, physically and logically, from public networks such as the Internet. Air-gapped networks are commonly used in military defense systems, critical infrastructure, banks and the financial sector, and others industries [1, 2].

But despite the high degree of isolation, air-gapped networks are not immune to breaches. In recent years it has been shown that even air-gapped networks can become compromised. In order to breach such networks, attackers have used complex attack vectors, such as supply chain attacks, malicious insiders, and social engineering. While the most well-known breach cases are Stuxnet [3] and agent.btz [4], other attacks have also been reported [3, 5–8].

1.1 Leaking Data Through an Air-Gap

While infiltrating air-gapped systems has been shown feasible in recent years, the exfiltration of data from systems without networking, physical access, or Internet connectivity is still considered a challenging task. Over the years, different types of air-gap covert channels (that is, covert channels aimed at leaking data from air-gapped computers) have been proposed. The electromagnetic emission from computer components is one type of covert channel that has been extensively studied. In this method, a malware controls the electromagnetic emission from computer parts, including the screen, cables, processors, and other peripherals [9–13]. Leaking data over ultrasonic waves [14, 15] and via thermal manipulations [16] has also been studied.

A few types of optical covert channels have been presented as well. In particular, leaking data via the blinks made by keyboard LEDs, or by inserting malicious hardware with controlled LEDs into an organization. However, these methods are not considered completely covert, since they can easily be detected by people who notice the anomalous LED blinking. Generally speaking, because optical and LED methods are considered less covert, they have not received as much attention from researchers.

1.2 Our Contribution

In this paper we present a method that enables malware to leak data from air-gapped computers using the HDD activity LED which is present in nearly all desktop and laptop computers today. A malware can manipulate the HDD LED and control its blinking period and speed by using certain HDD I/O operations, such as 'read' and 'write.' We show that arbitrary data can be modulated and transmitted over the optical signals.

Compared with existing optical methods, our method is unique in five ways:

- **Covertness**. Until now, leaking data through PC LEDs has not been considered covert – given the irregular and inconsistent nature of the blinking of keyboard and screen power LEDs, hence leaking data through these LEDs can easily be detected. In contrast, our method is considered covert, because unlike the keyboard and screen LEDs, HDD activity LEDs are frequently active, and manipulations of the blinking timing and speed may not draw special attention.

- **Speed**. Our measurements show that the HDD LED can be controlled and adjusted to operate at a relatively fast speed (over 6000 Hz). Therefore, we were able to transmit messages at a much faster speed than other LED methods were able to achieve. This rate allowed the exfiltration of an encryption key of 4096 bits in a matter of minutes (and even seconds), depending on the receiver.
- **Visibility**. When the HDD LED blinks for a short period of time, humans may not be able to perceive its activity [17]. Moreover, at high speeds (e.g., above 400 Hz), the LED flickering is invisible to humans, making the channel even more covert.
- **Availability**. Our method does not require any special hardware. It works with any computer that has an HDD activity LED. This component is found on most desktop PCs, laptops, and servers today.
- **Privilege level**. Activating the HDD LED can be initiated from an ordinary user-level code and does not require a special component in the OS kernel.

The rest of the paper is organized as follows. In Sect. 2 we present related work. Section 3 describes the adversarial attack model. Section 4 provides technical background. Data modulation and transmission are discussed in Sect. 5. Section 6 presents the evaluation and results. Countermeasures are discussed in Sect. 7, and we present our conclusions in Sect. 8.

2 Related Work

Leaking data from air-gapped computers via covert channels has been the subject of research for the past twenty years. Air-gap covert channels can be categorized as electromagnetic, acoustic, thermal, and optical channels.

2.1 Electromagnetic

In electromagnetic methods, the attacker modulates data over of the electromagnetic signals generated by various components within the computer. Back in 1998, Kuhn and Anderson [10] introduced the 'Soft Tempest' attack which involved hidden data transmission using electromagnetic emanations from a video cable. AirHopper [9], introduced in 2014, is a type of malware aimed at leaking data from air-gapped computers to a nearby mobile phone by generating FM radio signals from the video card. GSMem malware [13], presented in 2105, enables leaking data at cellular frequencies via electromagnetic emission generated by the computer RAM bus. More recently, researchers presented USBee [18] and Funthenna [19] which exploit the electromagnetic interference generated by the USB and GPIO buses, respectively. Matyunin et al. use the magnetic field sensors of mobile devices as a covert channel [20]. Other electromagnetic and magnetic covert channels are discussed in [21].

2.2 Sonic/Ultrasonic

Near ultrasonic methods for air-gap covert channels are discussed in a number of academic works. Hanspach and Goetz [22] present a method for near ultrasonic covert networking using speakers and microphones in laptops. The concept of communicating over inaudible sounds has been comprehensively examined by Lee et al. [23] and has also been extended for different scenarios using laptops and mobile phones [24]. Guri et al. introduced Fansmitter [25] and Disfiltration [26], new methods enabling acoustic data exfiltration from computers without speakers or audio hardware. The proposed methods utilized computer fans and the moving heads (the 'actuator arm') of hard drives to generate acoustic signals.

2.3 Thermal

BitWhisper [27], presented in 2015, is a unique air-gap covert channel, allowing bidirectional covert communication between adjacent air-gapped computers, using the computers' heat emissions and the built-in thermal sensors of the computers' motherboards. The two computers communicate by using so-called 'thermal pings' to exchange command and control data. Notably, such a thermal channel is relatively slow and hence relevant for brief commands and small amounts of data.

2.4 Optical

In the optical domain, Loughry and Umphress [28] and Sepetnitsky and Guri [29] discussed the risks of intentional information leakage through optical signals sent from keyboard and screen LEDs. They implemented malware that controls the keyboard and screen power LEDs to transfer data to a remote camera. The main drawback of these methods is that they are less covert: since the keyboard and screen LEDs don't blink typically, users can easily detect this type of communication. Shamir et al. demonstrated how to establish a covert channel with a malware over the air-gap using a blinking laser and standard all-in-one-printer [30]. However, this method is not covert and its success relies upon user absence. More recently, Lopes and Arana [31] presented a novel approach for air-gap data exfiltration using a malicious storage device which transmits data through blinking infrared LEDs. In this way, an attacker can leak sensitive data stored on the device, such as credentials and cryptographic keys, at a speed of 15 bit/s. The computer need not be infected with a malware, but this approach does require that the attacker finds a way to insert the compromised hardware implanted with infrared LEDs into the organization. Brasspup [32] demonstrated how to conceal secret images in a modified LCD screen. His method required removing the polarization filter of the LCD screen which makes it less practical for real world attacks. VisiSploit [33] is another optical covert channel in which data is leaked from the LCD screen to a remote camera via a so-called 'invisible image.' With this method, a remote camera can reconstruct an invisible QR code projected on the computer screen.

Table 1 provides a summary of the different types of existing air-gap covert channels, including their maximum bandwidth and effective distance.

Table 1. Different types of air-gap covert channels and distances

Method	Examples	Max bandwidth	Effective distance
Electromagnetic	AirHopper [9]	480 bit/s	~5–10 m
	GSMem [13]	1 to 1000 bit/s	
	USBee [18]	4800 bit/s	
	Funthenna [11]		
Acoustic	[14, 15, 23, 24, 34]	<100 bit/s	~15 m
	Fan noise (Fansmitter) [25]	900 bit/h	
	Hard disk noise (DiskFiltration) [26]	10 K bit/h	
Thermal	BitWhisper	1–8 bit/h	40 cm
Optical (LEDs)	Keyboard LEDs (unmodified) [28]	150 bit/s	Line of sight (0–30 m)
	Screen LEDs [29]	20 bit/s	
	Implanted infrared LEDs [31]	15 bit/s	
	Hard drive LED (this paper)	4000 bit/s	Line of sight

The method presented in this paper has two main advantages compared to other LED based methods: its covertness and its speed. The state of keyboard and screen power LEDs changes frequently, and it is likely that any blinking caused by tampering with this channel will be obvious to observers. On the other hand, the HDD activity LED blinks frequently (due to OS background operations), and hence the effects of communication via this channel (changes in the blinking pattern) will not arouse attention. By using the HDD LED we achieved an exfiltration speed of up to 4000 bit/s, more than 10 times faster than existing air-gap LED methods.

3 Adversarial Attack Model

The attack model consists of four phases: (1) infecting the target computer with a malware and collecting data, (2) transmitting the data through the HDD LED signals, (3) receiving the signals remotely, and (4) decoding the signals back into binary information.

Infection. As demonstrated in recent years, infecting a computer within a secure network can be accomplished. Attackers may employ supply chain attacks, use social engineering techniques, or launch hardware with preinstalled malware to obtain a foothold in the target machine [35–37]. The malware then gathers sensitive information from the user's computer (e.g., keystrokes, password, encryption keys, and documents).

Transmission. Eventually the malware starts transmitting the binary data through the blinking HDD LED using a selected encoding scheme. The data may be transmitted repeatedly at certain times, which are specified by the attacker.

Reception. The attack model requires a digital camera or optical sensor which has a line of sight with the compromised computer's front panel. We identify two scenarios in which this threat model is relevant: (1) the 'malicious insider' [38] (also known as the 'evil maid' [39] attack), in which a person carrying a hidden camera can obtain a line of sight with the compromised computer, and (2) a scenario involving a remote camera or optical sensor pointed at the compromised computer [40].

There are several types of equipment that can play the role of the receiver in this attack model.

- **Local hidden camera**. A hidden camera that has a line of sight to the front panel of the transmitting computer.
- **High resolution remote camera**. A high resolution camera (or other type of optical sensor) that is located outside the building, but positioned so it has a line of sight to the front panel of the transmitting computer.
- **Drone camera**. A camera installed on a versatile drone which is flown to a location which has a line of sight with the front panel of the transmitting computer, e.g., near the window. This type of receiver is relevant for leaking a small amount of data (e.g., leaking encryption keys). In practice, the drone attack might be used during the night hours or only for short transmission periods, to minimize the chance of being detected by humans.
- **Camera carried by a malicious insider**. A person that stands in close proximity to the computer and can position him/herself so as to have a line of sight with the front panel of the transmitting computer, carrying a smartphone or wearable video camera (e.g., hidden camera).
- **Compromised security camera**. A security camera positioned in a location where it has a line of sight with the front panel of the transmitting computer. In recent years, there were several cases in which security and surveillance cameras has been compromised by attackers [41, 42]. For example, in January 2017, two hackers were reportedly arrested in London on suspicion of hacking 70% of the CCTV cameras in Washington [43]. A comprehensive analysis of the threats, vulnerabilities, and attacks on video surveillance, closed-circuit TV, and IP camera systems was conducted by Costin in [40].
- **Optical sensors**. An optical sensor capable of sensing the light emitted from the HDD LED. Such sensors are used extensively in VLC (visible light communication) and LED to LED communication [44]. Notably, optical sensors are capable of sampling LED signals at high rates, enabling data reception at a higher bandwidth than a typical video camera. In the context of an attack model, optical sensors can be secretly installed within the room, e.g., in the walls or ceiling, within furniture, and so on. They can also be attached to a focusing optical lens with a line of sight with the transmitting computer placed remotely, inside or outside of the building.

Decoding. After receiving the digital videos or data sampled by the optical sensors, the information has to be demodulated and decoded back into the original binary form. This is done offline on the attacker's side by employing an appropriate decoding scheme.

Fig. 1. Example of the attack. A leaking HDD LED (the red LED at the center of the image) as captured by a hidden video camera located eight meters away from the transmitting computer. (Color figure online)

An example of the covert channel is provided in Fig. 1 in which sensitive data is encoded in binary form and covertly transmitted over a stream of HDD LED signals. A hidden video camera films the activity in the room, including the LED signals. The attacker can then decode the signals and reconstruct the modulated data.

4   Technical Background

LED (light emitting diode) is a two-lead semiconductor light source that illuminates when an electrical charge passes through it. LEDs are used as activity indicators in a wide range of electronic devices. In addition, LEDs of different sizes and colors are also used in various applications such as advertising, home lighting, the automotive industry, and traffic signals. The wavelength of the emitted light (which is indicated by its color) is determined by the material used in the semiconducting element within the LED. Generally, aluminum gallium indium phosphide (AlGaInP) is used in red, orange, and yellow LEDs, and indium gallium nitride (InGaN) is used in green, blue, and white LEDs.

LED indicators are commonly used in desktop and laptop computers and their peripheral hardware components. Computer LEDs include the power and keyboard LEDs, and many motherboards have an internal onboard power LED that indicates whether there are hardware errors.

4.1 HDD Activity LED

The HDD activity indicator is a small LED that blinks whenever the hard drive is active (being read from or written to). A schematic flow of the HDD activity LED's operation is provided in Fig. 2. Technically, internal hard disk drives in desktop and laptop computers are connected to the motherboard via a SATA/IDE interface or another type of mass storage device interface (Fig. 2-1). The motherboard hard drive controller sends signals via the HDD activity header pins over the standard 2-pin HDD LED extension cable (Fig. 2-2). These signals cause an LED on the front of a computer to flash when the drive is active. The signals are sent to the LED whenever 'read' or 'write' operations have been issued to the HDD. Some large computer cases (e.g., server PCs) have multiple hard disk activity LEDs to allow for the separate connection of a number of drives. External hard drives and flash drives are usually equipped with an activity LED as well. In these cases, the LED is connected to the embedded controller of the flash drive.

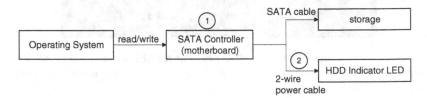

Fig. 2. Schematic flow of the HDD activity LED's operation.

On a desktop PC the HDD LED is located on the front panel of the computer. On a laptop the HDD LED is usually located on the front control bar (located above the keyboard) or on the front edge of the computer. The activity LED of an external HDD is usually located on the front of its case. The LED light may be any color, depending on the type of computer, but it is usually white, red, green, yellow, or blue.

4.2 HDD Activity LED Circuit Hardware

The HDD activity LED is connected to the motherboard circuit using a 2-pin extension cable. To activate the component, two parameters are needed: forward voltage of at least 2 V, and forward current of 20–130 mA, depending on type of LED. Digital output ports cannot provide the amount of current needed to operate the LED, and thus an extra electronic circuit, called an LED driver, is needed to meet this requirement. Figure 3 presents the two driver circuits commonly used in motherboards. The circuit in Fig. 3(a) is based on an NPN transistor connected in common emitter configuration. The circuit in Fig. 3(b) is based on an operational amplifier. Both circuits can provide the amount of current needed to operate the LED.

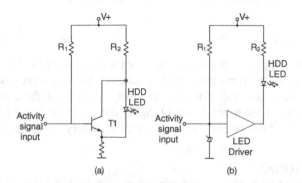

Fig. 3. The two common motherboard LED driver circuits. (a) A common emitter configuration with self-biasing implementation. (b) Operational amplifier based implementation.

The circuit presented in Fig. 3(a) is less expensive than the circuit in Fig. 3(b), and it has more limited current amplification (150–550). The more expensive circuit in Fig. 3(b) is based on an operational amplifier and has a comparator configuration with open loop amplification of 106, allowing faster responsivity to the input signal; in addition it has only two voltage levels (5 v and 0 v). This circuit also has better immunization to the input.

5   Data Transmission

In this section we present the data transmission. We discuss the basic signal generation and describe different modulation methods, along with their implementation details.

5.1   Signal Generation

In our method, the data carrier is the state of the HDD LED. The basic signal is generated by turning the LED on and off. Technically, the HDD LED is controlled directly by the motherboard chipset. We found that there is no reliable generic API that can be used to enable software to request the motherboard to turn on the HDD indicator LED. In order to generate the signal, we can indirectly control the LED by performing specific HDD 'read' or 'write' operations. These operations cause the motherboard to turn on the HDD LED for a specified amount of time, depending on the size of the buffer being read from or written to the storage device. Table 2 lists the OS level operations and the corresponding LED states, denoted as LED-ON and LED-OFF. As can be seen, reading or writing a buffer size S causes the HDD LED to be turned on for the time period of T_{on}. Sleeping for time T_{off} causes the HDD LED to be turned off for a period of T_{off}.

Table 2. Signal time

OS operation	HDD-LED state
Read/write (S)	LED-ON for time $T_{on}(S)$
Sleep (T_{off})	LED-OFF for time T_{off}

5.2 Data Encoding

The topic of visible light communication has been widely studied in the last decade. In particular, various modulations and encoding schemes have been proposed for LED to LED communication [44–46]. For our purposes, we present three basic encoding schemes which enable the transmission of digital data over the HDD LED: (1) on-off keying (OOK), (2) Manchester encoding, and (3) Binary Frequency Shift Keying (B-FSK).

On-Off keying (OOK)
This is the simplest form of the more general amplitude-shift keying (ASK) modulation. The presence of a signal for a certain duration encodes a logical one ("1"), while its absence for the same duration encodes a logical zero ("0"). In our case, LED-ON for a duration T_{on} encodes "1" and LED-OFF for duration of T_{off} encodes "0". Note that in the simple case $T_{on} = T_{off}$.

Manchester Encoding
In Manchester encoding each logical bit is sent using two physical bits. The sequence of physical bits "01" (LED-OFF, LED-ON) encodes a logical "0" and the sequence of physical bits "10" (LED-ON, LED-OFF) encodes a logical "1." Manchester encoding solves the LED flickering problem by sending an equal number of ones and zeroes. Manchester encoding's transfer rate is half of OOK's rate, since it uses two physical bits for each logical bit. This type of encoding is considered more reliable because of the redundancy of each transmitted bit; therefore it is heavily used in communication.

Binary Frequency Shift Keying (B-FSK)
In this encoding scheme both a logical "1" and "0" are encoded by LED-ON. We denote S_1 and S_0 as the size of buffer used for the transmission of logical "1"s and "0"s, respectively. A logical "1" is encoded by the LED-ON state for time duration of $T_{on}(S_1)$, and a logical "0" is encoded by the LED-ON state for time duration of $T_{on}(S_0)$. Each logical bit is followed by a guard interval (LED-OFF) for a time interval of T_{off}.

5.3 Bit Framing

We transmit the binary data in frames. The frames have two roles: (1) providing periodic synchronization signals to the receiver, and (2) providing a basic error check mechanism for each packet of bytes sent. We used two types of bit framing: (1) fixed length framing, and (2) variable length framing.

In fixed length framing (Table 3) the binary data is transmitted in small, fixed size packets. Each packet is composed of a preamble (8 bits), a payload (256 bits), and a checksum (16 bits). The preamble consists of a sequence of eight alternating bits

Table 3. Fixed length framing

8 bits	256 bits	16 bits
Preamble (10101010)	Payload	CRC

Table 4. Variable length framing

8 bits	16 bits	n bits	16 bits
Preamble (10101010)	Payload size (n)	Payload	CRC

('10101010') and is used by the receiver to periodically determine the channel timing (T_{on} and T_{off}). In addition, the preamble header allows the receiver to identify the beginning of a transmission and calibrate other parameters, such as the intensity and color of the transmitting LED. The payload is a chunk of 256 bits to be transmitted. We used a 16-bit CRC (cyclic redundancy check) for error detection. The CRC is computed on the payload and added to the end of the frame. The receiver calculates the CRC for the received payload, and if it differs from the received CRC, an error is detected. In variable length framing (Table 4) the binary data is transmitted in packets of varying length. The preamble is followed by 16 bits which determine the payload size. The payload size may differ between packets. Finally, the 16-bit CRC of the payload is added to the end of the frame.

Note that fixed length bit framing is more suitable for cases in which a small amount of fixed sized data is about to be transmitted (e.g., encryption keys and passwords). With a larger amount of data (e.g., files), variable length framing may be better, because it can transmit the entire amount of data in fewer packets, while saving on the overhead of the frame headers. However, in some circumstances larger frames are more wasteful, since a single bit error may corrupt the whole frame.

5.4 Transmission Overhead

The modulation schemes and bit framing add overhead on the transmitted data. Consequentially, the net payload can be considerably smaller than the amount of raw signals transmitted. The overhead for various modulation schemes and types of bit framing is summarized in Table 5.

The large amount of overhead associated with Manchester encoding is due to the state transition time required for every modulated bit. In our implementation, this doubles the amount of time required for the transmitted frame. In fixed length bit framing the source of

Table 5. Transmission overhead

Modulation/bit framing	Fixed length	Variable length
On-off keying (OOK)	8.5%	$\frac{100*40}{n+40}$%
Manchester encoding	58.5%	$50\% + \frac{100*40}{n+40}$%
Binary Frequency Shift Keying (B-FSK)	8.5%	$\frac{100*40}{n+40}$%

the overhead is associated with the preamble and the CRC (24 bits), and in variable length bit framing the source is due to the preamble, CRC, and the payload size (40 bits).

5.5   Implementation

We implemented a prototype of the transmitter for the Linux (Ubuntu 16.04 LTS, 64-bit) and Windows (Windows 10, professional 64-bit) OSs. We choose to use the read operation to turn on the HDD activity LED, because it leaves no traces on the file system. We executed a C program which uses the direct addressing system calls and the fseek(), fopen(), and fread() system calls [47, 48]. We also implemented a shell script version of the transmitter using the Linux dd command-line utility [49]. This is a low level utility of Linux that can perform a wide range of HDD operations (e.g., read or copy) at the file or block level. A pseudocode for on-off keying transmission (Linux version) is provided in Algorithm 1.

Algorithm 1. HDDLED_TransmitBit
1: procedure **transmitBits**(*bits, T0, ReadSize*)
2: sync(); //drop cache
3: hddDev = open(/dev/sda)
4: offset = 0
5: offsetIncrement = BLOCK_SIZE;
6: seek(hddDev, offset);
7: for(b in bits)
8:    if (b='0') then
9:       sleep (T0);
10: if (b='1') then
11:      seek(hddDev, offset);
12:      read(hddDev, *ReadSize*);
13:      offset += offsetIncrement
14: end for
15: return;

The procedure HDDLED_TransmitBit takes three parameters: the stream of bits to transmit (bits), time T_{off}(T0), and the size of the buffer for the read operation (ReadSize), which determines $T_{on}(S)$. Initially, the cache is cleared (line 2), and then we open the main hard drive for reading (line 3). Since the OS performs HDD reads in small sized blocks (BLOCK_SIZE), we must ensure that two consecutive reads are taken on different blocks in the HDD; otherwise, the second read operation will not generate HDD access (LED activity), because the block is already in the cache. For each bit in the bit stream, if the bit is '0,' we do nothing for time T0 (line 8–9). If the bit is '1,' a read operation is performed, and we advance to the next block (line 11–13).

5.6   Caching Avoidance

In order to efficiently modulate data over the LED signal, we need to precisely control the duration of the read operations. In particular, we need to be able to perform the read operation at a given time without delay. Modern OSs employ disk and file I/O caching mechanisms in their kernel or device drivers. Such caching can cause timing delays and inconsistencies in the generation of LED signals. For efficient and error-free signal generation, we must avoid any type of caching during the read operation. Before the transmissions, we turned off the disk caching using the /proc/sys/vm/drop_caches, in order to instruct the kernel to free the pagecache, dentries, and inodes. We also turned off the HDD write-back cache mechanism, using the hdparm command line tool [50]. In the shell script, we used the dd tool with 'direct' flag (use direct I/O for data), and 'sync' flag (use synchronized I/O for data). Note that employing a system-wide (e.g., to all processes) cache avoidance requires root privileges. Another option for bypassing OS caching that does not require root privileges is to specify appropriate flags in the file access related system calls invoked from the transmitting process. For example, the O_DIRECT flag for the open system call in Linux tries to minimize the cache effects of the I/O to and from a file [51]. In the Windows OS, the FILE_FLAG_WRITE_THROUGH and FILE_FLAG_NO_BUFFERING system call can be specified in the CreateFile API [52] to avoid some of the OS caching.

6   Evaluation

In this section we present the evaluation of the transmitter and its characteristics. Note that the concept of LED communication was the subject of a considerable amount of research in recent years. Today it is possible to transmit signals over LEDs at a rate of 500 Mbit/s [46, 53]. Other research shows that it is possible to decode LED signals from more than 30 m away [28]. Our evaluation focuses on the characteristics of the HDD LED and its rate. In our evaluation, we adopt the approach commonly used in visible light communication (VLC), which assumes a line of sight between the light source and the camera [28, 45].

6.1   Experimental Setup

The experimental setup consists of three off-the-shelf standard desktop PCs, each with a different type of HDD LED (Table 6). Note that although most HDD indication LEDs are red, many vendors today are using different colors. For the evaluation we used red, blue, and white types of HDD LEDs.

The main PC has an Infinity case with a Gigabyte H87 M-D3H motherboard with Intel H87 chipsets. We tested two hard drives. The first is the WD Blue 1 TB Desktop Hard Disk Drive - 7200 RPM SATA 6 Gb/s 64 MB Cache 3.5 in. Based on a benchmark that we conducted in our lab, this HDD has a read rate of 144.2 MB/s and an access time of 14.7 ms. We also tested the 240 GB Kingston HyperX Savage solid state drive (SSD). A small circular red HDD indicator LED is located on the front of the computer chassis. This LED is connected to two pins in the motherboard (HD LED

Table 6. PCs used in our experimental setup with red, blue, and white HDD indicator LEDs

#	Case type	LED	Motherboard	Hard drive
PC-1	Infinity	Red	Gigabyte H87 M-D3H	WD Blue 1 TB Desktop Hard Disk Drive - 7200 RPM SATA 6 Gb/s 64 MB Cache 3.5″ - Kingston HyperX Savage SSD, 240 GB
PC-2	Gigabyte	Blue	Gigabyte H77-D3H	Seagate Desktop HDD 1 TB 64 MB Cache SATA 6.0 Gb/s 3.5″
PC-3	Dell Optiplex 9020	White	Intel Q87 (LYNX POINT)	WD Blue 1 TB Desktop Hard Disk Drive - 7200 RPM SATA 6 Gb/s 64 MB Cache 3.5‴

pins), which supply its voltage. In terms of software, we used the user-level transmitting program described in the Implementation sub-section. This program receives the channel parameters (LED-ON and LED-OFF times) and the array of bits to transmit.

6.2 LED Measurement Setup

To evaluate the HDD LED at high speeds we designed a measurement setup based on photodiode light sensors.

Very simply, a photodiode is a semiconductor that converts light into electrical current. The measurement setup is shown in Fig. 4. The photodiode was connected to the charge configuration amplifier AD549 [54] (with 0.11 fA current noise density) and the data acquisition system. Data was collected with the NI cDAQ measurement system with a 16-bit ADC NI9223 measurement card [55] which is capable of 200 K samples per second. The system was driven by the LabVIEW dataflow visual programming language.

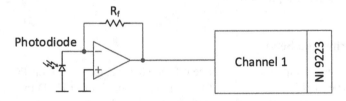

Fig. 4. The light measurement experimental setup, based on a photodiode and NI acquisition system with a high speed sampling rate.

We used two types of photodiodes: (1) SIEMENS photodiode SFH-2030 (Fig. 5 (a)), a device which is suitable for sensing light at wavelengths of 400–1100 nm, dark current of 1 nA, 55 nsec of current rise and fall time, and (2) Thorlabs PDA100A Si Switchable Gain Detector [56] (Fig. 5(b)), suitable for sensing light at wavelengths of 320–1100 nm, 2.4 MHz BW, 0.973–27 pW/Hz1/2 with a built-in amplifier.

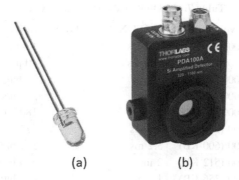

Fig. 5. (a) SIEMENS photodiode SFH-2030, and (b) Thorlabs PDA100A sensor.

The two sensors fit into different attack models. The SIEMENS photodiode circuit is a simple, small sensor that could be hidden in the room in which the transmitter computer is located. The Thorlabs PDA100A is a larger device with a built-in optimized amplifier and an option to connect an external lens used to magnify and focus the light signal. A larger sensor like this may be located remotely (e.g., outside the window), carried by human, or integrated on a flying drone.

Ambient Light

Our experiments took place in a typical office with six desktop workstations in the room. During the experiments, the room was illuminated by a fluorescent lamp. The room has a transparent glass window and a transparent glass door, so it is exposed to natural sunlight as well. The experiments described in this section were conducted in daylight (daytime hours) to simulate an attack environment. The room also included additional sources of light such as LCD screens and router LEDs.

6.3 Transmission and Reception

As mentioned, the HDD activity LED cannot be controlled directly by software. Instead, we perform the read operation from the OS, which in turn causes the HDD controller on the motherboard to turn on the HDD indication LED. We examine the correlation between S and $T_{on}(S)$, denoting the number of bytes we read as S and the time the LED was on as $T_{on}(S)$. This information is important, because it enables us to configure the parameters of the transmitting software. We also evaluate the channel boundaries to determine the maximum frequency on which the HDD LED can operate and the maximum bandwidth.

We configured the transmitter to perform the read operation, varying the number of bytes (S). Using the LED measurement setup described above, we measured the corresponding LED-ON time ($T_{on}(S)$). The photodiodes were positioned directly in front of the HDD LED and located a distance from zero to several meters away. Table 7 contains the main values of S and the corresponding $T_{on}(S)$, tested on PC-1.

Table 7. LED-ON measurements (PC-1)

Read volume (S)	LED-ON Time ($T_{on}(S)$)	Bit/s
60000000 (60 MB)	630 ms	1.6 bit/s
15120000 (15 MB)	250 ms	4 bps bit/s
80000000 (8 MB)	60 ms	16 bit/s
5120000 (5 MB)	32 ms	30 bit/s
1280000 (1.2 MB)	5 ms	180 bit/s
800000 (800 KB)	3.6 ms	277 bit/s
600000 (600 KB)	3.2 ms	312 bit/s
512000 (512 KB)	2 ms	500 bit/s
256000 (256 KB)	1.2 ms	833 bit/s
<4 KB	0.18 ms	4000 bit/s

Figures 6(a), (b), (c), and (d) show the waveforms of binary '101010...' (encoded in OOK modulation) transmitted at a rate of 1.6 bit/s, 30 bit/s, 277 bit/s, and 4000 bit/s, respectively. In this case, the transmitter is the PC-1 (red LED), and the receiver is the SIEMENS photodiode. Note that our LED-ON measurement includes a duty cycle of 50%. As can be seen, performing the SATA read operation on the 60 MB buffer causes an LED-ON time ($T_{on}(S)$) of 60 ms which implies a transmission rate of 1.6 bit/s. Performing the SATA read operation on buffers of 4 KB or less causes an LED-ON time ($T_{on}(S)$) of 0.18 ms which implies a transmission rate of 4000 bit/s. We identify two reasons for the effect of the lower limit of the transmission buffer and the corresponding $T_{on}(S)$ time. At the software layer, our transmission code operates from a user-level process. In modern operating systems such as Windows and Linux, the HDD I/O operations pass through a stack of drivers (e.g., file system drivers, volume drivers, disk port drivers, and so on). These drivers employ internal caching and scheduling mechanisms which deliver the I/O buffers to the hardware level in small packages. At the hardware layer, the use of small I/O blocks is enforced by the hardware itself. More specifically, reading and writing to HDDs is done in units of sectors which are the smallest storage unit of a hard drive. While the standard sector size is 512 bytes, newer HDDs use 4096-bytes (4 KB) sectors known as the Advanced Format (AF) [57]. In practice this means that in most cases HDDs will exchange (read or write) data in chunks of no less than 4 KB.

Figure 7 provides measurements for transmissions made from PC-1 (red LED), PC-2 (blue LED), and PC-3 (white LED). In this experiment we use the PDA100A sensor with $S = 4K$. PC-1 has a pulse width of 0.18 ms and an amplitude of 5.3 V. PC-2 has a pulse width of 0.12 ms and an amplitude of 0.71 V. PC-3 has a pulse width of 0.1 ms and an amplitude of 0.18 V. The amplitude represents the amount of charge converted to voltage with the electrical current amplifier. As can be seen, the blue LEDs produce the strongest optic signals.

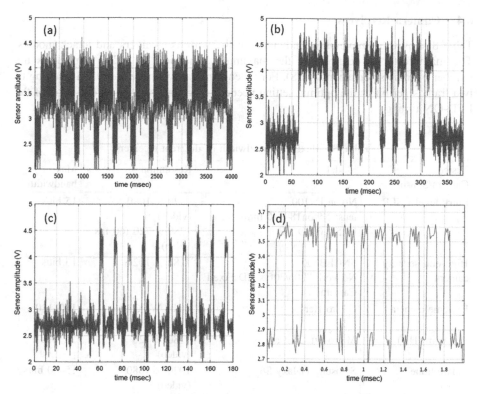

Fig. 6. PC-1 measurements with pulse width of (a) 680 ms ($S = 60$ MB), (b) 32 ms ($S = 5$ MB), (c) 3.6 ms ($S = 0.8$ MB), and (d) 0.18 ms ($S = 4$K).

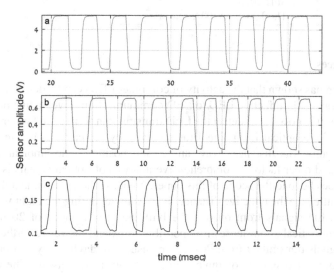

Fig. 7. Measurements for (a) PC-1 (red LED), (b) PC-2 (blue LED), and (c) PC-3 (white LED). (Color figure online)

6.4   Camera Receivers

Table 8 shows the maximum bandwidth for the various receivers and attack models. The main factor in determining the maximum bandwidth in video cameras is the number of frames per second (FPS). For video cameras, we have identified a setting of two frames per bit as the optimal setting needed to achieve successful detection of the LED-ON timing.

Table 8. Maximum bandwidth of different receivers

Tested Camera/Sensor	Model	Resolution	Max bandwidth
Entry-level DSLR	Nikon D7100. lens: Nikon18–140 mm F3.5-5.6 ED VR	1920 × 1080 (video) 1280 × 720 (60 fps video)	15 bit/s
High-end security camera	SNCEB600 Network 720p/30fps HD Fixed Camera	1280 × 1024	15 bit/s
Extreme camera	GoPro Hero5	4 K - WVGA	100–120 bit/s
Webcam (HD)	Microsoft LifeCam	1280 × 720 (video)	15 bit/s
Smartphone camera	Samsung Galaxy S6	1920 × 1080 (video)	15–60 bit/s
Wearable camera	Google Glass Explorer Edition	2528 × 1856 1280 × 720 (video)	15 bit/s
Photodiode sensors	SIEMENS photodiode SFH-2030 Thorlabs PDA100A sensor	–	<4000 bit/s

6.5   Distances

Other research has shown that the activity of computer LEDs can be detected from more than 30 m away [28]. In fact, in LED to LED communication, given a line of sight with the transmitter it is possible to detect the LED transmission from even farther away [45]. The quality of the optical LED signal (as received by the camera) is affected by the receiver's location (its distance away, angle, and position), the ambient light, LED wavelength, and other factors. Comprehensive analysis of optical signals is a complex task which goes beyond the scope of this paper. Notably, the environmental conditions can directly influence the effective distance. For example, during the night we were able identify the LED signals from outside the building at a distance of 20 m away. In addition, using optical zoom lenses it is possible to extend the range further. Figure 8 shows the signals transmitted from PC-1, as measured in daylight by an optical sensor within the room at distances of three, four, and five meters away. The amplitudes

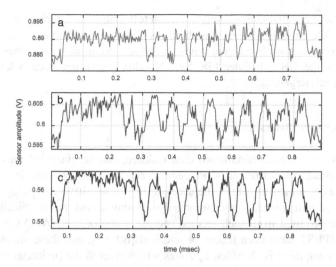

Fig. 8. Signals transmitted from PC-1, as measured in daylight by an optical sensor within the room at distances of (a) three, (b) four, and (c) five meters away. The amplitude represents the amount of charge converted to voltage with the current amplifier.

represent the amount of charge converted to voltage with the current amplifier. In this test the payload '010101010101010101' was transmitted with OOK modulation.

6.6 Signal Interferences

Because HDDs are shared access devices, it is possible (in multitasking OSs) that several processes will simultaneously access the HDD by performing read/write/seek operations. In the context of our proposed covert channel, the I/O operations performed by background processes can interfere with the I/O operations of the transmitting processes. Consequentially, the optical signals generated by the transmitting processes will be mixed with the optical signals generated by the background processes. Note that such interference is detected by the CRC calculations performed in every frame. We employed two strategies to eliminate the interference problems. We found that during the computer's 'idle' times (e.g., night hours) the interference caused by background processes is limited in practice. In particular, our evaluation shows that the interferences was limited to 1%, when no special user processes were running in the background (Table 9). By transmitting only during 'idle' times, the attacker may be able to minimize or eliminate the occurrences of interference.

Table 9. Interference in PC-1 with Linux Ubuntu 16.04 (64-bit)

Processes	Interference (per 10 s)
Compilation (GCC) + transmission	>%10
Browsing (Chrome) + transmission	~%5
Idle (default system processes) + transmission	<%1

Another solution that can be used to completely eliminate interference during both idle and non-idle periods is to execute the transmitting code from a kernel driver. The I/O operations performed in a kernel driver can be locked in such a way they will not be preempted by the OS scheduler [58, 59]. Notably, installing such a kernel driver requires root privileges.

7 Countermeasures

Countermeasures for emanation-based data leakage, can be classified into procedural and technological countermeasures. Procedural countermeasures may include organizational practices aimed to restrict the accessibility of sensitive computers by placing them in secured rooms where only authorized staff may access them; typically, all types of cameras are banned from such secured rooms. Some of the NATO standards concerning TEMPEST have been leaked or released [60, 61], and these standards define that certified equipment is classified by zones which refer to the perimeter that needs to be controlled to prevent signal leakage [62]. In these areas, the presence of surveillance cameras may serve as a deterrence measure. However, as mentioned previously in the attack model, the surveillance camera itself may be compromised by a malware [40, 63]. A less sophisticated countermeasure against LED attacks is to disconnect the HDD indication LED or cover it with black tape [28]. Equipment shielding is another countermeasure commonly recommended by TEMPEST standards. In the case of optical emanation, a special window film that prevents optical eavesdropping may be installed [64]; note that this type of countermeasure doesn't protect against cameras located within the building.

Technological countermeasures may include the detection of the presence of malware that triggers the HDD activity LED. However, practical implementation of such countermeasures appear to be nontrivial, since the read operation used for the LED control is commonly used by many processes running on the computer. Another possible countermeasure is video monitoring the computer's front panel in order to detect hidden signaling patterns. Again, practical implementation is nontrivial, because the HDD LED routinely blinks frequently due to read and write operations triggered by benign processes. Another interesting solution is to execute a background process that frequently invokes random read and write operations – that way, the signal generated by the malicious process will get mixed up with a random noise, limiting the attack's effectiveness. Another option is to limit the LED blinking frequency by adding a low pass filter (LPF) component. A simple LPF is built from a resistor and a capacitor, which is connected between the motherboard and the HDD LED. LPFs attenuate the output voltage above the cut off frequency and prevent the signal from passing through. Similarly, the blinking frequency can be limited by modifying the firmware within the HDD controller in the motherboard.

The list of countermeasures is summarized in Table 10.

Table 10. List of countermeasures

Type	Countermeasure	Cost
Procedural	Camera banning	Low
Procedural	LED covering	Low
Procedural	LED disconnecting	Low
Procedural	Window shielding	High
Technological	LED activity monitoring (software)	Low
Technological	LED activity monitoring (camera)	High
Technological	Signal jamming (software)	Low
Technological	Low pass filter (hardware)	Medium

8 Conclusion

We present a new method to leak data from air-gapped computers. Our method uses the HDD activity LED which is present in most PC workstations, laptops, and servers today. We show how the malware can indirectly control the status of the LED, turning it on and off for a specified amount of time, by invoking the hard drive's 'read' and 'write' operations. Our method is unique in two respects: it is covert and fast. It is covert, because the HDD activity LED routinely blinks frequently; hence, additional blinks caused by the attack may raise no suspicions. In terms of speed, our evaluation shows that the LED is capable of performing almost 6000 blinks per second, which enables a transmission rate of up to 4000 bit/s. This is 10 times faster than other air-gap covert channels relying on optical emissions. We examined the physical characteristics of HDD LEDs of different colors (red, blue, and white) and tested remote cameras, extreme cameras, security cameras, smartphone cameras, drone cameras, and optical sensors. Our results show that it is feasible to use this optical channel to efficiently leak different types of data (passwords, encryption keys, and files) from an air-gapped computer, via the HDD activity LED.

References

1. Federation of American Scientists. http://fas.org/irp/program/disseminate/jwics.htm
2. MCAFEE. Defending Critical Infrastructure Without Air Gaps and Stopgap Security, 14 August 2015. https://blogs.mcafee.com/executive-perspectives/defending-critical-infra structure-without-air-gaps-stopgap-security/
3. Karnouskos, S.: Stuxnet worm impact on industrial cyber-physical system security. In: IECON 2011-37th Annual Conference on IEEE Industrial Electronics Society (2011)
4. SECURELIST, Agent.btz: a Source of Inspiration? 12 March 2014. https://securelist.com/blog/virus-watch/58551/agent-btz-a-source-of-inspiration/

5. Knowlton, B.: Military Computer Attack Confirmed, 25 August 2010. http://www.nytimes. com/2010/08/26/technology/26cyber.html?_r=2&adxnnl=1&ref=technology&adxnnlx= 1423562532-hJL+Kot1FP3OEURLF9hjDw
6. Goodin, D., Group, K.E.: How "omnipotent" hackers tied to NSA hid for 14 years—and were found at last. ars technica (2015)
7. ICS-CERT. Malware infections in the conrol environment (2012)
8. Stasiukonis, S.: Social-Engineering-the-USB-Way (2006). http://www.darkreading.com/ attacks-breaches/social-engineering-the-usb-way/d/d-id/1128081?
9. Mordechai, G., Kedma, G., Kachlon, A., Elovici, Y.: AirHopper: bridging the air-gap between isolated networks and mobile phones using radio frequencies. In: 2014 9th International Conference on Malicious and Unwanted Software: The Americas (MAL-WARE), pp. 58–67. IEEE (2014)
10. Kuhn, M.G., Anderson, R.J.: Soft tempest: hidden data transmission using electromagnetic emanations. In: Aucsmith, D. (ed.) IH 1998. LNCS, vol. 1525, pp. 124–142. Springer, Heidelberg (1998). doi:10.1007/3-540-49380-8_10
11. Kuhn, M.G.: Compromising Emanations: Eavesdropping Risks of Computer Displays. University of Cambridge, Computer Laboratory (2003)
12. Vuagnoux, M., Pasini, S.: Compromising electromagnetic emanations of wired and wireless keyboards. In: USENIX Security Symposium (2009)
13. Guri, M., Kachlon, A., Hasson, O., Kedma, G., Mirsky, Y., Elovici, Y.: GSMem: data exfiltration from air-gapped computers over GSM frequencies. In: 24th USENIX Security Symposium (USENIX Security 15), Washington, D.C. (2015)
14. Hanspach, M., Goetz, M.: On covert acoustical mesh networks in air. J. Commun. **8**, 758–7647 (2013)
15. Halevi, T., Saxena, N.: A closer look at keyboard acoustic emanations: random passwords, typing styles and decoding techniques. In: ACM Symposium on Information, Computer and Communications Security (2012)
16. Guri, M., Monitz, M., Mirski, Y., Elovici, Y.: BitWhisper: covert signaling channel between air-gapped computers using thermal manipulations. In: 2015 IEEE 28th Computer Security Foundations Symposium (CSF) (2015)
17. Flicker fusion threshold. https://en.wikipedia.org/wiki/Flicker_fusion_threshold
18. Guri, M., Monitz, M., Elovici, Y.: USBee: air-gap covert-channel via electromagnetic emission from USB (2016). arXiv:1608.08397 [cs.CR]
19. Funtenna. https://github.com/funtenna
20. Matyunin, N., Szefer, J., Biedermann, S., Katzenbeisser, S.: Covert channels using mobile device's magnetic field sensors. In: 2016 21st Asia and South Pacific Design Automation Conference (ASP-DAC) (2016)
21. Kasmi, C., Esteves, J.L., Valembois, P.: Air-gap limitations and bypass techniques: command and control using smart electromagnetic interferences. In: Botconf (2015)
22. Hanspach, M., Goetz, M.: On covert acoustical mesh networks in air (2014). arXiv preprint arXiv:1406.1213
23. Lee, E., Kim, H., Yoon, J.W.: Attack, various threat models to circumvent air-gapped systems for preventing network. Inf. Secur. Appl. **9503**, 187–199 (2015)
24. O'Malley, S.J., Choo, K.-K.R.: Bridging the air gap: inaudible data exfiltration by insiders. In: Americas Conference on Information Systems (2014)
25. Guri, M., Solewicz, Y., Daidakulov, A., Elovici, Y.: Fansmitter: acoustic data exfiltration from (speakerless) air-gapped computers (2016). arXiv:1606.05915
26. Guri, M., Solewicz, Y., Daidakulov, A., Elovici, Y.: DiskFiltration: data exfiltration from speakerless air-gapped computers via covert hard drive noise (2016). arXiv:1608.03431

27. Guri, M., Kedma, G., Kachlon, A., Elovici, Y.: AirHopper: bridging the air-gap between isolated networks and mobile phones using radio frequencies. In: 9th IEEE International Conference on Malicious and Unwanted Software (MALCON 2014), Puero Rico, Fajardo (2014)

28. Loughry, J., Umphress, A.D.: Information leakage from optical emanations. ACM Trans. Inf. Syst. Secur. (TISSEC) 5(3), 262–289 (2002)

29. Sepetnitsky, V., Guri, M., Elovici, Y.: Exfiltration of information from air-gapped machines using monitor's LED indicator. In: Joint Intelligence & Security Informatics Conference (JISIC-2014) (2014)

30. S.G.SC Magazine UK. Light-based printer attack overcomes air-gapped computer security. 17 October 2014. http://www.scmagazineuk.com/light-based-printer-attack-overcomes-air-gapped-computer-security/article/377837/

31. Lopes, A.C., Aranha, D.F.: Platform-agnostic low-intrusion optical data exfiltration. In: 3rd International Conference on Information Systems Security and Privacy (ICISSP 2017), Porto (2016)

32. Griffith, S.: How to make a computer screen INVISIBLE, dailymail, October 2013. http://www.dailymail.co.uk/sciencetech/article-2480089/How-make-screen-INVISIBLE-Scientist-shows-make-monitor-blank-using-3D-glasses.html. Accessed May 2016

33. Guri, M., Hasson, O., Kedma, G., Elovici, Y.: VisiSploit: an optical covert-channel (2016). arXiv:1607.03946 [cs.CR]

34. Deshotels, L.: Inaudible sound as a covert channel in mobile devices. In: USENIX Workshop for Offensive Technologies (2014)

35. Gostev, A.: Agent.btz: a Source of Inspiration? SecureList, 12 March 2014. http://securelist.com/blog/virus-watch/58551/agent-btz-a-source-of-inspiration/

36. GReAT team. A Fanny Equation: I am your father, Stuxnet, Kaspersky Labs' Global Research & Analysis Team, 17 February 2015 https://securelist.com/blog/research/68787/a-fanny-equation-i-am-your-father-stuxnet/

37. Goodin, D.: Meet badBIOS, the mysterious Mac and PC malware that jumps airgaps. ars technica, 31 October 2013. http://arstechnica.com/security/2013/10/meet-badbios-the-mysterious-mac-and-pc-malware-that-jumps-airgaps/

38. Khimji, I.: TripWire. The Malicious Insider, March 2015. http://www.tripwire.com/state-of-security/security-awareness/the-malicious-insider/. Accessed 09 May 2016

39. TechTarget, Evil maid attack. http://searchsecurity.techtarget.com/definition/evil-maid-attack

40. Costin, A.: Security of CCTV and video surveillance systems: threats, vulnerabilities, attacks, and mitigations. In: TrustED '16 Proceedings of the 6th International Workshop on Trustworthy Embedded Devices, New York (2016)

41. 9 Investigates hacked surveillance cameras across Central Florida, 3 Nov 2016 http://www.wftv.com/news/9-investigates/9-investigates-hacked-surveillance-cameras-across-central-florida/463226966. Accessed 12 Apr 2017

42. Brant, T.: Samsung security cameras hacked again. pcmag, 18 January 2017. http://www.pcmag.com/news/351120/samsung-security-cameras-hacked-again. Accessed 12 Apr 2017

43. thehackernews. Two arrested for hacking washington CCTV cameras before trump inauguration. 02 February 2017. http://thehackernews.com/2017/02/cctv-camera-hacking.html

44. Schmid, S., Corbellini, G., Mangold, S., Gross, T.R.: An LED-to-LED visible light communication system with software-based synchronization. http://www.bu.edu/smartlighting/files/2012/10/Schmid_.pdf

45. Giustiniano, D., Tippenhauer, N.O., Mangold, S.: Low-complexity visible light networking with LED-to-LED communication. In: 2012 IFIP Wireless Days (WD) (2012)

184   M. Guri et al.

46. phys.org. Siemens Sets New Record for Wireless Data Transfer using White LEDs. 21 January 2010. https://phys.org/news/2010-01-siemens-wireless-white.html. Accessed 30 Jan 2017
47. http://man7.org/linux/man-pages/man3/fseek.3.html
48. http://man7.org/linux/man-pages/man3/fopen.3p.html
49. (Unix), dd. https://en.wikipedia.org/wiki/Dd_(Unix). Accessed 01 July 2016
50. sourceforge.net, 17 June 2015. https://sourceforge.net/projects/hdparm/. Accessed 01 July 2016
51. Linux Programmer's Manual. http://man7.org/linux/man-pages/man2/open.2.html
52. CreateFile function. MICROSOFT. https://msdn.microsoft.com/en-us/library/aa363858(VS.85).aspx
53. https://en.wikipedia.org/wiki/Visible_light_communication
54. http://www.analog.com/media/en/technical-documentation/data-sheets/AD549.pdf
55. NI-9223, C Series Voltage Input Module. http://sine.ni.com/nips/cds/view/p/lang/en/nid/209139
56. https://www.thorlabs.com/thorproduct.cfm?partnumber=PDA100A
57. http://www.seagate.com, http://www.seagate.com. SEGATE. http://www.seagate.com/em/en/tech-insights/advanced-format-4k-sector-hard-drives-master-ti/
58. Rubini, A., Corbet, J., Kroah-Hartman, J.: Interrupt handling. In: Linux Device Drivers. O'Reilly (2005)
59. Russinovich, M.E., Ionescu, A., Solomo, D.A.: Understanding the windows I/O system. MICROSOFT, 09 September 2012. https://www.microsoftpressstore.com/articles/article.aspx?p=2201309&seqNum=3
60. McNamara, J.: The complete, unofficial tempest information page (1999). http://www.jammed.com/~jwa/tempest.html
61. USAF. AFSSI 7700: Communications and information emission security. Secretary of the Air Force (2007)
62. Anderson, R.J.: Emission security. In: Security Engineering, 2nd edn. Wiley Publishing, Inc., pp. 523–546 (2008)
63. ZDNET. Surveillance cameras sold on Amazon infected with malware. April 2016. http://www.zdnet.com/article/amazon-surveillance-cameras-infected-with-malware/
64. https://www.signalsdefense.com/products

A Stealth, Selective, Link-Layer Denial-of-Service Attack Against Automotive Networks

Andrea Palanca[1](✉), Eric Evenchick[2](✉), Federico Maggi[3](✉),
and Stefano Zanero[1](✉)

[1] Dipartimento di Elettronica, Informazione e Bioingegneria,
Politecnico di Milano, Milan, Italy
andrea.palanca@mail.polimi.it, stefano.zanero@polimi.it
[2] Linklayer Labs, Toronto, Canada
eric@evenchick.com
[3] FTR, Trend Micro, Inc., Milan, Italy
federico_maggi@trendmicro.com

Abstract. Modern vehicles incorporate tens of electronic control units (ECUs), driven by as much as 100,000,000 lines of code. They are tightly interconnected via internal networks, mostly based on the CAN bus standard. Past research showed that, by obtaining physical access to the network or by remotely compromising a vulnerable ECU, an attacker could control even safety-critical inputs such as throttle, steering or brakes. In order to secure current CAN networks from cyberattacks, detection and prevention approaches based on the analysis of transmitted frames have been proposed, and are generally considered the most time- and cost-effective solution, to the point that companies have started promoting aftermarket products for existing vehicles.

In this paper, we present a selective denial-of-service attack against the CAN standard which does not involve the transmission of any complete frames for its execution, and thus would be undetectable via frame-level analysis. As the attack is based on CAN protocol weaknesses, all CAN bus implementations by all manufacturers are vulnerable. In order to precisely investigate the time, money and expertise needed, we implement an experimental proof-of-concept against a modern, unmodified vehicle and prove that the barrier to entry is extremely low. Finally, we present a discussion of our threat analysis, and propose possible countermeasures for detecting and preventing such an attack.

1 Introduction

The automobile, starting from the late seventies, has witnessed massive and radical changes over the years, due to the ever increasing addition of electronics and software. Almost every aspect of a car operation (e.g., steering, locks, windows, airbag deployment) is nowadays supervised by in-vehicle embedded systems, communicating among each other via an internal network typically

M. Polychronakis and M. Meier (Eds.): DIMVA 2017, LNCS 10327, pp. 185–206, 2017.
DOI: 10.1007/978-3-319-60876-1_9

based on the Controller Area Network (CAN) standard. The unavoidable consequence of this increased complexity and co-presence of electronic and computer-
based components is a wider digital attack surface. The feasibility of such
attacks has extensively been demonstrated by security researchers over the past
decade [4,10,13,14,26], to the point that "car hacking" is now being taken into
serious consideration by US government agencies [25], already acting toward
strengthening automotive cybersecurity regulations [1].

Most of the attacks demonstrated thus far leverage one or more vulnerabilities with the aim of indiscriminately sending messages into the car's internal
network and proving that it is possible to alter the behavior of safety-critical
elements such as engine, brakes or steering. The frame-based nature of these
attacks makes them effectively recognizable by proper intrusion detection or
prevention systems (IDSs/IPSs), which monitor all messages circulating on the
network and trigger countermeasures in case they detect that an attack is in
progress. Previous work [6,12,13,20,21,26,27] has shown the feasibility of porting classic intrusion detection methodologies to the automotive domain, and car
cybersecurity companies have already proposed aftermarket solutions for existing vehicles [2,17,23].

In this paper, we present a novel link-layer denial-of-service (DoS) attack
that is inherently harder to detect via frame-level analysis mechanisms, because
it does not require the transmission of *any* complete frame for its execution.

The attack is able to selectively cause malfunction or even a complete shut-
down of any CAN node connected to the bus, including safety-critical components
(e.g., electronic stability control, electric power steering). Since it exploits design
weaknesses of the CAN protocol standard, any implementation and manufacturer
is vulnerable, even beyond the automotive domain such as factory automation
(e.g., CANopen- or DeviceNet-based machinery), building automation (e.g., ele-
vator management), and hospitals (e.g., lights, beds, X-Ray machines).

The attack works locally, through the standard diagnostic port—which is
mandatory in essentially every country [19]—or via a tampered/counterfeited/
remotely-compromised replacement part. Therefore, the attacker model is rather
generic, including for example a malicious mechanic, a malicious over-the-air
(OTA) firmware upgrade, a malicious passenger or driver in a car sharing (or
even self-driving car) setting, and similar scenarios.

In order to precisely evaluate the required time, level of expertise and cost,
we concretely implemented a proof-of-concept of the attack against a modern,
unaltered production vehicle (an Alfa Romeo Giulietta), and prove that it can
be efficiently and conveniently mounted against a specific frame with 99.9974%
accuracy using a development board as simple as an Arduino Uno.

In the end, we discuss examples of possible threats to car occupants, examine
which are potential attack vectors and real-world scenarios where such attack
could be staged by attackers, and propose possible remediation approaches.

In summary, our paper makes the following contributions:

- We describe a stealth, denial-of-service attack against the CAN standard, to
  which all CAN bus implementations are vulnerable.

- We demonstrate the attack feasibility by implementing a low-cost proof-of-concept against an unmodified vehicle and release full source code to the community.
- We propose practical solutions for detecting the attack in existing CAN networks and discuss possible network modifications for preventing it in future vehicles.

2   Background

2.1   Controller Area Network (CAN) Bus

The Controller Area Network (CAN) bus is a multi-master asynchronous soft real-time serial bus standard designed for the interconnection of multiple components called *nodes*. It was designed and first developed by Robert Bosch GmbH, released in 1986, and standardized in 1993 as ISO 11898.

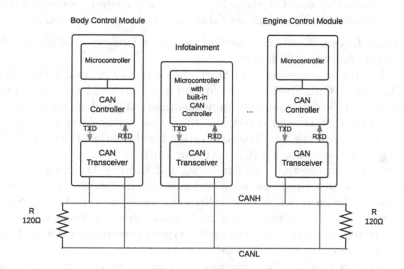

Fig. 1. Example architecture of a generic two-wire CAN network.

Physical Layer. ISO 11898 CAN buses are characterized by two wires, CANH (high) and CANL (low), terminated at each end by a 120 Ω resistor.

As shown in Fig. 1, each CAN node comprises three parts:

Microcontroller: is responsible for sending and processing complete CAN frames to and from the CAN controller and supervising the CAN controller operation.

CAN Controller: implements the CAN specification. It synchronizes with the CAN signal, sends and receives logical data to and from the CAN transceiver, automatically adds stuff bits, and performs error handling. Notably, in our attack we leverage such error handling mechanism. Therefore, we describe thoroughly in Sect. 3.

CAN Transceiver: serves as an interface between the CAN controller and the physical bus by translating logical signals coming from the CAN controller into bus electrical levels.

Stuff bits are added whenever a transmitter detects five consecutive identical bits to be sent. When this happens, the transmitter automatically inserts a subsequent complementary bit in the transmitter bit stream. This so-called *stuff rule* is necessary to keep the nodes synchronized. CAN buses have no clock sync signal, and use a Non Return to Zero encoding.

The CAN standard mandates that one of the two logical values shall be *dominant* over the other one. In case one "dominant" and one "recessive" bit are sent at the same time, the bus state—and thus the logical signal received by all CAN nodes—is "dominant." Most CAN bus implementations feature a wired-AND configuration, hence the dominant bit is the logical 0 whereas the recessive bit is the logical 1. The state read by the nodes is determined by the voltage measured between CANH and CANL lines; whenever it exceeds a certain threshold (usually 0.9 V), a dominant state is encoded (recessive otherwise).

Data Link Layer. The CAN standard describes four types of frames: data, remote, error, and overload frame.

The data frame is composed of Start of Frame, Arbitration Field, Control Field, Data Field, CRC Field, ACK Field, and terminates with the End of Frame. The Arbitration Field contains the Frame Identifier, which identifies the meaning of the message content, and determines the frame priority when two or more nodes are contending the bus. The Arbitration Field is either 11 or 29 bits long, depending on the specification (CAN 2.0A or 2.0B).

The error frame consists of an Error Flag and an Error Delimiter. The Error Flag is characterized by six consecutive identical bits (dominant or recessive, depending on the current CAN controller error state, as explained in Sect. 3), which violate the bit stuffing rule. A node sends an error frame whenever an error is detected. In particular, there exist 5 types of errors: bit error, stuff error, CRC error, form error, and acknowledgment error.

A message is valid for the transmitter if there is no error until the end of End of Frame. A message is valid for the receivers if there is no error until the last but one bit of End of Frame.

2.2 Applications of CAN Bus

The CAN bus standard has been designed specifically for the automotive domain, which is where it finds most applications.

Although other protocols have been proposed through years—e.g., Local Interconnect Network (LIN), Flexray—, CAN has been established as the *de-facto* standard by car manufacturers due to its general-purpose ability of carrying data for a great variety of applications [15] (which, for instance, LIN is not able to ensure due to its slow speed and master-slaves architecture [16]) while still preserving competitive prices (cost per node of a CAN bus network is approximately half the cost per node of a Flexray network [18]). In addition to that, some countries, such as the USA, recently started mandating the exclusive use of CAN for diagnostics purposes for all light duty cars sold on the market [24]: this further encouraged the majority of car makers into adopting CAN bus for the implementation of the entire car's internal network.

There are typically two types of CAN data frames in current automotive systems:

Standard messages: exchanged between two or more ECUs for regular communications, in order to coordinate for the correct execution of an application. For example, the frames sent from the engine control module to the instrument panel to display engine status.

Diagnostic messages: exchanged between diagnostic devices connected to the car internal network (e.g., via the on-board diagnostics OBD-II port) and one or more ECUs for diagnostic sessions. For example, for emission testing or, in case of malfunctioning vehicle, for checking diagnostic trouble codes.

One of the major applications of CAN bus standard messages in modern vehicles is for active safety systems, which reactively (and even proactively) intervene and correct car inputs in real time to avoid or minimize the effects of an accident, or to enhance the driving experience. In the past, active safety systems were included as standard equipment in luxury vehicles only; however, given the (measured) effectiveness of such systems in terms of road casualties and injuries reduction, governments started mandating a minimum set of active safety systems on all cars sold on their national market. At the same time, national crash-test evaluation agencies began fostering their adoption by means of safety ratings boosts. As a result, the majority of modern cars are equipped with on-board active safety systems.

Nevertheless, the CAN standard is not restricted to the automotive domain only. Beginning in 2002, with the Ducati 999, motorcycle manufacturers started adopting CAN buses, mainly due to the weight savings provided by the reduced wire harness requirements. The CAN standard is also employed for train-wide communication networks (e.g., linking door units, brake controllers coordination, passenger-counting units), maritime (e.g., controlled-by-wire ships), avionics (e.g., flight-state sensors, navigation systems, or communications with research PCs in the cockpit), or aerospace (e.g., fuel systems, pumps, or linear actuators). The CAN standard is also used for regulating CANopen- or DeviceNet-based machinery networks in industries (e.g., packaging machines, knitting systems or for semiconductor manufacturing), for managing operating rooms equipment in hospitals (e.g., lights, beds, X-Ray or other diagnostic machines), or for controlling elevators in modern, automated buildings.

2.3   Known Attacks

The constant addition and coupling of embedded systems inside vehicles and the inclusion of more and more interfaces with the outside world immediately raised concerns about the impact of vulnerabilities.

Researchers of ESCRYPT were the first to theoretically investigate the possible risks to which vehicles would be exposed in case of attack and to propose possible countermeasures [29].

Notably, starting from 2010, researchers have also been investigating *practical* attacks on CAN networks, especially focusing on frame-injection attacks because of their potential ability to deeply alter the vehicle's behavior. The authors of [8,10] first showed how a local attacker capable of injecting frames into the vehicle's network could control the majority of its subsystems, including safety-critical devices like engine or brakes, and even bypassing the driver inputs.

In the following years, the famous "Jeep hack" by Charlie Miller and Chris Valasek [14], anew completed via frame-injection attacks, further contributed to raising security awareness among car manufacturers.

2.4   Proposed Countermeasures

A survey conducted in March 2016 by the US Government Accountability Office [25] among major industry stakeholders identified the following countermeasures that could be applied to mitigate the impact of digital attacks against current and future cars:

Trusted Computing Base: hardware security modules or trusted software in order to preserve and guarantee ECUs integrity.
Network Segmentation: safety-critical ECUs decoupling from non safety-critical ECUs, or from ECUs featuring external interfaces, by confining them in different networks and restricting inter-networks communications via fire-walls/gateways.
Cryptography: by means of ECUs code signing or frames encryption and authentication.
Intrusion Detection or Prevention Systems (IDSs, IPSs): security appliances that monitor network traffic, try to establish if an attack is in progress and, in case of prevention systems, attempt to stop it automatically.

Among these, frame-analysis based detection or prevention systems are currently believed to be the most time- and cost-effective solution for circumventing security threats in CAN networks [6,12,13,20,21,26,27]. Indeed, frame-injection attacks are based either on the transmission of normal frames at a much higher rate than usual[1] or on the transmission of diagnostic frames that are not expected to be seen in standard circumstances. Hence, a proper detection system can recognize signs of such attacks. Moreover, the bus topology of CAN-based networks makes the deployment of IDSs or IPSs into current architectures effortless, to the point that companies have already developed aftermarket detection and prevention systems for current generation vehicles [2,17,23].

---

[1] The reason is that spoofed frames will be sent at the same time as legitimate frames. Thus, in order to trick the receiving ECU into considering only the maliciously crafted messages, these must be sent at a much faster rate with respect to the rightful ones.

2.5   Related Work

The idea of mounting denial-of-service attacks against CAN networks is not novel. In the aforementioned papers [8,10,14,26,29], several examples of DoS attacks via frames injection have been proposed (e.g., by sending frames that counteract driver inputs, or frames with the highest priority so as to indefinitely delay other nodes' transmissions). However, these kinds of attacks are effectively detected and stopped with frame-analysis based IDS/IPS approaches. Indeed, the essential aspect of such attacks is the injection of either unexpected frames or the transmission of frames at abnormal rates.

A more subtle denial-of-service attack exploiting CAN error handling and fault confinement protocols was published in July 2016 [5]. However, the attack is restricted to periodic messages only as it requires precise predictability of transmission instants of target frames, and it still involves the communication of a few complete messages for its execution. The attack presented in this paper, instead, is not affected by any restrictions and does not require any full message-sending capability at all.

These types of frame-less attacks were theorized in the past. For instance, in [29] the authors explore the feasibility of performing frame-less DoS attacks by sending well-directed error flags into the CAN network, forcing other nodes to reject a message. In [9] the authors briefly mention that similar situations could occur if a corrupted node started to upset CAN traffic bits. In [28] many bus networks (including CAN) are described as being vulnerable to "bit banging" attacks. However, all previous work described such attacks from a purely theoretical standpoint, without any proof-of-concept implementation nor in-depth threat-model analysis.

To the best of our knowledge, the only prior work which proposed an implementation of a mechanism capable of inserting faults in CAN networks is [7]. Yet, the research focused on injecting errors in CAN networks for pre-production testing purposes only, without covering any security considerations. Moreover, in order to perform such faults injection, the network had to be topologically altered to a non-ordinary star schema, tampering which a potential attacker is not expected to perform in a reasonable amount of time.

3   Protocol Analysis and Attack Description

In this section, we describe the two weaknesses that have been exploited by the proposed denial-of-service attack. The main one lies in how the CAN standard handles errors. A second weakness further exacerbates the impact of the first one, making its DoS capabilities more relevant. Finally, we present our attack, along with a description of its technical requirements.

3.1   CAN Error Handling Weakness

As mentioned in Sect. 2, there are five possible error types. For our attack, the relevant one is the bit error type.

By design, each node must monitor the bus signal every time it sends a frame. A bit error occurs (and must be detected within the sampling frequency) whenever a transmitting node notices that the logical value of the bus is different from the bit value that it is trying to send[2]. Should a node observe such condition, it must interrupt the frame transmission and send immediately an error frame, which breaks the stuff rule (or generates other errors) and causes all other nodes to reject the frame received up to this point, effectively denying the broadcast of that frame.

Therefore, considering that a dominant bit always overwrites a recessive bit, the transmission of just *one* single dominant bit, by *any* node, when a recessive bit is being transmitted, is enough to trigger a bit error, causing the other nodes to discard the current frame.

3.2   CAN Fault Confinement Weakness

The impact of bit errors is not limited to frame-wise DoS due to a second security weakness of the CAN standard induced by the automatic fault confinement protocol.

In order to automatically overcome node faults and avoid situations such as a malfunctioning node causing a complete bus failure, each CAN node can be in three distinct error states (Fig. 2), depending on how many errors a certain node has generated or observed:

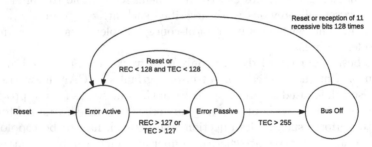

Fig. 2. CAN fault confinement finite state machine.

Error Active: the CAN node normally takes part in bus communications and sends an active error flag (six dominant bits) when it detects an error.
Error Passive: the CAN node can normally take part in bus communications, but can only send a passive error flag (six recessive bits) when it detects an error and must wait an additional 8-bit time before starting a new transmission.
Bus Off: the CAN node cannot take part in any bus communication, not even reading frames off the bus.

---

[2] With the exception of the Arbitration Field and the ACK Field, in which a bus value different than the transmitted one is an expected condition in regular CAN protocol operations.

Transitions between these three error states are determined by the values of two counters, the Transmit Error Count (TEC) and the Receive Error Count (REC). According to the protocol, whenever a transmitting node sends an error flag, its TEC must be increased by 8. This means that, after 16 invalid transmissions, an Error Active node with a zeroed TEC will go in Error Passive state ($TEC = 16 \times 8 = 128$), and after another 16 invalid transmissions it will enter the Bus Off state ($TEC = 256$), denying all bus communication until a bus idle condition or a reset command (or both) are observed. Unfortunately, forcing an idle condition is practically impossible, because it would mean disabling or disconnecting the majority of devices attached to the bus. Similarly, forcing a reset command, which can be done by the node's microcontroller, is problematic, because the Bus Off node could be a legitimate faulty node.

By means of the previous weakness, the practical consequence is that 32 straight bit overwrites on a frame sent by a node are sufficient for making that node unable to either send or receive any message on and off the bus, effectively denying the service that such node is implementing.

3.3 Technical Requirements

The attack is based on a deliberate violation of the CAN protocol, which mandates that all nodes that have lost arbitration shall in no way further interfere with CAN traffic.

The adversary must be able to directly read the RXD signal coming from the transceiver (which transports the current logical CAN bus value) and manipulate the TXD signal entering into the transceiver (which transports the logical value the CAN bus will be driven to), as depicted in Fig. 3. This requires the microcontroller to be directly attached to the transceiver, a common architecture among ECU manufacturers [11], such as in the case of the Renesas V850ES/FJ3

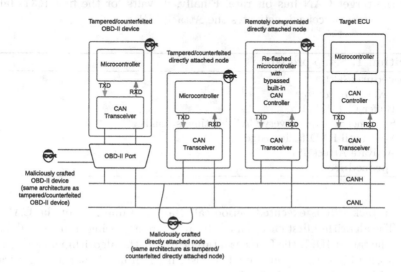

Fig. 3. Examples of attacking nodes architectures.

of the Jeep Cherokee's Uconnect [14], due to the induced cost-effectiveness and space-saving reasons.

The microcontroller is simply required to support pin-edge-change external interrupts and a timer that can be set to trigger at custom values (i.e., to match the CAN bus bit rate), both largely diffused features in modern microcontrollers (the aforementioned V850ES/FJ3 supports both). Obviously, the microcontroller must be fast enough to account for interrupt latency, pin read-write latency and compilation-induced overhead, a requirement which is nowadays not restricting thanks to the availability of low-price multi-core high-frequency microcontrollers (e.g., Parallax Propeller).

3.4   Proposed Attack Algorithm

The attack, which runs in a microcontroller attached to the CAN bus, consists of a setup phase (Algorithm 1), whose goal is to prepare the microcontroller for the attack execution, and an interrupt service routine (ISR) (Algorithm 2), which will monitor the bus and, when necessary, will execute the actual attack payload.

The setup algorithm is executed only once, when the microcontroller boots. The procedure consists in setting the TXD signal to recessive and initializing a buffer of size B—which, during the attack, will always contain the last B bits read from the CAN bus—with a series of 1s (as the ISR will start its execution after the first RXD falling edge for synchronization purposes, thus after a series of 1s have been transmitted on the bus). The size B of the buffer depends on the implemented CAN specification (11 bit or 29 bit): For instance, if the attacker wants to disable a node which is sending frames with a 29 bit ID, a buffer of at least $B = 29$ bits is needed. Then, the algorithm sets the timer expiration value—which regulates the rate at which the attack ISR will be executed—to match the target CAN bus bit rate. Finally, it waits for the first RXD falling edge and, when perceived, activates the Attack ISR.

Algorithm 1. Setup procedure

1: **procedure** SETUP
2:     TXD ← *Recessive*
3:     Buffer ← 111 ... 1
4:     Set timer to expire every CAN bit time seconds
5:     Wait until RXD falling edge
6:     Activate Attack ISR
7: **end procedure**

The attack ISR is executed periodically, at the same rate of the CAN bus signal. The algorithm first checks if the frame currently being transmitted on the bus has the target ID. If the frame is a target frame, the algorithm overwrites the first recessive bit with a dominant bit. Else, if the frame is not a target frame, the algorithm updates the buffer by sampling the bus signal and appending the sampled bus value to the buffer (Fig. 4).

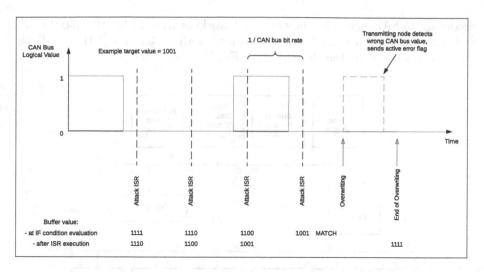

Fig. 4. Visualization of the proposed attack algorithm on a time graph.

Algorithm 2. Attack ISR
___

1: **procedure** ATTACK
2:     **if** Current frame in Buffer is a target frame **then**
3:         Wait until first recessive bit
4:         TXD ← *Dominant*
5:         Wait CAN bit time seconds
6:         TXD ← *Recessive*
7:     **else**
8:         Append RXD value to Buffer
9:     **end if**
10: **end procedure**

___

4   Experimental Proof-of-Concept Implementation and Testing

In this section we describe how an adversary can implement our attack. Our goal is twofold. First, we want to assess the technical feasibility of our attack and quantify its performance on a modern automobile. Secondly, we want to show how low the barrier to mount the attack is nowadays, given the ample availability of rapid-prototyping frameworks (e.g., Arduino).

A full demonstration video of the attack in action is available at https://www.youtube.com/watch?v=PmcqCbRMCCk and the source code running on the attacking device at https://github.com/stealthdos/CAN-Denial-of-Service.

4.1   Target Automobile

The automobile at our disposal for the test was a 2012 Alfa Romeo Giulietta 2.0 JTDm-2. The car features two CAN buses: a high-speed CAN (class C, according to SAE networks classification) working with 29 bit IDs (500 kbps), and a medium-speed CAN (class B) working with 29 bit IDs (50 kbps). Both lines are reachable via the OBD-II port (Fig. 5).

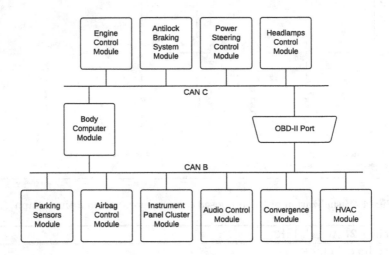

Fig. 5. Architecture of the 2012 Alfa Romeo Giulietta 2.0 JTDm-2 internal CAN networks.

For ethical reasons, we performed the proof-of-concept attack against a CAN B bus node, namely the parking sensors module. This choice is guided by the fact that CAN B buses typically do not connect safety-critical nodes: This should reduce the chances that, by simply reading this paper and taking our open-source prototype, a malicious attacker or a "script kiddie" could directly reuse our attack on safety-critical subsystems connected to CAN C buses. This does not imply any loss of generalization: bit rate apart, CAN Bs and CAN Cs operate identically.

4.2   CAN Traffic Analysis

In order to capture CAN traffic, we purchased for $30 a Scantool OBDLink SX USB-to-OBDII cable. The device features an embedded STN1130 micro-controller that, besides emulating the very common ELM327 1.3a AT instruction set, allows to capture even partial or erroneous CAN frames thanks to the additional ST commands. Moreover, it performs frame decoding automatically, writing ID-Data Length Code (DLC)-Data Field directly on the serial port.

We plugged the device into a laptop, then into the OBD-II connector, and we started listening on the serial port to capture all CAN messages sent on the bus for a fixed amount of time (until we noticed no different frames) in various conditions (e.g., with neutral gear, with reverse gear, with reverse gear and near an obstacle).

We filtered the captured CAN traffic and inspected it manually to remove uninteresting CAN frames. Eventually, we isolated the frame responsible for notifying the obstacle position, sent by the parking sensors module. Some examples of that frame follow:

```
CAN ID: 0x06314018;
Data Length Code: 8 bytes;
Data Field:
- Ignition off: frame not sent;
- On, N: C000000F0F000000;
- On, R, no obstacle: 0000000F0F000000;
- On, R, central obst: 0300000X0XY00000,
  X: chime sound frequency,
  Y: distance on driver's LCD.
```

An attacker who wants to target another device would have to either perform the same procedure offline, on another instance of the same car, or know the CAN ID in advance. Overall the whole procedure could require from minutes (e.g., for capturing the frame issued by a dashboard button) to hours or days (e.g., when trying to thoroughly reverse engineer a complex active safety protocol). The corner case is when the target CAN bus is not directly reachable via the OBD-II port. In this case, however, the attacker could simply reach the bus line by other means, as thoroughly discussed in Sect. 5.

4.3 Attacking Device Implementation

We implemented our attack as a hand-crafted OBD-II dongle, which can be physically plugged into the car's OBD-II port. Its architecture is reported in Fig. 6. We opted for an Arduino Uno Rev 3 and a Microchip MCP2551 E/P, the cheapest (total expense was around $25) and most common microcontroller and CAN transceiver available on the market which are capable of fulfilling the aforementioned minimum requirements.

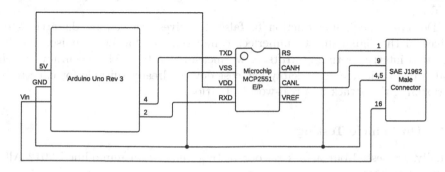

Fig. 6. Schematic of the crafted attacking device.

In order to execute the attack payload against the target vehicle, all it is necessary to do is plug the device into the car's OBD-II port. The operation requires less than 30 s, the device will be instantly powered by the 12 V battery and will immediately start the algorithm.

4.4   On Bench Testing

To adequately test our attacking device implementation and investigate its reliability, we implemented a bench test CAN bus.

On-bench Attack Test. In addition to the OBDLink SX and the attacking device, we used a breadboard and two 120 Ω resistors for creating a CAN network, a 12 V rechargeable battery for simulating the car battery, and a Linklayer Labs CANtact 1.0, an open-source, Python-scriptable, low-cost USB-to-CAN adapter. This setup ensured that we had at least two nodes, as required by the CAN specifications for correct operation.

First, we tested whether, without the attacking device, both nodes were able to correctly exchange messages with each other. Then, we connected the attacking device to the CAN bus and tried to send (target) CAN frames; first, from the OBDLink SX, then from the CANtact. In both cases the attacking device managed to correctly "kill" the target frames: The receiving nodes were not able to retrieve the message. Moreover, we confirmed that the CAN fault confinement weakness (Sect. 3.2) caused the CANtact node to enter the Bus Off state, after exactly 32 erroneous frames. Note that, being a mere testing tool, the OBDLink SX does not implement the CAN automatic fault confinement protocol, but retries to send an erroneous message for 160 times before halting the transmission.

Reliability Measurement. In order to investigate the reliability of our attacking device in a realistic scenario—comprising both target and non-target CAN frames—we developed a Python CAN-fuzzing script. The script automatically generates random, yet valid, CAN frames, sends them through the OBDLink SX, waits to receive them from the CANtact, and compares the received frames with the original ones. We left the script running for 24 h and report the results in Table 1.

Despite a negligible fraction of false negatives—caused by distortions or spikes in the signal due to imperfect connections or hardware noise, and by Arduino interrupts timing drifts—, we measured a 99.9974% accuracy, which makes our basic and remarkably low-cost device already suitable for effectively performing the attack in a real-world situation.

4.5   On Vehicle Testing

Finally, we tested our attack on our testing vehicle, an unmodified 2012 Alfa Romeo Giulietta.

Table 1. CAN fuzzer/checker test statistics.

Description	Value
Test duration	24 h
Total number of frames sent	9,403,842 frames
Average throughput	108.84 frames/s
Average frame length	101 bits
Average CAN utilization	0.21985834
Number of correctly processed frames	9,403,598 frames
Number of false positives	0 frames
Number of false negatives	244 frames
Accuracy	**0.99997405**

After plugging the attacking device to the OBD-II port, the parking sensors immediately stopped working altogether: Neither visual information nor warning proximity chime could be heard, even in the presence of a very close obstacle, and the dashboard display notified the driver about the malfunctioning subsystem (Fig. 7a and b).

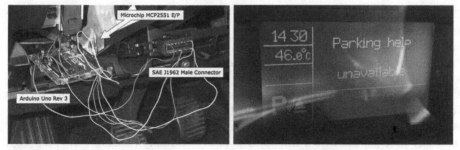

(a) The attacking device attached to the Giulietta's OBD-II port.

(b) The parking sensors malfunction reported on the driver's LCD.

Fig. 7. Our attack in action on a real-world modern vehicle.

The subsequent fabrication of an ad-hoc forked cable, which allowed to connect both the attacking node and the OBDLink SX to the OBD-II port at the same time, and the following CAN traffic capture also revealed that the parking sensors module reached the Bus Off state—only 32 transmission attempts were recorded—, without any doubt confirming the complete denial-of-service accomplishment.

5   Threat Model Discussion and Remediation Approach

5.1   Threat Assessment

In this section, we discuss the practical impact of our work in terms of threats arising if an adversary decides to mount this type of attack against a vehicle in the real world, even in the presence of frame-analysis based detection or prevention systems. In all cases, the envisioned attacker is only required to execute our denial-of-service attack. Therefore, differently than previous work, we do not require that the attacker has frame-injection capabilities.

Active Safety Systems Attacks. One of the main purposes of CAN standard messages is to support active safety systems communications. Despite their undeniable usefulness, active safety systems may induce double-edged sword situations while driving, especially when the drivers have grown accustomed to their presence, and begin to blindly rely on them. As a result, an abrupt malfunction in such systems may cause unpredictable and potentially dramatic consequences. Given this premise, a potential threat is that an adversary could start using our attack to induce specific "faults" in the CAN frames generated by active safety systems. For instance, mounting our attack on traction control systems may lead to perilous vehicles loss of control; on autonomous cruise control systems may lead to vehicles not autonomously stopping as expected by drivers, a failure which, last year, caused even fatal accidents [22].

Car Ransom. Although CAN is not suitable for supporting steer-by-wire or brake-by-wire functionalities, CAN has been employed in the past to carry throttle-by-wire messages. For instance, as described in [26], the 2010 Toyota Prius internal combustion engine throttle actuator is controlled by CAN frames sent from the power management control ECU to the engine control module. An adversary may use our attack against such frames, causing inability for the driver to control throttle position and thus to move the vehicle. Though this would not necessarily generate hazardous conditions, a financially motivated attacker, after exploiting a vulnerability in an externally reachable module (e.g., the infotainment system), could leverage the DoS to mount a ransomware-like attack and later show the classic message on the infotainment display, in an utter similar fashion to desktop computers ransomware. An analogous condition might also be caused by blocking the frames sent by the key-less access control unit at car startup to all other modules, preventing anti-theft systems from being disengaged and hence the car from being started.

Theft Support. Both the aforementioned attack scenarios, despite perfectly feasible, would require a previous substantial reverse-engineering effort. In this section we discuss a third option, focusing on resource-bound attackers. We also assume that the attacker has a very narrow time window to gain physical access to the target vehicle.

Most modern premium cars' door locks are controlled by CAN B-connected ECUs (for instance, the 2014 Jeep Cherokee [14]), which is typically accessible via the OBD-II port. Isolating the frames responsible for locking the doors is much simpler and faster than reverse-engineering active safety equipment messages. Indeed, the aforementioned door locks are under complete control of the user: A single press of the lock-unlock button on the driver's door corresponds exactly to one fixed set of frames issued to the door modules actuators. Therefore, in a matter of minutes, an adversary may isolate the frames responsible for doors locking, modify a software parameter in the attacking device in order to DoS locking frames, and then leave the device plugged into the car's OBD-II port, preventing car doors from being locked again after being unlocked. The attacking device architecture can be as simple as our experimental proof-of-concept or may include other components for additional functionality: For instance, GPS or GSM shields in order to track the vehicle position or command the attack payload execution remotely. The result of this attack is the ability, for the attacker, to gain cost-effective aposteriori access to the car, allowing her to subsequently steal any valuable goods or replacement part inside the vehicle.

5.2 Threat Vectors Analysis

After discussing the possible threats that a potential attacker may pose by selectively stopping specific CAN frames, we hereby examine the attack vectors that can be leveraged.

The easiest way by which the attack can be mounted is via a crafted device attached to the OBD-II port. As a matter of fact, in most vehicles the OBD-II port serves as a direct interface into all car internal buses, provides 12 V direct current output for powering connected devices, and is conveniently located underneath the steering wheel. Therefore, in a matter of seconds, an adversary with physical car access is able to install a working attacking device inside a car. Real-world scenarios in which this may happen are numerous, and include for instance valet parking, car sharing, car renting, car lending or self-driving car settings.

A similar situation may arise if the car owner decides to use a rogue (trojanized/counterfeited) aftermarket OBD-II device. The reasons for doing so could be various. For instance, the owner may opt for a low-cost "compatible" replacement part, be willing to obtain discounted fees from insurance companies by installing so-called "black boxes", could be interested in performing do-it-yourself car diagnostics, or simply for enriching car infotainment functionality.

Nonetheless, physical-access attacks are by no means limited to the diagnostic port. An adversary may or must opt for attaching and hiding the attacking device anywhere along the car internal network (see the attacker depicted under the two wires in Fig. 3). This, for instance, may happen in a malicious-mechanic scenario, while the car is undergoing tests or repair. The same holds for the installation of rogue replacement parts that require CAN bus connections for their operation, like aftermarket infotainment units, parking sensors modules, or anti-theft systems.

In addition, the denial-of-service attack may also be staged without requiring any physical interaction with the target vehicle at all. In this case, however, there must be an on-board CAN node with a fast-enough microcontroller that supports external and timer interrupts, and obviously there must be a vulnerability that allows an attacker to remotely re-flash the microcontroller firmware. Although this setting is certainly restrictive, in [14] the authors proved that, by leveraging a chain of vulnerabilities in the Harman Kardon Uconnect system of a 2014 Jeep Cherokee, it is possible to remotely re-flash the embedded Renesas V850ES/FJ3 microcontroller—responsible for the Uconnect CAN communications—with an ad-hoc firmware. Like many automotive-specific microcontrollers, the V850ES/FJ3 embeds an on-chip CAN controller—therefore, it is directly connected with CAN transceivers via re-programmable GPIO pins—and supports both edge-triggered and timer interrupts. As a consequence, the very same exploitation chain that led to the Cherokee remote compromise via CAN frames injection could be used for mounting our DoS attack as well.

In all depicted scenarios, the envisioned attacker is able to obtain persistent presence on the CAN network, even surviving through vehicle's power-cycles. In order to eliminate the threat, the vehicle's owner is required to physically disconnect the device from the vehicle's network in case of surreptitiously added or trojanized replacement part, or to reflash the compromised ECU with factory firmware in case of a remote reprogramming.

5.3   Detectability and Countermeasures

Last, we briefly compare our attack with detection approaches recommended so far in literature for identifying security incidents in current CAN networks, and propose possible detection and prevention solutions for recognizing and impeding the execution of the DoS, in the hope that car manufacturers would take them into account during the design of future vehicles' internal networks.

Comparison with Current Detection Mechanisms. CAN bus intrusion detection systems proposed up to now in literature are essentially based on the anomaly detection of a measure concerning well-formed frames, because, in the majority of attacks, in order to trigger actions on cyber-physical systems, a transmission of frames is required. The evaluated measures are the frequency of messages of a specific ID—such as in [13,21,26,27]—, the time differences of messages with a specific ID [20], the specification of the behavior of messages with a specific ID [12], or the clock skews of periodic frames, again given a fixed ID [6]. This attack, instead, is not based on the transmission of new frames, but on the transmission of bits concurrently to the transmission of a legitimate frame. If this is done as described in Sect. 3.4, there would not be anomalous activity such as, for instance, unexpected message transmissions or even something as subtle as spikes in the CAN signal: From the receiving devices' point of view, there would simply be a frame transmission interrupted by an error. In brief, a frame-analysis based IDS could only notice the effect of our attack, i.e. the lack of frames sent from a particular device, not the attack itself. At this point, it could effectively signal the anomaly to the driver, however the attack has already successfully taken place at least one time and the target device has already reached Bus Off state.

Attack Detection. The most problematic challenge to address is the detection of a forthcoming attack before the denial-of-service has been executed, as the attacking node will not participate in any way with the CAN activity but will remain completely silent to all other nodes.

To mitigate the surreptitious addition of rogue devices into the car's internal network, we propose a novel solution based on simple electronics principles. All CAN nodes are characterized by a differential internal resistance (Rdiff), within a standard interval according to the CAN specifications. Such Rdiff influences the total bus load that a transmitting unit must drive in order to correctly send a dominant or a recessive bit on the bus. Any additional node attached to the bus would change the load, and thus would change the necessary current flow for driving a dominant bit on the bus. Therefore, a detection mechanism could find out when a (new) node is connected by measuring the amount of current necessary for a dominant condition at each vehicle startup and comparing this value with the previously registered ones.

This mechanism, unfortunately, can by no means protect from remotely compromised nodes. However, a remote vector for our attack would require prior re-flashing of a node's microcontroller, thus altering its functionality. This opens the possibility for detecting signs of such alterations (e.g., via code-integrity checks) before the actual DoS attack takes place.

While the attack is in progress, a possible way to distinguish a deliberate DoS from an occasional node fault stands in the determinism by which errors are manifested. The malicious node that executes our attack will *always* send a dominant bit at a certain position of a specific frame, resulting in that frames regularly triggering bit errors in the same way. This is very unlikely to happen in the case of a fault. A detection approach could be to account for errors statistics for all frames and identify suspiciously correlated error scenarios.

Attack Prevention. Since our attack relies both on link-layer and physical-layer weaknesses proper of the CAN protocol, caused by a lack of consideration over security requirements at design time, preventing the DoS without a major nodes and network architecture revision is *hardly* feasible. Nevertheless, there exist a number of solutions that could be considered during the design of next-generation vehicles.

Network Segmentation. The main precondition of our attack is that the attacking node must be able to physically sense the target frame during its transmission. Should the target and attacking nodes be attached to *separate* CAN networks, the DoS would not be possible. Therefore, network segmentation by means of trusted mediators (e.g., CAN firewalls) is a viable solution. This approach would not prevent an attacker from physically connecting the attacking device directly on target CAN bus, but, at least, would very likely contain damages by possible counterfeited or remotely compromised nodes.

Network Topology Alteration. A more radical segmentation approach consists in changing the network topology from the current bus topology to a star topology, with a trusted network dispatcher in the middle, as proposed in a few prior studies [3,9]. Unfortunately, this solution would dramatically increase the wiring harness and limit the flexibility of the network, which was one of the core reasons which favored CAN bus adoption in the past.

Diagnostic Port Access Control. Another countermeasure consists in securing the access to the OBD-II port, which is the easiest attack vector. Apart from physical access prevention (e.g., via a separate hardware key), another approach is to rely on an authentication gateway between the OBD-II port and the other networks, designed to exclusively allow transmission of OBD-II PIDs data queries to unauthenticated users, and full CAN access to authenticated personnel only. This could deter both our attack as well as previous attacks based on frames injection, without breaking the OBD-II diagnostics capability.

Encryption. Another option is to implement encryption to the ID and Data Field of CAN frames (e.g., via stream ciphers or block ciphers in stream mode). The attacking node would not be able to distinguish target frames from unrelated ones and, thus, would be unable to selectively attack certain ones. This approach would not prevent the attacking node from brute-forcing the ID space to inject faults in the whole CAN traffic. Nevertheless, this would make the attacking node noisy and thus easier to detect.

Other Protocols. The ultimate solution for preventing this kind of attack in automotive networks would be to use non-vulnerable protocols. For instance, albeit not immune to other security issues [29], Flexray is not susceptible to our attack because both logical 0s and 1s are represented by dominant conditions on the bus.

6 Disclosure

An official disclosure to the Computer Emergency Response Team (CERT) of the attack and its impact has been performed, in the hope to reach the greatest number of members of the CAN bus community.

7 Conclusions

In this paper, we have presented and analyzed a novel design-level DoS attack against CAN buses. The attack does not require the transmission of any complete data frame. All it demands is the transmission of 1 bit, resulting in being potentially capable of deceiving all frame-analysis based detection and protection approaches, which are currently believed to be the most time- and cost-effective solution for securing CAN networks from digital attacks.

As the leveraged weaknesses lie in the CAN design, and are by no means implementation or manufacturer specific, all instances of CAN bus networks (including, but not limited to, land vehicles, maritime, avionic, medical or industrial applications) are vulnerable to this attack.

In our research we have focused on the impact on the automotive area. We implemented (and released to the public) an experimental proof-of-concept on a modern, unaltered vehicle, proving that the barriers for mounting the attack are slim. Then, we have described the possible threats against car owners and passengers descending from the discovery of our attack. Last, we have discussed the potential attack vectors, and proposed possible short- and long-term mitigation approaches.

The ultimate hope of the research is to instill awareness over the security risks that an aggressive and unrestricted interconnection approach of nodes—now equipped with external interfaces—via a fragilely security-wise designed network protocol such as CAN bus could pose, and propose practical solutions in order to ensure the security that a safety-critical components' backbone network is not expected to lack.

References

1. All bill information (except text) for s.1806 - SPY car act of 2015. https://www. congress.gov/bill/114th-congress/senate-bill/1806/all-info
2. Argussec: ARGUSidps. https://argus-sec.com/solutions/
3. Barranco, M., Rodriguez-Navas, G., Proenza, J., Almeida, L.: CANcentrate: an active star topology for CAN networks, pp. 219–228, September 2004. http://iestcfa.org/bestpaper/wfcs04/WFCS04_Barranco.pdf
4. Checkoway, S., et al.: Comprehensive experimental analyses of automotive attack surfaces. http://www.autosec.org/pubs/cars-usenixsec2011.pdf
5. Cho, K.T., Shin, K.G.: Error handling of in-vehicle networks makes them vulnerable. In: CCS 2016, USA, pp. 1044–1055 (2016). http://doi.acm.org/10.1145/2976749.2978302
6. Cho, K.T., Shin, K.G.: Fingerprinting electronic control units for vehicle intrusion detection, pp. 911–927. USENIX Association, Austin. https://www.usenix.org/conference/usenixsecurity16/technical-sessions/presentation/cho
7. Gessner, D., Barranco, M., Ballesteros, A., Proenza, J.: Designing sfiCAN: a star-based physical fault injector for CAN (2011). https://www.researchgate.net/profile/Julian_Proenza/publication/232259902_Designing_sfiCAN_A_star-based_physical_fault_injector_for_CAN/links/00b7d532161b659ee8000000.pdf
8. Hoppe, T., Kiltz, S., Dittmann, J.: Security threats to automotive CAN networks – practical examples and selected short-term countermeasures. In: Harrison, M.D., Sujan, M.-A. (eds.) SAFECOMP 2008. LNCS, vol. 5219, pp. 235–248. Springer, Heidelberg (2008). doi:10.1007/978-3-540-87698-4_21
9. Kammerer, R., Frömel, B., Wasicek, A.: Enhancing security in CAN systems using a star coupling router, pp. 237–246, June 2012. http://www.vmars.tuwien.ac.at/documents/extern/3116/canrouter_security.pdf
10. Koscher, K., et al.: Experimental security analysis of a modern automobile, May 2010. http://www.autosec.org/pubs/cars-oakland2010.pdf
11. Kvaser: Microcontrollers with CAN (2016). https://www.kvaser.com/about-can/can-education/can-controllers-transceivers/microcontrollers-with-can/

12. Larson, U.E., Nilsson, D.K., Jonsson, E.: An approach to specification-based attack detection for in-vehicle networks, June 2008. http://ieeexplore.ieee.org/document/4621263/

13. Miller, C., Valasek, C.: A survey of remote automotive attack surfaces, August 2014. http://illmatics.com/remote%20attack%20surfaces.pdf

14. Miller, C., Valasek, C.: Remote exploitation of an unaltered passenger vehicle, August 2015. http://illmatics.com/Remote%20Car%20Hacking.pdf

15. National Instruments: Controller area network (CAN) overview. http://www.ni.com/white-paper/2732/en/

16. National Instruments: Introduction to the local interconnect network (LIN) bus. http://www.ni.com/white-paper/9733/en/

17. NNG: Arilou cyber security. https://www.nng.com/arilou-cyber-security/

18. ON Semiconductor: Basics of in-vehicle networking (IVN) protocols. http://www.onsemi.com/pub/Collateral/TND6015-D.PDF

19. SAE International: Global OBD legislation update (worldwide requirements). http://www.sae.org/events/training/symposia/obd/presentations/2009/d1dave ferris.pdf

20. Song, H.M., Kim, H.R., Kim, H.K.: Intrusion detection system based on the analysis of time intervals of CAN messages for in-vehicle network, January 2016. http://ieeexplore.ieee.org/document/7427089/

21. Taylor, A., Japkowicz, N., Leblanc, S.: Frequency-based anomaly detection for the automotive CAN bus, December 2015. http://ieeexplore.ieee.org/document/7420322/

22. The Verge: Tesla driver killed in crash with autopilot active, NHTSA investigating, June 2016. http://www.theverge.com/2016/6/30/12072408/tesla-autopilot-car-crash-death-autonomous-model-s

23. Towersec: ECUShield. http://tower-sec.com/ecushield/

24. United States Environmental Protection Agency: Control of air pollution from new motor vehicles and new motor vehicle engines. http://www.epa.gov/fedrgstr/EPA-AIR/2005/December/Day-20/a23669.htm

25. United States Government Accountability Office: VEHICLE CYBERSECURITY - DOT and industry have efforts under way, but DOT needs to define its role in responding to a realworld attack, March 2016. http://www.gao.gov/assets/680/676064.pdf

26. Valasek, C., Miller, C.: Adventures in automotive networks and control units, August 2013. http://www.ioactive.com/pdfs/IOActive_Adventures_in_Automotive_Networks_and_Control_Units.pdf

27. Valdes, A., Cheung, S.: Communication pattern anomaly detection in process control systems, May 2009. http://ieeexplore.ieee.org/document/5168010/

28. Waibel, A.: The art of bit-banging: Gaining full control of (nearly) any bus protocol, June 2016. https://www.youtube.com/watch?v=sMmc0hSi5rs

29. Wolf, M., Weimerskirch, A., Paar, C.: Security in automotive bus systems (2004). http://citeseerx.ist.psu.edu/viewdoc/download?doi=10.1.1.92.728&rep=rep.1&type=pdf

Detection and Protection

Quincy: Detecting Host-Based Code Injection Attacks in Memory Dumps

Thomas Barabosch$^{(\boxtimes)}$, Niklas Bergmann, Adrian Dombeck, and Elmar Padilla

Fraunhofer FKIE, Zanderstrasse 5, 53177 Bonn, Germany
{thomas.barabosch,niklas.bergmann,
adrian.dombeck,elmar.padilla}@fkie.fraunhofer.de

Abstract. Malware predominantly employs code injections, which allow to run code in the trusted context of another process. This enables malware, for instance, to secretly operate or to intercept critical information. It is crucial for analysts to quickly detect injected code. While there are systems to detect code injections in memory dumps, they suffer from unsatisfying detection rates or their detection granularity is too coarse. In this paper, we present *Quincy* to overcome these drawbacks. It employs 38 features commonly associated with code injections to classify memory regions. We implemented *Quincy* for Windows XP, 7 and 10 and compared it to the current state of the art, *Volatility*'s *malfind* as well as *hollowfind*. For this sake, we created a high quality data set consisting of 102 current representatives of code injecting malware families. *Quincy* improves significantly upon both approaches, with up to 19.49% more true positives and a decrease in false positives by up to 94,76%.

Keywords: Malware · Memory forensics · Host-Based Code Injection Attacks · Machine learning

1 Introduction

Malware families implement many different behaviors such as form grabbing, information leakage, persistence or code injections. Host-Based Code Injection Attacks (HBCIA) are a family-inherit technique utilized to execute code in a trusted context of another process. There are two processes involved: the attacker process P_a and the victim process P_v, which both run on the same system. P_a injects code from its own process space into the one of P_v. Subsequently, P_a triggers the execution of this code within P_v. HBCIAs allow malware, for instance, to intercept critical information within a browser or to hide from antivirus software. A study indicates that almost two thirds of recent malware samples utilize this technique [7]. Amongst others, this includes prevalent families like *Dridex*, *Rovnix*, *Tinba* and *Zeus*. This points out the relevance of HBCIAs and renders them an interesting and valuable topic to investigate in order to detect and mitigate malware in general.

© Springer International Publishing AG 2017
M. Polychronakis and M. Meier (Eds.): DIMVA 2017, LNCS 10327, pp. 209–229, 2017.
DOI: 10.1007/978-3-319-60876-1_10

Analysts face HBCIAs on a daily basis. Forensic analysts are confronted with memory dumps of unknown systems and in case of a malware infection without an initial sample. Malware analysts continue to integrate forensic analyses in their work flow due to the improvement of memory forensic frameworks like *Volatility* [27]. In both cases, a fast and accurate initial detection of malicious code in a memory dump is crucial. There are systems such as *Volatility's malfind* [27], *hollowfind* [20] and *Membrane* [24] that support the detection of HBCIAs in memory dumps. However, they suffer from major drawbacks. Whereas *malfind* suffers from a high false positive rate, *hollowfind* detects only a subgroup of all relevant types of HBCIAs. For example, *malfind* fails to detect *Ponmocup*, driving one of the biggest botnets out in the wild [26]. It fails because it only considers two features: the access property of memory regions as well as the hiding of libraries. In contrast to *malfind* and *hollowfind*, *Membrane* is limited to a coarse grain detection, i.e. it detects infected processes instead of the actual malicious regions within a process. Although this reduces the size of the hay stack to search in, it does not pinpoint the malware exactly: for instance, the process *Explorer* contains 554 memory regions yielding 405 MB of data on an idling Windows 10 system.

In this paper, we overcome the limitations of the aforementioned systems by presenting *Quincy*. Its detection heuristic is based on 38 features from seven categories commonly associated with injected code. They include, among others, memory region permissions, memory region sparseness and the presence of shellcode. *Quincy* embeds these features in a vector space and classifies consecutive memory pages (in the following just *memory regions*) as either malicious or benign. We implemented *Quincy* for three Windows versions and released it as a *Volatility* plugin on our website [5]. Our evaluation with a set of 102 current malware families and 1794 benign programs shows that our system has a higher detection rate with only few false positives (up to 94,76%) and more true positives (up to 19,49%) when compared to *malfind* and *hollowfind*.

The contributions of this paper can be summarized as follows:

(I) **A novel approach for HBCIA detection**
We propose a fully-automated system to detect Host-Based Code Injection Attacks in memory dumps. *Quincy* has the idea of platform-independence in mind and hence focuses on concepts found among all modern multi-tasking operating systems. Our approach is based on supervised machine learning and utilizes a combination of 38 features to detect HBCIAs. This allows it to significantly improve upon the state of the art *malfind*.

(II) **Implementation and evaluation**
We implemented *Quincy* and released it as a *Volatility* plugin on our website [5]. We evaluated it in a systematic evaluation with current real world malware families and goodware. In addition, we compared it to *malfind* as well as *hollowfind* to prove that it significantly improves upon them.

(III) **Creation and publication of our data set**
During our investigation on HBCIAs in memory dumps, we gathered the most comprehensive data set of representatives of HBCIA-employing

malware families that is available today. We crafted YARA signatures for
each family to verify a successful infection and to ensure a precise ground
truth. We share this data set on our website [5].

2 Quincy

In this section, we present *Quincy*, our approach to detect HBCIAs in memory
dumps. At first, we give an overview of its architecture. The system consists
of the following phases: feature extraction, feature selection, embedding of these
features into a vector space, learning and classification. Subsequently, we describe
each of these phases in detail.

2.1 Overview

Figure 1 sketches *Quincy*'s work flow: first, it receives memory dumps as input
and closes the semantic gap, i.e. the gap between the binary representation of
data in a memory dump and its meaning to the operating system. Internally,
this is done by the memory forensic framework *Volatility* [27].

Second, it extracts low-level information, including processes, threads and
memory regions. The features are based on this low-level information. They are
closely related to HBCIAs such as memory region permissions, dynamic API
resolving and the presence of shellcode. *Quincy* extracts these features for each
region in a memory dump. A memory region is a set of consecutive pages within
a process. Whereas the typically page size is four kilobyte on x86, a memory
region consisting of many pages may have a size of several megabytes. *Virtual
Address Descriptor* (VADs) is the term for a memory region on Windows. Note
that such regions may be shared between processes, e.g. system libraries that
are mapped with *EXECUTE_WRITECOPY* permissions on Windows.

Third, *Quincy* embeds these features for every memory region in a multi-
dimensional vector space. Fourth, it induces a binary classifier. As a result, it
can classify previously unseen memory region as either malicious or benign.

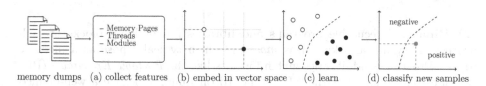

memory dumps   (a) collect features   (b) embed in vector space   (c) learn   (d) classify new samples

Fig. 1. The four phases of *Quincy*: it receives dumps with labeled memory regions
as input. Then, it extracts 38 HBCIA-related features, which are organized in seven
categories (a). Subsequently, it selects valuable features and embeds them in a multi-
dimensional vector space (b). It then induces a binary tree-based classifier (c). Finally,
it can classify previously unseen memory regions (d).

2.2 Feature Extraction

The following sections describe the 38 features organized in seven categories that *Quincy* may employ for classification. We engineered these features based upon domain knowledge in the fields of malware analysis and memory forensics. Table 1 summarizes the features. Later, we conduct a feature selection to discard less valuable features (see Sect. 4.1). Thereby, we create a feature set for each operating system. This optimizes our detection rate while minimizing the resources required.

(1) API. System interaction such as network communication and file access can only be accomplished through the operating system via syscalls. On most operating systems high-level APIs are available that are more comfortable to use. This included Windows. These APIs are an important keystone in the malware analysis process: the presence of certain function calls allows to draw conclusions about the behavior of a binary. For instance, we can deduce from a call to *CreateRemoteThread* that an *HBCIA* is likely to occur.

The feature $api_{general\_api\_strings}$ checks for the presence of API calls in general by scanning for common string prefixes such as *Create*, *Get* or *Open*. This enables us to differentiate memory regions that might communicate with the OS and the ones that might not. As a consequence this detects regions hosting executable files. The feature api_{hbcias} explicitly scans for a set of API calls that are related to HBCIAs such as *CreateToolhelp32Snapshot* and *ZwSetContextThread*.

Since the presence of API calls lessens the analyst's burden, malware authors obfuscate API names. Hence, they deobfuscate them just in time and dynamically resolve the pointers to the API code. This can also be done via a set of special functions. The feature $api_{dynamic\_loading}$ checks for the presence of such functions like *LoadLibrary* and *GetProcAddress*. A more sophisticated method is to manually resolve APIs by enumerating all libraries that are mapped into the process space. This requires access to process data structure, e.g. the *Process Environment Block* (PEB) on Windows. The feature $api_{hashing}$ searches for code patterns that access such data structures to detect code that implements api hashing.

(2) Binary. Executable programs and libraries are building blocks of each process. They are also known as *modules*, which typically pose as a memory region. Programs and libraries match formats like the *Portable Executable* (PE) standard on Windows or the *ELF* standard on Linux and have a well-defined header. The following features interpret header structures in memory regions in case they are available.

The feature $binary_{has\_header}$ checks if a memory region starts with a well-known header. However, malware may overwrite its header to impede its analysis. The feature $binary_{wiped\_header}$ covers this case by checking for a zeroed-out beginning of a memory region that is followed by code. Although benign programs come in the form of a stand-alone executable or a library, malware often

Table 1. Summary of the 38 features utilized by *Quincy*. The categories and features within them are alphabetically arranged. The rank of a feature is based on its importance determined in the feature selection on Windows XP/7/10. Note that the final models do not employ all features (see Sect. 4.6).

Overview of *Quincy* features			
Category	Feature	Rank	Description
(1) API	dynamic_loading	29/26/16	Presence of dynamic loading APIs
	general_api_strings	08/11/13	Common API call prefixes
	hashing	09/10/17	Code fragments related to API hashing
(2) Binary	exports	30/19/33	Exports API calls
	has_header	23/21/20	Starts with a header
	imports	35/33/28	Imports API calls
	is_dynamic_library	32/20/27	Has been loaded dynamically
	is_module	16/13/22	Registered module known to the OS
	is_pe_or_dll	14/16/10	A PE executable or shared library
	wiped_header	37/34/36	Executable header has been wiped
(3) Code	functions	10/08/18	Common assembler function prologues
	hooks	04/05/12	Memory region contains code hooks
	indirect_calls	05/03/05	Ratio of indirect calls to all calls
	indirect_jumps	12/04/07	Ratio of indirect jumps to all jumps
	shellcode	01/15/11	Shellcode patterns
(4) Cryptography	cipher	33/29/30	Constants of ciphers
	encoding	26/23/21	Constants of encoding schemes
	hashing	28/20/25	Constants of hashing algorithms
(5) Countermeasure detection	debugger	17/18/29	Strings and code patterns to detect debuggers
	sandbox	22/27/15	Strings and code patterns to detect sandboxes
	vm	36/36/35	Strings and code patterns to detect virtual machines
(6) Memory	embedded_exe	38/38/38	Embedded executable after header
	english_strings	27/35/23	Strings of Google's top 1000 English search terms
	high_entropy_areas	07/06/06	Areas of high entropy
	is_heap	34/32/32	Memory region is a heap
	is_sparse	03/01/02	Ratio of zero bytes
	mapped	15/37/37	Corresponds to a memory mapped file
	network_strings	06/07/14	Strings related to networking
	persistence	24/30/19	Strings related to persistence
	private	18/14/08	Tagged as private memory
	protection	13/17/01	Protection of memory region
	tag	20/09/05	Tagged by allocation functions
	threads	11/12/09	Count of threads originated in memory region
	victim_strings	19/31/26	Names of typical HBCIA victims
(7) Trojan	banking	25/28/31	Strings related to online banking
	cookies	21/23/24	Strings related to cookie stealing
	credentials	31/24/34	Strings related to credential stealing

injects shellcode into its victim processes. The feature $binary_{is\_pe\_or\_dll}$ checks if a memory region is a stand-alone executable or library by reading a field of the corresponding header. Benign executables and libraries are either loaded at process start or dynamically during runtime with the help of the OS, which keeps track of these modules. The feature $binary_{is\_module}$ encodes if a memory region is registered as an official module by parsing the PEB. Malware obfuscates its API usage and therefore imports few or none API functions. The feature $binary_{imports}$ encodes whether or not a memory region imports such functions. Malware may also inject entire libraries into victim processes. System libraries export up to several hundreds functions. In contrast, malware may only export a handful of functions, if any. The feature $binary_{exports}$ checks if a region has exported functions.

(3) Code. The following features scrutinize assembly code properties of a memory region. We assume that every meaningful program is split into several units of code, which is reflected by low-level assembly functions. Therefore, the feature $code_{functions}$ searches for patterns of common function prologues in memory regions. We assume these byte sequences to indicate code presence. Malware families like *GozNym* do not inject executable modules such as standalone executables and libraries but rather shellcode. On execution, this position-independent code has to determine its current address in memory to act. The feature $code_{shellcode}$ scans memory regions for code patterns that determine their position in memory. For example, it considers patterns like a call to the next instruction, followed by a pop to a register, which determines the current address in memory.

Due to position-independence and obfuscation reasons, malware contains significantly more branches with dynamically calculated targets in relation to direct calls and jumps. The features $code_{indirect\_calls}$ and $code_{indirect\_jumps}$ describe the ratio of indirect calls/jumps to all calls/jumps. The feature $code_{hooks}$ searches for code hooks that point from one memory region into another region. The presence of such hooks may reveal, for example, the presence of banking trojans that hook libraries in browsers to intercept banking credentials. On the downside, searching for hooks in memory dumps is computational expensive. For instance, *Volatility*'s *apihooks* may take up to a couple of minutes to scan a memory image. Therefore, we opted to scan memory regions for strings related to hooking of browser APIs functions like *Firefox*'s *Netscape Portable Runtime* (NSPR), which are commonly hooked by code-injecting banking trojans.

(4) Cryptography. Malware may try to hide its presence and communication by extensive use of cryptography, e.g. files are encrypted with *AES*, network traffic is encoded with *Base64* or network packets are hashed with *SHA256*. Usually malware does not rely on external libraries like Microsoft's Cryptographic API, but rather statically links the cryptographic algorithms into its binary in order to increase analysis costs. Features of this category look for constants or strings related to prominent encryption ($crypto_{cipher}$), encoding ($crypto_{encoding}$) and hashing algorithms ($crypto_{hashing}$).

(5) Countermeasure Detection. Malware authors want to postpone analysis as long as possible. Therefore, many malware families impede their analysis by including countermeasure techniques. We distinguish between three types: first, the feature $counter_{debugger}$ checks for traces of anti-debugging techniques that aim at manual analysis. These traces include code fragments, e.g. accessing the *beingDebugged* flag of the process space, and strings related to malware analysis tools such as debuggers and process inspectors. Second, the feature $counter_{sandbox}$ checks for the presence of certain sandbox related strings, e.g. such as *Anubis* or *Cuckoo*. Third, the feature $counter_{vm}$ scans for strings and code fragments that detect virtual machines, which are commonly employed in malware analysis. For example, malware can detect *VirtualBox* VMs due to its default MAC address prefix *0x080027*.

(6) Memory. The following features focus on the properties of memory regions themselves. They are arranged in three subcategories.

Statistical features: many memory regions are sparse, i.e. they have a high ratio of zero bytes. In contrast, memory regions of binaries are more densely filled with data. Therefore, the feature $memory_{is\_sparse}$ measures the ratio of zero bytes to find nearly empty regions.

Lyda et al. [18] proposed the entropy of data to detect compressed or encrypted data. *Quincy* leverages entropy analysis to detect areas of high entropy. We chose the area size to be four kilobyte as the typical page size on the Intel x86 architecture and the entropy threshold to be 6.5 as suggested by Lyda et al. [18]. The feature $memory_{high\_entropy\_areas}$ encodes the percentage of high entropy areas within a memory region.

Memory region properties: this subcategory considers mostly flags assigned to a memory region by the operating system: heap flag ($memory_{is\_heap}$), its protections ($memory_{protection}$) such as readable, writable or executable, memory mapped file flag ($memory_{mapped}$), private memory flag ($memory_{private}$) and memory allocation function tag ($memory_{tag}$). Furthermore, the feature $memory_{threads}$ determines if any thread has been started within a region.

Strings: whereas strings may be obfuscated on hard disk, there are surprisingly many strings in memory. This also holds for malware employing executable packing. The feature $memory_{english\_strings}$ matches a word frequency list of the thousand most frequent search terms on *Google* consisting of more than three characters. We assume that this may help to identify rather benign regions. The feature $memory_{network\_strings}$ detects memory regions that contain networking vocabulary such as *HTTP* or *POST* since network communication is an integral part of today's malware. HBCIA-employing malware prefers certain victim processes [7]. The feature $memory_{victim\_strings}$ searches for victim names in regions such as *explorer.exe* or *svchost.exe* to identify memory regions of HBCIA-employing malware. The feature $memory_{persistence}$ detects strings related to persistence, e.g. the Windows registry key $\ldots\backslash CurrentVersion\backslash Run$ to find code that may have achieved persistence on the system.

(7) Trojan. One reason to inject code into another process is to intercept information. Therefore, code injections are especially important to trojans like *GozNym, Xswkit* or *KINS*. Since the main objective of banking trojans is to divert money in banking sessions, the feature $trojans_{banking}$ scans every memory region for a comprehensive list of financial vocabulary and bank names. Furthermore, they target cookies and general credentials such as *Facebook* or *LinkedIn* accounts. The two features $trojans_{cookies}$ and $trojans_{credentials}$ scan for strings related to cookies and credentials correspondingly.

2.3 Feature Selection and Embedding in Vector Space

Before utilizing machine learning, we select a set of appropriate features and embed them in a vector space without standardization. We employ machine learning algorithms that are unaffected by varying feature scales (tree-based algorithms, see next section). Most features are of binary nature, e.g. the feature $memory_{embedded\_executable}$. However, there are also continuous features such as $memory_{high\_entropy\_areas}$ and $code_{indirect\_calls}$.

Initially, the vector space has 38 dimensions. We carry out a *recursive feature elimination* (RFE) as proposed by Guyon et al. [16]. RFE employs an external estimator that weights features based on their importance. It is recursively trained with decreasing feature sets, where it prunes the weakest feature in each iteration. For this sake, we employ *Random Forests* as external estimator as proposed by Genuer et al. [13].

2.4 Learning and Classification

Quincy learns a model to classify memory regions either as malicious or benign. There are several classes of machine learning algorithms for classification problems such as *Support Vector Machines, Logistic Regression* and *Decision Tree-based algorithms*. Tree-based algorithms pose several advantages including the comprehensibility of predictions, the simplicity of the algorithms and the minimal effort required in data preparation. Therefore, we opt for *Decision Tree-based algorithms*, considering *CART-Decision Trees* [10], *Random Forests* [9], *Extremely Randomized Trees* [14], *AdaBoost* [11] and *GradientBoosting* [12].

2.5 Implementation

We implemented *Quincy* in *Python*. It leverages the memory forensic framework *Volatility* [27] to extract features and *scikit-learn* [3] to learn. Our implementation analyzes all Windows NT versions from Windows XP onwards.

To speed up the analysis process, Quincy copies memory images to a RAM disk and conducts the feature extraction in memory. Hence, the read speed of the machine's memory is crucial to the general runtime. Furthermore, *Quincy*'s feature extraction is single-threaded. Therefore, we expect further speed up by parallelizing the feature extraction.

3 Data Set Creation

We follow the advices of Rossow et al. [25], based on the fact that an evaluation requires a comprehensive data set. This section describes how we created the data set for our evaluation and what kind of data it comprises. First, we describe the considered binaries and how we generated memory dumps from them for the evaluation. Next, we show how we properly labeled the memory regions to ensure a reliable ground truth. Finally, we conduct an initial data analysis of the extracted data.

3.1 Data Set

We require an evaluation data set to contain:

R1 a considerable amount of HBCIA-employing malware families
R2 recent malware families
R3 only Windows malware
R4 goodware programs to estimate false positives

The data set should contain a considerable amount of different families to evaluate the systems with different code injection techniques (**R1**). Next, we want to ensure that our evaluation results are valid for recent malware (**R2**) that runs on the prevalent target Microsoft Windows (**R3**). Finally, the set should contain goodware programs to estimate false positives (**R4**). Table 2 matches these four requirements to three publicly available data sets. *cwsandbox* as well as *malicia* contain only older malware strains and hence violate requirement **R2**. *Malware Classification Challenge* consists of a considerable amount of samples. However, they belong to less than ten families, not all of which employing code injections. Since none of these data sets matches our requirements, we opted to create our own and contribute it to the research community.

Table 2. Matching of publicly available data sets to our four requirements to an evaluation data set discussed in Sect. 3.1

Data set	Year	Publication	R1	R2	R3	R4
cwsandbox	2007	[29]	✗	✗	✓	✗
Malicia	2013	[21]	✗	✗	✓	✗
Malware Classification Challenge	2015	[19]	✓	✗	✓	✗

We considered 1794 benign as well as 102 malicious binaries and generated a memory dump for each of them. Memory dumps of malware contain benign and malicious memory regions, while dumps generated with benign binaries are assumed to contain only benign regions. In the following sections, we describe which binaries we considered in detail.

Benign Binaries. Benign binaries comprise software included in Windows and other widespread programs. For this sake, we extracted programs from the system directory of Windows XP, 7 and 10. Additionally, we collected binaries of widespread programs from an archive of portable freeware applications [1]. In total, we collected 1794 benign binaries. However, the programs that we were able to execute varied among Windows versions. Some programs were not compatible with each version. Moreover, we did not execute system programs of one version on another to ensure compatibility. A list of all benign binaries and their hashes is provided on our website [5].

Malicious Binaries. Our set of malicious binaries consist of 102 representatives of HBCIA employing malware families. Barabosch et al. [6] showed that HBCIAs are an inherent malware family feature, i.e. it is unlikely to change between versions and variants of a family. Therefore, it is sufficient to consider one representative per family. Note that this minimizes family specific overfitting by focusing on the employed HBCIA techniques. We gathered family representatives over the last months. On the one hand, we consulted IT security blogs, e.g. of antivirus companies, that carried out in-depth analysis of malware families. On the other hand, we included families that we internally analyzed at our institute. Later, we manually verified the HBCIA capability of the obtained families (see Sect. 3.3). The set of malicious families contains a wide range of current malware that represent today's threat landscape, for instance, viruses (*Sality*), banking trojans (*Xswkit*), spamming bots (*Cutwail*) and droppers (*Nymaim*). Some samples are not compatible with every Windows version, therefore the number of executable families varies. We share the malicious binaries on our website [5].

3.2   Creation of Memory Dumps

We generated memory dumps for Windows XP SP3, Windows 7 SP1 and Windows 10. We automated the memory dump generation process with a tool, which is based on the virtualization software *VirtualBox* [22]. First, it creates an ISO image containing the sample. Then, it starts the virtual machine in a predefined state and mounts the ISO image on the virtual CD Drive. The guest system runs a script, which executes the sample with administrator privileges. We grant each sample two minutes to initialize, which is a common timeout of sandboxing systems. At the end, it dumps the memory state of the virtual machine to a file.

The virtual machines were not connected to the Internet during the infection, since no command and control server communication was required. They were hardened against several virtual machine detection techniques, since malware may be environment sensitive [17]. First, we utilized the tool *Pafish* [23] to find ways to detect our VMs. Subsequently, we hardened detection points, e.g. by removing strings of the hypervisor from the registry. Note that sometimes hardening is not feasible. For instance, fixing subtle differences between a real x86 CPU and the implementation provided by *VirtualBox* are out of scope for this work.

Table 3. Data distribution of benign and malicious binaries as well as benign and malicious memory regions for all three considered Windows versions.

OS	Binaries		Memory regions	
	Benign	Malicious	Benign	Malicious
Windows XP	1205	71	2729563	398
Windows 7	1264	72	5306368	319
Windows 10	977	73	7266226	710
Total (unique)	1794	102	15302157	1427

3.3 Establishing a Ground Truth

A proper labeling of the data set is essential for a reliable evaluation of our model and comparison with the state of the art *malfind* [27] and *hollowfind* [20]. We established our labeling as follows: we assumed all memory regions of goodware dumps as benign. We can not make a similar assumption for malware dumps: the regions may be malicious or benign. Therefore, we opt to employ *YARA* signatures [2] to reliably detect malicious artifacts in memory dumps. For this sake, we manually reverse engineered the malware families and wrote signatures for each of them. Even though some preliminary work on automatic signature generation exists [15], it is limited to static signatures. However, malware usually is packed, i.e. the original binary and the executed code in memory significantly differ.

We estimated the detection rates of *malfind* and *hollowfind* by interpreting their results as follows: in case they did not mention a memory region then it was labeled as benign. In the other case, it was labeled as malicious.

3.4 Initial Data Analysis

We conducted an initial analysis of the extracted data to get a first impression. According to Table 3, it exhibits a skewed class distribution. The benign binaries outnumber the malicious binaries by an order of magnitude. Benign binaries are easier to access than properly labeled representatives of HBCIA-employing malware. Thereby, the distribution is even more skewed in the case of benign and malicious memory regions, because there are typically more benign processes and hence more benign memory regions than infected processes and malicious regions, respectively. Nevertheless, we argue that this is exactly the haystack scenario that detection systems face in the wild.

4   Model Evaluation

We select features and conduct an optimization and evaluation of our model in Sects. 4.1–4.3. This is followed by the evaluation of our optimized model and a comparison with *malfind* as well as *hollowfind* in Sect. 4.4. Then, we conduct a temporal analysis to estimate how well *Quincy* detects future malware families in Sect. 4.5. Section 4.6 summarizes the final models that we learned on the whole data sets. Finally, we discuss evasion strategies for *Quincy* in Sect. 4.7.

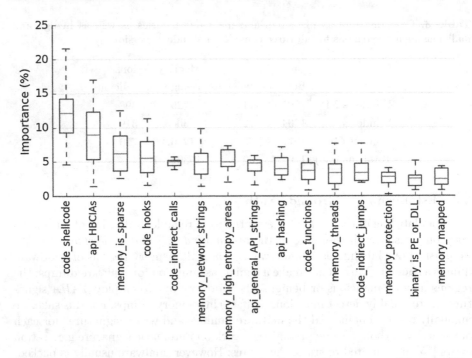

Fig. 2. Relative feature importance in percent for the top 15 features on Windows XP. We obtained these values during the recursive feature elimination phase in the model learning stage. They are based on the estimation of the *Random Forests*.

4.1   Methodology of the Model Evaluation

We did the following ten times for each data set of the three Windows versions, in a cross-validation loop in order to cope with variance.

At first, we randomly split the whole data set consisting of the malicious and benign memory regions into two sets. The first set is the training set d_{train} and the second set is the validation set $d_{validation}$. d_{train} was utilized in model training and model optimization, whereas $d_{validation}$ was exclusively utilized to estimate the final performance of our optimized model. Therefore, we evaluated our optimized model on unseen data to estimate its potential for generalization. Please note that we split the data set such that the malicious regions of one family were either in d_{train} or in $d_{validation}$ but never in both sets. This ensured that our model did not face malicious regions of one family in training and validation.

We showed that the class distribution is heavily skewed in our initial data analysis (see Sect. 3.4). Machine learning algorithms may perform poorly and misclassify many minority class instances due to optimizing the overall accuracy and hence shifting their focus to the majority class. Therefore, we treated the two classes separately. We split malicious regions with a ratio of 60%/40% into d_{train} and $d_{validation}$ and benign regions with a ratio of 10%/90%. On the one hand, this ensured that there are sufficient malicious samples in d_{train}. On the other hand, this added noise in form of benign regions to $d_{validation}$. Noise that *Quincy*, *malfind* and *hollowfind* are confronted with in the real world.

We selected the optimal set of features on d_{train} using *Recursive Feature Elimination* (RFE) with Random Forests. Afterwards, we trained and optimized several tree-based models on d_{train} for comparing them later. The model optimization took place on the whole set of d_{train} and was carried out in form of a randomized grid search. Finally, we evaluated the optimized models together with *malfind* and *hollowfind* on $d_{validation}$.

4.2   Feature Selection

The feature selection took place on d_{train} using *Recursive Feature Elimination* (RFE) with Random Forests. Figure 2 shows the relative feature importance on Windows XP. Note that the results are similar on Windows 7 and Windows 10. Table 1 lists the ranking of the features for the three operating systems.

There are only a few features that significantly contribute to the model with an average of more than 5%. The top three features are $code_{shellcode}$, $memory_{contains\_HBCIA\_strings}$ and $memory_{is\_sparse}$. Whereas the first two features directly aim at detecting malicious memory regions, the third feature detects close to empty and hence probably benign memory regions. Surprisingly, $memory_{contains\_HBCIA\_strings}$ performs well even though it scans for strings. Furthermore, all features of the categories *code* and *API* as well as one half of the features of *memory* are contained within the top 15 features. They cover the two integral parts of a code injection: the injected code and its execution context. In contrast, the two categories *trojan* and *cryptography* do not perform as expected. The assumptions on which these two categories are based did not hold. Whereas in the case of *cryptography* we assumed that malware prefers to statically link cryptographic algorithms, in the case of *trojan* we assumed that data theft related vocabulary is present in many malware strains.

There are few features that have an importance of less than one percent. They are either rare cases like $memory_{embedded\_executable}$ and $binary_{wiped\_header}$ or they are common in regular programs like $crypto_{cipher}$. The feature $memory_{protection}$ on which *malfind* heavily relies on is only of medium importance to our model.

4.3   Optimization of Hyperparameters

The optimization of hyperparameters is an important step towards an optimal model. They are defined outside of the machine learning algorithm, e.g. maximal tree depth or the number of base estimators in a learning ensemble. We opted for a randomized grid search to optimize the hyperparameters of our tree-based models. It does not search over every grid point of the hyperparameter space, instead it randomly samples grid points and evaluates the model with them. Bergstra et al. [8] showed that randomized grid search is more effective than exhaustive grid search as it converges to a close-to-optimum solution at a high rate. We sampled 64 grid points in total as suggested by Bergstra et al. [8] and

Table 4. Hyperparameters to optimize and their value ranges for the five tree-based machine learning algorithms. f denotes the total number of features.

Algorithm	Trees	Learning rate	Max. features	Tree depth
AdaBoost [11]	[10,400]	[0.1, 1.0]	–	–
CART [10]	1	–	$\sqrt{|f|}, |f|$	$[3, 12] + \infty$
Extremely Randomized Trees [14]	[10,400]	–	$\sqrt{|f|}, |f|$	–
GradientBoosting [12]	[10,400]	[0.1, 1.0]	–	[4, 8]
Random Forest [9]	[10,400]	–	$\sqrt{|f|}, |f|$	–

conducted a 10-fold cross validation for every sampled grid point. We chose the best performing parameters for our final model. The evaluation metric was the area under the receiver operating characteristic curve (ROC AUC score).

We considered five algorithms: *CART-Decision Trees, Random Forests, Extremely Randomized Trees, AdaBoost* and *GradientBoosting*. All of them have several hyperparameters: some of these hyperparameters affect the whole ensemble like the learning rate and some of them affect the individual trees like the maximal tree depth. Optimizing all of these parameters is computationally expensive. Therefore, we decided to optimize only the most significant four hyperparameters and set the others to *scikit-learn*'s [3] default values. Table 4 lists the hyperparameters and their respective value ranges.

4.4 Model Evaluation

After having trained and optimized our models, we evaluated their final performance on unseen data to estimate how well they generalize. In addition, we compared them to the state of the art approach *malfind* in version 2.5 [27] as well as *hollowfind* [20], the Volatility plugin contest winner of 2016. *malfind* extensively focuses on memory region related features like memory region permissions. *hollowfind* detects process hollowing by finding discrepancies in process data structures. For an exact description of *malfind* and *hollowfind* see Sect. 5.

We evaluated *Quincy* with five tree-based machine learning algorithms. The following holds true for all three operating systems: the standard decision tree algorithm *CART* yields more true positives than *malfind* but comes with an order of magnitude more false positives. *AdaBoost* and *GradientBoosting* detect less false positives than *malfind*, however they also detect less malicious regions, resulting in an overall worse performance. These two algorithms exhibit far better results than non-boosting algorithms on the training data, which lets us conclude that they most likely overfit. The two best performing algorithms are *Random Forests* and *Extremely Randomized Trees*. Both algorithms are bagging-based. They dominate *malfind* in all cases, with *Extremely Randomized Trees* being the most successful. *Quincy* and *malfind* dominated *hollowfind* in all cases, which showed only slightly better performance than throwing a coin.

Table 5. Final data of the evaluation of *Quincy* with *Extremely Randomized Trees*, *malfind* and *hollowfind* on $d_{validation}$: Area Under Curve (AUC), True Positives (TP) and False Positives (FP).

Windows	Quincy			Malfind			Hollowfind		
	AUC	TP	FP	AUC	TP	FP	AUC	TP	FP
XP	93.8%	149.1	813.5	90.2%	137.9	15538.3	52.24%	7.7	1306.4
7	88.5%	94.4	547.3	80.4%	76.0	7488.0	52.70%	6.6	9176.8
10	84.4%	187.3	1828.5	81.9%	175.6	3672.0	51.57%	8.8	110.1

Table 5 lists the final results of *Quincy* with *Extremely Randomized Trees*, *malfind* and *hollowfind*. All values represent the mean of the 10-fold cross validation. Our system dominates *malfind* when comparing their area under the ROC curve. Its highest score is 93,8% on Windows XP. The greatest difference between their AUC scores can be observed on Windows 7 with 8,09%. Both *Quincy* and *malfind* outperform *hollowfind*, which only detects process hollowing. This is a special case of HBCIAs.

Quincy with *Extremely Randomized Trees* detects more true positives than *malfind* with up to 19,49% on Windows 7. Since *Quincy* incorporates one of *malfind*'s two features, we assumed equal performance at least. However, our system considers more features and detects more malicious memory regions. In contrast to *malfind*, it detects, for instance, malware families like Ponmocup and Dridex, which inject libraries into their victim processes.

Quincy has also less false positives than *malfind* with up to 94,76% on Windows XP. *malfind* considers every non-empty memory area with *RWX* permissions as malicious. Malware authors might forget to cover their traces or the architecture (e.g. shellcode) demands these permissions. This allows *malfind* at least to partially detect a family. However, once these permissions are adjusted well (i.e. only *RX* permissions are set), *Quincy* outperforms *malfind* due to its comprehensive set of other features. False positives of our approach include programs like *Dropbox Portable* that exhibit similar signs like the malicious regions: high entropy areas (probably due to packing), presence of shellcode to determine its position in memory, *RWX* memory permissions and extensive use of cryptography. This results in similar features like of malicious regions. They are therefore falsely classified as malicious. Another observation is that falsely assumed malicious regions decrease with more modern Windows versions. Therefore, *malfind* false positive rate decreases, however our system benefits from this as well.

Table 6 shows the family detection and family completeness. We consider a family *detected* if one approach detects at least one of the family's memory regions. Note that a malware infection may result in many distinctive memory regions distributed over several processes. A detection is considered *complete* when all memory regions are detected. On average, *Quincy* detects more malware families on Windows 7 than *malfind*. Even though both exhibit a similar family detection on Windows XP and Windows 10, *malfind* often just detects small

Table 6. Family detection and family completeness of *Quincy* with *Extremely Randomized Trees*, *malfind* and *hollowfind* on $d_{validation}$.

Windows	Families	Quincy		Malfind		Hollowfind	
		Detection	Complete	Detection	Complete	Detection	Complete
XP	29	24.3	20.9	24.4	19.5	4.7	0
7	29	26.4	18.1	24.3	11.9	4.6	0
10	30	23.7	18.1	23.6	15.2	4.9	0

malicious regions with *RWX* permissions but misses on the main module of the malware family. While this may confirm an infection, it does not yield the main payload responsible for the infection, which is essential to carry out further investigations. This assumption is also supported by the family completeness. On average, our system completely detects more families since it does not solely focus on memory region permissions. *hollowfind* detected only the families that employ process hollowing and none of them completely. Overall our proposed model dominates the other approaches in all evaluation metrics.

4.5   Temporal Evaluation

After evaluating *Quincy* with *malfind* and *hollowfind* and showing its superiority, we conducted a temporal evaluation of these three systems. The objective was to evaluate how well they perform in a temporal setting, i.e. training them on older, historical data and evaluating them on recent data. This evaluation proceeds similar to the general one, limited to one iteration of the cross validation loop. The chronological order is based on a family's first occurrence in the wild. For this sake, we queried *VirusTotal* [4] to arrange the malware in chronological order and split it with a 60%/40% ratio.

Figure 3 shows the final performance as ROC curve of the three approaches averaged over all three operating systems. It documents the superiority of *Quincy* in the temporal evaluation comparing an AUC score of 90.9% versus 87.6% of *malfind* and 54.3% of *hollowfind*. An interesting finding is that the ways of injecting code, e.g. hollowing processes by using memory mapped files or creating a remote thread, do not substantially differ in the two data sets, meaning that newer families exhibit similar injection traces as older families. An explanation may be that malware authors tend to copy from each other.

4.6   Final Models

We precomputed three models based on the full data sets, which we distribute with *Quincy*'s source code [5]. Therefore, we chose *Extremely Randomized Trees* as learning algorithm based on its performance. Moreover, we carried out a feature selection using *RFE* with *Random Forests* and optimized the hyperparameters *number of trees* and *maximal number of considered features*. Table 7 presents the number of selected features and the final hyperparameters.

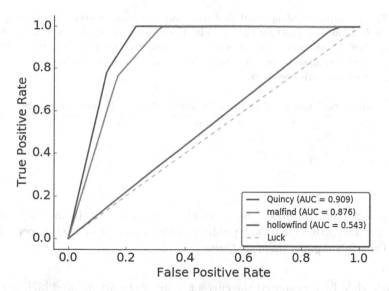

Fig. 3. Final performance of *Quincy* (green), *malfind* (orange) and *hollowfind* (red) in temporal evaluation illustrated as ROC curves averaged over all three evaluated operating systems (XP, 7, 10) (Color figure online)

4.7 Discussion of Evasion

As with every detection system, an adversary can try to understand and circumvent its detection heuristic. However, we utilize 38 features from seven categories. These categories scrutinize several aspects of a memory region, from its memory properties to its embedded code. An adversary may try to circumvent some features, e.g. by bloating the code with zeros to resemble a sparse region, but there are still other features like $code_{functions}$ that would indicate that the region may contain relevant code. The number of different features and their correlations increases the challenge to circumvent our system, when compared to other systems like *malfind* or *hollowfind*.

But there are HBCIAs that might not be detectable during a post-mortem memory dump analysis. Several operating systems offer the possibility to load arbitrary libraries into a process during its creation, e.g. *AppInit DLLs* on Windows. If malware employs such means then detection may fail for several reasons. Foremost, the library has been loaded by the system loader in the same fashion as a regular library. Such modules have therefore the same permissions or they are listed in the same data structures as regular system libraries. In the case of the absence of other indicators these injections are especially difficult to detect.

5 Related Work

There are four systems allowing forensic detection of HBCIAs in memory dumps, which are closely related to our approach: *malfind* [27], *hollowfind* [20],

Table 7. The number of optimal features and hyperparameters for *Quincy* with *Extremely Randomized Trees* on the evaluated operating systems. The number of features describes the amount of features that were selected during the feature selection. The two hyperparameters were selected during a randomized grid search on the whole data set of each operating system.

Windows	Number of features	Number of trees	Maximal features
XP	27	445	$\sqrt{|f|}$
7	34	475	$\sqrt{|f|}$
10	23	435	$\sqrt{|f|}$

Membrane [24] and *Hashtest* [28]. All of them are based on the memory forensic framework *Volatility*. There are public implementations of each except *Membrane*. Table 8 compares them to *Quincy*.

Malfind. Hale Ligh proposed the current state of the art *malfind* [27]. It implements a combination of two features to classify memory regions. At first, it marks entirely empty regions as benign. Pages with *RWX* protections and unlinked libraries (from the PEB) are marked as malicious. Furthermore, it detects wiped PE headers in *RWX*-protected memory regions. The remaining regions are assumed to be benign. Its detection heuristic may be completely circumvented by not utilizing *RWX* permissions and not unlinking libraries. Lassalle proposed *malfinddeep* [27], an improvement to *malfind* that utilizes whitelisting of memory regions based on ssdeep hashes. We did not evaluate *malfinddeep* since there is no official whitelist available. Our work significantly improves upon *malfind*, as shown in the evaluation. *Quincy* considers a superset of *malfind*'s features adding many more in order to decrease false positives, increase true positives and render evasion more difficult.

Hollowfind. The volatility plugin *hollowfind* [20] detects process hollowing, which is a code injection technique, replacing code of a legitimate process and manipulating the initial thread to execute malicious code. The behavior of the malware blends in a trusted process, e.g. *svchost.exe*. *hollowfind* detects process hollowing by comparing two process management data structures for discrepancies. It considers the *Process Environment Block* (PEB), which amongst others list the loaded modules with their paths. Furthermore, it considers a data structure in kernel space (VAD structure), which contains information about the modules' paths. If *hollowfind* finds a discrepancy for a process, then it assumes it to be hollowed out and outputs its memory regions with *RWX* protection like *malfind* does. Its heuristic may be circumvented by not using process hollowing or by removing the discrepancies from the PEB. Overall, the scope of *hollowfind* is narrower than *Quincy*'s. Our system detects HBCIAs in general, a superset including process hollowing.

Table 8. Comparison of related approaches. $XP+$ implies that the approach runs on every Windows version since Windows XP.

Approach	Heuristic	Features	Granularity	Compatibility
malfind [27]	Rule-based	2	Memory region	XP +
hollowfind [20]	Rule-based	2	Memory region	XP +
Membrane [24]	*Random Forrest*	23/28ª	Process	XP and 7
Hashtest [28]	Hash comparison	1	Memory region	XP and 7
Quincy	*Extremely Randomized Trees*	38	Memory region	XP +

ª*Membrane* considers 23 features on Windows XP and 28 features on Windows 7.

Membrane. Pek et al. propose *Membrane* [24]. It reconstructs low-level memory paging information of Windows's software memory management unit (MMU) and leverages this information to detect HBCIAs. Based on domain knowledge, they identified 23 features on Windows XP and 28 features on Windows 7 and applied a *Random Forest* classifier to detect HBCIAs on process-granularity.

There are overlappings between *Quincy* and *Membrane* such as the implementation as a *Volatility* plugin and the utilization of one common feature ($memory_{mapped}$). However, *Quincy* significantly differs from *Membrane*. First, *Quincy*'s detection is finer. Whereas *Membrane* detects HBCIAs on process-granularity, *Quincy* detects them on memory region-granularity. Therefore, a direct comparison between them is not possible. Second, Pek et al.'s approach is very prone to noise. Their results drastically decline from 98% accuracy on Windows XP to 73% on Windows 7. We assume that on Windows 10 this problem gets even worse since the noise level increases with every Windows version as our evaluation showed. Third, they implemented their approach for two older Windows versions (XP and 7). Quincy is not limited to a certain Windows version, hence it also runs on the latest version. Fourth, *Membrane* is based on low-level features. The authors had to reverse engineer parts of the Windows kernel to implement their system. Porting *Membrane* to a new Windows version or even new OS requires tedious reverse engineering.

Hashtest. White et al. present *Hashtest* [28]. They detect HBCIAs by hashing memory regions and subsequently searching for these hashes in a previously built hash database. This reduces the amount of memory regions to analyze. *Quincy* does not rely on whitelisting. Therefore, our approach generalizes better and can deal with previously unseen data.

6   Conclusion

Host-Based Code Injection Attacks (HBCIAs) play an important role in modern malware with at least two thirds employing them [7]. A fast initial detection of injected malicious code in memory dumps is crucial. Therefore, we presented *Quincy*, a system for detecting these attacks on memory region basis. It is based

on supervised machine learning, utilizing 38 HBCIA-related features, selecting
the optimal feature set, embedding these features in a vector space and training a tree-based model for classification. The evaluation showed that *Extremely
Randomized Trees* fit especially well to the problem.

We evaluated our system on Windows XP, 7 and 10. For this purpose, we created a data set according to the best practices and published the data set online.
We generated memory dumps for more than one thousand benign and malicious
binaries and created a comprehensive data set of benign and malicious memory
regions based on a sound ground truth. Based on this data set, we evaluated
Quincy and compared it to the current state of the art *malfind* and *hollowfind*.
Our results show that *Quincy* significantly improves upon them. It has less false
positives as well as more true positives and dominates the other approaches on
all three considered Windows versions. Finally, we enable practitioners to take
advantage of our findings by publishing our implementation [5].

References

1. The Portable Freeware Collection. http://www.portablefreeware.com. Accessed 24
   Apr 2017
2. YARA. https://plusvic.github.io/yara/. Accessed 24 Apr 2017
3. scikit-learn (2016). http://scikit-learn.org. Accessed 24 Apr 2017
4. VirusTotal. https://www.virustotal.com. Accessed 24 Apr 2017
5. Barabosch, T., Bergmann, N., Dombeck, A., Padilla, E.: Quincy Project Site.
   https://net.cs.uni-bonn.de/wg/cs/staff/thomas-barabosch/. Accessed 24 Apr 2017
6. Barabosch, T., Eschweiler, S., Gerhards-Padilla, E.: Bee master: detecting host-
   based code injection attacks. In: Dietrich, S. (ed.) DIMVA 2014. LNCS, vol. 8550,
   pp. 235–254. Springer, Cham (2014). doi:10.1007/978-3-319-08509-8_13
7. Barabosch, T., Gerhards-Padilla, E.: Host-based code injection attacks: a popular
   technique used by malware. In: Malicious and Unwanted Software (MALCON)
   (2014)
8. Bergstra, J., Bengio, Y.: Random search for hyper-parameter optimization. J.
   Mach. Learn. Res. (JMLR) **13**, 281–305 (2012)
9. Breiman, L.: Random forests. Mach. Learn. **45**, 5–32 (2001)
10. Breiman, L., Friedman, J., Stone, C.J., Olshen, R.A.: Classification and Regression
    Trees. CRC Press, Boca Raton (1984)
11. Freund, Y., Schapire, R.E.: A desicion-theoretic generalization of on-line learning
    and an application to boosting. In: Vitányi, P. (ed.) EuroCOLT 1995. LNCS, vol.
    904, pp. 23–37. Springer, Heidelberg (1995). doi:10.1007/3-540-59119-2_166
12. Friedman, J.H.: Greedy function approximation: a gradient boosting machine. Ann.
    Stat. **29**, 1189–1232 (2001)
13. Genuer, R., Poggi, J.-M., Tuleau-Malot, C.: Variable selection using random
    forests. Pattern Recognit. Lett. **31**(14), 2225–2236 (2010)
14. Geurts, P., Ernst, D., Wehenkel, L.: Extremely randomized trees. Mach. Learn.
    63, 3 (2006)
15. Griffin, K., Schneider, S., Hu, X., Chiueh, T.: Automatic generation of string sig-
    natures for malware detection. In: Kirda, E., Jha, S., Balzarotti, D. (eds.) RAID
    2009. LNCS, vol. 5758, pp. 101–120. Springer, Heidelberg (2009). doi:10.1007/
    978-3-642-04342-0_6

16. Guyon, I., Weston, J., Barnhill, S., Vladimir, V.: Gene selection for cancer classification using support vector machines. Mach. Learn. **46**, 389–422 (2002)
17. Lindorfer, M., Kolbitsch, C., Milani Comparetti, P.: Detecting environment-sensitive malware. In: Sommer, R., Balzarotti, D., Maier, G. (eds.) RAID 2011. LNCS, vol. 6961, pp. 338–357. Springer, Heidelberg (2011). doi:10.1007/978-3-642-23644-0_18
18. Lyda, R., Hamrock, J.: Using entropy analysis to find encrypted and packed malware. Secur. Priv. (S&P) (2007)
19. Microsoft: Microsoft Malware Classification Challenge (BIG 2015) (2015). https://www.kaggle.com/c/malware-classification. Accessed 24 Apr 2017
20. Monnappa, K.A.: Detecting deceptive process hollowing techniques using hollowfind volatility plugin (2016). https://cysinfo.com/detecting-deceptive-hollowing-techniques/. Accessed 24 Apr 2017
21. Nappa, A., Rafique, M.Z., Caballero, J.: The MALICIA dataset: identification and analysis of drive-by download operations. Int. J. Inf. Secur. 1–19 (2014)
22. Oracle: VirtualBox. https://www.virtualbox.org. Accessed 24 Apr 2017
23. Ortega, A.: Pafish. https://github.com/a0rtega/pafish. Accessed 24 Apr 2017
24. Pék, G., Lázár, Z., Várnagy, Z., Félegyházi, M., Buttyán, L.: Membrane: a posteriori detection of malicious code loading by memory paging analysis. In: Askoxylakis, I., Ioannidis, S., Katsikas, S., Meadows, C. (eds.) ESORICS 2016. LNCS, vol. 9878, pp. 199–216. Springer, Cham (2016). doi:10.1007/978-3-319-45744-4_10
25. Rossow, C., Dietrich, C.J., Grier, C., Kreibich, C., Paxson, V., Pohlmann, N., Bos, H., Van Steen, M.: Prudent practices for designing malware experiments: status quo and outlook. In: Security and Privacy (SP) (2012)
26. van Dantzig, M., Heppener, D., Frank Ruiz, Y.K., Hu, Y.Z., de Jong, E., de Mik, K., Haagsma, L.: Ponmocup - a giant hiding in the shadows (2015). https://foxitsecurity.files.wordpress.com/2015/12/foxit-whitepaper_ponmocup_1_1.pdf. Accessed 24 Apr 2017
27. Volatility Foundation: The Volatility Framework (2015). http://www.volatilityfoundation.org. Accessed 24 Apr 2017
28. White, A., Schatz, B., Foo, E.: Integrity verification of user space code. In: Digital Forensic Research Workshop (DFRWS) (2013)
29. Willems, C., Holz, T., Freiling, F.: Toward automated dynamic malware analysis using cwsandbox. In: Proceedings of the 28th Symposium on Security and Privacy (S&P) (2007)

SPEAKER: Split-Phase Execution of Application Containers

Lingguang Lei[1,3(✉)], Jianhua Sun[2], Kun Sun[3], Chris Shenefiel[5], Rui Ma[1], Yuewu Wang[1], and Qi Li[4]

[1] Institute of Information Engineering, Chinese Academy of Sciences, Beijing, China
[2] College of William and Mary, Williamsburg, USA
[3] George Mason University, Fairfax, USA
llei2@gmu.edu, leilingguang@iie.ac.cn
[4] Tsinghua University, Beijing, China
[5] Cisco Systems, Inc., Raleigh, USA

Abstract. Linux containers have recently gained more popularity as an operating system level virtualization approach for running multiple isolated OS distros on a control host or deploying large scale microservice-based applications in the cloud environment. The wide adoption of containers as an application deployment platform also attracts attackers' attention. Since the system calls are the entry points for processes trapping into the kernel, Linux seccomp filter has been integrated into popular container management tools such as Docker to effectively constrain the system calls available to the container. However, Docker lacks a method to obtain and customize the set of necessary system calls for a given application. Moreover, we observe that a number of system calls are only used during the short-term booting phase and can be safely removed from the long-term running phase for a given application container. In this paper, we propose a container security mechanism called SPEAKER that can dramatically reduce the number of available system calls to a given application container by customizing and differentiating its necessary system calls at two different execution phases, namely, booting phase and running phase. For a given application container, we first separate its execution into booting phase and running phase and then trace the invoked system calls at these two phases, respectively. Second, we extend the Linux seccomp filter to dynamically update the available system calls when the application is running from the booting phase into the running phase. Our mechanism is non-intrusive to the application running in the container. We evaluate SPEAKER on the popular web server and data store containers from Docker hub, and the experimental results show that it can successfully reduce more than 50% and 35% system calls in the running phase for the data store containers and the web server containers, respectively, with negligible performance overhead.

Keywords: Container · System call · Seccomp

M. Polychronakis and M. Meier (Eds.): DIMVA 2017, LNCS 10327, pp. 230–251, 2017.
DOI: 10.1007/978-3-319-60876-1_11

1   Introduction

Linux containers have emerged as one popular operating system level virtualization approach, and state-of-the-art container managers such as Docker [2] and Rocket [13] are enabling the wide adoption of Linux containers. Recently, major cloud providers are adding support for Docker containers on Linux VMs [8,19,49]. In general, there are two types of Linux containers, *OS container* and *application container*. OS containers are useful for running identical or different flavors of an OS distro. Basically, they are designed to run multiple processes and services. Container technologies, such as LXC [21], OpenVZ [48], Linux VServer [32], BSD Jails [25] and Solaris zones [40], are suitable for creating OS containers. In contrast, application containers are designed to package and run a single service. Platforms for creating and deploying application containers include Docker [2] and Rocket [13]. The idea behind application containers is to create different containers for each of the components in a specific application. This approach works especially well when it comes to deploy a distributed, multi-component system using the microservices architecture.

In traditional hypervisor-based virtualization technologies, virtual machines (VMs) are presented with a hardware abstraction layer created by the hypervisor. Direct communications between the processes in the VMs and the host hardware are mediated by the hypervisor. In comparison, Linux containers, as one OS level virtualization technology, relies on security primitives such as *namespace* and *cgroups* provided by the Linux kernel to achieve the isolation among containers. A container can be considered as a group of processes sharing a bunch of isolated but dedicated Linux kernel resources. Therefore, applications running in the containers can achieve near native performance. Essentially, all containers share the same host OS kernel. Unfortunately, this sharing also exposes the entire host kernel interface to malicious processes running in any one of the containers. It has been demonstrated that an unwary container process can manage to escape into the host kernel space [7].

A number of security mechanisms have been proposed or adopted to enhance the security of containers [6,9,14,20,36,37,44,48]. Since the system calls are the entry points for processes in the container trapping into the kernel, seccomp [6] has been integrated into the popular container management tools such as Docker to effectively constrain the system calls available to the container. For instance, Docker provides a whitelist of available system calls. However, Docker lacks a method to obtain and customize the set of system calls in the seccomp profile for a given application. Instead, it only provides a coarse-grained setting recommendation for all application containers.

We observe that an application container usually requires different sets of available system calls at different phases during the lifetime of its execution. Since most of the application containers are used to run long-term services such as web servers and database servers, the lifetime of those containers can be generally divided into two phases, namely, the *booting phase* and the *running phase*. The booting phase is responsible for setting the container environment and initializing the service within a couple of minutes. In the long-term running phase, the container service begins to accept service requests and send back responses. Due to the different sets of functions demanded in these two phases, a number of system calls invoked in the booting phase may no longer be needed and thus can be removed in the running phase. For instance, compared to the default 313 available system calls through the entire lifetime of a Docker container, our experiments show only 116 system calls are invoked in the booting phase and 58 system calls are needed in the running phase of the MySQL database server.

In this paper, we develop a split-phase container execution mechanism called SPEAKER to dramatically reduce the number of necessary system calls during the lifetime of an application container's execution. For a given application container, it first profiles the two sets of system calls required for the booting phase and the running phase, respectively. Based on the profiling results, it can constrain the available system calls accordingly. Both system call profiling and constraint setting run outside the container, so it requires no changes on the image of the container.

To profile the system calls required in either booting phase or running phase, we first need to find a time point to separate the two phases. We provide a polling-based method to identify an accurate phase splitting time point for a given container image. In addition, we implement a coarse-grained phase separation approach, which can find a generic separation time point for application containers running on a specific platform. After obtaining the phase splitting time point, we perform dynamic program analysis to record the system calls invoked during the container booting and running phases.

For the split-phase container execution, we statically configure the set of available system calls in the booting phase and then dynamically change the available system calls when the container switches from the booting phase into the running phase. In the Linux kernel, the available system call list can be represented as a seccomp filter of one process, which can be set by two system calls `prctl()` and `seccomp()`. However, they can only be called to install the seccomp filters onto the calling process, but we need to change the seccomp filters of the processes inside the container from another process outside the container. Otherwise, a malicious process with the root privilege inside the container may be able to disable the constraints on the system calls. Since all processes inside one container share the same seccomp filter, we can change the seccomp filter of one process to update the available system calls for the entire container. To modify a container's seccomp filter from outside, we need to fill the semantic gap to find and change the data structures of seccomp filter.

The most popular usage of Docker containers is to deploy web applications [11], so we apply our mechanism on two closely related categories of application containers from Docker hub, namely, *web server containers* and *data store containers*. We study the top four web server container images (i.e., nginx, Tomcat, httpd, and php) and the top four data store container images (i.e., MySQL, Redis, MongoDB, and Postgres). The experimental results show that SPEAKER can reduce more than 50% and 35% system calls in the running phase for the data store containers and the web server containers, respectively. The number of system calls for web server containers may vary when deploying different web applications; however, they share most of system calls since the primary functions of web servers such as processing HTTP requests and web pages are the same. Actually, for all website applications tested in our experiments, about 80% system calls will be invoked for just fetching one web page.

In summary, we make the following contributions.

- We develop a split-phase execution mechanism called SPEAKER to minimize the system call interface in one container at two different execution phases. It can successfully reduce the attack surface of containers by removing unnecessary system calls that may be misused by malicious processes in the container.
- We develop an out-of-the-box method to profile the necessary system calls for a given application container in the booting phase and the running phase, respectively.
- We develop a new method to dynamically change the sets of available systems calls by filling the semantic gap on the data structure of seccomp filter. SPEAKER does not require any modifications to the existing container management software or the application images.
- We implement SPEAKER as a tool set and evaluate its effectiveness on the popular container images downloaded from Docker hub. The experiments show that SPEAKER can effectively reduce the number of available system calls for both data store containers and web server containers with negligible performance overhead.

2 Background

In this section, we provide some background on namespace and seccomp mechanisms, which are highly related to our system design and implementation.

2.1 Linux Namespace

Namespace is one core mechanism that allows isolation of an application's view of system resources within a container. Linux kernel utilizes six types of namespaces: pid, user, uts, mnt, net, and ipc. Specifically, pid namespace isolates the process ID number space, which means each container may have a process whose PID is 1 and processes in different pid namespace can have the same PID value. In addition, all processes inside a container have a mapping PID on the Linux Kernel host outside the container. For instance, the process with PID 1 in one container could be the process on the host with PID 1001. In this paper, we use this mapping to help profile container's system calls from outside.

2.2 Seccomp

Secure computing (seccomp) is a sandboxing tool in the Linux kernel to restrict a process from making certain system calls. Since the system calls provide entry points for the processes in one container into the host kernel, a malicious app may misuse system calls to disable all the security measures and escape out of the container [52]. Seccomp can be used to reduce the number of entry points into the kernel space, thereby reducing the kernel attack surface. Since Docker version 1.11.0, a `--security-opt seccomp` option is supported to set a seccomp profile when the container is launched. It allows the user to set the list of system calls available to be called inside the container. Currently the default seccomp profile by Docker has 313 available system calls [5].

Seccomp has three working modes: *seccomp-disabled*, *seccomp-strict*, and *seccomp-filter*. The seccomp-filter mode allows a process to specify a filter for the incoming system calls. Linux kernel provides two system calls, `prctl()` and `seccomp()`, to set the seccomp filter mode. However, they can only be used to change the seccomp filter mode of the calling thread/process and cannot set the seccomp filter mode of other processes.

3   Design and Implementation

Figure 1 shows the architecture of SPEAKER, which consists of two major modules, *the Tracing Module* and *the Slimming Module*, working in five sequential steps. For a given application container, the tracing module is responsible for profiling the available system calls in the booting phase and the running phase, respectively. The tracing module shares the system call lists with the slimming module, which is responsible for constraining the available system calls when the container boots up and runs. Both modules run outside of application containers as root-privileged processes in the host OS. SPEAKER is non-intrusive, so it does not require any modification to the applications or the container deployment tool.

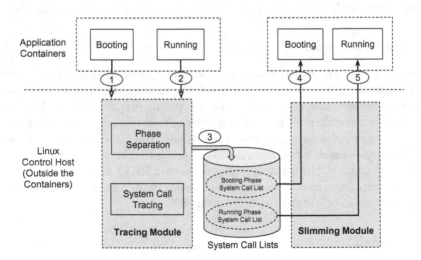

Fig. 1. SPEAKER architecture

3.1 Tracing Module

This module is to generate system call sets for the booting phase and the running phase, respectively. It is transparent to the applications inside the container and consists of two components, *phase separation* and *system call tracing*.

Phase Separation. The phase separation is in charge of separating the execution of the application containers into two phases, namely, the booting phase and the running phase. Though the booting phase is short, it may require a number of extra system calls to setup the execution environments, and those system calls are no longer necessary in the running phase. Moreover, the running phase may require some extra system calls to support the service's functions. Thus, it is important to find the running point that separates these two phases in order to profile their system calls. For instance, in the booting phase of the Apache web server, the container and the web server are booted and all modules needed for the service execution, such as mod_php and mod_perl, are loaded. In the running phase, the Apache web server accepts and handles the requests and generates the responses.

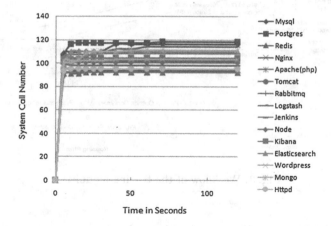

Fig. 2. Number of system calls invoked over container execution time.

We can achieve a reliable phase separation through a polling-based method, which can find the splitting time point by continuously checking the status changes of the running service. Once the booting up finishes, the service enters the running status. Most current Linux distributions provide a service utility to uniformly manage various services, such as apache, mysql, nginx etc. Therefore, our polling-based method can find the split-phase time point by checking the service status through running the service command with status option. This method works well when the service creates its own /etc/init.d script.

We also develop a coarse-grained phase separation approach, which is generic and service independent. This method is based on two observations. First, the container and service booting can finish quickly in tens of seconds. Second, the number of invoked system calls keeps increasing during the booting phase and becomes stable after the booting process ends and the container enters an idle running state. We verify both observations using the 15 most popular application container images in the Docker hub. Figure 2 shows that the numbers of system calls increase quickly in the first 10 s after the container starts to boot for all the 15 containers, and the number of system calls becomes stable after 70 s when all 15 containers enter the idle running state. Therefore, we can choose a rough time point (e.g., 100 s) for all containers. This time point may be different for other services on different hardware platform; however it should not be larger than a couple of minutes. Though it may include some extra system calls invoked in the service idle state into the whitelist of booting phase, since the booting phase is short, the chance for those extra system calls being misused by attackers is minor.

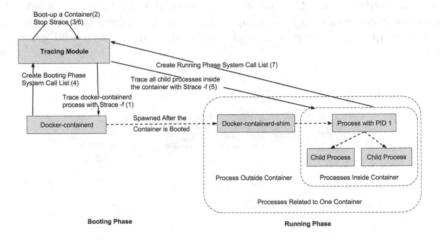

Fig. 3. Workflow of the tracing module.

System Call Tracing. The system call tracing component is responsible for tracing the execution of the container as well as the hosted application to obtain the necessary system calls used in each phase. In most cases, multiple processes may be running inside a container even if only one service is hosted. Therefore, the system call tracing needs to ensure that all the processes inside the container are correctly identified to adequately collect the invoked system calls.

System call tracing can be done either using a static analyzer to extract all the system calls used from a container image or using a dynamic analyzer to collect the system calls invoked during the container booting and running stages. We choose to use the Linux *strace* tool to dynamically trace the necessary system calls for a given application container. We solve the challenge of tracing container processes from outside the container through utilizing the process mapping between the container and the host OS.

As shown in Fig. 3, the tracing process consists of 7 steps, where steps 1 to 4 target at creating the booting phase system call list and steps 5 to 7 are to generate the running phase system call list. To guarantee the completeness of the tracing results, we enable the -f option of *strace* to trace the children of the processes currently being traced.

Since a container is a group of processes sharing the same set of kernel resources, a process inside a container is a normal process with different attributes such as pid, uid, and gid when viewed from the host OS. For example, each container contains a process with PID 1, but the same process may have a PID larger than 1000 on the host OS. Therefore, instead of running *strace* to trace the processes inside one container, we can trace the same process on the host OS using a different PID.

The arrowed dash lines in Fig. 3 demonstrate the parent-child relationship among the container processes from the host's point of view. We can see that each container contains a *docker-containerd-shim* process, which is the parent of all the remaining container processes. All the *docker-containerd-shim* processes are spawned from the process *docker-containerd*. Therefore, we can obtain the booting phase system call list through tracing the process *docker-containerd*. Similarly, the running phase system call list can be obtained through tracing all processes inside the container when the booting is finished, which refer to the child processes of the container's *docker-containerd-shim* process.

3.2   Slimming Module

The slimming module is responsible for monitoring the execution of the container and dynamically changing the available system call list for all processes inside one container during the different execution phases. It restricts the container to use only system calls in the booting phase system call list during the booting phase. During the running phase, it only allows system calls in the running phase system call list, which may add new system calls and remove old system calls in the booting phase system call list. Note we cannot rely on one process inside the container to implement the slimming module, otherwise, a malicious process with the root privilege in the container may also be able to manipulate the slimming module to disable the constraints on the system calls. To solve this problem, we put the slimming module out of the target container.

The slimming module is implemented as a user space program on the host OS with root privilege. Since it is based on the seccomp mechanism in Linux kernel, we first introduce some detailed internal design of the seccomp mechanism and then present our implementation details.

A seccomp filter records an available system call list. In Linux, it is possible for a process to be attached with multiple seccomp filters, and all seccomp filters are organized in an one-way linked list. Each seccomp filter is implemented as a program code composed of seccomp instructions, which is represented as a bpf_prog structure. Each seccomp_filter structure has a prog pointer pointed to the bpf_prog structure. Each instruction is a 4-tuple structure that includes the actual filter code, the jump offset when the filter codes returns true, the jump offset when `false` is returned, and a generic value. Figure 4 shows an example of a process attached with two seccomp filters. The first filter restricts the process to use the system calls `read()`, `write()`, `rt_sigreturn()` and `exit()`, as shown in the right-bottom `bpf_prog` structure. The k values in the `bpf_prog` structure correspond to the system call numbers of these four system calls. The second seccomp filter in the left bottom of Fig. 4 restricts the process to use only `read()` and `write()` system calls.

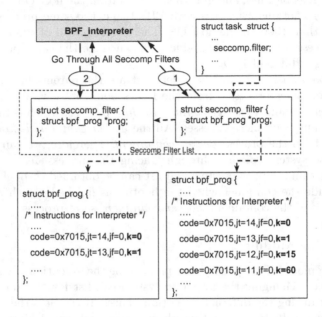

Fig. 4. Seccomp data structure in Linux kernel

Seccomp Filters in Linux Kernel. Seccomp mechanism restricts the set of system calls available to a process. The list of available system calls is represented as a *seccomp filter* data structure, as shown in Fig. 4. Each process has a `task_struct` structure that contains an `seccomp` structure, which defines the seccomp state of the process. If the process is being protected by seccomp, the `filter` field of the `seccomp` structure points to the first seccomp filter defined as a `seccomp_filter` structure.

The *BPF_interpreter* running in the Linux kernel is in charge of enforcing the system call filtering. When the process invokes a system call, it goes through all the seccomp filters attached to this process. As long as one seccomp filter does not include this system call, this process is not allowed to invoke this system call. Now let's see an example in Fig. 4. When a `rt_sigreturn()` system call is invoked by the process, the BPF_interpreter first checks the seccomp filter on the right bottom and finds that the `rt_sigreturn()` system call is allowed. However, when it continues to check the second seccomp filter on the left-bottom, it finds that `rt_sigreturn()` system call is not allowed. After combining these two results, the BPF_interpreter denies the `rt_sigreturn()` system call.

Linux kernel provides two system calls `prctl()` and `seccomp()` to change the seccomp filters of one process. However, we cannot directly use them to dynamically change the seccomp filters of one container. First, they can only install the seccomp filters onto the calling process, but we need to change the seccomp filters of the processes inside the container from outside the container. Second, after one seccomp filter is installed, it cannot be removed or changed when the process is running. In other words, we can use these two system calls to add new seccomp filters but cannot remove any existing filters. Meanwhile, our experimental results show that some system calls used in the running phase are not necessary for the booting phase, and vice versa. Therefore, we choose to locate the memory address of the seccomp filters and directly modify their contents in the memory. It requires us to fill the semantic gaps on recovering the seccomp filter related data structures.

Workflow of Slimming Module. The basic idea of the slimming module is to first construct a new `bpf_prog` struct in the memory based on the available system call list, and then redirect the `prog` pointer to it. The slimming module workflow consists of three steps, as shown in Fig. 5. First, the container is booted with the system calls in the booting phase system call list. Second, we develop a *Seccomp Filter Constructor* to generate a `bpf_prog` struct that records the seccomp instructions according to the running phase system call list. The third and final step is changing the seccomp filters of all the processes inside a container to the newly crafted one.

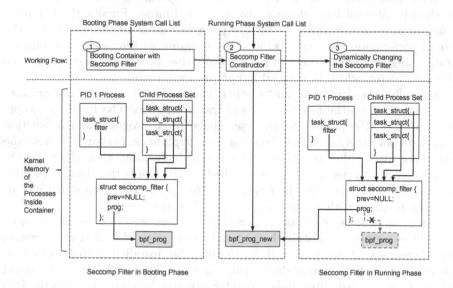

Fig. 5. Workflow of the slimming module.

Booting Container with Seccomp Filter. As shown in Fig. 3, before a container is created, a *docker-containerd-shim* process is spawned. It is the parent process of all the remaining processes inside the container. The seccomp filter for the booting phase can be enabled to protect the booting phase once the *docker-containerd-shim* process has been created. Alternatively, we can transform the booting phase system call list into a Docker seccomp profile and utilize the Docker *"–security-opt seccomp"* optional function to launch the container by the command *"docker run -id –security-opt seccomp:booting-phase-system-call-profile.json image_name"*. This approach is less secure than the first one, since the seccomp filter may not be enabled immediately after the container starts to boot. However, this time gap is small.

Seccomp Filter Constructor. We develop a seccomp filter constructor to generate the kernel data structure of the seccomp filter for a given system call list. The constructor is composed of a user level process called *UIApp* and a Linux kernel module to perform a three-step transformation, as shown in Fig. 6. First, the UIApp takes the system call list as the input and generates the corresponding bpf filter program. We use the libseccomp [12] library to convert one available system call list to the bpf filter instructions. Particularly, we use the `seccomp_rule_add()` method from the libseccomp library to add all available system calls and use the `seccomp_export_bpf()` method to export the resulting bpf filter program. Next, the bpf filter program generated in the user space is passed into the kernel module, which converts the program into a seccomp filter. Since some *code* of the bpf filter program is specific to seccomp filter, they are slightly different from those in the classic bpf filters. Finally, the `bpf_prog` structure is generated, that is the `bpf_prog_new` structure in Fig. 5. For the sake of performance, in Linux kernel a bpf program with a new instruction set totally different from the ones in the seccomp filter program is accepted by the BPF_interpreter, which is included in `bpf_prog` structure.

Normally, we can use an internal kernel function `bpf_prog_create_from_user()` to do the last two steps of transformation. The function accepts two parameters, a pointer to the user space filter program and a function pointer to an internal kernel function `seccomp_check_filter()`. First, the user space filter buffer is copied into a kernel buffer, and then the passed-in `seccomp_check_filter()` function is called to transform the classic bpf filter program into a seccomp bpf filter program. Finally, the `bpf_prog` struct including a bpf program with a new instruction set is generated.

`bpf_prog_create_from_user()` is an internal non-exported kernel function. In addition, when we install the kernel module with the `system('`insmod kernel-module`')` function call in UIApp, the installed kernel module is not running in the same address space as the UIApp. Therefore, we could not pass user space filter buffer pointer created in step one directly into `bpf_prog_create_from_user()`. In our implementation, we directly pass the data content of the user space bpf filter into kernel module as the kernel module parameter, and create a copy one in the kernel. Then we change bpf_prog_create_from_user() slightly to enable it accept the kernel buffer filter data, and incorporate it into our kernel module. In addition, the function seccomp_check_filter() is not exported too. Thus, we extract all related code and implement the function of seccomp_check_filter() as a kernel module.

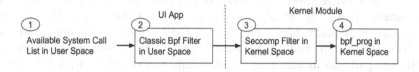

Fig. 6. Seccomp filter constructor.

Dynamically Changing the Seccomp Filter. With the new bpf_prog_new structure, we can dynamically change the seccomp filters of all the container processes to enforce the available system calls in the running phase. When the container is successfully booted, usually more than one process will be running inside the container. For example, 6 processes will be created after the Apache service is launched in the container. Therefore, we need to change the seccomp filter for all processes. The inheritance attribute of the seccomp filter indicates that a forked child process will inherit the seccomp filter of its parent. As shown in Fig. 5, when the service and the container is booted through command *"docker run -id –security-opt seccomp"*, the first process in the container has only one seccomp filter. All its child processes inherit this seccomp filter and contain the same pointer pointing to the bpf_prog structure. When we change the bpf_prog structure of one process in the container, the seccomp filters of all processes will be changed. In Fig. 5, initially all processes possess the same bpf_prog struct in the booting phase. After changing the system call list, all the processes now share the new bpf_prog_new structure, which records the running phase system call list. In brief, the kernel module in Fig. 6 first locates the task_struct of the first process inside the container through its PID, which is the process with PID 1 in Fig. 3. Next, it finds the pointer of bpf_prog through the task_struct, as shown in Fig. 5 and then modifies the pointer to point to the new constructed bpf_prog_new structure.

4   Experimental Results

We apply the SPEAKER toolkit on the popular web server containers and data store containers downloaded from Docker hub. We measure its effectiveness on reducing the number of available system calls from the default setting. We observe minimal performance overhead triggered by our system. Our experiments are conducted on the machine with a 4-core 1.6 GHz Intel i5 CPU and 8 GB of RAM. We use the Ubuntu 15.10 Desktop Edition with Docker 1.11.0 installed.

4.1 System Call Reduction

We evaluate both web server containers and data store containers, which count around half of the deployed Docker application containers in real world.

Web Server Containers. We study four popular web server images in Docker Hub, namely, *nginx, php, httpd,* and *tomcat.* Httpd is the Apache HTTP server and php is the Apache httpd server with PHP installed. Therefore, we only need to evaluate php, nginx, and tomcat. For all three web server containers, we directly pull the images from Docker hub and deploy a wiki software on it. For Tomcat a JSP-based open source wiki software JSPWIKI is deployed. Nginx and php are web servers with PHP installed, so we deploy the PHP-based open source wiki application DOKUWIKI. Since the available system calls in the running phase vary among different applications, we deploy a popular bulletin board system PHPBB3 on the Apache php web server. The installed software versions are Nginx web server 1.4.6 with PHP 5.5.34, Apache web server 2.4.10 with PHP 5.6.20, and Apache Tomcat 8.0.33 with JVM 1.7.0.

We use the HTTPERF [39] tool to access the web server continuously with increasing numbers of requests per second. We also scan the web servers using Skipfish in order to exercise as many code paths as possible. Skipfish is a tool conducting automated security check for the web applications by recursive crawl and dictionary-based probes, hence exercising many edge-cases. In addition, we manually access the websites to trigger all popular functions.

Table 1. System call reduction on web servers.

Server name	Booting & running	Booting phase	Running phase
Nginx	124	107 (86.3%)	79 (63.7%)
Tomcat	111	106 (95.5%)	46 (41.4%)
Php(Apache)DOKUWIKI	117	102 (87.2%)	70 (59.8%)
Php(Apache)PHPBB3	112	102 (91.1%)	67 (59.8%)

Table 1 shows the tracing results. We can see that the number of system calls invoked in the booting phase ranges from 90 to 120, but a large fraction of these system calls are not needed in the running phase. Moreover, accessing the web server through HTTPS does not incur substantially more system calls compared to the case of accessing through HTTP. By default, all the system calls needed in both the booting phase and the running phase must be enabled when the container enters the running phase. In contrast, SPEAKER can significantly reduce the system calls in the running phase by dynamically changing the seccomp filter. At the running phase, the system call reduction rates are 36.3%, 58.6%, 40.2%, and 40.2% for nginx, tomcat, php with DOKUWIKI, and php with PHPBB3, respectively.

Though the system call numbers may vary when deploying different web applications, the primary functions on processing HTTP requests and rendering web pages are similar in web servers. For all four web applications tested, about 80% system calls are invoked when just fetching one page through WGET and HTTPERF [39]. Moreover, half of the remaining 20% are file-operation-related system calls such as chmod(), ftruncate(), rename(), unlink(), sendfile(), dup(), pread64() etc. All three PHP-enabled applications invoke 61 identical system calls, which occupy 77.21%, 87.14%, and 91.04% of the total running phase system calls for three web applications, respectively. It means the system calls invoked are more affected by the programming language used rather than the functions of the applications. The number of system calls does not correlate with the complexity of the web application, and we see that the seemingly more complicated bulletin board system invokes less system calls than DOKUWIKI.

Table 2. System call reduction on DB servers.

Server name	Booting & running phase	Booting phase	Running phase
Redis	102	92 (90.2%)	42 (41.2%)
MongoDB	116	110 (94.8%)	55 (47.4%)
MySQL	118	116 (98.3%)	58 (50.0%)
Postgres	118	116 (98.3%)	52 (44.1%)

Data Store Containers. We evaluate four data store containers, namely, Redis server v3.2.0, MongoDB v3.2.6, MySQL v5.7.12, and Postgres v9.5.3, directly pulled from the Docker hub. The last three are traditional database platforms, while Redis is an in-memory data structure store that can serve as the database, cache and message broker. Since the operations on the data store containers are more deterministic when comparing to the web application containers. We generate their workloads in three aspects. First, we exercise the commands manually according to the official manual references of each data store [4,15,38,45]. Second, we utilize the load testing tools to test the case when accessing these platforms concurrently. The load testing and benchmarking tool HammerDB is used to exercise on Postgres, MySQL, and Redis. For MongoDB, we use Cloud System Benchmark provided by Yahoo. Third, we use penetration testing tools to enumerate all the data in the data store platforms, (e.g., databases and tables in MySQL). As our purpose is to simulate normal user behavior, other penetration tests such as attacks exploiting are not triggered. SQLMap is used on sql-based databases including MySQL and Postgres, while NoSQL-Exploitation-Framework and NoSQLMap are used for Redis and MongoDB, respectively.

Table 2 shows the experimental results for the data store containers. We observe that the number of system calls necessary for the container booting ranges from 90 to 120, and more than half of the system calls invoked in the booting phase are not needed in the running phase. The system call reduction achieved by SPEAKER is above 50% for all data store containers.

4.2 Performance Overhead

We evaluate the performance impacts of SPEAKER on the running containers. In general, our system introduces negligibly small overhead on both system
resource and application performance. Since all the processes in one container
share the same set of seccomp filter, when updating the system call whitelist, we
only need to add one new bpf_prog struct to record bpf instructions and release
the old bpf_prog struct. Since the seccomp filter is enabled by default for Linux
application containers, the changes of the filtering rules can barely have impacts
on application performance. For a list with 116 system calls, it only takes around
41 ms to change the seccomp filter, and it only occurs once. For the Apache web
server container, we measure the throughput using HTTPERF [39]. For the
MySQL data store container, we use benchmark tools coming with the MySQL
to measure the response delay. Figure 7 shows that the performance differences
on request throughput are minor when we enable either Docker default seccomp
profile or SPEAKER.

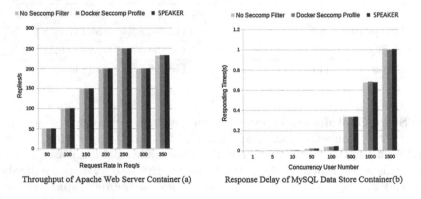

Fig. 7. Performance overhead.

We implement the tracing module as a bash script with 570 SLOC. The
slimming module is written in C language, consisting of a user level code with
2256 SLOC for converting the system call lists into Bpf filter format and a kernel
module with 1088 SLOC for dynamically updating the seccomp filter.

5   Security Analysis

Since containers share the same kernel, it is critical to constrain the available
system calls for each container to reduce the attack surface. Our security analysis
mainly targets at the system calls being removed in our experiments, so those
system calls not invoked by the containers (e.g., seteuid() and setegid())
are out of the scope. For the containers we tested in kernel 4.2, the number of
available system calls during both booting and running phases could be reduced

from 370 to 111–124. By separating running phase from the booting phase our method can further reduce the number of available system calls. In the long-term running phase, we reduce the number of system calls to 46–79 out of 111–124.

By shrinking the number of available system calls, we can efficiently reduce the attack surface of the host OS and lower the risk that a malicious process may escape from the container and gain control of the host OS. On the one hand, we can remove the system calls which are vulnerable due to lack of sanity checking and thus may be misused by attackers. For instance, among the 47 system calls removed from the running phase of the Apache web server with DOKUWIKI, we found 14 vulnerable system calls with CVE security level MEDIUM or above, including `getrlimit()`, `listen()`, `sigaltstack()`, `socketpair()`, `prctl()`, `setsid()`, `setsockopt()`, `uname()` etc. Similarly, 23 vulnerable system calls can be prevented after we remove 60 unnecessary system calls in the running phase of the MySQL server, including `bind()`, `brk()`, `chdir()`, `epoll_ctl()`, `execve()`, `io_setup()`, `socketpair()`, `setsid()`, `listen()`, `setgroups()`, `setgid()`, `uname()`, `setuid()`, etc. Among those removed vulnerable system calls, 6 and 12 system calls may be exploited to achieve privilege escalation for Apache and MySQL containers, respectively. On the other hand, since attackers may misuse some high-privileged system calls (e.g., `fchown()`, `fchmodat()`, `mknodat()`) to launch attacks, we can reduce the attack surface by removing those high-privileged system calls. For instance, among the removed system calls, around 25% may be called to gain full control of the system [10,35].

Particularly, `setuid()` is a dangerous system call frequently used in shell-code, it is eliminated from all data store containers we tested. And we remove the `exec` family of system calls such as `execve()` from the running of MySQL server. `execve()` system call is usually used to run a binary executable after creating a new process, and it may be misused by attackers to create a shell. By default, Docker seccomp profile has all the `exec` system calls enabled. After eliminating `execve()` from the system call interface, we can at least increase the difficulty on exploiting *shellshock* vulnerability. As another example, when the `setsockopt()` system call is eliminated from the Apache server with DOKUWIKI, we remove potential vulnerabilities that can be exploited by `setsockopt()` for launching heap memory corruption and denial of service attack against the host.

Our mechanism targets at reducing the attack surface; however, since the available system call list may still contain vulnerable system calls, we cannot prevent attackers from exploiting those remaining system calls. For the Apache web server container with Dokuwiki, 22 out of the total 70 available system calls may expose vulnerabilities. Similarly, for the MySQL server container, 16 out of the 58 available system calls may expose some vulnerabilities. To further constrain those vulnerable system calls, we can combine SPEAKER with careful sanity checking on the parameters of system calls [23,28,34] and strict resource access control [16,17,26,41,53]. For example, we can combine our SPEAKER system and the Linux capability mechanism [20] to block the exploitation of vulnerability CVE-2016-9793 [1], which requires both CAP_NET_ADMIN capability and `setsockopt()` system call. When `setsockopt()` cannot be removed from some containers, we still can prevent this vulnerability by removing the CAP_NET_ADMIN capability from the vulnerable processes in the container.

Since we cannot change the container processes' seccomp filter inside the container, we rely on a kernel module to dynamically change the seccomp filter from outside of an container. The kernel module does not export any APIs, and it can be removed from the system once the container enters the running phase and the seccomp filter has been changed. Therefore, it can hardly be misused by malicious processes in the container. In addition, it is difficult, if not impossible, for the attackers in the container to modify the seccomp filter through direct memory overwriting. First, it is difficult for the user processes in the containers to understand and locate the seccomp filter related structures in the kernel space. Second, even if the programs in the user space could resolve the semantic gap and locate the seccomp filter related structures, they cannot write into the kernel space memory.

6   Limitations and Discussion

System Call Tracing Completeness. We trace system calls involved in the container boot-up phase and application running phase using both automatic workload generation tools and manual operations. However, this tracing process may still be incomplete. First, different versions of the services on different platforms may use various kinds of system calls, which greatly increases the complexity of the tracing procedure. Second, some corner cases may exist and may not be accounted in our tracing process. For example, the Apache web server can exhibit abnormal running patterns when experiencing extremely large amount of request traffic. As SPEAKER is a tool transparent to the applications running inside the container, we can combine the system call tracing phase with the `testing` process [24] of the application development to better trace the system call profile of a specific application. In addition, the static analysis approach (e.g., [50,54]) can be integrated to further improve the profiling accuracy. We consider them as our future work to enhance our toolkit. Third, the existence of dynamically generated scripts such as PHP script can make the tracing more complicated, as these scripts can arbitrarily invoke certain system calls. A reiterative method can be adopted to add new available systems calls during a longer trace and verification stage.

System Call Control Granularity. We adopt a simple container-specific whitelist model to reduce the unnecessary system calls, which is easy for deployment with its near zero overhead, comparing to the sophisticated and costly FSA or PDA [18,47,50] models based system call intrusion detection system. As other stateless model [54], SPEAKER also suffers a risk of system call misuse attacks, such as mimicry attack [51], which transforms a malicious attack sequence to a seemingly valid sequence by inserting `no-op` system calls. However, Kruegel et al. [27] and Zeng et al. [54] work illustrates that a stateful FSA or PDA model is actually not much better than the stateless whitelist model, as it is easy and can be automated for a mimicry attack to evade FSA models.

To achieve a more fine-grained protection of the system calls, we could integrate the system call interposition based approach such as MBox [26] or the argument constraint solutions [23,28,34]. We leave it as our future work.

Deployment Extensibility. We divide one container's lifetime into the booting phase and the running phase; however, the same paradigm can be extended to achieve multiple phase execution. Moreover, for those application containers deployed using tools other than Docker, our approach works well as long as the container execution can be dissected into separated phases. SPEAKER can be smoothly integrated into the container management services, such as Amazon EC2 container service (Amazon ECS) [8], Docker Datacenter [3], and OpenShift Enterprise [22] to prevent malicious applications in one container from escaping into the hosting virtual machine (VM).

Phase Separation Efficiency. We provide a polling-based method and coarse-grained timing-based method for phase separation. However, the timing-based solution might cause some extra system calls invoked in the service idle state being added into the whitelist of booting phase. While the polling-based method will subject to the implementation constraints of the services, e.g. it will not work well for the services without their own /etc/init.d scripts. We can adopt a binary-based execution partition scheme [31] to achieve a fine-grained phase separation. It is based on one observation that most long running applications include an initialization phase followed by certain event-handling loops for processing inputs/requests. Thus, by locating those loops, we can separate the initialization phase (booting phase) from the running phase. We leave it as one of our future work.

Diversity of the Container Evaluation. Our current evaluation focuses on two most popular categories of Application containers, i.e. web server container and data store container, which count for half of all real deployed containers. A more variety of application containers could boost the impact of the proposed approach. We will leave it as our future work to perform evaluation on other types of containers, such as RabbitMQ, Redis, Node.js, Logstash etc.

7 Related Work

Linux Kernel Security Primitives. Linux kernel provides other primitives which can be utilized to enhance container security. *CGroups* can be used for fine-grained limitation and prioritization of resources. By setting up a quota of the maximum resources available to a container, cgroups can be utilized to mitigate the resource exhaustion attacks initiated from inside a compromised container. *Mandatory Access Control* (MAC) refers to the access control enforced at the kernel level based on a predefined set of rules. By default, Docker on Ubuntu uses Apparmor, and Docker on Redhat uses SELinux. *Discretionary access control* (DAC) mechanisms can be used to protect kernel resources from malicious containers. DAC mainly involves capabilities and file mode access control. In the docker container, by default only 14 out of the 38 capabilities are allowed [20].

Contrary to MAC, for DAC the access is determined by the owner of the object or resource in question.

Container Security. Reshetova et al. [46] gives a comparative study of several OS-level virtualization systems and identify the gaps in current security solutions based on a spectrum of attack models. [14] analyzes the security level of Docker containers and how Docker interact with the security features of Linux kernel. However, they only talk about how container isolation is achieved through namespaces and cgroups. An extension to the *Dockerfile* is proposed in [9] to ship a specific SELinux policy for processes running in a Docker image, which incurs great burden for container image maintainers to build up a dedicated policy module. In contrast, we have designed a practical, non-intrusive, and systematic framework to enhance the security of application containers. [36] proposes an approach that combines customized AppArmor/SELinux rules based on container operation tracing with host-based intrusion detection. However, we focus on proactively eliminating the unnecessary system calls to reduce the potential vulnerabilities exploitable by malicious containers.

Application Sandboxing. System call interposition based application sandboxing [16] regulates and monitors application behavior by intercepting each system call according to a predefined policy profile. Our system traces the execution of the running application to create a tailored seccomp policy instead of intercepting every system call. MBOX [26] is a lightweight sandboxing mechanism that interposes on a sandboxed program's system calls to layer a sandbox filesystem on the host filesystem. Similarly, we also utilize seccomp/BFP as a means for interposing system calls invoked by processes in the containers. The Capsicum sandboxing framework [53] isolates processes from global kernel resources by disabling system calls which address resources via global namespaces. Their approach is different from ours as we utilize the seccomp mechanism. *Systrace* [41] is a solution that confines multiple applications running according to accurate policies. We have adopted its tracing capability to generate audit logs for execution of container processes. Moreover, some other system call monitoring based anomaly detection and prevention solutions have been proposed [18,33,47,50] and may be integrated to further enhance the container security.

Attack Surface Reduction. Seccomp [6] allows a process to restrict a set of system calls it can execute. Although our system is built on seccomp, we aim to adjust the set of available system calls for the entire application container instead of letting the process to determine the policy itself. In addition, we split the container execution into two different phases and dynamically change the seccomp filters from outside the container to further reduce the attack surface. Cimplifier [43] and Docker-slim [42] use dynamic or static analysis to identify a minimal set of resources for running a specific application, thereby greatly reducing the size of application container images. However, our approach can dynamically adjust the runnable system call list during various phases of container booting and running. A different approach for system hardening is trimming [29,30], which effectively reduces the attack surface by removing or preventing the execution of unused kernel code sections. Specifically, they are able to remove unnecessary features through automated compile-time kernel configuration tailoring. This approach can serve as a complement to our system to guarantee the general security of the container host.

8 Conclusions

In this paper, we design and develop a system call reduction mechanism called SPEAKER to reduce the attack surface of Linux application containers. It works by first tracing the available system calls necessary for the booting phase and the running phase of the application containers, and then dynamically changing the seccomp filter to update the available system calls for each phase. SPEAKER runs outside the container and is completely non-intrusive to the application containers. Our evaluation results show that SPEAKER can significantly reduce the system call interface and incurs almost no performance overhead.

Acknowledgments. We would like to thank our shepherd Andrea Lanzi and our anonymous reviewers for their valuable comments and suggestions. We would also like to thank Xianchen Meng, Chong Guan, Yue Li, and Shengye Wan for their feedback and advice. This work is partially supported by U.S. ONR grants N00014-16-1-3216 and N00014-16-1-3214, the National Basic Research Program of China under GA No. 2013CB338001 (973 Program), the National Key Research & Development Program of China under GA No. 2016YFB0800102, and a Cisco award.

References

1. CVE-2016-9793 Detail. https://nvd.nist.gov/vuln/detail/CVE-2016-9793
2. Docker. https://www.docker.com/
3. Docker Datacenter. https://www.docker.com/products/docker-datacenter
4. PostgreSQL 9.5.3. http://www.postgresql.org/docs/current/static/sql-commands.html
5. Seccomp security profiles for Docker. https://github.com/docker/docker/blob/master/docs/security/seccomp.md
6. SECure COMPuting with filters. https://www.kernel.org/doc/Documentation/prctl/seccomp_filter.txt
7. Vulnerability summary for CVE-2014-9357. https://web.nvd.nist.gov/view/vuln/detail?vulnId=CVE-2014-9357
8. AWS: Amazon EC2 container service. https://aws.amazon.com/ecs/
9. Bacis, E., Mutti, S., Capelli, S., Paraboschi, S.: DockerPolicyModules: mandatory access control for docker containers. In: 2015 IEEE Conference on Communications and Network Security (CNS), pp. 749–750. IEEE (2015)
10. Bernaschi, M., Gabrielli, E., Mancini, L.V.: Enhancements to the Linux kernel for blocking buffer overflow based attacks. In: Annual Linux Showcase & Conference (2000)
11. Boettiger, C.: An introduction to docker for reproducible research. ACM SIGOPS Oper. Syst. Rev. **49**(1), 71–79 (2015)

12. Bruno, L.: Libseccomp: an enhanced seccomp (mode 2) helper library. https://github.com/seccomp/libseccomp
13. Bruno, L.: rkt - app container runtime. https://github.com/coreos/rkt
14. Bui, T.: Analysis of docker security. arXiv preprint arXiv:1501.02967 (2015)
15. Oracle Corporation: Mysql 5.7 reference manual. http://dev.mysql.com/doc/refman/5.7/en/tutorial.html
16. Garfinkel, T., Pfaff, B., Rosenblum, M., et al.: Ostia: a delegating architecture for secure system call interposition. In: NDSS (2004)
17. Garfinkel, T., et al.: Traps and pitfalls: practical problems in system call interposition based security tools. In: NDSS. vol. 3, pp. 163–176 (2003)
18. Giffin, J.T., Jha, S., Miller, B.P.: Detecting manipulated remote call streams. In: USENIX Security Symposium, pp. 61–79 (2002)
19. Google: Container engine on Google cloud platform. https://cloud.google.com/container-engine/
20. Hallyn, S.E., Morgan, A.G.: Linux capabilities: making them work. In: Linux Symposium, vol. 8 (2008)
21. Helsley, M.: LXC: Linux container tools. IBM devloperWorks Technical Library (2009)
22. Red Hat Inc.: Red Hat OpenShift Container Platform. https://www.openshift.com/enterprise/trial.html
23. Jachner, J., Agarwal, V.K.: Data flow anomaly detection. IEEE Trans. Softw. Eng. 4, 432–437 (1984)
24. Jacobson, I., Booch, G., Rumbaugh, J., Rumbaugh, J., Booch, G.: The Unified Software Development Process, vol. 1. Addison-Wesley, Reading (1999)
25. Kamp, P.H., Watson, R.N.: Jails: confining the omnipotent root. In: The 2nd International SANE Conference, vol. 43, p. 116 (2000)
26. Kim, T., Zeldovich, N.: Practical and effective sandboxing for non-root users. In: USENIX Annual Technical Conference, pp. 139–144 (2013)
27. Kruegel, C., Kirda, E., Mutz, D., Robertson, W., Vigna, G.: Automating mimicry attacks using static binary analysis. In: Proceedings of the 14th Conference on USENIX Security Symposium, p. 11. USENIX Association (2005)
28. Kruegel, C., Mutz, D., Valeur, F., Vigna, G.: On the detection of anomalous system call arguments. In: Snekkenes, E., Gollmann, D. (eds.) ESORICS 2003. LNCS, vol. 2808, pp. 326–343. Springer, Heidelberg (2003). doi:10.1007/978-3-540-39650-5_19
29. Kurmus, A., Sorniotti, A., Kapitza, R.: Attack surface reduction for commodity OS kernels: trimmed garden plants may attract less bugs. In: Proceedings of the Fourth European Workshop on System Security, p. 6. ACM (2011)
30. Kurmus, A., Tartler, R., Dorneanu, D., Heinloth, B., Rothberg, V., Ruprecht, A., Schröder-Preikschat, W., Lohmann, D., Kapitza, R.: Attack surface metrics and automated compile-time OS kernel tailoring. In: NDSS (2013)
31. Lee, K.H., Zhang, X., Xu, D.: High accuracy attack provenance via binary-based execution partition. In: NDSS (2013)
32. des Ligneris, B.: Virtualization of Linux based computers: the Linux-Vserver project. In: HPCS 2005, pp. 340–346. IEEE (2005)
33. Linn, C., Rajagopalan, M., Baker, S., Collberg, C.S., Debray, S.K., Hartman, J.H.: Protecting against unexpected system calls. In: Usenix Security (2005)
34. Maggi, F., Matteucci, M., Zanero, S.: Detecting intrusions through system call sequence and argument analysis. IEEE Trans. Dependable Secure Comput. 7(4), 381–395 (2010)

35. Martignoni, L., Christodorescu, M., Jha, S.: Omniunpack: fast, generic, and safe unpacking of malware. In: Twenty-Third Annual Computer Security Applications Conference, 2007. ACSAC 2007, pp. 431–441. IEEE (2007)
36. Mattetti, M., Shulman-Peleg, A., Allouche, Y., Corradi, A., Dolev, S., Foschini, L.: Securing the infrastructure and the workloads of Linux containers. In: 2015 IEEE Conference on Communications and Network Security (CNS) (2015)
37. Menage, P., Jackson, P., Lameter, C.: Cgroups. https://www.kernel.org/doc/Documentation/cgroup-v1/cgroups.txt
38. MongoDB, I.: Mongodb manual reference. https://docs.mongodb.com/manual/reference/command/
39. Mosberger, D., Jin, T.: Httperf: a tool for measuring web server performance. ACM SIGMETRICS Perform. Eval. Rev. **26**(3), 31–37 (1998)
40. Price, D., Tucker, A.: Solaris zones: operating system support for consolidating commercial workloads. In: Proceedings of the 18th USENIX Conference on System Administration. LISA (2004)
41. Provos, N.: Improving host security with system call policies. In: USENIX Security, vol. 3, p. 19 (2003)
42. Quest, K.C.: docker-slim: lean and mean docker containers. https://github.com/docker-slim/docker-slim
43. Rastogi, V., Davidson, D., De Carli, L., Jha, S., McDaniel, P.: Towards least privilege containers with cimplifier. arXiv preprint arXiv:1602.08410 (2016)
44. RedHat: Docker selinux security policy. https://access.redhat.com/documentation/en/red-hat-enterprise-linux-atomic-host/7/container-security-guide/chapter-6-docker-selinux-security-policy
45. Redislabs: Redis commands reference. http://redis.io/commands
46. Reshetova, E., Karhunen, J., Nyman, T., Asokan, N.: Security of OS-level virtualization technologies. In: Bernsmed, K., Fischer-Hübner, S. (eds.) Nord-Sec 2014. LNCS, vol. 8788, pp. 77–93. Springer, Cham (2014). doi:10.1007/978-3-319-11599-3_5
47. Sekar, R., Bendre, M., Dhurjati, D., Bollineni, P.: A fast automaton-based method for detecting anomalous program behaviors. In: Proceedings of IEEE Security and Privacy, pp. 144–155 (2001)
48. Soltesz, S., Pötzl, H., Fiuczynski, M.E., Bavier, A., Peterson, L.: Container-based operating system virtualization: a scalable, high-performance alternative to hypervisors. In: ACM SIGOPS Operating Systems Review, pp. 275–287. ACM (2007)
49. van Surksum, K.: Microsoft announces support for docker container virtualization for next version of windows server (2014)
50. Wagner, D., Dean, R.: Intrusion detection via static analysis. In: Proceedings of the 2001 IEEE Symposium on Security and Privacy (2001)
51. Wagner, D., Soto, P.: Mimicry attacks on host-based intrusion detection systems. In: Proceedings of the 9th ACM Conference on Computer and Communications Security, pp. 255–264. ACM (2002)
52. Walsh, D.J.: Docker security in the future. https://opensource.com/business/15/3/docker-security-future
53. Watson, R.N., Anderson, J., Laurie, B., Kennaway, K.: Capsicum: practical capabilities for UNIX. In: USENIX Security Symposium, vol. 46, p. 2 (2010)
54. Zeng, Q., Xin, Z., Wu, D., Liu, P., Mao, B.: Tailored application-specific system call tables. Technical report, Pennsylvania State University (2014)

Deep Ground Truth Analysis
of Current Android Malware

Fengguo Wei[1]([⊠]), Yuping Li[1], Sankardas Roy[2], Xinming Ou[1], and Wu Zhou[3]

[1] University of South Florida, Tampa, FL, USA
fwei@mail.usf.edu
[2] Bowling Green State University, Bowling Green, OH, USA
[3] Didi Labs, Mountain View, CA, USA

Abstract. To build effective malware analysis techniques and to evaluate new detection tools, up-to-date datasets reflecting the current Android malware landscape are essential. For such datasets to be maximally useful, they need to contain reliable and complete information on malware's behaviors and techniques used in the malicious activities. Such a dataset shall also provide a comprehensive coverage of a large number of types of malware. The Android Malware Genome created circa 2011 has been the only well-labeled and widely studied dataset the research community had easy access to (As of 12/21/2015 the Genome authors have stopped supporting the dataset sharing due to resource limitation). But not only is it outdated and no longer represents the current Android malware landscape, it also does not provide as detailed information on malware's behaviors as needed for research. Thus it is urgent to create a high-quality dataset for Android malware. While existing information sources such as VirusTotal are useful, to obtain the accurate and detailed information for malware behaviors, deep manual analysis is indispensable. In this work we present our approach to preparing a large Android malware dataset for the research community. We leverage existing anti-virus scan results and automation techniques in categorizing our large dataset (containing 24,650 malware app samples) into 135 varieties (based on malware behavioral semantics) which belong to 71 malware families. For each variety, we select three samples as representatives, for a total of 405 malware samples, to conduct in-depth manual analysis. Based on the manual analysis result we generate detailed descriptions of each malware variety's behaviors and include them in our dataset. We also report our observations on the current landscape of Android malware as depicted in the dataset. Furthermore, we present detailed documentation of the process used in creating the dataset, including the guidelines for the manual analysis. We make our Android malware dataset available to the research community.

1 Introduction

The Android platform continues to dominate the smartphone market with more than 80% share according to the study by International Data Corporation [8]

© Springer International Publishing AG 2017
M. Polychronakis and M. Meier (Eds.): DIMVA 2017, LNCS 10327, pp. 252–276, 2017.
DOI: 10.1007/978-3-319-60876-1_12

and Gartner [29]. Over the last five years, the Android world has been changing dramatically with more features added, and more sensitive operations (*e.g.*, banking and wallet) becoming popular on smartphones. Along with the Android platform's popularity, the Android malware has been growing as well, with more complex logic and anti-analysis techniques.

As expected, research groups across academia and industry put enormous effort to design novel methods to detect Android malware. However, the above effort is adversely affected by the lack of clear understanding of the latest Android malware landscape. A reliable ground truth dataset is essential for building effective malware analysis techniques and verifying the validity of new detection methods. For understanding the nefarious techniques used in the state-of-the-art malware apps, **detailed behavior profiles for each malware variety must be provided in such a dataset**. While creating such a dataset is a must-do ground work, this task is extremely difficult. In particular, **to provide the rich information for malware behaviors, manual analysis is indispensable.** However it is not feasible to manually analyze all Android malware at our hands (we have 24,650 from various sources). Thus the first step is to categorize the samples into semantically equivalent groups; then we only need to study a few samples from each group.

One can use AV scanning service like VirusTotal [7] to group malware samples into families; however, the family labels returned are often inconsistent [16,25]. Moreover, we observe that malware samples within one family may actually contain different varieties with different behaviors. Thus we cannot simply rely upon the grouping provided by AV products, even after being refined by tools like AVclass [25]. Even if grouping has been done perfectly, the amount of work of manually analyzing representative apps from each malware variety is still daunting. Advanced obfuscation methods are widely adopted in recent Android malware apps, further complicating the manual analysis process.

Due to the above reasons, there has not been any effort on creating such a rich Android malware dataset, except for the Android Malware Genome [34] project. The Android Malware Genome dataset is no longer available to researchers due to resource limitations.

It provided a malware dataset containing 1260 malware samples categorized in 49 families, discovered in 2010 and 2011. We have collected a more recent Android malware dataset from several sources (VirusShare, Google Play and third party security companies). The malware in this collection were discovered between 2010 and 2016. We made comparative study of the Genome dataset with our malware samples of 2011 and later, and found that the majority of the threats in those newer samples are not captured by the Genome samples. As a result, we not only need a more up-to-date malware dataset for Android, we also need one with much richer semantic information than what the Genome dataset provided.

The main contributions of this work are as follows

1. We present a systematic method of analyzing large volumes of Android malware samples with high confidence, which helps us prepare a large ground

truth Android malware dataset with rich profile information. This method addresses the scalability challenge by leveraging a two-step grouping technique followed by a systematic and deep manual analysis.

2. We present a detailed guideline for performing the manual analysis so other researchers can replicate the process on other Android malware samples in their possession. Our manual analysis provides profiles for each variety of the Android malware regarding their behaviors. This provides insights into the landscape of the current Android malware.

3. We prepare a comprehensive dataset which contains 24,650 labeled Android malware samples that are classified in 135 varieties within 71 families, whose discovery dates range from 2010 to 2016. We publish detailed reports including behavior information for each malware variety at our Android malware website http://amd.arguslab.org/. We are sharing the whole dataset with the research community.

The rest of the paper is organized as follows. Section 2 discusses the process of preparing the dataset. Section 3 discusses in details the behaviors and techniques of malware in our dataset, and Sect. 4 discusses our analysis and observation of the malware evolution trends. We discuss related research in Sect. 5, and conclude in Sect. 6.

2 Methodology

We collect Android malware apps from multiple sources, analyze the samples, and report their detailed behaviors. Figure 1 illustrates the pipeline of the methodology, which consists of a two-step grouping process followed by a manual procedure: (a) Group malware samples with the same family name, (b) Categorize each family into semantically different varieties using a customized clustering analysis, (c) Conduct a systematic and deep manual analysis for each variety of malware samples to obtain the accurate and detailed behavior information for the malware.

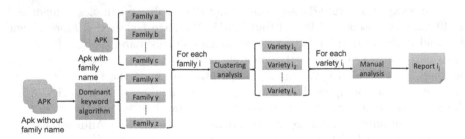

Fig. 1. Methodology pipeline: After malware families are identified, each family is categorized into semantically different varieties. For each variety we generate a malware behavior report, which is available at our Android malware website.

2.1   Identifying Malware Families

After raw malware samples are collected, it is an industry common practice to assign a family name to each app and group malware into families. The family name typically indicates the origin of the malware samples, such as in terms of the malware writer, malicious campaign, individual characteristics, *etc.*

We collect sample apps from multiple sources, including VirusShare, Google Play[1], and third party security companies. Most of the malware do not have an assigned malware family name. For such "unassigned" apps, the first step is to identify the family name.

Challenge. Existing state-of-the-art malware scanning service such as Virus-Total often provides multiple labels when it lists the scan result for an app using different anti-virus tools. However, due to inconsistent naming schemes from different anti-virus vendors [20,21], how to reliably identify a family name for a malware sample is a challenge.

Solution. We collected 1,464,590 unassigned app samples, and applied the following two steps:

(a) For each app x we get scan results of 55 antivirus products from VirusTotal (each result is either a candidate label or not-a-malware). If at least 50% of anti-virus products used in the VirusTotal recognize app x as a malware, we mark x as malware and move to the second step to obtain the family name. After this step, out of the collected apps, 1,216,885 are not labeled as malware by any AV product; about 195,185 are labeled as malware by some AV but did not reach the 50% threshold. We have 52,520 apps left.

(b) We obtain the family name of app x using a "dominant keyword algorithm" as follows. First, take the scanning results of app x from VirusTotal as label candidates. Second, normalize all the label candidates into individual English keywords, and meanwhile remove generic English keywords if any, *e.g.*, Trojan, Android, A, B, *etc.* There are a few hundred English keywords extracted and we identify the generic terms manually. Finally, we use the *dominant keyword* among the remaining labels as the family name. A keyword is dominant when: (a) the count of the keyword is greater than 50% of the anti-virus products used in the VirusTotal result; (b) the count of the most popular keyword is equal or more than twice of any other keyword, *i.e.*, there are no ambiguous labels that are highly popular at the same time. If for an app no dominant family name is found, we filter out the app from our dataset.

This process is very similar to *AVclass* [25], although we developed the approach independently without the knowledge of the AVclass work. An example is illustrated in Fig. 2, in which (1) We show VirusTotal result for an app (to save space we show only 10 anti-virus products' candidate labels for this app) (2) We

---

[1] Some malware can get pass Google's vetting system and end up in Google Play.

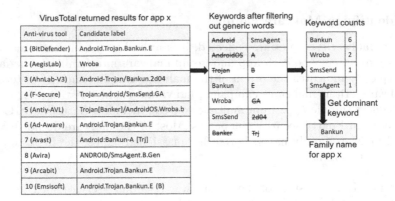

Fig. 2. Dominant keyword algorithm: identifying the malware family name of app x from VirusTotal scan results of app x. Not all AV tools are listed here to save space

extract the keywords from each of the result, and get a list of keywords such as *Android, AndroidOS, Bankum, Wroba, etc.* We filter out the generic keywords such as *Android, AndroidOS*, and *Trojan*. (3) We count the remaining keywords, and get *Bankun* as the dominant keyword, which is thus considered the family name. In particular, *Bankun* appeared 6 times, which is greater than 50% of the total results ($6 > 10 \times 50\%$), and more than twice of the count of the second dominant keyword *Wroba* ($6 > 2 \times 2$).

Out of the 52,520 apps obtained from step (1), we have 24,650 samples left after step (2). The rest are filtered out due to inconsistent family labels.

Discussion. Our goal is to provide a reliable ground truth dataset that presents insights into the up-to-date landscape of Android malware. The more anti-virus companies agree with the labeling for a malware sample, the more popular such family is and thus it is a more important representative to serve our purpose. We leave as future work to analyze those apps that as of now have no dominant family names.

2.2 Identifying Malware Behavior Groups – Varieties

It will not be feasible to perform deep manual analysis on each of the sample apps due to the large number of samples. How to reduce the amount of labor while maintaining the reliability of the result is a big challenge. While one may think that samples under the same family name should have similar behaviors, the reality is that the family name of a malware typically does not carry much semantic information. Anti-virus scanners name a malware with different and often inconsistent conventions [16]. Sometimes, a scanner names a malware after the malware writer Id; Other times the assigned family name is to highlight the main activities of the app (*e.g.*, *FakePlayer*) or main goal of the app (*e.g.*, *BankBot*), and so on. A malware app can achieve a goal through different schemes. Thus the samples of a malware family can be very different in terms of their behaviors. Hence, we have to categorize the family members into semantically different groups which we call *varieties*. During our study, we observed that many families have more than one varieties.

This motivates us to apply a clustering analysis for a malware family to categorize the samples into different varieties. For a given family malware apps, we use a Android malware clustering analysis tool [18] to further categorize the labeled malicious apps into multiple varieties (Fig. 1). Each variety of apps reported by the clustering algorithm contains a unique version of malicious payload. Then, we only need to study a few representatives of each variety (not all apps therein) in the later manual analysis phase. This makes the whole manual analysis process scale. Details of the clustering algorithm can be found in our technical report [18].

2.3 Manual Analysis

We manually analyze each variety of malware samples. If a variety contains more than three samples, we randomly select three of them for manual analysis. Otherwise, we analyze all samples in the variety. Through a systematic study of the samples, we generate a detailed report on the malware variety's behavior.

Challenges

(a) Manually analyzing a malware sample warrants a systematic strategy; without a strategy it is nearly impossible to understand the comprehensive picture of a malware's behaviors.
(b) Anti-analysis/obfuscation techniques are commonly used in Android apps as well as in malware payloads, which has an adverse impact both on static analysis tools and to the analyst who wants to understand the semantics of the given app.
(c) The malware app itself may not always contain the full information. Many components could be fetched from a remote server while the malware runs on the infected device, and those servers may have already been taken down after the malware app was identified. Thus it may be impossible for us to obtain those missing parts for analysis.

Assistance Tools. When manually analyzing malware apps, we leverage available tools and frameworks wherever they are relevant and helpful. A static analysis tool with capability of collecting apk information and performing reachability analysis can help the analyzer quickly prioritize the analysis process. An appropriate tool can help obtain the trace to critical APIs. For instance, when analyzing renamed obfuscated apps, we cannot easily guess the semantics of the classes and methods. In that case, we should locate the critical API calls (*e.g.*, openConnection, sendTextMessage) and perform reachability analysis to understand from which component this API gets invoked, and track the call chain to get a more clear picture of what the app is doing. To serve this purpose, we leverage Amandroid [28] which is a publicly available[2] comprehensive static analysis framework for analyzing Android apps.

In addition, an IDE-like editor that provides functionality of class hierarchy resolution, def-use chain building, method invocation tracing in the decompiled IR (intermediate representation) is also to the human analysts to understand the code flow. We built such an analysis tool for this purpose[3].

An Android app development environment is also important for manual analysis. An analyst may need to "re-implement" certain parts of the malware to test the real functionality, or to get the runtime value of certain variables. For instance, many malware apps encrypt the string constant and the malicious payloads to avoid detection. When analyzing such a malware, we first identify the decryption routine, extract and load it in a separate app, and then provide the encrypted content to get the plaintext information.

The Overall Strategy of Manual Analysis. With the help from the aforementioned assistance tools, we performed manual analysis of 405 Android malware samples representing 135 varieties. Here we present a systematic way of how to manually analyze Android malware, which serves as a guideline for other people who want to reproduce our analysis results, or to analyze other Android malware apps.

Identifying Malicious Components. An Android app is organized as a collection of components. To understand the behavior of a given malware sample we have to identify which components belong to the malware payload, or whether the whole app is a standalone malware. As the clustering analysis (CA) tool [18] we use is imperfect, the payload it outputs for each variety could be the full payload or a partial payload. For the latter case, we need more effort to identify the full payload. We get help from the following observations: (1) Since a component is the basic functional block for an Android app, we can expect that the full component is likely to belong to the payload, if a few of the component's methods or reachable methods appear in the CA-extracted payload; (2) In most cases, the package name is a good indicator; if some of a package's classes appear in the CA-extracted malicious payload, then the whole package is very likely to belong to the payload. Malware writers could also instrument the benign part of the repackaged malware to initialize the payload, so we should also search for any use of payload package names inside the benign components. This will enrich our understanding of the activation strategy for this malware.

Prioritizing Component Analysis. We should not start the analysis from a random component as that will not put the analysis in a meaningful context. After obtaining the malicious components using the CA tool, we follow a triaging scheme, and analyze the components in the following sequence:

---

[2] Tool website: http://pag.arguslab.org/argus-saf.
[3] Tool website: http://pag.arguslab.org/argus-cit.

(a) Event handlers: Event handlers mostly serve as the entry points in an Android app. More specifically, the main Activity and the BroadcastReceiver receiving "android.intent.action.BOOT_COMPLETED" event (BootReceiver) is the initializer, which can be used to start the core component (*e.g.*, monitor service) of the malware, so it should be analyzed first. Other event handlers are mainly related to monitoring user information and the environment of infected device. They also can be considered as entry points of certain malware. Take as example a BroadcastReceiver which receives "android.provider.Telephony.SMS_RECEIVED". This component is used to listen to any new incoming SMS message for this device. When we analyze such a component, we should check how it handles the message, whether it performs some operation related to the device inbox, if it matches the incoming message phone number with some list (*e.g.*, bank phone numbers, vendor phone numbers, *etc.*), and aborts the SMS using abortBroadcast() method call.

(b) The services that are started by initializers normally contain the main logic of the malware (monitor service); thus they need to be analyzed as soon as possible. It is the core component for most malware, which the malware will try to keep running as long as possible. It is common to see that many entry point components or scheduled tasks will start such service. The monitor service normally is used to fetch and reply to commands from a command and control server. It is also common to schedule some TimerTask or BroadcastReceiver to constantly check the internet connectivity, whether an anti-virus product is running, whether itself is still alive, and so on.

(c) All remaining components. The purpose of those components vary. The guideline is to start from such a component and trace all the reachable code to understand: (i) what role the component plays, (ii) which other components this component communicates with, (iii) which BroadcastReceiver this component registers, (iv) whether this component starts some thread or AsyncTask and what is the purpose.

Building the Behavior Report. After we analyze all the relevant components, we generate a report that includes an inter-component graph where a node represents a component (present in the malicious payload) or a worker thread loaded by such a component, and an edge represents the communication/interaction between two nodes. The graph also illustrates behavior description for each node and edge, such as the activation method, communication message, C&C commands, *etc.* This gives us a comprehensive picture of the malware on top of which we can understand its richer behavior, *e.g.*, what is the monetizing method, how it maintains the persistence, its main goal, and so on. The behavior report including the inter-component graph for each malware variety is available at the Android malware website.

Handling Anti-analysis/Obfuscation

(a) Renaming: Class name, method name and field name are important hints for understanding the malware's purpose. Renaming them to meaningless words makes manual analysis difficult. We can get help from static analysis tools to perform a reachability analysis to see all the reachable methods from a given component. This can help us locate the interesting APIs (as the system API names cannot be renamed). We follow the call trace to understand how an API gets invoked and how the calling parameters are prepared.

(b) String encryption: Oftentimes, we understand the malware behavior based on the strings used in the code, like URL, C&C command, class names, phone number, *etc.* If those strings are encrypted, it is very difficult to understand the semantics of those actions. To address this issue, we analyze the malware code to figure out the decryption routine and key. We then re-implement it in a separate app to decrypt the strings.

(c) Dynamic loading: Malware may hide its functionality in a separate apk/dex file and load it dynamically at runtime. Even worse, apk/dex file may be encrypted. To handle such cases, we first retrieve the decryption routine to decrypt the apk/dex file. For either case we decompile the code to study it as a regular app, which adds to our understanding of the malware.

(d) Native payload: Most Android static analysis tools do not handle native code. Thus malware writers like to put some core function or data in the native payload. For us to understand how the native payload works, we use standard binary reverse-engineering tools including IDA [5] and hex-dump [4].

Handling Missing Contents. Sometimes, we may not be able to obtain the full payload of the malware, but we still have ways to maximize our understanding. The basic idea is to understand how the malware leverages the missing content. For instance, if we observe that the malware downloads an apk file, we could see whether this malware sends an installation request for this apk or it uses *DexClassLoader* to load some new classes. In the first case, we could check the description of the installation request (which will show up on the screen to the device user) to understand the purpose of such action. For example, this description may say "Crucial update found for xxx." Then we know it is misleading the user to install a malware. In the second case, we know this malware is dynamically loading some code; we should expect to see multiple java reflection calls to such code, and from those reflection calls we could infer what role it plays.

Discussion. One may wonder what is the benefit of our study given the fact that after a malware family is discovered, anti-virus companies usually publish a report/bulletin on a sample app from that family. In fact, for each family under our study (71 in total), we did find such reports on the web. However, such reports usually only highlight the security breaches and main activities of the malware family and do not describe the malware behaviors in details. This is not sufficient for malware research. In addition, those reports do not provide the varieties for each family and the different malware behaviors from those varieties.

3 Android Malware Profiling

We present an overview of our Android malware dataset, and discuss the detailed profiles for the samples along two main dimensions: behaviors and monetization methods. The detailed information of each malware variety can be found at our Android malware website.

3.1 Malware Dataset Overview

Table 1 provides an overview of the malware families in our dataset. For each family we show the time it was first discovered. The malware type roughly indicates the main purpose of the family. The table shows the number of samples, and the number of varieties in each family. The dataset consists of 24,650 malware samples categorized in 135 varieties within 71 families.

Table 1. Dataset overview.

Family	Type	Samples	Variety	Detection	Family	Type	Samples	Variety	Detection
Lnk	Trojan	5	1	07/2010	Minimob	Adware	203	1	09/2013
FakePlayer	Trojan-SMS	21	2	08/2010	Tesbo	Trojan-SMS	5	1	09/2013
DroidKungFu	Backdoor	546	6	05/2011	Gumen	Trojan-SMS	145	1	10/2013
GoldDream	Backdoor	53	2	07/2011	Svpeng	Trojan-Banker	13	1	11/2013
GingerMaster	Backdoor	128	7	08/2011	Spambot	Backdoor	15	1	12/2013
Boxer	Trojan-SMS	44	1	09/2011	Utchi	Adware	12	1	02/2014
Zitmo	Trojan-Banker	24	2	10/2011	Airpush	Adware	7843	1	03/2014
SpyBubble	Trojan-SMS	10	1	11/2011	FakeAV	Trojan	5	1	04/2014
Fjcon	Backdoor	16	1	11/2011	Koler	Ransom	69	2	05/2014
Steek	Trojan-Clicker	12	1	01/2012	SimpleLocker	Ransom	173	4	06/2014
FakeTimer	Trojan	12	2	01/2012	Cova	Trojan-SMS	17	2	06/2014
Opfake	Trojan-SMS	10	2	01/2012	Jisut	Ransom	560	1	06/2014
FakeAngry	Backdoor	10	2	02/2012	Univert	Backdoor	10	1	07/2014
FakeInst	Trojan-SMS	2172	5	05/2012	Aples	Ransom	21	1	07/2014
FakeDoc	Trojan	21	1	05/2012	Finspy	Trojan-Spy	9	1	08/2014
MobileTX	Trojan	17	1	05/2012	Erop	Trojan-SMS	46	1	08/2014
Nandrobox	Trojan	76	2	07/2012	Andup	Adware	45	1	11/2014
Mmarketpay	Trojan	14	1	07/2012	Ramnit	Trojan-Dropper	8	1	11/2014
UpdtKiller	Trojan	24	1	07/2012	Kuguo	Adware	1199	1	02/2015
Vidro	Trojan-SMS	23	1	08/2012	Youmi	Adware	1301	1	02/2015
SmsZombie	Trojan-Spy	9	1	08/2012	Dowgin	Adware	3385	1	02/2015
Lotoor	HackerTool	333	15	09/2012	Fobus	Backdoor	4	1	03/2015
Penetho	HackerTool	18	1	10/2012	BankBot	Trojan-Banker	740	8	03/2015
Ksapp	Trojan	36	1	01/2013	Roop	Ransom	48	1	05/2015
Winge	Trojan-Clicker	19	1	01/2013	Ogel	Trojan-SMS	6	1	06/2015
Mtk	Trojan	67	3	02/2013	Mecor	Trojan-Spy	1820	1	07/2015
Kyview	Adware	175	1	04/2013	Ztorg	Trojan-Dropper	20	1	08/2015
SmsKey	Trojan-SMS	165	2	04/2013	Gorpo	Trojan-Dropper	37	1	08/2015
Obad	Backdoor	9	1	06/2013	Leech	Trojan-SMS	128	3	09/2015
Vmvol	Trojan-Spy	13	1	06/2013	Fusob	Ransom	1277	2	10/2015
AndroRAT	Backdoor	46	1	07/2013	Kemoge	Trojan-Dropper	15	1	10/2015
Stealer	Trojan-SMS	25	1	07/2013	SlemBunk	Trojan-Banker	174	4	12/2015
Boqx	Trojan-Dropper	215	2	07/2013	Triada	Backdoor	210	1	03/2016
Bankun	Trojan-Banker	70	4	07/2013	RuMMS	Trojan-SMS	402	4	04/2016
Mseg	Trojan	235	1	08/2013	VikingHorde	Trojan-Dropper	7	1	05/2016
FakeUpdates	Trojan	5	1	08/2013	Total: 71		24650	135	

3.2 Malware Behaviors

Table 2 illustrates the behaviors of malware families[4] we analyzed. Due to space constraint we only present part of the analysis result. The more detailed information can be found at our Android malware website. Behavior tags in one category may not be mutually-exclusive — some apps may present multiple behaviors in a category.

Composition. There are three ways an Android malware is composed: a **stand-alone** app where the malware was written from scratch, a **repackaged** app where the malware was repackaged within a legitimate app, and **library** where the malicious components exist in the library code of an otherwise legitimate app. For the library case, this is the common way adware gets on the user's device. The difference between this method and repackaging is that the malicious payload here may get tagged on the app by the app developer (who may not be aware of the malicious activity inside the library) as opposed to being repackaged by a malware writer.

In our dataset, we observe that 63% of malware varieties and 35% of malware apps (shorthanded 63%/35% thereafter) are standalone, 30%/7% of malware are repackaged, and in 7%/58% of malware the malicious payload is installed as a library of the "legitimate" app. This means repackaging is no longer the dominant method for composing Android malware. The reason could be that malware writers nowadays put more effort in Android, and have started to design more comprehensive and sophisticated malware from scratch. For instance, *FakeAV* is a fake anti-virus family; its behavior looks exactly the same as a typical anti-virus application and its appearance looks very professional. *Bankun* masquerades as the legitimate Korean bank app – in fact it looks exactly the same as the legitimate one.

Even in decline repackaging is still frequently used in distributing malware. We define two types of repackaging: *isolated* repackaging and *integrated* repackaging.

Isolated repackaging means the malware payload is packaged into a legitimate application x but not in any way connected with x's original functionality. It declares its own event handler as the activation component, and does all the malicious tasks on its own without affecting x's functionality.

Integrated repackaging is the more advanced way where the malware author modifies the workflow of (or injects code into) the host app, and lets the payload run together with the host app. This makes the malware more stealthy, and more likely to be activated. For instance, *VikingHorde* [22] replaces the app's launcher Activity with its own launcher; the launcher will activate its monitoring service and then start the host app's launcher component.

---

[4] Table 2 aggregates the behaviors over all malware varieties in a family. The more specific per-variety breakdown can be found at our Android malware website.

Deep Ground Truth Analysis of Current Android Malware

Table 2. Malware behaviors.

Legend		
Composition	Standalone (ST)	Repackaging (RPKG): Isolated (O), Integrated (T) Library (LIB)
Activation	Event (EV)	By Host App (BHA) Scheduling (SC)
Persistence	Stealthy (TH):	Block (BL), Clean (CL), Hide Icon (HI), Rootkit (RK)
	Prevent destroy (PD):	Hide Admin (HA), Kill AV (KA), Lock Device (LD), Monitor Destroy Action (MDA), Reinstall (RI), System App (SYS)
Privilege	Request Admin (RA)	Root Exploit (RE)
C&C	Internet (IN)	Command Encoding (CE): JSON (J), Java Script (JS), XML (X), Custom Protocol (P)
Anti-analysis	Renaming (RN)	String Encryption (SE) Dynamic Loading (DL) Native Payload (NP)
	Evade Dynamic Analysis (EDA):	Check Device Info (CDI), Encrypt Communication (EC), Check Installed App (CIA)

Installation: Drop (DR) Drive-by Download (DD) — Info Stealing: Device Info (DI) Personal Info (PI)

Family	ST	RPKG	LIB	DR	DD	EV	BHA	SC	DI	PI	TH	PD	RA	RE	IN	SMS	CE	RN	SE	DL	NP	EDA
Airpush			✓	✓		✓		✓	✓	✓			✓				J	✓				
AndroRAT	✓			✓		✓			✓	✓			✓				P					
Andup			✓	✓		✓	✓		✓	✓								✓	✓			
Aples	✓					✓			✓	✓		LD	✓				P					
BankBot	✓			✓	✓	✓		✓	✓	✓	BL&HI	MDA	✓			✓	J&P	✓	✓	✓		CDI
Bankun	✓			✓	✓	✓		✓	✓	✓	BL&HI		✓				J&X					CDI
Boqx		O		✓		✓			✓	✓											✓	
Boxer	✓				✓	✓			✓									✓	✓			
Cova	✓			✓		✓			✓	✓	BL		✓				JS	✓	✓			
Dowgin			✓	✓		✓	✓		✓	✓			✓				J	✓	✓	✓		EC
DroidKungFu	✓	O&T		✓		✓		✓	✓	✓		KA	✓	✓		✓	J&P	✓	✓	✓	✓	
Erop	✓					✓				✓	BL		✓									
FakeAV	✓					✓			✓		BL											
FakeAngry		O				✓			✓	✓							P	✓	✓			
FakeDoc	✓			✓		✓			✓	✓	BL		✓									
FakeInst	✓			✓		✓			✓		BL						J&P	✓	✓			
FakePlayer	✓					✓					BL											
FakeTimer	✓					✓			✓										✓			
FakeUpdates		T		✓		✓	✓	✓	✓								X	✓	✓			
Finspy	✓					✓			✓	✓	HI		✓				P		✓			EC
Fjcon		O				✓			✓		BL						X					
Fobus	✓					✓			✓		BL&HI		✓				X	✓	✓			EC
Fusob	✓					✓		✓	✓	✓		LD&MDA	✓				J	✓	✓			
GingerMaster		O&T		✓		✓		✓	✓	✓				✓		✓	P	✓	✓			
GoldDream	✓	T		✓		✓			✓	✓			✓				P					
Gorpo		O		✓		✓			✓				✓	✓		✓	J	✓	✓			EC
Gumen		T		✓		✓	✓		✓	✓	BL		✓				X				✓	DI
Jisut	✓					✓						LD										
Kemoge		O		✓		✓			✓				✓	✓		✓	P					
Koler	✓			✓		✓			✓	✓		LD&MDA	✓				JS&P	✓				CDI
Ksapp		T		✓		✓	✓	✓	✓	✓			✓				P					EC
Kuguo			✓	✓		✓			✓	✓			✓				P	✓				
Kyview			✓	✓	✓	✓			✓	✓							J	✓	✓			
Leech		T		✓		✓	✓	✓	✓	✓	BL	MDA	✓			✓	J	✓	✓	✓		EC
Lnk		T				✓			✓					✓								
Lotoor	✓			✓		✓												✓		✓	✓	
Mecor	✓					✓			✓	✓							JS					
Minimob					✓	✓			✓	✓			✓				J	✓				
Mmarketpay		O		✓		✓		✓	✓	✓	BL						P					
MobileTX	✓					✓			✓	✓												
Mseg		O	✓	✓		✓			✓	✓	BL						P					
Mtk		O&T		✓		✓			✓		BL						P	✓	✓	✓		
Nandrobox		T		✓	✓	✓	✓		✓	✓	BL						J					
Obad	✓			✓	✓	✓			✓	✓	BL&HI	HA	✓			✓	J	✓	✓			CDI&EC
Ogel	✓					✓			✓		BL						P	✓			✓	
Opfake	✓			✓		✓			✓	✓	BL&CL&HI						P		✓			
Penetho	✓					✓																
Ramnit		T					✓															
Roop	✓					✓			✓		HI	LD	✓				JS					
RuMMS	✓			✓		✓		✓	✓	✓	BL&HI		✓				J	✓	✓	✓		
SimpleLocker	✓					✓			✓		HI	LD	✓			✓	J&P	✓				
SlemBunk	✓			✓	✓	✓		✓	✓	✓	BL&HI		✓			✓	J		✓	✓	✓	
SmsKey		T				✓	✓											✓				
SmsZombie	✓			✓		✓			✓	✓	BL&CL		✓			✓	X					
Spambot	✓					✓					BL		✓									
SpyBubble	✓			✓		✓			✓		BL&CL						X					
Stealer	✓			✓		✓			✓	✓	BL	MDA	✓				JS					
Steek	✓					✓																
Svpeng	✓			✓	✓	✓			✓	✓	BL	LD	✓	✓			P	✓				CDI
Tesbo		O				✓			✓		BL&CL		✓				X	✓	✓			
Triada	✓			✓		✓		✓	✓	✓	CL&RK	SYS	✓				P	✓	✓	✓		CDI&CIA
Univert	✓					✓			✓		BL		✓				J					
UpdtKiller		T				✓	✓	✓	✓		BL	KA&MDA	✓				X	✓			✓	
Utchi				✓	✓	✓			✓	✓			✓				J					
Vidro	✓					✓			✓		BL		✓				J					
VikingHorde		T				✓			✓	✓		RI	✓				J				✓	
Vmvol	✓			✓		✓			✓	✓	BL&CL		✓				J					
Winge		O		✓		✓			✓	✓							X	✓				
Youmi			✓	✓	✓	✓			✓	✓			✓				P	✓				
Zitmo	✓					✓	✓		✓	✓	BL&HI						P	✓				
Ztorg		T		✓		✓			✓	✓			✓	✓		✓		✓	✓	✓	✓	EC
Total families:	41	24	9	40	9	64	20	34	39	58	34	15	15	8	50	9	53	39	22	11	8	14
Total varieties:	85	40	9	76	15	120	23	58	92	61	53	27	30	32	83	12	86	64	35	13	19	15
Total apps:	8567	1833	14231	9231	1218	14980	14687	12341	21333	15035	2839	3549	2823	1061	22108	367	22145	18143	7211	5072	972	4051
Malware	ST	RPKG	LIB	DR	DD	EV	BHA	SC	DI	PI	TH	PD	RA	RE	IN	SMS	CE	RN	SE	DL	NP	EDA
	Composition			Installation		Activation			Info Stealing		Persistence		Privilege		C&C			Anti-analysis				

Installation. Besides being installed by users, there are a couple other ways Android malware get on a victim's device.

Drop: There are more than 56%/37% of malware that try to download and install applications on the victim's device; the downloaded application could be the malware's real payload, upgraded version, or other risky applications. There are different ways malware use to install applications on victim's device. ***Vmvol***

will show a dialog with critical update message to trick the victim user to install the payload as an update.

Drive-by Download: We adopt the following definition for Drive-by download [3]: (1) Downloads which a person authorized but without understanding the consequences; and (2) Any download that happens without a person's knowledge. As one example, *SlemBunk* [31, 33] gets on the device when the user visits some porn website. The website will show a prompt that asks the user to upgrade the Flash Player; if the user chooses to upgrade, it will actually download the Slembunk malware. Another example: *Bankun* will collect victim's contacts, and send a message saying "*We will send you a mobile birthday invitations* http://vik6.pw" to each of the contacts. As people normally trust what they get from their friends, the friend will likely click on the link, and the malware will be downloaded.

Activation. Android Malware Genome only reported event-based activation methods. Our analysis found two more options: **by-host-app** and **scheduling**.

The by-host-app option is closely related to the integrated repackaging method, where the attacker instruments code into the host app to activate the malware together with the host app. This is the typical way for activating adware, which we will discuss in Sect. 3.3.

The scheduling option is also frequently used to start their monitoring or data collection in a periodic manner. Typically, the malware registers a Timer task thread, or uses Android's AlarmManager with PendingIntent. When certain time goes by, the malware's monitor service is activated to get new commands from the C&C server. One extreme use of scheduling is in ransomware. Some ransomware apps schedule a periodic task using a very short interval, making the victim device non-responding. We discuss this more in Sect. 3.3.

Information Stealing. In our dataset, more than 68%/87% malware collect users' device information, such as international mobile station equipment identity (IMEI), international mobile subscriber identity (IMSI), kernel version, phone manufacturer, network operator, *etc.* We observe that information items such as IMEI and IMSI are unique for each device and thus could be used as an identifier to register the compromised device with the C&C server. Other device information items, such as the OS version, the baseband version, the OS language, and installed applications give the C&C server some idea of the target device's specification, based on which the C&C server can decide the strategy for using the compromised device.

Persistence. In our dataset, 48%/22% malware use at least one persistence technique, which shows that persistence is one of the important attributes the malware writers consider in the app design. The longer the malware can stay in the victim's device, the more revenue they can produce for the adversary. Persistence can be achieved over multiple dimensions, including:

(a) Making malware's presence stealthy. We observed multiple stealthy methods malware use to hide evidence of malicious activity: (a) Blocking the appearance of items such as audio, call, notification, or SMS, (b) Cleaning items such as call log and SMS history – important for the malware since the automatically added messages or phone records may alert the victim user that something wrong may have happened, (c) Hiding the malware's launcher icon despite the malware's background service running, (d) Hooking system APIs to mask its existence.
(b) Preventing itself from being destroyed by the system, anti-virus product, or the user via techniques such as hiding itself from appearing in the device administrator list, killing AV process, locking device, *etc.*

Privilege Escalation. Obtaining admin privilege can make the malware much harder to remove, and can allow the malware to perform privileged operations such as changing lock-screen pin code, locking device, wiping device data, *etc.* More and more malware these days try to acquire admin-privilege. *Obad* leverages admin-privilege to make it disappear. Another notable malware family is *Fobus*. Once *Fobus* gets admin-privilege, it will listen to the *DEVICE_ADMIN_DISABLE_REQUESTED* event. If the user tries to disable admin-privilege for this malware, it will lock the screen before the user can click the confirm button. Even if the user is fast enough to click the confirm button, it will display a message saying that if the user continues, the malware will do a factory reset of the device resulting in all the user's data being lost. Users usually know that granting admin-privilege is risky. Nevertheless, malware apps always try to convince the victim that they are security related services (*e.g.*, *Updtkiller*), or they can make the device more efficient (*e.g.*, *Fobus*). If the victim does not grant admin-privilege, many malware apps (*e.g.*, *SmsZombie*) will aggressively ask for it, which annoys the victim and makes the device unusable.

Lotoor is a generic name for a collection of hacking tools that exploit vulnerabilities to root a device and perform privileged actions by leveraging the root privilege. Our dataset has 15 varieties of different hacking tools under the name *Lotoor*. Those tools either help user root their device, or perform actions needing root privilege. Most rooter malware contain one to three root exploits targeting 2.x Android devices. The mostly used root exploits are *Exploid*, *RageAgainstTheCage (RATC)*, and *GingerBreak*. However, *Lotoor.FramaRoot* changes the story – it is the most comprehensive hacking tool containing at least eleven exploits that target devices with all kinds of processors (*e.g.*, *Exynos*, *Qualcomm*, *Mediatek*, *etc.*) ranging from 2.x to 4.x. *Lotoor.MasterKey* does not use any root exploit, but leverages a MasterKey vulnerability to hide its payload in a system app and bypasses the Android cryptographic verifier to infect the victim's device up to 4.x.

At the end of 2014 malware with root exploits appeared again while they still targeted devices before 4.x. *Leech*, *Ztorg*, *Gorpo* work together [13] and form a kind of "malvertising botnet." They leverage root privilege to drop new malware on the "network" of infected devices. For instance, *Triada* is dropped by this network. **Triada** has some interesting behaviors. It is a modular malware (with well-defined interfaces) with active use of root privilege. Once it is installed on the rooted device, it will try to exchange a configuration file with the C&C server, which contains the communication rate, the modules that need to be downloaded, *etc.* The modules include downloader, SMS trojan, and banking trojan. **Triada** is as sophisticated as traditional PC malware, which raises the alert that Android malware are evolving from the more primitive form to the next level.

Kaspersky reports [14] that Android devices running versions higher than 4.4.4 have much fewer exploitable vulnerabilities. This may explain why malware with root exploits are becoming less popular than reported in Android Malware Genome. However, there are still about 60% devices running old versions of Android that are vulnerable to rooting attack. Thus root exploit is still a major threat to Android devices.

Command and Control (C&C). 64%/90% have C&C servers. C&C increases the functionality and flexibility of the malware, helps it adapt to its running environment, continuously monitors the victim, and makes the best strategy to generate revenue. A C&C module generally contains a message builder and a command handler. Android malware have a variety of ways to transmit the collected items to the server. For example, **SmsZombie** builds a formatted text message and sends it to the server via SMS; one version of **FakeAngry** builds a URL like *http://l.anzhuo7.com:8097/getxml.do?flagid=-500&mediaver=7&channel=202_109&imei=xxx&...* which contains information items as the parameters; a newer version of **FakeAngry** puts the data into the HTTP POST request entity; **SpyBubble** stores all the messages into an XML file; **RuMMS** [32] encodes data into JSON format.

Upon receiving a command from the C&C server, the malware will perform certain actions according to the command. We observe that there are at least the following ways by which a command handler is designed.

(a) Commands can be in a standard formatted such as XML or JSON. The decoding routine reads contents from the command and perform the tasks accordingly.

(b) Android *Webview* allows the developer to specify a Javascript to Java bridge interface [1]; when the server sends javascript code back to the *Webview*, it will automatically be mapped to the corresponding Java method to perform the task.

(c) Many malware varieties use plain text or a self-defined protocol for the command format. A custom protocol is not necessarily less sophisticated than the other types. One of the most notable is **Ksapp**, which uses a self-designed language MDK as the command. In the malware payload, it contains a full interpreter of MDK including a lexer, a parser, and an MDK to Java type mapper. Whenever the malware receives a new command file, it will first parse it, generate a function table, and start executing from a predefined entry point function "start." In the execution, the MDK will map MDK types to Java types, and for the invocation, MDK will issue the invocation in JVM via reflection. When analyzing this kind of malware, analysts cannot see any functionality in the malware payload, but the malware can perform whatever actions allowed by permissions specified in the AndroidManifest.

Anti-analysis Techniques. We observe that 63%/79% of malware use at least one anti-analysis technique.

Renaming is one of the most adopted obfuscation techniques. It translates the original meaningful package, class, method, field, and parameter names into some meaningless or unreadable form. This makes the manual analysis much harder. However, it does not impact static analysis tools, and API calls cannot be renamed.

String Encryption is also widely found in malware. Strings in the code like server URL, JSON/XML key values, intent action, component name strings, or reflection strings can help anti-virus product or analysts identify the malware. Malware can use string encryption to change the constant strings to ciphertext, which increases the difficulty of understanding the malware behavior. Normally, malware uses the following ways or their combination to encrypt the string: byte permutation, one-time pad, base64 encoding, DES/AES, *etc.* To manually inspect those malware, we had to reimplement the decryption/decoding routine and map the ciphertext back to the plaintext form to understand their behavior.

```
ComponentName v0_3 = this.getComponentName();
Object[] v2_2 = new Object[3];
v2_2[2] = 1;
v2_2[1] = 2;
v2_2[0] = v0_3;
Context v1_1 = this.getApplicationContext();
Object v1_2 = Class.forName(IljIllj.IliijIIl(IljIllj.IliijIIl[104],
    IljIllj.IliijIIl[33] + 1, IljIllj.IliijIIl[26]))
    .getMethod(IljIllj.IliijIIl(IljIllj.IliijIIl[20],
    IljIllj.IliijIIl[20] | 14, 183), null)
    .invoke(v1_1, null);
Class<?> v0_2 = Class.forName(IljIllj.IliijIIl(IljIllj.IliijIIl[107],
    IljIllj.IliijIIl[107] | 24, 79));
int v3 = IljIllj.IliijIIl[138];
int v4 = IljIllj.IliijIIl[127] - 1;
v0_2.getMethod(IljIllj.IliijIIl(v3, v4, v4 | 69),
    Class.forName(IljIllj.IliijIIl(IljIllj.IliijIIl[7],
    IljIllj.IliijIIl[33] + 1, 136)), Integer.TYPE, Integer.TYPE)
    .invoke(v1_2, v2_2);
```

```
ComponentName v0_3 = this.getComponentName();
Context v1_1 = this.getApplicationContext();
PackageManager v1_2 = v1_1.getPackageManager();
v1_2.setComponentEnabledSetting(v0_3,
    PackageManager.COMPONENT_ENABLED_STATE_DISABLED,
    PackageManager.DONT_KILL_APP);
```

Fig. 3. Obad Code Snippet. The obfuscated code is on the top; the de-obfuscated version is at the bottom.

One notable family that extensively adopts renaming and string encryption techniques is *Obad*. Figure 3 shows the code snippets in *Obad* and the corresponding translation. We can see that, the obfuscation renames all classes, methods, fields to human unreadable forms (*e.g.*, *IljIllj*, *IliijIIl*, etc.). Furthermore, all invoke statements in the unobfuscated bytecode are translated to java reflection in the obfuscated version, and the name strings of such reflection are further encrypted and stored in a byte array list "IliijIIl." The decrypting method "*IljIllj.IliijIIl*" takes the byte array from "IliijIIl" and decrypts it and makes the reflection call. This clearly shows that the obfuscation can make both manual analysis and static analysis extremely difficult.

Dynamic Loading dex file becomes more popular nowadays. Normally it contains a dropper payload, which is lightweight and looks benign. But this dropper payload will then load the real payload from its assets or resource folder (*e.g.*, *RuMMS*), or download the real payload from internet (*e.g.*, *SlemBunk*). To further complicate the analysis, the real payload can even be encrypted (*e.g.*, *Fobus*).

Native Payload: Most of the static analysis tools focus on Dalvik bytecode. So the native library seems to be a good place to hide malware behavior. In our analysis, we observed that native payloads are becoming more popular. Malware apps not only hide functionalities, but also hide sensitive strings, like server URL, premium numbers in the native code.

Evade Dynamic Analysis: The basic idea of evading dynamic analysis is to detect the malware's current running environment. For example, when *BankBot* [26] gets activated, it will check whether IMEI, MODEL, FINGERPRINT, MANUFACTURE, BRAND and DEVICE are of certain value. If the running environment satisfies the condition, it will act benignly and stop itself. *Triada* will check if IMEI matches some pattern, and check whether "com.qihoo.androidsandbox" is installed. To thwart dynamic analysis that monitors the communication channel (*e.g.*, Internet, SMS.) of the malware, many malware encrypt communication with their C&C servers.

Many of these anti-analysis techniques involve encryption; thus how to obtain the key is important to the analyst. In most of the cases, the key is just hardcoded in the application code. Some malware put the key in the manifest, a resource XML file, or in the native payload. We also observed a few smart ways to hide or generate the keys. *Fobus* reads the JVM stack trace and uses the class and method name of the fourth entry in the stack to construct the key. *Obad* obtains its key by requesting a webpage from Facebook, and reads certain location from that webpage to generate the key.

3.3   Monetization
We observe that many malware attempt to make money from the victims as Table 3 illustrate.

Premium Service Subscription. Subscribing to a premium service is one of the main ways cybercriminals use to make money. In general, subscribing to

Table 3. Monetization techniques.

Family	Premium Service Subscription	Bank	Ransom	Aggressive Advertising	Family	Premium Service Subscription	Bank	Ransom	Aggressive Advertising
Airpush	Dynamic			✓	Minimob	Dynamic			✓
AndroRAT	Dynamic				Mmarketpay	Dynamic			
Andup				✓	MobileTX	Static			
Aples			✓		Mseg	Dynamic			
BankBot		✓			Mtk				
Bankun		✓			Nandrobox	Static			
Boqx					Obad	Dynamic			
Boxer	Static				Ogel				
Cova	Dynamic&Static				Opfake	Dynamic&Static	✓		
Dowgin				✓	Penetho				
DroidKungFu					Ramnit				
Erop	Static				Roop			✓	
FakeAV		✓			RuMMS	Dynamic	✓		
FakeAngry					SimpleLocker			✓	
FakeDoc	Static				SlemBunk		✓		
FakeInst	Dynamic&Static				SmsKey	Static			
FakePlayer	Static				SmsZombie			✓	
FakeTimer					Spambot	Static			
FakeUpdates					SpyBubble				
Finspy					Stealer	Dynamic			
Fjcon	Dynamic				Steek				
Fobus	Dynamic				Svpeng	Dynamic	✓	✓	
Fusob			✓		Tesbo				
GingerMaster					Triada	Dynamic	✓		
GoldDream	Dynamic				Univert	Dynamic			
Gorpo				✓	UpdtKiller	Dynamic			
Gumen	Dynamic				Utchi				✓
Jisut			✓		Vidro	Dynamic			
Kemoge					VikingHorde				✓
Koler			✓		Vmvol	Dynamic			
Ksapp					Winge	Dynamic			
Kuguo				✓	Youmi				✓
Kyview				✓	Zitmo		✓		
Leech				✓	Ztorg				✓
Lnk					Total families:	30	9	8	12
Lotoor					Total varieties:	41	27	13	13
Mecor					Total apps:	11839	1652	2166	14336

a premium service requires the malware app to send a request to the service provider. The premium service sends back a confirmation message, which has to be entered back to finish the subscription process. A comprehensive premium-service-subscription module includes a premium service requester and an incoming message handler. The service requester makes phone calls, sends SMS or network request to the premium service. After that, the malware waits for the services to reply with confirmation message. The incoming message handler intercepts the confirmation message and parses it. It then applies a handler logic based on different subscription routines, and cleans any evidence that might alert the victim user.

In our analysis, we found the following ways to obtain the premium numbers and handler logic: hard coded into the bytecode, hidden in the resource XML files or native library, encrypted, and dynamically configured from C&C server.

Banking Trojan. Online payment and mobile wallet are becoming more popular nowadays. Cybercriminals are also putting much effort to increase their revenue by designing banking trojans. In 2013, banking trojan *Bankun* came into picture. Once activated this trojan will check the compromised device for installed Korean banking applications, and try to replace them with fake ones.

Newer versions of banking trojans are capable of overlaying the on-screen display of a legitimate banking app with a phishing window. *Slembunk* falls into this category. When this malware is activated, it will schedule a

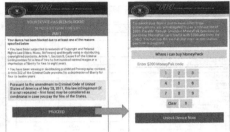

Fig. 4. Slembunk Phishing Windows   **Fig. 5.** Ransom Windows by Aples

java.lang.Runnable every 4 seconds to monitor the current running applications by looking at the Activity at the top of the Activity stack. If the current running Activity belongs to certain banking application, it will overlay a phishing window on top of the screen. Figure 4 shows what the phishing window looks like for different banking applications. As an example, if the current application is *com.android.vending* the left top window will be popped, and so on. **Slembunk** not only overlays phishing windows, it is also capable of forwarding phone calls and SMS from bank numbers, and applying the response logic. To effectively conceal the arrival of text messages or phone calls from banks, it will mute the device's audio system. Later versions of **Slembunk** even apply most sophisticated string encryption and dynamic loading obfuscation techniques (Sect. 3.2). Recently, IBM and FireEye report [9,17] that the source code of **SlemBunk** was leaked, which could result in the emergence of more variants.

Ransom. Ransomware locks the victim device by making it non-responsive or encrypting its data, and then coerces the victim to pay for the restoration.

Device Locking Techniques

Svpeng is both a banking trojan and ransomware. If its C&C server sends a command "forceLock," it will lock the infected device by using SYSTEM_ALERT_WINDOW permission and *WindowManager LayoutParams* with certain flags (*e.g.*, FLAG_SCREEN, FLAG_LAYOUT_IN_SCREEN, FLAG_WATCH_OUTSIDE_TOUCH, *etc.*) to achieve an unremovable full screen floating window.

Aples first appeared in 2014 – when activated, it will schedule a *Runnable* in every 0.1 second to load the threatening window with flag FLAG_ACTIVITY_NEW_TASK which looks like Fig. 5. Clicking on "PRO-CEED" at the first window will lead to the second window that asks the victim user to fill in a $300 MoneyPark code to unlock. Another malware family *SimpleLocker* has applied similar techniques, at the same time also encrypting all the data in the compromised device's external storage using AES with a hard-coded key.

Jisut once activated will launch a ransom window, and override *onKeyDown* method of *Activity* to redirect key press event (*e.g.*, return key, volume key, menu key, *etc.*) to some meaningless action to achieve the lock screen purpose.

Device UnLocking Techniques. After the victim has paid the money, the cybercriminal will tell the victim how to unlock the device or unlock it remotely. The most common way is to type in the pin. The pin in one variety of *SimpleLocker* is generated by obtaining a serial number at beginning (which is a random number), then uses some calculation logic (in one sample, the logic is *key = (serial_number - 2016)*2 + 2016*). The second way is using remote control. For instance, *Koler* uses network command to clear a lock tag at the malware's shared preference. The third way is by installing an unlock app. One variety of *Jisut* constantly checks whether an app with package "*tk.jianmo.study*" is installed or not; if yes, it will release the lock.

Aggressive Advertising. Mobile advertising is the main revenue source for app developers as well as malware writers. Advertising in malware is usually more aggressive, and this kind of apps are called adware.

Potentially Unwanted Application (PUA). A PUA adware performs tasks such as monitoring victim's personal data, showing unwanted advertisement content, annoying victim user with aggressive advertisement push, showing and tempting the victim to download and install potential harmful applications. *Dowgin* is one adware app. It will be activated once the device connectivity changes, user comes into presence, or a new application is installed or deleted. Once activated, it will display unwanted advertisements in the system's notification bar. If the victim clicks on this notification, it will show an application wall which attracts the victim to install new applications. At the same time, it will send device information and the list of installed apps to a remote C&C server using JSON, and receive commands for showing a new advertisement, uploading client info *etc.* Many other adwares have similar behaviors, *e.g.*, *Airpush*, *Kuguo*, *Youmi*.

Malware Dropper. *Gorpo*, *Kemoge* [30], *Leech* and *Ztorg* are some examples. Their task is to gain the root privilege on the infected device as discussed in Sect. 3.2, and then silently drop all the active malware apps that are available on the "malvertising campaign network" to the infected device. *VikingHorde* is running in two modes: rooted and not-rooted. If the device is not rooted, it performs in a regular fashion: uploading victim's data, fetch command from C&C to execute, *etc.* If the device is rooted, it will install some additional components, which are capable of constantly and silently downloading new malware onto the device. We include this as part of aggressive advertising even though their main purpose is spreading malware.

4   Evolution

We have performed a longitudinal study of our malware dataset with an attempt to discover the trend of malware behaviors and techniques used over the years from 2010 to 2016. For each type of behaviors and techniques, we observe the trend in terms of percentage of malware varieties manifesting a specific behavior/technique within a year. Figure 6 presents the results.

Figure 6a shows that the repackaging usage was growing until 2012, but later standalone malware became dominant. The reason could be that there are many effective anti-repackaging solutions made available during the last few years, which gives cybercriminals less incentive to use such techniques. On the other hand, the bad guys are putting more effort into designing comprehensive and sophisticated malware apps from scratch, and their malware design skill has matured.

Not surprising to see in Fig. 6b that listening to system events to activate malware's functional units is the main trick given the nature of Android system design. Scheduling a task to periodically start its functional unit is an alarmingly growing trend. By scheduling timer task or leveraging the *AlarmManager* the malware can constantly upload victim's information to or retrieve commands from the C&C server; in the ransomware apps, it is also one of the techniques to lock victim's device.

We observe that persistence has become a core feature of Android malware apps. Figure 6c shows that malware apps are evolving to be harder to notice by the victim, and harder to be destroyed by the system, anti-virus solutions, or users.

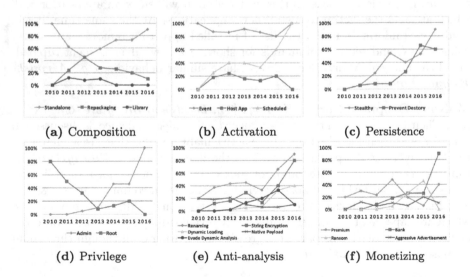

(a) Composition   (b) Activation   (c) Persistence

(d) Privilege   (e) Anti-analysis   (f) Monetizing

Fig. 6. Malware behavior trends

Root exploit is becoming less popular as we have discussed in Sect. 3.2, but obtaining device-admin-privilege seems to have become popular as seen in Fig. 6d.

The anti-analysis techniques are one of the key weapons of cybercriminals in the battle against security analysts. From Fig. 6e we can see that renaming and string encryption are the most growing techniques; dynamic loading and evading dynamic analysis are catching up while the practice of hiding behaviors in native payload is staying at the similar level.

Figure 6f shows that banking malware is becoming the main channel for cybercriminals to make money. Ransomware is a new threat that has started an uptick.

5   Related Work

The Android Malware Genome [34] was the first research project that has provided the community an Android malware dataset. This dataset has been the only well-labeled one and has been widely studied and used by the research community. Unfortunately, it has not been updated after its creation time around 2011. We comparatively studied this dataset with the new malware samples we have, and found that the Genome dataset does not include many of the new threats, which motivated us to carry out this work. Our dataset also provides much more detailed information on Android malware behaviors than that in Genome. Moreover, we provide detailed documentation of the process used in creating the dataset, including the guidelines for the manual analysis, to help other researchers do the same.

Recently, the *AndroZoo* [10] dataset has been published, which contains more than 3 million Android apps from Google Play, other smaller markets, and app repositories. *AndroZoo*'s goal is to create a comprehensive app collection for software engineering studies. Our goal is different and we focus on (only) malware apps to study their security related behaviors. Our dataset provides malware labels and detailed behavior information of the malware.

There are a few other repositories for Android malware apps which researchers can use, such as *Contagio Minidump* [2] and *VirusShare* [6]. However, they do not provide a comprehensive malware collection or comprehensive label and behavior information on the malware.

The *ANDRUBIS* [19] combines static and dynamic analysis to automatically extract feature and behaviors from Android apps, and studies the changes in the malware threat landscape and trends among "goodware," or benign apps, developers. However, as many behaviors are either unknown or can evade the automated analysis method, this work cannot give a comprehensive understanding of the malware landscape as we produced through the systematic and deep manual analysis.

AVclass [25] provides a method to extract malware family name by processing the AV labels obtained from VirusTotal. We adopted a similar approach for identifying malware family label. Our work is focused on deep manual analysis of malware samples from different malware varieties, and reporting the detailed behavioral profiles for Android malware.

There has been quite some work on how to detect malicious apps. The *Drebin* [11] work applies machine learning (ML) techniques to Android malware detection. The authors made the set of *feature vectors* used in the ML work available to the community. More recently, *MassVet* [15] provides a method to detect malware apps by observing the repackaging traits (if any) compared to that of other apps. Rastogi, *et al.* [24] conducted research on identifying adware tricks and drive-by-download techniques. *Harvestor* [23] attempts to extract the *run-time* values from obfuscated apps to detect malware. Researchers have identified ways in which Android users can be deceived to misidentify a malicious app window as a legitimate app's [12]. Moreover, *CopperDroid* [27] is a dynamic analysis system which attempts to reconstruct the behaviors of Android malware. Our work complements these and other Android malware analysis work by providing a comprehensive dataset of Android malware with detailed label and behavior information, which can facilitate future research in this area.

6   Conclusion

We created a large volume of well-labeled and well-studied Android malware dataset containing 24,650 samples, categorized in 135 varieties among 71 families ranging from 2010 to 2016. For each variety of this dataset we conduct a comprehensive study to profile their behaviors and evolution trends. We document in details the process of creating this dataset to enable other researchers to replicate the process. We observe that Android malware are evolving towards monetization, and becoming sophisticated and persistent. The extensive usage of anti-analysis techniques in the malware samples shows the urgent need for advanced de-obfuscation and dynamic analysis methods. We will make the dataset available to research community.

Acknowledgment. This research is partially supported by the U.S. National Science Foundation under Grant No. 1622402. Any opinions, findings and conclusions or recommendations expressed in this material are those of the authors and do not necessarily reflect the views of the National Science Foundation. This research is also partially supported by David and Amy Fulton Grant received by co-author Roy at Bowling Green State University.

References

1. Building Web Apps in WebView. https://developer.android.com/guide/webapps/webview.html
2. Contagio Mobile Malware Mini Dump. http://contagiominidump.blogspot.com/
3. Drive-by Download. https://en.wikipedia.org/wiki/Drive-by_download
4. hexdump. https://www.freebsd.org/cgi/man.cgi?query=hexdump&sektion=1
5. IDA. https://www.hex-rays.com/products/ida/index.shtml
6. VirusShare. https://virusshare.com/

7. VirusTotal. https://www.virustotal.com/
8. IDC: Smartphone OS Market Share 2015, 2014, 2013, and 2012 (2015). http://www.idc.com/prodserv/smartphone-os-market-share.jsp
9. A Growing Number of Android Malware Families Believed to Have a CommonOrigin: A Study Based on Binary Code (2016). https://community.fireeye.com/external/1438
10. Allix, K., Bissyand, T.F., Klein, J., Le Traon, Y.: AndroZoo: collecting millions of android apps for the research community. In: Proceedings of the Mining Software Repositories (MSR) (2016)
11. Arp, D., Spreitzenbarth, M., Hubner, M., Gascon, H., Rieck, K.: Drebin: effective and explainable detection of android malware in your pocket. In: Proceedings of the NDSS (2014)
12. Bianchi, A., Corbetta, J., Invernizzi, L., Fratantonio, Y., Kruegel, C., Vigna, G.: What the app. is that? deception and countermeasures in the android user interface. In: Proceedings of the IEEE S&P (2015)
13. Nikita Buchka. Taking root (2015). https://securelist.com/blog/mobile/71981/taking-root/
14. Buchka, N., Kuzin, M.: Attack on Zygote: a new twist in the evolution of mobile threats (2016). https://securelist.com/analysis/publications/74032/attack-on-zygote-a-new-twist-in-the-evolution-of-mobile-threats/
15. Chen, K., Wang, P., Lee, Y., Wang, X., Zhang, N., Huang, H., Zou, W., Liu, P.: Finding unknown malice in 10 seconds: mass vetting for new threats at the google-play scale. In: Proceedings of the USENIX Security Symposium, pp. 659–674 (2015)
16. Hurier, M., Allix, K., Bissyandé, T.F., Klein, J., Le Traon, Y.: On the lack of consensus in anti-virus decisions: metrics and insights on building ground truths of android malware. In: Caballero, J., Zurutuza, U., Rodríguez, R.J. (eds.) DIMVA 2016. LNCS, vol. 9721, pp. 142–162. Springer, Cham (2016). doi:10.1007/978-3-319-40667-1_8
17. Kessem, L.: Android Malware About to Get Worse: GM Bot Source Code Leaked (2016). https://securityintelligence.com/android-malware-about-to-get-worse-gm-bot-source-code-leaked/
18. Li, Y., Jang, J., Hu, X., Ou, X.: Android Malware Clustering through Malicious Payload Mining. Technical Report 2017–1, Argus Cybersecurity Lab, University of South Florida (2017). http://www.arguslab.org/tech_reports/2017-1
19. Lindorfer, M., Neugschwandtner, M., Weichselbaum, L., Fratantonio, Y., Van Der Veen, V., Platzer, C.: ANDRUBIS - 1,000,000 apps later: a view on current android malware behaviors. In: 2014 Third International Workshop on Building Analysis Datasets and Gathering Experience Returns for Security (BADGERS), pp. 3–17. IEEE (2014)
20. Maggi, F., Bellini, A., Salvaneschi, G., Zanero, S.: Finding non-trivial malware naming inconsistencies. In: Jajodia, S., Mazumdar, C. (eds.) ICISS 2011. LNCS, vol. 7093, pp. 144–159. Springer, Heidelberg (2011). doi:10.1007/978-3-642-25560-1_10
21. Mohaisen, A., Alrawi, O.: AV-Meter: an evaluation of antivirus scans and labels. In: Dietrich, S. (ed.) DIMVA 2014. LNCS, vol. 8550, pp. 112–131. Springer, Cham (2014). doi:10.1007/978-3-319-08509-8_7
22. Polkovnichenko, A., Koriat, O., Horde, V.: A New Type of Android Malware on Google Play (2016). http://blog.checkpoint.com/2016/05/09/viking-horde-a-new-type-of-android-malware-on-google-play/

23. Rasthofer, S., Arzt, S., Miltenberger, M., Bodden, E.: Harvesting runtime values in android applications that feature anti-analysis techniques. In: Proceedings of the NDSS (2016)

24. Rastogi, V., Shao, R., Chen, Y., Pan, X., Zou, S., Riley, R.: Are these ads safe: detecting hidden attacks through the mobile app-web interfaces. In: Proceedings of the NDSS (2016)

25. Sebastián, M., Rivera, R., Kotzias, P., Caballero, J.: AVCLASS: a tool for massive malware labeling. In: Monrose, F., Dacier, M., Blanc, G., Garcia-Alfaro, J. (eds.) RAID 2016. LNCS, vol. 9854, pp. 230–253. Springer, Cham (2016). doi:10.1007/978-3-319-45719-2_11

26. Shatilin, I.: Banking Trojans: mobile's major cyberthreat. https://blog.kaspersky.com/android-banking-trojans/9897/

27. Tam, K., Khan, S.J., Fattori, A., Cavallaro, L.: CopperDroid: automatic reconstruction of android malware behaviors. In: Proceedings of the NDSS (2015)

28. Wei, F., Roy, S., Ou, X., Robby: Amandroid: a precise and general inter-component data flow analysis framework for security vetting of android apps. In: Proceedings of the CCS (2014)

29. Woods, V., van der Meulen, R.: Gartner Says Emerging Markets Drove Worldwide Smartphone Sales to 15.5 Percent Growth in Third Quarter of 2015 (2015). http://www.gartner.com/newsroom/id/3169417

30. Zhang, Y.: Kemoge: Another Mobile Malicious Adware Infecting Over 20 Contries (2015). https://www.fireeye.com/blog/threat-research/2015/10/kemoge_another_mobi.html

31. Zhou, W., Chen, Z., Su, J., Xie, J., Huang, H.: SlemBunk: An Evolving Android Trojan Family Targeting Users of Worldwide Banking Apps (2015). https://www.fireeye.com/blog/threat-research/2015/12/slembunk_an_evolvin.html

32. Zhou, W., Deyu, H., Jimmy, S., Yong Kang, R.: The Latest Family of Android Malware Attacking Users in Russia via SMS Phishing (2016). https://www.fireeye.com/blog/threat-research/2016/04/rumms-android-malware.html

33. Zhou, W., Huang, H., Chen, Z., Xie, J., Su, J.: SlemBunk Part II: Prolonged Attack Chain and Better-Organized Campaign (2016). https://www.fireeye.com/blog/threat-research/2016/01/slembunk-part-two.html

34. Zhou, Y., Jiang, X.: Dissecting android malware: Characterization and evolution. In: Proceedings of the IEEE S&P (2012)

Code Analysis

HumIDIFy: A Tool for Hidden Functionality Detection in Firmware

Sam L. Thomas$^{(\boxtimes)}$, Flavio D. Garcia, and Tom Chothia

School of Computer Science, University of Birmingham, Birmingham B15 2TT, UK
{s.l.thomas,f.garcia,t.p.chothia}@cs.bham.ac.uk

Abstract. This paper presents a semi-automated approach to detect hidden functionality (such as backdoors) within binaries from consumer off-the-shelf (COTS) embedded device firmware. We build a classifier using semi-supervised learning to infer what kind of functionality a given binary has. We then use this classifier to identify binaries from firmware, so that they may then be compared to an *expected* functionality profile, which we define by hand for a range of applications. To specify these profiles we have developed a domain specific language called Binary Functionality Description Language (BFDL), which encodes the static analysis passes used to identify specific functionality traits of a binary. Our tool, HumIDIFy achieves a classification accuracy of 96.45% with virtually zero false positives for the most common services. We demonstrate the applicability of our techniques to large-scale analysis by measuring performance on a large data set of firmware. From sampling that data set, HumIDIFy identifies a number of binaries containing unexpected functionality, notably a backdoor in router firmware by Tenda. In addition to this, it is also able to identify backdoors in artificial instances known to contain unexpected functionality in the form of backdoors.

1 Introduction

Embedded devices are not only part of our everyday life but also part of our critical infrastructure. Internet routers, network switches, sensors and actuators assembled overseas are part of our electricity, banking and telecommunication infrastructure. When introducing a new device in a security critical environment you are implicitly trusting the device manufacturer together with the whole production and distribution chain.

In recent years there have been a number of incidents where hidden, unexpected functionality has been detected in both the software (firmware) [1,13] and hardware [18] of embedded devices. In many cases, this additional functionality is often referred to as a backdoor. In other cases, this functionality is considered undocumented functionality; but both types of functionality can manifest as real-world threats. Additional functionality inserted into hardware is notoriously hard to detect, but requires a much more powerful adversary – such as a nation-state, or chip manufacturer. Conversely, inserting hidden functionality into binary software, while still difficult to detect is much easier for an adversary. The most common types of such functionality found in the real-world are

M. Polychronakis and M. Meier (Eds.): DIMVA 2017, LNCS 10327, pp. 279–300, 2017.
DOI: 10.1007/978-3-319-60876-1_13

authentication bypass vulnerabilities and additional, undocumented functionality added to common services that weaken a system's security – such as so-called *debugging interfaces* (arguably) left over from development. This work focuses on the detection of the latter threat class.

Many companies and governmental organisations need to 'manually' analyse the firmware used in devices which are to be deployed in security-critical locations. This is a tedious and time-consuming task which requires highly-skilled employees. When we say a piece of software contains unexpected functionality, or a backdoor we require context to make this statement. Certain behaviour found in one piece of software that is considered *abnormal*, might be considered standard functionality in another. The formalisation of this notion of expected functionality inevitably requires a degree of human intervention, but the thorough analysis of the whole firmware can, to a large extent, be automated. One big challenge in developing techniques to perform this automation is the huge diversity in the binaries themselves that arise from having different embedded architectures, operating system versions, compiler options and optimisation levels. Another challenge is the fact that a large portion of the firmware which is readily available online only consist of partial updates, containing just modified files and not a complete system image. A further challenge is the sheer quantity of firmware available. In this paper we aim to provide a useful tool to automate as much of the process of finding hidden/unexpected functionality as possible, that is able to handle different architectures and compiler optimisations and is lightweight enough to scale to analyse large amounts of firmware in reasonable time. The approach we propose is nessessarily semi-automated and requires a human analyst to confirm identified *abnormalities*; despite this, when compared to manual analysis alone, we find the overall time taken to analyse firmware is greatly reduced.

1.1 Our Contribution

This paper presents a novel approach to detect unexpected, hidden functionality within embedded device firmware by using a hybrid of machine learning and human knowledge. Our techniques support an expert analyst in a semi-automated fashion: automatically detecting where common binaries from Linux-based embedded device firmware deviate from their expected functionality. While the proof-of-concept tool supports only Linux-based firmware, the techniques we present can easily be generalised to support other systems. Concretely our tool, HumIDIFy implements the following components which are used to identify unexpected functionality:

- A classifier for common classes of binaries contained within COTS embedded device firmware images, that is resilient to the heterogeneity of device architectures, including those binaries that contain unwanted data due to the current deficiencies in firmware extraction methods.
- A domain-specific language, BFDL and a corresponding evaluator for specification of so–called functionality profiles that encode expert human knowledge to aid with the identification of hidden/unexpected functionality in binaries.

HumIDIFy takes as input a firmware image, which it unpacks and runs each binary extracted through the (previously trained) classifier in order to infer what kind of well-known services it provides, e.g., FTP, HTTP, SSH, Telnet, etc. The classifier will assign to each binary file a *functionality category* label and a confidence value – representing the degree of certainty that the binary contains functionality associated with the assigned category.

The binary file is then subject to static analysis against the functionality profile corresponding to its assigned functionality category. This profile is defined by a human for each functionality category in our domain-specific language. In this way we provide enough flexibility for the tool to capture a wide range of abnormalities and allow it to be refined and adapted to the evolving threats.

We have collected a data set of 15,438 firmware images for COTS embedded devices from 30 different vendors. Of this dataset a total of 800 were selected uniformly at random to train a semi-supervised classifier. An additional 100 were selected to be a hold-out test set to evaluate the performance of the final classifier.

The classifier has been developed from extensive evaluation of a suite of 17 existing supervised learning algorithms alongside an adaptation of the semi-supervised self-training [21] algorithm which we show produces a classifier with significantly better performance than supervised learning alone.

In addition to real-world sample binaries, we evaluated the effectiveness of HumIDIFy on binaries we have embedded hidden functionality into. These were produced using the methodology proposed in [16] and manifested as backdoors in both the mini_httpd web server and the utelnetd Telnet daemon. In both cases HumIDIFy was able to accurately flag the binaries as containing hidden functionality – across both different architectures and differing compiler optimisation levels. Finally we used a further random sample of 50 firmware images which HumIDIFy was executed on resulting in detection of 9 binaries potentially containing hidden functionality one of which being a previously discovered backdoor present within Tenda routers[1].

We intend to release HumIDIFy as an open source tool under the LGPL v2.1 licence.

1.2   Expectations of Our Approach

Our approach does not claim to solve the problem of automating the identification of unexpected, hidden functionality within firmware, rather it lessens the effort of an analyst by automating as much of the process as possible.

Further, we do not claim to detect all kinds of hidden functionality such as authentication bypass vulnerabilities (like Firmalice [17]), cryptographic backdoors, highly complex backdoors [19] or functionality that is hidden due to obfuscation. From our analysis, complex and cryptographic backdoors on embedded devices are non-existent and thus, we conjecture are very rare.

---

[1] http://www.devttys0.com/2013/10/from-china-with-love/.

We note that on many devices, the mere presence of a Telnet or SSH daemon should signify a real threat—a large portion of firmware does not contain firewall rules for protecting such services—many of which, are Internet-facing. In addition, we have found that on many devices, user accounts generally have weak passwords—some not even protected by cryptographic hashing and on almost all devices, the only user available has privileges equivalent to the `root` user on UNIX-like systems. Again, we do attempt to detect such threats with our approach.

A generic approach to detecting all kinds of hidden, potentially backdoor-like functionality is infeasible for any approach. Instead we focus on a class of threat that covers hidden, additional functionality that deviates from the expected functionality of a binary.

Finally, we do not evaluate the effectiveness of our approach in the case of an adversary introducing the hidden functionality; we address the problem of detecting if device vendor, deliberately or otherwise has inserted unexpected functionality into common firmware services.

1.3 Related Work

Schuster and Holz [16] propose a dynamic analysis technique based on delta debugging to identify regions within binaries which may contain backdoors. They illustrate this technique by introducing backdoors in popular software tools such as ProFTPD and OpenSSH and then apply their methodology to identify them. Zaddach et al. [20] describe their framework, Avatar which allows for semi-automatic analysis of embedded device firmware. The framework is capable of performing complex dynamic analysis which is facilitated by insertion of a minimal debugger stub into the firmware itself and thus requires a live system; for this reason Avatar requires physical access to the device under analysis. Avatar relies on KLEE [4], where execution is performed both on commodity hardware through emulation, symbolic execution and in a *standard* manner upon the device itself. FIE, a tool developed by Davidson et al. [8] is also based upon KLEE and is designed to locate vulnerabilities in embedded microcontrollers by means of symbolic execution. FIRMADYNE [5] is another framework proposed by Chen et al., which like Avatar, allows for dynamic analysis via emulation of embedded device firmware. However, by restricting itself to Linux-based firmware mitigates the need for physical access to the device under analysis; as a result, a higher degree of automation is possible when compared to Avatar.

Costin et al. [6] presented the first large-scale simple static analysis of embedded device firmware whereby they studied 32,000 firmware images. Their analysis technique is based upon a variant of fuzzy hashing and what essentially amounts to pattern matching. These techniques are ineffective in identifying binary similarities when modifications are more widespread, for example, different compiler optimisation levels. Shoshitaishvili et al. [17] present Firmalice, which focuses on the identification of firmware authentication bypass backdoors—in contrast to the potential backdoors identified by the system presented in this paper—which focuses on backdoors that manifest as hidden functionality. We also note that our tool HumIDIFy is better suited to larger scale analysis due to the inherent complexity of identifying authentication bypass backdoors.

Pewny et al. [14] propose a method to identify bugs and vulnerabilities over multiple CPU architectures. They apply their technique to firmware from various vendors. Similarly, Eschweiler et al. [9] also devise a method of cross-architecture discovery of known bugs within binaries, and [6,7] provide details of a large-scale analysis of consumer embedded device firmware, however restricts itself specifically to the identification of web-frontend vulnerabilities.

2 Overview of HumIDIFy

Figure 1 provides an overview of our system architecture. Our system takes as input a firmware image as obtained directly from a device vendor or a compressed file system extracted from a device, then:

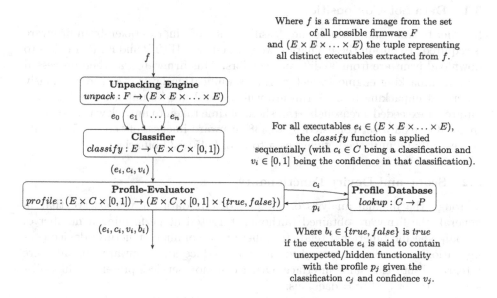

Where f is a firmware image from the set of all possible firmware F and $(E \times E \times \ldots \times E)$ the tuple representing all distinct executables extracted from f.

Unpacking Engine
$unpack : F \to (E \times E \times \ldots \times E)$

For all executables $e_i \in (E \times E \times \ldots \times E)$, the $classify$ function is applied sequentially (with $c_i \in C$ being a classification and $v_i \in [0,1]$ being the confidence in that classification).

Classifier
$classify : E \to (E \times C \times [0,1])$

Profile-Evaluator
$profile : (E \times C \times [0,1]) \to (E \times C \times [0,1] \times \{true, false\})$

Profile Database
$lookup : C \to P$

Where $b_i \in \{true, false\}$ is $true$ if the executable e_i is said to contain unexpected/hidden functionality with the profile p_j given the classification c_j and confidence v_j.

Fig. 1. HumIDIFy system architecture

1. We use our unification of unpacking tools (BinWalk[2], Firmware Mod Kit[3] and Binary Analysis Toolkit[4]) with the improvements detailed in Sect. 3.5. This process yields a file-system which we scan for ELF binaries; these binaries are used as input to both the classifier and the profile evaluator.

---

[2] https://github.com/devttys0/binwalk.
[3] https://code.google.com/p/firmware-mod-kit/.
[4] http://www.binaryanalysis.org/en/home.

2. The classifier takes as input a binary executable and outputs a corresponding category label and confidence value. The set of categories match one-to-one with possible functionality profiles of the profile evaluator and represent general functionality classes such as *web-server* or *secure-shell daemon*. The executable, label and confidence value are used as input to the profile evaluator.
3. The profile evaluator first locates the appropriate profile description for the input category from the profile database. It then performs static analysis passes upon the input binary dependent on the given profile. If hidden/unexpected functionality is detected, it is reported along with the confidence in the assigned label to the analyst.

The output of HumIDIFy for a firmware image is a list of binaries that contain potential hidden/unexpected functionality along with the assigned classification label and the classifier's confidence in that assigned label.

3   Classification of Binaries

3.1   Data Set Composition

In order to train and evaluate the classifier, a set of binaries taken from firmware is required. To obtain these binaries, we built custom HTTP and FTP crawlers to download firmware from 30 different vendors. This firmware was then processed by our unpacking engine—which acts as a unification layer over the previously described unpacking tools. Firmware which could not be unpacked due to tool failure, or exceeded a reasonable threshold of time taken to unpack was discarded. In total our data set consisted of 15,438 firmware images, of those 7,590 could successfully be unpacked; giving us a total of 2,451,532 binaries.

3.2   Scope and Device Functionality

Through the manual analysis of samples of our data set we observe that in general, the firmware obtained (although targeted at performing a number of domain-specific functions) tends to adhere to a common structure: device configuration is usually performed via a web-interface and firmware upgrades are integrated into this same interface. Other common services present include file-servers, Telnet and SSH daemons.

A major problem in the analysis of binaries within embedded device firmware is the heterogeneousness of the architectures they are compiled for. Unlike more traditional malware analysis, where the predominant architectures are x86 and x86-64 which have been studied extensively in the literature, embedded devices are deployed on more esoteric architectures such as ARM, MIPS and PowerPC. Further, the predominant deployment Operating Systems are variants of Linux— so, the possibility to utilise existing tooling across such platforms is significantly hampered. Our implementation targets the predominant architectures: ARM and MIPS and restricts itself to Linux-based firmware. Although these choices may appear as limitations in our approach, we observe that the vast majority of firmware falls within these boundaries, as highlighted in [6].

3.3   Choice of Classification Domain

A naïve approach would be to classify binaries based on their filename: for example, FTP daemons might be called `ftpd`, `vsftpd`, etc. However, a significant amount of the firmware we examined does not unpack cleanly, that is we could extract files, but not the filenames. Additionally, for firmware that did unpack cleanly we saw a range of names for the same service. For example, we saw web servers called `webs`, `httpd`, `mini_httpd`, `goahead` and `web_server`. Having attempted to use just filenames initially, we found the classifer constructed overfit the data set with bias towards detecting services from particular vendors.

We considered two approaches to classifier construction: supervised learning and semi-supervised learning. Supervised learning demands a subset of the input data set be labelled, and a reasonable number of examples collected for each such label. Thus, the labels chosen for classification do not cover all possible binary types found within firmware. From a manual analysis of 100 firmware images we create an initial data set with 24 labels. This process yields an inital set of 419 unique binaries to train from; cryptographic hashing is used to ensure the uniqueness of the binaries. A number of labels we construct are meta-labels in that they encode a particular functionality: one such label is *web-server* which itself covers a number of distinct example binaries within our data set: from very simple servers such as `uhttpd` to more complex such as `lighttpd`; the reasoning for this is that we wish to construct a classifier that is robust to different, not seen before examples of labels. While we acknowledge our initial training set is relatively small in proportion to the overall number of firmware images collected, manual analysis of binaries is very time consuming for a human analyst and one of the problems we attempt to address with this work.

An alternative to the techniques proposed in this paper would be to follow the example of others (such as [15]) who use supervised learning to classify binaries as anomalous. While this approach is applicable for binaries on commodity systems due to exsitence of large, balanced data sets of malicious binaries; such large data sets do not exist for binaries found on embedded systems. Further, supervised learning requires roughly equal sized input sets for each label; in the case of binaries for embedded device firmware this is also not possible to construct due to the relatively small number of binaries known to contain hidden functionality or backdoors on such systems.

Our approach overcomes the issues with supervised learning by employing semi-supervised learning to classify binaries based on general classes—using machine learning as a filter to aid in more precise, targeted static analysis—which can be used to detect anomalous binaries irrespective of the inital number of anomalous binaries known.

We use IDA Pro[5] to manually analyse the binaries used to construct the initial data set. Those binaries analysed are used to derive set of labels. The set of labels corresponds to those services that are prevalent amongst our initial data set.

---

[5] https://www.hex-rays.com/products/ida/.

3.4 Attribute Selection

To perform both attribute selection and construction of the classifier, we utilise the open-source machine learning toolkit WEKA [11].

Since our technique aims to extend to multiple architectures, we restrict the possible attributes to those that are homogeneous among binaries across different architectures. These consist of high-level meta-information: strings and the contents of function import and export tables, these are obtained using IDAPython. Our technique demonstrates that this meta-information is sufficient to derive a classifier capable of inferring the general class of an arbitrary binary taken from a firmware image with high precision.

Although the number of possible attribute types that are considered for constructing the classifier is small, the number of distinct values associated with each class of attributes is impractically large. To overcome this, we apply feature selection methods to remove needless, non-discriminating attributes that do not characterise a general category.

We use two passes of attribute filtering. The first pass filters attributes based on their association with a given class. For each binary of a given class, if an attribute is to be included in the set of all possible attributes, it must be present in a relatively high proportion of examples of that given class. For example, for web servers, the string GET / HTTP/1.1 is included in a large proportion of examples whereas, in those same binaries there exist unique compiler strings which are irrelevent. Thus we define a threshold delta to filter the initial features: this delta is selected based upon constructing a supervised classifier using the BayesNet classifier (chosen arbitrarily and kept consistent for uniform results) and seeing which delta produces the best performing classifier when evaluating using 10-fold cross validation. Concretely the selected delta that performed best (in respect to maximising the precision of the classifier) was 0.6 when used as input to the second stage of attribute selection. Figure 2 details the quantities of remaining features for each evaluated value for the delta.

The second pass utilises a standard feature selection algorithm found in WEKA. From evaluation of all algorithms available, we found CfsSubsetEval combined with the BestFirst ranker using default parameters performed best. Figure 3 outlines the results of this evaluation; the overall evaluation was performed with data sets produced using thresholds from 0 to 0.7 from the first stage of processing and utilisation combined with attribute selection algorithms. In the interest of space, we omit the results of evaluation of all but CfsSubsetEval; the remaining algorithms used (CorrelationAttributeEval, GainRatioAttributeEval, InfoGainAttributeEval, OneRAttributeEval,- ReliefAttributeEval, SymmetricUncertAttributeEval all used with Ranker) resulted in classifiers that perfomed considerably worse than those trained following use of CfsSubsetEval and BestFirst ranking. We also note that we did not evaluate the performance of those processed data sets from the first stage of attribute selection due to the absence of API features.

The CfsSubsetEval algorithm outlined in [12] evaluates the merit of subsets of features by correlating the predictive nature of individual features with respect

Threshold	API count	String count
0.0	2391	38040
0.1	1688	14328
0.2	1513	11074
0.3	1209	8522
0.4	442	5624
0.5	442	4843
0.6	231	3001
0.7	14	2020
0.8	0	1920
0.9	0	1830
1.0	0	1790

Threshold	Correct (%)
0.1	87.8788
0.2	87.8788
0.3	87.8788
0.4	87.8788
0.5	85.4545
0.6	**88.4848**
0.7	85.4545

Fig. 2. First stage attribute filtering

Fig. 3. Second stage attribute filtering with `CfsSubsetEval`

to the relative redundancy amongst the subset. Those subsets that are highly correlated with a given class whilst maintaining a low degree of intercorrelation are considered the most useful. The `BestFirst` ranking algorithm searches the subsets of features by hill climbing; that is, starting from an inital solution attempts to find a better solution incrementally by changing a single element upon each iteration until a fix point is reached. For `BestFirst`, hill climbing is performed in a greedy manner with backtracking.

Our feature, or attribute vectors as input to the classification algorithm consist of nominal attributes representing if a given API name or string is present in the binary being represented. That is, for each attribute a_i within the feature vector: $a_i \in \{0, 1\}$ with 1 representing inclusion and 0 the converse. As a specific example, suppose the API names: `socket`, `bind` and `puts` are selected as attributes and a given training instance is given the label *web-server*, importing only the first two API names, we would represent its corresponding feature vector as: $\langle 1, 1, 0, web\text{-}server \rangle$.

3.5 Construction of the Classifier

Prior to classifier construction, we evaluated an extensive set of supervised learning algorithms on the initally labelled set following processing from attribute selection. We attempt to maximise the precision of the classifier in assigning labels: maximising the number of correctly classified instances and minimising the number of incorrectly classified instances, whilst attempting to minimise the time taken to train the classifier. We note that minimisation of the traning time for semi-supervised learning is particularly important: training is an iterative process with each iteration processing more input data. Concretely, we trained each classifier upon the same labelled data set, and evaluated using 10-fold cross-validation; Fig. 4 details the results.

Classifier	Correct (%)	Time (s)	Classifier	Correct (%)	Time (s)
BayesNet [10]	88.4848	0.00	ZeroR	10.9091	0.00
NaiveBayes	79.3939	0.01	DecisionStump	20.6061	0.00
IBk	84.2424	0.00	HoeffdingTree	79.3939	0.00
KStar	84.2424	0.00	J48	76.9697	0.00
LWL	51.5152	0.00	LMT	85.4545	0.90
DecisionTable JRip	66.6667	0.08	RandomForest [2]	88.4848	0.11
OneR	21.2121	0.00	RandomTree	78.7879	0.00
PART	77.5758	0.04	REPTree	64.8485	0.03

Fig. 4. Supervised learning algorithm evaluation

Amongst the possible choices for classification algorithm, the two best performing in terms of optimising the number of correctly/incorrectly classified instances were BayesNet and RandomForest. Of those, the time taken to train the BayesNet classifier was less than that using RandomForest: 0.00 s compared to 0.11 s.

From the inital classifier, we used binaries from a further 700 firmware images as input to construct the final classifier; all of which were previously unlabelled. Final evaluation of the classifier was performed on an additional set of labelled binaries from 100 firmware images. We adapted the self-training algorithm as outlined in [21] using the BayesNet classifier as the supervised learning algorithm and a threshold bound on the iteration. We detail that algorithm in Algorithm 1. The number of iterations required to reach our chosen threshold bound of 0.05 was 8 iterations; that is between the 7th and 8th iterations the percentage difference was less than 0.05% we count the inital supervised learning step as the first iteration. We use a value of 0.9 as the required confidence bound to move a given binary from the set of unclassified data to the set of classified data; a value less than 1.0 is required in order to avoid over-fitting the training data. A value of 1.0. would produce a classifier that after being trained over multiple iterations would learn to only correctly classify instances that were of high similarity to those used to initially train the supervised classifier. After running the first stage of semi-supervised learning on a range of values we found 0.9 to be the most suitable—lower values in fact produced classifiers that performed worse when using 10-fold cross-validation. Figure 5 details the monotonic nature of the number of correctly classified instances at each iteration of training. The final classifier acheived a correct classification rate of 99.3691% when evaluated using 10-fold cross-validation. Evaluation on a completely unseen hold-out test set of labelled binaries resulted in the correctly classified rate dropping marginally to 96.4523%. The resulting drop in performance is observed due to a number of instances being mislabelled; of those instances mislabelled the maximum confidence the classifier supplied in the label it assigned was 0.65 which resulted in a binary manually labelled as a *dhcp-daemon* being incorrectly classified as a *upnp-daemon*.

Algorithm 1. Bounded self-training

---

function BOUNDEDSELFTRAINING(labelledData, unlabelledData, v, bound)
    L ← labelledData, U ← unlabelledData, k ← 0
    loop
        train f from L using supervised learning
        (k', L', U') ← apply f to unlabelled instances in U where u ∈ U' if CONFI-
DENCE(f(u)) ≥ v
            if U = U' ∨ k' − k ≤ bound **then return** f
            end if
            k ← k', L ← L', U ← U'
    end loop
end function

Iteration	1	2	3	4	5	6	7	8
Correct (%)	88.4848	95.4819	97.0760	97.9021	98.5462	99.2366	99.3256	99.3691

Fig. 5. Semi-supervised iterations

Avoiding Over-Fitting. As with any use of machine learning, over-fitting can become a problem when the classifier becomes biased to the data presented to it during the training phase, and thus, the chance of introducing such a bias needs to be minimised in order to produce a useful classifier. In the case of identifying classes of binaries, we identify two sources of bias. The first, is that by only using firmware from a small subset of vendors, which generally use the same web servers, Telnet daemons, and so on, on their devices our classifier shall be biased towards identifying a limited number of binaries from each class. Further, by using only particular types of firmware, for example for routers or IP cameras, the aforementioned problem manifests in that the types of service present in such firmware would be non-representative of those found if all possible types of firmware was considered. Thus, in training our classifier we ensure that our data set is representative of the overall state of COTS embedded device firmware in terms of vendor and device type selection. We do this by random sampling of the firmware data set. Additionally, our data set includes firmware from some 30 device vendors and includes firmware from all embedded devices they produce, thus has sufficient representation.

Overcoming Limitations in the Classification Method. A limitation in the classification method selected is the fact that a label must be assigned to every input instance; thus, if a binary that contains functionality never seen before is presented to the classifier, rather than returning an *unknown* classification label, it must assign a known label. We overcome this deficiency by using the confidence value in the results returned by our system. Namely, an analyst is able to see those binaries classified as a given label with low confidence not matching their functionality profiles are less likely to contain unexpected functionality and require further manual analysis. Conversely those labelled with high confidence not matching their expected functionality profiles are likely to contain additional functionality.

Overcoming Limitations in Data Collection. Our system can handle binaries that are carved from raw binary files—which do not have an assigned file name. We observe that `BinWalk` fails to correctly extract binaries in cases such as that shown in Fig. 6.

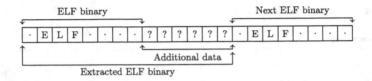

Fig. 6. ELF binary carving

`BinWalk` operates by identifying contiguous files by locating so-called "magic numbers". Unfortunately if it happens that an ELF binary is followed by a chunk of data that does not contain a "magic number" that data is appended to the binary. Thus, when we extract strings from the binary additional strings found within the appended data can potentially corrupt the classification result. We overcome this by parsing the ELF file header and calculating the correct file size: if the calculated size is smaller than the extracted binary we remove the additional data.

4   Hidden and Unexpected Functionality Detection

The result of the classification method we described in the last section is a tuple, (e_i, c_i, v_i), where e_i is the binary itself from the firmware image, c_i is an identifier representing the label assigned by the classifier and v_i represents the confidence of the classifier in the assigned label. We have built functionality profiles p_i for all classification labels, these are obtained via a lookup into a profile database P. Generation of these profiles has been performed manually. Adding additional binary classes to the system assumes a knowledgeable analyst capable of describing the expected functionality of that binary class. Hence when a binary being analysed does not conform to the expected functionality profile, potential unexpected functionality has been detected. As a concrete example, suppose a given binary has been classified as a *web-server*, then an analyst might expect that is a TCP-only service—something classified as a *web-server* additionally performing UDP networking should then (in this case) be considered as unexpected and further analysed to ascertain if this additional functionality is malicious or benign.

4.1   Binary Functionality Description LanguAge

We encode the description of the expected functionality of a given class of binaries using our domain specific language. The syntax of our Binary Functionality Description Language (BFDL) is shown in Fig. 7. A functionality profile for a given class of binary is defined by the use of the **rule** top-level expression, where the name supplied corresponds to the class of binary. The body of these rules will evaluate to true if the binary matches the profile, and it will evaluate to false if the binary shows evidence of deviating from the profile. Rules may additionally be parametrised; making available parameter names as bound variables within the body of the rule. Rules may also be used to define reusable components that can be used within multiple other rules. The **import** keyword allows for further rule reuse: it allows rules to be defined within separate files—essentially providing a facility to implement libraries of predefined rules for common static analysis passes.

$\langle$top-level$\rangle$ ::= **rule** $\langle$ident$\rangle$($\langle$arg-list$\rangle$) = $\langle$expr$\rangle$
 | **import** $\langle$string$\rangle$

$\langle$expr$\rangle$ ::= $\langle$rule$\rangle$($\langle$values$\rangle$)
 | **let** $\langle$ident$\rangle$ = $\langle$expr$\rangle$ **in** $\langle$expr$\rangle$
 | **if** $\langle$expr$\rangle$ **then** $\langle$expr$\rangle$ **else** $\langle$expr$\rangle$
 | **!** $\langle$expr$\rangle$
 | $\langle$expr$\rangle$ $\langle$logic-op$\rangle$ $\langle$expr$\rangle$
 | $\langle$value$\rangle$ $\langle$comp-op$\rangle$ $\langle$value$\rangle$
 | **forall** $\langle$ident$\rangle$($\langle$arg-list$\rangle$) $\Rightarrow$ $\langle$expr$\rangle$
 | **exists** $\langle$ident$\rangle$($\langle$arg-list$\rangle$) $\Rightarrow$ $\langle$expr$\rangle$

$\langle$type-name$\rangle$ ::= **bool** | **int** | **string**

$\langle$arg$\rangle$ ::= $\langle$ident$\rangle$: $\langle$type-name$\rangle$
$\langle$arg-list$\rangle$ ::= ε | $\langle$arg-list1$\rangle$
$\langle$arg-list1$\rangle$ ::= $\langle$arg$\rangle$ | $\langle$arg$\rangle$, $\langle$arg-list1$\rangle$

$\langle$narg$\rangle$ ::= _ | $\langle$arg$\rangle$
$\langle$narg-list$\rangle$ ::= ε | $\langle$narg-list1$\rangle$
$\langle$narg-list1$\rangle$ ::= $\langle$narg$\rangle$ | $\langle$narg$\rangle$, $\langle$narg-list1$\rangle$

$\langle$value$\rangle$ ::= $\langle$const$\rangle$
 | $\langle$variable$\rangle$
 | $\langle$value$\rangle$ $\langle$arith-op$\rangle$ $\langle$value$\rangle$

$\langle$rule$\rangle$ ::= $\langle$base-rule$\rangle$
 | $\langle$ident$\rangle$

$\langle$base-rule$\rangle$ ::= **import_exists**
 | **export_exists**
 | **string_exists**
 | **function_ref**
 | **string_ref**
 | **architecture**
 | **endianness**

$\langle$const$\rangle$ ::= $\langle$bool$\rangle$
 | $\langle$int$\rangle$
 | $\langle$string$\rangle$
 | **error**

$\langle$arith-op$\rangle$ ::= + | − | × | ÷ | % | & | ˆ | | | ~ | << | >>
$\langle$comp-op$\rangle$ ::= == | != | < | > | <= | >=
$\langle$logic-op$\rangle$ ::= || | &&

Fig. 7. BFDL language specification

The key feature of the language are the built-in rules that test specific properties of binaries. The most primitive are: **import_exists**, **export_exists** and **string_exists**. These rules do not constitute program analysis per se, rather, their results are derived from parsing the underlying binary file format. Both **import_exists** and **export_exists** check for the existence of strings representing imported or exported function names within the import and export tables of the ELF file format. **string_exists** disregards the file format entirely—essentially searching for a given string within the entire binary file. The **architecture** takes a case-insensitive string argument representing the architecture name—evaluating to true if the binary under analysis is indeed of said architecture, otherwise false—this rule allows for architecture-specific analysis passes to be performed.

For implementation of more complex analysis rules, we leverage both BAP [3]—a binary analysis library for the OCaml language which supports code–lifting, disassembly and CFG recovery functionality, and IDA Pro—a state of the art commercial disassembler. To ascertain if a function is called within the binary we provide a rule named **function_ref**. It operates first by inspection of the call graph of the binary, and attempts to verify the existence of an incoming edge to the node representing the function name being searched for; if such a relation does not exist, then a search is made for references to the function— which could indicate the use of the function as a callback, or indirect use such as via a function pointer. For example, the expression **function_ref**("listen") can be used to check if the binary makes a call to the listen function in order to open an incoming socket. In a similar fashion, **string_ref** searches for references to a given string within the binary—this is implemented in the same manner as the aforementioned method of locating potential indirect uses of functions.

The **forall** and **exists** keywords allow us to quantify over the parameters of a function call made by the binary, and allow us to define constraints on these arguments. As an example of the use of these rules, we could check that a binary makes a call to the socket function with the *type* argument equal to 2 using the following expression:

$$\textbf{exists} \ \text{socket}(\textit{domain: int, type: int, protocol: int}) \Rightarrow \textit{type} == 2$$

We use BAP as a basis for writing binary analysis routines to estimate the arguments passed as part of function invocations. In the case where a function is passed constants or static data that is independent of prior branching constructs, this always succeeds. In order to statically compute the constant arguments we first determine the function boundaries; that is, the start and end addresses of the functions deemed to contain calls to the function of interest. For each of the boundaries found we take the start address and perform disassembly, deriving a control flow graph to the granularity of basic blocks. In the interest of maintaining reasonably lightweight analysis we make the assumption that the basic block containing the call to the function of interest shall contain all of the argument loading instructions for that given call and any argument loading instructions related to the call in parent blocks are conditional and hence cannot be determined without further processing of the disassembled code. Since for both the ARM and MIPS instruction sets, argument passing is implemented by passing values in registers, we are able to estimate integer constants and string references to the data section of the binary by examination of load operations into registers. Concretely, for integer constants, the implementation is trivial as both instruction sets have instructions for loading constant integers directly into registers. For strings, the implementation is more difficult, we first identify loads into registers from the data section and then verify the data is a string: we perform this by checking for a consecutive block of ASCII characters followed by a terminating NULL byte (i.e., a C-style string). From manual analysis, C-style strings are found to be used in the vast majority of binaries from embedded device firmware, hence we check for those exclusively for efficiency. Inputs into the analysis pass are the function name and a list of arguments, which may either be constants or variable names. The expression specified following the function name and arguments defines a constraint over such variables used as arguments. If the arguments of a function are the result of a complex calculation (more complex than constant propagation and folding) our system will not find them. To represent such a failure at the language level, we augment each type with an additional value $\perp$ which is represented by the error keyword; a comparison with error that is not itself an error value will always result in false. In a boolean context when used as part of a logical expression error is automatically coerced into the boolean value false.

To compose expressions, BFDL supports all of C's logical and equality operators. It implements conditionals by way of an **if** expression, and allows for binding names to values through the **let** keyword—the semantics of which follow that of ML-like languages. The expected behaviour may be encoded in a number of ways: some rules make it possible to estimate "behaviour" in a manner that has a bias towards minimising the execution time of the profile evaluator, while others trade execution time and resources for greater precision. BFDL supports a number of primitive data types: strings, integers, booleans.

Figure 8 illustrates an excerpt from our standard prelude included with BFDL. It shows how both socket and file (stream) behaviour is encoded within the language. We note that these rules do not provide an absolute check of the behaviour being tested for example, uses_udp() checks if the socket API is used with an appropriate parameter (2 for MIPS, 1 for other architectures) as a value our analysis tools can detect. It would be possible for a program to implement its own version of UDP, which this rule would not detect, or it would be possible for a program to generate the traffic type parameter as a result of a complex calculation. So what this rule tests is if UDP is used in the standard way, rather than if UDP is used at all.

```
rule uses_udp() = exists socket(domain, type, protocol) ⇒
    if architecture("MIPS") then type == 2 else type == 1

rule may_read_files() = exists fopen(filename, mode) ⇒
    (mode == "r" || mode == "r+" || mode == "w+" || mode == "a+")
```

Fig. 8. An excerpt of BFDL rules from our standard prelude.

Figure 9 shows toy examples of how one might encode the functionality profiles for a *web-server* and *telnet-daemon*. As in this example, we are primarily interested in detecting unexpected functionality, these rules are focused on checking that the binaries conform to their expected network and file behaviour.

import "prelude.bfdl"

rule web_server() = uses_tcp() && !uses_udp() && may_read_write_files()
                        && !outgoing_socket()

rule telnet_daemon() = uses_tcp() && !(read_write_files() || uses_udp())

Fig. 9. Toy example profiles for web servers and Telnet daemons

They emphasise how basic rules may be composed to implement a more complex analysis.

As evidenced in the examples, the functionality profiles do not specify how a particular service might work, rather, what given the assumed behaviour in a given service might be deviation from the *norm*.

5   Experimental Results

In this section we evaluate the separate components of our contribution according to the points outlined in Sect. 1.1. First, we examine the performance of the classifier on a new hold-out set of manually labelled binaries. We then evaluate the entire system using a set of binaries known to have hidden functionality embedded within them, we then evaluate the tool on a sample of binaries taken from real-world firmware images. Following this, we examine the run-time performance of our tool and demonstrate its applicability to large-scale analysis. Finally we look at how one might attempt to evade our techniques within the limitations outlined in Sect. 1.1 and possible way to mitigate such attempts.

5.1   Evaluation of Classifier

As outlined in Sect. 3.5, our classifier was trained on a data set consisting of binaries from 800 firmware images and subsequently tested against an additional (separate, manually labelled) data set of binaries from 100 firmware images. It achieves a correct classification rate of 99.3691% on the training set using 10-fold cross-validation and a correct classification rate of 96.4523% on the independent test set which in total consisted of 451 individual binaries that exactly matched the functionality labels. The overall TP (true positive) rate over all 24 classes on the test set was 0.965 while the FP (false positive) rate was 0.002. Of those instances that were incorrectly classified seven labels were involved. Figure 10 outlines the TP/FP rates as well as the precision and recall rates for those labels.

These results show that for the most commonly found services, our classifier is highly effective in assigning the correct labels to services – irrespective of their origin (i.e. they are new instances of common services).

In the test set gathered, we found a single instance that corresponded directly to the label *cron-daemon*, this can be explained by the existence of busybox on

Label	TP rate	FP rate	Precision	Recall
cron-daemon	0.000	0.002	0.000	0.000
dhcp-daemon	0.636	0.002	0.875	0.636
ftp-daemon	1.000	0.002	0.929	1.000
ntp-client	1.000	0.002	0.933	1.000
nvram-get-set	1.000	0.011	0.750	1.000
ping	0.667	0.002	0.667	0.667
tcp-daemon	0.000	0.000	0.000	0.000
telnet-daemon	0.800	0.000	1.000	0.800
upnp-daemon	0.739	0.005	0.895	0.739
web-server	0.939	0.010	0.886	0.939

Fig. 10. Statistics for labels that were misclassified

the majority of those firmware images which includes the functionality for cron; we found what should have been labelled a *web-server* was mislabelled in this case. The mislabelled *cron-daemon* was labelled as a *dhcp-daemon*. We similarly found four instances of *dhcp-daemon* (of eleven) mislabelled; they received the labels: *ftp-daemon*, *nvram-get-set*, *ping* and *upnp-daemon*. A single instance of the *ping* utility was mislabelled as *nvram-get-set*; the small number of binaries corresponding to the *ping* label (three) was again due to its functionality being implemented within busybox; this was also the case for the *tcp-daemon* label. Of the mislabelled *telnet-daemon* label, one was labelled as *nvram-get-set*. Of the two (of thirty-three) mislabelled *web-server* instances, one was labelled as *upnp-daemon* while the other was labelled as *cron-daemon*; we see similarity in the API used by these services which led to the mislabelling. The *upnp-daemon* label was mislabelled in six instances (of twenty-three) as *web-server* in four cases (for the reasons previously described); the remaining two were mislabelled as *nvram-get-set*.

We note that the *nvram-get-set* label represents binaries that include general functionality to access and modify the non-volatile storage of the embedded device. Thus, of all labels we would expect it to induce the highest FP rate. On many devices there exist binaries specifically for NVRAM interaction (commonly called nvram-get and nvram-set), however we have found some instances whereby NVRAM interaction is implemented directly rather than in a separate utility, hence the possibility of mislabelling.

While a number of FP results exist, for the most pervasive services found within firmware, the classifier is highly successful in assigning the correct label to binaries.

5.2 Performance on New Artificial Instances

In this section we assess the ability of the whole system to recognise hidden functionality in well-known application modified by ourselves to contain additional, unexpected functionality.

We modified the source code of two services – `mini_httpd` and `utelnetd` – two of the most common services found in embedded device firmware from all device vendors. The hidden functionality takes the form of a remote control backdoor and is implemented using the same methodology proposed in [16].

Our tests consisted first of running the two services, unmodified through our system (acting as a base-line); each was classified correctly with a confidence value of 1.000 and said to not contain additional functionality. Then, each modified binary was run through our system; in all cases each binary was assigned the correct classification label with a confidence of 1.000 – the feature vectors remained unchanged between the base-line and each modified binary indicating the features chosen to define binary functionality for the classes chosen are discriminating enough to represent the core functionality for those labels. Similarly, in all cases, the profiling engine correctly identified all modified binaries as containing unexpected functionality.

This evaluation demonstrates both the effectiveness of our system in identifying hidden functionality and the generality of our approach to extend to multiple device architectures and different compiler optimisations.

5.3   Real-World Performance Using Sampling

In this section we evaluate the performance of our system using real-world data. The number of binaries within our data set is too large to feasibly evaluate manually, therefore we use a random sample of 50 firmware images from our data set. This yields a total of 15,507 binaries to use as input to HumIDIFy. A confidence value threshold of 0.9 was chosen to determine if a binary is evaluated by the functionality profiler of HumIDIFy; we selected this value for two reasons: it maintains consistency with the value chosen to train the classifier, and those binaries that are classified with confidence above this threshold value are likely to match the functionality of their assigned label with a (known) high probability (96.4523%).

For the purposes of our experiment, binaries processed that are assigned a label with a confidence value below 0.9 are considered to be classified as *unknown*.

From the 15,507 binaries, 4,012 were classified with a confidence value of 0.9 or greater. After removing duplicates, 425 unique binaries were classified with a confidence value equal to or above 0.9. From manual analysis, 392 were classified correctly, and of those classified correctly nine were flagged by HumIDIFy as potentially containing unexpected functionality.

Of those nine binaries, six of them were found within the *web-server* class, one within the *ssh-daemon* class, one within the *telnet-daemon* class and one within the *tcp-daemon* class.

HumIDIFy identified a *web-server* binary that contained a previously documented backdoor; it manifests as an embedded *management* interface which provides shell execution upon the device. It is found within the firmware of a number of devices from Tenda.

Another contained a built-in DNS resolver—which was unexpected. Two instances contained the same unexpected feature: an undocumented internal interface for device configuration listening on a non-default port; this interface provides privileged access to anyone with shell access on the device in question.

The *telnet-daemon* identified was implemented in a non-standard manner and thus, was flagged as containing unexpected functionality.

A binary appearing as an *ssh-daemon* in the first stage of classification mismatched the second stage of processing due to being statically linked. The first stage of classification was correct as the classifier was able to correctly label the instance based upon string features alone.

A further *web-server* was found to interact with the Syslog daemon over UDP to perform logging, and hence failed to match its expected functionality profile which assumes only TCP based networking. Another example was a custom application implementing HTTP proxy functionality; this was actually middleware for Trend Micro kernel engine. It was classified as containing unexpected functionality as not only does it implement HTTP request processing using TCP, it also provides additional functionality via UDP.

Another custom service was detected by HumIDIFy that serves as an Internet telephony proxy that was classified as a *tcp-daemon*; the service additionally supports UDP as a means of data transmission; thus, is classified as containing unexpected functionality.

We observe that our method not only supports finding instances of services that are strictly adhereing to the original set of functionality labels, but also those services that share the same core functionality with additional features; this is indeed useful for an analyst as it allows them to filter those services that are known but contain unexpected functionality and those services that may be of interest that contain functionality unknown to HumIDIFy.

In this evaluation we have demonstrated both the flexibility and effectiveness of our system: an analyst wanting to evaluate a firmware image in a more "paranoid" mindset can set the confidence threshold for classifier label assignment to a low value to have the system identify a larger amount of potential hidden, unexpected functionality, whereas an analyst wishing to analyse a large amount of firmware quickly can set this confidence threshold to a high value to limit the amount of manual analysis required. On real-world data our system with a modest confidence threshold was able to sucessfully identify a number of binaries containing unexpected functionality, some of which representing a real-world threat.

Our BFDL language is relatively high-level in terms of the checks that can be defined and performed on binaries – this allows us to perform lightweight analysis. This is however at some the cost to the accuracy and ability to check for precise, lower-level functionality that could eliminate some of the misclassified results in this section.

5.4   Run-Time Performance

In this section we examine the run-time performance of our analysis approach. For a single binary, the average time taken to perform feature extraction is 1.31 s. The average time taken to classify a single binary is 0.291 s (not including the time taken to invoke the Java virtual machine in order to run WEKA). The time taken to execute a profile is dependent upon the complexity of that profile. In the worst case (where we reconstruct function CFGs) the average time taken is 1.53 s; this value is proportional to the number of functions present within the binary under analysis. A single firmware image contains around 310 binaries; thus the average time to process a single firmware image assuming the worst case scenario—the classifier assumes a confidence threshold of 0.0 in which every binary passes through each stage of analysis is 970.61 s. We note that this evaluation does not take into account the time taken to perform the final stage of analysis—that performed by a human to manually analyse the binaries containing unexpected functionality.

In contrast to other work, such as Firmalice [17] – which has similar goals, but identifies binaries containing authentication bypass vulnerabilities as opposed to hidden, unexpected functionality, HumIDIFy performs well. Processing an entire firmware image on average in roughly the same time taken to process a single binary with Firmalice. From this analysis, we demonstrate the feasibility for our techniques to be used on a large-scale.

5.5   Security Analysis of HumIDIFy

HumIDIFy relies on certain meta–data: both strings and imported symbol names. While strings are present within all binaries, imported symbol names are only present within dynamically—linked binaries. Thus, when classifying a binary that does not contain all of the required meta—data incorrect labelling will occur and thus lead to false positives (i.e. the binary will be reported as containing unexpected functionality). Since our technique is intended to reduce the time taken for manual analysis, as opposed to being completely automated, reporting the binary as potentially containing unexpected functionality and therefore prompting manual analysis is the correct behaviour. From manual analysis of a large number of firmware images, we have found that an overwhelming majority use dynamic—linking; we attribute this to the general lack of storage space available on embedded devices and the space savings afforded by utilising dynamic–linking.

An attempt to evade the classifier, with for example a binary that is inherently a web-server manifesting as say, a Telnet daemon, HumIDIFy would still detect the binary as containing unexpected functionality due to the two-stage classification mechanism: the expected profile of a Telnet daemon would obviously be quite different from that of a web-server and thus fail to match. Thus, our overall approach is robust inspite of potential limitations in the individual components.

6   Conclusion

We have presented a semi-automated framework for detecting hidden and unexpected functionality in firmware. At the heart of our approach is a hybrid of machine learning and human knowledge encoding within our domain specific language, BFDL. As we have shown, this is a highly effective method for detecting unexpected functionality and (in some cases) backdoors in firmware.

References

1. Bradbury, D.: SCADA: a critical vulnerability. Comput. Fraud Secur. **2012**(4), 11–14 (2012)
2. Breiman, L.: Random forests. Mach. Learn. **45**(1), 5–32 (2001)
3. Brumley, D., Jager, I., Avgerinos, T., Schwartz, E.J.: BAP: a binary analysis platform. In: Gopalakrishnan, G., Qadeer, S. (eds.) CAV 2011. LNCS, vol. 6806, pp. 463–469. Springer, Heidelberg (2011). doi:10.1007/978-3-642-22110-1_37
4. Cadar, C., Dunbar, D., Engler, D.: KLEE: unassisted and automatic generation of high-coverage tests for complex systems programs. In: Proceedings of the 8th USENIX Conference on Operating Systems Design and Implementation, OSDI 08. USENIX Association (2008)
5. Chen, D.D., Egele, M., Woo, M., Brumley, D.: Towards automated dynamic analysis for linux-based embedded firmware. In: Network and Distributed System Security (NDSS) Symposium, NDSS 2016 (2016)
6. Costin, A., Zaddach, J., Francillon, A., Balzarotti, D., Antipolis, S.: A large scale analysis of the security of embedded firmwares. In: USENIX Security 2014. USENIX Association (2014)
7. Costin, A., Zarras, A., Francillon, A.: Automated dynamic firmware analysis at scale: a case study on embedded web interfaces. In: 11th ACM Asia Conference on Computer and Communications Security (AsiaCCS), ASIACCS 2016 (2016)
8. Davidson, D., Moench, B., Ristenpart, T., Jha, S.: Fie on firmware: Finding vulnerabilities in embedded systems using symbolic execution. In: 22nd USENIX Security Symposium (USENIX Security 2013) (2013)
9. Eschweiler, S., Yakdan, K., Gerhards-Padilla, E.: discovRE: efficient Cross-Architecture Identification of Bugs in Binary Code (2016)
10. Friedman, N., Geiger, D., Goldszmidt, M.: Bayesian network classifiers. Mach. Learn. **29**(2–3), 131–163 (1997)
11. Hall, M., Frank, E., Holmes, G., Pfahringer, B., Reutemann, P., Witten, I.H.: The weka data mining software: An update. SIGKDD Explor. Newsl. **11**(1), 10–18 (2009)
12. Hall, M.A.: Correlation-based Feature Subset Selection for Machine Learning. Ph.D. thesis, University of Waikato, Hamilton, New Zealand (1998)
13. Koscher, K., Czeskis, A., Roesner, F., Patel, S., Kohno, T., Checkoway, S., McCoy, D., Kantor, B., Anderson, D., Shacham, H., Savage, S.: Experimental security analysis of a modern automobile. In: 31th IEEE Symposium on Security and Privacy (S&P 2010) (2010)
14. Pewny, J., Garmany, B., Gawlik, R., Rossow, C., Holz, T.: Cross-architecture bug search in binary executables. In: 2015 IEEE Symposium on Security and Privacy (2015)
15. Rieck, K., Holz, T., Willems, C., Düssel, P., Laskov, P.: Learning and classification of malware behavior. In: Zamboni, D. (ed.) DIMVA 2008. LNCS, vol. 5137, pp. 108–125. Springer, Heidelberg (2008). doi:10.1007/978-3-540-70542-0_6
16. Schuster, F., Holz, T.: Towards reducing the attack surface of software backdoors. In: Proceedings of the 2013 ACM SIGSAC Conference on Computer & Communications Security. ACM (2013)

17. Shoshitaishvili, Y., Wang, R., Hauser, C., Kruegel, C., Vigna, G.: Firmalice - automatic detection of authentication bypass vulnerabilities in binary firmware (2015)
18. Skorobogatov, S., Woods, C.: Breakthrough silicon scanning discovers backdoor in military chip. In: Prouff, E., Schaumont, P. (eds.) CHES 2012. LNCS, vol. 7428, pp. 23–40. Springer, Heidelberg (2012). doi:10.1007/978-3-642-33027-8_2
19. Wysopal, C., Eng, C., Shields, T.: Static detection of application backdoors. Datenschutz und Datensicherheit - DuD **34**(3), 149–155 (2010)
20. Zaddach, J., Bruno, L., Francillon, A., Balzarotti, D.: Avatar: a framework to support dynamic security analysis of embedded systems' firmwares. In: Proceedings of the 21st Symposium on Network and Distributed System Security (2014)
21. Zhu, X., Goldberg, A.B.: Introduction to semi-supervised learning. Synth. Lect. Artif. Intell. Mach. Learn. **3**(1), 1–130 (2009)

BinShape: Scalable and Robust Binary Library Function Identification Using Function Shape

Paria Shirani[✉], Lingyu Wang, and Mourad Debbabi

Concordia University, Montreal, Canada
p_shira@encs.concordia.ca

Abstract. Identifying library functions in program binaries is important to many security applications, such as threat analysis, digital forensics, software infringement, and malware detection. Today's program
binaries normally contain a significant amount of third-party library
functions taken from standard libraries or free open-source software packages. The ability to automatically identify such library functions not only
enhances the quality and the efficiency of threat analysis and reverse engineering tasks, but also improves their accuracy by avoiding false correlations between irrelevant code bases. Existing methods are found to either
lack efficiency or are not robust enough to identify different versions of
the same library function caused by the use of different compilers, different compilation settings, or obfuscation techniques. To address these
limitations, we present a scalable and robust system called *BinShape* to
identify standard library functions in binaries. The key idea of *BinShape*
is twofold. First, we derive a robust signature for each library function
based on heterogeneous features covering CFGs, instruction-level characteristics, statistical characteristics, and function-call graphs. Second,
we design a novel data structure to store such signatures and facilitate
efficient matching against a target function. We evaluate *BinShape* on a
diverse set of C/C++ binaries, compiled with GCC and Visual Studio
compilers on x86-x64 CPU architectures, at optimization levels $O0 - O3$.
Our experiments show that *BinShape* is able to identify library functions
in real binaries both efficiently and accurately, with an average accuracy
of 89% and taking about 0.14 s to identify one function out of three
million candidates. We also show that *BinShape* is robust enough when
the code is subjected to different compilers, slight modification, or some
obfuscation techniques.

1 Introduction

Binary code analysis is an essential security capability with extensive applications, ranging from threat analysis, reverse engineering, cyber forensics, recognizing copyright infringement, to malware analysis. However, today's reverse
engineers still largely rely on manual analysis with only limited support from
automated tools, such as IDA Pro [4]. Such manual analysis is typically tedious
and error-prone due to the complex code transformation performed by the compilers, which usually involves highly optimized control flows, varying registers,

© Springer International Publishing AG 2017
M. Polychronakis and M. Meier (Eds.): DIMVA 2017, LNCS 10327, pp. 301–324, 2017.
DOI: 10.1007/978-3-319-60876-1_14

and the assignment of memory locations based on the CPU architectures and optimization settings [19]. Therefore, automated tools are highly desirable to assist reverse engineers in binary code analysis, which is especially relevant to security applications where the source code is unavailable.

Since modern software typically contain a significant number of library functions, identifying such functions in a binary file can offer a vital help to threat analysts and reverse engineers in many practical security applications. Further, it has a strong positive impact in various applications such as clone detection [9,10,14,20,27], function fingerprinting [38], authorship attribution [8,45], vulnerability analysis [12,13,19,40,47], and malware analysis [32,34,48]. Since it helps to filter out those library functions and focus on the analysis of user functions. In addition, the labeled library functions could provide valuable insights about the functionality of program binaries. Hence, the ability to automatically identify library functions cannot only enhance the efficiency of such threat analysis and reverse engineering tasks, but also improve the accuracy.

Automating the process of accurately identifying library functions in binary programs poses the following challenges: *(i) Robustness:* the distortion of features in the binary file may be attributed to different sources arising from the platform, the compiler, or the programming language, which may change the structures, syntax, or sequences of features. Hence, it is challenging to extract robust features that would be less affected by different compilers, slight changes in the source code as well as obfuscation techniques. *(ii) Efficiency:* another challenge is to efficiently extract, index, and match features from program binaries in order to detect a given target function within a reasonable time, considering the fact that many known matching approaches imply a high complexity [36]. *(iii) Scalability:* due to the dramatic growth of software packages as well as malware binaries, threat analysts and reverse engineers deal with large numbers of binaries on a daily basis. Therefore, designing a system that could scale up millions of binary functions is an absolute necessity. Accordingly, it is important to design efficient data structures to store and match against a large number of candidate functions in a repository.

To address the library identification problem, security researchers elaborated techniques to automatically identify library functions in binaries. For instance, the widely-used IDA FLIRT [3,15] applies signature matching to patterns generated according to the first invariant byte sequence of the function. This simple method is indeed very efficient but the robustness is a major issue. It suffers from the limitation of signature collisions and might require a new signature for each new version as the result of a slight modification, since various compilers and build options usually would affect byte-level patterns. Similarly, most other existing methods, e.g., UNSTRIP [28], which is based on the interaction of wrapper functions with the system call interfaces, and LIBV [41], which employs data flow analysis and graph isomorphism, also rely on one type of features and thus might also be easily affected by compiler families and compilation settings. Furthermore, these methods are usually not as efficient as FLIRT due to the need for complex operations, e.g., graph isomorphism testing.

In this paper, we aim to address aforementioned challenges and limitations of existing works. Specifically, we focus on following research problems. *Can we generate a "robust" signature for each library function to be resilient against compiler effects and obfuscation techniques? Can we rely on only those features who extraction, indexing, and matching can be performed in an efficient manner? Can we design an efficient data structure to allow a target function be matched against millions of candidate functions stored in a repository in a short time (e.g., less than a second)?* The key idea of *Binshape* is twofold. First, we derive a robust signature for each library function, called the shape of function, based on heterogeneous features covering CFGs, instruction-level features, statistical features, and function-call graphs. The shape of a library function captures a collection of most segregative characteristics along one or more dimensions of the features, which is automatically determined using selection evaluators, such as mutual information-based feature ranking and decision tree learning. Second, the shapes of library functions are extracted and stored in a repository and indexed using a novel data structure based on B^+trees for efficiently matching against a target function.

The main advantages of our approach are as follows: First, by relying mostly on lightweight features and the proposed data structure, our technique is *efficient*, and outperforms other techniques that rely on time-consuming computations such as graph isomorphism. Second, incorporating different types of features significantly reduces the chance of signature collisions compared to most existing works which rely on a single type of features. Therefore, by extracting the aforementioned heterogeneous features and furthermore selecting the best features amongst them, our approach achieves a great deal of *robustness*. As demonstrated by the experimental results, there is only a slight drop in accuracy when the code is generated by different compilers or has been moderately modified. Third, our technique is general in the sense that it is not limited to a particular type of functions, e.g., the wrapper functions provided by standard system libraries [28]. Finally, testing against a large number (over a million) of functions in a repository confirms the *efficiency* and *scalability* of our system.

Contribution. In summary, our main contributions are enlisted as follows:

- **Extracting Heterogeneous Features:** To the best of our knowledge, this is the first effort in employing a diverse collection of features, including graph features, instruction-level characteristics, statistical characteristics, and function-call graphs, for library function identification.
- **Generating a Robust Signature:** The novel concept of function shape induces a single robust signature based on heterogeneous features, which allows our system to produce good accuracy even when the code is compiled with different compilers and compilation settings, and is subjected to slight modifications and some obfuscation techniques.
- **Proposing a Scalable Technique:** By designing a novel data structure and using filters to prune the search space, our system demonstrates superior performance and provides a practical framework for large scale applications with millions of indexed library functions.

2   Overview

This section illustrates our motivating example, explains the threat model, and finally provides an overview of our system.

2.1   Motivating Example

Most of the existing works rely on a particular type of features (a review of related works is given in Sect. 6), and they typically organize those features as a vector. In addition, for every version of the function a new signature must be generated and indexed in the repository. Our first observation here is that, instead of using one type of features as in FLIRT, the diverse nature of library functions demands a rich collection of features in order to increase the robustness of detection. In addition, as will be demonstrated shortly in Fig. 1, the most segregative features for different library functions will likely be different, and therefore a feature vector may not be the best way for representing a signature. Specifically, the CFGs of _memmove, _memchr, and _lock_file functions are depicted in Fig. 1. We observe that two graph features of _memmove function are enough to be distinguishable from others in our repository. On the other hand, the CFG of _lock_file function contains smaller number of nodes (i.e., five), and the CFG of _memchr function is almost flat. Therefore, the best features to identify two different functions, one with few basic blocks and one with a large and complex CFG, would be very different; for instance, basic block level features for the former, and graph features for the latter.

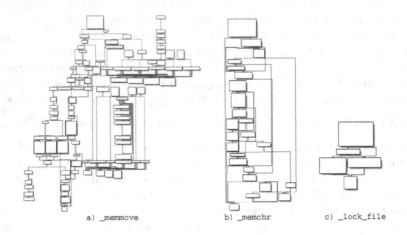

a) _memmove   b) _memchr   c) _lock_file

Fig. 1. CFGs of three library functions

2.2   Threat Model

In designing the features and the methodology of our system, we take into consideration several ways by which adversaries may attempt to evade detection by our system. First, adversaries may intentionally apply obfuscation techniques (discussed in more details below) to alter the syntax of binary files. Second, since the syntax of a program binary can be significantly altered by simply changing the compilers or compilation settings, adversaries may adopt such strategies to evade detection. Finally, attackers may slightly modify the source code of library functions and reuse them so as to evade detection. However, our system is not intended to replace threat analysts or reverse engineers. Thus, it is not designed to overcome the hurdles imposed by packers, obfuscation, or encryption. Therefore, the scope of our work is limited to function identification, and our tool is designed to work together with other reverse engineering tools or efforts [16,37] (e.g., those for de-obfuscation) instead of replacing them completely.

In general, obfuscation techniques may be applied to three types of binary analysis platforms: disassemblers, debuggers, and virtual machines [49]. Since we perform static analysis, the anti-disassembler category, which includes a variety of techniques such as dead code insertion, control flow obfuscation, instruction aliasing, binary code compression, and encryption will be considered in this work.

2.3   Approach Overview

Our approach is divided into two phases: offline preparation (indexing) and online search (detection). As illustrated in the upper part of Fig. 2, the offline preparation includes: (1) feature extraction; (2) feature selection, which includes feature ranking to extract the elements of the function shape, as well as best feature selection; and (3) signature generation to index the functions in a repository. The lower part of Fig. 2 depicts online search, which includes: (A) feature extraction; (B) filtration; and (C) detection components.

First, the binaries in our training set are disassembled by IDA Pro disassembler. Second, the graph features along with the instruction-level features, statistical features, and function-call graphs (explained in Sects. 3.1, 3.2, 3.3 and 3.4 respectively) are extracted. To select subsets of the features that are

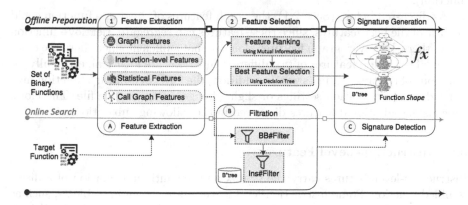

Fig. 2. Approach overview

useful to build the best signature, mutual information (Sect. 3.5) is employed on the extracted features. The top-ranked features are fed into a decision tree [22], and the outcome of the decision tree is stored in a data structure (Sect. 4.1) to form a signature for each library function. In addition to such signatures, we also store the top-ranked features that compose the signature of each function. For detection, all the features are extracted from a given target binary, two filters (Sect. 4.2) based on the number of basic blocks ($BB\#$) and the number of instructions ($Ins\#$) are used to prune the search space. Consequently, a set of candidate functions are returned as the result of filtration. Finally, the best matches are returned as the final results.

3   Feature Extraction

This section first describes different types of features, then presents feature selection, and finally defines the so-called function shape.

3.1   Graph Feature Metrics

We extract the control flow graph (CFG) of a binary function. To extract the best features for each library function and to describe the shape of a function, we extract graph features based on different characteristics of the CFG. Among existing graph metrics [24], we only employ those which are inexpensive to extract. The selected graph features are listed in Table 1. Below we show an example to illustrate the application of graph features to two functions. Our graph metrics are applied to two different library functions, memcpy_s and strcpy_s, as listed in Table 1. The corresponding CFGs have identical feature values for some metrics; for instance, *numnodes*, *numedges*, and *cc* values are equal, while other metrics such as *graph_energy*, and *pearson* (shown in boldface) are different and can be used to distinguish between them in this example (more generally, we will certainly need more features to uniquely characterize a function).

As discussed before (Sect. 2.1), the graph features of _memmove function could be part of the best features, since these features can segregate _memmove function from others. However, graph features alone are not sufficient since there are cases where all the graph features of two different functions are identical, especially for functions of relatively small sizes. In addition, the CFG of a library function may differ due to compilation settings or slight changes in the source file. Therefore, we consider additional features discussed in the following subsections.

3.2   Instruction-Level Features

Instruction-level features carry the syntax and semantic information of a disassembled function. Some instruction-level features are shown in Table 2a, such as the number of constants (*#constants*), and the number of callees (*#call list*). In addition, inspired by [33], we categorize the instructions according to their operation types, as shown in Table 2b. We record the frequency of each instruction category as a feature. By enriching standard CFGs with such information as different colors, there is a better chance to distinguish two functions even if they have the same CFG structure. Since these categories carry some information about the functionality of a program; for instance, encryption algorithms perform more logical and arithmetic operations.

3.3 Statistical Features

Statistical analysis of binary code can be used to capture the semantics of a function. Several works have applied opcode analysis to binary code; for instance, opcode frequencies are used to detect metamorphic malware in [42,46]. Therefore, each set of opcodes that belong to a specific function will likely follow a specific distribution according to the functionality they implement. For this

Table 1. Comparing graph features of _memcpy_s and _strcpy_s

Graph metric	Description	_memcpy_s	_strcpy_s
n, numnodes	Number of nodes	13	13
e, numedges	Number of edges	18	18
p, num_conn_comp	Number of connected components	1	1
CC	Cyclomatic complexity: $e - n + 2p$	7	7
num_conn_triples	Number of connected triples	6	6
num_loop	Number of independent loops	6	6
leaf_nodes	Number of leaves	7	7
average_degree	$2 * e/n$	2.7692	2.7692
ave_path_length	Average distance between any two nodes	**2.2308**	**2.5**
r, graph_radius	Minimum vertex eccentricity	**5**	**6**
link_density	$e/(n(n-1)/2)$	0.2308	0.2308
s_metric	Sum of products of degrees across all edges	**150**	**159**
rich_club_metric	Extent to which well-connected nodes also connect to each other	**0.2778**	**0.2778**
graph_energy	Sum of the absolute values of the real components of the eigenvalues	**18.7268**	**18.0511**
algeb_connectivity	2nd smallest eigenvalue of the Laplacian	**1**	**0.3820**
pearson	Pearson coefficient for degree sequence of all edges	**0.4635**	**0.3415**
weighted_clust_coeff	Maximum value of the vector of node weighted clustering coefficients	**0.3334**	**0.5**

Table 2. An example of instruction-level features and mnemonic groups

Feature	Description	Group	Description
retType	return type	DTR	Data transfer operations (e.g., mov)
declaration	declaration type	STK	Stack operations (e.g., push, pop)
argsnum	number of arguments	CMP	Compare operations (e.g., cmp, test)
argsize	size of arguments	ATH	Arithmetic operations (e.g., add, sub)
localvarsize	size of local variables	LGC	Logical operations (e.g., and, or)
instrnum	number of instructions	CTL	Control transfer (e.g., jmp, jne)
numReg	number of registers	FLG	Flag manipulation (e.g., lahf, sahf)
#mnemonics	number of mnemonics	FLT	Float operations (e.g., f2xm1, fabs)
#operand	number of operands	CaLe	System and interrupt operations (e.g.,
#constants	number of constants		sysexit)
#strings	number of strings		
#call list	number of callees		

(a) Example of Instruction-level Features   (b) Mnemonic groups

purpose, we calculate the *skewness* and *kurtosis* measures to convert these distributions into scores by the following formulas [6]:

$$Sk = (\frac{\sqrt{N(N-1)}}{N-1})(\frac{\sum_{i=1}^{N}(Y_i - \overline{Y})^3/N}{s^3}), Kz = \frac{\sum_{i=1}^{N}(Y_i - \overline{Y})^4/N}{s^4} - 3$$

where Y_i is the frequency of each opcode, $\overline{Y}$ is the mean, s is the standard deviation, and N is the number of data points. Similarly, we calculate *z-score* [50] for each opcode, where the corpus includes all the functions in our repository.

Normalization. Each assembly instruction consists of a mnemonic and a sequence of up to three operands. The operands can be classified into three categories: memory references, registers, and constant values. We may have two fragments of a code that are both structurally and syntactically identical, but differ in terms of memory references, or registers [20]. Hence, it is essential that the assembly code be normalized prior to comparison. Therefore, the memory references and constant values are normalized to MEM and VAL, respectively. The registers can be generalized according to the various levels of normalization. The top-most level generalizes all registers regardless of types to REG. The next level differentiates General Registers (e.g., eax, ebx), Segment Registers (e.g., cs, ds), and Index and Pointer Registers (e.g., esi, edi). The third level breaks down the General Registers into three groups by size - namely, 32, 16, and 8-bit registers.

3.4   Function-Call Graph

Function-call graph is a structural representation that abstracts away instruction-level details, and can provide an approximation of a program functionality. Moreover, function-call graph is more resilient to instruction-level obfuscation that usually are employed by malware writers to evade the detection systems [23]. In addition, it offers a robust representation to detect variants of malware programs [26]. Hence, the caller-callee relationship of the library functions is extracted.

The derived function-call graphs from those relationships are directed graphs containing a node corresponding to each function and edges representing calls from callers to callees. For labeling the nodes to exploit properties shared between functions, a neighbor hash graph kernel (NHGK) is applied to subsets of the call graph [25]. Those subsets include library functions and their neighbor functions (callees and callers). The function G maps the features of function f_k to a bit vector of length l, where l is the number of mnemonic categories (9) as shown in Table 2. Function G checks each value of the mnemonic groups of a function; if the value is greater than 0, the corresponding bit vector is set to 1; otherwise, it would be 0.

$$G : f_k \rightarrow v_k = \{0,1\}^l$$

The neighborhood hash value h for a function f_i and its set of neighbor functions N_{f_i} can be computed using the following formula [23]:

$$h(f_i) = shr_1(G(f_i)) \oplus (\oplus_{f_j \in N_{f_i}} G(f_j))$$

where shr_1 denotes a one-bit shift right operation and $\oplus$ indicates a bit-wise XOR. The time complexity of this computation is constant time, $O(ld)$, where d is the summation of outdegrees and indegrees, and l is the length of bit vector. For instance, suppose f_i is called by two other functions f_1 and f_2, and calls one function f_3. Therefore, the bit vectors based on the mnemonic group values of each function are generated (by the function G) to construct the set of neighbor function $N_{f_i} = \{v_1, v_2, v_3\}$. Finally, the hash value $h(f_i)$ would be equal to $(shr_1(v_i) \oplus (v_1 \oplus v_2 \oplus v_3))$.

3.5   Feature Selection

After extracting all the aforementioned features, we will end up with a number of features among which some might be the most relevant ones - those that appear more frequently and are most segregative in one function. Therefore, a feature selection process is conducted to reduce the number of features as well as to find the best ones. Our feature selection phase contains two major steps: feature ranking and best feature selection, which are described as follows.

Feature Ranking. We measure the relevance of the aforementioned features based on the frequency of their appearance in each library function. Mutual information [39] represents the degree depending on which the uncertainty of knowing the value of a random variable is reduced given the value of another variable. To this end, we employ a Mutual Information (MI) measure to indicate the dependency degree between features X and library function labels Y as follows:

$$MI = \sum_{x \in X} \sum_{y \in Y} p(x,y) log_2 \frac{p(x,y)}{p(x)p(y)}$$

where x is the feature frequency, y is the class of library function (e.g., memset), $p(x,y)$ is the joint probability distribution function of x and y, and $p(x)$ and $p(y)$ are the marginal probability distribution functions of x and y. The main intention of this feature ranking is to shorten the training time and to reduce overfitting. We measure mutual-information-based feature ranking on all categories of aforementioned features. In addition to mutual information, we apply feature selection evaluators including *ChiSquared* [43], *GainRatio* [43], and *Info-Gain* [44] using WEKA [7] on our features. Finally, we select the top-ranked features of our training dataset based on the MI.

Best Feature Selection. Our aim is to build a classification system which separates library functions from non-library functions. As such, we choose to apply a decision tree classifier on the top-ranked features obtained from the feature ranking process. Each library function is passed through the decision tree and the best provided features for that specific function are recorded. This automated task is performed on all library functions to create a signature for each. For instance, according to our dataset, the best features for _strstr function are *#DataTransConv*, *instrnum*, *algeb_connectivity*, *#id_to_constants*, and *average_degree* as shown in Listing 1.1.

Listing 1.1. _strstr best feature selection

```
#DataTransConv > 32.500
| instrnum > 237: other {_strstr=0,other=69}
| instrnum ? 237: _strstr {_strstr=11,other=0}
#DataTransConv ? 32.500
| algebraic_connectivity > 2.949
| | #id_to_constants > 3
| | | average_degree > 2.847: other {_strstr=0,other=591}
| | | average_degree ? 2.847
| | | |   instrnum > 171: _strstr {_strstr=1,other=0}
| | | |   instrnum ? 171: other {_strstr=0,other=48}
| | #id_to_constants ? 3: _strstr {_strstr=2,other=0}
| algebraic_connectivity ? 2.949:other{_strstr=0,other=4745}
```

4   Detection

Given a target binary function, the disassembled function is passed through two filters to obtain a set of candidate functions from the repository. The classical approach to detection would be to employ the closest Euclidean distances [18] between all top-ranked features of target function and candidate functions. However, such an approach may not be scalable enough for handling millions of functions. Therefore, we design a novel data structure, called B^{++}tree, to efficiently organize the signatures of all the functions, and to find the best matches. Our experimental results (Sect. 5) confirm the scalability of our method.

4.1   B^{++}tree Data Structure

Due to the growing number of free open-source libraries and the fact that binaries and malware are becoming bigger and more complex, indexing the signatures of millions of library functions to enable efficient detection has thus become a demanding task. One classical approach is to store $(key, value)$ pairs as well as the indices of best features; however, the time complexity of indexing/detection would be $O(n)$, where n is the number of functions in the repository. To reduce the time complexity, we design a data structure, called B^{++}tree, that basically indexes the best feature values of all library functions in the repository in separate B^+trees, and links those B^+tree to corresponding features and functions. We also augment the B$^+$tree structure by adding *backward* and *forward* sibling pointers attached to each leaf node, which points to the previous and next leaf nodes, respectively. The number of neighbors is obtained by a user-defined *distance*. Consequently, slight changes in the values that might be due to the compiler effects or the slight changes in the source code is captured by the modified structure. Therefore, the indexing/detection time complexity will be reduced to $O(log(n))$, which is asymptotically better.

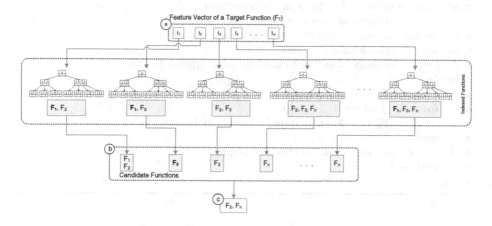

Fig. 3. Indexing and detection structure

We explain the B^{++}tree structure with a small example illustrated in Fig. 3. The best features of all library functions in our repository are indexed in B$^+$trees depicted in the middle box. For instance, the best features of library function F_1 are f_1, f_2 and f_m; hence, these three feature values linked to the function F_1 are indexed in the corresponding B^+trees (shown in boldface). For the purpose of detection, (a) all the features of a given target function are extracted. For each feature value, a lookup is performed on the corresponding B^+tree, and (b) a set of candidate functions based on the closest values and the user-defined *distance* are returned (we assume that $\{F_1, F_2, F_3, F_n\}$ are returned as the set of candidate functions). For instance, one match is found for the f_2 feature with the second feature of function F_3 (shown in boldface in part b), whereas this feature is indexed as the best feature for F_1 function as well. Finally, the candidate functions are sorted based on the distance and total number of matches: $\{F_2, F_n, F_1, F_3\}$. If we consider the first most frequent functions ($t = 1$), the final candidates would be $\{F_2, F_n\}$ functions.

The details are shown in Algorithm 1. Let f_T be the target function, and F retains the set of candidate functions and their frequency as output. First, all top-ranked features are extracted from the given target binary f_T (line 6). By performing m (total number of features) lookups in each B^+trees (line 7), a set of candidate functions will be returned (line 8). In order to choose the top t functions, the most t frequent functions are returned as the final set of matched functions (line 10).

Algorithm 1. Function Detection

Input: f_T : Target function.
Output: F : Set of candidate functions.
Initialization
1 $m \leftarrow$ total number of features;
2 $n \leftarrow$ total number of functions in the repository;
3 $F_c \leftarrow \{\}$; dictionary of candidate functions ;
4 $t \leftarrow$ number of most frequent functions to be considered;
5 $distance \leftarrow$ user-defined distance;
6 $feature[m] \leftarrow$ array of size m to hold all the extracted features;
  begin
7 | feature[] = featureExtraction(f_T);
8 | **foreach** $feature[i] \subset F_T$ **do**
9 | | $F_c = F_c + B^+TreeLookup(feature[i], distance)$;
10 | **end**
11 | $F = t\_most\_frequent\_functions(F_c, t)$;
12 | **return** F;
13 **end**

4.2 Filtration

To address the scalability issue of dealing with large datasets, a filtration process is necessary. Instead of a pairwise comparison, we prune the search space by excluding functions that are unlikely to be matched. In the literature, DISCOVRE [19] applies the k-Nearest Neighbors algorithm (kNN) on numerical features as a filter to find similar functions. However, GENIUS [21] re-evaluates DISCOVRE, and illustrates that pre-filtering significantly reduces the accuracy of DISCOVRE. To this end, two simple filters are used in our work, which are described hereafter.

Basic Blocks Number Filter (BB#). It is unlikely that a function with four basic blocks can be matched to a function with 100 basic blocks. In addition, due to the compilation settings and various versions of the source code, there exist some differences in the number of basic blocks. Thus, a user-defined threshold value (γ) is employed, which should not be too small or too large to prevent discarding the correct match. Therefore, given a target function f_T, the functions in the repository which have $\gamma\%$ more or less basic blocks than the f_T are considered as candidate functions for the final matching. Based on our experiences with our dataset, we consider $\gamma = \pm 35$.

Instruction Number Filter (Ins#). Similarly, given a target function f_T, the differences between the number of instructions of target function f_T and the functions in the repository are calculated; if the difference in the number of instructions is less than a user-defined threshold value λ, then the function is considered as a candidate function. According to our dataset and experiments, we consider $\lambda = 35\%$.

5   Evaluation

In this section, we present the evaluation results of proposed technique. First, we explain the environment setup details followed by the dataset description. Then, the main accuracy results of library function identification are presented. Furthermore, we study the impact of different obfuscation techniques as well as the impact of compilers on the proposed approach and discuss the results. Additionally, we examine the effect of feature selection on our accuracy results. We then evaluate the scalability of *BinShape* on a large dataset. Finally, we study the effectiveness of *BinShape* on a real malware binary.

5.1   Experiment Setup

We develop a proof-of-concept implementation in python to evaluate our technique. All of our experiments are conducted on machines running Windows 7 and Ubuntu 15.04 with Core i7 3.4 GHz CPU and 16 GB RAM. The Matlab software has been used for the graph feature extraction. A subset of python scripts in the proposed system is used in tandem with IDA Pro disassembler. The *MongoDB* database [5] is utilized to store our features for efficiency and scalability purposes. For the sake of usability, a graphical user interface in which binaries can be uploaded and analyzed is implemented. Any particular selection of data may not be representative of another selection. Hence, to mitigate the possibility that results may be biased by the particular choice of training and testing data, a $C4.5(J48)$ decision tree is evaluated on a $90:10$ training/test split of the dataset.

5.2   Dataset Preparation

We evaluate our approach on a set of binaries, as detailed in Table 3. In order to create the ground truth, we download the source code of all C-library functions [1], as well as different versions of various open-source applications, such as

Table 3. An excerpt of the projects included in our the dataset

Project	Version	No. Fun.	Size(kb)	Project	Version	No. Fun.	Size(kb)
7zip/7z	15.14	133	1074	nspr	4.10.2.0	881	181
7zip/7z	15.11	133	1068	nss	27.0.1.5156	5979	1745
7-Zip/7zg	15.05 beta	3041	323	openssl	0.9.8	1376	415
7-Zip/7zfm	15.05 beta	4901	476	avgntopensslx	14.0.0.4576	3687	976
bzip2	1.0.5	63	40.0	pcre3	3.9.0.0	52	48
expat	0.0.0.0	357	140	python	3.5.1	1538	28070
firefox	44.0	173095	37887	python	2.7.1	358	18200
fltk	1.3.2	7587	2833	putty/putty	0.66 beta	1506	512
glew	1.5.1.0	563	306	putty/plink	0.66 beta	1057	332
jsoncpp	0.5.0	1056	13	putty/pscp	0.66 beta	1157	344
lcms	8.0.920.14	668	182	putty/psftp	0.66 beta	1166	352
libcurl	10.2.0.232	1456	427	Qt5Core	2.0.1	17723	3987
libgd	1.3.0.27	883	497	SQLite	2013	2498	1006
libgmp	0.0.0.0	750	669	SQLite	2010	2462	965
libjpeg	0.0.0.0	352	133	SQLite	11.0.0.379	1252	307
libpng	1.2.51	202	60	TestSSL	4	565	186
libpng	1.2.37	419	254	tinyXML	2.0.2	533	147
libssh2	0.12	429	115	Winedt	9.1	87	8617
libtheora	0.0.0.0	460	226	WinMerge	2.14.0	405	6283
libtiff	3.6.1.1501	728	432	Wireshark	2.0.1	70502	39658
libxml2	27.3000.0.6	2815	1021	Wireshark/libjpeg	2.0.1	383	192
Notepad++	6.8.8	7796	2015	Wireshark/libpng	2.0.1	509	171
Notepad++	6.8.7	7768	2009	xampp	5.6.15	5594	111436

7-zip. The source code are compiled with Microsoft Visual Studio (VS 2010, and 2012), and GNU Compiler Collection (GCC 4.1.2) compilers, where the /MT and -static options, respectively, are set to statically link C/C++ library. In addition, the $O0 - O3$ options are used to examine the effects of optimization settings. Program debug databases (PDBs) holding debugging information are also generated for the ground truth. Furthermore, we obtain binaries and corresponding PDBs from their official websites (e.g., WireShark); the compiler of these binaries are detected by a packer tool called EXEINFOPE [2]. Finally, the prepared dataset is used as the ground truth for our system, since we can verify our results by referring to source code. In order to demonstrate the effectiveness of our approach to identify library functions in malware binaries, we additionally choose Zeus malware version 2.0.8.9, where the source code was leaked in 2011 and is reused in our work[1].

---

[1] https://github.com/Visgean/Zeus.

5.3   Function Identification Accuracy Results

Our ultimate goal is to discover as many relevant functions as possible with less concern about false positives. Consequently, in our experiments we use the F-measure, $F_1 = 2 \cdot \frac{P \cdot R}{P + R}$, where P is the precision, and R is the recall. Additionally, we show the ROC curve for each set of features used by *BinShape*. To evaluate our system, we split the binaries in the ground truth into ten sets, reserving one as a testing set and using the remaining nine as training sets. We repeat this process 1000 times and report the results that are summarized in Fig. 4.

We obtain a slightly higher true positive rate when using graph features (including function-call graph feature) and statistical features. This small difference can be inferred due to the graph similarity between two library functions that are semantically close. Similarly, statistical features convey information related to the functionality of a function, which cause a slight higher accuracy. On the other hand, instruction-level features return lower true positive rate. How-

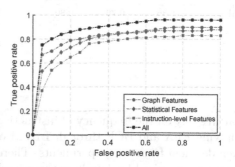

Fig. 4. ROC curve for *BinShap* features

ever, when all the features are combined together, our system returns an average F_1 measure of 0.89.

5.4   Impact of Obfuscation

In the second scenario, we investigate the impact of obfuscation techniques on *BinShape* as well as FLIRT and LIBV approaches. Our choices of obfuscation techniques are based on the popular obfuscator LLVM [29] and DaLin [35], which include *control flow flattening* (FLA), *bogus control flow* (BCF), *instruction substitution* (SUB), *register renaming* (RR), *instruction reordering* (IR), and *dead code insertion* (DCI). Other obfuscation techniques, such as *code compression* and *encryption*, will be investigated in our future work.

For this purpose, we collect a random set of files (i.e., 25) compiled with compilers. The binaries are converted into assembly files through disassembler, and the code is then obfuscated using DaLin. We initially test the original selected files and report accuracy measurements. The obfuscation is then applied and new accuracy measurements are obtained. The effectiveness of obfuscation is shown in Table 4. As can be seen, *BinShape* can tolerate some obfuscation techniques. The accuracy remains the same when RR and IR techniques are applied, while it is reduced slightly in the case of DCI and SUB obfuscations. The reason is that most of the features which are not extracted from the instruction-level features (e.g., graph features), are not significantly affected by these techniques. In addition, normalizing the assembly instructions eliminates the effect of RR, whereas, statistical features are more affected by DCI and SUB techniques, since these

Table 4. F-measure before/after (F_1/F_1^*) applying obfuscation

Obfus. Tech.	BinShape	FLIRT	LIBV
	$F_1 = 0.89$	$F_1 = 0.81$	$F_1 = 0.84$
	F_1^*	F_1^*	F_1^*
RR	0.89	0.81	0.84
IR	0.89	0.78	0.82
DCI	0.88	0.80	0.82
SUB	0.86	0.79	0.80
All	0.86	0.76	0.80

Table 5. Impact of compiler versions (Ver.), Optimizations (Opt.), and compilers (Com.)

Project	Ver.		Opt.		Com.	
	Prec.	Rec.	Prec.	Rec.	Prec.	Rec.
bzip2	1.00	0.98	0.90	0.85	0.82	0.80
OpenSSL	0.93	0.78	0.91	0.80	0.83	0.78
Notepad++	0.98	0.97	0.95	0.82	0.84	0.72
libpng	1.00	1.00	0.91	0.74	0.81	0.72
TestSTL	0.98	1.00	0.90	0.84	0.81	0.75
libjpeg	0.93	0.90	0.88	0.76	0.81	0.69
SQLite	0.91	0.87	0.89	0.85	0.78	0.71
tinyXML	1.00	0.99	0.90	0.82	0.84	0.79

features rely on the frequency of instruction. However, the accuracy results after applying FLA and BCF through LLVM obfuscator are not promising, and we exclude them from our experiments. Therefore, additional de-obfuscation techniques are required for handling these kinds of obfuscations.

5.5 Impact of Compilers

In this section, we examine the effects of compilers on a random subset of binaries as follows. (i) *The impact of compiler version (Ver.)*. We train our system with binaries compiled with VS 2010 ($O2$) and test it with binaries compiled with VS 2012 ($O2$). (ii) *The impact of optimization levels (Opt.)*. We train our system with binaries compiled with VS 2010 at optimization level $O1$, and test it under the same compiler at optimization level $O2$. (iii) *The impact of different compilers (Com.)*. We collect binaries compiled with VS 2010 ($O2$) as training dataset, and test the system with binaries compiled with GCC 4.1.2 compiler ($O2$). The obtained precision and recall for the scenarios are reported in Table 5. We observe that our system is not affected significantly by changing either the compiler versions or the optimization levels. However, different compilers affect the accuracy. Examining the effects of more possible scenarios, such as comparing binaries compiled with the same compiler and at optimization levels $O1$ and $O3$, is one of the subjects of our feature work.

5.6 Impact of Feature Selection

We carry out a set of experiments to measure the impact of feature selection process, including top-ranked feature selection as well as best feature selection. First, we test our system to determine the best threshold value for top-ranked features as shown in Fig. 5. We start by considering five top-ranked featrures and report the F_1 measure of 0.71. We increment the number of top-ranked features by five each time. When the number of top-ranked features reaches 35 classes, the F_1 measure is increased to 0.89 and it remains almost constant afterwards. Based on our findings, we choose 35 as the threshold value for the top-ranked feature classes.

Next, we pass the top-ranked features into the decision tree in order to select the best features for each function. The goal is to investigate whether considering the subset of best features would be enough to segregate the functions. In order to examine the effect of best features, we perform a breadth first search (BFS) on the corresponding trees to sort best features based on their importance in the function; since the closer the feature is to the root, the more it is segregative. Our experiments examine the F_1 measure while varying the percentage of best features. We start by 40% of the top-ranked best features and increment them by 10% each time. Figure 6 shows the relationship between the percentage of best features and the F_1 measure. Based on our experiments, we find that 90% of the best features results in an F_1 measure of 0.89. However, for the sake of simplicity, we consider all the selected best features in our experiments.

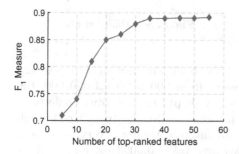
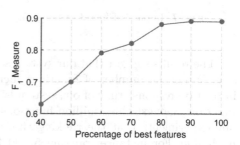

Fig. 5. Impact of top-ranked features   **Fig. 6.** Impact of best features

5.7 Impact of Filtration

We study the impact of the proposed filter (e.g., $BB\#$ and $Ins\#$) on the accuracy of BinShape. For this purpose, we perform four experiments by applying: (i) no filtering (ii) $BB\#$ filter, (iii) $Ins\#$ filter, and (iv) the two filters. As shown in Fig. 7, the drop in the accuracy caused by the proposed filters is negligible. For instance, when we test our system with two filters, the highest drop in accuracy is about 0.017. We observe through this experiment that $Ins\#$ filter affects accuracy more than $BB\#$ filter.

5.8 Scalability Study

To evaluate the scalability of our system, we prepare a large collection of binaries consisting of different '.exe' or '.dll' files (e.g., msvcr100.dll) containing more than 3,020,000 disassembled functions. We gradually index this collection of functions in a random order, and query the `7-zip` binary file of version 15.14 on our system at an indexing interval of every $500,000$ assembly functions. We collect the average indexing time for each function to be indexed, as well as the average time it takes to respond to a function detection. The indexing time includes feature extraction and storing them in the B^+trees. Figure 8 depicts the average indexing and detection time for each function.

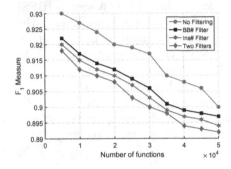

Fig. 7. Impact of filtration

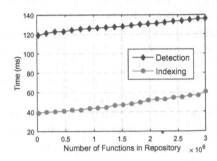

Fig. 8. Scalability study

The results suggest that our system scales well with respect to the repository size. When the number of functions increases from $500,000$ to $3,020,000$, the impact on response time of our system is negligible (0.14 s on average to detect a function amongst three million functions in the repository). We notice through our experiments that the ranking time and filtering time are very small and negligible. For instance, ranking $5,000$ features takes 0.0003 ms, and to filter high likely similar functions in the repository to a function having 100 basic blocks and $10,000$ instructions, takes 0.009 ms.

5.9   Application to Real Malware

We are further interested in studying the practicability and applicability of our tool in identifying library functions in malware binaries. However, one challenge is the lack of ground truth to verify the results due to the nature of malware. Consequently, we consider `Zeus` version 2.0.8.9, where the leaked source code is available. First, we compile the source code with VS and GCC compilers, and keep the

Table 6. Function identification in `Zeus`

Library	No. of functions	*BinShape*	
		Found	FP
`UltraVNC`	20	28	11
`info-zip`	30	27	0
`xterm`	17	18	2
`BEAEngine`	21	20	0

debug information for the purpose of verification. Second, we compile `UltraVNC`, `info-zip`, `xterm` and `BEAEngine` libraries with VS and GCC compilers and index inside our repository. We choose the aforementioned libraries based on the technical report [30] that reveals which software components are reused by Zeus. Finally, we test the compiled binaries of Zeus to find the similar functions with the functions in our repository. By manually examining the source code as well as the debug information at binary level, we are able to verify the results listed in Table 6. We observe through our experiments that the statistical features as well as graph features are the most powerful features in discovering free open-source library functions.

6 Related Work

Various approaches for library function identification have been proposed. The well-known FLIRT [3] technique builds the signatures from the first invariant byte sequence of the function. However, the main limitations of FLIRT are signature collision as well as requiring a new signature even for slight changes in a function. UNSTRIP [28] employs pattern matching to identify wrapper functions in the GNU C library based on their interaction with the system call interface. However, UNSTRIP is limited to the wrapper functions. In LIBV [41], a graph isomorphism is applied on execution dependence graphs (EDGs) to identify both full and inline functions. However, various library functions may have the same EDGs. In addition, compiler optimization might affect the instructions of inline functions. The well-known BINDIFF [14] technique and BINSLAYER [11] (inspired by BINDIFF), perform a graph isomorphism on function pairs in two differing but similar binaries. However, these approaches are not designed to label library functions and rely on graph matching, which is expensive to be applied to large scale datasets. Moreover, a few binary code search engines have been proposed. For instance, RENDEZVOUS [31] extracts multiple features, such as n-grams and control flow subgraphs, to form the tokens and query terms in order to construct the search query. However, this approach is sensitive to structural changes. TRACY [13] decomposes the CFG into small tracelets and uses longest common subsequence algorithm to align two tracelets. However, much structure information may be lost by breaking down the CFGs into tracelets. In addition, TRACY is suitable for the functions with more than 100 basic blocks [13].

Some cross-architecture approaches for searching known bugs in firmware images have been proposed. For instance, DISCOVRE [19] extracts structural features and applies maximum common subgraph (MCS) isomorphism on the CFGs to find similar functions. This approach utilizes pre-filtering on statistical features in order to perform subgraph isomorphism efficiently. However, the effectiveness of the proposed pre-filtration is evaluated in GENIUS [21] and demonstrates that it can cause significant reduction in accuracy. Inspired by DISCOVRE, GENIUS [21] extracts statistical and structural features, generates codebooks from annotated CFGs, converts the codebooks into high-level numeric feature vectors (feature encoding), and finally compares the encoded features using locality sensitive hashing (LSH) in order to tackle scalability issues. However, the authors mentioned that codebook generation may be expensive, and also some changes in the CFG structures affect the accuracy of GENIUS.

Table 7. Comparing different existing solutions with *BinShape*. The symbol (•) indicates that proposal offers the corresponding feature, otherwise it is empty. We use following abbreviations for different methods: (PM) Pattern Matching, (GI) Graph Isomorphism, (GED) Graph Edit Distance, (LSH) Locality Sensitive Hashing, (LCS) Longest Common Subsequence, (MCS) Maximum Common Subgraph Isomorphism, (SPP) Small Primes Product, Symbolic Execution (SE), Data Flow Analysis (DFA), Jaccard Distance (JD), and VLAD (Vector of Locally Aggregated Descriptors).

PROPOSALS	Feature				Ana.		Method	Arch.			Compiler				Obfusc.			
	Syntactic	Semantic	Structural	Statistical	Static	Dynamic		x86-64	ARM	MIPS	VS	GCC	ICC	Clang	RR	IR	DCI	SUB
FLIRT [3]	•				•		PM	•	•	•	•	•			•			
UNSTRIP [28]		•			•		PM, SE	•				•			•	•	•	•
LIBV [41]		•	•		•		GI, DFA	•					•		•	•	•	•
BINDIFF [14]		•	•		•		GI, SPP	•	•	•	•	•			•	•		
BINSLAYER [11]		•	•		•		GI, GED	•	•			•			•	•		
RENDEZVOUS [31]	•		•		•		GI	•				•				•		
TRACY [13]		•	•		•		LCS, DFA	•				•			•	•	•	•
BLEX [17]		•				•	JD	•				•	•	•	•	•	•	•
DISCOVRE [19]			•	•	•		MCS, JD	•	•	•					•	•		
GENIUS [21]			•	•	•		VLAD, LSH, JD	•	•	•		•		•	•	•		
BinShape	•	•	•	•	•		B⁺tree	•				•	•		•	•	•	•

All of the aforementioned approaches employ static analysis, however, there exist other techniques which perform dynamic analysis. For instance, a binary search engine called Blanket Execution (BLEX) [17], executes functions for several calling contexts and collects the side effects of functions; two functions with similar side effects are deemed to be similar. However, dynamic analysis approaches are often computationally expensive, and rely on architecture-specific tools to run executables. As a result, they are inherently difficult to support other architectures [19].

We compare *BinShape* with aforementioned proposals in Table 7. A direct comparison between GENIUS [21] and *BinShape* is not possible, since the authors have not made GENIUS prototype available. However, a high-level comparison has been done as follows. GENIUS is designed to identify known bugs in firmware images, while the goal of *BinShape* is to identify library functions in program binaries and malware samples. GENIUS extracts few statistical and structural features where some salient features might be missing, while a richer set of features (in terms of types and numbers) is extracted by *BinShape*. GENIUS detects a function out of three million functions in about 0.007 s, whereas 0.14 s takes for *BinShape*. However, in the preparation time (which includes codebook generation) reported by GENIUS, the number of functions is not indicated to be compared with *BinShape*. Based on the provided ROC curve in GENIUS [21] we have obtained the average true positive rates of 0.96, while that of *BinShape* is equal to 0.91. In summary, *BinShape* differs from existing works as follows. *BinShape* extracts a rich set of heterogeneous features, which could overcome some code changes; *BinShape* supports large scale of dataset and does not involve expensive computation methods; Finally, *BinShape* can be extended easily to support other compilers or architectures.

7   Conclusion

Limitations. Our work has the following limitations: (i) We have not scrutinized the impact of inline functions. (ii) Our system is able to tackle some code transformation such as instruction reordering, however, some other obfuscation techniques, such as control flow flattening, affect the accuracy of *BinShape*. In addition, our system is not able to handle the packed, encrypted, and obfuscated binaries. (iii) We have tested *BinShape* with VS and GCC compilers, however, binaries compiled with ICC and Clang have not been examined. (iv) We have not investigated the impact of hardware architectures such as MIPS in this study. These limitations are the subjects of our future work.

Concluding Remarks. In this paper, we have conducted the first investigation into the possibility of representing a function based on its shape. We have proposed a robust signature for each library function based on diverse collection of heterogeneous features, covering CFGs, instruction-level characteristics, statistical features, and function-call graphs. In addition, we have designed a novel data structure, which includes B^+tree, in order to efficiently support accurate and scalable detection. Experimental results have been demonstrated the practicability of our approach.

Acknowledgment. We would like to thank our shepherd, Dr. Cristiano Giuffrida, and the anonymous reviewers for providing us very precious comments. This research is the result of a fruitful collaboration between the Security Research Center (SRC) of Concordia University, Defence Research and Development Canada (DRDC) and Google under a National Defence/NSERC Research Program.

References

1. C Language Library. http://www.cplusplus.com/reference/clibrary/
2. Exeinfo PE. http://exeinfo.atwebpages.com
3. HexRays: IDA F.L.I.R.T. Technology. https://www.hex-rays.com/products/ida/tech/flirt/in_depth.shtml
4. HexRays: IDA Pro. https://www.hex-rays.com/products/ida/index.shtml
5. MongoDB. https://www.mongodb.com/
6. NIST/SEMATECH e-Handbook of Statistical Methods. http://www.itl.nist.gov/div898/handbook/
7. WEKA. https://weka.wikispaces.com/
8. Alrabaee, S., Saleem, N., Preda, S., Wang, L., Debbabi, M.: OBA2: an Onion approach to binary code authorship attribution. Digital Invest. **11**, S94–S103 (2014)
9. Alrabaee, S., Shirani, P., Wang, L., Debbabi, M.: SIGMA: a semantic integrated graph matching approach for identifying reused functions in binary code. Digital Invest. **12**, S61–S71 (2015)

10. Alrabaee, S., Wang, L., Debbabi, M.: BinGold: towards robust binary analysis by extracting the semantics of binary code as semantic flow graphs (SFGs). Digital Invest. **18**, S11–S22 (2016)
11. Bourquin, M., King, A., Robbins, E.: BinSlayer: accurate comparison of binary executables. In: Proceedings of the 2nd ACM SIGPLAN Program Protection and Reverse Engineering Workshop, p. 4. ACM (2013)
12. David, Y., Partush, N., Yahav, E.: Statistical similarity of binaries. In: Proceedings of the 37th ACM SIGPLAN Conference on Programming Language Design and Implementation (PLDI), pp. 266–280. ACM (2016)
13. David, Y., Yahav, E.: Tracelet-based code search in executables. In: ACM SIGPLAN Notices, vol. 49, pp. 349–360. ACM (2014)
14. Dullien, T., Rolles, R.: Graph-based comparison of executable objects (English version). SSTIC **5**, 1–3 (2005)
15. Eagle, C.: The IDA Pro Book: The Unofficial Guide to the World's Most Popular Disassembler. No Starch Press, San Francisco (2011)
16. Egele, M., Scholte, T., Kirda, E., Kruegel, C.: A survey on automated dynamic malware-analysis techniques and tools. ACM Comput. Surv. (CSUR) **44**(2), 6 (2012)
17. Egele, M., Woo, M., Chapman, P., Brumley, D.: Blanket execution: dynamic similarity testing for program binaries and components. In: Usenix Security, pp. 303–317 (2014)
18. Elmore, K.L., Richman, M.B.: Euclidean distance as a similarity metric for principal component analysis. Mon. Weather Rev. **129**(3), 540–549 (2001)
19. Eschweiler, S., Yakdan, K., Gerhards-Padilla, E.: discovRE: efficient cross-architecture identification of bugs in binary code. In Proceedings of the 23th Symposium on Network and Distributed System Security (NDSS) (2016)
20. Farhadi, M.R., Fung, B.C., Fung, Y.B., Charland, P., Preda, S., Debbabi, M.: Scalable code clone search for malware analysis. Digital Invest. **15**, 46–60 (2015)
21. Feng, Q., Zhou, R., Xu, C., Cheng, Y., Testa, B., Yin, H.: Scalable graph-based bug search for firmware images. In: Proceedings of the 2016 ACM SIGSAC Conference on Computer and Communications Security (CCS), pp. 480–491. ACM (2016)
22. Frank, E., Wang, Y., Inglis, S., Holmes, G., Witten, I.H.: Using model trees for classification. Mach. Learn. **32**(1), 63–76 (1998)
23. Gascon, H., Yamaguchi, F., Arp, D., Rieck, K.: Structural detection of android malware using embedded call graphs. In: Proceedings of the 2013 ACM Workshop on Artificial Intelligence and Security (AISec), pp. 45–54. ACM (2013)
24. Griffin, C., Theory, G.: Penn State Math 485 Lecture Notes (2012). http://www.personal.psu.edu/cxg286/Math485.pdf
25. Hido, S., Kashima, H.: A linear-time graph kernel. In: Ninth IEEE International Conference on Data Mining, ICDM 2009, pp. 179–188. IEEE (2009)
26. Hu, X., Chiueh, T.-C., Shin, K.G.: Large-scale malware indexing using function-call graphs. In: Proceedings of the 16th ACM Conference on Computer and Communications Security (CCS), pp. 611–620. ACM (2009)
27. Huang, H., Youssef, A.M., Debbabi, M.: BinSequence: fast, accurate and scalable binary code reuse detection. In: Proceedings of the 2017 ACM on Asia Conference on Computer and Communications Security (ASIA CCS), pp. 155–166. ACM (2017)
28. Jacobson, E.R., Rosenblum, N., Miller, B.P.: Labeling library functions in stripped binaries. In: Proceedings of the 10th ACM SIGPLAN-SIGSOFT Workshop on Program Analysis for Software Tools (PASTE), pp. 1–8. ACM (2011)

29. Junod, P., Rinaldini, J., Wehrli, J., Michielin, J.: Obfuscator-LLVM: software protection for the masses. In: Proceedings of the 1st International Workshop on Software PROtection (SPRO), pp. 3–9. IEEE Press (2015)
30. Khoo, W.M.: Decompilation as search. Technical report, University of Cambridge, Computer Laboratory (2013)
31. Khoo, W.M., Mycroft, A., Anderson, R.: Rendezvous: a search engine for binary code. In: Proceedings of the 10th Working Conference on Mining Software Repositories (MSR), pp. 329–338. IEEE Press (2013)
32. Kolbitsch, C., Holz, T., Kruegel, C., Kirda, E.: Inspector gadget: automated extraction of proprietary gadgets from malware binaries. In: 2010 IEEE Symposium on Security and Privacy (SP), pp. 29–44. IEEE (2010)
33. Kruegel, C., Kirda, E., Mutz, D., Robertson, W., Vigna, G.: Polymorphic worm detection using structural information of executables. In: Valdes, A., Zamboni, D. (eds.) RAID 2005. LNCS, vol. 3858, pp. 207–226. Springer, Heidelberg (2006). doi:10.1007/11663812_11
34. Kührer, M., Rossow, C., Holz, T.: Paint it black: evaluating the effectiveness of malware blacklists. In: Stavrou, A., Bos, H., Portokalidis, G. (eds.) RAID 2014. LNCS, vol. 8688, pp. 1–21. Springer, Cham (2014). doi:10.1007/978-3-319-11379-1_1
35. Lin, D., Stamp, M.: Hunting for undetectable metamorphic viruses. J. Comput. Virol. **7**(3), 201–214 (2011)
36. Livi, L., Rizzi, A.: The graph matching problem. Pattern Anal. Appl. **16**(3), 253–283 (2013)
37. Martignoni, L., Christodorescu, M., Jha, S.: Omniunpack: fast, generic, and safe unpacking of malware. In: Twenty-Third Annual Computer Security Applications Conference, ACSAC 2007, pp. 431–441. IEEE (2007)
38. Nouh, L., Rahimian, A., Mouheb, D., Debbabi, M., Hanna, A.: BinSign: fingerprinting binary functions to support automated analysis of code executables. In: IFIP International Information Security and Privacy Conference (IFIP SEC). Springer (2017)
39. Peng, H., Long, F., Ding, C.: Feature selection based on mutual information criteria of max-dependency, max-relevance, and min-redundancy. IEEE Trans. Pattern Anal. Mach. Intell. (TPAMI) **27**(8), 1226–1238 (2005)
40. Pewny, J., Garmany, B., Gawlik, R., Rossow, C., Holz, T.: Cross-architecture bug search in binary executables. In: 2015 IEEE Symposium on Security and Privacy (SP), pp. 709–724. IEEE (2015)
41. Qiu, J., Su, X., Ma, P.: Using reduced execution flow graph to identify library functions in binary code. IEEE Trans. Softw. Eng. (TSE) **42**(2), 187–202 (2016)
42. Rad, B.B., Masrom, M., Ibrahim, S.: Opcodes histogram for classifying metamorphic portable executables malware. In: 2012 International Conference on e-Learning and e-Technologies in Education (ICEEE), pp. 209–213. IEEE (2012)
43. Ramaswami, M., Bhaskaran, R.: A study on feature selection techniques in educational data mining. arXiv preprint arXiv:0912.3924 (2009)
44. Roobaert, D., Karakoulas, G., Chawla, N.V.: Information gain, correlation and support vector machines. In: Guyon, I., Nikravesh, M., Gunn, S., Zadeh, L.A. (eds.) Feature Extraction. STUDFUZZ, vol. 207, pp. 463–470. Springer, Heidelberg (2006)
45. Rosenblum, N., Zhu, X., Miller, B.P.: Who wrote this code? identifying the authors of program binaries. In: Atluri, V., Diaz, C. (eds.) ESORICS 2011. LNCS, vol. 6879, pp. 172–189. Springer, Heidelberg (2011). doi:10.1007/978-3-642-23822-2_10
46. Toderici, A.H., Stamp, M.: Chi-squared distance and metamorphic virus detection. J. Comput. Virol. Hacking Tech. **9**(1), 1–14 (2013)

47. van der Veen, V., Göktas, E., Contag, M., Pawoloski, A., Chen, X., Rawat, S., Bos, H., Holz, T., Athanasopoulos, E., Giuffrida, C.: A tough call: mitigating advanced code-reuse attacks at the binary level. In: 2016 IEEE Symposium on Security and Privacy (SP), pp. 934–953. IEEE (2016)
48. Yokoyama, A., et al.: SandPrint: fingerprinting malware sandboxes to provide intelligence for sandbox evasion. In: Monrose, F., Dacier, M., Blanc, G., Garcia-Alfaro, J. (eds.) RAID 2016. LNCS, vol. 9854, pp. 165–187. Springer, Cham (2016). doi:10.1007/978-3-319-45719-2_8
49. Zeng, J., Fu, Y., Miller, K.A., Lin, Z., Zhang, X., Xu, D.: Obfuscation resilient binary code reuse through trace-oriented programming. In: Proceedings of the 2013 ACM SIGSAC Conference on Computer & Communications Security (CCS), pp. 487–498. ACM (2013)
50. Ziegel, E.R.: Probability and Statistics for Engineering and the Sciences. Technometrics (2012)

SCVD: A New Semantics-Based Approach for Cloned Vulnerable Code Detection

Deqing Zou[1], Hanchao Qi[1], Zhen Li[1,2(✉)], Song Wu[1], Hai Jin[1],
Guozhong Sun[3], Sujuan Wang[1], and Yuyi Zhong[1]

[1] Services Computing Technology and System Lab,
Big Data Technology and System Lab, Cluster and Grid Computing Lab,
School of Computer Science and Technology,
Huazhong University of Science and Technology, Wuhan 430074, China
lizhen_hbu@126.com
[2] School of Computer Science and Technology,
Hebei University, Baoding 071002, China
[3] Dawning Information Industry (Beijing) Co., Ltd., Beijing 100193, China

Abstract. The behavior of copying existing code to reuse or modify
its functionality is very common in the software development. However,
when developers clone the existing code, they also clone any vulnerabilities in it. Thus, it seriously affects the security of the system. In this
paper, we propose a novel semantics-based approach called SCVD for
cloned vulnerable code detection. We use the full path traversal algorithm to transform the *Program Dependency Graph* (PDG) into a tree
structure while preserving all the semantic information carried by the
PDG and apply the tree to the cloned vulnerable code detection. We
use the identifier name mapping technique to eliminate the impact of
identifier name modification. Our key insights are converting the complex graph similarity problem into a simpler tree similarity problem and
using the identifier name mapping technique to improve the effectiveness
of semantics-based cloned vulnerable code detection. We have developed
a practical tool based on our approach and performed a large number of
experiments to evaluate the performance from three aspects, including
the false positive rate, false negative rate, and time cost. The experiment
results show that our approach has a significant improvement on the vulnerability detection effectiveness compared with the existing approaches
and has lower time cost than subgraph isomorphism approaches.

Keywords: Vulnerability detection · Cloned code · Semantics

1 Introduction

Developers often copy the existing code to reuse or modify its functionality in
the software development. The behavior of copying similar or exactly the same
code from the existing code is called *code clone*. There are a lot of cloned code
segments in the large software development. Examples are abundant: 22.3% of

© Springer International Publishing AG 2017
M. Polychronakis and M. Meier (Eds.): DIMVA 2017, LNCS 10327, pp. 325–344, 2017.
DOI: 10.1007/978-3-319-60876-1_15

Linux kernel source code was reported as the reused code, even a small number of code segments were copied at least 8 times [21]; 145 unpatched cloned vulnerable code were confirmed in the Linux kernel 2.6.6 of Debian Squeeze packages [10]. If the cloned code is vulnerable, it might result in the vulnerability prevalence problem [20] because the published vulnerability probably exists in other software but cannot be patched completely. Utilizing the information of published vulnerabilities, an attacker could exploit unpatched cloned code and produce disastrous influence on the software system. Therefore, we urgently need an accurate and efficient method to detect the cloned vulnerable code.

Many approaches have been proposed for cloned vulnerable code detection [16], such as CP-Miner [21], Deckard [11], and CBCD [19]. In these approaches, token-based approaches leverage lexical analysis to generate the token collection from source code, and find similar sub-sequences in the target token collection for the cloned vulnerable code detection. Syntax-based approaches parse the *Abstract Syntax Tree* (AST) [14] from the vulnerable code, and then use the AST as vulnerability feature to detect cloned vulnerable code. However, token-based and syntax-based approaches cannot be used to detect the code clones which are only functionally similar without being textually similar. In fact, these code clones can be applied to semantics-based approaches.

Program Dependency Graph (PDG) is a typical representative of the semantics-based approaches. Finding the subgraph isomorphism in the PDG can be used to detect cloned code segments [17], but the subgraph isomorphism problem is a NP-complete problem [23]. In order to reduce the performance impact of the subgraph isomorphism as far as possible, Gabel et al. [9] mapped the PDG to the corresponding AST tree, and used the similarity of AST to replace the similarity of PDG to find the clone code. However, the process of transformation loses part of the semantic information, which leads to the incomplete semantic comparison. CBCD [19] adopted four optimizations to reduce the size of PDG before the subgraph query by removing irrelevant nodes and edges or splitting the source code with too many lines. Although it could improve the efficiency of the cloned vulnerable code detection, it does not solve the subgraph isomorphism problem directly. Especially the simply source code splitting separates the complete semantics which might produce more false positives. Consequently, we aim to optimize the NP-complete problem of subgraph isomorphism and present a practical cloned vulnerable code detection approach with both high accuracy and low time cost.

In this paper, we propose a novel lightweight semantics-based approach called SCVD for cloned vulnerable code detection which can be used for the large-scale software. The approach converts the PDG into a program feature tree by full path traversal from PDG while ensuring the integrity of the semantic information of the PDG, and searches subtree in the program feature tree to detect the cloned vulnerable code. Specifically, we have the following three contributions:

- **Convert the PDG into program feature tree to reduce the execution time cost.** We generate the program feature tree by parsing the PDG and convert complex graphs into relatively simple trees while preserving the semantic information of the PDG. More importantly, we use program feature tree for the cloned vulnerable code detection, thus the subgraph isomorphism problem is bypassed.

- **Apply program syntax information and the identifier mapping technique to improve the accuracy.** While using the semantics-based program feature tree, we also deal with the vertex code values in the program feature tree at the syntax level. Through the fuzzification of the identifier names in the program, we make the semantics-based approaches be able to deal with the case of modified identifiers in the cloned vulnerable code effectively.
- **Develop a lightweight cloned vulnerable code detection tool for large programs.** Based on our approach, we develop a lightweight practical tool for the cloned vulnerable code detection of large programs, and perform a comprehensive performance evaluation. The experiment results show that our approach has a significant improvement on the vulnerability detection effectiveness compared with the existing approaches and has lower time cost than subgraph isomorphism approaches.

The rest of this paper is structured as follows. We first present a detailed design of our approach and explain the important principles with typical examples (Sect. 2). Then we describe the implementation of SCVD (Sect. 3) and discuss the evaluation of SCVD (Sect. 4). After that, we discuss the limitations of our approach (Sect. 5) and summarize the related work (Sect. 6). Finally, we conclude the present work with a discussion of future work (Sect. 7).

2 Design

2.1 Overview

Figure 1 shows the overview of SCVD. In general, SCVD is divided into five steps: (1) Select the vulnerability diff hunks and the target program as the raw input data; (2) process the raw input data to obtain the valid input data; (3) generate the PDGs for vulnerability program and target program respectively; (4) convert each PDG into program feature tree; and (5) detect the cloned vulnerable code

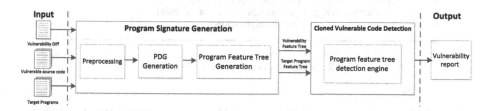

Fig. 1. Overview of SCVD. The program signature generation phase generates program feature tree from the raw input data. The cloned vulnerable code detection phase searches similar sub-trees in the target program feature trees to detect the cloned vulnerable code.

from target programs by program feature sub-tree matching. In the following subsections, we introduce the details of these five main parts: preparing the input, preprocessing, PDG generation, program feature tree generation, and program feature tree detection engine.

2.2 Preparing the Input

For the vulnerability signature generation, we select the *diff* which is used to patch the vulnerability and the corresponding original source code as the vulnerability raw input. *Diff* is a formatted text file for code modification which is applied to popular revision control systems. As shown in Fig. 2, a *diff* consists of a series of diff hunks. Each diff hunk starts with a header containing the modified function name and followed by a series of formatted code. In these formatted code, each line is prefixed by a "+" symbol, "−" symbol, or no symbol which represents line addition, line deletion, and no change, respectively. Therefore, the vulnerability diff hunk records the changes from the vulnerable piece of code to the patched one. Thus the vulnerable piece of code from the diff can be used to generate the PDG of vulnerability.

```
diff --git a/libavformat/rtsp.c b/libavformat/rtsp.c
index 1a545c7..f1e0780 100644 (file)

--- a/libavformat/rtsp.c
+++ b/libavformat/rtsp.c
@@ -1668,7 +1668,8 @@ int ff_rtsp_connect(AVFormatContext *s)
       return AVERROR(EIO);

    if (!rt->protocols) {
-        rt->protocols = ffurl_get_protocols(NULL, NULL);
+        rt->protocols = ffurl_get_protocols(s->protocol_whitelist,
+                                            s->protocol_blacklist);
       if (!rt->protocols)
          return AVERROR(ENOMEM);
    }
@@ -2252,7 +2253,8 @@ static int sdp_read_header(AVFormatContext *s)
       return AVERROR(EIO);

    if (!rt->protocols) {
-        rt->protocols = ffurl_get_protocols(NULL, NULL);
+        rt->protocols = ffurl_get_protocols(s->protocol_whitelist,
+                                            s->protocol_blacklist);
       ...
```

Fig. 2. A diff file commited in ffmpeg.git

For the target program signature generation, we represent source code function as a basic unit of target program and search the cloned vulnerable code in these functions.

2.3   Preprocessing

We use the diff and the vulnerable source code as the raw inputs of vulnerable program. Combined with the vulnerability information, we analyze the vulnerability diff and extract the diff hunks that are directly related to fixes. If the source code extracted directly from the diff hunks has the incomplete syntax structure and the fragmentary context, it may lead to wrong results. Therefore, we need to do the following preprocessing.

First, extract the vulnerable code fragment. We can obtain the vulnerable code fragment from the diff by extracting the lines prefixed by a "−" symbol and the lines with no prefix. Second, process the whitespace, format, and comment. These meaningless modifications in the diff hunk may impact the result of cloned vulnerable code detection. Therefore, we need to filter them out. Third, complete the structure of code fragment. A diff hunk is a snippet of code and may lose the necessary context in some cases. For example, the code fragment might only have "if" statement but have no execution statement block. In the case of no complete context, it is difficult to describe the characteristics of the vulnerability accurately. For this reason we compare the vulnerable code fragment with the original function source code to complement enough context for all incomplete structures.

We also need to process the target program. The target software source code is relatively integrity, therefore we only need to complete the first two steps in the preprocessing phase.

2.4   PDG Generation

We use the open source platform *Joern* [27] to generate the PDG. On the one hand, each vertex in the PDG is a code entity such as a statement, a predicate expression, or an operand. It records the source code text, the location of source code, and the vertex type such as declaration or control-point. On the other hand, the PDG uses the data dependency edges to reflect the data transfer between two vertexes and uses control dependency edges to reflect the change of the program execution process.

After obtaining the PDG, what we need to do next is to identify the identifiers in each vertex and map the identifier names. We realize that the semantics-based approaches use the code value in vertex as the conditions to decide whether the two vertexes are the same. However, using this comparison method is unable to detect the modification of the identifier name in the cloned vulnerable code. In fact, according to our statistics in the *Vulnerability Code Instance Database* (VCID) [20] which contains code reuse instances of vulnerabilities, there are 26.5% of these code reuse instances contained local modifications, such as variable name or function name modifications. Therefore, the locally modified code-clone is very necessary to be solved. Through mapping all variables (or functions) to a same name, or mapping the same type of variables to a same name, we eliminate the differences in identifier names and preclude the false negatives due to the identifier name modification.

2.5   Program Feature Tree Generation

In this subsection, we present the details of program feature tree generation. It is known that subgraph isomorphism algorithm is too inefficient to be used for the vulnerability detection of large-scale programs directly. Therefore, we use the program feature tree to describe the feature of program. The program feature tree consists of a control dependency tree converted from the control dependence part of PDG and a set of data dependency edges extracted from the data dependence part of PDG.

We use the full path traversal algorithm to generate the program feature tree from the PDG. The main idea of the full path traversal algorithm is to use depth-first traversal in the PDG and ensure all reachable paths are accessed. In the PDG, the vertex represents the code entity and the edge indicates the relationship between two vertexes. Through traversing all reachable paths and recording the vertexes and edges encountered during the traversal, we can obtain all the program semantic information carried in the PDG. The process is elucidated in the following Algorithm 1. There are three steps.

First, we record all the real entrance vertexes into a set (lines 4–8). In the PDG, there is a virtual vertex named "Entry". The "Entry" vertex connects each vertex directly which has no previous vertex, consequently these vertexes are the real entrances of the PDG. We traverse from the "Entry" vertex of the PDG and record all the real entrance vertexes into a set. Second, starting with each vertex in the set, we traverse all the reachable paths in the PDG (lines 9–25). Third, during the traversal, we apply all the vertexes and the control dependency edges to construct the control dependency tree, and store all the data dependency edges in the other set (lines 18–20). Thus, we divide the program feature tree into two parts after the traversal. The first part is the control dependency tree consisting of vertexes and the control dependency edges from the PDG, and it is used to find the candidate matched tree. The second part is the set of data dependent edges of the PDG, and this part is used to confirm the existence of the cloned vulnerable code.

It is important to note that the traversal only has two conditions to backtrack to the upper level. One condition is when the current vertex has no successor vertex. This is an obvious condition. The other condition is when the traversal returns to the entrance vertex of a circle once again. PDG, as a directed graph, could form a circle because of the existence of data dependency edges and control dependency edges. When a traversed vertex is encountered in the current traversal path, we deem that the vertex is an entrance vertex in a circle. Then the traversal begins backtracking. In this way, all the reachable paths are traversed until all of them have been visited.

Considering that the "Entry" node of PDG is a meaningless node and just connects the PDG nodes that have no parent nodes, we remove the "Entry" node and get a forest consisting of many program feature trees after traversing the PDG. Thus the large-scale program feature tree is transformed into some smaller trees which makes the subtree searching cheaper.

Algorithm 1. The full path traversal algorithm

Input: A graph G = $\{graphNodes, graphEdges\}$, where $graphNodes$ =
             $(node_1, node_2, \ldots, node_n)$ is a set of nodes in the graph and $graphEdge$ =
             $(edge_1, edge_2, \ldots, edge_m)$ is a set of edges in the graph
Output: A set of program feature tree $Trees = \{tree_1, tree_2, tree_3, \ldots\}$, where each tree in
             it is a tree-like data structure

```
 1: Trees ← ∅
 2: EntryNodeStack ← ∅
 3: EntryNode ← Entry {refer to the EntryNode as the "Entry" vertex in the PDG}
 4: for each node_i ∈ graphNodes do
 5:    if node_i = EntryNode then
 6:       consider node_i as the real entrance of the PDG and push it into EntryNodeStack
 7:    end if
 8: end for
 9: while EntryNodeStack is not empty do
10:    set curEntryNode ← EntryNodeStack.topNode()
11:    curGraphNode ← curEntryNode
12:    Tree ← ∅
13:    curTreeNode ← create a new tree node for curGraphNode
14:    add curTreeNode into Tree
15:    repeat
16:       if  curGraphNode has already been traversed in this path or curGraphNode has no
          successor node then
17:          backtrace and reset curGraphNode as the upper level node
18:       else if curGraphNode has successor node to traverse then
19:          select one successor graph node node_i and set curGraphNode ← node_i
20:          curTreeNode ← create a new tree node for curGraphNode
21:          add curTreeNode and relevant edge information into Tree
22:       end if
23:    until curGraphNode = curEntryNode
24:    got an independent tree, and then add Tree into Trees
25:    EntryNodeStack.pop()
26: end while
27: return Trees
```

The full path traversal algorithm requires special emphasis on two points. The first point is that the data dependencies and control dependencies are separated in the program feature tree, and the second point is the full path traversal algorithm eliminates the inconsistent traversal order caused by the different entries for a circle traversal.

Separation of data dependency and control dependency. For the separation of data dependency and control dependency, we are based on the following two considerations.

First, the number of data dependency edges may be several times larger than the number of control dependency edges in many cases (the explosion problem of data dependency edges). Such a large number of edges will seriously reduce the execution efficiency of the approach. We randomly selected 1000 functions from the source code of Wireshark 2.2.4 and found that there were 12% functions in which the number of data dependency edges is at least 5 times more than the number of control dependency edges.

Second, data dependency edges are more sensitive to program modification. Data dependency edges are more sensitive for subtle changes in the program than control dependency edges. For example, the addition of an assignment statement in a consecutive code fragment could cause a huge increase of the data dependency edges. However, many of these edges are irrelevant to vulnerability feature. Thus these irrelevant data dependency edges pose a challenge to our approach of the discontinuous cloned vulnerable code.

In order to solve the first problem as much as possible, we divide the process of vulnerability detection into two steps. First, we compare the similarities of the control dependency tree which consists of control dependency edges and vertexes to search for matching candidate subtree. Second, we compare the similarity of the parts of data dependency edges between the candidate subtree and the vulnerability program feature tree. If there are no candidate subtrees in the target program feature tree, then we will no longer compare the similarity of data dependency edges. Thus we use two separated steps to eliminate the impact from the explosion problem of data dependency edges.

To solve the second problem, our approach does not require data dependency edges exactly the same, but rather we set a threshold to indicate the similarity of data dependency edges. If the data dependency edges similarity between the candidate subtree and vulnerability feature tree is higher than the threshold, then we conclude that this is a cloned vulnerable code.

Elimination of the inconsistent traversal order caused by the different entries in a circle traversal. It is known that the different traversal order will be obtained if the traversal starts from different entries of a circle. In this situation, it is difficult for us to find the isomorphic subgraphs containing the circles.

However, the full path traversal algorithm can solve this problem. As shown in Fig. 3 there is a circle consisting of three vertexes: C, D, and E. The circle has two entries C and D. We use two different types of lines to distinguish two different vulnerability PDGs. It is obvious that these two vulnerabilities can enter the same circle from different entries. In this condition, different traversal entries will produce completely different trees. From the target program control dependency tree obtained using the full path traversal algorithm, we can see that no matter which entry the traversal starts from, we can always find the subtree which matches with the vulnerability control dependency tree.

From the above example, we can easily see that although the approach can ensure the integrity of paths, it will produce a lot of redundant nodes. We use the shared node technique to optimize this problem. Despite the graph vertex may generate multiple tree nodes after traversal, we do not copy all information from the graph vertex to each tree node. Instead, in each tree node we use a pointer to point out the original graph vertex. This makes all the redundant tree nodes share the information of the original graph vertex. The use of share node technique not only reduces the large amount of memory overhead caused by these redundant nodes, but also retains all the information in the PDG at the maximum degree, which is also helpful in the process of vulnerability detection.

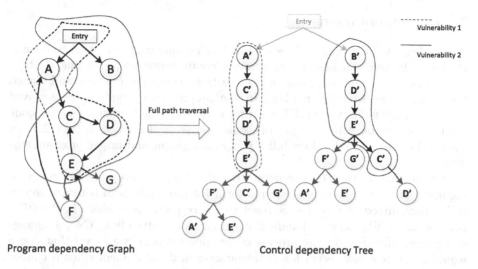

Program dependency Graph   **Control dependency Tree**

Fig. 3. Full path traverse algorithm. We use depth-first traversal policy and ensure all reachable paths are accessed.

2.6   Program Feature Tree Detection Engine

The program feature tree detection engine is responsible for finding cloned vulnerable code using program feature tree. Specifically, our cloned vulnerable code detection process can be divided into the following three steps.

First, find all the matched candidate root nodes. We first find all the candidate nodes in the target program data dependency tree. These candidate nodes match with the root node of vulnerability data dependency tree in both the code text and the type of node, and are used for matching subtree. Then we filter the candidate root nodes which have less successor nodes than the vulnerability data dependency tree's root node. Because this kind of node must have no subtrees matching the vulnerability data dependency tree, we use the number of sub-nodes to filter completely impossible candidate nodes.

Second, search the matched candidate subtree. For each node obtained in the previous step, we find the subtree which matches the vulnerability control dependency tree in the target software control dependency tree as the candidate tree. Two nodes are considered to be matched if both the vertex code value and vertex type are the same.

Third, confirm the matching subtree using data dependency edges. For each candidate subtree, we compare data dependency edges between these matching nodes and compute the similarity of data dependency edges. If the similarity value is higher than the threshold which we set in advance, then we record it as a cloned vulnerable code. Finally, we output the information of target program into the detection result report file, such as the similarity value and the location of matching code.

3   Implementation

We implemented our approach as a cloned vulnerable code detection tool using Python. The tool consists of four primary components: preprocessing module, PDG generation module, program feature tree generation module, and cloned vulnerable code detection module. In the preprocessing module, we received the vulnerability diff, vulnerability source code and target program source code as the raw inputs. After a series of extraction steps described in Sect. 2.3, we obtained the formatted vulnerability program segment and target program segment.

We utilized *Joern* [27] to generate the PDG for the preprocessed program segment. *Joern* is a code analysis platform for the analysis of software source code programmed by C/C++. Subject to the restrictions of Joern in the PDG generation, SCVD can only handle the source code written in C/C++ language at present. Moreover, in the process of our development, we found that Joern would generate a new vertex for each character in the statement when it cannot parse the statement. In this situation, hundreds of thousands of meaningless vertexes will be generated by Joern, which leads to a serious impact on the subsequent vulnerability detection. In view of the limitation of Joern, we monitor the occurrence of such a situation, and once it happens we will terminate the PDG generation directly.

After the PDG generation, we generated the program feature tree by using full path traversal algorithm. In order to make the semantics-based approach deal with the variable (or function) name modification, we mapped the identifier name in each vertex of the PDG. Thus we reset all variable (or function) name to the same value so that we can quickly complete the identifier mapping in a very short time.

The redundant nodes generated in the full path traversal bring challenges to our implementation. A large number of redundant nodes will not only cause memory wasting, but more importantly, it will make the vulnerability searching process extremely complex. In order to solve this problem, we used share node technique when we designed the data structure for the program feature tree. In our design, all the original information retained in the original PDG nodes and all the tree nodes shared the data through one pointer. Thus each tree node only needs to carry their own unique information instead of copying all the information in graph nodes. More importantly, all the redundant nodes can share the information through the corresponding graph nodes. As a result, once the state of the node has been changed, we only need to modify the original graph node data. Then all the tree nodes created by the graph node can perceive the change of the information. Thus we can avoid a lot of inefficient data modification and prevent the possible repetitive traversal.

4   Evaluation

We evaluated our approach SCVD in three open-source software including FFm-peg, Wireshark, and Linux kernel. Moreover, we evaluated the performance of

SCVD from three aspects: false positive rate, false negative rate, and time cost. In this section, we first describe the experimental setup, then show the results of our experiments.

4.1 Experimental Setup

We evaluated the performance of the approach on a Centos 7/64bit with two 2 GHz Intel Xeon processors and 8 GB of memory. In order to obtain the original test case, we chose three software from *Vulnerability Patch Database* (VPD) and *Vulnerability Code Instance Database* (VCID) [20]. VPD contains 3454 diff hunks and these diff hunks correspond to 1761 vulnerabilities in 19 products. VCID contains 455 code reuse instances of vulnerabilities. The main reasons why we choose these three software are as follows.

- *Joern* [27] can only generate the PDG for software written in C/C++, thus we have to choose the software programmed in these languages.
- The software should have sufficient number of vulnerability test cases (vulnerability diff hunks and vulnerability source function code) and code reuse instances. We must ensure that there are enough test cases to evaluate the performance accurately.
- The types of vulnerabilities in the test cases and the ways to fix them should be comprehensive. If we only use a single test case type, the results cannot fully reflect the performance of the approach in a various aspects.

Finally, we selected 832 vulnerability diff hunks from VPD to evaluate the false positive rate, including 117 vulnerabilities of FFmpeg, 169 vulnerabilities of Wireshark, and 546 vulnerabilities of Linux kernel. We selected 230 code reuse instances from VCID to evaluate the false negative rate, including 14 vulnerabilities of FFmpeg, 15 vulnerabilities of Wireshark, and 201 vulnerabilities of Linux kernel. We randomly selected 2000 functions from FFmpeg, Wireshark, and Linux kernel, respectively, and used these 6000 functions to test the time cost.

We compared the false positive rate and the false negative rate among CBCD [19], Deckard [11], ReDeBug [10], and our approach SCVD. For the false positive rate, we used the patched vulnerability code as the target program. If we find the matching part in the target program, we deem this is a false positive test case. For the false negative rate, we used the code reuse instances as the target program. If we do not find the matching part in the target program, we deem this is a false negative test case.

In order to compare our approach with other types of approaches, we also used the same data to test CBCD (Semantics-based), Deckard (AST-based), and ReDeBug (Token-based). According to the default value of CBCD, we set the parameter as 8 lines when the vulnerability source code was split to subsegments. For Deckard, we set the parameters *min_tokens* to 3, *stride* to 2, and the similarity threshold to 0.95. For ReDeBug, we set the parameter *ngram_size* to 4 when the number of lines for the vulnerable code is greater than or equal to 4, and set *ngram_size* to 1 when the number of lines is less than 4. For SCVD, we set the data dependency edges similarity threshold to 0.8, which was an empirical value obtained by a number of experiments.

We compared the time cost of our approach with the subgraph isomorphism function *get_subisomorphisms_vf2*() provided by *igraph* [6]. The function uses VF2 [5] algorithm as the implementation. VF2 is recognized as the best graph similarity detection algorithm. CBCD also uses the function in the subgraph isomorphism matching. The reason why we do not compare the time cost with CBCD and Deckard directly is that SCVD mainly focuses on converting the PDG into program feature tree to bypass the NP-complete subgraph isomorphism. However, CBCD is committed to accelerate vulnerability detection by reducing the size of the PDG before the subgraph isomorphism operation. It is believed that if SCVD uses the methods proposed in CBCD to reduce the size of the PDG before the vulnerability detection, it will get faster than it does now.

4.2   Experimental Results

We describe the results of evaluation in this subsection, including false positive rate, false negative rate, and time cost.

False Negative Rate.   Figure 4 shows the false negative rate of three approaches for software FFmpeg, Wireshark, and Linux kernel. Compared with CBCD, Deckard, and ReDeBug, it is obvious that SCVD has a significant decrease in the false negative rate. Especially for FFmpeg, the false negative rate of SCVD is only 14.2%, while that of CBCD is 64.2%, and that of Deckard and ReDeBug even reaches as high as 85.7%.

Though both SCVD and CBCD are semantics-based approaches, SCVD has a much lower false negative rate because it has mapped the identifiers. The existing PDG-based cloned vulnerable code detection approaches could tolerate the replacement of program control statements, but could not identify the variable name modification effectively. For example, 44% of the false negative test cases for CBCD are due to the variable name modification. However, we use the identifier name mapping technique, which maps all the variable (or functions) name to the same value and eliminates the difference between the identifier names. Thus our approach obtains a lower false negative rate.

It is not surprising that SCVD has a lower false negative rate than Deckard. First of all, SCVD is semantics-based, and it maps the variable name in the syntax level. Therefore, SCVD could fully consider the syntax and semantic information of the code in the cloned vulnerable code detection. Although Deckard also considers the syntax information using AST, it ultimately uses the generated vectors for each node in the AST to detect the code similarity. In this way, Deckard might have a faster execution speed, but it greatly reduces the accuracy of the approach. Second, compared with the semantics-based approach, Deckard has a great dependence on the syntax of the code, which is very sensitive to the code modification. As a result, Deckard cannot identify some situations of code

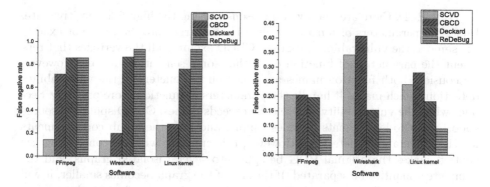

Fig. 4. False negative rate   **Fig. 5.** False positive rate

modifications robustly, such as re-ordered statement clones and non-contiguous clones. In fact, Li et al. [19] also compare CBCD and Deckard in their experimental results and show the similar problems of Deckard.

For ReDeBug, the hash value for the n-token window is used for the code similarity comparison. Thus, any modification can change the hash value, which results in the false negatives directly. However, almost all of the code reuse instances we use involve identifier modifications. Therefore, the false negative rate of ReDeBug is very high. This also shows that ReDeBug can hardly detect the cloned vulnerable code except non-substantive modifications such as comments and whitespaces.

We also analyze the false negative test cases in SCVD and find out a disadvantage of the semantics-based clone detection approach, that is, the changes of macro variables. In general, we always prefer to use macros to replace the hard-coding numbers. Because these hard-coding numbers called magic numbers can cause a lot of problems in the code maintenance. However, *Joern* cannot identify macros correctly at the time of writing, thus the macros are treated as a general variable in the PDG generation. For example, the vulnerability in our test case, which named CVE-2014-8544 in NVD, modifies the hard-coded function return value "−1" to the macro variable "AVERROR_INVALIDDATA". This is a typical example of code reuse instances, but the semantics-based approach cannot handle correctly.

False Positive Rate. Figure 5 shows the false positive rate of the three approaches for software FFmpeg, Wireshark, and Linux kernel. The false positive rate of our approach is lower than that of CBCD, but higher than that of Deckard and ReDeBug. The reason why Deckard and ReDeBug have a relatively low false positive rate is that it is more sensitive to the code modification. Thus they report the cloned vulnerable code only when the two code fragments are highly consistent. However, it is also the reason why Deckard and ReDeBug have a fairly high false negative rate which is unacceptable in practice.

For CBCD, there are mainly two reasons causing the high false positive rate. First, the parameters of functions called in the target program are not exactly the same as the vulnerability program. CBCD exempts all the vertexes that represent the parameters of function calls, thus some semantics are lost. However, we consider both function names and function parameters in the vulnerability detection, which makes it handle the parameters of function more precisely. Second, when the vulnerability source code exceeds 8 lines, CBCD splits the source code to sub code segments by lines simply, and uses these sub code segments for the vulnerability detection. However, this splitting without considering the context makes the original PDG be split into several isolated graphs, and the complete semantics be separated. If the size of the graph becomes smaller, it will increase the possibility of finding a complete matching graph, but also lead to an increase in the false positive rate undoubtedly.

For our approach SCVD, two main situations causing false positives are as follows. First, the coarse-grained identifier mapping leads to the false positives. In some target programs, there are exactly the same structure as the vulnerability program, but only the name of the variable is different. We map all the variables (or functions) to the same value. Therefore, SCVD gets two identical programs, but that is not the case actually. Second, a common approach to vulnerability patching is checking the validity of variable before using it. The changes of PDG in this situation is adding the control vertex and the corresponding edges in the periphery of the vulnerability PDG. As a result, the original PDG becomes the subgraph of the new PDG, thus the matching will be reported when the target program is detected, which leads to the emergence of false positives. For example, CVE-2013-3674 is a buffer overflow vulnerability caused by the function call ignoring the check of parameter size. Figure 6 clearly shows that the patching of CVE-2013-3674 is adding the validity check for the parameters of the function. Because the original statements still exist, SCVD reports the existence of the vulnerability falsely.

These two situations mentioned above make the false positive rate of SCVD a little high. In fact, these two situations in the actual applications are either unusual or very easy to exclude, therefore the false positive rate of SCVD will be lower than that shown in Fig. 5 actually. Compared with Deckard and ReDeBug which have a low false positive rate and a very high false negative rate, SCVD is obviously more practical and effective.

Time Cost. Table 1 shows the time cost of each step in SCVD and the subgraph isomorphism function $get\_subisomorphisms\_vf2()$ provided by $igraph$ [6]. We use a total of 6000 functions to test the time cost, that is, we randomly select 2000 functions from FFmpeg, Wireshark, and Linux kernel, respectively. Because the running time of the program is affected by many factors, we test ten times and take their average values as the final experimental results. For software FFmpeg, Wireshark, and Linux kernel, we can clearly see that SCVD is faster than the approach using sub-graph isomorphism algorithm. Although converting PDG into the program feature tree also spends extra time, it can significantly improve

```
@@ -289,7 +289,9 @@ static int cdg_decode_frame(AVCodecContext *avctx,
    ...
1:    inst   = bytestream_get_byte(&buf);
2:    inst   &= CDG_MASK;
3:    buf += 2;  // skipping 2 unneeded bytes
4: -  bytestream_get_buffer(&buf, cdg_data, buf_size - CDG_HEADER_SIZE);
5: +
6: +  if (buf_size > CDG_HEADER_SIZE)
7: +      bytestream_get_buffer(&buf, cdg_data, buf_size - CDG_HEADER_SIZE);
8:    if ((command & CDG_MASK) == CDG_COMMAND) {
9:    ...
```

Fig. 6. The diff hunk of CVE-2013-3674

the performance of approach on the whole. Considering that CBCD is optimized before the PDG comparison, we believe that SCVD will have a more significant improvement in accuracy and execution speed if the optimization operations proposed in CBCD are used to reduce the size of PDG before converting.

Table 1. Time Cost (ms)

Target software	Step 1	SCVD			$get\_subisomorphisms\_vf2()$
		Step 2	Step 3	Total	
FFmepg	850789	1526	307697	309223	468446
Wireshark	788126	758	433485	434243	681094
Linux kernel	663011	903	545041	545944	892744

In addition, we also list the time cost of each step during the execution of SCVD in Table 1. We divide the execution process of SCVD into three steps. Step 1 is the PDG generation for two input programs. We can see that this step is very time-consuming, especially for larger programs. But every semantic-based algorithm goes through this step, and it uses either *Joern* as we do or other program-analysis tools such as *CodeSurfer* [2]. Step 2 in SCVD is the program feature tree generation. From the implementation point of view, using the full path traversal algorithm to convert PDG into a program feature tree might be very complex. However, from the experimental results, we are surprised to find that this part of time cost is very little, almost negligible. Step 3 in SCVD is the program feature tree detection. Compared with step 1, this step also costs very little time. Although the generation of PDG takes a lot of time, the generated PDG can be reused. For this reason, we are not take the generation of PDG into account when comparing the execution time of the SCVD with $get\_subisomorphisms\_vf2()$.

In theory, the time complexity of SCVD is not less than the subgraph isomorphism algorithm. However, SCVD is indeed faster than subgraph isomorphism algorithm in actual test results. There are mainly three reasons. First, the large-scale tree is transformed into some smaller trees after removing the "Entry" node of PDG. This makes the subtree searching cheaper. Second, the separation of data dependency and control dependency improves the efficiency of execution. By filtering the dissimilar subtrees in the control dependency part in the first step, we can save considerable time for the data dependency comparison. Third, we use the shared node technique in the implementation to reduce the impact of redundant nodes on both time complexity and space complexity to a certain extent.

5   Limitations

In the following, we discuss the limitations of our approach. First, although SCVD performed very well in experimental results, there are still many places in the implementation of SCVD to be optimized. Specifically, we need to optimize the implementation of the program feature tree detection engine to improve the execution efficiency of the approach.

Second, the coarse-grained identifier mapping leads to the increase of false positive rate. Considering the mapping efficiency, we map all variables (or functions) to a same name. Unfortunately, as shown in Sect. 4.2, this coarse-grained identifier mapping leads to the increase of false positive rate. It is possible that two pieces of code with the same structure but different variables will become exactly the same after the coarse-grained identifier mapping. Therefore, we need to refine the granularity of the identifier mapping in the future. We can divide the identifiers into several categories, such as variable, const variable, macro, or different type of variable, then map the same category of variables to a same name.

Third, our experiments focuses on C/C++ open source software. This is because SCVD is implemented by *Joern* in the PDG generation and *Joern* can only generate the PDG for software written in C/C++. While SCVD is language agnostic, experiments need to be conducted to analyze target programs written in other languages.

6   Related Work

In this section, we discuss the related work about the cloned vulnerable code detection. The approaches can be classified into four categories: token-based approach, string-based approach, syntax-based approach, and semantics-based approach.

The *token-based* approaches [10,15,21,24] firstly generate the token sequence collection from the source code by lexical analysis. Then they find the similar subsequences in the target token collection to detect the vulnerable code. The suffix tree algorithm is the most commonly used technique in these approaches such as CCFinder [15]. Besides, CP-Miner [21] utilized the frequent subsequence mining technique to find the subsequence. Sajnani et al. [24] used MapReduce parallel processing techniques to improve the efficiency of token comparisons.

The token-based approach is language agnostic and it always has a highly efficiency in the cloned vulnerable code detection. But these methods cannot tolerate the modification in the cloned vulnerable code, such as inserting or deleting some code lines.

The *string-based* approaches [7, 12, 13] compare the source code strings for the cloned vulnerable code detection. Generally, the direct source code comparison is very inefficient, thus the raw strings tend to be processed before the comparison. Johnson [13] first proposed a text-based cloning detection method using hash technique, and leveraged the incremental hash function to find the code segment which had the same hash value. In his another article [12], the Karp-Rabin Fingerprinting technology was used to process the source code strings. Ducasse et al. [7] developed a language independent cloned vulnerable code detection tool. They put every line of source code as a code segment, and transformed the entire source code into an ordered set of code segments as the matching target before the direct string matching. The string-based approaches use the string matching in the cloned vulnerable code detection, so it is only efficient for the exactly identical cloned vulnerable code.

The *syntax-based* approaches [1, 3, 4, 11, 18, 22, 26] suggest that similar code segments should have similar syntax structures. The AST and parse tree are the most commonly used structures for syntax-based cloned vulnerable code detection. Baxter [4] first applied the AST technique to this field. However, it is inefficient to generate the AST for large programs and look for vulnerabilities in the AST tree directly. As a result, the syntax-based approaches, such as Deckard [11] and CloneDR [1], used the hash to speed up the execution of the approach. For example, Deckard generated a subtree-type vector for each node of the AST, and then used the local sensitive hash technique to calculate the similarity between the generated vectors. Mayrand et al. [22] extracted 21 kinds of metrics from the generated AST, and compared the vectors of these metrics from four aspects to check the similarity of the source code. In addition, White et al. [26] utilized the machine learning to establish the vulnerability pattern on the syntactic level to determine the existence of the clone vulnerability code.

The *semantics-based* approaches [8, 9, 17, 19, 25] compare the similarity of the code from the semantic level. Most of these approaches are represented by PDG. Ferrante et al. [8] proposed the PDG which combined data dependence and control dependence for all operations in a program. Komondoor et al. [17] proposed that looking for isomorphism PDG subgraph could be used to find the clone code segment. Sheneamer et al. [25] proposed a machine learning framework to classify vulnerabilities by different characteristics in the cloned vulnerable code detection. In fact, semantics-based approaches consider the similarity of code from the semantic of the program, which makes it more robust than the above three approaches.

However, the subgraph isomorphism is a NP-complete problem, the time cost could hardly be tolerated for the large scale programs. To solve this problem, CBCD [19] reduced the size of PDG before the subgraph isomorphism execution by removing irrelevant nodes and edges, or splitting the source code which has too many lines. The optimization approach could reduce the size of PDG effectively and improve the efficiency of the cloned vulnerable code detection, but the subgraph isomorphism problem still existed. Gabel et al. [9] joined the PDG on the basis of Deckard. They mapped the PDG to the corresponding AST tree and then replaced PDG with AST to calculate the similarities between two programs. In this way they could speed up the PDG-based approach, but the process of transformation lost part of the semantic information which could lead to a wrong comparison result. Unlike CBCD and Gabel et al.'s work, we converted the PDG into program feature tree, while preserving all the semantics information in PDG. Using program feature tree to represent program features, we could solve the subgraph isomorphism problem directly and ensure the accuracy of the algorithm at the same time.

Recently, there are some token-based, syntax-based, or semantics-based vulnerability detection approaches [24–26] using machine learning or distributed techniques. Indeed, these approaches improved the efficiency to some extent, but we did not compare the performance with these approaches. The reason is that these approaches required a lot of vulnerability data for training, while our approach focused on the situation that a vulnerability should be detected even if it matched with one case in the past.

7   Conclusion

In this paper, we have proposed a novel semantics-based cloned vulnerable code approach SCVD. We use the full path traversal algorithm to transform the PDG into program feature tree for the cloned vulnerable code detection. The algorithm can preserve all the semantic information carried by PDG, and use the simple tree searching to detect the cloned vulnerable code instead of the NP-complete subgraph searching. We also apply the program syntax information and the identifier mapping technique to improve the accuracy.

We have developed a cloned vulnerable code detection tool and evaluated the performance by a large number of experiments. Our experimental results indicate that the program feature tree generated by the full path traversal could replace the PDG for cloned vulnerable code detection completely. SCVD has a significant improvement on the vulnerability detection effectiveness compared with the existing approaches such as CBCD, Deckard, and ReDeBug, and has lower time cost than subgraph isomorphism approaches.

For future research, it is interesting to address the limitations mentioned above and strive to detect the cloned vulnerable code more effectively. In addition, we will try to integrate the optimization methods proposed in CBCD into our approach to further reduce the time cost.

Acknowledgments. This paper is supported by the National Science Foundation of China under grant No. 61672249, the National Basic Research Program of China (973 Program) under grant No. 2014CB340600, the National Key Research & Development (R&D) Plan of China under grant No. 2016YFB0200300, and the Natural Science Foundation of Hebei Province under grant No. F2015201089.

References

1. CloneDR. http://www.semdesigns.com/Products/Clone/
2. CodeSurfer. https://www.grammatech.com/products/codesurfer
3. Baker, B.S.: On finding duplication and near-duplication in large software systems. In: Proceedings of 2nd Working Conference on Reverse Engineering, pp. 86–95. IEEE (1995)
4. Baxter, I.D., Yahin, A., Moura, L., Sant'Anna, M., Bier, L.: Clone detection using abstract syntax trees. In: Proceedings of International Conference on Software Maintenance, pp. 368–377 (1998)
5. Cordella, L.P., Foggia, P., Sansone, C., Vento, M.: An improved algorithm for matching large graphs. In: Proceedings of 3rd IAPR-TC15 Workshop on Graph-Based Representations in Pattern Recognition, pp. 149–159 (2001)
6. Csardi, G., Nepusz, T.: The igraph software package for complex network research. Int. J. Complex Syst. **1695**(5), 1–9 (2006)
7. Ducasse, S., Rieger, M., Demeyer, S.: A language independent approach for detecting duplicated code. In: Proceedings of the International Conference on Software Maintenance (ICSM), pp. 109–118. IEEE (1999)
8. Ferrante, J., Ottenstein, K.J., Warren, J.D.: The program dependence graph and its use in optimization. ACM Trans. Program. Lang. Syst. (TOPLAS) **9**(3), 319–349 (1987)
9. Gabel, M., Jiang, L., Su, Z.: Scalable detection of semantic clones. In: Proceedings of ACM/IEEE 30th International Conference on Software Engineering (ICSE), pp. 321–330. IEEE (2008)
10. Jang, J., Agrawal, A., Brumley, D.: ReDeBug: finding unpatched code clones in entire OS distributions. In: Proceedings of IEEE Symposium on Security and Privacy (SP), pp. 48–62. IEEE (2012)
11. Jiang, L., Misherghi, G., Su, Z., Glondu, S.: Deckard: scalable and accurate tree-based detection of code clones. In: Proceedings of the 29th International Conference on Software Engineering, pp. 96–105. IEEE Computer Society (2007)
12. Johnson, J.H.: Identifying redundancy in source code using fingerprints. In: Proceedings of the 1993 Conference of the Centre for Advanced Studies on Collaborative Research, pp. 171–183. IBM Press (1993)
13. Johnson, J.H.: Substring matching for clone detection and change tracking. In: Proceedings of the International Conference on Software Maintenance (ICSM), vol. 94, pp. 120–126 (1994)
14. Jones, J.: Abstract syntax tree implementation idioms. In: Proceedings of the 10th Conference on Pattern Languages of Programs (PLoP). p. 26 (2003)
15. Kamiya, T., Kusumoto, S., Inoue, K.: CCFinder: a multilinguistic token-based code clone detection system for large scale source code. IEEE Trans. Softw. Eng. **28**(7), 654–670 (2002)
16. Kim, M., Sazawal, V., Notkin, D., Murphy, G.: An empirical study of code clone genealogies. In: ACM SIGSOFT Software Engineering Notes, vol. 30, pp. 187–196. ACM (2005)
17. Komondoor, R., Horwitz, S.: Using slicing to identify duplication in source code. In: Cousot, P. (ed.) SAS 2001. LNCS, vol. 2126, pp. 40–56. Springer, Heidelberg (2001). doi:10.1007/3-540-47764-0_3
18. Koschke, R., Falke, R., Frenzel, P.: Clone detection using abstract syntax suffix trees. In: Proceedings of the 13th Working Conference on Reverse Engineering (WCRE), pp. 253–262. IEEE (2006)

344   D. Zou et al.

19. Li, J., Ernst, M.D.: CBCD: cloned buggy code detector. In: Proceedings of 34th International Conference on Software Engineering (ICSE), pp. 310–320. IEEE (2012)
20. Li, Z., Zou, D., Xu, S., Jin, H., Qi, H., Hu, J.: VulPecker: an automated vulnerability detection system based on code similarity analysis. In: Proceedings of the 32nd Annual Conference on Computer Security Applications (ACSAC), pp. 201–213. ACM (2016)
21. Li, Z., Lu, S., Myagmar, S., Zhou, Y.: CP-Miner: finding copy-paste and related bugs in large-scale software code. IEEE Trans. Softw. Eng. **32**(3), 176–192 (2006)
22. Mayrand, J., Leblanc, C., Merlo, E.: Experiment on the automatic detection of function clones in a software system using metrics. In: Proceedings of International Conference on Software Maintenance (ICSM), p. 244 (1996)
23. Read, R.C., Corneil, D.G.: The graph isomorphism disease. J. Graph Theory **1**(4), 339–363 (1977)
24. Sajnani, H., Saini, V., Lopes, C.: A parallel and efficient approach to large scale clone detection. J. Softw. Evol. Process **27**(6), 402–429 (2015)
25. Sheneamer, A., Kalita, J.: Semantic clone detection using machine learning. In: Proceedings of 15th IEEE International Conference on Machine Learning and Applications, pp. 1024–1028. IEEE (2016)
26. White, M., Tufano, M., Vendome, C., Poshyvanyk, D.: Deep learning code fragments for code clone detection. In: Proceedings of the 31st IEEE/ACM International Conference on Automated Software Engineering, pp. 87–98. ACM (2016)
27. Yamaguchi, F., Golde, N., Arp, D., Rieck, K.: Modeling and discovering vulnerabilities with code property graphs. In: Proceedings of IEEE Symposium on Security and Privacy (SP), pp. 590–604. IEEE (2014)

Web Security

On the Privacy Impacts of Publicly Leaked Password Databases

Olivier Heen[(✉)] and Christoph Neumann

Technicolor, Rennes, France
{olivier.heen,christoph.neumann}@technicolor.com

Abstract. Regularly, hackers steal data sets containing user identifiers and passwords. Often these data sets become publicly available. The most prominent and important leaks use bad password protection mechanisms, e.g. rely on unsalted password hashes, despite longtime known recommendations. The accumulation of leaked password data sets allows the research community to study the problems of password strength estimation, password breaking and to conduct usability and usage studies. The impact of these leaks in terms of privacy has not been studied.

In this paper, we consider attackers trying to break the privacy of users, while not breaking a single password. We consider attacks revealing that distinct identifiers are in fact used by the same physical person. We evaluate large scale *linkability* attacks based on properties and relations between identifiers and password information. With these attacks, stronger passwords lead to better predictions. Using a leaked and publicly available data set containing 130×10^6 encrypted passwords, we show that a privacy attacker is able to build a database containing the multiple identifiers of people, including their secret identifiers. We illustrate potential consequences by showing that a privacy attacker is capable of deanonymizing (potentially embarrassing) secret identifiers by intersecting several leaked password databases.

1 Introduction

Data sets containing user identifiers and password related information are regularly published. In general, these data sets have been hijacked by some hackers, who then published the data on the Internet. The list of such leaks is quite long and only a small fraction of it is listed in Table 1. Taken all together this constitutes a large corpus of personal information. Two factors are worrying in this context. First, the size of the leaks tends to increase, putting more and more users at risk. Second, the passwords are often insufficiently protected, despite long time known recommendations.[1] The most prominent and important leaks over the last years - some of which are listed in Table 1 - use bad password protection mechanisms.

It is commonly accepted that insufficiently protected passwords - e.g. relying on unsalted password hashes or using the same encryption key - have weak

---

[1] Such as recalled in the OWASP Password Storage Cheat Sheet.

© Springer International Publishing AG 2017
M. Polychronakis and M. Meier (Eds.): DIMVA 2017, LNCS 10327, pp. 347–365, 2017.
DOI: 10.1007/978-3-319-60876-1_16

Table 1. Large leaked password databases. Most of them use password-equivalents.

Top 5 confirmed password leaks on "';–have i been pwned?"[a] in February 2017				
Site	#identifiers	Year[b]	Protection	Password-equivalent?
MySpace	360 million	2008 (2016)	hash, sha1	yes
LinkedIn	164 million	2012 (2016)	hash, sha1	yes
Adobe	153 million	2013	encryption, 3des	yes
VK	100 million	2012 (2016)	plaintext	yes
Rambler	100 million	2014 (2016)	plaintext	yes
Data sets used in this paper				
Name	#identifiers	Category	Protection	Password-equivalent?
A	1,5 million	Adult	Plaintext	yes
B	1 million	Social network	salt + hash, md5	no
C	164 million	Social network	hash, sha1	yes
D	153 million	Software company	encryption, 3des	yes

[a] https://haveibeenpwned.com/PwnedWebsites - retrieved February 2017.
[b] If the release year is different from the hack year, the release year is provided in parenthesis.

security properties and ease the breaking of passwords. Still, in the light of the important number of leaks that actually use a bad password protection mechanism, it is important to understand all the different types of attacks - including privacy attacks - that an attacker can perform.

These last few years, research focused on password user studies [1,5,25], password breaking [18,26] and estimation of password strength [1–3,6,13,15, 24]. Most existing attacks apply to passwords that are used by an important number of users. E.g. dictionary attacks or grammar based attacks [26] focus on passwords that a human would generate. Password popularity is also used to measure the strength of a password [7,14,24]. The intuition is that the more frequent a password is, the less secure it is. Conversely, rare password are found to be more secure. The popularity distribution of passwords typically follows a Zipf law [7,14] - meaning that the frequency of a password is inversely proportional to its rank - as exemplified for the data set D used in our study in Fig. 1. Related work mainly concentrates on frequent passwords represented on the left hand side of this figure.

In this work, we focus on rare passwords (i.e. supposedly secure passwords), corresponding to the heavy tail of the password distribution. In our example distribution (Fig. 1), this corresponds to the passwords located at the bottom right of the curve. We worry about the information that a privacy attacker can find automatically *without* recovering the password clear text. Data sets with insufficiently protected passwords provide *password-equivalents* that can be reused in subsequent attacks, even though the corresponding clear text password

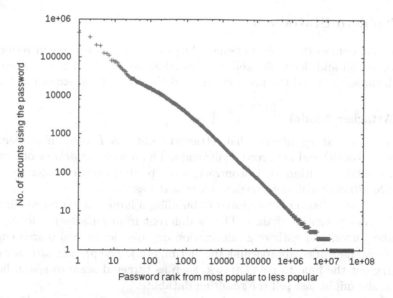

Fig. 1. Distribution of passwords in the data set D used in our study. For each password appearing in the data set we compute its rank in the data set (horizontal axis) and its number of occurrences (vertical axis). The relatively flat aspect on a log/log representation is characteristic of a Zipf law [21].

is never disclosed. Typical password-equivalents are unsalted password hashes and passwords encrypted with a fixed unknown key.

Contributions. We introduce a model for leaked identifier and password data sets regarding privacy matters. We formalize the notion of *password-equivalents*. We further describe the privacy attacker and define the tools and relations she will operate on identifier names and passwords.

We present classifiers for linking identifiers and revealing secret links, i.e. links that people do not reveal publicly. Using these classifiers, for a subset of these secret links the privacy attacker is able to deanonymize the associated secret identifiers.

We use a publicly leaked data set (named D in this paper) to evaluate our classifiers. It is one of the largest publicly available data set in its kind containing 153×10^6 identifiers and 130×10^6 encrypted passwords. With this dataset we show that a privacy attacker can link millions of identifiers, and deanonymize hundreds of thousands secret identifiers. Having no ground truth (for obvious privacy reasons), we estimate the precision of the classifiers through indirect measurements. Finally, we illustrate the consequences of a privacy attack that deanonymizes secret identifiers appearing in a data set related to adult content (denoted A in this paper), by intersecting A with D.

2 Problem Statement

This section defines the problem being addressed by our work. We introduce the attacker model and define linkability properties. We finish with a note on legal and ethical aspects and the precautions used throughout our experiments.

2.1 Attacker Model

We consider a *privacy attacker* that retrieved a data set D containing identifiers (e.g. *name@mail*) and password-equivalents. The *privacy attacker*'s objective is to link identifiers within D. In contrast, most related work consider the *confidentiality attacker* willing to retrieve clear text passwords.

The *privacy attacker* is interested in building a large database revealing sensitive links of potential victims. This is different from an attacker focusing on a specific person and gathering information on this victim (via search engines, online social networks, approaching the victim, etc.). The *privacy attacker* might not carry out the final targeted attack, such as targeted scam or spam, herself. Instead, she might just sell the resulting database.

The privacy attacks presented in this paper target the passwords that are less sensitive to password breaking. Consequently, users that are subject to the privacy attacker are not necessarily subject to the confidentiality attacker and vice-versa.

2.2 Model and Definitions

Throughout the paper, we use the privacy related notions defined hereafter.

Definition 1. *A **password-equivalent** is the output of a function $f(p)$ applied to a plain-text password p. $f(p)$ is a function in its strict sense, meaning that each plain-text password is related to exactly one password-equivalent.*

With this definition a password-equivalent encompasses unsalted hash values such as $sha1(p)$, hash values with a fixed salt such as $sha1(p.\ "0xdeadbeef")$, unsalted encrypted values such as $3DES(p, S)$ where S is a secret key, etc. This excludes outputs of randomized hash-functions as in [11]. In this paper, we consider $f(p)$ to be injective; we are thus neglecting collisions of hashes.

Consistently with [19], we define linkability and k-linkability.

Definition 2. *Identifiers x and y are **linked**, denoted $L(x, y)$, if x and y are identifiers of the same real person.*

We also introduce the informal notions of *secret link* and *secret identifier*.

$L'(x, y)$ is a *secret link* if the attributes of x provide no information about y. Informally, x and y hide their connection, e.g. by using identifier names that are sufficiently different to not reveal the link.

x is a *secret identifier* of y (i) if there exists a secret link $L(x, y)$ and (ii) if the identifier x does not reveal the identity of the person (the identity being e.g. the person's family name or the URL of a public profile page) while the identifier y does.

Definition 3. *Given a data set D of identifiers, a person is k-**linkable** in D if there exists a subset $\hat{D}$ of D such that $L(x_i, x_j); \forall x_i, x_j \in \hat{D}$ and $|\hat{D}| = k$.*

In this work, we evaluate a linkability attack on the data set D. This linkability attack infers links between identifiers, and we provide a lower bound probability p that identifiers are indeed linked. More formally, we define p as $Pr[L(x_i, x_j); \forall x_i, x_j \in \hat{D}] \geq p$. In Sect. 5, we provide estimates and statistics for k and p.

The *privacy attacker* employs similarities to compare identifiers. One first similarity, denoted $ls(x, y)$, is the complement of the normalized Levenshtein distance between character strings x and y. A second similarity, denoted $jw(x, y)$, is the Jaro-Winkler similarity. The Jaro-Winkler similarity was created for reconciliating user names from heterogeneous databases, the so-called *record linkage problem*. The Jaro-Winkler similarity provides good results for short strings such as names [4]. Noticeably, $jw(x, y)$ is generally higher than $ls(x, y)$ for pairwise comparisons of strings such as: "ic", "icomputing", "ingrid.computing", "computing.ingrid".

Last, the *privacy attacker* computes the sets defined below.

Definition 4. *For any identifier x in D, let $sp(x) = \{y | y \in D$ and $pwd(y) = pwd(x)\}$, the **Same Rare Password** function is:*

$$srp_r(x) = \begin{cases} sp(x) \text{ if } |sp(x)| = r \\ \emptyset \text{ otherwise} \end{cases}$$

The extension of srp_r to subsets of D is $srp_r(\{x_1, \ldots, x_n\}) = \bigcup_{i=1}^n srp_r(x_i)$

In practice, we consider values in the range $2 \leq r \leq 9$.

2.3   Note on Ethics

Dealing with passwords and personal identifiers raises legal and ethical concerns. Accordingly, we took a set of considerations and employed appropriate precautions.

The objective of this work is to understand, as researchers, the privacy implications of password leaks, poor password storage practices, and to raise awareness amongst colleagues, administrators and the community at large.

As a first precaution, all our results are non-nominative, i.e., they do not include any real personal identifiers. In particular, in this paper, we build examples such that: (i) the exemplified property is still clear, (ii) no single element leads back to any real identifier attribute. The example names, emails and encrypted passwords are invented, such as "ingrid.computing" in Table 2.

As a second precaution, for all treatments not requiring word distance computations or requiring the detection of some pattern, we anonymize the name part of the account using a keyed SHA256 function. For all treatments requiring word distance computations or requiring the detection of some pattern (e.g. detection of separators) we perform the same anonymization operation just after

```
10...89-|--|-ingrid.computing@comp.com-|-32gt...dfmQhQa...Dzfl==-|-same|--
13...25-|--|-0628...09@mail.uk-|-32gt...dfmQhQa...Dzfl==-|-usual|--
```

uid	pwdl	pwdr	name	mail	hint
10...89	gt...dfm	Qa...D	ingrid.computing	comp.com	same
13...25	gt...dfm	Qa...D	0628...09	mail.uk	usual

Fig. 2. Top: original text. Bottom: result after normalization. *uid*: internal user identifier zero-padded to 9 digits. *pwdl*: significant bytes of the encrypted left part of the password. *pwdr*: significant bytes of the encrypted right part of the password if any. *name*: identifier before '@' if any. *mail*: identifier after '@'. *hint*: hint string.

the distance computation or pattern detection. These precautions guarantee that no real identity appears as a result of a treatment.

As a third precaution, we key-hashed the passwords regardless whether there were already protected or not in their initial dataset. None of our treatments require the knowledge of the real password.

In addition, we took classical security measures to protect and clean the files and the programs used for this study.

Our results rely on leaked and publicly available password data sets, and there is a debate whether researchers should use such data sets (see [8]). Still, there exists an important body of related work that already rely on such type of data sets [2,3,5–7,14,23,26]. Individuals willing to know if their accounts appear in publicly leaked datasets may use online services such as haveibeenpwned.com or sec.hpi.uni-potsdam.de/leak-checker.

We would also like to emphasize our ethics regarding identifier providers. While we use publicly available data sets leaked from real organizations, our conclusion are not targeted against these organization. Our conclusions apply to *any* identifier provider using password-equivalents. Even though it is easy to reconstruct which data set we used, we anonymized the names of the related organizations or companies in this paper.

3   Description of the Databases

In this section, we describe the databases that we use for our study. We use four leaked password databases that we call A, B, C and D. Table 1 summarizes some characteristics of these data sets. We set emphasis on the database D as it is our main data set for this paper.

3.1   Data Set D

In October 2013, a password and identifier database - denoted D in the rest of the paper - was stolen from a software company and publicly released. At the time of its release, D was the largest data set in its kind, with 153×10^6 identifiers (including email addresses) and 130×10^6 encrypted passwords. The company quickly reacted by warning users and locking accounts. Anticipating contagion due to password reuse [5,9], other identifier providers promptly asked their users to change their password.

D was probably used by an authentication server used to access numerous products and services offered by the software company. D covers a long time span of 12 years; the first identifiers were created in 2001. It seems that are very large and diverse set of services and applications of that company relied on the identifiers and passwords in D. While we do not know the exact list of services and applications that use D, they certainly include many standard applications provided by this software company. Users showing up in D may also just have tried once an application, on a PC, on a phone, on a tablet, or registered to some web service (possible third party). Because of the above reasons a given user might have multiple identifiers and forgotten identifiers in D.

Analysts focused on password retrieval from D. Despite 3DES encryption, some passwords could be recovered because of three main reasons: (i) D contains user provided hints in the clear, (ii) the passwords are encrypted with an unsalted 3DES, allowing comparison across different users, (iii) the encryption mode is Electronic Code Book, allowing the comparison of independent ciphertexts blocks of 8 characters. This combination of factors leads to an online "crossword" game for retrieving weak passwords[2]. D has long been searchable through sites like pastebin.com and it is still accessible through peer-to-peer downloads.

The raw file contains 153 004 874 lines. We removed irregularities such as absurdly long or short lines, empty lines every 10 000 records, etc. In order to ease subsequent searches, we normalized the fields. Figure 2 shows the result of the normalization. The password equivalents in D have the following structure: $pwdl = 3DES(left, S)$, $pwdr = 3DES(right, S)$ where $left$ is the first 8 characters of the clear password, $right$ is the next 8 characters. S is a 3DES key only known by the software company. Only the owner of S is able to formally verify clear passwords. In contrast, password equivalents made from unsalted hashes allow public verification. Without the key S, only an accumulation of evidences will reveal possible pairs of clear text passwords and password equivalents. Typical evidences are explicit *hint* such as: 'my password is frog35', 'frog + 7x5', '53gorf reverse'.

3.2   Other Password Databases

Data Set C - A Social Network. The leaked data set contains 164×10^6 identifiers of a social network. The data set stores the users email address ($name@mail$) and a non-salted password hash. An entry in the data set C is associated with a profile page on the social network.

---

[2] See game http://zed0.co.uk/crossword and picture http://xkcd.com/1286.

Data Set B - A Social Network. The leaked data set contains 1 057 596 identifiers of a social network. This data set stores the users email address (*name@mail*) and a salted and hashed password. The data set includes URLs towards public profile pages (Facebook, Twitter, LinkedIn, Yahoo) if provided by the user.

Data Set A - An Adult Content Site. The leaked data set contains 1 504 128 identifiers of an adult content site. This data set stores the users email address (*name@mail*) and a password in clear-text.

4 Privacy Attacks

In this section we describe three privacy attacks on D. We propose a set of classifiers that reveal potential links and secret links in Sects. 4.1 and 4.2 respectively. We also describe a method to deanonymize potentially secret identifiers in Sect. 4.3. Throughout this section we depict our classifiers and methods using the examples of Table 2 ($k = 2$) and Table 3 ($k = 4$).

We evaluate, extend and discuss the presented classifier and methods in Sect. 5.

Table 2. Example case for 2-linkability.

uid	pwdl	pwdr	name	mail	hint
042...89	gt...dfm	Qa...D	ingrid.computing	mycompany.com	as usual
151...06	gt...dfm	Qa...D	sexy_single_69	somedatingsite.com	

4.1 Revealing Links

Let us consider the fictive case of Ingrid Computing as shown in Table 2. The privacy attacker will notice that only two identifiers in D have the same password cipher "gt...dfm Qa...D". The attacker suspects a link between the two identities ingrid.computing@mycompany.com and sexy_single_69@somedatingsite.com. Both identifiers may of course relate to different persons, in which case the attacker makes a false positive in assessing a link. A motivated attacker may use external sources (search engines, OSN etc.) to collect more evidences, which is out of our scope. The above imaginary example depicts our first simple classifier for revealing links that we describe below.

A classifier for 2-linkability: The classifier tells that $L(x, y)$ (i.e. x and y are *linked*) if $\{x, y\} \in srp_2(D)$. $srp_2(D)$ is the set of identifiers having encrypted passwords appearing only twice in D.

The above classifier can be extended to k-linkability, i.e. to cases of password ciphers appearing exactly k times in D. An illustrative example for $k = 4$ is provided in Table 3.

A classifier for k-linkability: The classifier tells that $x_1, x_2 \ldots x_k$ are *k-linked* if $\{x_1, x_2 \ldots x_k\} \in srp_k(D)$. $srp_k(D)$ is the set of identifiers having encrypted passwords appearing exactly k times in D.

4.2 Revealing Secret Links

Secret links are a subset of links. Coming back to the example shown in Table 2 the attacker might suspect a *secret link* since the *name* of both identifiers have nothing in common (have a small similarity). We propose the following classifier for secret links:

A classifier for secret links for $k = 2$: The classifier tells that $L(x, y)$ is a *secret link* if $\{x, y\} \in srp_2(D)$ and $jw(x, y) < s$ with a small s. jw is the Jaro-Winkler similarity as defined in Sect. 2.2.

We also propose a classifier for secret links for cases where $k > 2$. We consider the cases where $k-1$ identifiers employ similar names and the remaining identifier is either a pseudonym of the same user or a different user. An example is provided in Table 3.

A classifier for secret links for $3 \leq k \leq 9$: We consider identifiers $x \in D$ such that $srp_k(x) \neq \emptyset$ and having the following properties: (i) $k - 1$ identifiers in $srp_k(x)$ have similar *name*, for a chosen similarity and a threshold s, (ii) the remaining single identifier in $srp_k(x)$ does not have a similar name to any of the $k - 1$ identifiers.

Table 3. Example data for a secret link with $k = 4$.

uid	pwdl	pwdr	name	mail	hint
05	G...F		ic.computing	email.xx	1st cat
05	G...F		0699999996	telco.xx	1st cat
06	G...F		computing.ic	telco.xx	kitty
15	G...F		iccomputing	corp.xx	kitty

We use the Stochastic Outlier Selection (SOS) [12] method to automate and build the above classifier. SOS is an unsupervised outlier-selection algorithm that provides an outlier probability for each data point. In our case the outlier is the remaining single identifier, which uses a *name* very different from the $k - 1$ others. We apply SOS on $srp_k(x)$ and keep all sets of linked identifiers that exhibit a single and clear outlier. We conservatively consider an outlier to be an outlier if the SOS outlier probability is at least 0.98. Privacy attackers may adjust the threshold differently, according to their needs and resources.

4.3 Deanonymizing Secret Identifiers

Secret links can be used to deanonymize *secret identifiers*. Within the sets of identifiers that have a secret link, we search for sets of identifiers where at least one identifier reveals an identity, while the other linked identifiers do not. In the example of Table 2 the attacker might suspect that both identifiers relate to the same person, the first revealing a person's identity (the name of the person) while the second by itself does not reveal the person's identity (thus being a *secret identifier*). Similarly in Table 3, the phone number might be a *secret identifier* of a person which identity is revealed by the *name* of the other identifiers. We employ three heuristics, described below, to determine if an identifier reveals an identity of a person or not.

Social network B: The first heuristic uses the leaked data set B of a social network. We consider that an identifier reveals an identity of a person if there exists an URL to a public profile page in the data set B. The data sets D and B both store the users email address ($name@mail$), allowing us to calculate joins of the two data sets.

Social network C: The second heuristic uses the leaked data set C of a social network. An identifier in the data set C is associated with a profile page on the associated social network, and we therefore consider that it reveals the identity of a person. The data sets D and C both store the users email address ($name@mail$), allowing us to calculate joins of the two data sets.

US census: The last heuristic verifies if the *name* part by itself reveals the identity of its owner. We use surnames provided by the US census[3]. We consider that an identifier reveals its owner's identity if the *name* contains a substring of at least four characters long equal to any surname occurring 100 or more times in the US. This heuristic is not very strict and may therefore include many false positives.

5   Evaluation

5.1   Evaluating Classifiers for Links

One objective of our analysis is to demonstrate k-linkability in D, and to provide an estimate of the probability p that identifiers are actually linked. The main obstacle in such an analysis is the lack of ground truth. This prevents us from evaluating the results of our classifiers (e.g. calculate accuracies, false positives etc.) as it is done classically with machine learning problems. From a user perspective, the lack of such widely available ground truth in this domain is good news.

   Instead of ground truth we use a set of heuristics on the password, the identifier name and the password hint. We also analyze the frequencies of these features to provide further evidence that two identifiers are in fact linked.

2-Linkability. We first evaluate the classifier for 2-linkability proposed in Sect. 4.1. The cumulated number of identifiers returned by this classifier is 13 507 724 (6 753 862 identifier pairs), representing 8.8% of identifiers out of D.

   To estimate p (the probability that two identifiers are actually linked) we use the heuristic that two identifiers link to the same person if the *name* fields are

---

[3] See https://www.census.gov/genealogy/www/data/2000surnames.

similar, i.e. $jw(x, y) \geq s$ or $ls(x, y) \geq s$. The strict equality ($s = 1$) provides a lower bound for p. The strict equality on the *name* field e.g. establishes that ingrid.computing@gmail.com and ingrid.computing@hotmail.com are the same person. The intuition is that the probability that two different users use the same *rare* password and the same *name* is almost zero. 10% identifier pairs have identical *name* in $srp_2(D)$. We consider this value as a pessimistic lower bound for p, i.e. $p \geq 0.1$.

By decreasing s we obtain more optimistic values for p (e.g. establishing that ingrid.computing@gmail.com and i.computing@hotmail.com are the same person). At the same time we may introduce more false positives. Figure 3 plots the cumulative distribution function of similarities of identifier pairs in $srp_2(D)$ for ls and jw-similarities. Using a rather strict value for $s = 0.7$, we increase the proportion of linked identifiers to 23% with ls-similarity and 29% with jw-similarities. While we cannot provide more precise evidence, we strongly suspect that identifiers in $srp_2(D)$ are 2-linkable with probability p greater than the pessimistic value 0.29.

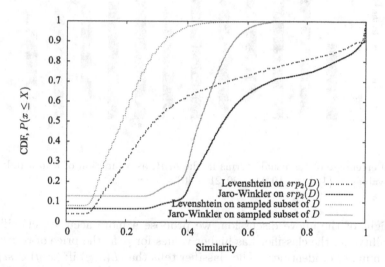

Fig. 3. Cumulative distribution function of similarities in srp_2 and in randomly sampled pairs of identifiers of D.

We now compare the similarities of *name* between randomly sampled pairs out of D (supposedly not linked) and identifier pairs in $srp_2(D)$ (supposedly linked). Figure 3 plots the cumulative distribution function of the similarities for both sets. We notice that the similarities are in general higher in $srp_2(D)$; the mean ls-similarity in $srp_2(D)$ is 0.42 versus 0.19 for random pairs. Similarly, the mean jw-similarity in $srp_2(D)$ is 0.58 versus 0.40 for random pairs. Finally, the proportion of random identifier pairs having identical *name* is in the range of 0.003%, compared to 10% in $srp_2(D)$. These numbers confirm the *name* is in general closer between identifier pairs in $srp_2(D)$, than any other random identifier pair.

As a further indirect evidence, we show that the propensity of a user to reuse passwords is much higher within $srp_2(D)$. We use the *hint* field to estimate the propensity of a user to reuse passwords. More precisely, we count the number of *hint* fields containing terms indicating password reuse: 'as usual', 'always', etc. See Appendix A.1 for the full list. The result is shown in Fig. 4. Among the 66 493 790 identifiers with unique passwords within D, 435 842 identifiers (0.7%) have a 'as usual' kind of hint. Among the 13 507 724 identifiers that share their password exactly once with some other identifier, 173 272 (1.3%) have a 'as usual' kind of hint. The proportion almost doubles, confirming the higher propensity of users in $srp_2(D)$ to reuse passwords.

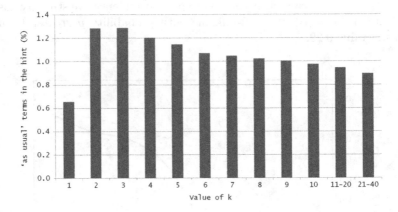

Fig. 4. Percentage of "as usual" terms in the *hint*, as a function of k in k-linkability. k takes values in $\{1, 2, \ldots, 10, 11 - 20, 21 - 40\}$.

In light of the above discussion, we propose a more accurate classifier for 2-linkability, i.e. the classifier has higher values for p, at the price of returning a smaller number of identifiers. The classifier tells that $L(x, y)$ if: $(x, y) \in srp_2(D)$ and $jw(x, y) \geq s$ for a similarity parameter s. With $s = 1$, we link 683 722 identifier pairs of D with a p close to 1. As discussed before, decreasing s increases the number of linked identifiers but decreases p. The precision of this classifier can be further extended by adding the condition that the *hint* indicates password reuse.

K-Linkability. Figure 5 shows the number of *k-links* (being $|srp_k(D)|$) revealed by the classifier for k-linkability of Sect. 4.1. Table 4 provides the cumulative number of links for $k = 2 \ldots 9$. We can observe, that the number of revealed *k-links* gradually decreases with k. As discussed in Sect. 5.1, the probability p that the corresponding identifiers are linked to a same user should decrease when k increases. To demonstrate this trend we consider the propensity of a user to reuse a password (Fig. 4). The ratio of *hints* indicating password reuse is similar with $k = 3$ and $k = 2$. For $k > 3$ this ratio regularly decreases, indicating that p also decreases.

The absolute numbers of *k-links* of Fig. 5 are difficult to interpret, particularly because it is difficult to estimate the probability p. Still, the results of the *k-link* classifier can be further filtered and refined to reveal *secret links* and *secret identifiers*.

5.2   Evaluating Classifiers for Secret Links and Secret Identifiers

We now evaluate the classifier for *secret links* and *secret identifiers* proposed in Sects. 4.2 and 4.3. *Secret links* and *secret identifiers* are supposed to be *secret* and it is even more difficult to find ground truth than with *links* (e.g. the secret links will in general not appear on Google, Facebook or LinkedIn profile pages). We therefore first provide global results and numbers and then focus on a corner-case experiment consisting in deanonymizing role based emails. We also intersect the revealed *secret identifiers* with external data sets (A) and discuss the potential impacts.

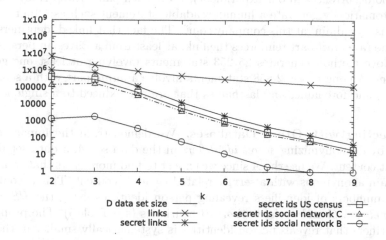

Fig. 5. Number of *links*, *secret links* and *secret identifiers* in D for k between 2 and 9.

Secret Links and Secret Identifiers Global Results. For *secret links*, we set $s = 0.4$ (as defined in Sect. 4.2) and therefore require that $jw(x, y) < 0.4$. This threshold corresponds to the first "elbow" in Fig. 3. Doing so, we estimate that an attacker would reveal 1 million potential *secret links*. Figure 5 also shows the number of revealed potential *secret links* with $k > 2$; Table 4 provides the cumulative numbers. While it is difficult to assess the p of this classifier, we know that we can increase p by adding the condition that the *hint* indicates password reuse. Figure 5 and Table 4 further shows the number of *secret identifiers* we could deanonymize in D, according to the three deanonymization heuristics proposed in Sect. 4.3.

Table 4. Cumulative number of *links*, *secret links* and *secret identifiers* in D for k between 2 and 9.

#*links*	11 038 079
#*secret links*	1 937 634
#*secret identifiers using US census*	763 348
#*secret identifiers using social network C*	348 892
#*secret identifiers using social network D*	4 003
in comparison: size of D	153 004 874

Deanonymizing Role-Based Emails. The classifiers may discover real names behind generic email addresses like support, admin, security, etc. An attacker can use this knowledge to bypass an 'administrator' or 'support' email address and directly contact the real person in charge. For this application, we select pairs of identifiers in $srp_2(D)$ such that: (i) one *name* is generic (see Appendix A.2), (ii) both identifiers have the same *mail* part, (iii) the *mail* part is rare within D (less than 100 occurrences in our experiment). From such pairs, the privacy attacker can automatically generate a human readable statement such as: "Ingrid Computing is 'sysadmin' at this-company.com". The fact that linked identifiers have the same rare *mail* part reinforces the link, at least from a Bayesian perspective. The above method generates 25 253 statements involving at least one generic identifier. Among those, 2 858 statements involve a *name* part with a separator (".","_") and forenames and lastnames that are not reduced to a single letter.

Intersecting with Other Databases. We demonstrate the impact of our attack by deanonymizing *secret identifiers* in the data set A, a data set related to adult content. We use the A since we expect to find more users that would like to remain anonymous with a service related to adult content. This is confirmed by the numbers of identifiers revealing person identities using the *US census*, *social network C* and *social network B* heuristics (see Table 5). The proportion of identifiers that reveals person identities is systematically smaller in the data set A.

We deanonymize a *secret identifier* in the data set A by (i) extracting all *secret identifiers* in D and (ii) keeping only the *secret identifiers* (*name@mail*) that also appear in A. The data sets A, B, C and D all include email addresses

Table 5. Proportion of identifiers in D and A revealing person identities according to different heuristics.

	US census	Social network C	Social network B
D	93.83 %	8.33 %	0.07 %
A	78.03 %	3.91 %	0.02 %

Table 6. Number of deanonymized secret identifiers in A, and number of secret links according to different criterions

Deanonymized secret identifiers			Secret links			
US census	Social network C	Social network B	All	Corporate	Gov.	Univ.
851	337	5	2979	3	4	104

($name@mail$), allowing us to calculate joins. Table 6 reports the number of deanonymized identifiers.

We further highlight the existence of embarrassing *secret links*. In Table 6, we report the number of *secret links* between an identifier in A and identifiers that verify a set of criteria: *(all)* no restriction on the mail address, *(corporate)* corporate mail addresses from major companies, *(gov)* mail addresses from government agencies, *(univ)* mail addresses from universities.

6 Related Work

Related work focuses on password cracking, password strength, password user studies and deanonymization of public data sets.

The most common password cracking attacks are the brute-force and dictionary attacks using popular tools such as John the Ripper. Many improvements for password cracking have been proposed: using rainbow tables [22], using Markov models [18], using probabilistic context-free grammars [26], etc.

Some works try to assess or measure the strength of a password [1,2,6,7,13, 15,24]. In this context, password meters are supposed to help users to improve their password. However, Ur et al. [25] show that in general password meters only marginally increase the resistance to password cracking. Only very strict password meters tend to increase the password strength [3,25]. Password popularity is also used to measure the strength of a password [7,14,24]. To strengthen a password, Schechter et al. [24] use the quite simple idea of discouraging the use of popular passwords. This latter approach is clearly beneficial for the privacy attacker of this work. The above works often use well-known password data sets to evaluate their performance.

Other work considered user behavior regarding passwords [5,9,15]. [5,9] study the problem of password reuse across sites. Both show that the reuse of the same or a similar password is a predominant practice for end-users. In particular, [5] studies how users transform their password for different online accounts. Both papers focus on an attacker breaking passwords, e.g. [5] builds a password guessing algorithm based on the observed user behavior. These works do not consider the privacy attacker which does not require to break passwords.

Most privacy attacks focus on the deanonymization of social networks and rating systems. [19] deanonymizes the public Netflix data set, by matching movie ratings provided by users of the Internet Movie Database. [20] re-identifies users of an anonymized Twitter graph, matching them against Twitter and Flicker identifiers. [17] identifies anonymous online authors by comparing writing styles. [16] links reviewers of community review sites. We consider a radically different type of data set that has not been studied in terms of privacy so far.

To the best of our knowledge, the work that comes closest to ours is [23]. The authors use identifier names to link or uniquely identify users. They further leverage textual similarities between identifier names for estimating the linkability probabilities. Our work is different as (i) we use encrypted information rather than textual information and (ii) we link to secret identifiers that are – by definition – very dissimilar from their linked identifiers.

7   Discussion and Conclusion

We presented linkability attacks based on password equivalents in leaked identifier and password data sets. The attacks do not require breaking a single password, and the efficiency increases with the password strength. Having no ground truth, which is expected in this domain, we provided indirect assessment of the performance of our classifiers. We demonstrated the consequences of our attack by showing that a privacy attacker can reveal sensitive private information such as secret identifiers. In particular, we evaluated how privacy attackers can deanonymize secret identifiers of users of adult content sites. State of the art attacks analyzing online social networks do not reveal this kind of information.

7.1   Tractability of Privacy Attacks

We would like to emphasize several risks for people's privacy. First, the presented privacy attacks require little computation resources. For instance, the k-linkability analysis on D took only 400 cumulated computation hours. The complexity of most treatments does not exceed $O(n.log(n))$. The attacker does not need to break any password, which saves a lot of resources. Further, the attacks can be performed using publicly available data sets. There is no need to crawl social networks or to have access to a social network graph. These two facts make our attacks tractable to most individuals without requiring any specific privileges or computing power. Finally, D is much larger than other data sets in this domain. This allows retrieving a fair amount of results, typically thousands, even when using multiple refinement requests. The number and size of publicly available data sets of that kind tends to increase, meaning that the number of retrieved results will also further increase over time.

7.2   Mitigations

The mitigations and countermeasures are rather classical. End-users achieve best results in terms of both privacy and security by using a strong and different password for each service. Since it might be difficult for a user to remember all these passwords, we recommend users to segment linkability according to their estimated privacy needs. Users should use unique passwords for the few services that they never want to be linked to. For other non-privacy critical services, users may use a password based on one single root (e.g. *frog35!*), and prefix the password with a character or string related to the service (e.g. *FB* for Facebook, *LI* for LinkedIn). This "poor man's salt" does not reinforce the security of the password, but decreases the impact of linking attacks. Password managers that generate randomized passwords also provide an efficient countermeasure. Finally, identifier providers should use salted hashing functions. These recommendations have been published several years ago and still, numerous leaked files reveal bad practices. In addition, we encourage identifier providers to encrypt both the hints and the email addresses. Obviously the hints are private, while massively leaked email addresses are a gift to spammers. Finally, identifier providers should avoid incremental uid's and use random numbers [10].[4]

Table 7. Probable history of a user w.r.t data set *D*.

uid	pwdl	pwdr	name	mail	hint
06...83	hc...si		joe.target	corp1.com	
10...68	sj...f2	Tr...G	joe_target	corp2.com	
16...80	sj...f2	Tr...G	tryjoe	isp.com	usual
17...22	Fg...st		tryjtarget	corp3.uk	other

7.3 Future Work

We found several cases where additional private information can be inferred from the available data sets. For instance, a privacy attacker could deduce people "histories" from the set of successive identifiers of a same person. Table 7 shows one example. Using time reconciliation this history reads: "In 2001, Joe was at corp1, he joined corp2 before mid-2008, then he went to corp3 before 2012". Building such histories requires linking identifiers through names [23], in addition to the links established through passwords. The first entry in Table 7 is linked to the second via distances introduced in [23]. The second entry is linked to the third entry via the password. The fourth item is linked to all others via a combination of both techniques.

Acknowledgements. We thank the Program Committee and reviewers for the many valuable comments that significantly improved the final version of this paper.

---

[4] The *uid* of *D* increases monotonically with the time of creation of the identifier. It allows the reconstruction of a timeline, by e.g. using creation dates of some identifiers or by searching in the fields *name* and *hint* for events having a worldwide notoriety.

A   Appendix

A.1   Terms for 'as usual'

always, usual, the rest, for all, normal, same as, standard, regular, costumbres, siempre, sempre, wie immer, toujours, habit, d'hab, comme dab, altijd.

A.2   List of generic email addresses

abuse admin administrator contact design email info intern it legal kontakt mail marketing no-reply office post press print printer sales security service spam support sysadmin test web webmaster webmestre.

References

1. Bonneau, J.: The science of guessing: analyzing an anonymized corpus of 70 million passwords. In: IEEE Symposium on Security and Privacy (2012)
2. Bonneau, J.: Statistical metrics for individual password strength. In: 20th International Workshop on Security Protocols, April 2012
3. Castelluccia, C., Dürmuth, M., Perito, D.: Adaptive password-strength meters from markov models. In: Network and Distributed System Security (NDSS) Symposium (2012)
4. Cohen, W.W., Ravikumar, P., Fienberg, S.E.: A comparison of string distance metrics for name-matching tasks. In: KDD Workshop on Data Cleaning and Object Consolidation (2003)
5. Das, A., Bonneau, J., Caesar, M., Borisov, N., Wang, X.: The tangled web of password reuse. In: Network and Distributed System Security (NDSS) Symposium (2014)
6. Dell'Amico, M., Michiardi, P., Roudier, Y.: Password strength: an empirical analysis. In: IEEE INFOCOM (2010)
7. Ding, W., Wang, P.: On the implications of zipf's law in passwords. In: ESORICS (2016)
8. Egelman, S., Bonneau, J., Chiasson, S., Dittrich, D., Schechter, S.: It's not stealing if you need it: a panel on the ethics of performing research using public data of illicit origin. In: Blyth, J., Dietrich, S., Camp, L.J. (eds.) FC 2012. LNCS, vol. 7398, pp. 124–132. Springer, Heidelberg (2012). doi:10.1007/978-3-642-34638-5_11
9. Florencio, D., Herley, C.: A large-scale study of web password habits. In: ACM WWW (2007)
10. Gambs, S., Heen, O., Potin, C.: A comparative privacy analysis of geosocial networks. In: 4th ACM SIGSPATIAL International Workshop on Security and Privacy in GIS and LBS, SPRINGL 2011 (2011)
11. Halevi, S., Krawczyk, H.: Strengthening digital signatures via randomized hashing. In: Dwork, C. (ed.) CRYPTO 2006. LNCS, vol. 4117, pp. 41–59. Springer, Heidelberg (2006). doi:10.1007/11818175_3
12. Janssens, J., Huszßr, F., Postma, E., van den Herik, J.: TiCC TR 2012–001, Stochastic Outlier Selection. Technical report, Tilburg University (2012)
13. Kelley, P.G., Komanduri, S., Mazurek, M.L., Shay, R., Vidas, T., Bauer, L., Christin, N., Cranor, L.F., Lopez, J.: Guess again (and again and again): Measuring password strength by simulating password-cracking algorithms. In: IEEE Symposium on Security and Privacy (2012)

14. Malone, D., Maher, K.: Investigating the distribution of password choices. In: ACM WWW, pp. 301–310. ACM (2012)
15. Mazurek, M.L., Komanduri, S., Vidas, T., Bauer, L., Christin, N., Cranor, L.F., Kelley, P.G., Shay, R., Ur, B.: Measuring password guessability for an entire university. In: ACM CCS (2013)
16. Almishari, M., Tsudik, G.: Exploring linkability of user reviews. In: Foresti, S., Yung, M., Martinelli, F. (eds.) ESORICS 2012. LNCS, vol. 7459, pp. 307–324. Springer, Heidelberg (2012). doi:10.1007/978-3-642-33167-1_18
17. Narayanan, A., Paskov, H., Gong, N.Z., Bethencourt, J., Stefanov, E., Shin, E.C.R., Song, D.: On the feasibility of internet-scale author identification. In: IEEE Symposium on Security and Privacy (2012)
18. Narayanan, A., Shmatikov, V.: Fast dictionary attacks on passwords using time-space tradeoff. In: ACM CCS (2005)
19. Narayanan, A., Shmatikov, V.: Robust de-anonymization of large sparse datasets. In: IEEE Symposium on Security and Privacy (2008)
20. Narayanan, A., Shmatikov, V.: De-anonymizing social networks. In: IEEE Symposium on Security and Privacy (2009)
21. Newman, M.E.: Power laws, pareto distributions and zipf's law. Contemp. Phys. **46**(5), 323–351 (2005)
22. Oechslin, P.: Making a faster cryptanalytic time-memory trade-off. In: Boneh, D. (ed.) CRYPTO 2003. LNCS, vol. 2729, pp. 617–630. Springer, Heidelberg (2003). doi:10.1007/978-3-540-45146-4_36
23. Perito, D., Castelluccia, C., Kaafar, M.A., Manils, P.: How unique and traceable are usernames? In: Fischer-Hübner, S., Hopper, N. (eds.) PETS 2011. LNCS, vol. 6794, pp. 1–17. Springer, Heidelberg (2011). doi:10.1007/978-3-642-22263-4_1
24. Schechter, S., Herley, C., Mitzenmacher, M.: Popularity is everything: a new approach to protecting passwords from statistical-guessing attacks. In: USENIX HotSec (2010)
25. Ur, B., Kelley, P.G., Komanduri, S., Lee, J., Maass, M., Mazurek, M., Passaro, T., Shay, R., Vidas, T., Bauer, L., et al.: How does your password measure up? The effect of strength meters on password creation. In: USENIX Security (2012)
26. Weir, M., Aggarwal, S., de Medeiros, B., Glodek, B.: Password cracking using probabilistic context-free grammars. In: IEEE Symposium on Security and Privacy (2009)

Unsupervised Detection of APT C&C Channels using Web Request Graphs

Pavlos Lamprakis[1], Ruggiero Dargenio[1], David Gugelmann[1],
Vincent Lenders[2], Markus Happe[1], and Laurent Vanbever[1](✉)

[1] ETH Zurich, Zurich, Switzerland
lvanbever@ethz.ch
[2] Armasuisse, Thun, Switzerland

Abstract. HTTP is the main protocol used by attackers to establish a command and control (C&C) channel to infected hosts in a network. Identifying such C&C channels in network traffic is however a challenge because of the large volume and complex structure of benign HTTP requests emerging from regular user browsing activities. A common approach to C&C channel detection has been to use supervised learning techniques which are trained on old malware samples. However, these techniques require large training datasets which are generally not available in the case of advanced persistent threats (APT); APT malware are often custom-built and used against selected targets only, making it difficult to collect malware artifacts for supervised machine learning and thus rendering supervised approaches ineffective at detecting APT traffic.

In this paper, we present a novel and highly effective unsupervised approach to detect C&C channels in Web traffic. Our key observation is that APT malware typically follow a specific communication pattern that is different from regular Web browsing. Therefore, by reconstructing the dependencies between Web requests, that is the Web request graphs, and filtering away the nodes pertaining to regular Web browsing, we can identify malware requests without training a malware model.

We evaluated our approach on real Web traces and show that it can detect the C&C requests of nine APTs with a true positive rate of 99.5–100% and a true negative rate of 99.5–99.7%. These APTs had been used against several hundred organizations for years without being detected.

Keywords: Malware detection · Web request graph · Command and control channel · Click detection · Graph analysis · Advanced persistent threat

1 Introduction

An increasing number of high-profile cyber attacks against companies and governments were reported in the last years. In contrast to untargeted attacks that aim at infecting as many hosts in the Internet as possible, these so called

© Springer International Publishing AG 2017
M. Polychronakis and M. Meier (Eds.): DIMVA 2017, LNCS 10327, pp. 366–387, 2017.
DOI: 10.1007/978-3-319-60876-1_17

Advanced Persistent Threats (APTs) target a certain organization over long periods of time, focus on a specific objective and are conducted by adversaries with significant resources in a stealthy way [11,28]. Because these APT campaigns are supposed to run for a long time, the malware used is often tailored-made and attackers take great care in hiding its traces. This makes it difficult to obtain APT malware samples for analysis—in contrast to general purpose malware that can, due to their widespread presence[1], easily be collected and analyzed. As a result, traditional signature-based threat protection solutions and supervised learning techniques struggle to identify APT malware. As an example, the Swiss defense contractor RUAG had been compromised for at least one year until an external organization provided information that lead to the detection of the HTTP C&C channel [1].

Once in place, APT malware typically rely on HTTP-based Command & Control (C&C) channels [1,12–14,21,24,35,39]. Using HTTP provides the attacker with two main advantages. First, this C&C channel is widely available as most organizations allow their employees to browse the Web. Second, normal Web browsing generates a huge amount of requests destined to a large number of servers. This makes it very difficult to tell apart benign HTTP requests caused by employees' browsing from malicious activity, allowing attackers to hide their communication in plain sight.

Detecting and blocking C&C channels under these constraints is challenging. Indeed, the large number of Web servers contacted daily makes it impractical to operate with a default-block policy and a whitelist for Web browsing. Therefore, most organizations use a default-accept policy in combination with a blacklist to detect C&C channels in the Web traffic of internal clients. The employed blacklists typically combine the Indicators Of Compromise (IOC) from different commercial and freely available intelligence feeds, such as abuse.ch, cymon.io, autoshun.org, and www.openbl.org. Unfortunately, since the target scope of APT malware is very narrow, traces of APT samples are often only detected by accident and it can take years until corresponding malware samples are recovered and IOC are added to intelligence feeds. Furthermore, the fact that there are only few APT malware samples available makes it difficult to apply supervised learning techniques for the detection of APT campaigns.

In this paper, we propose an unsupervised detection approach that does not need any malware samples for training. Our one-class classifier only requires labeled benign traces for training. Our approach is built around the observation that C&C channels typically follow a specific communication pattern that is unrelated to regular Web browsing. Therefore, after analyzing and reconstructing all the artifacts caused by human Web browsing, i.e., creating the Web request graph of the recorded Web traffic [25,42], the malicious requests to C&C servers stand out because they do not have any dependency or interaction with other Web requests; they are so-called unrelated nodes in the Web request graph. The key challenge behind this approach is that simply relying on the HTTP

---

[1] 430 million malware samples have been released in 2015 according to Symantec's Internet security threat report [37].

referrer for Web request dependency reconstruction, such as done by [17,42], results in many unrelated benign nodes. For this reason, we studied the Web traffic caused by benign browsing in detail and introduce several new heuristics to reconstruct missing links in the request graph. For instance, if the requested URL of an unrelated node can be found in the HTML source code of a recently accessed Web page, we can connect both requests. In combination with a small whitelist of benign services causing unrelated requests, such as OCSP servers and software update services, this approach allows us to identify C&C requests with high accuracy—after running the link completion process and applying the whitelist, all remaining requests are considered as suspicious.

This paper provides the following key contributions:

- *Link completion heuristics* that extend and complete the request graph generated in our previous work Hviz [17] by linking unrelated Web requests to their most likely parent. Link completion reduces the number of unrelated nodes in benign Web traffic by a factor of 8–30.
- A *malware detection approach* that marks non-whitelisted, unrelated Web requests in (completed) request graphs as malicious. Our whitelist only contains certificate authority domains and the update server of the operating system.
- A *comprehensive evaluation* in which we evaluate the performance of our approach by randomly inserting C&C traces covering the activities of trojan horses, exploit kits, botnets, ransomware and APTs into benign Web traffic traces[2]. We detect 99.5% of all malicious C&C requests (true positive rate) while falsely labeling 0.3–0.5% of the benign requests as malicious (false positive rate).

The rest of this paper is structured as follows. Section 2 presents our malware detection approach that applies a click detection classifier and link completion heuristics to connect unrelated, benign Web request to their most likely parent. Section 3 evaluates our approach and Sect. 4 discusses our results. Section 5 compares our approach to related work and Sect. 6 concludes the paper.

2   Approach

Our three-step malware detection approach is shown in Fig. 1. It detects C&C channels of APT malware (used in targeted attacks) and 'general purpose' malware (used in untargeted attacks). In a first step, we extract the (incomplete) request graph from Web traffic logs. In a second step, we complete the request graph by (i) click detection (see Sect. 2.3) and (ii) link completion (see Sect. 2.4). In a third step, we filter the remaining unrelated requests. The remaining unrelated requests are considered as suspicious unless the contacted server is whitelisted. We use Bro IDS [31] and Hviz [17] to create the request graph.

---

[2] We use benign Web traffic generated by scripts accessing the top 250 Web sites for Switzerland and user traffic logs from ClickMiner [25].

In the following we first give an overview on request graphs in Sect. 2.1, which are the base for our detection approach. Section 2.2 describes the idea behind our approach in more detail and the applied click detection and link completion are discussed in Sects. 2.3 and 2.4, respectively.

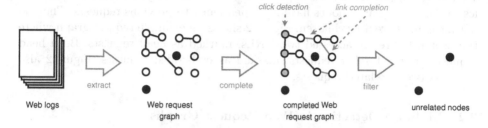

Fig. 1. Our malware detection approach: First, we extract the request graph from Web traffic logs. Second, we complete the request graph by (i) click detection and (ii) link completion. Third, we filter the remaining unrelated requests that are not whitelisted.

2.1 Background on Web Request Graphs

Web traffic logs store HTTP requests and corresponding responses. The requests can be connected to a request graph. In a request graph, a node corresponds to an HTTP request and its response. Two nodes i and j can be connected using a directed edge (i, j) if the request j has been issued by the response of i. For most HTTP requests, these links can be derived from the referrer field in request j, which points to i. If there is a directed edge (i, j) from i to j, then i is the parent of j and j is the child of i. If there are two edges (i, j_1) and (i, j_2) then j_1 and j_2 are siblings. Unfortunately, the referrer is not always set. Therefore, request graphs are often incomplete if they are constructed solely based on the referrer information.

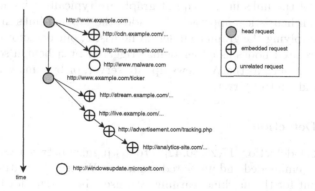

Fig. 2. Example request graph

We distinguish between three types of requests: 'head', 'embedded' and 'unrelated' requests, as can be seen in Fig. 2. Head requests are requests that have been issued by the user directly, for example by typing an URL into the browser, clicking on a link, a browser bookmark or submitting a Web form. Embedded requests are generated as a result of head requests. For instance, accessing a Web page triggers embedded requests to content delivery networks and analytics services. Unrelated nodes have no dependency to previous requests. They do not have any parent or children. Figure 2 shows an example request graph where the user has directly accessed two URLs, marked as head requests. Both head requests trigger further requests, marked as embedded requests. Figure 2 also contains two unrelated requests.

2.2   Malware Detection in Web Request Graphs

Our detector is based on the idea that any HTTP request must have one of the following root causes:

1. *Triggered by users' Web browsing:* The request is directly or indirectly triggered by a user's Web browsing. These requests are part of a larger graph component that represents Web browsing.
2. *Triggered by benign software applications:* Many benign software applications running on end hosts issue HTTP requests, for example to check for updates or load information. These requests are unrelated to a user's Web browsing and thus classified as "unrelated". End hosts in larger organizations typically run a pre-build image that contains a limited number of benign software applications. Thus the Web services that are contacted by valid application software can easily be whitelisted.
3. *Triggered by malicious software:* Any request not being part of one of the previous categories falls into this category.

The assumption behind this scheme is that regular Web browsing results in perfectly connected request graphs. However, as we will show in Sect. 3.2 between 2.6% and 9% of the links in the request graph are typically missing. Therefore we introduce an heuristical approach that adds the missing links in the request graph. After applying the graph completion heuristic, our detector considers all remaining unrelated nodes as either being triggered by a benign software that accesses a server, such as the Windows update server, or by a malware accessing a command and control server.

2.3   Click Detection

The goal of click detection [17,25,40,42] is to distinguish between *user clicks* and *other requests* (embedded and unrelated requests). We use the features shown in Table 1 as input for the machine learning. We use labeled data for training, but we only train on benign traces. Hence, we do not require any labeled malware trace. After evaluating different machine learning classifiers using Python scikit-learn [32], we found that a random forest classifier performs best, which is in-line with the work of Vassio et al. [40]. The detailed results are shown in our evaluation in Sect. 3.1.

Table 1. Feature set for click detection

#	Feature	Description
F1	Content type	Content type such as text/html or image/jpeg
F2	Response length	Number of bytes of the HTTP response body
F3	Number of referrals	Number of children in request graph
F4	Time gap	Time gap between current and parent request
F5	URL length	Number of characters of the URL
F6	Advertisement	Is the request an advertisement (in EasyList)?
F7	Presence of parent	Does the node have a parent node (referrer)?

2.4 Link Completion

The goal of our link completion algorithm is to add missing edges to the request graph. Referrer-based request graphs of benign Web browsing contain many unrelated nodes. In the following we discuss the primary reasons we have observed in our traces:

- *Certificate status checks*: The Online Certificate Status Protocol (OCSP) [18] is an Internet protocol which is used as an alternative to certificate revocation lists (CRLs). It allows applications to determine the validity of a digital certificate. An OCSP client (e.g., the browser) issues a status request to the Certificate Authority (CA). The browser suspends the acceptance of the certificate until it receives a response from the CA. Those requests/responses do not have a referrer header set and do not cause any embedded requests. Thus, the nodes corresponding to them are unrelated. The same is happening with the usual transfer of certificates and CRLs. These requests can be identified by their content type which is *application/ocsp-response*, *application/pkix-cert* and *application/pkix-crl*. However, note that we can not simply whitelist all requests with these content types, as this would make it very easy for attackers to hide their HTTP requests by including a corresponding (fake) header.
- *Favicons*: We observed that whenever Firefox sends an HTTP request to retrieve the favicon of a website, it does not include the referrer field in the HTTP request headers. As it turned out, this happens due to the *link rel='icon'* tag found in the HTML source code of web pages. There is a known bug associated with the above behavior [9] which has been resolved but not fixed yet. The same bug is not present in Google Chrome.

- *Privacy*: There are cases where the referrer header can affect the user's privacy. For instance, a URL might contain personal information in its query strings in case of a GET request. For example, this was the case with Facebook in 2010 [20]. More specifically, advertisers could identify users who clicked on their advertisement since their user ID was contained in the referrer header. Thus, security-aware developers remove this information from the referrer by specifying referrer policies [41], which were recently developed by the World Wide Web Consortium (W3C). These referrer policies allow developers to limit the referrer to only the visited domain of the origin website or to even remove referrers completely. Another case which results in a missing referrer is the transition from an object loaded via HTTPS to an HTTP object (downgrade). The main reason for this behavior is to avoid leaking sensitive information in the plain-text HTTP request.

- *Cross-Origin Resource Sharing (CORS)* [3]: When browsers make cross-domain HTTP requests, the referrer can be missing while the origin header is set. For example, this can happen when an OPTIONS preflight request is being sent, in order "to determine the options and/or requirements associated with a resource before performing the actual HTTP request" [4]. Firefox does not set the referrer header when performing this kind of requests, in contrast to Chrome. As a result, nodes that relate to this HTTP method become unrelated in Firefox.

- *Invalid Referrer*: The referrer header can have an invalid value which means that it does not correspond to a request URI of any previous node in the graph. A possible reason for this behavior could be bugs in the software.

- *Redirect Implementation*: There are several different ways for a user to be redirected from a source to a destination website. Firstly, the recommended way is to provide a 302 HTTP status code combined with the Location value in the HTTP response headers. Another way is to send a regular 200 HTTP status code and set the Refresh header or an HTML meta tag. In addition, a user can be redirected using Javascript. Depending on the implementation of the redirection, there are different behaviors of browsers to either keep or suppress the referrer [20].

The link completion algorithm completes the request graph to reduce the number of unrelated nodes in benign traffic. Our algorithm, which is depicted in Fig. 3, takes as main input an unrelated node n and a request graph G. The output is the most likely parent in the graph or False if the node does not fit into the graph sequence.

Firstly, the algorithm uses a whitelist in order to filter requests from benign software that can be running on the host (step 1). The whitelist consists of 37 entries and includes OS update domains as well as Certificate Authorities. The latter domains can be reduced since companies usually set up their own OCSP responder which acts as an OCSP proxy server. Further, domains and IP addresses contacted by deployed software can be added to this list. We argue that the overhead for maintaining a corresponding whitelist is small, primarily because of two reasons: *(I)* Even if an organization does not use an OCSP proxy

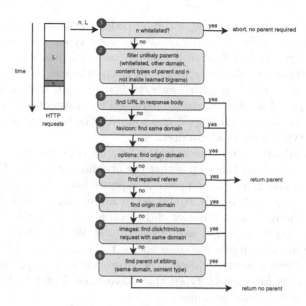

Fig. 3. The link completion algorithm tries to find the most likely parent of a node n inside a request list L. L is sorted by time and only contains the previous requests of a given time window. Steps 3–5 are processed twice, first for the click requests and second for the embedded requests in L.

server, the number of contacted OCSP servers is limited as certificate issuers typically only operate few OCSP servers and there are publicly available lists of these servers. *(II)* Security-aware organizations should already be aware of the software deployed in their network and the corresponding external servers contacted by the software, which allows them to add the corresponding domains and IP addresses either proactively or reactively to the whitelist. In fact, our approach can be helpful to identify software that has been installed without authorization because most software includes an update process that operates over HTTP(S). The corresponding requests will most likely be unrelated such that our system will trigger an alert when the software contacts its update server.

If the node is not whitelisted, its possible parent is predicted as follows (step 2): Based on the fact that the HTTP requests of an unrelated node's possible parents were performed before it, we create a list with all the candidate nodes falling into a time window covering few seconds before the analyzed request. The time window's length is not fixed and can be provided as input to the algorithm. Before adding a possible parent node in the list, the algorithm confirms that it is a candidate depending on its content type. There are certain content types which have much more embedded objects (and therefore cause child requests) than others. For instance, an HTML document is more likely to perform more requests to load additional content (e.g., third-party content) than a Javascript file. In contrast, a node representing a request to a PNG image should not have any children since it is not rational for this type of content to make additional requests. The algorithm encodes the knowledge on likely and unlikely parent-child relations as bigrams of content types. For instance, a node whose content type is *text/html* will usually have children with content types *image/jpeg*, *text/css*, *application/javascript*, etc., whereas a *text/css* object is more likely to have children with *image/png*, *image/gif*, *application/font-woff* etc. content types. The bigrams are constructed by traversing all the graphs of the network traces in the training set and counting the top length-two sequences of the content types with most children.

For each candidate parent node in the list, its response body is examined (step 3). The idea behind this step is that the absolute or relative URLs of child objects are often contained in the parent's response body. For example,the URL of a displayed image is typically contained in an *src* attribute in the webpage embedding the image and if the user clicked on a link, then the corresponding URL often previously appeared as *href* attribute. While this method is quite accurate, it requires complete response bodies to be stored, which can be large – especially if users consume videos. Therefore, we only apply this approach to response bodies for content types that have been found to have the most children, such as *text/html* responses.

Favicons can partially be linked using the above methods, but there is also a more accurate way (step 4): If the unrelated node's request URI is www.example. com/favicon.ico then, the parent's should be www.example.com. By default the favicon is placed in the root directory of the web page and browsers know where to find it. However, it is a common practice that developers place their favicons in other directories. In that case, the algorithm finds the parent based on the domain name and the content type of the possible parent nodes. Further, if a request's HTTP method is *OPTIONS* and the origin header value is set, then the parent is identified based on this value (step 5).

The steps 3–5 are run twice. In a first run, only nodes in the time window L that the click detection identified as head nodes are considered. If no parent has been found in the first run, then a second run is started which considers all nodes in the time window L. This way, identified clicks have a higher priority.

In order to handle requests with invalid referrers, the algorithm extracts the domain of the invalid referrer and searches for the parent that is closest in the time domain (step 6). The algorithm connects requests according to the origin header field, if the header field is available (step 7). If a request's content type relates to an image, then the time windows L is traversed and the first parented node that is either a head node, a node with *text/html* or *text/css* content is returned (step 8).

Finally, the algorithm matches nodes of the same content type and domain to the same parent (step 9). In other words, the algorithm tries to find the closest sibling *s*, which has the same content type and domain as the analyzed node *n*, and connects *n* to the parent of its closest sibling *s*.

3   Evaluation

For our evaluation we have merged benign Web browsing traces with malicious C&C requests. We have two types of benign Web traces, script-generated traces and user traffic collected by Neasbitt et al. [25]. We collected C&C requests from general purpose malware and APT malware samples from Weblogs [2,5–7]. We only use the post infection traffic of that general purpose/APT malware samples.

Table 2 shows our benign datasets. We have generated datasets S_1 and S_2 with a python script that emulates the Web browsing behavior of users by accessing the Alexa top 250 websites of Switzerland. Our script is based on the Selenium WebDriver [36]. It visits each of the top 250 websites in random order. We have removed websites with adult content from that list. The script makes five clicks per average on each website and stays on each resulting page for a random time interval. The time spent on each page has an upper bound of 30 s. We record only unencrypted HTTP traffic. This is achieved by visiting the HTTP versions of the websites included in the input list. In case the website is forcing SSL by redirecting the client to its secure version, the connection is terminated and the next URL in the list is fetched.

Table 2. Benign Web traffic: S_1 and S_2 have been generated by a script and C_1 has been taken from the ClickMiner dataset [25]

ID	Data source	Browser	#traces	# train requests	# test requests
S_1	script	Firefox 46.0.1	10	132k	278k
S_2	script	Chrome 54.0.2840.71	10	112k	257k
C_1	ClickMiner	Firefox 14.0.1	24	-	74k

We recorded 10 browsing traces using Mozilla Firefox as a browser and 10 browsing traces using Google Chrome. The user clicks have been recorded in order to train and evaluate the click detection classifier. Three out of the ten traces are used for training the click detection classifier. The other seven traces are used for testing in click detection, link completion and malware detection.

For evaluation we additionally used a third benign dataset C_1 that contains traffic from real users. The dataset has been published together with the Click-Miner paper [25] and contains 24 traces. These traces were accumulated from a user study with 21 participants. Each participant was requested to browse any website they wished for twenty minutes while preserving their privacy.

Table 3 summarizes the general purpose malware samples that have been collected from Contagiodump [2], Malware-traffic-analysis [6], the malware capture facility project [5] and pcapanalysis.com [7]. We labeled the C&C requests of these 49 malicious traces manually. We used a variety of general purpose malware that can be categorized in five malware families: botnets, exploit kits, trojan horses, sality and ransomware.

Table 3. C&C requests from published general purpose malware traces [2,5–7].

id	Malware type	#traces	#C& C requests
M_1	Botnet	6	478
M_2	Exploit Kit	13	357
M_3	Trojan	25	274
M_4	Sality	3	155
M_5	Ransomware	2	3

Table 4 lists our APT malware samples. Again, we labeled the C&C requests manually. Section 3.4 explains the APTs in more detail. Unfortunately, some of the APT malware traces only consist of few HTTP samples. We decided to include these traces in our evaluation in order to investigate whether our approach mistakenly connects these requests to benign traffic or not.

Table 4. C&C requests collected from published APT malware traces [2].

id	APT type	#traces	#C& C requests	APT report
A_1	TrojanCookies	1	720	[24]
A_2	Lagulon	1	561	[12]
A_3	Taidoor	1	35	[39]
A_4	Netraveler	1	11	[21]
A_5	Tapaoux	1	8	[23]
A_6	Sanny	1	6	[14]
A_7	Taleret	1	1	[13]
A_8	Likseput	1	1	[24]
A_9	Darkcomet	1	1	[35]

3.1   Click Detection

The information gain of each feature F1–F7 for click detection is depicted in Fig. 4 for the datasets S_1 and S_2 separately. It can be seen that the results are similar for both tested browser types. The content type (F1) has the highest information gain. Most user clicks are performed on a text/html content type, while embedded requests often contain images, scripts, style sheets but also text/html. The response length contains more bytes for user clicks than for embedded requests (F2). The number of referrals (F3) is higher for user clicks since the accessed websites often trigger many embedded requests that refer to the clicked website. The time gap (F4) between a request and its parent is usually longer for user clicks since they are manually triggered as compared to embedded requests that are automatically generated. The URL length (F5) of user clicks are longer than the one of embedded requests. Users do not often directly access servers that are listed on EasyList as advertisement sites (F6). The presence of a parent feature (F7) provides only limited information gain.

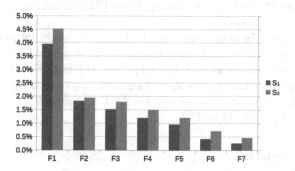

Fig. 4. Information gain per feature.

We have evaluated click detection for the datasets S_1 and S_2 separately. A separate investigation shows us, how well the approach works for different browsers. We have tested Mozilla Firefox in S_1 and Google Chrome in S_2, which are two of the most popular Web browsers. For both datasets, we used the same testing methods. We randomly selected three out of ten traces for training and used the remaining seven traces for testing. The actual user clicks have been recorded while capturing the network traffic. We assume that every access to a Web server that is listed in our recorded click database is a user click. We have evaluated various machine learning approaches and found that a random forest classifier with 1000 estimators shows the best performance. A decision tree was the runner up.

The results of the random forest classifier are listed in Table 5. The trained random forest classifier has a recall of 0.96 for both browsers. The precision is higher for Google Chrome with 0.96 as compared to Mozilla Firefox with 0.94. The resulting f1 score is therefore slightly better for Google Chrome. Our click detection performance is comparable to the one published by Vassio et al. [40]. We refer to Vassio et al. [40] for a more detailed analysis of click detection based on a random forest classifier.

Table 5. Click detection classification results

Dataset	Recall	Precision	f1 score
S_1	0.96	0.94	0.95
S_2	0.96	0.96	0.96

In the following, all presented results are based on Web request graphs that have been updated by the click detection classifier, such that only requests that have been classified as user clicks are marked as head nodes. The remaining results are only based on the test datasets of S_1, S_2 and C_1. We have also applied click detection to the Web request graphs of the ClickMiner dataset. We have used the trained classifier of S_1, since ClickMiner has used (a previous version of) Mozilla Firefox.

We have merged the malicious datasets M_{1-5} randomly into the benign test datasets S_1, S_2 and C_1 to evaluate our approach for general-purpose malware. The merged datasets are labeled as $\{S_1, M\}$, $\{S_2, M\}$ and $\{C_1, M\}$. Similarly, we have merged the malicious traces A_{1-9} randomly into the benign test datasets S_1, S_2 and C_1 to evaluate our approach for APT malware. The merged datasets are named $\{S_1, A\}$, $\{S_2, A\}$ and $\{C_1, A\}$.

3.2 Link Completion

Table 6 gives an overview of our results for link completion and malware detection for all merged datasets. It can be seen that the malicious requests are mostly unrelated. Only six requests from general-purpose malware are related. When we only rely on the referrer, we see that the vast majority of the unrelated requests

Table 6. Statistics on the number of related/unrelated and benign/malicious requests for all merged datasets. The majority of the requests are benign for all datasets. Our approach significantly reduces the number of unrelated benign requests without reducing the number of unrelated malicious requests.

Datasets	$\{S_1, M\}$	$\{S_2, M\}$	$\{C_1, M\}$	$\{S_1, A\}$	$\{S_2, A\}$	$\{C_1, A\}$
# benign	278 367	257 123	74 037	278 367	257 123	74 037
# malicious	1 267	1 267	1 267	1 344	1 344	1 344
Referrer-based approach						
# related	253 239	250 490	70 851	253 233	250 484	70 845
# unrelated	26 395	7 900	4 453	26 478	7 983	4 536
# related malicious	6	6	6	0	0	0
# unrelated malicious	1 261	1 261	1 261	1 344	1 344	1 344
# related benign	253 233	250 484	70 845	253 233	250 484	70 845
# unrelated benign	25 134	6 639	3 192	25 134	6 639	3 192
Our approach: click detection and link completion						
# related	277 551	256 411	73 650	277 545	256 405	73 644
# unrelated	2 083	1 979	1 654	2 166	2 061	1 737
# related malicious	6	6	6	0	0	0
# unrelated malicious	1 261	1 261	1 261	1 344	1 344	1 344
# related benign	277 545	256 405	73 644	277 545	256 405	73 644
# unrelated benign	822	718	393	822	718	393

is benign (72–95%). After applying click detection and link completion, only 23–39% of the remaining unrelated requests are benign.

We evaluated our link completion algorithm with the test datasets S_1, S_2 and C_1. The results are depicted in Fig. 5. We can see that the S_2 dataset has less unrelated nodes as compared to dataset S_1 before applying link completion. Chrome produces a more complete request graph as compared to Firefox since it sets the referrer header more often than Firefox as explained in Sect. 2.4. Our link completion algorithm decreased the number of unrelated nodes by an average factor of 30 for S_1 dataset, nine for S_2 and eight for ClickMiner. After applying link completion, each test dataset contains between 0.28–0.53% unrelated nodes.

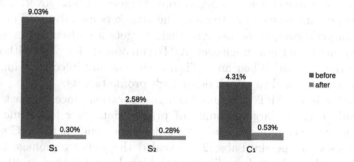

Fig. 5. Share of unrelated nodes before and after link completion. Link completion decreases the number of unrelated nodes by an average factor of 30 for S_1, nine for S_2 and eight for C_1.

3.3 General Purpose Malware Detection

We evaluated the ability of the algorithm to perform malware detection over the above metrics using the merged datasets in the following way. For each data source we randomly merged its traces with malicious ones by injecting the whole malicious graphs inside the benign graph at random timestamps. This would simulate a real case scenario where a user browses the Web and at the same time a general purpose malware is running in the background (e.g., exfiltrating data to the C&C server). We run the algorithm on each merged trace for each data source and the results can be seen in Table 7. 99.5% of the C&C requests were successfully detected while 0.5% were missed, independently of the benign dataset used. The true negative and false positive rates are the same as shown in Fig. 5. Hence, we can see that the link completion algorithm does not falsely connect benign and malicious nodes. The false positive rate is a bit different for each dataset and relates to the benign nodes (requests/responses) that the algorithm was not able to connect in the graph.

Table 7. Malware detection results.

Data set	TPR	FPR	TNR	FNR
$\{S_1, M\}$	0.995	0.005	0.995	0.005
$\{S_2, M\}$	0.995	0.003	0.997	0.005
$\{C_1, M\}$	0.995	0.003	0.997	0.005

3.4   Advanced Persistent Threat Malware Detection

Advanced persistent threats employ targeted malware. They are hard to detect, because they only attack selected high-profile targets, such as governments, military, diplomats and research institutes. The attackers use advanced methods to infect the target's computers, because their targets are often better protected against malware than the average user. APTs can operate for years without being noticed by the victims. When an APT has successfully infected a high-profile target, it is often reused to attack other high-profile targets.

Nettraveler is an APT that has been in operation since at least 2005. It automatically extracts large amounts of private data over long time periods. The APT malware compresses the private data and sends it to C&C servers in HTTP requests. Kaspersky Labs [21] revealed this cyber espionage campaign in 2013. More than 350 high-profile targets have been attacked in 40 countries during this campaign. When Kaspersky revealed the campaign, 22 GB of stolen data was still on the C&C servers. However, it is likely that stolen data had been removed from the servers during the campaign. Therefore the total amount of stolen data cannot be estimated.

The attackers send spear phishing e-mails to selected users. The Nettraveler APT malware is hidden inside a Microsoft Office document. The APT malware takes advantage of one of two vulnerabilities in Microsoft Office that can lead to remote code execution. Both vulnerabilities have been patched in the mean time, the vulnerability CVE-2010-3333 in 2010 and the vulnerability CVE-2012-0158 in 2012. Interestingly, this APT has been recently used to attack high-profile targets in Russia, Mongolia, Belarus and other European countries in 2016 [34]. This indicates that even high-profile targets do not continuously and consistently apply critical software updates on their computers. Hence, attackers can still find a machine that can be attacked in order to get access to the corporate network.

We have also investigated malicious samples of the following APTs.

- *Likseput* (trace A_8) is an APT malware which was used by a government-sponsored Chinese APT group, called APT1, in order to control compromised systems in cyber espionage campaigns that took place since at least 2006. APT1 has already extracted hundreds of terabytes from at least 141 organizations according to the Mandiant report [24].
- *TrojanCookies* (trace A_1) is another APT malware used by APT1. It communicates with the C&C server by encoding the commands as well as the responses in the cookie using base64 and a single-byte xor obfuscation.

- *Lagulon* (trace A_2) was used in several targeted campaigns performed by an Iranian group, named Cleaver, in 2013. The APT malware can log the user's keystrokes, download and execute code, take screenshots and periodically exfiltrate data to a remote HTTP-based C&C server. The attackers gained highly sensitive information from government agencies and infrastructure companies in many countries [12].
- *Sanny* (trace A_6) was used in targeted attacks primarily against major industries in Russia. It was detected in 2012. The attackers sent a malicious Microsoft Word document via spear phishing emails. The APT malware profiles the victims regarding their region and language. It extracts credentials such as saved passwords in applications [14].
- *Taidoor* (trace A_3) APT malware, a remote access trojan, was used to compromise targets since at least 2008. The threat actors sent out spear phishing emails to Taiwanese government email addresses [39].
- *Taleret* (trace A_7) APT malware was also used in the Taidoor campaign. Unlike Taidoor, it connected to Yahoo blogs to retrieve a list of C&C servers [13].
- *Tapaoux* (trace A_5) is an APT malware used by the Darkhotel APT campaign which appeared to have been active for seven years since 2007 [23]. The attackers also used spear phishing with advanced zero-day exploits.
- *Darkcomet* (trace A_9) is a remote access trojan, which was developed in 2008. The Syrian government used it to spy on dissidents during the Syrian Civil war in 2014 according to Fidelis Security [35]. It was also associated with operation hangover, a cyber espionage campaign against Pakistani organizations that took place from 2010 until 2013 [29].

We have evaluated our malware detection approach on malicious traces for all nine mentioned advanced persistent threats, see Table 4. All of these APTs have lead to severe damages on high-profile targets as described before. We randomly integrated the C&C requests and responses of A_{1-9} to the benign test data sets S_1, S_2 and C_1. Our malware detection approach successfully detects all C&C requests, as can be seen in Table 8. Therefore, the true positive rate is one and the false negative rate is zero for all tested data sets. The false positive rate has not changed as compared to Table 7.

Table 8. Advanced persistent threat detection results.

Data set	TPR	FPR	TNR	FNR
$\{S_1, M\}$	1.000	0.005	0.995	0.000
$\{S_2, M\}$	1.000	0.003	0.997	0.000
$\{C_1, M\}$	1.000	0.003	0.997	0.000

4   Discussion

In total 2605 of 2611 C&C requests (99.8%) are unrelated in the Web request graphs of the malicious datasets of general purpose malware M_{1-5} and APT malware A_{1-9}. Only six C&C requests are related. There are three traces that each contain a pair of related C&C requests. Each pair of C&C requests happens due to an URL redirection. Table 9 shows the three traces that contain related C&C requests. It can be seen that the HorstProxy trace is the only tested trace without any unrelated C&C request. All other 57 traces contain unrelated C&C requests, which are identified by our approach. This means that our approach detects C&C traffic in 57 out of 58 malicious traces (including APT traces).

Table 9. Malicious traces with false negatives

Set	Trace	# related	# unrelated
M_3	HorstProxy_EFE5529D697174914938F4ABF115F762-2013-05-13 [7]	2	0
M_5	BIN_sality_CEAF4D9E1F408299144E75D7F29C1810 [7]	2	6
M_5	InvestigationExtraction-RSA_Sality [2]	2	8

Our experiments show that most C&C requests are indeed unrelated and are correctly identified as malicious. Only HTTP redirects of malicious requests are not identified. Such redirects could be merged in a request graph to single nodes. In this case, we would have identified the redirected C&C requests as malicious. However, we did not combine redirections and redirection targets into single nodes in this work as this could result in additional false positives if the benign requests have no relation to other nodes in the Web graph.

Our approach works on single clients and equally good for general purpose and APT malware. This is a strong result considering the fact that some of the considered APTs were active for years without being noticed. Our approach would have detected the general purpose/APT malware in few minutes. We consider 30 s time windows, this means that a real-time implementation of the detection approach can react in a granularity of 30 s to a C&C request. Our C&C detection approach can significantly improve the response time to attacks, which might last for several years until the vulnerability has been identified and patched.

As with any malware detection approach, attackers might change their behavior in order to better obfuscate their activities and circumvent detection. However, the fact that the investigated malware traces caused considerable damage, clearly shows that there is need for an approach like ours. We see several future challenges for our approach. Firstly, the C&C traffic can be adapted such that it sends related requests that mimic benign Web browsing traffic. Fake referrers could be detected by analyzing the popularity of links in the request tree, as outlined in our previous work [17]. Further, click detection could be used to analyze the sites visited by users. In case malware builds its own sequence of related requests, this could still identify the C&C channel since it is a Web site that is visited repeatedly.

Secondly, C&C requests can set a referrer to a benign request in order to better hide inside Web browsing. In this scenario, one has to take the referrer field into question. One will look at other features such as the timing behavior between related requests in order to see, whether the general purpose/APT malware performs the requests in the same manner as a Web browser.

Thirdly, the number of false positives might increase in future due to a growing complexity of Web request graphs and removal of referrers due to privacy constraints. In this case, one can develop further heuristics to improve the link completion. Furthermore, one could reduce the number of detection alerts by summarizing the unrelated requests on domain level. One can send a detection alert whenever a server has been contacted with unrelated requests for at least a given number of times. This should significantly reduce the number of alerts.

Finally, benign and malicious Web traffic might mostly consist of HTTPS connections instead of HTTP. This challenge can be overcome by using man-in-the-middle proxies, which allows a network application to inspect the otherwise encrypted traffic. This is already done in many companies and other high-profile targets.

5   Related Work

Supervised malware detection: Most related approaches that detect C&C channels in network traffic use supervised machine learning that trains on labeled malware samples. For instance, Perdisci et al. [33] propose a scalable malware clustering system for HTTP-based malware, which has a detection rate of 65%–85%. BotFinder [38] creates botnet traffic inside a controlled environment in order to learn bot detection models with a detection rate of 80%. ExecScent [26] learns adaptive control protocol templates in order to determine a good trade-off between true and false positive rates. DISCLOSURE [8] detects C&C traffic using a large-scale NetFlow analysis that relies on labeled training samples. Their detection rate is about 90%. They use external reputation scores to reduce the false positive rate.

HAS-Analyzer [22] uses a random forest classifier with an accuracy of 96% and a false positive rate of 1.3% without using any whitelist. JACKSTRAWS [19] correlates host behavior with network traffic to detect C&C channels of botnets. The authors use machine learning with labeled malicious samples and achieve a detection rate of 81.6% at a false positive rate of 0.2%. In contrast to [8,19,22, 26,27,33,38], our detector works without learning from malware samples while providing a very high true positive rate and a low false positive rate.

Our link completion algorithm uses similar techniques as the ones developed by Nelms et al. [27] for the WebWitness system. WebWitness classifies the infection method as malicious drive-by, social engineering and update/drop downloads. However, in contrast to our approach, Nelms et al. do not build a malware detector, instead they focus on enabling forensic investigations of already identified malware infections.

Unsupervised malware detection: BotSniffer [16] presents an unsupervised network-based anomaly detector without prior knowledge of the malware. The detection rate is 100% with a false positive rate of 0.16%. BotMiner [15] clusters communication patterns and malicious activities traffic and identifies botnets due to a cross cluster correlation. The detection rate is 100% for HTTP bots with a false positive rate of 0.003%. However, BotSniffer and BotMiner only work on network level with multiple infected hosts. BotSniffer takes advantage of the observations that bots communicate in a similar spatial-temporal behavior to the malicious server. However, these approaches do not work for APTs, which only infect a single computer.

Burghouwt et al. [10] and Zhang et al. [43] correlate Web request graphs with user interactions to detect malware. Burghouwt et al. achieve a detection rate of 70%–80% with a false positive rate of 0.17%, Zhang et al. achieve an accuracy of 96%. In contrast to our approach, they continuously record user interactions such as clicks and keystrokes. We only record the accessed domains in an initial training stage for click detection. After training is completed, we do not need to record any user interaction. Furthermore, [10,43] do not employ link completion.

Oprea et al. [30] propose a graph-theoretic framework based on belief propagation to detect early-stage APT campaigns. Unlike our approach, they do not fully rely on the network traffic but also collect registration information of the accessed domains. Furthermore, their approach only works on the enterprise network level, while our approach also works for single hosts.

6   Conclusion

We propose a novel APT and general purpose malware detection approach that identifies command and control channels in Web request graphs. Our approach relies on the observation that malware communicates to malicious servers periodically with single, unrelated HTTP requests. This communication pattern is different from Web browsing where page requests usually result in several requests that are related to each other. Software applications and the operating system also send single, unrelated request to dedicated servers. Their traffic patterns are similar to C&C requests. However, we assume that these servers are well known and can be whitelisted. In our experiments, we whitelist 37 update servers and certificate authorities.

Our malware detection approach improves the request graphs of related work by automatically detecting user clicks (click detection) and restoring dependencies between unconnected requests (link completion). In a first step, we use a random forest classifier to detect user clicks inside request graphs. Our classifier relies on seven features on node and graph level, such as content type (node level) and number of children (graph level). We evaluate our click detection classifier with generated benign browsing traffic that accesses the Alexa top 250 of Switzerland. Our classifier has a f1 score of 95% for Firefox and 96% for Chrome.

In a second step, we connect unrelated nodes to their most likely parent. We evaluated link completion on the script-generated traffic and real user traffic provided by ClickMiner [25]. We find that 91–97% of the HTTP requests in Web browsing are already connected to other requests after extracting the request graphs with Hviz [17]. Our heuristic algorithm, called link completion, connects unrelated requests to their most likely parent. Our experiments show that link completion adds many missing links to the request graph. Between 99.5% and 99.7% of the benign nodes are connected after link completion.

We have evaluated our detection approach for 49 general purpose malware and nine APT malware packet traces, which are publicly available. The post-infection C&C traffic of these traces consists of 99.8% unrelated requests and 0.2% related requests. When we randomly merge these requests to benign Web browsing traffic, we can detect 99.5% of the malware and 100% of the APT C&C requests while having a false positive rate of 0.3–0.5%. Our approach can be applied in real-time at the granularity of single clients. This means that C&C traffic can be recognized in the order of 30 s. The Web request graphs can be tracked and completed on a per client base. This allows the proposed algorithm to scale horizontally as well as vertically. We hope that our findings will help to significantly shorten the timespan until new pieces of malware, especially those used by APTs, are discovered.

References

1. APT Case RUAG. Technical Report. GovCERT.ch, 23 May 2016. https://www.melani.admin.ch/dam/melani/en/dokumente/2016/technical%20report%20ruag.pdf.download.pdf/Report_Ruag-Espionage-Case.pdf
2. Contagiodump Blog. http://contagiodump.blogspot.com. Accessed Jan 2017
3. HTTP Access Control. https://developer.mozilla.org/en-US/docs/Web/HTTP/Access_control_CORS. Accessed Jan 2017
4. HTTP Method Definitions. https://www.w3.org/Protocols/rfc2616/rfc2616-sec9.html. Accessed Jan 2017
5. Malware Capture Facility Project. http://mcfp.weebly.com. Accessed Jan 2017
6. Malware-Traffic-Analysis Blog. http://www.malware-traffic-analysis.net. Accessed Jan 2017
7. pcapanalysis. http://www.pcapanalysis.com. Accessed Jan 2017
8. Bilge, L., Balzarotti, D., Robertson, W., Kirda, E., Kruegel, C.: Disclosure: detecting botnet command and control servers through large-scale netflow analysis. In: Proceedings of the Annual Computer Security Applications Conference, ACSAC 2012, pp. 129–138. ACM (2012)
9. Bugzilla: Bug 1282878. https://bugzilla.mozilla.org/show_bug.cgi?id=1282878. Accessed Feb 2017
10. Burghouwt, P., Spruit, M., Sips, H.: Detection of covert botnet command and control channels by causal analysis of traffic flows. In: Wang, G., Ray, I., Feng, D., Rajarajan, M. (eds.) CSS 2013. LNCS, vol. 8300, pp. 117–131. Springer, Cham (2013). doi:10.1007/978-3-319-03584-0_10
11. Chen, P., Desmet, L., Huygens, C.: A study on advanced persistent threats. In: Decker, B., Zúquete, A. (eds.) CMS 2014. LNCS, vol. 8735, pp. 63–72. Springer, Heidelberg (2014). doi:10.1007/978-3-662-44885-4_5

12. Cylance: Operation cleaver report. http://cdn2.hubspot.net/hubfs/270968/assets/Cleaver/Cylance_Operation_Cleaver_Report.pdf. Accessed Feb 2017
13. FireEye: Evasive Tactics: Taidoor. https://www.fireeye.com/blog/threat-research/2013/09/evasive-tactics-taidoor-3.html. Accessed Feb 2017
14. FireEye: To Russia With Targeted Attack. https://www.fireeye.com/blog/threat-research/2012/12/to-russia-with-apt.html. Accessed Feb 2017
15. Gu, G., Perdisci, R., Zhang, J., Lee, W.: Botminer: clustering analysis of network traffic for protocol- and structure-independent botnet detection. In: Proceedings of the USENIX Security Symposium. USENIX Security 2008 (2008)
16. Gu, G., Zhang, J., Lee, W.: Botsniffer: detecting botnet command and control channels in network traffic. In: Proceedings of the Network and Distributed System Security Symposium (NDSS 2008) (2008)
17. Gugelmann, D., Gasser, F., Ager, B., Lenders, V.: Hviz: Http(s) traffic aggregation and visualization for network forensics. In: Proceedings of the DFRWS Europe (DFRWS 2015 Europe) Digital Investigation 12, Supplement 1, pp. 1–11 (2015)
18. IETF: Online Certificate Status Protocol - OCSP. https://tools.ietf.org/html/rfc6960. Accessed Feb 2017
19. Jacob, G., Hund, R., Kruegel, C., Holz, T.: Jackstraws: picking command and control connections from bot traffic. In: Proceedings of the USENIX Security Symposium. USENIX Security 2011 (2011)
20. Jones, M.: Protecting privacy with referrers (2010). https://www.facebook.com/notes/facebook-engineering/protecting-privacy-with-referrers/392382738919/. Accessed Feb 2017
21. Lab, K.: The Nettraveler (aka 'Travnet'). https://kasperskycontenthub.com/wp-content/uploads/sites/43/vlpdfs/kaspersky-the-net-traveler-part1-final.pdf. Accessed Jan 2017
22. Kim, S.J., Lee, S., Bae, B.: Has-analyzer: detecting http-based c&c based on the analysis of http activity sets. TIIS 8(5), 1801–1816 (2014)
23. Lab, K.: The Darkhotel APT, a story of unusual hospitality. https://securelist.com/files/2014/11/darkhotel_kl_07.11.pdf. Accessed Feb 2017
24. Mandiant: APT1 - Exposing One of China's Cyber Espionage Units. https://www.fireeye.com/content/dam/fireeye-www/services/pdfs/mandiant-apt1-report.pdf. Accessed Feb 2017
25. Neasbitt, C., Perdisci, R., Li, K., Nelms, T.: Clickminer: towards forensic reconstruction of user-browser interactions from network traces. In: Proceedings of the ACM CCS 2014, pp. 1244–1255. ACM (2014)
26. Nelms, T., Perdisci, R., Ahamad, M.: Execscent: mining for new c&c domains in live networks with adaptive control protocol templates. In: Proceedings of the USENIX Security Symposium, pp. 589–604. USENIX, Washington, D.C. (2013)
27. Nelms, T., Perdisci, R., Antonakakis, M., Ahamad, M.: Webwitness: investigating, categorizing, and mitigating malware download paths. In: Proceedings of the USENIX Security Symposium, pp. 1025–1040. USENIX (2015)
28. NIST: Managing Information Security Risk. http://nvlpubs.nist.gov/nistpubs/Legacy/SP/nistspecialpublication800-39.pdf, nIST Special Publication 800–39
29. Norman: Operation Hangover. http://enterprise-manage.norman.c.bitbit.net/resources/files/Unveiling_an_Indian_Cyberattack_Infrastructure.pdf. Accessed Feb 2017
30. Oprea, A., Li, Z., Yen, T.F., Chin, S.H., Alrwais, S.: Detection of early-stage enterprise infection by mining large-scale log data. In: Proceedings of the IEEE/IFIP Int. Conf. on Dependable Systems and Networks, DSN 2015, pp. 45–56. IEEE Computer Society (2015)

31. Paxson, V.: Bro: a system for detecting network intruders in real-time. Comput. Netw. **31**(23–24), 2435–2463 (1999)
32. Pedregosa, F., Varoquaux, G., Gramfort, A., Michel, V., Thirion, B., Grisel, O., Blondel, M., Prettenhofer, P., Weiss, R., Dubourg, V., Vanderplas, J., Passos, A., Cournapeau, D., Brucher, M., Perrot, M., Duchesnay, E.: Scikit-learn: machine learning in Python. J. Mach. Learn. Res. **12**, 2825–2830 (2011)
33. Perdisci, R., Ariu, D., Giacinto, G.: Scalable fine-grained behavioral clustering of http-based malware. Comput. Netw. **57**(2), 487–500 (2013)
34. Proofpoint: Nettraveler apt targets russian, european interests. https://www.proofpoint.com/us/threat-insight/post/nettraveler-apt-targets-russian-european-interests. Accessed Jan 2017
35. Security, F.: Looking at the Sky for a DarkComet. https://www.fidelissecurity.com/sites/default/files/FTA_1018_looking_at_the_sky_for_a_dark_comet.pdf. Accessed Feb 2017
36. SeleniumHQ: http://www.seleniumhq.org. Accessed Jan 2017
37. Symantec: Internet security threat report. Technical Report 21, Symantec, April 2016. https://www.symantec.com/security-center/threat-report
38. Tegeler, F., Fu, X., Vigna, G., Kruegel, C.: Botfinder: finding bots in network traffic without deep packet inspection. In: Proceedings of the International Conference on Emerging Networking Experiments and Technologies (CoNEXT), pp. 349–360. ACM (2012)
39. TrendMicro: The Taidoor Campaign. https://www.trendmicro.de/cloud-content/us/pdfs/security-intelligence/white-papers/wp_the_taidoor_campaign.pdf. Accessed Feb 2017
40. Vassio, L., Drago, I., Mellia, M.: Detecting user actions from HTTP traces: toward an automatic approach. In: International Wireless Communications and Mobile Computing Conference (IWCMC), pp. 50–55 (2016)
41. W3C: Referer Policy. https://w3c.github.io/webappsec-referrer-policy. Accessed Feb 2017
42. Xie, G., Iliofotou, M., Karagiannis, T., Faloutsos, M., Jin, Y.: Resurf: reconstructing web-surfing activity from network traffic. In: Proceedings of the International Conference on Networking, IFIP (2013)
43. Zhang, H., Banick, W., Yao, D., Ramakrishnan, N.: User intention-based traffic dependence analysis for anomaly detection. In: IEEE Symposium on Security and Privacy Workshops, pp. 104–112, May 2012

Measuring Network Reputation
in the Ad-Bidding Process

Yizheng Chen[1]([✉]), Yacin Nadji[2], Rosa Romero-Gómez[2], Manos Antonakakis[2],
and David Dagon[1]

[1] School of Computer Science, Georgia Institute of Technology,
Atlanta, Georgia
yzchen@gatech.edu, dagon@sudo.sh
[2] School of Electrical and Computer Engineering, Georgia Institute of Technology,
Atlanta, Georgia
{yacin,rgomez30,manos}@gatech.edu

Abstract. Online advertising is a multi-billion dollar market, and therefore a target for abuse by Internet criminals. Prior work has shown millions of dollars of advertisers' capital are lost due to ad abuse and focused on defense from the perspective of the end-host or the local network egress point. We investigate the potential of using public threat data to measure and detect adware and malicious affiliate traffic from the perspective of demand side platforms, which facilitate ad bidding between ad exchanges and advertisers. Our results show that malicious ad campaigns have statistically significant differences in traffic and lookup patterns from benign ones, however, public blacklists can only label a small percentage of ad publishers (0.27%), which suggests new lists dedicated to ad abuse should be created. Furthermore, we show malicious infrastructure on ad exchanges can be tracked with simple graph analysis and maliciousness heuristics.

1 Introduction

On-line advertisement is a complex ecosystem that enables one of the most prosperous Internet businesses. Naturally, it has become the target of abuse. Only in the last few years are we beginning to grasp the scale of the economic loss for advertisers from ad abuse [10,15,24,28]. Using armies of compromised machines (i.e., botnets), sophisticated affiliate programs, and ad injection techniques, millions of dollars are stolen from advertisers. If we want to reduce abuse on the Internet, we will have to eliminate the monetization opportunities attackers use.

For almost a decade, security researchers and network operators have studied how to detect and stop advertisement abuse. The focus of past research efforts has been on detecting ad abuse at the edge (i.e., the infected host), at the egress point of a network, or "outside" of the ad ecosystem. Little is known, however, about the network policies that are being enforced *within* the ad ecosystem, especially during the ad bidding process. Advertisers do not want to display ads on low quality publishers that may include automated visits from adware

M. Polychronakis and M. Meier (Eds.): DIMVA 2017, LNCS 10327, pp. 388–409, 2017.
DOI: 10.1007/978-3-319-60876-1_18

and affiliate marketing entities, and thus they need to selectively respond to ad bidding requests based on the reputation of the publishers. Unfortunately, little work has been done to measure reputation of publisher domains.

In this paper, we examine if open source intelligence data from the security community can be used to ascertain publisher reputation. To this end, we analyze anonymized ad bidding requests between a large demand side platform (DSP) in North America and six ad exchanges over a period of three months. Using open source intelligence from public blacklists and malware execution traces, we investigate the reputation properties of publishers in the *advertisement bidding process* (Sect. 5). Our study makes the following key observations:

- We explain the ad bidding process and measure it in detail to improve the network and security communities' understanding of the advertising ecosystem. These measurements include bidding request traffic from six large ad exchanges for request volume, publisher domains, and client distribution. We find that malicious publisher domains tend to be present on more ad exchanges and reach more clients than non-blacklisted publisher domains on average. These differences are statistically significant and suggest that reputation systems for advertisement publishers are possible.
- We identify that of all publisher domains seen in the DSP, 13,324 (0.27%) are on blacklists, which generate only 1.8% of bid requests, and 134,262 (2.74%) are queried by malware. This underestimates the amount of ad abuse based on other studies [14,16], which has been measured as high as 30%. This also indicates that traditional sources of maliciousness used in the security community are insufficient to understand ad abuse seen from DSPs.
- Using graph analysis, we demonstrate how to track advertising infrastructure over time. To focus on potentially malicious campaigns, we use a simple suspiciousness heuristic based on open-source intelligence feeds. Using this technique, we identify case studies that show ad network domains support Potentially Unwanted Programs (PUP), rely on domain name generation algorithms, and are occasionally used to distribute malware.

2   Background

In this section, we briefly describe the key components of the ad ecosystem and the real-time bidding process.

2.1   Ad Ecosystem

Figure 1 gives an overview of the online advertising ecosystem. When a user visits a publisher webpage (step 1, Fig. 1) its elements are loaded (step 2), during which the iFrame representing the *ad inventory* requests the ad server for an ad to display (step 3). The ad server asks for an ad from the ad network (step 4), and reports ad metrics for payment logging. An ad network can also sell ad inventories to an ad exchange (step 5). If an ad request cannot be fulfilled, it will be relayed to a Demand Side Platform provider (DSP) (step 6), and then advertisers who work with the DSP can purchase the impression (scenario A). The advantage of using a DSP is that advertisers will have access to multiple ad exchanges. In this paper, we focus on the vantage point of a DSP (scenario A).

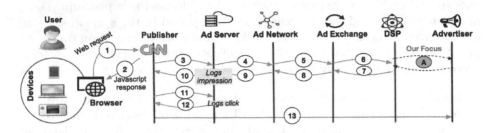

Fig. 1. An overview of the online advertising ecosystem.

The DSP, ad exchanges, and ad networks consolidate advertisers' audience target and budget information, and show the optimal ad back to the publisher's page (step 7 to 10). An impression is therefore fulfilled and logged. Impressions are often charged according to the CPM (Cost Per Mille, or cost per thousand impression). If the ad is clicked, the ad server will log it (step 11), and redirect the user (step 12) to the page of the advertiser (step 13). In such an event, the advertiser is charged for the click. The CPC (Cost Per Click) varies according to the keywords of the webpage and the user category.

Publishers can resell (*syndicate*) the ads to other publishers. In turn, these publishers can sell (*subsyndicate*) the ads further to other publishers. Syndication enables the ads to reach a wider audience. Thus, there can be several redirections among publishers before an ad request reaches the ad server (step 3).

2.2 Real-Time Bidding

Figure 2 shows a simplified view of the Real-Time Bidding (RTB) process. The JavaScript from the publisher page requests an ad through a *bid request*. In a request, the publisher includes information such as category of the page, size of the ad space, country, user's browser and OS version, cookie, etc., and sends it to the ad exchange (step 1).

Once the ad exchange receives the bid request from a seller, it then consolidates the request into seller site information (e.g., URL of the publisher page), device information, and user data. The ad exchange sends the bid request to its buyer applications (step 2), for instance, through a DSP.

After receiving the bid request, the buyer replies with a bid response containing the ad URL and the markup price (step 3). The RTB protocol typically waits for a fixed amount of time (e.g., 100 ms) to collect bids, and then chooses the winning bid under the auction's rules (e.g., OpenRTB [27]). The ad exchange then notifies the winner and returns the ad to the publisher (step 4).

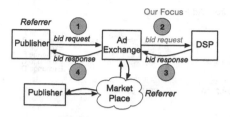

Fig. 2. A simplified view of the Real-Time Bidding process.

Table 1. Summary of all datasets.

	Date range	Size
DSP traffic	12/10/14–3/24/15	2.61 T
Blacklists	12/9/09–1/15/16	22 G
Malware	1/1/11–11/17/15	136 G
DNS	12/10/14–3/24/15	1.54 T

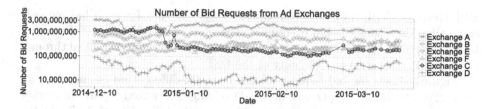

Fig. 3. Number of daily bid requests from ad exchanges seen in the DSP.

In the aforementioned example, the bid request comes from the publisher directly. Therefore, the publisher page is the *referrer* for the bid request. Very often, the bid request comes from the market place, where the original request was purchased and resold by many intermediaries. In that case, the *referrer* is the last entity that sold the ad inventory to the ad exchange. Ad exchanges do not have visibility of the user-side publisher if the request comes from the market place. This is one of the challenges for ad exchanges to detect and stop fraud.

3   Datasets

In this section, we describe the datasets we obtained including Demand Side Platform provider (DSP) traffic, public blacklist data, and malware domain data. Table 1 provides a brief summary of the datasets.

3.1   DSP Traffic

The DSP provides ad bidding logs extracted from step 3 of Fig. 2. The traffic is aggregated into eight fields per hour every day: the **ad exchange** that issued the bid request, the **publisher domain name** of the referrer URL, the **hashed IP address** of the user, the **country code** and **autonomous system number** of the IP address, the hourly **timestamp** of when the bid request was sent, and lastly the **number of bid requests** seen within the specific hour that match all the previous fields. Within the fields, the **publisher domain name** represents either the webpage that users saw, or the last traffic reseller before the bid request reached the ad exchange. Next, we describe DSP traffic using the volume of bid requests and publisher domain names.

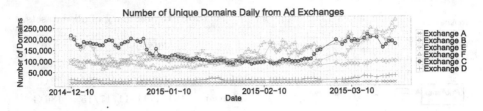

Fig. 4. Number of daily publisher domains from ad exchanges seen in the DSP.

Bid Request Volume. It is reasonable to assume that for each bid request, some advertiser wins the bid eventually. Therefore, the bid request volume can be considered to be the number of ad inventories purchased and shuffled through the ad exchanges from the visibility of the DSP.

Figure 3 shows the bid request volume from six different ad exchanges from 12/10/2014 to 3/24/2015. One of these ad exchanges is ranked top five in market share. On average, there are 3.45 billion bid requests daily in total. Individually, Exchange A processed the most bid requests of all, with an average of 1.77 billion requests per day. Exchange B comes next, with an average of 695 million requests per day. In addition, Exchange E, Exchange F, and Exchange C received bid requests on the order of hundreds of millions. Finally, Exchange D had an average of 30 million bid requests daily, which fluctuated the most compared to other ad exchanges.

Comparing the volume of the last day from the DSP traffic (3/24/2015) with that of the first day (12/10/2014), there is a decline in the overall bid request volume from Exchange A (63.2%), Exchange B (34.3%), Exchange C (83.2%), and Exchange D (31.2%). However, the volume increased for Exchange E (18.34%) and Exchange F (64.26%). Our DSP confirmed that this was not a traffic collection problem but could not identify the root cause of these changes.

Publisher Domains. The publisher domain field in the DSP traffic indicates the source of an ad request. It is either the publisher website where the ad will be shown, or the reseller domain redirected from some previous publisher.

An average of 391,430 total publisher domains were seen from all ad exchanges every day. Figure 4 shows the number of unique publisher domains from each ad exchange. Although Exchange A had the highest number of bid requests (Fig. 3), it represented the lowest number of unique domains (average: 955) per day. It is likely that many of them are traffic resellers. For instance, `coxdigitalsolutions.com` is a subsidiary of Cox specializing in buying and selling digital media. It is the most popular publisher domain in Exchange A, generating more than 20% of all bid requests. The small set of publisher domains of Exchange A is quite stable. There were no new publishers in 39 days out of three months, and an average of 91 new publisher domains on the other days. Exchange D has the fewest bid requests and also had very few publisher domains, an average of 14,732 every day. If an ad exchange works with few publishers, it is easier to provision them and block malicious traffic. On the other hand, it is harder to know the source of ad inventories from reseller publishers, meaning detection may need to happen at the reseller's perspective.

Two ad exchanges saw the largest number of new publisher domains. Exchange E had an average of 22,647 new publisher domains, while Exchange F had an average of 23,405 new publisher domains daily. Towards the end of March 2015 in Fig. 4, there were as many as 35,794 new domains from Exchange E and 56,151 new domains from Exchange F. Both ad exchanges also increased the volume of bid requests during the same time period in Fig. 3. The churn rates of the publisher domain names in these two ad exchanges were quite high. This presents a challenge for ad exchanges to track the reputation of new publishers.

Lastly, Exchange B had a stable number of publisher domains every day, on the order of 100,000. There was a decrease in the number of daily publisher domains seen from Exchange C around the end of 2014, and then the number increased again, reaching the 150,000 mark towards the end of March 2015.

3.2   Other Datasets

In order to measure reputation in the DSP bid request traffic, we also obtained other datasets that provide threat information, which includes public blacklists and dynamic malware execution traffic. Both provide insight into known abuse in the ad exchanges. We crawled seven public blacklists [2–5,7,8,39] daily from 12/9/2009 to 1/15/2016. In total, 1.92 million unique domains appeared on the public blacklists. Dynamic malware execution feeds are from one university [20] and two industry partners. The binaries were each executed for five minutes in a controlled environment. We extracted date, malware md5, and the domain names queried during the execution of the binaries. The feeds are collected from 1/1/2011 to 11/17/2015. There are 77.29 million unique malware md5s, querying a total of 14.3 million domain names. We use PBL to denote the public blacklists dataset and $Md5$ to denote the malware domains dataset.

Lastly, we collected DNS resolution data every day from a passive DNS repository in North America between 12/10/2014 to 3/24/2015. The dataset contains domain name, query type, and resolved data every day for A, NS, CNAME, and AAAA query types. We observed a daily average of 891 million unique mappings between domain names. On average, the DNS resolution dataset matches 71.56% of all publisher domain names seen in the DSP in the same day. Among the 28.55% publisher domains from DSP not seen in passive DNS, the majority of them are long tail content sites. For example, unpopular blog sites, user's own fantasy sport pages, customized lists pages, etc. Long tail content can be specific to certain users' interests and not commonly accessed across different networks. In full disclosure, this is perhaps the only not fully open source intelligence source we used in our experiments. However, commercial passive DNS offerings are very simple to obtain today [6]. We will use the resolution information to construct infrastructure graphs and track them over time in Sect. 6.

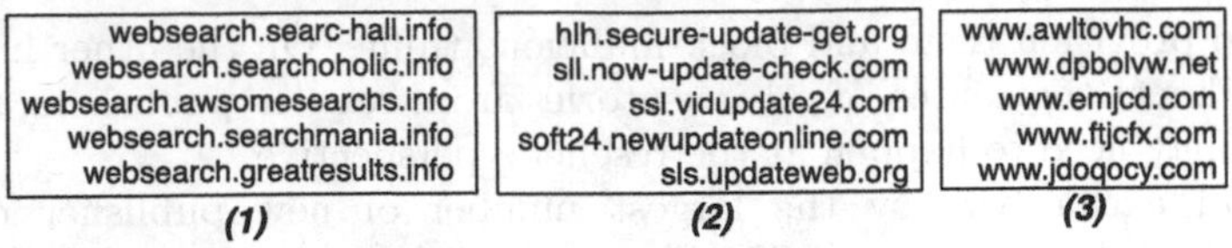

websearch.searc-hall.info	hlh.secure-update-get.org	www.awltovhc.com
websearch.searchoholic.info	sll.now-update-check.com	www.dpbolvw.net
websearch.awsomesearchs.info	ssl.vidupdate24.com	www.emjcd.com
websearch.searchmania.info	soft24.newupdateonline.com	www.ftjcfx.com
websearch.greatresults.info	sls.updateweb.org	www.jdoqocy.com
(1)	*(2)*	*(3)*

Fig. 5. Examples of blacklisted publisher domains seen in the DSP traffic.

4   Fraudulent Publisher Domains

In this section we provide examples of blacklisted publisher domains that generated ad bidding requests through the ad exchanges. These domains are from adware and affiliate marketing programs.

4.1   Case 1: PUP

Blacklisted publisher domains can be generated by Potentially Unwanted Programs (PUP) such as browser hijacker and pop-up ads.

Figure 5(1) shows domain names of pattern websearch.*.info that are used by browser hijackers [22]. The adware forces the user to use a different search engine to steal impressions that would have otherwise been delivered through typical search engines (e.g., Google, Bing, Yahoo, etc.). The adware hijacks user search queries and makes ad bidding requests from these publisher domains to generate revenue.

Figure 5(2) shows "update" domains used by pop-up ads. The adware shows pop-up ads that masquerade as fake updaters for legitimate software, such as Windows, Flash, and video players [23]. These publisher domains make ad bidding requests from pop-up windows generated by the adware.

4.2   Case 2: Affiliate Marketing

Blacklisted publisher domains may represent affiliate marketing domains. These affiliate domains request ads through ad exchanges on behalf of adware or malware. We manually analyzed network traces from dynamic execution of malware md5s that contained domains in Fig. 5(3). The malware uses fake referrers to send HTTP GET requests through domains in Fig. 5(3). Then the requests go through a chain of redirections until finally receiving an ad to generate revenue.

5   Measurement

We first discuss client IP location distribution in DSP traffic in Sect. 5.2. Then, we perform reputation analysis of publisher domains by correlating them with blacklists and malware domains in Sect. 5.3.

Fig. 6. Distributions of client IP address locations.

5.1 Summary of Findings

In summary, we found that:

- There are 13,324 (0.27%) known malicious domains generating bid request traffic through the ad exchanges in our datasets. On average, they generate 1.8% of overall bid requests daily, much less than previously published values [14,16]. However, 68.28% of blacklisted domains were identified by public blacklists before they appeared in DSP traffic. This suggests traditional sources of maliciousness are valuable, but insufficient to understand ad-abuse from the perspective of DSPs.
- On average, blacklisted publisher domains tend to use more ad exchanges (average: 1.85) and reach more clients (average: 5109.47) compared to non-blacklisted domains (average ad exchanges: 1.43, average hashed client IP addresses: 568.78) (Sect. 5.3). This suggests reputation systems for ad publishers are possible.
- Contrary to the observation of blacklisted publisher domains, malware domains use a similar number of ad exchanges (average: 1.44), but are seen from more hashed client IP addresses (average: 2310.75), compared to publisher domains never queried by malware (average ad exchanges: 1.43, average hashed client IP addresses: 485.36) (Sect. 5.3).

5.2 Client Analysis

We observed 436 million hashed client IPs that sent bid requests for ads. According to information provided by the DSP, the hashed client IP addresses are from 37,865 different Autonomous Systems in 234 different countries.

Table 2a shows the top six countries where hashed client IP addresses reside. Nearly 40% of clients are located in the United States. Next, it is the United Kingdom with 8% of hashed IP addresses. The top six countries also include Germany (7.11%), Canada (4.82%), France (3.90%), and Mexico (2.98%). There is a long tail of 228 other countries for the remaining clients. Overall the top six countries account for 66.75% of all the hashed client IP addresses seen in DSP. Figure 6 shows the country distribution of hashed client IP address locations.

Table 2. a: The top six countries for 66.75% of hashed client IP addresses. b: The top six Autonomous System Names for 17.66% of hashed client IP addresses.

Country	Hashed IPs millions	AS Names	Hashed IPs millions
US	174 (39.91%)	Comcast	18 (4.13%)
GB	35 (8.03%)	AT&T	17 (3.90%)
DE	31 (7.11%)	Deutsche Telekom	14 (3.21%)
CA	21 (4.82%)	MCI	12 (2.75%)
FR	17 (3.90%)	Verizon	9 (2.06%)
MX	13 (2.98%)	Uninet	7 (1.61%)
Other	103 (23.62%)	Other	359 (82.34%)
Unknown	42 (9.63%)	Unknown	42 (9.63%)
Total	**436 (100.00%)**	**Total**	**436 (100.00%)**
(a) Client Location		(b) AS Name	

Table 2b presents the top six Autonomous System Names (ASNs) for hashed client IP addresses. The ASN distribution is less biased compared to the country distribution. Comcast, AT&T, and Deutsche Telekom are the top three ASNs, each with under 5% of all hashed IP addresses. There are 37,859 different ASNs in the long tail of the distribution, which contains 82.34% of all hashed IPs.

5.3   Reputation Analysis

In this section, we explain how we intersect publisher domains from DSP traffic with blacklists and malware domains to perform reputation analysis.

Public Blacklist Traffic. Since 89.87% of the domains on the blacklists we collected do not have semantic information, we filter them to ensure they are bad publishers with high confidence. We want to be conservative about what we keep, so we choose the following filters. First, we obtained all the domains that appeared on the Alexa [11] top one million list for every day from 12/10/2014 to 3/24/2015. We excluded those consistent Alexa domains because they are unlikely to be malicious. Second, we excluded all domains under the ad server category of EasyList [1], because malware conducting impression fraud or click fraud can generate traffic that goes through ad servers. Lastly, we excluded a hand curated a whitelist of CDN effective second level domains (e2lds) and we excluded all fully qualified domain names that overlapped with these e2lds.

Observation 1: **0.27% publisher domains appeared in DSP traffic were blacklisted by the security community. They generated 1.8% of all bid requests daily**

   We observed 4,905,224 unique domains in the DSP traffic from 12/10/2014 to 3/24/2014. Among them, 13,324 (0.27%) domains were blacklisted some time between 12/9/2009 and 1/15/2016. Blacklisted domains were responsible for an

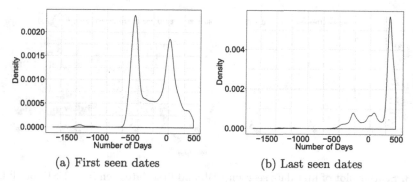

(a) First seen dates   (b) Last seen dates

Fig. 7. Density plot of first seen date date on PBL - first date seen from DSP (7a) and last seen date on PBL - last date seen from DSP (7b).

average of 1.8% of all bid requests every day. Previous studies estimate nearly 30% of bid requests are malicious [14,16], which suggests this is only a fraction of the actual abuse. While there are many potential causes, such as referrer spoofing or lack of ad-abuse investigations, these findings show simply relying on blacklists from the security community is insufficient to study and combat abuse. While they are few, we investigated the potential to automatically detect these abusive domains.

Observation 2: **68.28% of blacklisted publisher domains were known to the security community before they appeared in DSP traffic**

Figure 7a shows the density distribution for the difference of days between when a domain was first blacklisted and when it was seen in DSP traffic. The zero value in this case means that the domain name was blacklisted on the same day as it was seen in the ad exchanges. Similarly, a value of −500 means that the domain was blacklisted 500 days before it ever appeared in the datasets from the DSP. The plot shows that 68.28% (9,097) of all blacklist domains were known to the security community prior to they started requesting for ads in the DSP traffic. Moreover, 32.49% (4,329) of blacklisted publisher domains were labeled more than 535 days before they were seen in the DSP datasets. The peaks of the distribution reflects several blacklists update events. One event was a major update of 4,031 domains on 6/23/2013, which corresponds to the −535 days in Fig. 7a. Another update event on 12/4/2014 was reflected around −6 days in the plot. Eighty domains were blacklisted on 1/15/2011, which makes up the small bump around −1500 days in the plot.

Figure 8 is a scatter plot of the first date a domain is blacklisted (x-axis) and its corresponding first seen date in the DSP (y-axis). The size of the point represents the number of domains in these dates. The points in the bottom side of the plot are large because this is the first date we had the DSP data. The vertical group of points represent domains being updated in the blacklist in the same day. We highlighted a few days when blacklisted domains from the DSP traffic were first labeled. The plot is more dense on the right side since 2013-06-23. We

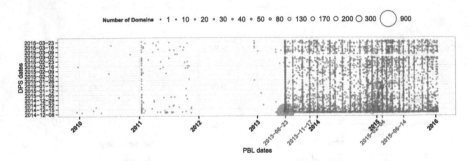

Fig. 8. Scatter plot of first date seen on PBL and first date seen from DSP for all DSP domains that were on PBL.

increased the number of blacklists to crawl from 3 to 7 on that day, which resulted in more domain names in PBL dataset and more overlap with the DSP traffic from that point on. On 2013-11-17, the blacklists updated many domain names including websearch.*.info used by browser hijackers. On 2015-02-04, there were a lot of "update" domains used by pop-up ads added to the blacklists, e.g., soft12.onlineupdatenow.com. On 2015-06-14, the blacklists updated a group of algorithmically generated domains with sub domains freempr#.

Observation 3: **Most (77.01%) blacklisted publisher domains remained on blacklists after they were last seen in DSP traffic**

We would like to see whether the publisher domains remained on the blacklists after they were seen in the DSP. We plotted the density distribution for the number of days when a domain was last seen on blacklists minus when it last appeared in the DSP (Fig. 7b). The distribution has shifted a lot towards the right part of the x-axis this time. Figure 7b shows that the majority (77.01%) of blacklisted domains were still on blacklists after they were seen in the DSP. A total of 14.06% (1,873) of them remained on blacklists more than a year after they were last seen in the DSP datasets. The peak of Fig. 7b reflects the last date (1/15/2016) of our blacklist dataset. Overall 8,051 DSP domains belong to this peak in the plot.

Observation 4: **Blacklisted publisher domains tend to use more ad exchanges and reach more hashed client IP addresses than those that have never been blacklisted**

Each day, we separate the publisher domains into two groups: those that were seen in PBL (True) and not in PBL (False). For each group, we compute the average number of distinct ad exchanges and the number of hashed client IPs that a publisher domain was seen from, as well as the variance within the group. We visualize the results in Fig. 9a–d.

Figure 9a shows the density distributions of the daily average number of ad exchanges for the PBL group and non-PBL group across the entire DSP dataset. The PBL group were seen from an average of 1.7 to 2 ad exchanges, more than the non-PBL group. We perform a two-sample Kolmogorov-Smirnov

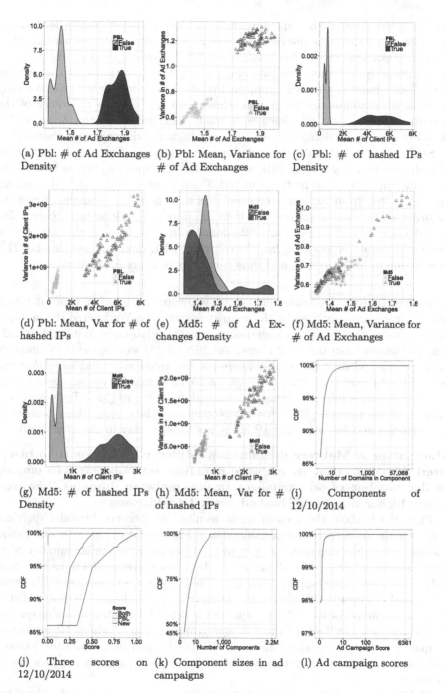

(a) Pbl: # of Ad Exchanges Density

(b) Pbl: Mean, Variance for # of Ad Exchanges

(c) Pbl: # of hashed IPs Density

(d) Pbl: Mean, Var for # of hashed IPs

(e) Md5: # of Ad Exchanges Density

(f) Md5: Mean, Variance for # of Ad Exchanges

(g) Md5: # of hashed IPs Density

(h) Md5: Mean, Var for # of hashed IPs

(i) Components of 12/10/2014

(j) Three scores on 12/10/2014

(k) Component sizes in ad campaigns

(l) Ad campaign scores

Fig. 9. 9a to 9d are PBL plots. 9e to 9h are Md5 plots. 9i to 9l are CDFs for number of publisher domains forming components of 12/10/2014 (9i), three scores for components seen on 12/10/2014 (9j), number of components in ad campaigns (9k) and ad campaign scores (9l).

test (K-S test) where the null hypothesis is that x=y, i.e., that the datasets are drawn from the same distribution. The K-S test demonstrates we can reject this null hypothesis ($p - value < 2.22 * 10^{-16}$). Therefore, the two distributions are significantly different. We also plot the mean and variance of the average ad exchange number for each group in Fig. 9b. The figure shows that not only do non-PBL domains use fewer ad exchanges in general, the difference of the measure between non-PBL domains is small, as reflected by the variance. On the other hand, PBL domains have relatively higher variance among themselves.

Similarly, we plot the density distribution for number of average hashed client IP addresses in a day for the PBL and non-PBL groups (Fig. 9c), as well as the mean and variance of the metric (Fig. 9d). These figures show that PBL domains tend to be seen from more hashed client IPs than non-PBL domains. Since the majority of the content on the web is in the unpopular "long tail", only a few hashed client IPs visit any non-PBL domain in general, and the variance of number of clients is low (Fig. 9d). In contrast, PBL domains seen in the RTB process aim to make money, and thus spread to as many hosts as possible.

Malware Traffic. Domains queried by malware are another type of threat information commonly used by the security community. We filtered the malware domains using the same three methods as in the PBL case. Within 4,905,224 unique domains from the DSP traffic, 134,262(2.74%) were queried by malware samples collected over five years. *There are ten times more publisher domains queried by malware than from those on blacklists.* Similarly, we can separate the publisher domains into two groups: malware domain group (Md5 True) and non-malware domain group (Md5 False). We computed the average daily number of ad exchanges and hashed client IP addresses for each day in the DSP traffic.

Observation 5: **Malware domains have different behavior than blacklisted domains. That is, malware domains were observed to employ similar number of ad exchanges to non-malware domains, however, with a higher number of hashed client IP addresses**

Figure 9e–h show the measurement results. We observe bimodal distributions of malware vs. non-malware domains in Fig. 9e and g. Figure 9e and f show that publisher domains queried by malware tend to use a similar number of ad exchanges. In addition, the distributions between malware domains and non-malware domains overlapped much more than when we compared PBL group with non-PBL group. Therefore, the number of ad exchanges is not a distinguishing attribute for the MD5 group. On the other hand, DSP domains queried by malware were still seen from a larger group of hashed client IP addresses, compared to the rest of domains never queried by malware. Malware domains that interact with ad ecosystem are relatively more popular than non-malware domains.

Malware query non-malicious domains for various reasons, and only a few of the domains are fraudulent publishers. Recall that when malware interacts with the ad ecosystem from the client side (Fig. 1), there may be syndicated publishers, or benign ad servers contacted by the malware, in order to reach ad exchanges. Despite our filtering efforts, it is likely that there are still numerous benign domains in the malware domain set. Additionally, domains could remain on blacklists after they become inactive or parked, which results in false positives when using blacklists. These findings all point to the need for better ad-abuse ground truth datasets.

6   Infrastructure Tracking

In this section, we show that traditional DNS infrastructure features can be used to extend the ground truth set, discover new ad abuse cases and track the threat evolution over time. This can be used by any entity in the ad ecosystem with visibility of bidding requests to track advertising campaign infrastructure—focusing on those that are likely to be malicious in intent. While we acknowledge that the word "campaign" has an overloaded meaning, we define it in the following way and only in the context of ad abuse: *a campaign will be defined as the set of domain names that can be linked together over time based on their IP infrastructure properties.*

At a high level, we construct graphs of the relationship between the domain name of the ad publisher and the infrastructure the domain name uses. By building and merging these graphs over time, we can track the infrastructure and focus on those campaigns that may be malicious, e.g., domains known to have been blacklisted, queried by malware, or have never been seen before. We present case studies based on this process in Sect. 7.

6.1   Constructing Infrastructure Graphs

An *infrastructure graph* is an undirected graph G, defined by its set of vertices V and edges E. A *disconnected* graph is made up of multiple *components* or subgraphs with no adjacent edges between them. These components correspond to advertising campaigns that are tracked over time. Vertices in infrastructure graphs are domain names or the RDATA the domain names resolve to. RDATA can be an IPv4/IPv6 address (A/AAAA), a canonical name (CNAME), or a nameserver (NS). Two vertices are adjacent if and only if exactly one is a domain name, and the domain name resolved to the RDATA of one of the aforementioned query types (A/AAAA/CNAME/NS) during time t when the domain name appeared as a publisher for a bid request.

A Demand Side Platform provider (DSP) can build infrastructure graphs by performing the following steps. First, the DSP collects all publisher domain names D_p from the bid requests seen on day t. Second, the DSP resolves all domain names $d \in D_p$, which results in zero or more domain name and IP address tuples. More formally, resolving d will yield $[(d, rdata_0), \cdots, (d, rdata_N)]$ if d resolves to N different IPs, CNAMEs, or NSes on day t. Each of these tuples corresponds to an edge in our graph G. Finally, after G is built for day t, G is decomposed into its *connected components* C, where each component $c \in C$ is ranked and tracked over time as a specific ad campaign. While we experimented

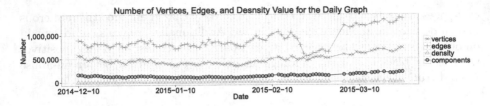

Fig. 10. Number of vertices, edges and density values for the graph every day.

with more sophisticated community discovery or spectral methods, the benefits gained were disproportional to the add-on complexity. Thus, we decided to select the simplest and most straightforward way to mine the graph for campaigns.

Since the DSP bidding request traffic did not include DNS resolution information, we chose to correlate that with the DNS dataset obtained from a passive DNS database from a North American ISP (Table 1). By combining the DNS resolution seen in the same day in the ISP with the publisher domains from the bidding request traffic, we were able to construct daily infrastructure graphs. Next, we discuss how we analyze the produced graphs.

Graph Analysis. We study the infrastructure graphs using some basic graph analysis metrics. Specifically, we first analyze overall graph properties including vertices, edges and density measures. Then, we examine the connected components of the graphs every day and over time. These analytics help us understand the infrastructure of the publisher domains, and give us insights about how to rank components based on how suspicious they are and track them over time.

First, we discuss three properties of daily infrastructure graphs. Figure 10 shows three statistics for graphs generated every day: number of vertices (V), number of edges (E), and the density measure. We use the following formula to compute the *graph density D*:

$$D = \frac{2E}{V(V-1)} \tag{1}$$

On average, there are 472 thousand vertices, and 883 thousand edges every day. The graphs are extremely sparse and the daily density is only $8.35 * 10^{-6}$. In fact, the majority of the edges only connect two vertices. There are 566,744 vertices on 12/10/2014, and it dropped to 342,426 (by 39.58%) on 1/29/2015. Then the number of vertices slowly increased to 727,501 on 3/24/2015. Since vertices include publisher domains and DNS resolution data, the change in the number of vertices over time is largely consistent with the observation of how the number of daily publisher domains changed (Fig. 4). On the other hand, the change in the number of edges per day is different. The number of daily edges decreased since 2/17/2015, and dropped to the lowest number 542,945 on 2/21/2015, before it jumped up to 1,203,202 on 3/5/2015. Through manual analysis, we concluded that this was not caused by any single domain name. There were fewer resolved data per domain in general in these days.

Second, we study properties of connected components in the infrastructure graphs. Figure 10 shows the number of connected components over time that were in the daily infrastructure graphs. On average, there are 127,513 connected components in a day. Figure 9i demonstrates that the daily infrastructure graph is highly disconnected. The cumulative distribution for the size of the components in a day follows the Zipf's law. For instance, CDF in 12/10/2010 shows that 86% of connected components have only one publisher domain in it. Fewer than 0.7% components have more than ten publisher domains.

6.2 Identifying Suspicious Components

The number of graph components based on the results from Sect. 6.1 can be hundreds of thousands in a day (Fig. 10), which is likely too many for manual analysis. However, the measurement from Sect. 5 suggests we can prioritize components that are likely to be interesting from a security perspective. We know publisher domain names differ in behavior when they are known to appear on blacklists. Conversely the subset of malware domains seen in DSP are very noisy, and thus it is not a good metric to use for prioritizing components. We also hypothesize that never-before-seen domains deserve close scrutiny as they may represent infrastructure changing to avoid detection. The question remains if these are indicative of true malicious behavior. To find out, we rank publisher components by their domain names, specifically, if they are on blacklists, if the domains have never been seen before and a combination of these two measures.

For each publisher component $c \in C$ we compute two values β_c and ν_c that correspond to the proportion of domains in c that appear on blacklists, and are under brand new from the perspective of the DSP, respectively. Intuitively, the first one indicates an association with known malicious activity, and the last suggests the potential threat may have just begun. Specifically, the way we compute each value of a component is smoothed.

$$\beta_c = \frac{\# \ of \ blacklisted \ publisher \ domains - 1}{Total \ \# \ of \ publisher \ domains} \tag{2}$$

$$\nu_c = \frac{\# \ of \ brand \ new \ publisher \ domains - 1}{Total \ \# \ of \ publisher \ domains} \tag{3}$$

We offset the numerator count by one based on results of the infrastructure graph analysis from Sect. 6.1. Since the majority of components have only one publisher domain name in it, they are isolated singletons and do not provide any information to other unlabeled domains from infrastructure point of view. We prefer not to prioritize these singletons among all components even if they are already blacklisted or brand new. Equations 2 and 3 give singleton components both zero values. Moreover, we judge whether a domain name is "brand new" using the effective second-level domains (e2ld) according to public suffix list [9]. An e2ld is the smallest registrable unit of a domain name and two domains under an e2ld are likely operated by the same individual. Therefore, a new domain under a new e2ld is more interesting to us.

After getting these two values β_c and ν_c, we also compute the linear combination of these: $\iota_c = \frac{1}{2}(\beta_c + \nu_c)$. Finally, we reversely sort the components in a day based on the ι_c score. Within a day, ι_c can range between 0 and 1. A component with higher ι_c will be prioritized over a component with lower ι_c for inspection. Figure 9j presents cumulative distributions of the proportion of pbl-related, never-before-seen domains and a linear combination of the two for a day per component. A total of 98% of the components have zero PBL score because they do not have any blacklisted domains, and 14% of the components have a score for having new domains. The final component score combining the two falls in between the two distributions.

6.3   Tracking Campaigns over Time

Building infrastructure graphs for an individual day is useful, but tracking the ad campaigns over time will yield more comprehensive coverage of ad campaigns, as well as advanced warning of potentially malicious ones. First, if an ad campaign is determined to be malicious, tracking them over time through small infrastructure changes will enable more comprehensive blacklists to be built. Second, if a tracked ad campaign is known to be malicious, newly added infrastructure can be more pro-actively blacklisted. Finally, tracking infrastructure over time allows us to build ground truth to eventually model malicious and benign advertising campaign infrastructure. In our future work we plan to experiment with predicting fraudulent publishers.

To unify ad campaigns across multiple infrastructure graphs, we simply join ad campaigns that share IP addresses, canonical names, and name servers that are the same. This allows us to not only construct graphs within days, but also across time. We will show that this simple tracking method works well in practice. While on average there are 127 K connected components every day, only 10 K of them form new ad campaigns. A DSP can choose to only go through top-ranked new components if there is limited time available for threat analysts.

ι_{ad} is used to sort advertising campaigns to identify case studies. It is calculated by adding up all the interesting scores of individual components ι_c belonging to that campaign. After we sort the ad campaigns by ι_c, we then examine the distribution of the interesting scores and number of components in the campaigns. Figure 9l shows the cumulative distribution of ad campaign scores. Also, Fig. 9k shows the CDF of the number of components in an ad campaign. Overall 99.99% ad campaigns have fewer than 1,000 components. The ad campaign with the largest number of components (2.2 million in Fig. 9k) has the highest ad campaign score. Domains in this campaign resolved to several parking, and sinkholing IP addresses, as well as common names servers like GoDaddy. This is the reason that this noisy campaign is not representative of maliciousness or freshness of the domains. Starting from the second ad campaign, the interesting score indicate suspicious activities in the ad exchanges. We now describe the case studies this measure uncovers in Sect. 7.

7   Case Studies

Among the campaigns with highest (top 0.1%) interesting scores, we found new cases including Potentially Unwanted Programs (PUP), algorithm generated domains and malware sites.

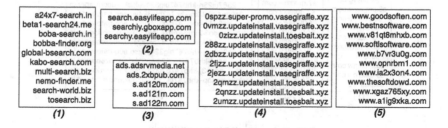

Fig. 11. Publisher domain examples.

7.1   Case 1: PUP

Among advertising campaigns with the highest interesting scores, one category of publisher domains are generated by Potentially Unwanted Programs (PUP). For example, domains in Fig. 11(1)–(5).

A VirusTotal report [35] suggests a machine communicating with domain names in Fig. 11(1) (ι_{ad} ranked the 3rd highest) is likely infected with a trojan known as LEMIR or Win32.BKClient by the AV industry. The malware has many capabilities including changing default search engines to generate revenue, disabling Windows AV, Firewall and Security Center notifications, and can drop additional malicious binaries [33]. Similarly, ad campaigns with 2nd and 4th highest ι_{ad} (Fig. 11(2) and (3)) are generated by ad injections of certain browser extension. Different malware families communicate with domains in Fig. 11(3) including Win.Trojan.Symmi [36]. These publisher domains may not be malicious, but they are strongly associated with monetization behavior of malware. These are interesting cases as traditional malware are involved in an area where we would expect to see only adware or "potentially unwanted programs." This shows that malware uses advertising fraud to monetize infections and malware can also be identified from the vantage point of a DSP.

In addition, several Pop-up Ads campaigns exhibit high level of agility similar to traditional malware. The ad campaign ranked $1,184^{th}$ (Fig. 11(4)) uses domain fluxing, likely to avoid browser extension detection systems. In total, we observed more than 26,000 unique domain names from this campaign in three months of DSP traffic. Moreover, the ad campaign in Fig. 11(5) not only uses domain fluxing, it also uses the Amazon EC2 cloud to further decrease the chance of detection. Each of these domains resolved into an EC2 cloud domain representing a unique Virtual Machine (VM), when active. The VM domains also change according to the domains that point to them. This shows that miscreants are constantly employing fresh VMs to perform ad fraud. Since traditional detection systems often use reputation of IP addresses of domains and URLs, using cloud machines makes this campaign harder to be detected.

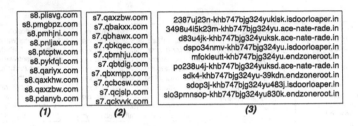

Fig. 12. Malware site example.

7.2 Case 2: Algorithm Generated Domains

Figure 12(1) and (2) shows two ad campaigns of algorithm generated domains we found in the DSP traffic (ranked 142th and 183th), containing at least 195 domains. None of the domains were blacklisted, but a high percentage of brand new domains results in a high score. A new group of domains appear everyday, pointing to the same IP address. These publisher domains are suspicious. Although no open threat analysis evidence is available to date, it is reasonable to assume that anything that changes so often must be trying to evade a detection process. With infrastructure tracking, ad exchanges or DSP can keep a close eye on such campaigns to proactively deal with potential ad abuse.

7.3 Case 3: Malware Site

Figure 12(3) shows a group of malware site domains (ranked $1,484^{th}$ campaign) seen from DSP traffic, none of which appeared on blacklists. A Virustotal report [37] shows that the IP address these domains resolved to, had other similar domains pointing to it during the week ending on 3/24/2015. Related URLs were detected as malware sites by several URL scanners from the AV industry. This group uses domain fluxing with both the second level domain zone, and the child labels. We saw other groups of domains tracked separately, with similar domain name patterns, and short lifetime. However, they were not grouped into one big campaign, because different groups were using different IP addresses. In other words, this campaign uses both domain fluxing and IP address fluxing. Since we only used exact the same IP address match to form a campaign, we will need other information to further analyze campaigns like this.

8 Related Work

Previous research has studied behavior of click bots [17,18,26]. The bots mimic human behavior by generating fake search queries and adding jitters to click delay. More advanced bots hijacked users' original clicks and replaced the ads [12, 18,28?]. The ZeroAccess botnet cost advertisers $100,000 per day [28] and the TDSS/TDL4 botnet cost advertisers at least $346 million in total. Ad fraud detection work mainly focused on click fraud [19,25,32].

Impression fraud is harder to detect than click fraud. Springborn et al. [29] studied pay-per-view networks that generated fraudulent impressions from invisible iFrames and caused advertisers millions of dollars lost. Advertisers can purchase *bluff ads* to measure ad abuse [18] and compare charged impressions with valid impressions. The adware and ad injection problem has been systematically studied by static and dynamic analysis of web browser extensions [21,31,38]. From within the ad ecosystem, Stone-Gross et al. [30] used ad hoc methods to study specific attacks faced by ad exchanges, including referrer spoofing and cookie replay attacks. Google also documented what they consider to be invalid traffic in [34] but did not disclose the details of their traffic filters.

9 Conclusion

In this study, we measured ad abuse from the perspective of a Demand Side Platform (DSP). We found that traditional sources of low reputation, such as public blacklists and malware traces, greatly underestimate ad-abuse, which highlight the need to build lists catered towards ad-abuse. The good news, however, is malicious publishers that participate in ad-abuse can likely be modeled at the DSP level based on their behavioral characteristics. Finally, malicious campaigns can be tracked using graph analysis and simple heuristics, allowing DSPs to track suspicious infrastructure.

Acknowledgements. We would like to thank TAPAD and in particular their CTO, Dag Liodden, for his invaluable help throughout this project. This material is based upon work supported in part by the US Department of Commerce grant 2106DEK, National Science Foundation (NSF) grant 2106DGX and Air Force Research Laboratory/Defense Advanced Research Projects Agency grant 2106DTX. Any opinions, findings, conclusions, or recommendations expressed in this material are those of the authors and do not necessarily reflect the views of the US Department of Commerce, National Science Foundation, Air Force Research Laboratory, or Defense Advanced Research Projects Agency.

References

1. EasyList. https://easylist-downloads.adblockplus.org/easylist.txt
2. Hphosts List. http://hosts-file.net/?s=Download
3. I.T. Mate List. http://vurldissect.co.uk/daily.asp
4. Malc0de Database. http://malc0de.com/bl/BOOT

5. Malware Domain List. https://www.malwaredomainlist.com/
6. PassiveTotal: RiskIQ. https://www.passivetotal.org/
7. sagadc.org list. http://dns-bh.sagadc.org/domains.txt
8. SANS ISC Feeds. https://isc.sans.edu/feeds/
9. Mozilla Public Suffix List (2015). https://publicsuffix.org/list/
10. Advertising Age. Ad Fraud Will Cost $7.2 Billion in 2016, ANA Says, Up Nearly $1 Billion. http://bit.ly/1Qe21C2
11. Alexa: The web information company (2007). http://www.alexa.com/
12. Alrwais, S.A., Gerber, A., Dunn, C.W., Spatscheck, O., Gupta, M., Osterweil, E.: Dissecting ghost clicks: ad fraud via misdirected human clicks. In: Proceedings of the 28th Annual Computer Security Applications Conference. ACM (2012)
13. Antonakakis, M., Demar, J., Stevens, K., Dagon, D.: Unveiling the network criminal infrastructure of tdss/tdl4 dgav14: a case study on a new tdss/tdl4 variant. Technical Report, Damballa Inc.,Georgia Institute of Technology (GTISC) (2012)
14. Association of National Advertisers: The Bot Baseline: Fraud in Digital Advertising. http://bit.ly/1PKe769
15. Chen, Y., Kintis, P., Antonakakis, M., Nadji, Y., Dagon, D., Lee, W., Farrell, M.: Financial lower bounds of online advertising abuse. In: International conference on Detection of Intrusions and Malware, and Vulnerability Assessment (2016)
16. ClickZ. Fake Display Ad Impressions Comprise 30% of All Online Traffic [Study]. http://bit.ly/2e3HdCZ
17. Daswani, N., Stoppelman, M.: The anatomy of Clickbot.A. In: The First Workshop on Hot Topics in Understanding Botnets. USENIX Association (2007)
18. Dave, V., Guha, S., Zhang, Y.: Measuring and fingerprinting click-spam in ad networks. In: Proceedings of the ACM SIGCOMM 2012 Conference on Applications, Technologies, Architectures, and Protocols for Computer Communication (2012)
19. Dave, V., Guha, S., Zhang, Y.: Viceroi: catching click-spam in search ad networks. In: 2013 ACM SIGSAC Conference on Computer & Communications Security (2013)
20. Department of Homeland Security: Trusted Cyber Risk Research Data Sharing. https://www.dhs.gov/csd-impact
21. Kapravelos, A., Grier, C., Chachra, N., Kruegel, C., Vigna, G., Paxson, V.: Hulk: eliciting malicious behavior in browser extensions. In: 23rd USENIX Security Symposium (USENIX Security) (2014)
22. Malware Tips: How to remove Websearch.searc-hall.info. http://bit.ly/2e9qyKw
23. Malware Tips: Remove Sl.now-update-check.com virus. http://bit.ly/2dm1LWp
24. Meng, W., Duan, R., Lee, W.: DNS Changer Remediation Study. In: M3AAWG 27th General Meeting (2013)
25. Metwally, A., Agrawal, D., El Abbadi, A.: Detectives: detecting coalition hit inflation attacks in advertising networks streams. In: Proceedings of the 16th International Conference on World Wide Web, pp. 241–250. ACM (2007)
26. Miller, B., Pearce, P., Grier, C., Kreibich, C., Paxson, V.: What's clicking what? Techniques and innovations of today's clickbots. In: Detection of Intrusions and Malware, and Vulnerability Assessment (2011)
27. openrtb.info: OpenRTB: Documentation and Issue tracking for the OpenRTB Project (2014). http://openrtb.github.io/OpenRTB/
28. Pearce, P., Dave, V., Grier, C., Levchenko, K., Guha, S., McCoy, D., Paxson, V., Savage, S., Voelker, G.M.: Characterizing large-scale click fraud in zeroaccess. In: 2014 ACM SIGSAC Conference on Computer and Communications Security (2014)
29. Springborn, K., Barford, P.: Impression fraud in online advertising via pay-per-view networks. In: Proceedings of the 22nd USENIX Security Symposium (2013)

30. Stone-Gross, B., Stevens, R., Zarras, A., Kemmerer, R., Kruegel, C., Vigna, G.: Understanding fraudulent activities in online ad exchanges. In: Proceedings of the 2011 ACM SIGCOMM Conference on Internet Measurement Conference (2011)
31. Thomas, K., Bursztein, E., Grier, C., Ho, G., Jagpal, N., Kapravelos, A., McCoy, D., Nappa, A., Paxson, V., Pearce, P., et al.: Ad injection at scale: assessing deceptive advertisement modifications. In: 2015 IEEE Symposium on Security and Privacy (2015)
32. Tian, T., Zhu, J., Xia, F., Zhuang, X., Zhang, T.: Crowd fraud detection in internet advertising. In: Proceedings of the 24th International Conference on World Wide Web, pp. 1100–1110. ACM (2015)
33. TrendMicro, Inc.: Threat Encyclopedia: TROJ_LEMIR.CS (2012). https://goo.gl/8ryRjK
34. Tuzhilin, A.: The Lane's Gift v. Google Report (2006)
35. VirusTotal: Antivirus scan (2014). https://goo.gl/jU0b0b
36. VirusTotal: Antivirus scan (2015). https://goo.gl/s97XI5
37. VirusTotal: IP address information (2015). https://goo.gl/ifLvT5
38. Xing, X., Meng, W., Lee, B., Weinsberg, U., Sheth, A., Perdisci, R., Lee, W.: Understanding malvertising through ad-injecting browser extensions. In: Proceedings of the 24th International Conference on World Wide Web (2015)
39. Zeus Tracker: Zeus IP & domain name block list. https://zeustracker.abuse.ch

Author Index

Akritidis, Periklis 48
Anand, Kapil 97
Antonakakis, Manos 388

Barabosch, Thomas 209
Barua, Rajeev 97
Bergmann, Niklas 209
Buettner, Daniel 97

Chen, Yizheng 388
Choi, Jin-Young 48
Chothia, Tom 279
Continella, Andrea 73

D'Alessio, Stefano 73
Dagon, David 388
Dargenio, Ruggiero 366
Debbabi, Mourad 301
Doerr, Christian 141
Dombeck, Adrian 209

Eckert, Claudia 119
Elovici, Yuval 161
ElWazeer, Khaled 97
Evenchick, Eric 185

Fontana, Lorenzo 73

Garcia, Flavio D. 279
Gritti, Fabio 73
Gruss, Daniel 3
Gugelmann, David 366
Guri, Mordechai 161

Hanif, Zachary D. 119
Happe, Markus 366
Heen, Olivier 347

Jin, Hai 325

Kim, Danny 97
Kirsch, Julian 119
Kolosnjaji, Bojan 119

Lamprakis, Pavlos 366
Lei, Lingguang 230
Lenders, Vincent 366
Li, Qi 230
Li, Yuping 252
Li, Zhen 325
Luchs, Mark 141

Ma, Rui 230
Maggi, Federico 185
Majlesi-Kupaei, Amir 97
Mangard, Stefan 3
Mariani, Sebastiano 73
Maurice, Clémentine 3

Nadji, Yacin 388
Nam, Myoung Jin 48
Nam, Wonhong 48
Neumann, Christoph 347

Ou, Xinming 252

Padilla, Elmar 209
Palanca, Andrea 185
Polino, Mario 73

Qi, Hanchao 325

Romero-Gómez, Rosa 388
Roy, Julien 97
Roy, Sankardas 252

Saxena, Prateek 25
Schwarz, Michael 3
Shenefiel, Chris 230
Shirani, Paria 301

Sun, Guozhong   325
Sun, Jianhua   230
Sun, Kun   230

Thomas, Sam L.   279
Tople, Shruti   25

Vanbever, Laurent   366
von Pentz, Christian   119

Wang, Lingyu   301
Wang, Sujuan   325

Wang, Yuewu   230
Webster, George D.   119
Wei, Fengguo   252
Weiser, Samuel   3
Wu, Song   325

Zadov, Boris   161
Zanero, Stefano   73, 185
Zarras, Apostolis   119
Zhong, Yuyi   325
Zhou, Wu   252
Zou, Deqing   325

Printed in the United States
By Bookmasters